PARADISE LOST

AN AUTHORITATIVE TEXT
BACKGROUNDS AND SOURCES
CRITICISM

SECOND EDITION

A NORTON CRITICAL EDITION

John Milton

PARADISE LOST

AN AUTHORITATIVE TEXT
BACKGROUNDS AND SOURCES
CRITICISM

SECOND EDITION

Edited by

SCOTT ELLEDGE

CORNELL UNIVERSITY

W • W • NORTON & COMPANY • *New York* • *London*

Copyright © 1993, 1975 by W. W. Norton & Company, Inc.

Printed in the United States of America

The text of this book is composed in Electra with the display set in Bernhard Modern. Composition by PennSet, Inc. Manufacturing by Courier. Book design by Antonina Krass.

Library of Congress Cataloging-in-Publication Data
Milton, John, 1608–1674.
Paradise lost : an authoritative text, backgrounds and sources, criticism / John Milton ; edited by Scott Elledge. — 2nd ed.
      p.   cm. — (A Norton critical edition)
Includes bibliographical references.
1. Fall of man—Poetry. 2. Milton, John, 1608–1674. Paradise
lost. 3. Fall of man in literature. I. Elledge, Scott. II. Title.
                    PR3560.A2E45 1993
821'.4—dc20   92-9988

ISBN 0-393-96293-8

W. W. Norton & Company, Inc., 500 Fifth Avenue, New York, N.Y. 10110
W. W. Norton & Company Ltd., 10 Coptic Street, London WC1A 1PU

2 3 4 5 6 7 8 9 0

Contents

Preface

The chief innovations in this second edition of the first Norton Critical Edition of *Paradise Lost* are the addition of a short, slightly revised version of a biography of Milton written by Milton's greatest biographer, David Masson; an abridgment of the first edition of Milton's *Doctrine and Discipline of Divorce*; five of Milton's sonnets; and several recent essays about *Paradise Lost* whose presence increases the variety of critical approaches represented. To make room for all this, I deleted from the first edition an intrusive introduction, further abridged the selections from *Christian Doctrine*, and regretfully deleted several excellent critical essays simply because they seemed less likely to interest students and teachers today than they did seventeen years ago.

The text of the poem is that of my first edition (see A Note on the Text, p. 302), and the only substantial change in the footnotes is the addition of references to Homer, Virgil, and Ovid in sufficient number to suggest the nature and extent of the part their poems played in Milton's conception and composition of his epic. Echoes of Dante, Spenser, and other poets can be detected with pleasure by readers who know well the passages Milton echoes or alludes to, but, as I said in the first edition, pointing out such "sources" or allusions to readers unacquainted with the originals seems to me supererogatory.

Andrew Marvell's commendatory poem should have been included in the first edition (Milton included it in his second edition), and I thank Professor Steven Knapp for pointing that out, as well as for suggesting other improvements. In addition to him I am greatly indebted to Professors Ellen H. Brinkley, Norman Carlson, Frank Morral, Mary Ann Radzinowicz, Owen Jenkins, Gordon Teskey, and M. H. Abrams.

SCOTT ELLEDGE

The Text of
PARADISE LOST

A Note on the Footnotes

Some excellent editions of *Paradise Lost* have many fewer footnotes than this one, and some have many, many more. This edition was made for undergraduates, not necessarily English majors, reading the poem in various kinds of courses, who will welcome a certain amount of aid in understanding and enjoying the poem. For them I have (1) called attention to derivations and obsolete or uncommon meanings of words, (2) supplied illustrative citations to the Bible and to passages in Milton's *Christian Doctrine* that bear on the original story and important theological questions, and (3) explained allusions to myths, history, geography, and other things an educated undergraduate might very well never have heard of.

Since my aim is to relieve frustration, I hope that the presence of the notes will not distract anyone. No one, I think, should interrupt his or her first reading of a poem, or a substantial part of it, by looking to the bottom of the page for help. The best way to read is to listen to the poet, the way one listens to someone speaking; then, if one is attracted to what one hears, or is curious about it, one can go back over the poem, or a passage in it, consulting the notes. In my opinion one should read a poem before one begins to study it.

Like previous editors of *Paradise Lost*, I have made use of the work of my predecessors. I have not acknowledged specific debts to eighteenth-, nineteenth-, and early-twentieth-century editors, but I have at appropriate places given credit to the original contributions of more recent editors: Merritt Y. Hughes, *John Milton: Complete Poems and Major Prose* (New York, 1957); Douglas Bush, *The Complete Poetical Works of John Milton* (Boston, 1965); Alastair Fowler, *Paradise Lost* (London, 1971).

The following abbreviations appear in the footnotes:

In the derivations of words: D = Dutch, Fr = French, Gk = Greek, It = Italian, L = Latin, LL = Late Latin, ME = Middle English, ML = Medieval Latin, OE = Old English, OF = Old French.

Aen.	Virgil's *Aeneid*, trans. H. Rushton Fairclough (1930).
CD	Milton's *Christian Doctrine*.
Il.	Homer's *Iliad*, trans. Andrew Lang, Walter Leaf, and Ernest Myers, rev. ed. (1892).
Met.	Ovid's *Metamorphoses*, trans. Frank Justin Miller (1916).
NEB	*The New English Bible, with the Apocrypha* (Oxford, 1970). Biblical quotations not so indicated are from the Authorized King James Version.
NT	New Testament.
Od.	Homer's *Odyssey*, trans. S. H. Butcher and A. Lang (1921).
OED	*The Oxford English Dictionary.*
OT	Old Testament.
PL	*Paradise Lost.*
PR	*Paradise Regained.*
Prose	*Complete Prose of John Milton*, 8 vols. (New Haven, 1953–82).

Paradise Loſt.

A POEM

IN TWELVE BOOKS.

The Author
JOHN MILTON.

𝔗𝔥𝔢 𝔖𝔢𝔠𝔬𝔫𝔡 𝔈𝔡𝔦𝔱𝔦𝔬𝔫
Reviſed and Augmented by the
ſame Author.

LONDON,
Printed by *S. Simmons* next door to the
Golden Lion in *Alderſgate-ſtreet,* 1674.

A.[NDREW] M.[ARVELL]

On *Paradise Lost*†

When I beheld the poet blind, yet bold,
In slender book his vast design unfold—
Messiah crowned, God's reconciled decree,
Rebelling angels, the forbidden tree,
Heaven, hell, earth, chaos, all—the argument   5
Held me a while misdoubting his intent,
That he would ruin (for I saw him strong)
The sacred truths to fable and old song
(So Samson groped the temple's posts in spite),
The world o'erwhelming to revenge his sight.   10
   Yet as I read, soon growing less severe,
I liked his project, the success did fear—
Through that wide field how he his way should find
O'er which lame faith leads understanding blind;
Lest he perplexed the things he would explain,   15
And what was easy he should render vain.
   Or if a work so infinite he spanned,
Jealous I was that some less skilful hand
(Such as disquiet always what is well,
And by ill imitating would excel)   20
Might hence presume the whole creation's day
To change in scenes, and show it in a play.
   Pardon me, mighty poet, nor despise
My causeless, yet not impious, surmise.
But I am now convinced, and none will dare   25
Within thy labors to pretend a share.
Thou hast not missed one thought that could be fit,
And all that was improper dost omit;
So that no room is here for writers left,

---

† This commendatory poem by Milton's friend Andrew Marvell first appeared in the second
edition of *PL* (1674).
17–22. When John Dryden, about the time he was appointed poet laureate, read the first edition
of *PL* (1667), he is said to have cried out, "This man cuts us all out, and the ancients too."
When he called on Milton some time later, he asked Milton for permission to turn the epic
into an opera, with dialogue in rhymed couplets; and Milton is reported to have given the
popular poet leave to "tag his verses" or (in another version) "to tag his points." Milton's
meaning is illuminated by lines 45–50, below. Dryden's *State of Innocence, and the Fall of
Man* (1677), like some of Dryden's plays, was written in rhyme (heroic couplets), which had
become a popular verse form after the Restoration, partly beause of Dryden's skillful use of it.
In 1674, when Milton's second, revised edition appeared, Marvell may have heard that Dryden
was writing or had written *The State of Innocence*.
27. *fit:* appropriate.

But to detect their ignorance or theft.   30
  The majesty which through thy work doth reign
Draws the devout, deterring the profane.
And things divine thou treat'st of in such state
As them preserves, and thee, inviolate.
At once delight and horror on us seize,   35
Thou sing'st with so much gravity and ease;
And above human flight dost soar aloft
With plume so strong, so equal, and so soft.
The bird named from that Paradise you sing
So never flags, but always keeps on wing.   40
  Where could'st thou words of such a compass find?
Whence furnish such a vast expense of mind?
Just Heav'n, thee like Tiresias to requite,
Rewards with prophecy thy loss of sight.
  Well might'st thou scorn thy readers to allure   45
With tinkling rhyme, of thy own sense secure;
While the Town-Bayes writes all the while and spells,
And like a pack-horse tires without his bells.
Their fancies like our bushy points appear;
The poets tag them, we for fashion wear.   50
I too, transported by the mode, offend,
And, while I meant to *praise* thee, must *commend*.
Thy verse created like thy theme sublime,
In number, weight, and measure, needs not rhyme.

                                                 A.M.

30. *detect*: expose.
39–40. According to folklore, birds of paradise had no legs and were therefore always in flight.
47. *Town-Bayes*: Dryden. *spells*: talks.
49–50. A *point* was a ribbon or cord (like a modern shoelace), whose ends were kept from raveling by a *tag*, a little band of soft metal. Points were used to lace one's hose to one's doublet (or jacket) in Shakespeare's time as well as in Dryden's Restoration days, when it became fashionable to attach decorative tags to the ends of their (already functionally tagged) points—such as tassels—which would make them *bushy points*. Marvell's criticism is consistent with the meaning of Milton's witty reply to Dryden: rhyme words come in pairs, at the ends of lines of verse, are nonfunctional decoration, call attention to themselves, and are fashionable.

The Verse

The measure is English heroic verse without rhyme, as that of Homer in Greek and of Virgil in Latin; rhyme being no necessary adjunct or true ornament of poem or good verse, in longer works especially, but the invention of a barbarous age, to set off wretched matter* and lame meter; graced indeed since by the use of some famous modern poets, carried away by custom, but much to their own vexation, hindrance, and constraint to express many things otherwise, and for the most part worse than else they would have expressed them. Not without cause therefore some both Italian and Spanish poets of prime note have rejected rhyme both in longer and shorter works, as have also long since our best English tragedies, as a thing of itself, to all judicious ears, trivial and of no true musical delight; which consists only in apt numbers, fit quantity of syllables, and the sense variously drawn out from one verse into another, not in the jingling sound of like endings, a fault avoided by the learned ancients both in poetry and all good oratory. This neglect then of rhyme so little is to be taken for a defect, though it may seem so perhaps to vulgar readers, that it rather is to be esteemed an example set, the first in English, of ancient liberty recovered to heroic poem from the troublesome and modern bondage of rhyming.

---

* *wretched matter:* perhaps the bawdy content of the Latin songs composed by Goliardic poets of the Middle Ages, whose singsong meter and stressed rhyme they learned from medieval hymns.

Book I

The Argument

This first book proposes, first in brief, the whole subject, man's disobedience, and the loss thereupon of Paradise wherein he was placed: then touches the prime cause of his fall, the Serpent, or rather Satan in the Serpent; who revolting from God, and drawing to his side many legions of angels, was by the command of God driven out of heaven with all his crew into the great deep. Which action passed over, the poem hastes into the midst of things, presenting Satan with his angels now fallen into hell, described here, not in the center (for heaven and earth may be supposed as yet not made, certainly not yet accursed) but in a place of utter darkness, fitliest called Chaos: here Satan with his angels lying on the burning lake, thunderstruck and astonished, after a certain space recovers, as from confusion, calls up him who next in order and dignity lay by him; they confer of their miserable fall. Satan awakens all his legions, who lay till then in the same manner confounded; they rise, their numbers, array of battle, their chief leaders named, according to the idols known afterwards in Canaan and the countries adjoining. To these Satan directs his speech, comforts them with hope yet of regaining heaven, but tells them lastly of a new world and new kind of creature to be created, according to an ancient prophecy or report in heaven; for that angels were long before this visible creation, was the opinion of many ancient Fathers. To find out the truth of this prophecy, and what to determine thereon he refers to a full council. What his associates thence attempt. Pandemonium the palace of Satan rises, suddenly built out of the deep: the infernal peers there sit in council.

Of man's first disobedience, and the fruit \ |
Of that forbidden tree, whose mortal taste

---

1. Argument. *the center* i e, of the earth. *heaven and earth*: the created universe. *yet not made*. I.e., chaos and hell existed before the Creation. *utter*: outer, extreme, complete. *Canaan*: Palestine. *Fathers*: early Christian theologians.

1–5. These five lines state the *argument* (see 24), or subject of the epic, just as the opening lines of Homer's *Il.* and *Od.* and Virgil's *Aen.* announce the subjects of those classical epics: "Sing, goddess, the wrath of Achilles that brought innumerable woes on the Achaians and hurled into Hades many strong souls of heroes"; "Tell me, Muse, of that man [Odysseus, the hero], so ready at need, who wandered far and wide, after he had sacked the sacred city of Troy, . . . and many were the woes he suffered"; "Arms I sing and the man [Aeneas] who first from the coasts of Troy, exiled by fate came to Italy . . .; much buffeted on sea and land . . . much enduring in war, till he should build a city . . . ; whence came the Latin race . . . and the lofty walls of Rome." Milton's readers would notice that the fall of mankind is to be the subject of this poem, and mankind itself, the hero. This statement of subject is full of double meanings: the Hebrew name *Adam* means man: *first* may mean in time and in importance; *fruit* means profit or enjoyment and result or consequence, as well as apple; *mortal* means deadly as well as human. *Eden* means the garden of Eden, or Paradise, but it also means heavenly perfection. Being both man and god, Jesus Christ was *a greater Adam*, and, some say, the *greater* hero.

Brought death into the world, and all our woe,
With loss of Eden, till one greater Man
Restore us, and regain the blissful seat,   5
Sing Heav'nly Muse, that on the secret top
Of Oreb, or of Sinai,didst inspire
That shepherd, who first taught the chosen seed,
In the beginning how the heav'ns and earth
Rose out of chaos: or if Sion hill   10
Delight thee more, and Siloa's brook that flowed
Fast by the oracle of God; I thence
Invoke thy aid to my advent'rous song,
That with no middle flight intends to soar
Above th' Aonian mount, while it pursues   15
Things unattempted yet in prose or rhyme.
And chiefly thou O Spirit, that dost prefer
Before all temples th' upright heart and pure,
Instruct me, for thou know'st; thou from the first

6. With the verb *sing* (meaning "sing through me") Milton invokes the aid of a superhuman inspiration, as did the epic poets before him; but Milton's Muse is not one of the nine pagan Muses—it is an abstraction of the wisdom and power of the Judeo-Christian divinity, identified here as the Muse that inspired Moses, who was then believed to have been the author of the first five books of the Bible. Milton's allusion conflates Moses the lawgiver, who received the ten commandments on Mount Horeb (Deut. 4.10) or on Mount Sinai (Exod. 19.20), with Moses the literal shepherd and figurative pastor, and with Moses as a kind of bard, or inspired singer, who may teach the past and reveal the future. See "Truth and Poetry," pp. 473–74.
10–15. By adding that the Muse may prefer to dwell on Mount Zion in Jerusalem, near *Siloa's brook*, Milton invites a comparison with the Greek Muses, who also favored mountains and their nearby fountains or streams. The oracle of Delphi was by the Castalian Spring on the side of Mount Parnassus, sacred to the Muses and to Apollo, the god of light, music, poetry,and prophecy; the *oracle of God* was near a spring (*Siloa's brook*) which was near Mount Zion (*Sion Hill*), where God spoke to his people through priests and prophets. Cf. Isa. 2.3: "Come ye, and let us go up to the mountain of the Lord . . . and he will teach us of his ways . . . for out of Zion shall go forth the law." In Greece the Muses were thought to live also near the spring Hippocrene, on the side of Mount Helicon (*th'Aonian mount*), a spring created by the hoof-stamp of Pegasus, a winged horse that symbolized poetic inspiration because he could fly to the top of Mount Olympus, the home of the gods. The earth, in Milton's time, was believed to be covered with three layers of atmosphere, the second of which ("middle region") reached to the top of mountains. The highest heaven of the pagan gods, Mount Olympus, was in the *middle air* (see 514–17); and it is above this region that Milton's Pegasus must carry him on his *no middle flight*, since Milton intends to sing of true heaven, which is far above the universe. See "The Universe," pp. 461–63. *pursues*: tries to accomplish.
16. This line is a translation of a line in Ariosto's Renaissance epic *Orlando Furioso*. Milton is not boasting; he is emphasizing the greatness and seriousness of his undertaking—a heroic poem that makes the ways of God seem just—a poem that makes man's fate seem reasonable and psychologically satisfying, an epic in which the hero is not an active warrior but patient (or suffering) mankind, including the first and second Adams. *rhyme*: Gk *rythmos*, verse.
17–22. *And chiefly thou O Spirit* may not refer to the same being as the Heavenly Muse, but the difference, if any, is slight. Here Milton emphasizes the creative power and wisdom needed for such great undertakings as creating the world and writing this definitive poem, and he calls, not upon the third person of the Trinity, but upon God. *Dove-like*. In the Gospels the Holy Spirit is said to have assumed the shape of a dove when it descended to earth. *sat'st*. The King James Version reads (Gen. 1.2) "moved," but the original Hebrew word means "hovered" or "brooded." *Abyss* (Gk *abyssos* without bottom) is a synonym for "the deep" of Gen. 1.2. V*ast* implies "waste" as well as "large," and helps to suggest the chaos out of which Milton says the world was made. *Brooding . . . mad'st it pregnant* is not, according to Fowler, a mixed metaphor, but "a deliberate allusion to the Hermetic doctrine that God is both masculine and feminine."

Wast present, and with mighty wings outspread   20
Dove-like sat'st brooding on the vast abyss
And mad'st it pregnant: what in me is dark
Illumine, what is low raise and support;
That to the highth of this great argument
I may assert Eternal Providence,   25
And justify the ways of God to men.
    Say first, for heav'n hides nothing from thy view
Nor the deep tract of hell, say first what cause
Moved our grand parents in that happy state,
Favored of Heav'n so highly, to fall off   30
From their Creator, and transgress his will
For one restraint, lords of the world besides?
Who first seduced them to that foul revolt?
Th' infernal Serpent; he it was, whose guile
Stirred up with envy and revenge, deceived   35
The mother of mankind, what time his pride
Had cast him out from heav'n, with all his host
Of rebel angels, by whose aid aspiring
To set himself in glory above his peers,
He trusted to have equaled the Most High,   40
If he opposed; and with ambitious aim
Against the throne and monarchy of God
Raised impious war in heav'n and battle proud
With vain attempt. Him the Almighty Power
Hurled headlong flaming from th' ethereal sky   45
With hideous ruin and combustion down
To bottomless perdition, there to dwell
In adamantine chains and penal fire,

24. *to the highth of*: as far as is possible by means of.
25. *assert*: (L *asserere* to put one's hand on the head of a slave to set him free or protect or defend him) take the part of, champion. *Eternal*: without beginning or end. *Providence*: (L *pro* before + *videre* to see; foresight) foreknowing, beneficent, and efficient concern. Cf. other uses of the word in the poem: I.162; II.559; XII.564, 647.
28. *what cause*. This opening question is an epic convention. Homer and Virgil both began by asking the Muse to tell which gods (or why a god) had caused the events of the story.
29. *grand*: supremely deserving of the title (equivalent to the prefix *arch-*).
32. *For*: because of. *besides*: otherwise.
34–49. Cf.Isa. 14.12–15, p. 444.
43. *impious*. The L word means disrespectful of one's parents or one's country as well as of one's god.
45. *ethereal*: (Gk *aithein* to ignite, blaze) of the ether, the element supposed to fill the outer regions of the universe; not earth, air, fire, or water, it was not earthly but heavenly, and eternal.
46. This image of a meteorite is more distinct in the description of Satan's fall at 745 ("like a falling star"). *hideous*: Causing dread or horror. *ruin*: (L *ruere* to fall violently) ruins, rubble; fall, destruction. *combustion*. Cf. *combustible*, line 233.
48. *adamantine*: like or made of adamant (from Gk. *adamas*, "invincible"), originally emery, a very hard stone used as whetstones. By the fourth century B.C. *adamas* also meant steel as hard as adamant. When Plato wrote that the concentric spheres of the universe turned on an axle

Who durst defy th' Omnipotent to arms.
Nine times the space that measures day and night   50
To mortal men, he with his horrid crew
Lay vanquished, rolling in the fiery gulf
Confounded though immortal: but his doom
Reserved him to more wrath; for now the thought
Both of lost happiness and lasting pain   55
Torments him; round he throws his baleful eyes
That witnessed huge affliction and dismay
Mixed with obdúrate pride and steadfast hate:
At once as far as angels ken he views
The dismal situation waste and wild,   60
A dungeon horrible, on all sides round
As one great furnace flamed, yet from those flames
No light, but rather darkness visible
Served only to discover sights of woe,
Regions of sorrow, doleful shades, where peace   65
And rest can never dwell, hope never comes
That comes to all; but torture without end
Still urges, and a fiery deluge, fed
With ever-burning sulphur unconsumed:
Such place Eternal Justice had prepared   70
For those rebellious, here their prison ordained
In utter darkness, and their portion set

---

of adamant, he may have meant very hard steel, not stone. And in the opening lines of
Prometheus, a tragedy of the fifth century B.C., "adamantine chains" means chain made of
adamantine steel. A few centuries later, however, *adamas* became the name for diamond, the
hardest mineral known, able to withstand very high temperatures. Virgil (*Aen.* 6.439) and
Milton (*PL* 2.436) described the pillars of the gates of hell as made of adamant. In Milton's
time, *adamant* was the scientific word for diamond, and at 2.466 he refers to "admantine
rock." See also 3.506–7: "a kingly palace gate/With frontispiece of diamond."

53. *confounded*: (L *con.* together + *fundere* to pour; *confundere* to mix up, confuse) ruined,
    routed; spoiled, corrupted.
53. *doom*: sentence of punishment.
56. *baleful*: full of suffering; of pernicious influence.
57. *witnessed*: expressed, revealed.
60. *dismal*: calamitous, as well as depressingly dark.
63. *darkness visible*. Cf. Job 10.20–22: "Let me alone, that I may take comfort a little, before I
    go whence I shall not return, even to the land of darkness, and the shadow of death; a land
    of darkness, as darkness itself; and of the shadow of death, without any order, and where the
    light is as darkness."
68. *Still*: constantly. *urges*: stimulates, excites, provokes. The idea is antithetical to that of *rest*,
    and the word was often used in a context of fire, as in "urge like fire."
70. *Such place*. The biblical authority for Milton's location and description of hell is cited in
    CD I.XXXIII.
72. *utter darkness*. Speaking of the faith of some gentiles and the lack of faith among his own
    people, Christ said (Matt. 8.11–12): "Many shall come from the east and west and shall sit
    down with Abraham, and Isaac, and Jacob, in the kingdom of heaven. But the children [who
    were born to the kingdom—(*NEB*)] shall be cast out into outer darkness [the place of
    wailing—(*NEB*)] and gnashing of teeth." But the basic English meaning of *utter* is "complete."

As far removed from God and light of heav'n
As from the center thrice to th' utmost pole.
O how unlike the place from whence they fell!   75
There the companions of his fall, o'erwhelmed
With floods and whirlwinds of tempestuous fire,
He soon discerns, and welt'ring by his side
One next himself in power, and next in crime,
Long after known in Palestine, and named   80
Beëlzebub. To whom th' Arch-Enemy,
And thence in heav'n called Satan, with bold words
Breaking the horrid silence thus began.
    "If thou beest he; but O how fall'n! how changed
From him, who in the happy realms of light   85
Clothed with transcendent brightness didst outshine
Myriads though bright: if he whom mutual league,
United thoughts and counsels, equal hope
And hazard in the glorious enterprise,
Joined with me once, now misery hath joined   90
In equal ruin: into what pit thou seest
From what highth fall'n, so much the stronger proved
He with his thunder: and till then who knew
The force of those dire arms? Yet not for those,
Nor what the potent victor in his rage   95
Can else inflict, do I repent or change,
Though changed in outward luster, that fixed mind
And high disdain, from sense of injured merit,
That with the mightiest raised me to contend,
And to the fierce contention brought along   100
Innumerable force of Spirits armed
That durst dislike his reign, and me preferring,
His utmost power with adverse power opposed
In dubious battle on the plains of heav'n,
And shook his throne. What though the field be lost?   105
All is not lost; the unconquerable will,
And study of revenge, immortal hate,

73–74. From hell to earth (*the center*) is twice as far as from earth to heaven, which lies just
beyond the outer shell of the universe. *utmost pole*: the end of the axis of the universe. See
"The Universe," pp. 461–63. Cf. *Aen.* 6.578, where Virgil gives the same relative distances.
78. *welt'ring*: rolling in the waves.
81. *Beëlzebub* is called "the prince of the devils" in Matt. 12.24, and the name may have been
a synonym for Satan. Its meaning, "lord of the flies," suggests a mythical origin in the worship
of a god who delivered men from insects or of one who was himself infested by flies (Hughes).
But according to Fowler, Milton's portrayal of him "seems rather to be based on an allegorization
invented by St. Jerome," in which the fly is a symbol of pertinacity. Beëlzebub "never ceases
to infest the human race in every way."
82. *Satan*: the Hebrew word for adversary.
84. Cf. Isa. 14.12: "How art thou fallen from heaven, O Lucifer, son of the morning!"
98. *injured*: done an injustice to. *merit*: just claim to reward.
104. *dubious*: of uncertain outcome.
107. *study of*: application of thought to; zealous effort to achieve.

And courage never to submit or yield:
And what is else not to be overcome?
That glory never shall his wrath or might   110
Extort from me. To bow and sue for grace
With suppliant knee, and deify his power
Who from the terror of this arm so late
Doubted his empire, that were low indeed,
That were an ignominy and shame beneath   115
This downfall; since by fate the strength of gods
And this empyreal substance cannot fail,
Since through experience of this great event
In arms not worse, in foresight much advanced,
We may with more successful hope resolve   120
To wage by force or guile eternal war
Irreconcilable, to our grand foe,
Who now triúmphs, and in th' excess of joy
Sole reigning holds the tyranny of heav'n."
    So spake th' apostate angel, though in pain,   125
Vaunting aloud, but racked with deep despair:
And him thus answered soon his bold compeer.
    "O Prince, O Chief of many thronèd Powers,
That led th' embattled Seraphim to war
Under thy conduct, and in dreadful deeds   130
Fearless, endangered heav'ns perpetual King;
And put to proof his high supremacy,
Whether upheld by strength, or chance, or fate;
Too well I see and rue the dire event,
That with sad overthrow and foul defeat   135
Hath lost us heav'n, and all this mighty host
In horrible destruction laid thus low,
As far as gods and heav'nly essences
Can perish: for the mind and spirit remains
Invincible, and vigor soon returns,   140
Though all our glory extinct, and happy state
Here swallowed up in endless misery.
But what if he our conqueror (whom I now
Of force believe almighty, since no less

109. I.e.: What else does 'not being overcome' mean?
114. *Doubted*: feared for.
116. *fate*. PL is a Christian definition of fate as Providence, but Satan thinks of fate as a power
  greater than God. Cf. *CD*, p. 402, and other uses of the word in the poem: I.133; II.197,
  232, 393, 550, 559, 560, 809; III.120; V.527; VI.869; IX.689, 885, 927; X.265, 480; XI.181.
  Gods. It is true that God refers to the angels as *gods* (III.341), but Satan's intent here may be
  to suggest that God is just another angel.
117. *empyreal*: (Gk *empyros* in fire, fiery) of the empyrean, the highest heaven; heavenly. See
  "The Universe," pp. 461–63.
128–29. *Powers, Seraphim*. See "Angels," pp. 466–68.
134. *event*: (L *e* out + *venire* come) outcome.
141. *extinct*: (be) put out.
144. *of force*. May modify *believe* or *almighty*.

Than such could have o'erpow'red such force as ours)   145
Have left us this our spirit and strength entire
Strongly to suffer and support our pains,
That we may so suffice his vengeful ire,
Or do him mightier service as his thralls
By right of war, whate'er his business be   150
Here in the heart of hell to work in fire,
Or do his errands in the gloomy deep;
What can it then avail though yet we feel
Strength undiminished, or eternal being
To undergo eternal punishment?"   155
Whereto with speedy words th' Arch-Fiend replied.
    "Fall'n Cherub, to be weak is miserable
Doing or suffering: but of this be sure,
To do aught good never will be our task,
But ever to do ill our sole delight,   160
As being the contrary to his high will
Whom we resist. If then his providence
Out of our evil seek to bring forth good,
Our labor must be to pervert that end,
And out of good still to find means of evil;   165
Which ofttimes may succeed, so as perhaps
Shall grieve him, if I fail not, and disturb
His inmost counsels from their destined aim.
But see the angry victor hath recalled
His ministers of vengeance and pursuit   170
Back to the gates of heav'n: the sulphurous hail
Shot after us in storm, o'erblown hath laid
The fiery surge, that from the precipice
Of heav'n received us falling, and the thunder,
Winged with red lightning and impetuous rage,   175
Perhaps hath spent his shafts, and ceases now
To bellow through the vast and boundless deep.
Let us not slip th' occasion, whether scorn,
Or satiate fury yield it from our foe.
Seest thou yon dreary plain, forlorn and wild,   180
The seat of desolation, void of light,
Save what the glimmering of these livid flames
Casts pale and dreadful? Thither let us tend
From off the tossing of these fiery waves,

148. *suffice*: satisfy.
149–52. Cf. *CD*, pp. 412–13.
157. *Cherub*: sing. of *cherubim*.
167. *fail*: err.
172. *laid*: calmed.
178. *slip*: let pass by.
182. *livid*: blue, the color of burning sulphur.

There rest, if any rest can harbor there,   185
And reassembling our afflicted powers,
Consult how we may henceforth most offend
Our enemy, our own loss how repair,
How overcome this dire calamity,
What reinforcement we may gain from hope,   190
If not what resolution from despair."
Thus Satan talking to his nearest mate
With head uplift above the wave, and eyes
That sparkling blazed, his other parts besides
Prone on the flood, extended long and large   195
Lay floating many a rood, in bulk as huge
As whom the fables name of monstrous size,
Titanian, or Earth-born, that warred on Jove,
Briareos or Typhon, whom the den
By ancient Tarsus held, or that sea-beast   200
Leviathan, which God of all his works
Created hugest that swim th' ocean stream:
Him haply slumb'ring on the Norway foam
The pilot of some small night-foundered skiff,
Deeming some island, oft, as seamen tell,   205
With fixèd anchor in his scaly rind
Moors by his side under the lee, while night
Invests the sea, and wishèd morn delays:
So stretched out huge in length the Arch-Fiend lay
Chained on the burning lake, nor ever thence   210
Had ris'n or heaved his head, but that the will
And high permission of all-ruling Heaven
Left him at large to his own dark designs,
That with reiterated crimes he might
Heap on himself damnation, while he sought   215
Evil to others, and enraged might see
How all his malice served but to bring forth
Infinite goodness, grace and mercy shown

186. *afflicted*: overthrown. *powers*: army.
187. *offend*: (L *offendere* to hit, strike, dash against) harm, wound, pain; vex, annoy, displease
    Cf. VIII.379.
195. *large*: broad.
196. *rood*: a quarter of an acre.
197–200. In pagan mythology the gods were attacked by the Titans (the twelve children of Heaven
    and Earth) and their offspring, the Giants (partly human monsters, whose feet were serpents).
    Briareos was a rebellious monster with one hundred hands and Typhon was another, with one
    hundred serpent heads and fiery eyes. According to Hesiod Jove attacked Typhon with lightning,
    set him on fire, and hurled him into Tartarus (hell); according to Pindar Jove imprisoned him
    in a cave near *Tarsus* in Asia Minor. Christian mythographers moralized the revolt of Typhon
    as an analogy to the proud revolt of Satan.
200–208. *Leviathan* is an enemy of the Lord (Isa. 27.1) described as an amphibious behemoth,
    a huge crocodilelike dragon, in Job 40.15–41.34. He was identified by commentators with
    Satan, as was the whale. The story of the deceived sailor was common and had been moralized.
207. *under the lee*: out of the wind.
208. *Invests*: covers.

On man by him seduced, but on himself
Treble confusion, wrath and vengeance poured.   220
Forthwith upright he rears from off the pool
His mighty stature; on each hand the flames
Driv'n backward slope their pointing spires, and rolled
In billows, leave i' th' midst a horrid vale.
Then with expanded wings he steers his flight   225
Aloft, incumbent on the dusky air
That felt unusual weight, till on dry land
He lights, if it were land that ever burned
With solid, as the lake with liquid fire,
And such appeared in hue; as when the force   230
Of subterranean wind transports a hill
Torn from Pelorus, or the shattered side
Of thund'ring Etna, whose combustible
And fueled entrails thence conceiving fire,
Sublimed with mineral fury, aid the winds,   235
And leave a singèd bottom all involved
With stench and smoke: such resting found the sole
Of unblest feet. Him followed his next mate,
Both glorying to have scaped the Stygian flood
As gods, and by their own recovered strength,   240
Not by the sufferance of supernal power.
    "Is this the region, this the soil, the clime,"
Said then the lost Archangel, "this the seat
That we must change for heav'n, this mournful gloom
For that celestial light? Be it so, since he   245
Who now is sovran can dispose and bid
What shall be right: farthest from him is best
Whom reason hath equaled, force hath made supreme
Above his equals. Farwell happy fields

220. *confusion:* (L *confundere* to pour together) ruin, discomfiture, overthrow.
224. *horrid:* bristling (with the *spires* of flame).
226. *incumbent:* lying on.
229. As usual Milton's images are more factual than fanciful. The idea of the burning lake probably comes from accounts of the Dead Sea, on which floated a bituminous marl (see 296n), whose hydrocarbons furnished both an asphaltic mortar (as used in the Tower of Babel) and the "naphtha and asphaltus" that were burned for light in Pandemonium (see 728). The *solid* fire is explained in the note to line 296.
230–37. *Pelorus:* a promontory near Mount Etna in Sicily. *Sublimed:* vaporized. *mineral fury:* deeply buried energy, violence. Sublimed sulphur is produced by the spontaneous combustion of coal seams containing pyrites. *involved:* enveloped. *stench:* in this case, of sulphur dioxide. Cf. *Aen.* 3.570–77: "Aetna thunders with terrifying crashes, and now hurls forth to the sky a black cloud, smoking with pitch-black eddy and glowing ashes, and uplifts balls of flame and licks the stars—now violently vomits forth rocks, the mountain's uptorn entrails, and whirls molten stone skyward with a roar, and boils up from its lowest depths."
238. *unblest:* no longer blessed or enjoying the bliss of heaven.
239. *Stygian flood:* Styx-like gulf, lake, ocean.
243. *seat:* residence, especially a sumptuous one, a country estate.
244. *change:* exchange.

Where joy for ever dwells: hail horrors, hail   250
Infernal world, and thou profoundest hell
Receive thy new possessor: one who brings
A mind not to be changed by place or time.
The mind is its own place, and in itself
Can make a heav'n of hell, a hell of heav'n.   255
What matter where, if I be still the same,
And what I should be, all but less than he
Whom thunder hath made greater? Here at least
We shall be free; th' Almighty hath not built
Here for his envy, will not drive us hence: 260
Here we may reign secure, and in my choice
To reign is worth ambition though in hell:
Better to reign in hell, than serve in heav'n.
But wherefore let we then our faithful friends,
Th' associates and copartners of our loss   265
Lie thus astonished on th' oblivious pool,
And call them not to share with us their part
In this unhappy mansion, or once more
With rallied arms to try what may be yet
Regained in heav'n, or what more lost in hell?"   270
    So Satan spake, and him Beëlzebub
Thus answered. "Leader of those armies bright,
Which but th' Omnipotent none could have foiled,
If once they hear that voice, their liveliest pledge
Of hope in fears and dangers, heard so oft   275
In worst extremes, and on the perilous edge
Of battle when it raged, in all assaults
Their surest signal, they will soon resume
New courage and revive, though now they lie
Groveling and prostrate on yon lake of fire,   280
As we erewhile, astounded and amazed,
No wonder, fall'n such a pernicious highth."
    He scarce had ceased when the superior Fiend
Was moving toward the shore; his ponderous shield
Ethereal temper, massy, large and round,   285
Behind him cast; the broad circumference
Hung on his shoulders like the moon, whose orb

257. *all but less than:* barely less than, all but equal to; but the *OED* gives no examples.
260. *for his envy:* out of envy; i.e., "because he liked the place."
261. *secure:* L *sine* without + *cura* care, anxiety.
262. *ambition:* L *ambitio* great exertion.
266. *astonished:* stunned. *oblivious pool:* lake of forgetfulness.
268. *mansion:* dwelling place. Cf. John 14.2: "In my Father's house are many mansions: . . . I [Christ] go to prepare a place for you."
276. *edge:* a critical position or moment; front line of battle (like L *acies*).
282. *pernicious:* (L *per* + *nec-, nex* violent death) destructive.
283–313. See Harold Bloom's discussion of this passage on pp. 559ff., below.
285. *Ethereal.* See 45n.

Through optic glass the Tuscan artist views
At evening from the top of Fesole,
Or in Valdarno, to descry new lands, 290
Rivers or mountains in her spotty globe.
His spear, to equal which the tallest pine
Hewn on Norwegian hills, to be the mast
Of some great ammiral, were but a wand,
He walked with to support uneasy steps 295
Over the burning marl, not like those steps
On heaven's azure; and the torrid clime
Smote on him sore besides, vaulted with fire;
Nathless he so endured, till on the beach
Of that inflamèd sea, he stood and called 300
His legions, angel forms, who lay entranced
Thick as autumnal leaves that strow the brooks
In Vallombrosa, where th' Etrurian shades
High overarched embow'r; or scattered sedge
Afloat, when with fierce winds Orion armed 305
Hath vexed the Red Sea coast, whose waves o'erthrew
Busiris and his Memphian chivalry,
While with perfidious hatred they pursued
The sojourners of Goshen, who beheld
From the safe shore their floating carcasses 310
And broken chariot wheels. So thick bestrown
Abject and lost lay these, covering the flood,
Under amazement of their hideous change.
He called so loud, that all the hollow deep
Of hell resounded. "Princes, Potentates, 315
Warriors, the flow'r of heav'n, once yours, now lost,

288–91. When Milton visited him in 1638 Galileo was living in Tuscany, near Florence, which is in the valley of the Arno River below the hills of Fiesole (*Fesole*). Galileo, an *artist* because he knew the art of astronomy, had published in 1610 his descriptions of the mountains on the moon as seen through a telescope.
292. *to equal:* compared with.
292–94. Cf. *Aen.* 3.659: "In his hand a lopped pine guides and steadies his steps."
294. *ammiral:* admiral—a flagship.
296. *burning marl:* Milton's paraphrase of *brimstone* (ME *birnen* or *brinnen* to burn + *ston* stone), which is sulphur, an element commonly found in certain forms of calcium carbonates (or *marls*). From such sulphur-bearing marls the element is extracted by melting it in the intense heat generated by burning some of the sulphur itself. Cf. 350 and 562, below.
299. *Nathless:* nevertheless.
302. Cf. *Aen.* 6.309–10: "thick as the leaves of the forest that at autumn's first frost dropping fall."
303. Homer, Virgil, and Dante had compared the numberless dead with fallen leaves. *Vallombrosa* (literally "shady valley," with pun on *shades* as "spirits" or "souls") is a vale near Florence; Etruria was the classical name for the region that embraces modern Tuscany.
304–11. The Hebrew word for the Red Sea means "sedgy sea." *Orion*, a constellation configuring an armed man, was supposed to be a sign of stormy weather. When the Israelites (*sojourners of Goshen*) were fleeing from the Egyptians, God parted the waters of the Red Sea, let his people pass, and then let the waters flow together over the pursuing Egyptian army. See Exod. 14.5–31, pp. 434–35. Memphis was once the capital of Egypt. In Greek myth *Busiris*, son of Poseidon, was king of Egypt. Fowler notes that Christian mythographers had identified *Busiris* as the Pharaoh of Exod. 1. And early theologians had seen Pharaoh as a type of devil.

If such astonishment as this can seize
Eternal Spirits: or have ye chos'n this place
After the toil of battle to repose
Your wearied virtue, for the ease you find   320
To slumber here, as in the vales of heav'n?
Or in this abject posture have ye sworn
To adore the conqueror? who now beholds
Cherub and Seraph rolling in the flood
With scattered arms and ensigns, till anon   325
His swift pursuers from heav'n gates discern
Th' advantage, and descending tread us down
Thus drooping, or with linkèd thunderbolts
Transfix us to the bottom of this gulf.
Awake, arise, or be for ever fall'n."   330
      They heard, and were abashed, and up they sprung
Upon the wing, as when men wont to watch
On duty, sleeping found by whom they dread,
Rouse and bestir themselves ere well awake.
Nor did they not perceive the evil plight   335
In which they were, or the fierce pains not feel;
Yet to their general's voice they soon obeyed
Innumerable. As when the potent rod
Of Amram's son in Egypt's evil day
Waved round the coast, up called a pitchy cloud   340
Of locusts, warping on the eastern wind,
That o'er the realm of impious Pharaoh hung
Like night, and darkened all the land of Nile:
So numberless were those bad angels seen
Hovering on wing under the cope of hell   345
'Twixt upper, nether, and surrounding fires;
Till, as a signal giv'n, th' uplifted spear
Of their great Sultan waving to direct
Their course, in even balance down they light
On the firm brimstone, and fill all the plain;   350
A multitude, like which the populous North

319. *repose:* (L *reponere* to replace) restore.
320. *virtue:* power inherent in supernatural beings; physical strength; valor.
325. *ensigns:* military banners.
339. *Amram:* Moses's father; the plague of locusts is described in Exod. 10.12–15.
340. *coast:* region.
341. *warping:* moving in a swarm.
345. *cope:* vaulted ceiling.
351. The barbarian invasion of the civilized Roman Empire, which brought on the so-called Dark Ages, was something like the Flood (cf. *deluge*) of OT history. The Rhine and Danube rivers, which freeze in winter, form two sides of a triangle that can be seen as an emblem of the part of the human body covered by a loincloth (*loins* means generally the organs of reproduction). From this geographic region came the Vandals, who *poured* south into Italy and southwest through France and Spain to Gibraltar, then by sea to the coast of North Africa north of the Lybian desert. Cf. Job 38.29: "Out of whose womb came the ice? and the hoary frost of heaven, who hath gendered it?"

Poured never from her frozen loins, to pass
Rhene or the Danaw, when her barbarous sons
Came like a deluge on the South, and spread
Beneath Gibraltar to the Libyan sands.   355
Forthwith from every squadron and each band
The heads and leaders thither haste where stood
Their great commander; godlike shapes and forms
Excelling human, princely dignities,
And powers that erst in heaven sat on thrones;   360
Though of their names in heav'nly records now
Be no memorial, blotted out and razed
By their rebellion, from the Books of Life.
Nor had they yet among the sons of Eve
Got them new names, till wand'ring o'er the earth,   365
Through God's high sufferance for the trial of man,
By falsities and lies the greatest part
Of mankind they corrupted to forsake
God their Creator, and th' invisible
Glory of him that made them, to transform   370
Oft to the image of a brute, adorned
With gay religions full of pomp and gold,
And devils to adore for deities:
Then were they known to men by various names,
And various idols through the heathen world.   375
Say, Muse, their names then known, who first, who last,
Roused from the slumber on that fiery couch,
At their great emperor's call, as next in worth
Came singly where he stood on the bare strand,
While the promiscuous crowd stood yet aloof.   380
The chief were those who from the pit of hell
Roaming to seek their prey on earth, durst fix
Their seats long after next the seat of God,
Their altars by his altar, gods adored
Among the nations round, and durst abide   385

362. *razed:* erased.
363. *Books of Life:* God's records of those who will escape damnation. Cf. Rev. 21.27.
372. *gay religions:* showy, specious, (perhaps) immoral rites.
374f. Cf. *Aen.* 7.641ff. and *Il.* 2.484 (lists of warriors and leaders gathering together for battle).
376–521. See "Angels," pp. 466–68. In adapting to his own purposes the epic device of listing names of famous warriors, Milton identifies certain fallen angels as spirits who later became the false gods of Israel's neighboring nations. Bush notes that the catalogue "recalls places where the enemies of God and Israel were overthrown [and] relates [Milton's] fable to the corrupted world of history."
380. *promiscuous:* of various kinds mixed together. *aloof:* (related to *luff.* "To stand aloof" meant to head into the wind and stand clear of the shore) at a distance.
383–87. *the seat of God:* generally, the court or residence of his power and presence; but *Jehovah* was specifically *throned* in his *sanctuary,* the Holy of Holies, within the Temple, on the "mercy-seat" (cf. XI.2n), the solid gold cover on the Ark of the Covenant, at opposite ends of which were golden *Cherubim* facing one another, their outspread wings above their heads forming a canopy.

Jehovah thund'ring out of Zion, throned
Between the Cherubim; yea, often placed
Within his sanctuary itself their shrines,
Abomination; and with cursèd things
His holy rites, and solemn feasts profaned,   390
And with their darkness durst affront his light.
First Moloch, horrid king besmeared with blood
Of human sacrifice, and parents' tears,
Though for the noise of drums and timbrels loud
Their children's cries unheard, that passed through fire   395
To his grim idol. Him the Ammonite
Worshiped in Rabba and her wat'ry plain,
In Argob and in Basan, to the stream
Of Utmost Arnon. Nor content with such
Audacious neighborhood, the wisest heart   400
Of Solomon he led by fraud to build
His temple right against the temple of God
On that opprobrious hill, and made his grove
The pleasant valley of Hinnom, Tophet thence
And black Gehenna called, the type of hell.   405
Next Chemos, th' obscene dread of Moab's sons,
From Aroer to Nebo, and the wild
Of southmost Abarim; in Hesebon

387–91. For example, King Manasseh "did what was wrong in the eyes of the Lord. . . . He rebuilt the hill-shrines which his father Hezekiah had destroyed. . . . He built altars in the house of the Lord. . . . and the image he had made of the goddess Asherah he put in the house. . . ." [NEB] 2 Kings 21.2–7.

392–405. The brass idols of *Moloch* (whose name means "king") represented him with the head of a calf and arms outstretched to receive the *children* sacrificed to him. He was the god of the Ammonites, whose capital city, *Rabba* (modern Amman, in Jordan), was called the city of waters. He was also worshipped in neighboring countries. *Gehenna*, meaning *valley of Hinnom*, became a synonym for hell. The place was also called *Tophet*, a word whose root is Hebrew *toph*, meaning *"drum,"* perhaps in reference to the drums that were beaten to drown out the cries of the children being sacrificed. Cf. 1 Kings 11.1–7 [NEB]: "King Solomon was a lover of women, and besides Pharaoh's daughter he married many foreign women . . . from the nations with whom the Lord had forbidden the Israelites to intermarry, 'because,' he said, 'they will entice you to serve their gods.' But Solomon was devoted to them. . . . When he grew old, his wives turned his heart to follow other gods, and he did not remain wholly loyal to the Lord his God. . . . He built a hill-shrine for Kemosh, the loathsome god of Moab, on the height to the east of Jerusalem, and for Moloch, the loathsome god of the Ammonites." The Egyptian name for the planet Mars was *Moloch*, and Milton may have known of this association when he conceived of *Moloch* as warlike. *Argob, Basan,* and *Arnon* were lands east of the Dead Sea.

406–17. *Chemos* is the Kemosh for whom Solomon built a shrine beside the one for *Moloch*, on the *hill of scandal* (*opprobrious hill*), i.e., the Mount of Olives. A god of the Moabites (whose kingdom extended from the city of *Aroer* on the north, to *Nebo* on the east, to the mountains of *Abarim* on the south, to the Dead Sea, or *Asphaltic Pool* on the west), *Chemos* was thought by St. Jerome to be the same god as Priapus, the classical god of fertility represented as a grotesque figure with a prominent phalus. Cf. Num. 25.1–9 [NEB]: "When the Israelites were in Shittim [on their way from Egyptian captivity to the Promised Land], the people began to have intercourse with Moabite women, who invited them to the sacrifices offered to their gods; and they ate the sacrificial food and prostrated themselves before the Gods of Moab. The Israelites joined in the worship of the Baal of Peor. . . . One of the Israelites brought a Midianite woman into his family in open defiance of Moses and all the community of Israel, while they were weeping by the Tent of the Presence. Phinehas son of Eleazar, son of Aaron the priest,

And Horonaim, Seon's realm, beyond
The flow'ry dale of Sibma clad with vines,   410
And Elealè to th' Asphaltic Pool.
Peor his other name, when he enticed
Israel in Sittim on their march from Nile
To do him wanton rites, which cost them woe.
Yet thence his lustful orgies he enlarged   415
Even to that hill of scandal, by the grove
Of Moloch homicide, lust hard by hate;
Till good Josiah drove them thence to hell.
With these came they, who from the bord'ring flood
Of old Euphrates to the brook that parts   420
Egypt from Syrian ground, had general names
Of Baalim and Ashtaroth, those male,
These feminine. For Spirits when they please
Can either sex assume, or both; so soft
And uncompounded is their essence pure,   425
Not tied or manacled with joint or limb,
Nor founded on the brittle strength of bones,
Like cumbrous flesh; but in what shape they choose
Dilated or condensed, bright or obscure,
Can execute their airy purposes,   430
And works of love or enmity fulfill.
For those the race of Israel oft forsook
Their Living Strength, and unfrequented left
His righteous altar, bowing lowly down
To bestial gods; for which their heads as low   435
Bowed down in battle, sunk before the spear
Of despicable foes. With these in troop
Came Astoreth, whom the Phoenicians called
Astartè, queen of heav'n, with crescent horns;
To whose bright image nightly by the moon   440
Sidonian virgins paid their vows and songs,

saw him. He stepped out from the crowd and took up a spear, and he went into the inner room after the Israelite and transfixed the two of them, the Israelite and the woman, pinning them together. Thus the plague, which had attacked the Israelites, was brought to a stop, but twenty-four thousand had already died."

418. *Josiah.* Cf. 2 Chron. 34.3 [NEB]: "In the eighth year of his reign, when he was still a boy, he began to seek guidance of the God of his forefather, David; and in the twelfth year he began to purge Judah and Jerusalem of the hill-shrines and the sacred poles, and the carved idols and the images of metal. He saw to it that the altars for the Baalim were destroyed."

422. *Baalim* (pl. of Baal) and *Ashtaroth* (pl. of Ashtoreth) were collective names for sun gods and moon goddesses of Phoenicia (Syria) and Palestine.

423–31. See "Angels," pp. 466–68.

437–46. King Josiah also desecrated "on the east of Jerusalem, to the south of the Mount of Olives . . . the hillshrines which Solomon the king of Israel had built for Ashtoreth the loathsome goddess of the Sidonians" (2 Kings 23.13, NEB). Sidon was a rich trading city of the Phoenicians on the coast of Syria. *Astarte*, a fertility goddess represented as a woman with the head of a bull whose horns resembled a crescent moon, was the Phoenician version of Aphrodite. *heart though large.* Cf. 1 Kings 4.29: "God gave Solomon . . . largeness of heart [the translators' word for the Hebrew word for intellect]."

In Sion also not unsung, where stood
Her temple on th' offensive mountain, built
By that uxorious king, whose heart though large,
Beguiled by fair idolatresses, fell   445
To idols foul. Thammuz came next behind,
Whose annual wound in Lebanon allured
The Syrian damsels to lament his fate
In amorous ditties all a summer's day,
While smooth Adonis from his native work   450
Ran purple to the sea, supposed with blood
Of Thammuz yearly wounded: the love-tale
Infected Sion's daughters with like heat,
Whose wanton passions in the sacred porch
Ezekiel saw, when by the vision led   455
His eye surveyed the dark idolatries
Of alienated Judah. Next came one
Who mourned in earnest, when the captive ark
Maimed his brute image, head and hands lopped off
In his own temple, on the grunsel edge,   460
Where he fell flat, and shamed his worshipers:
Dagon his name, sea monster, upward man
And downward fish: yet had his temple high
Reared in Azotus, dreaded through the coast
Of Palestine, in Gath and Ascalon   465
And Accaron and Gaza's frontier bounds.
Him followed Rimmon, whose delightful seat
Was fair Damascus, on the fertile banks
Of Abbana and Pharphar, lucid streams.

446–57. Cf. Ezek. 8.12–14 [NEB]: " 'Man,' he said to me, 'do you see what the elders of Israel
are doing in darkness, each at the shrine of his own carved image? . . . You will see,' he said,
'yet more monstrous abominations which they practise.' Then he brought me to that gateway
of the Lord's house which faces north; and there I saw women sitting and wailing for Tammuz."
Thammuz was the Phoenician name for Adonis, a very ancient god presiding over the cycle
of death and rebirth of vegetation. He was the beloved of Aphrodite. Adonis was killed by a
wild boar in Lebanon, where rises the river Adonis, whose waters, reddish from the soil they
carried, were believed by the *Syrian damsels* to be colored by the blood of the god.
457–66. The mourning for *Thammuz* was insincere compared with *Dagon's* mourning for his
own fate. He was the god of the Israelites' enemy, the Philistines, whose chief cities were the
five named in 464–66. Cf. 1 Sam. 5.1–5 [NEB]: "After the Philistines had captured the Ark
of God, they brought it from Eben-ezer to Ashdod; and there they carried it into the temple
of Dagon and set it beside Dagon himself. When the people of Ashdod rose next morning,
there was Dagon fallen face downwards before the Ark of the Lord; so they took him and put
him back in his place. Next morning when they rose, Dagon had again fallen face downwards
before the Ark of the Lord, with his head and his two hands lying broken off beside his platform.
This is why . . . the priests of Dagon . . . do not set foot on Dagon's platform." For *platform*
the King James Version reads *threshold*, Milton's *grunsel*.
467–76. *Rimmon*, a Phoenician god, had a temple in the fabulously beautiful city of *Damascus*.
When Naaman, a commander of the Syrian army, came to Israel in search of a cure for his
leprosy, Elisha told him to wash in the river Jordan. Naaman at first indignantly refused: were
not *Abbana* and *Pharphar* "better than all the waters of Israel"? But he finally consented, was
cured, and renounced his allegiance to *Rimmon* (2 Kings 5.1ff.). King Ahaz, the Israelite
conqueror of Damascus, on the other hand, was much taken by an altar to *Rimmon*, sent
sketches of it back home with orders to have it reproduced, and on his return worshipped the
foreign god (2 Kings 16.10–18). *sottish*: ME *sot*, a fool.

He also against the house of God was bold: 470
A leper once he lost and gained a king,
Ahaz his sottish conqueror, whom he drew
God's altar to disparage and displace
For one of Syrian mode, whereon to burn
His odious off'rings, and adore the gods   475
Whome he had vanquished. After these appeared
A crew who under names of old renown,
Osiris, Isis, Orus and their train
With monstrous shapes and sorceries abused
Fanatic Egypt and her priests, to seek   480
Their wand'ring gods disguised in brutish forms
Rather than human. Nor did Israel scape
Th' infection when their borrowed gold composed
The calf in Oreb: and the rebel king
Doubled that sin in Bethel and in Dan,   485
Lik'ning his Maker to the grazèd ox,
Jehovah, who in one night when he passed
From Egypt marching, equaled with one stroke
Both her first-born and all her bleating gods.
Belial came last, than whom a Spirit more lewd   490
Fell not from heaven, or more gross to love
Vice for itself: to him no temple stood
Or altar smoked; yet who more oft than he
In temples and at altars, when the priest
Turns atheist, as did Eli's sons, who filled   495
With lust and violence the house of God.
In courts and palaces he also reigns
And in luxurious cities, where the noise
Of riot ascends above their loftiest tow'rs,
And injury and outrage: and when night   500
Darkens the streets, then wander forth the sons

476–89. According to Ovid (*Met.* 5.319ff.), when the Giants invaded Olympus some of the gods fled in terror to Egypt, wandering there *disguised* as various animals. *Osiris*, in the image of a bull, and his wife, *Isis*, represented as a cow, were (among other things) fertility gods. *Orus* was their son. By killing in one night the firstborn of all the Egyptian people and of all their cattle (*bleating gods*), Jehovah forced the Pharaoh to free the captive Israelites; but first he told the Israelites to "borrow" (NEB: "ask for") gold and silver jewelry from their "well-disposed" Egyptian neighbors. Later, on the journey home, while Moses was on Mount *Oreb* receiving God's word, the Israelites, impatient at his failure to return promptly, melted down their gold, made an image of a bull-calf, worshipped it, and "gave themselves up to revelry" [NEB]. Much later in the history of the nation, King Jeroboam, who had been in exile in Egypt before he led a successful revolution, set up two golden calves in *Bethel* and *Dan*, the two extremities of the kingdom of Israel. Cf. Exod. 11, 12, 32 and 1 Kings 12. *abused:* deceived.

490–505. *Belial* in Hebrew means simply "wickedness," but the phrases "children of belial" and "sons of belial," as they are used in the OT led to personification, as in Paul's second letter to the Corinthians: "What concord hath Christ with Belial?" (6.15), and Christians came to think of "him" as a devil. Milton conceived of *Belial* as a "sensualist . . . the fleshliest incubus," "to vice industrious" (*PR*, II.150–52. and *PL*, I.116). The sons of Eli were priests who corrupted the ceremony of sacrifice and "lay with the women who were serving at the entrance of the [Tabernacle]" (1 Sam. 2.12–25). The references to *Sodom* (Gen. 19) and *Gibeah* (Judg. 19) identify homosexual rapists as men of *Belial*.

Of Belial, flown with insolence and wine.
Witness the streets of Sodom, and that night
In Gibeah, when the hospitable door
Exposed a matron to avoid worse rape.   505
These were the prime in order and in might;
The rest were long to tell, though far renowned,
Th' Ionian gods, of Javan's issue held
Gods, yet confessed later than Heav'n and Earth
Their boasted parents; Titan Heav'n's first-born   510
With his enormous brood, and birthright seized
By younger Saturn, he from mightier Jove
His own and Rhea's son like measure found;
So Jove usurping reigned: these first in Crete
And Ida known, thence on the snowy top   515
Of cold Olympus ruled the middle air
Their highest heav'n; or on the Delphian cliff,
Or in Dodona, and through all the bounds
Of Doric land; or who with Saturn old
Fled over Adria to th' Hesperian fields,   520
And o'er the Celtic roamed the utmost isles.
All these and more came flocking; but with looks
Downcast and damp, yet such wherein appeared
Obscure some glimpse of joy, to have found their chief
Not in despair, to have found themselves not lost   525
In loss itself; which on his count'nance cast
Like doubtful hue: but he his wonted pride
Soon recollecting, with high words, that bore
Semblance of worth, not substance, gently raised
Their fainting courage, and dispelled their fears.   530
Then straight commands that at the warlike sound
Of trumpets loud and clarions be upreared
His mighty standard; that proud honor claimed
Azazel as his right, a Cherub tall:
Who forthwith from the glittering staff unfurled   535
Th' imperial ensign, which full high advanced

502. *flown:* (archaic past participle of *flow*) filled to excess; therefore, swollen—as well as *flushed*, a word from the same L stem as *flow*.
508–21. Biblical commentators had suggested that the Greeks (*Ionians*) were the descendants of the biblical *Javan*, a grandson of Noah. Of the various versions available to him Milton chose the story that *Saturn*, youngest of the *Titan* sons of *Heaven* and *Earth*, overthrew his oldest brother to seize the throne, and that he in turn was overthrown by his own son *Jove*, who reigned on Mount Ida in *Crete*, then in various other places in Greece till he had to flee over the Adriatic to Italy, France, and Great Britain (*the utmost isles*).
516. *middle air.* See 10–15n.
523. *damp:* stupefied.
528. *recollecting:* recovering, rallying.
532. *clarions:* shrill trumpets used in war.
534. *Azazel.* See "Angels," pp. 466–68.
535–39. This flag of the empire of hell contained the coats of arms of the various orders of the fallen angels as well as devices memorializing the battles they had fought.

Shone like a meteor streaming to the wind
With gems and golden luster rich emblazed,
Seraphic arms and trophies: all the while
Sonorous metal blowing martial sounds: 540
At which the universal host upsent
A shout that tore hell's concave, and beyond
Frighted the reign of Chaos and old Night.
All in a moment through the gloom were seen
Ten thousand banners rise into the air   545
With orient colors waving: with them rose
A forest huge of spears: and thronging helms
Appeared, and serried shields in thick array
Of depth immeasurable: anon they move
In perfect phalanx to the Dorian mood   550
Of flutes and soft recorders; such as raised
To highth of noblest temper heroes old
Arming to battle, and instead of rage
Deliberate valor breathed, firm and unmoved
With dread of death to flight or foul retreat,   555
Nor wanting power to mitigate and swage
With solemn touches, troubled thoughts, and chase
Anguish and doubt and fear and sorrow and pain
From mortal or immortal minds. Thus they
Breathing united force with fixèd thought   560
Moved on in silence to soft pipes that charmed
Their painful steps o'er the burnt soil; and now
Advanced in view they stand, a horrid front
Of dreadful length and dazzling arms, in guise
Of warriors old with ordered spear and shield,   565
Awaiting what command their mighty chief
Had to impose: he through the armèd files
Darts his experienced eye, and soon traverse
The whole battalion views, their order due,
Their visages and stature as of gods,   570
Their number last he sums. And now his heart
Distends with pride, and hard'ning in his strength
Glories: for never since created man,
Met such embodied force, as named with these

542. *concave:* commonly meant "the vault of heaven," as Fowler notes.
546. *orient:* sparkling.
548. *serried:* pressed close together.
550. *perfect phalanx:* "a square battle formation common in Milton's time" (Fowler). *Dorian mood:* one of the three musical modes in ancient Greece (the others. Phrygian and Lydian). It was distinguished for its manly and grave style. To such music the Spartans marched to battle.
563. *horrid:* bristling.
567–69. Satan reviews the troops rank (*traverse*) and *file.*

Could merit more than that small infantry   575
Warred on by cranes: though all the giant brood
Of Phlegra with th' heroic race were joined
That fought at Thebes and Ilium, on each side
Mixed with auxiliar gods; and what resounds
In fable or romance of Uther's son   580
Begirt with British and Armoric knights;
And all who since, baptized or infidel
Jousted in Aspramont or Montalban,
Damascó, or Marocco, or Trebisond,
Or whom Biserta sent from Afric shore   585
When Charlemain with all his peerage fell
By Fontarabbia. Thus far these beyond
Compare of mortal prowess, yet observed
Their dread commander: he above the rest
In shape and gesture proudly eminent   590
Stood like a tow'r; his form had yet not lost
All her original brightness, nor appeared
Less than Archangel ruined, and th' excess
Of glory obscured: as when the sun ris'n
Looks through the horizontal misty air   595
Shorn of his beams, or from behind the moon
In dim eclipse disastrous twilight sheds
On half the nations, and with fear of change
Perplexes monarchs. Darkened so, yet shone
Above them all th' Archangel: but his face   600
Deep scars of thunder had intrenched, and care
Sat on his faded cheek, but under brows
Of dauntless courage, and considerate pride
Waiting revenge: cruel his eye, but cast
Signs of remorse and passion to behold   605

575. *small infantry*: the Pygmies referred to by Homer (*Il.* 3.6) and described by Pliny as little people (note Milton's pun on *infant*) living in India. Hughes cites Wm. Cunningham's *Cosmographical Glasse* (London, 1559), where they are said to be about eighteen inches high and to ride on goats in battle against cranes.
577. *Phlegra*: a place in Thessaly where, in Greek myth, the Giants battled the gods. But Milton may allude to the Phlegraean plains near Mt. Vesuvius, where in Roman myth Jupiter fought the Giants with thunderbolts that left the region a volcanic desert, like hell.
578. *Thebes and Ilium*. Milton refers to the great epic stories of the war between the sons of Oedipus at Thebes and the war between the Greeks and the Trojans at Troy, in which various gods assisted certain of the heroes.
579–87. *Uther's son*: King Arthur. *Armoric*: from Brittany. *Aspramont and Montalban* are castles in Ariosto's *Orlando Furioso*. Damascus and *Trebisond* were scenes of tournaments in the wars between the Christians and the Saracens. *Bsierta* in Tunis was a Saracen city. In the *Song of Roland* Roland (not *Charlemain*) died at Roncevalles, not far from *Fontarrabia*.
588. *observed*: acknowledged the authority, superiority, of.
592. *her*. L *forma* (feminine) means shape, appearance, beauty, pattern, nature—cf. Gk *idea*. See VII.557n.
594. *glory*: splendor. *obscured*: darkened.
597. *disastrous*: (L *dis* + *astrum* star) astrologically unfavorable.
603. *considerate*: (L *considerare*, literally, to observe the stars) circumspect, wary.
605. *remorse*: (L *remordere* to bite again) pangs of conscience. *passion*: suffering. The emphasis is on Satan's pain, not his love.

The fellows of his crime, the followers rather
(Far other once beheld in bliss) condemned
For ever now to have their lot in pain,
Millions of Spirits for his fault amerced
Of heav'n, and from eternal splendors flung   610
For his revolt, yet faithful how they stood,
Their glory withered: as when heaven's fire
Hath scathed the forest oaks, or mountain pines,
With singèd top their stately growth though bare
Stands on the blasted heath. He now prepared   615
To speak; whereat their doubled ranks they bend
From wing to wing, and half enclose him round
With all his peers: attention held them mute.
Thrice he assayed, and thrice in spite of scorn,
Tears such as angels weep, burst forth: at last   620
Words interwove with sighs found out their way.
　　"O myriads of immortal Spirits, O Powers
Matchless, but with th' Almighty, and that strife
Was not inglorious, though th' event was dire,
As this place testifies, and this dire change   625
Hateful to utter: but what power of mind
Foreseeing or presaging, from the depth
Of knowledge past or present, could have feared,
How such united force of gods, how such
As stood like these, could ever know repulse?   630
For who can yet believe, though after loss,
That all these puissant legions, whose exile
Hath emptied heav'n, shall fail to reascend
Self-raised, and repossess their native seat?
For me, be witness all the host of heav'n,   635
If counsels different, or danger shunned
By me, have lost our hopes. But he who reigns
Monarch in heav'n, till then as one secure
Sat on his throne, upheld by old repute,
Consent or custom, and his regal state   640
Put forth at full, but still his strength concealed,
Which tempted our attempt, and wrought our fall.
Henceforth his might we know, and know our own
So as not either to provoke, or dread
New war, provoked; our better part remains   645
To work in close design, by fraud or guile
What force effected not: that he no less

609. *amerced*: fined; i.e., punished by being deprived.
619. *Thrice . . . thrice*: cf. *Il.* 21.176–77, *Od.* 11.206–7, *Aen.* 6.700–701.
624. *event*: outcome.
636. *different*: differing.
646. *close*: concealed.

At length from us may find, who overcomes
By force, hath overcome but half his foe.
Space may produce new worlds; whereof so rife   650
There went a fame in heav'n that he ere long
Intended to create, and therein plant
A generation, whom his choice regard
Should favor equal to the sons of heaven:
Thither, if but to pry, shall be perhaps   655
Our first eruption, thither or elsewhere:
For this infernal pit shall never hold
Celestial Spirits in bondage, not th' abyss
Long under darkness cover. But these thoughts
Full counsel must mature: peace is despaired,   660
For who can think submission? War then, war
Open or understood must be resolved."
    He spake: and to confirm his words, out flew
Millions of flaming swords, drawn from the thighs
Of mighty Cherubim; the sudden blaze   665
Far round illumined hell: highly they raged
Against the Highest, and fierce with graspèd arms
Clashed on their sounding shields the din of war,
Hurling defiance toward the vault of heav'n.
    There stood a hill not far whose grisly top   670
Belched fire and rolling smoke; the rest entire
Shone with a glossy scurf, undoubted sign
That in his womb was hid metallic ore,
The work of sulphur. Thither winged with speed
A numerous brígade hastened. As when bands   675
Of pioneers with spade and pickax armed
Forerun the royal camp, to trench a field,
Or cast a rampart. Mammon led them on,
Mammon, the least erected Spirit that fell
From heav'n, for ev'n in heav'n his looks and thoughts   680
Were always downward bent, admiring more
The riches of heav'n's pavement, trodden gold,
Than aught divine or holy else enjoyed

650–54. Milton does not say how the rumor got started. In VII.150–61, God implies that the
    creation of man was a consquence of the revolt of the angels. See CD, I.vii.
653. *generation:* (L *genus* stock, race) family, breed, race. *choice:* discriminative.
656. *eruption:* (L *erumpere* to break out, burst forth) sallying forth (as of soldiers from a fort),
    escape (as from a prison); outbreak (as of a disease or a volcano).
662. *understood:* undeclared.
672–74. *scurf:* a hard crust made of a volcanic mixture of hydrocarbons and sulphur. Alchemists
    believed that sulphur was the "father" of all metals.
676. *pioneers:* military engineers.
679. The word *mammon,* meaning "riches," appears in Matt. 6.24: "Ye cannot serve God and
    mammon." Commentators identified the "prince of this world" (John 12.31) as Mammon,
    and this personification became a kind of Christian equivalent of Plutus. The angelologists
    made him prince of the lowest order of angels.
682. *gold.* Cf. Rev. 21.2

In vision beatific: by him first
Men also, and by his suggestion taught,   685
Ransacked the center, and with impious hands
Rifled the bowels of their mother earth
For treasures better hid. Soon had his crew
Opened into the hill a spacious wound
And digged out ribs of gold. Let none admire   690
That riches grow in hell; that soil may best
Deserve the precious bane. And here let those
Who boast in mortal things, and wond'ring tell
Of Babel, and the works of Memphian kings,
Learn how their greatest monuments of fame,   695
And strength and art are easily outdone
By Spirits reprobate, and in an hour
What in an age they with incessant toil
And hands innumerable scarce perform.
Nigh on the plain in many cells prepared,   700
That underneath had veins of liquid fire
Sluiced from the lake, a second multitude
With wondrous art founded the massy ore,
Severing each kind, and scummed the bullion dross:
A third as soon had formed within the ground   705
A various mold, and from the boiling cells
By strange conveyance filled each hollow nook,
As in an organ from one blast of wind
To many a row of pipes the soundboard breathes.
Anon out of the earth a fabric huge   710

684. *vision beatific*: a theological term meaning the mystical experience of seeing God in the glory of heaven.
685–88. Cf. *Met.* 1.138ff.: "they delved as well into the very bowels of the earth; and the wealth which the creator had hidden away and buried deep amidst the very Stygian shades, was brought to light, wealth that pricks men on to crime."
690. *ribs*: the solid parts of a vein of ore (technical term). *admire*: wonder.
692. *bane*: (OE. *bana* murderer) what destroys life, deadly poison, ruin, cause of ruin.
694. The tower of *Babel* is described in Gen. 11.1–9, p. 433. *works*: i.e., the Pyramids.
697. *reprobate*: (L *reprobare* to disapprove, from *re* + *probare* to test, prove) condemned.
703–4. *founded*: melted. *massy*: of high specific gravity. *Severing*: separating. *bullion*: (L to be in bubbling motion) of unrefined gold. *dross*: scum produced by boiling impure metals.
710–30. The exterior of a classical temple in the Doric style (like the Parthenon—or the Pantheon, in Rome, which fits Milton's description in detail) consisted of a row of fluted columns supporting (*overlaid With*) an entablature of three layers of stone: the *architrave*, sometimes covered with gold leaf; the *frieze*, a row of figures carved (embossed, *bossy*) in relief; and the *cornice*, a thin band of stone, sculptured or otherwise ornamented. Within this outer row of columns was an inner wall whose surface was interrupted by *pilasters*, rectangular columns partially projecting from the wall surface. *Pandemonium* (756) is a building (*fabric*) of monumental architecture for political congresses, and in the Argument Milton calls it the Palace of Satan; but by describing it in terms of a classical temple and contrasting it with Assyrian and Egyptian shrines, Milton suggests its religious as well as political functions. This mixture of worldly and spiritual powers might remind Milton's readers of St. Peter's in Rome. And though the pure Doric style of Pandemonium may have been more to Milton's taste than the art of *Babylon* and Memphis (*Alcairo*), still the emphasis on its magnificence would have made it seem sinful to Puritans, who believed, with Milton, that God preferred "Before all temples th' upright heart and pure." *fretted*: richly ornamented. *Belus or Serapis*: alternate names for Baal and Osiris. *cressets*: iron baskets holding coal or pitched rope burnt for illumination.

Rose like an exhalation, with the sound
Of dulcet symphonies and voices sweet,
Built like a temple, where pilasters round
Were set, and Doric pillars overlaid
With golden architrave; nor did there want   715
Cornice or frieze, with bossy sculptures grav'n;
The roof was fretted gold. Not Babylon,
Nor great Alcairo such magnificence
Equaled in all their glories, to enshrine
Belus or Serapis their gods, or seat   720
Their kings, when Egypt with Assyria strove
In wealth and luxury. Th' ascending pile
Stood fixed her stately highth, and straight the doors
Opening their brazen folds discover wide
Within, her ample spaces, o'er the smooth   725
And level pavement: from the archèd roof
Pendent by subtle magic many a row
Of starry lamps and blazing cressets fed
With naphtha and asphaltus yielded light
As from a sky. The hasty multitude   730
Admiring entered, and the work some praise
And some the architect: his hand was known
In heav'n by many a towered structure high,
Where sceptered angels held their residence,
And sat as princes, whom the Súpreme King   735
Exalted to such power, and gave to rule,
Each in his hierarchy, the orders bright.
Nor was his name unheard or unadored
In ancient Greece and in Ausonian land
Men called him Mulciber; and how he fell   740
From heav'n, they fabled, thrown by angry Jove
Sheer o'er the crystal battlements: from morn
To noon he fell, from noon to dewy eve,
A summer's day; and with the setting sun

Among the arts incorporated in this description of the building of Pandemonium are two Milton may have observed. One is that of casting large ornamental iron or bronze gates, doors, railings, etc. Milton imagines the temple as one gigantic casting made by pouring molten metal into an intricate mold dug out of the earth. The other is stagecraft: when the building rose out of the earth it did so as buildings were made, by means of elaborate machinery, to rise out of the stage in masques designed by Inigo Jones for great court performances.
726–30. Cf. *Aen.* 1.725–27: "A din arises in the palace and voices roll through the spacious halls; lighted lamps hang down from the fretted roof of gold, and flaming torches drive out the night."
732–51. *Mulciber*, meaning "one who refines ore by melting it and pouring it into a mould," was another name for Vulcan, a Roman fire god, or god of smiths, identified with the Greek god of fire and arts, Hephaestus, the son of Hera, who is said to have thrown him out of heaven because he was born lame, and Zeus (*Jove*), who in another version is said to have thrown him out because in a quarrel between his parents he took his mother's side. Homer (*Il.* 1.590) says the fall lasted a day and ended on Lemnos. *Ausonian land*: Italy.

Dropped from the zenith like a falling star,   745
On Lemnos th' Aégean isle: thus they relate,
Erring; for he with this rebellious rout
Fell long before; nor aught availed him now
To have built in heav'n high tow'rs; nor did he scape
By all his engines, but was headlong sent   750
With his industrious crew to build in hell.
Meanwhle the wingèd heralds by command
Of sovran power, with awful ceremony
And trumpet's sound throughout the host proclaim
A solemn council forthwith to be held   755
At Pandemonium, the high capitol
Of Satan and his peers: their summons called
From every band and squarèd regiment
By place or choice the worthiest; they anon
With hundreds and with thousands trooping came   760
Attended: all access was thronged, the gates
And porches wide, but chief the spacious hall
(Though like a covered field, where champions bold
Wont ride in armed, and at the Soldan's chair
Defied the best of paynim chivalry   765
To mortal combat or career with lance)
Thick swarmed, both on the ground and in the air,
Brushed with the hiss of rustling wings. As bees
In springtime, when the sun with Taurus rides,
Pour forth their populous youth about the hive   770
In clusters; they among fresh dews and flowers
Fly to and fro, or on the smoothèd plank,
The suburb of their straw-built citadel,

746–47. The poet's Muse, or Milton as bard, comments. On Milton's Christian views of the truth of pagan myths see "Truth and Poetry," pp. 473–74.
750. *engines*. Vulcan was a man of ingenuity—inventor of things as well as of tricks.
756. *Pandemonium*. Milton invents a Gk name from *pan* all + *daimonion* (evil) spirits, demons—analogous with *pantheion* temple of all the gods. *capitol*. In the ms. of Bk. I *Capitoll* was corrected to *Capitall*, as it appears in the first and second editions. But, as Helen Darbishire pointed out, Milton probably meant *capitol*, which comes from L *capitolium*, the temple of Jupiter on the Capitoline Hill, and means a building in which a legislative body meets.
759. *By place or choice*: ex officio or by election. *worthiest*: highest-ranking.
760. *hundreds*. Milton called for this spelling in the list of *errata* added to a later printing of the first edition.
764. *Wont*: were wont to. *Soldan's*: Sultan's.
765. *paynim*: pagan.
768–88. Bee similes were commonplace in the epic tradition from Homer through the Renaissance. Milton characteristically enriched the significance of his version with meaningful detail. Instead of wild bees (as in Homer and others) Milton refers to a domestic swarm, housed in a man-made work of art—a hive of woven straw set on a plank that the beekeeper has made glassy smooth with the same kind of balsam gum bees themselves use to smooth any rough place on which they congregate. The dome of St. Peter's is shaped like a hive; St. Peter's Square is like the plank; when Milton was in Rome, the Pope's personal insignia was a bee and his followers were called "bees." The grand irony is perhaps in God as beekeeper, but the strawbuilt citadel and the smooth, balm-rubbed plank are typical of Milton's sardonic humor. Cf. *Il.* 2.87–90: "Even as when the tribes of thronging bees issue from some hollow rock, ever in

New rubbed with balm, expatiate and confer
Their state affairs. So thick the aery crowd   775
Swarmed and were straitened; till the signal giv'n,
Behold a wonder! they but now who seemed
In bigness to surpass Earth's giant sons
Now less than smallest dwarfs, in narrow room
Throng numberless, like that Pygmean race   780
Beyond the Indian mount, or fairy elves,
Whose midnight revels, by a forest side
Or fountain some belated peasant sees,
Or dreams he sees, while overhead the moon
Sits arbitress, and nearer to the earth   785
Wheels her pale course: they on their mirth and dance
Intent, with jocund music charm his ear;
At once with joy and fear his heart rebounds.
Thus incorporeal Spirits to smallest forms
Reduced their shapes immense, and were at large,   790
Though without number still amidst the hall
Of that infernal court. But far within
And in their own dimensions like themselves
The great Seraphic Lords and Cherubim
In close recess and secret conclave sat   795
A thousand demi-gods on golden seats,
Frequent and full. After short silence then
And summons read, the great consult began.

Book II

The Argument

The consultation begun, Satan debates whether another battle be to
be hazarded for the recovery of heaven: some advise it, others dissuade:
a third proposal is preferred, mentioned before by Satan, to search the
truth of that prophecy or tradition in heaven concerning another world,

---

fresh procession, and fly clustering among the flowers of spring, and some on this hand and
some on that fly thick . . ." and *Aen.* 1.430–36: "Even as bees in early summer, amid flowery
fields, ply their task in sunshine, when they lead forth the full-grown young of their race, or
pack the fluid honey and strain their cells to bursting with sweet nectar, or receive the burdens
of incomers, or in martial array drive from their folds the drones, a lazy herd; all aglow is the
work and the fragrant honey is sweet with thyme." *with Taurus rides:* is in the sign of Taurus.
expatiate: walk about (suggesting "to expatiate upon"). *confer:* discuss. *Earth's giant sons:* the
Titans of Greek mythology. *Pygmean race.* See I.575n. *arbitress:* presiding authority (over the
fairy revels).
795. *close recess:* secret place. *conclave:* L word meaning "a room that can be locked." The
meeting of Cardinals at which the Pope is elected is called a conclave.
797. *Frequent and full:* (an idiom) crowded together in great numbers.
798. *consult:* a meeting for consultation; in the seventeenth century, often a secret, seditious
meeting.·

and another kind of creature equal or not much inferior to themselves, about this time to be created: their doubt who shall be sent on this difficult search: Satan their chief undertakes alone the voyage, is honored and applauded. The council thus ended, the rest betake them several ways and to several employments, as their inclinations lead them, to entertain the time till Satan return. He passes on his journey to hell gates, finds them shut, and who sat there to guard them, by whom at length they are opened, and discover to him the great gulf between hell and heaven; with what difficulty he passes through, directed by Chaos, the power of that place, to the sight of this new world which he sought.

High on a throne of royal state, which far
Outshone the wealth of Ormus and of Ind,
Or where the gorgeous East with richest hand
Show'rs on her kings barbaric pearl and gold,
Satan exalted sat, by merit raised   5
To that bad eminence; and from despair
Thus high uplifted beyond hope, aspires
Beyond thus high, insatiate to pursue
Vain war with Heav'n, and by success untaught
His proud imaginations thus displayed.   10
   "Powers and Dominions, deities of heaven,
For since no deep within her gulf can hold
Immortal vigor, though oppressed and fall'n,
I give not heav'n for lost. From this descent
Celestial Virtues rising, will appear   15
More glorious and more dread than from no fall,
And trust themselves to fear no second fate:
Me though just right, and the fixed laws of heav'n
Did first create your leader, next, free choice,
With what besides, in counsel or in fight,   20
Hath been achieved of merit, yet this loss
Thus far at least recovered, hath much more
Established in a safe unenvied throne
Yielded with full consent. The happier state
In heaven, which follows dignity, might draw   25
Envy from each inferior; but who here
Will envy whom the highest place exposes
Foremost to stand against the thunderer's aim

II.1–485. Cf. *Il.* 1.54ff. (councils of leaders as in many epics).
2. *Ormus:* Hormuz, trading town on the Persian Gulf, then famous for spices, drugs, diamonds, and pearls. *Ind:* India.
5. *merit:* that for which a person deserves reward or punishment. Cf. I.98; II.21; III.309.
6. *eminence:* (L *eminere* to project) height, rank.
9. *success:* (L *succedere* to follow after) outcome. But, as with *merit*, the normally positive connotation produces Milton's characteristic irony.
10. *imaginations:* schemes, plots.
11. *Dominions:* synonym for *Dominations*, one of the angelic orders. See "Angels," pp. 466–68.
15. *Virtues:* another angelic order.

Your bulwark, and condemns to greatest share
Of endless pain? Where there is then no good   30
For which to strive, no strife can grow up there
From faction; for none sure will claim in hell
Precédence, none, whose portion is so small
Of present pain, that with ambitious mind
Will covet more. With this advantage then   35
To union, and firm faith, and firm accord,
More than can be in heav'n, we now return
To claim our just inheritance of old,
Surer to prosper than prosperity
Could have assured us; and by what best way,   40
Whether of open war or covert guile,
We now debate; who can advise, may speak."
    He ceas'd, and next him Moloch, sceptered king
Stood up, the strongest and the fiercest Spirit
That fought in heav'n; now fiercer by despair: 45
His trust was with th' Eternal to be deemed
Equal in strength, and rather than be less
Cared not to be at all; with that care lost
Went all his fear: of God, or hell, or worse
He recked not, and these words thereafter spake.   50
    "My sentence is for open war: of wiles,
More unexpert, I boast not: them let those
Contrive who need, or when they need, not now.
For while they sit contriving, shall the rest,
Millions that stand in arms, and longing wait   55
The signal to ascend, sit lingering here
Heav'n's fugitives, and for their dwelling-place
Accept this dark opprobrious den of shame,
The prison of his tyranny who reigns
By our delay? No, let us rather choose   60
Armed with hell flames and fury all at once
O'er heav'n's high tow'rs to force resistless way,
Turning our tortures into horrid arms
Against the torturer; when to meet the noise
Of his almighty engine he shall hear   65
Infernal thunder, and for lightning see
Black fire and horror shot with equal rage
Among his angels; and his throne itself

50. *recked*: took heed. *thereafter*: accordingly.
51. *sentence*: opinion.
52. *unexpert*: inexperienced.
63. *horrid*: bristling.
65. *engine*: machine of war; i.e., thunder.
68–69. The throne of God was "like the fiery flame" (Dan. 7.9), a pure fire that Moloch proposes
    to adulterate with fires of hell.

Mixed with Tartarean sulfur, and strange fire,
His own invented torments. But perhaps   70
The way seems difficult and steep to scale
With upright wing against a higher foe.
Let such bethink them, if the sleepy drench
Of that forgetful lake denumb not still,
That in our proper motion we ascend   75
Up to our native seat: descent and fall
To us is adverse. Who but felt of late
When the fierce foe hung on our broken rear
Insulting, and pursued us through the deep,
With what compulsion and laborious flight   80
We sunk thus low? Th' ascent is easy then;
Th' event is feared; should we again provoke
Our stronger, some worse way his wrath may find
To our destruction: if there be in hell
Fear to be worse destroyed: what can be worse   85
Than to dwell here, driven out from bliss, condemned
In this abhorrèd deep to utter woe;
Where pain of unextinguishable fire
Must exercise us without hope of end
The vassals of his anger, when the scourge   90
Inexorably, and the torturing hour
Calls us to penance? More destroyed than thus
We should be quite abolished and expire.
What fear we then? What doubt we to incense
His utmost ire? which to the highth enraged,   95
Will either quite consume us, and reduce
To nothing this essential, happier far
Than miserable to have eternal being:
Or if our substance be indeed divine,
And cannot cease to be, we are at worst   100
On this side nothing; and by proof we feel
Our power sufficient to disturb his heav'n,
And with perpetual inroads to alarm,

69. *Tartarean*: of Tartarus, a region of Hades (the "lower world" of classical myth) where the most guilty were punished. *strange fire*. Cf. Lev. 10.1–2: ". . . the sons of Aaron . . . offered strange fire before the Lord, which he commanded them not. And there went out fire from the Lord, and devoured them. . . ."
73. *drench*: potion; large draught.
74. *forgetful lake*. Cf. "oblivious pool," I.266.
75. I.e.: it is our nature to ascend.
77. *adverse*: contrary to our nature.
79. *Insulting*: (L *insultare* to spring upon) triumphantly scorning.
82. *event*: outcome.
89. *exercise*: L *exerceo* to vex or plague, as in the baiting of wild beasts.
90. *vassals*: slaves.
94. *doubt we*: makes us hesitate.
97. *essential*: essence.

Though inaccessible, his fatal throne:
Which if not victory is yet revenge."　　　　　　　　　105
　　He ended frowning, and his look denounced
Desperate revenge, and battle dangerous
To less than gods. On th' other side up rose
Belial, in act more graceful and humane;
A fairer person lost not heav'n; he seemed　　　　　110
For dignity composed and high exploit:
But all was false and hollow; though his tongue
Dropped manna, and could make the worse appear
The better reason, to perplex and dash
Maturest counsels: for his thoughts were low;　　　115
To vice industrious, but to nobler deeds
Timorous and slothful: yet he pleased the ear,
And with persuasive accent thus began.
　　"I should be much for open war, O Peers,
As not behind in hate; if what was urged　　　　　120
Main reason to persuade immediate war,
Did not dissuade me most, and seem to cast
Ominous conjecture on the whole success:
When he who most excells in fact of arms,
In what he counsels and in what excels　　　　　　125
Mistrustful, grounds his courage on despair
And utter dissolution, as the scope
Of all his aim, after some dire revenge.
First, what revenge? The tow'rs of heav'n are filled
With armèd watch, that render all access　　　　　130
Impregnable; oft on the bordering deep
Encamp their legions, or with óbscure wing
Scout far and wide into the realm of Night,
Scorning surprise. Or could we break our way
By force, and at our heels all hell should rise　　135
With blackest insurrection, to confound
Heav'n's purest light, yet our great enemy
All incorruptible would on his throne
Sit unpolluted, and th' ethereal mold
Incapable of stain would soon expel　　　　　　　140
Her mischief, and purge off the baser fire
Victorious. Thus repulsed, our final hope
Is flat despair: we must exasperate
Th' almighty victor to spend all his rage,

104. *fatal:* established by fate; also, deadly.
106. *denounced:* portended.
109. *Belial.* See I.490–505n above and "Angels," pp. 466–68. *humane:* civil, polite.
114. *reason:* argument.
124. *fact:* feat.
127. *scope:* target, range, extent.
139. *ethereal mold:* heavenly substance (i.e., pure fire).

And that must end us, that must be our cure,   145
To be no more; sad cure; for who would lose,
Though full of pain, this intellectual being,
Those thoughts that wander through eternity,
To perish rather, swallowed up and lost
In the wide womb of uncreated night,   150
Devoid of sense and motion? And who knows,
Let this be good, whether our angry foe
Can give it, or will ever? How he can
Is doubtful; that he never will is sure.
Will he, so wise, let loose at once his ire,   155
Belike through impotence, or unaware,
To give his enemies their wish, and end
Them in his anger, whom his anger saves
To punish endless? 'Wherefore cease we then?'
Say they who counsel war, 'We are decreed,   160
Reserved and destined to eternal woe;
Whatever doing, what can we suffer more,
What can we suffer worse?' Is this then worst,
Thus sitting, thus consulting, thus in arms?
What when we fled amain, pursued and strook   165
With Heav'n's afflicting thunder, and besought
The deep to shelter us? This hell then seemed
A refuge from those wounds: or when we lay
Chained on the burning lake? That sure was worse.
What if the breath that kindled those grim fires   170
Awaked should blow them into sevenfold rage
And plunge us in the flames? Or from above
Should intermitted vengeance arm again
His red right hand to plague us? What if all
Her stores were opened, and this firmament   175
Of hell should spout her cataracts of fire,
Impendent horrors, threat'ning hideous fall
One day upon our heads; while we perhaps
Designing or exhorting glorious war,
Caught in a fiery tempest shall be hurled   180
Each on his rock transfixed, the sport and prey

---

148. *wander*. Milton may have wanted to make Belial unintentionally ironic with a word that also means to stray, or err.
156. *Belike through impotence*: perhaps through lack of self-control.
165. *amain*: with full speed.
170. Cf. Isa. 30.33: "The breath of the Lord, like a stream of brimstone, doth kindle [the fire of Tophet]." Cf. I.404–5.
173. *intermitted*: suspended.
174. *red right hand*. Horace refers to Jupiter, the hurler of thunderbolts, as having a red right hand.
176. *cataracts*: waterspouts.
180–82. Cf. *Aen.* 1.44–45: "but him, as with pierced breast he breathed forth flame, she caught in a whirlwind and impaled on a spiky crag."

Of racking whirlwinds, or for ever sunk
Under yon boiling ocean, wrapped in chains;
There to converse with everlasting groans,
Unrespited, unpitied, unreprieved,   185
Ages of hopeless end; this would be worse.
War therefore, open or concealed, alike
My voice dissuades; for what can force or guile
With him, or who deceive his mind, whose eye
Views all things at one view? He from heav'n's highth   190
All these our motions vain, sees and derides;
Not more almighty to resist our might
Than wise to frustrate all our plots and wiles.
Shall we then live thus vile, the race of heav'n
Thus trampled, thus expelled to suffer here   195
Chains and these torments? Better these than worse
By my advice; since fate inevitable
Subdues us, and omnipotent decree,
The victor's will. To suffer, as to do,
Our strength is equal, nor the law unjust   200
That so ordains: this was at first resolved,
If we were wise, against so great a foe
Contending, and so doubtful what might fall.
I laugh, when those who at the spear are bold
And vent'rous, if that fail them, shrink and fear   205
What yet they know must follow, to endure
Exile, or ignominy, or bonds, or pain,
The sentence of their conqueror: This is now
Our doom; which if we can sustain and bear,
Our Súpreme foe in time may much remit   210
His anger, and perhaps thus far removed
Not mind us not offending, satisfied
With what is punished; whence these raging fires
Will slacken, if his breath stir not their flames.
Our purer essence then will overcome   215
Their noxious vapor, or inured not feel,
Or changed at length, and to the place conformed
In temper and in nature, will receive
Familiar the fierce heat, and void of pain;
This horror will grow mild, this darkness light,   220

182. *racking*: pulling, straining, torturing.
184. *converse*: converse; also, dwell.
190–91. Cf. Ps. 2.4: "He that sitteth in the heavens shall laugh; the Lord shall have them in
    derision."
191. *motions*: proposals.
199–203. I.e.: We are able to take as much punishment as we are able to inflict (and the natural
    law that makes that true is not unfair). If we were wise, we agreed upon that before we undertook
    to contend against so great a foe, since we were so uncertain of the outcome.
212–13. *what is punished*: (L syntax) the punishment.
216. *inured*: accustomed to.

Besides what hope the never-ending flight
Of future days may bring, what chance, what change
Worth waiting, since our present lot appears
For happy though but ill, but ill not worst,
If we procure not to ourselves more woe."   225
   Thus Belial with words clothed in reason's garb
Counseled ignoble ease, and peaceful sloth,
Not peace: and after him thus Mammon spake.
   "Either to disenthrone the King of heav'n
We war, if war be best, or to regain   230
Our own right lost: him to unthrone we then
May hope when everlasting fate shall yield
To fickle chance, and Chaos judge the strife:
The former vain to hope argues as vain
The latter: for what place can be for us   235
Within heav'n's bound, unless heav'n's Lord supreme
We overpower? Suppose he should relent
And publish grace to all, on promise made
Of new subjection; with what eyes could we
Stand in his presence humble, and receive   240
Strict laws imposed, to celebrate his throne
With warbled hymns, and to his Godhead sing
Forced hallelujahs; while he lordly sits
Our envied Sovran, and his altar breathes
Ambrosial odors and ambrosial flowers,   245
Our servile offerings. This must be our task
In heav'n, this our delight; how wearisome
Eternity so spent in worship paid
To whom we hate. Let us not then pursue
By force impossible, by leave obtained   250
Unacceptable, though in heav'n, our state
Of splendid vassalage, but rather seek
Our own good from ourselves, and from our own
Live to ourselves, though in this vast recess,
Free, and to none accountable, preferring   255
Hard liberty before the easy yoke
Of servile pomp. Our greatness will appear
Then most conspicuous, when great things of small,
Useful of hurtful, prosperous of adverse
We can create, and in what place soe'er   260
Thrive under evil, and work ease out of pain

223–24. I.e.: Though our present lot, considered for its happiness, seems an ill one, when
    considered as an ill lot, it seems not the worst.
243. *hallelujahs:* songs of praise. The Hebrew word means: Praise ye the Lord (i.e., *Jah*, or
    Jehovah).
245. *Ambrosial:* (Gk *ambrosia* immortality; elixir of life) of the fragrance (or flavor) of a food (or
    drink) worthy of the gods; divinely fragrant.

Through labor and endurance. This deep world
Of darkness do we dread? How oft amidst
Thick clouds and dark doth heav'n's all-ruling Sire
Choose to reside, his glory unobscured,   265
And with the majesty of darkness round
Covers his throne; from whence deep thunders roar
Must'ring their rage, and heav'n resembles hell?
As he our darkness, cannot we his light
Imitate when we please? This desert soil   270
Wants not her hidden luster, gems and gold;
Nor want we skill or art, from whence to raise
Magnificence; and what can heav'n show more?
Our torments also may in length of time
Become our elements, these piercing fires   275
As soft as now severe, our temper changed
Into their temper; which must needs remove
The sensible of pain. All things invite
To peaceful counsels, and the settled state
Of order, how in safety best we may   280
Compose our present evils, with regard
Of what we are and where, dismissing quite
All thoughts of war: ye have what I advise."
     He scarce had finished, when such murmur filled
Th' assembly, as when hollow rocks retain   285
The sound of blust'ring winds, which all night long
Had roused the sea, now with hoarse cadence lull
Seafaring men o'erwatched, whose bark by chance
Or pinnace anchors in a craggy bay
After the tempest: such applause was heard   290
As Mammon ended, and his sentence pleased,
Advising peace: for such another field
They dreaded worse than hell: so much the fear
Of thunder and the sword of Michaël
Wrought still within them; and no less desire   295
To found this nether empire, which might rise
By policy, and long process of time,
In emulation opposite to heav'n.
Which then Beëlzebub perceived, than whom,
Satan except, none higher sat, with grave   300

263–67. Cf. Ps. 18.11: "He made darkness his secret place; his pavilion round about him were
   dark waters and thick clouds. . . ."
271. *Wants*: lacks.
276. *temper*: (L *temperare* to mix) nature, constitution; see theory of humors in "Physiology and
   Psychology," pp. 463–64, below.
278. *sensible*: physical part.
281. *Compose*: come to terms with. *evils*: misfortunes.
288–89. *bark*: ship. *pinnance*: boat.
292. *field*: battle.
294. *Michael*. See "Angels," pp. 466–68.
297. *policy*: statecraft.

Aspect he rose, and in his rising seemed
A pillar of state; deep on his front engraven
Deliberation sat and pubic care;
And princely counsel in his face yet shone,
Majestic though in ruin: sage he stood   305
With Altantean shoulders fit to bear
The weight of mightiest monarchies; his look
Drew audience and attention still as night
Or summer's noontide air, while thus he spake.
    "Thrones and imperial Powers, offspring of heav'n,   310
Ethereal Virtues; or these titles now
Must we renounce, and changing style be called
Princes of hell? for so the popular vote
Inclines, here to continue, and build up here
A growing empire; doubtless; while we dream,   315
And know not that the King of heav'n hath doomed
This place our dungeon, not our safe retreat
Beyond his potent arm, to live exempt
From Heav'n's high jurisdiction, in new league
Banded against his throne, but to remain   320
In strictest bondage, though thus far removed,
Under th' inevitable curb, reserved
His captive multitude: for he, be sure,
In highth or depth, still first and last will reign
Sole king, and of his kingdom lose no part   325
By our revolt, but over hell extend
His empire, and with iron scepter rule
Us here, as with his golden those in heav'n.
What sit we then projecting peace and war?
War hath determined us, and foiled with loss   330
Irreparable; terms of peace yet none
Vouchsafed or sought; for what peace will be giv'n
To us enslaved, but custody severe,
And stripes, and arbitrary punishment
Inflicted? And what peace can we return,   335
But to our power hostility and hate,
Untamed reluctance, and revenge though slow,
Yet ever plotting how the conqueror least

302. *front:* forehead, face.
306. *Atlantean.* When with other Titans, Atlas unsuccessfully revolted against the gods, he was
    punished by being forced to hold up the heavens on his shoulders.
312. *style:* official titles.
324–25. Cf. Rev. 22.13: "I am Alpha and Omega, the beginning and the end, the first and the
    last."
327–28. Cf. Ps. 2.9, p 439: "Thou shalt break them with a rod of iron; thou shalt dash them
    in pieces, like a potter's vessel."
330. *determined:* (L to enclose within boundaries) put an end or limit to.
336. *to:* to the limit of.
337. *reluctance:* L *reluctare* to struggle against.

May reap his conquest, and may least rejoice
In doing what we most in suffering feel?   340
Nor will occasion want, nor shall we need
With dangerous expedition to invade
Heav'n, whose high walls fear no assault or siege,
Or ambush from the deep. What if we find
Some easier enterprise? There is a place   345
(If ancient and prophetic fame in heav'n
Err not) another world, the happy seat
Of some new race called Man, about this time
To be created like to us, though less
In power and excellence, but favored more   350
Of him who rules above; so was his will
Pronounced among the gods, and by an oath,
That shook heav'n's whole circumference, confirmed.
Thither let us bend all our thoughts, to learn
What creatures there inhabit, of what mold,   355
Or substance, how endued, and what their power,
And where their weakness, how attempted best,
By force or subtlety: though heav'n be shut,
And heav'n's high arbitrator sit secure
In his own strength, this place may lie exposed   360
The utmost border of his kingdom, left
To their defense who hold it: here perhaps
Some advantageous act may be achieved
By sudden onset, either with hell fire
To waste his whole creation, or possess   365
All as our own, and drive as were driven,
The puny habitants, or if not drive,
Seduce them to our party, that their God
May prove their foe, and with repenting hand
Abolish his own works. This would surpass   370
Common revenge, and interrupt his joy
In our confusion, and our joy upraise
In his disturbance; when his darling sons
Hurled headlong to partake with us, shall curse
Their frail original, and faded bliss,   375
Faded so soon. Advise if this be worth

341. *want:* be lacking.
346. *fame:* rumor. Cf. I.650–54n.
349–51. Cf. Ps. 8.5 "For thou [O Lord] hast made him [man] a little lower than the angels, and
hast crowned him with glory and honor."
352–53. Cf. *Il.* 1.530: "Kronion spake, and . . . he made great Olympus quake." Also *Aen.*
9.106: "he nodded assent, and with the nod made all Olympus tremble."
357. *attempted:* tempted; seduced; assaulted.
367. *puny:* Fr *puis né* born since.
368–70. Cf. Gen. 6.7 "And the Lord said, I will destroy man whom I have created from the
face of the earth . . . for it repenteth me that I have made [him and all the other creatures]."
374. *partake:* share.
376. *Advise:* consider.

Attempting, or to sit in darkness here
Hatching vain empires." Thus Beëlzebub
Pleaded his devilish counsel, first devised
By Satan, and in part proposed: for whence,   380
But from the author of all ill could spring
So deep a malice, to confound the race
Of mankind in one root, and earth with hell
To mingle and involve, done all to spite
The great Creator? But their spite still serves   385
His glory to augment. The bold design
Pleased highly those infernal States, and joy
Sparkled in all their eyes; with full assent
They vote: whereat his speech he thus renews.
  "Well have ye judged, well ended long debate,   390
Synod of gods, and like to what ye are,
Great things resolved, which from the lowest deep
Will once more lift us up, in spite of fate,
Nearer our ancient seat; perhaps in view
Of those bright confines, whence with neighboring arms   395
And opportune excursion we may chance
Re-enter heav'n; or else in some mild zone
Dwell not unvisited of heav'n's fair light
Secure, and at the bright'ning orient beam
Purge off this gloom; the soft delicious air,   400
To heal the scar of these corrosive fires
Shall breathe her balm. But first whom shall we send
In search of this new world, whom shall we find
Sufficient? Who shall tempt with wand'ring feet
The dark unbottomed infinite abyss   405
And through the palpable obscure find out
His uncouth way, or spread his aery flight
Upborne with indefatigable wings
Over the vast abrupt, ere he arrive
The happy isle; what strength, what art can then   410
Suffice, or what evasion bear him safe

379–80. See I.650–56.
382. *confound*: (L. *confundere* to pour together, confuse—see *mingle* and *involve* two lines below)
    ruin.
387. *States*: statesmen; representatives of the ruling classes met in political assembly.
404. *tempt*: try; risk the perils of.
406. *palpable obscure*. Cf. Exod. 10.21: "And the Lord said unto Moses, Stretch out thine hand
    toward heaven, that there may be darkness over the land of Egypt, even darkness which may
    be felt."
407. *uncouth*: unknown.
409. *abrupt*: L *abrumpere* to break off. Milton uses the adjective for a noun, as with *obscure*,
    line 406.
410. *The happy isle*. In early Greek mythology the Islands of the Blest, where the gods sent those
    whom they wished to reward with immortality, were located in the West, in Oceanus, a river
    thought to encircle the flat continent of the world. The irony, of course, is Milton's, not
    Beëlzebub's.

Through the strict senteries and stations thick
Of angels watching round? Here he had need
All circumspection, and we now no less
Choice in our suffrage; for on whom we send,   415
The weight of all and our last hope relies."
 This said, he sat; and expectation held
His look suspense, awaiting who appeared
To second, or oppose, or undertake
The perilous attempt: but all sat mute,   420
Pondering the danger with deep thoughts; and each
In other's count'nance read his own dismay
Astonished: none among the choice and prime
Of those heav'n-warring champions could be found
So hardy as to proffer or accept   425
Alone the dreadful voyage; till at last
Satan, whom now transcendent glory raised
Above his fellows, with monarchal pride
Conscious of highest worth, unmoved thus spake.
 "O progeny of heav'n, empyreal Thrones,   430
With reason hath deep silence and demur
Seized us, though undismayed: long is the way
And hard, that out of hell leads up to light;
Our prison strong, this huge convex of fire,
Outrageous to devour, immures us round   435
Ninefold, and gates of burning adamant
Barred over us prohibit all egress.
These passed, if any pass, the void profound
Of unessential night receives him next
Wide gaping, and with utter loss of being   440
Threatens him, plunged in that abortive gulf.
If thence he scape into whatever world,
Or unknown region, what remains him less
Than unknown dangers and as hard escape?
But I should ill become this throne, O Peers,   445
And this imperial sovranty, adorned
With splendor, armed with power, if aught proposed
And judged of public moment, in the shape
Of difficulty or danger could deter

415. *Choice:* discrimination. *suffrage:* vote.
423. *Astonished:* struck with fear.
431. *demur:* hesitation.
432–33. Cf. *Aen.* 6.126–29: "easy is the descent to Avernus: night and day the door of gloomy Dis stands open; but to recall thy steps and pass out to the upper air, this is the task, this the toil!"
434–37. In the *Aen.*, Hell, or Hades, was surrounded by the *ninefold* river Styx, and the pillars of the gate to Tartarus, or deepest hell, were made of *adamant. burning:* incandescent.
438–41. *the void profound* is literally the bottomless emptiness of a night that has no essence or being. Such a *gulf* would be an *abortive* womb because it could not hold anything. *unessential:* having no real substance.

Me from attempting. Wherefore do I assume   450
These royalties, and not refuse to reign,
Refusing to accept as great a share
Of hazard as of honor, due alike
To him who reigns, and so much to him due
Of hazard more, as he above the rest   455
High honored sits? Go therefore mighty Powers,
Terror of heav'n, though fall'n; intend at home,
While here shall be our home, what best may ease
The present misery, and render hell
More tolerable; if there be cure or charm   460
To respite or deceive, or slack the pain
Of this ill mansion: intermit no watch
Against a wakeful foe, while I abroad
Through all the coasts of dark destruction seek
Deliverance for us all: this enterprise   465
None shall partake with me." Thus saying rose
The monarch, and prevented all reply,
Prudent, lest from his resolution raised
Others among the chief might offer now
(Certain to be refused) what erst they feared;   470
And so refused might in opinion stand
His rivals, winning cheap the high repute
Which he through hazard huge must earn. But they
Dreaded not more th' adventure than his voice
Forbidding; and at once with him they rose;   475
Their rising all at once was as the sound
Of thunder heard remote. Towards him they bend
With awful reverence prone; and as a god
Extol him equal to the Highest in heav'n:
Nor failed they to express how much they praised,   480
That for the general safety he despised
His own: for neither do the Spirits damned
Lose all their virtue; lest bad men should boast
Their specious deeds on earth, which glory excites,
Or close ambition varnished o'er with zeal.   485
Thus they their doubtful consultations dark
Ended rejoicing in their matchless chief:
As when from mountain tops the dusky clouds

451. *royalties*: royal prerogatives (*splendor, power,* line 447).
452. *Refusing*: if I refuse.
457. *intend at*: turn (your) thoughts to.
461. *respite*: relieve. *deceive*: beguile.
468. *raised*: roused.
478. *awful*: full of awe.
483–85. I.e.: Lest bad men take pride in virtuous deeds performed for selfish motives, [God ordained that] even the devils in hell retain *that* kind of virtue.
485. *close*: hidden.

Ascending, while the north wind sleeps, o'erspread
Heav'n's cheerful face, the louring element   490
Scowls o'er the darkened landscape snow, or show'r;
If chance the radiant sun with farewell sweet
Extend his evening beam, the fields revive,
The birds their notes renew, and bleating herds
Attest their joy, that hill and valley rings.   495
O shame to men! Devil with devil damned
Firm concord holds, men only disagree
Of creatures rational, though under hope
Of heavenly grace: and God proclaiming peace,
Yet live in hatred, enmity, and strife   500
Among themselves, and levy cruel wars,
Wasting the earth, each other to destroy:
As if (which might induce us to accord)
Man had not hellish foes enow besides,
That day and night for his destruction wait.   505
    The Stygian council thus dissolved; and forth
In order came the grand infernal peers:
Midst came their mighty paramount, and seemed
Alone th' antagonist of Heav'n, nor less
Than hell's dread emperor with pomp supreme,   510
And god-like imitated state; him round
A globe of fierty Seraphim enclosed
With bright emblazonry and horrent arms.
Then of their session ended they bid cry
With trumpet's regal sound the great result: 515
Toward the four winds four speedy Cherubim
Put to their mouths the sounding alchemy
By herald's voice explained; the hollow abyss
Heard far and wide, and all the host of hell
With deaf'ning shout, returned them loud acclaim.   520
Thence more at ease their minds and somewhat raised

489. Cf. *Il.* 5.524: "while the might of the north wind sleepeth . . ."
490. *element:* sky.
496. *O shame to men!* This speech of the bard on the ways of men is like the lament of an OT
    prophet, but more like the bardic asides that became conventional after Virgil.
504. *enow:* enough.
508. *paramount:* supreme ruler.
511. *state:* magnificence.
512. *globe:* perhaps literally three-dimensional, though the L word also meant a compact body
    of persons, a crowd.
513. *emblazonry:* the brightly colored coats of arms that were painted on shields; here, the armor
    itself. *horrent:* bristling.
516–18. When Christ told his disciples about his second coming, he said (Matt. 24.30–31): "And
    then shall appear the sign of the Son of man in heaven: and then shall all the tribes of the
    earth mourn, and they shall see the Son of man coming in the clouds of heaven with power
    and great glory. And he shall send his angels with a great sound of a trumpet, and they shall
    gather together his elect from the four winds, from one end of heaven to the other." *alchemy:*
    goldlike metal; brass. Heralds *explained* the meaning of the trumpets' *sound*.
521–628. Cf. *Il.* 23.257f.; *Aen.* 5.104f.; 577ff. (epic convention of games in honor of a dead
    hero).

By false presumptuous hope, the rangèd powers
Disband, and wand'ring, each his several way
Pursues, as inclination or sad choice
Leads him perplexed, where he may likeliest find   525
Truce to his restless thoughts, and entertain
The irksome hours, till his great chief return.
Part on the plain, or in the air sublime
Upon the wing, or in swift race contend,
As at th' Olympian games or Pythian fields;   530
Part curb their fiery steeds, or shun the goal
With rapid wheels, or fronted brígades form.
As when to warn proud cities war appears
Waged in the troubled sky, and armies rush
To battle in the clouds, before each van   535
Prick forth the aery knights, and couch their spears
Till thickest legions close; with feats of arms
From either end of heav'n the welkin burns.
Others with vast Typhoean rage more fell
Rend up both rocks and hills, and ride the air   540
In whirlwind; hell scarce holds the wild uproar.
As when Alcides from Oechalia crowned
With conquest, felt th' envenomed robe, and tore
Through pain up by the roots Thessalian pines,
And Lichas from the top of Oeta threw   545
Into th' Euboic sea. Others more mild,
Retreated in a silent valley, sing
With notes angelical to many a harp
Their own heroic deeds and hapless fall
By doom of battle; and complain that fate   550
Free virtue should enthrall to force or chance.
Their song was partial, but the harmony
(What could it less when Spirits immortal sing?)

526. *entertain:* while away.
528. *sublime:* borne aloft; on high.
530. *Pythian fields.* The Pythian games, held at Delphi, were like the ancient Olympic games.
531. *Shun the goal:* Come close but not hit the pole around which a charioteer had to turn in a race.
536. The language of chivalric tournaments. *prick:* advance on horseback.
538. *welkin:* vault of heaven.
539. *Typhoean rage.* See I.199n.
542–46. When Hercules (*Alcides*) defeated the king of *Oechalia,* and prepared to sacrifice the king's daughter, Hercules' wife mistook his intention and sent him, by his friend *Lichas,* a sacrificial robe smeared with the blood of a centaur (whom Hercules had killed some time before), thinking it would work like a love potion and insure her husband's constancy. Instead, it was a burning poison and stuck to him so firmly that he could not remove it. In his torment he seized Lichas and threw him into the sea *from the top of Oeta,* a mountain in Thessaly. Cf. *Met.* 9.134ff.
546–49. Cf. *Aen.* 6.637ff.
550. *doom:* decision.
552. *partial:* prejudiced; possibly a pun on "in parts," or "polyphonic."

Suspended hell, and took with ravishment
The thronging audience. In discourse more sweet   555
(For eloquence the soul, song charms the sense)
Others apart sat on a hill retired,
In thoughts more elevate, and reasoned high
Of providence, foreknowledge, will, and fate,
Fixed fate, free will, foreknowledge absolute,   560
And found no end, in wand'ring mazes lost.
Of good and evil much they argued then,
Of happiness and final misery,
Passion and apathy, and glory and shame,
Vain wisdom all, and false philosophy: 565
Yet with a pleasing sorcery could charm
Pain for a while or anguish, and excite
Fallacious hope, or arm th' obdurèd breast
With stubborn patience as with triple steel.
Another part in squadrons and gross bands,   570
On bold adventure to discover wide
That dismal world, if any clime perhaps
Might yield them easier habitation, bend
Four ways their flying march, along the banks
Of four infernal rivers that disgorge   575
Into the burning lake their baleful streams:
Abhorrèd Styx the flood of deadly hate,
Sad Acheron of sorrow, black and deep;
Cocytus, named of lamentation loud
Heard on the rueful stream; fierce Phlegethon   580
Whose waves of torrent fire inflame with rage.
Far off from these a slow and silent stream,

---

554. *took. Ravish, rapture,* and *rape* all come from L *rapere* take, seize, rob.
555–65. As God in the OT holds his enemies in derision, so the poet's irony mocks the philosophers of hell—making their discussions sound like a parody of high talk by ignorant men on popular theological and philosophical topics. *Passion and apathy* may be an allusion to the stoic belief that men should try to avoid all feeling, and *glory and shame* to an opposing pagan philosophy of heroic action. *PL* is in part a definition of Christian patience and Christian heroism.
559. *foreknowledge.* See CD, pp. 404–5; other uses of the word in the poem: III.116, 118, and IX.768; and "God," pp. 468–69.
560. *free will:* God-given, autonomous faculty by which one chooses and proposes. Cf. CD, pp. 404 and 420, and other uses of the phrase in the poem: IV.66; V.236; VIII.636; IX.1174; X.9, 46.
568. *obdured:* hardened. An example of prolepsis, a figure in which the adjective describes the state yet to be produced by the action signified by the verb.
570. *gross:* compact.
575–86. A *burning lake* is mentioned in Rev. 20.10. The five rivers are classical, but their confluence into a lake is Milton's idea. Each of the descriptions of the rivers is a translation of their Greek names. In Dante's *Inferno, Lethe* is said to be *far off* from the other rivers. *baleful:* of deadly influence. Cf. *Aen.* 6.265: "Thou, Chaos, and thou, Phlegethon, ye broad, silent tracts of night!" and 6.295–97: "Hence a road leads to the waters of Tartarean Acheron. Here, thick with mire and of fathomless flood, a whirlpool seethes and belches into Cocytus all its sand," and 6.323: "thou seest the deep pools of Cocytus and the Stygian marsh, by whose power the gods fear to swear falsely," and 6.439: "the unlovely mere with its dreary water enchains them and Styx imprisons with his ninefold circles."

Lethe the river of oblivion rolls
Her wat'ry labyrinth, whereof who drinks,
Forthwith his former state and being forgets,   585
Forgets both joy and grief, pleasure and pain.
Beyond this flood a frozen continent
Lies dark and wild, beat with perpetual storms
Of whirlwind and dire hail, which on firm land
Thaws not, but gathers heap, and ruins seems   590
Of ancient pile; all else deep snow and ice,
A gulf profound as that Serbonian bog
Betwixt Damiata and Mount Casius old,
Where armies whole have sunk: the parching air
Burns frore, and cold performs th' effect of fire.   595
Thither by harpy-footed Furies haled,
At certain revolutions all the damned
Are brought: and feel by turns the bitter change
Of fierce extremes, extremes by change more fierce,
From beds of raging fire to starve in ice   600
Their soft ethereal warmth, and there to pine
Immovable, infixed, and frozen round,
Periods of time, thence hurried back to fire.
They ferry over this Lethean sound
Both to and fro, their sorrow to augment,   605
And wish and struggle, as they pass, to reach
The tempting stream, with one small drop to lose
In sweet forgetfulness all pain and woe,
All in one moment, and so near the brink;
But fate withstands, and to oppose th' attempt   610
Medusa with Gorgonian terror guards
The ford, and of itself the water flies
All taste of living wight, as once it fled
The lip of Tantalus. Thus roving on
In cónfused march forlorn, th' advent'rous bands   615
With shudd'ring horror pale, and eyes aghast
Viewed first their lamentable lot, and found

586–95. The notion that hell provides both cold and hot tortures "goes back to OT apocryphal
writings" (Fowler).
591. *pile:* building.
592–94. Lake Serbonis, near the city of *Damiata,* on one of the eastern mouths of the Nile,
was surrounded by high dunes, whose sand, blown to the shore, formed quicksand.
595. *frore:* frozen.
596. In Greek mythology *harpies* were birdlike creatures with faces and breasts of women, thought
to be spirits of the dead who returned to earth to carry off the living. The *Furies,* or Eumenides,
were winged women, born of Uranus, whose function it was to avenge crimes. *haled:* hauled,
pulled.
597. *revolutions:* recurrent periods of time.
600. *starve:* to kill or make numb with cold.
611–14. *Medusa:* one of three Gorgons, the snaky-haired children of the goddess Ge (Earth) who
could turn to stone anyone who looked them in the eye.
614. *Tantalus:* a mythological character condemned eternally to fail in his effort to drink from
the pool in which he was set.
617–18. Cf. Matt. 12.43: "When the unclean spirit is gone out of a man, [it] walketh through
dry places, seeking rest, and findeth none."

No rest: through many a dark and dreary vale
They passed, and many a region dolorous,
O'er many a frozen, many a fiery alp,   620
Rocks, caves, lakes, fens, bogs, dens, and shades of death,
A universe of death, which God by curse
Created evil, for evil only good,
Where all life dies, death lives, and nature breeds,
Perverse, all monstrous, all prodigious things,   625
Abominable, inutterable, and worse
Than fables yet have feigned, or fear conceived,
Gorgons and Hydras, and Chimeras dire.
    Meanwhile the Adversary of God and man,
Satan with thoughts inflamed of highest design,   630
Puts on swift wings, and towards the gates of hell
Explores his solitary flight; sometimes
He scours the right-hand coast, sometimes the left,
Now shaves with level wing the deep, then soars
Up to the fiery concave tow'ring high.   635
As when far off at sea a fleet descried
Hangs on the clouds, by equinoctial winds
Close sailing from Bengala, or the isles
Of Ternate and Tidore, whence merchants bring
Their spicy drugs: they on the trading flood   640
Through the wide Ethiopian to the Cape
Ply stemming nightly toward the pole. So seemed
Far off the flying Fiend: at last appear
Hell bounds high reaching to the horrid roof,
And thrice threefold the gates; three folds were brass,   645
Three iron, three of adamantine rock,
Impenetrable, impaled with circling fire,

624. *nature*. See CD, pp. 401–2 and 414–15. and other uses of this word in the sense of a
    creative and ordering power (as distinct from the sense of the products of that power): III.49,
    455; IV.207, 242, 314; V.24, 45, 181, 294, 318; VII.482; VIII.26, 459, 534, 541, 561; IX.624;
    X.805; XI.49, 602; XII.29, 578.
628. *Hydras*: poisonous water snakes whose multiple heads were regenerative. A *Chimera* had
    the head of a lion, the body of a goat, and the tail of a dragon.
629. *Adversary*. See I.82n.
632. *Explores his solitary flight*: puts his lonely flight to the test.
633. *scours*: passes rapidly along in search of something.
636–42. *discried*: seen from far off. *Hangs*: seems suspended. *equinoctial*: in the region on either
    side of the equator, where the trade winds blow in a general direction towards the equator.
    trading flood: the sea where the trade winds blow: here the Indian Ocean (*Ethiopian*). *Close
    sailing* ("close hauled"), *ply* ("steer" and "work to windward"), and *stemming* ("making headway
    against the wind") emphasize Satan's struggle and are true to the facts of the simile, for in the
    south Indian Ocean, ships sailing SW toward the *Cape* (of Good Hope) would, from April to
    September, when nights in the southern hemisphere are long (*nightly*), be sailing into the
    prevailing SW monsoons. *Bengala*: Bengal. *Ternate, Tidore*: islands in the Moluccas, or Spice
    Islands.
646. Adamant, or diamond, was an especially suitable building material in hell because it burns
    only at very high temperatures.
647. *impaled*: enclosed, as with stakes.

Yet unconsumed. Before the gates there sat
On either side a formidable shape;
The one seemed woman to the waist, and fair,   650
But ended foul in many a scaly fold
Voluminous and vast, a serpent armed
With mortal sting: about her middle round
A cry of hell-hounds never ceasing barked
With wide Cerberean mouths full loud, and rung   655
A hideous peal: yet, when they list, would creep,
If aught disturbed their noise, into her womb,
And kennel there, yet there still barked and howled,
Within unseen. Far less abhorred than these
Vexed Scylla bathing in the sea that parts   660
Calabria from the hoarse Trinacrian shore:
Nor uglier follow the night-hag, when called
In secret, riding through the air she comes
Lured with the smell of infant blood, to dance
With Lapland witches, while the laboring moon   665
Eclipses at their charms. The other shape,
If shape it might be called that shape had none
Distinguishable in member, joint, or limb,
Or substance might be called that shadow seemed,
For each seemed either; black it stood as night,   670
Fierce as ten Furies, terrible as hell,
And shook a dreadful dart; what seemed his head
The likeness of a kingly crown had on.
Satan was now at hand, and from his seat
The monster moving onward came as fast   675
With horrid strides, hell trembled as he strode.
Th' undaunted Fiend what this might be admired,
Admired, not feared; God and his Son except,
Created thing naught values he nor shunned;
And with disdainful look thus first began.   680
    "Whence and what art thou, execrable shape,
That dar'st, though grim and terrible, advance
Thy miscreated front athwart my way
To yonder gates? Through them I mean to pass,

648–66. At the doors of the hell Aeneas visited in Virgil's poem there were "stalled" horrible
beasts, including "doubled-shaped Scyllas." *Scylla*, the daughter of *Hecate*, goddess of night
and the lower world (the *night-hag* of 662), was turned into a monster with a waist of dogs'
heads, above which she had the body of a young woman, and below, the tail of a dolphin.
From her cave on the Straits of Messina (between *Calabria* and the *Trinacrian shore*) opposite
the whirlpool of Charybdis, she preyed on sailors passing through that dangerous channel.
Cerberus was the multiheaded watchdog of Hades. *voluminous:* manycoiled. *Lapland* was
famous for witchcraft. *laboring:* L *laborare* to be in distress, difficulty (said of a moon in eclipse
because it suffers from the loss of the sun's light).
654. *cry:* pack.
662–63. *called/In secret:* conjured.
665. *laboring:* suffering eclipse.
677. *admired:* wondered.

That be assured, without leave asked of thee: 685
Retire, or taste thy folly, and learn by proof,
Hell-born, not to contend with Spirits of heav'n."
    To whom the goblin full of wrath replied:
"Art thou that traitor angel, art thou he,
Who first broke peace in heav'n and faith, till then   690
Unbroken, and in proud rebellious arms
Drew after him the third part of heav'n's sons
Conjured against the Highest, for which both thou
And they outcast from God, are here condemned
To waste eternal days in woe and pain?   695
And reckon'st thou thyself with Spirits of heav'n,
Hell-doomed, and breath'st defiance here and scorn,
Where I reign king, and to enrage thee more,
Thy king and lord? Back to thy punishment,
False fugitive, and to thy speed add wings,   700
Lest with a whip of scorpions I pursue
Thy ling'ring, or with one stroke of this dart
Strange horror seize thee, and pangs unfelt before."
    So spake the grisly terror, and in shape,
So speaking and so threat'ning, grew tenfold   705
More dreadful and deform: on th' other side
Incensed with indignation Satan stood
Unterrified, and like a comet burned,
That fires the length of Ophiuchus huge
In th' arctic sky, and from his horrid hair   710
Shakes pestilence and war. Each at the head
Leveled his deadly aim; their fatal hands
No second stroke intend, and such a frown
Each cast at th' other, as when two black clouds
With heav'n's artillery fraught, come rattling on   715
Over the Caspian, then stand front to front
Hov'ring a space, till winds the signal blow
To join their dark encounter in mid-air:
So frowned the mighty combatants, that hell
Grew darker at their frown, so matched they stood;   720
For never but once more was either like
To meet so great a foe: and now great deeds

686. *taste.* This important word in *PL* meant in Milton's time, "to learn by proof, test, or
    experience," as well as "to try, examine, or explore by touch," "to handle," and "to have carnal
    knowledge of." It also meant "to perceive by the sense of taste or smell."
692. *the third part.* Cf. Rev. 12.4.
693. *Conjured:* (L *con* together + *jurare* swear) conspired; perhaps also bewitched (see 662–63n).
701. Cf. 1 Kings 12.11: ". . . my father hath chastened you with whips, but I will chastise you
    with scorpions [whips with metal studs]."
709. *Ophiuchus:* "the serpent-bearer," a large constellation.
710. *horrid hair.* Comet comes from Gk *komētēs* long-haired. Comets portended horrible events.
    Horrid comes from L *horrere* to bristle.
718. *mid-air.* See "The Universe," pp. 461–63.
721–22. Christ would finally destroy them.

Had been achieved, whereof all hell had rung,
Had not the snaky sorceress that sat
Fast by hell gate, and kept the fatal key,   725
Ris'n, and with hideous outcry rushed between.
   "O father, what intends thy hand," she cried,
"Against thy only son? What fury O son,
Possesses thee to bend that mortal dart
Against thy father's head? And know'st for whom;   730
For him who sits above and laughs the while
At thee ordained his drudge, to execute
Whate'er his wrath, which he calls justice, bids,
His wrath which one day will destroy ye both."
   She spake, and at her words the hellish pest   735
Forbore, then these to her Satan returned.
   "So strange thy outcry, and thy words so strange
Thou interposest, that my sudden hand
Prevented spares to tell thee yet by deeds
What it intends; till first I know of thee,   740
What thing thou art, thus double-formed, and why
In this infernal vale first met thou call'st
Me father, and that phantasm call'st my son?
I know thee not, nor ever saw till now
Sight more detestable than him and thee."   745
   T' whom thus the portress of hell gate replied:
"Hast thou forgot me then, and do I seem
Now in thine eye so foul, once deemed so fair
In heav'n, when at th' assembly, and in sight
Of all the Seraphim with thee combined   750
In bold conspiracy against heav'n's King,
All on a sudden miserable pain
Surprised thee, dim thine eyes, and dizzy swum
In darkness, while thy head flames thick and fast
Threw forth, till on the left side op'ning wide,   755
Likest to thee in shape and count'nance bright,
Then shining heav'nly fair, a goddess armed
Out of thy head I sprung: amazement seized
All th' host of heav'n; back they recoiled afraid
At first, and called me Sin, and for a sign   760
Portentous held me; but familiar grown,
I pleased, and with attractive graces won
The most averse, thee chiefly, who full oft
Thyself in me thy perfect image viewing

---

739. *Prevented:* held back.
749–61. Zeus swallowed his wife fearing she would give birth to a son greater than he, but a
    daughter—Athena, goddess of wisdom—sprang full grown from his head. The story of the
    birth of Eve furnishes an even greater ironic contrast to that of Sin. Milton's genealogy of Sin
    and Death comes ultimately from James 1.15: "Then when lust hath conceived, it bringeth
    forth sin; and sin, when it is finished, bringeth forth death."

Becam'st enamored, and such joy thou took'st   765
With me in secret, that my womb conceived
A growing burden. Meanwhile war arose,
And fields were fought in heav'n; wherein remained
(For what could else) to our almighty foe
Clear victory, to our part loss and rout   770
Through all the empyrean: down they fell
Driv'n headlong from the pitch of heaven, down
Into this deep, and in the general fall
I also; at which time this powerful key
Into my hand was giv'n, with charge to keep   775
These gates for ever shut, which none can pass
Without my op'ning. Pensive here I sat
Alone, but long I sat not, till my womb
Pregnant by thee, and now excessive grown
Prodigious motion felt and rueful throes.   780
At last this odious offspring whom thou seest
Thine own begotten, breaking violent way
Tore through my entrails, that with fear and pain
Distorted, all my nether shape thus grew
Transformed: but he my inbred enemy   785
Forth issued, brandishing his fatal dart
Made to destroy: I fled, and cried out 'Death';
Hell trembled at the hideous name, and sighed
From all her caves, and back resounded 'Death.'
I fled, but he pursued (though more, it seems,   790
Inflamed with lust than rage) and swifter far,
Me overtook his mother all dismayed,
And in embraces forcible and foul
Engend'ring with me, of that rape begot
These yelling monsters that with ceaseless cry   795
Surround me, as thou saw'st, hourly conceived
And hourly born, with sorrow infinite
To me, for when they list, into the womb
That bred them they return, and howl and gnaw
My bowels, their repast; then bursting forth   800
Afresh with conscious terrors vex me round,
That rest or intermission none I find.
Before mine eyes in opposition sits
Grim Death my son and foe, who sets them on,
And me his parent would full soon devour   805
For want of other prey, but that he knows

772. *pitch*: zenith.
782. *Thine own begotten*: an ironic echo of "For God so loved the world that he gave his only
    begotten son . . ." (John 3.16). Cf. 728: *thy only son.*
795ff. Milton's allegory is not specific, but the consequences of Sin's second incest, or act of
    perversion, are torments that may include disease, as well as the guilt and fear that Fowler
    suggests.

His end with mine involved; and knows that I
Should prove a bitter morsel, and his bane,
Whenever that shall be; so fate pronounced.
But thou O father, I forewarn thee, shun   810
His deadly arrow; neither vainly hope
To be invulnerable in those bright arms,
Though tempered heav'nly, for that mortal dint,
Save he who reigns above, none can resist."
    She finished, and the subtle Fiend his lore   815
Soon learned, now milder, and thus answered smooth.
"Dear daughter, since thou claim'st me for thy sire,
And my fair son here show'st me, the dear pledge
Of dalliance had with thee in heav'n, and joys
Then sweet, now sad to mention, through dire change   820
Befall'n us unforeseen, unthought of, know
I come no enemy, but to set free
From out this dark and dismal house of pain,
Both him and thee, and all the heav'nly host
Of Spirits that in our just pretenses armed   825
Fell with us from on high: from them I go
This uncouth errand sole, and one for all
Myself expose, with lonely steps to tread
Th' unfounded deep, and through the void immense
To search with wand'ring quest a place foretold   830
Should be, and, by concurring signs, ere now
Created vast and round, a place of bliss
In the purlieus of heav'n, and therein placed
A race of upstart creatures, to supply
Perhaps our vacant room, though more removed,   835
Lest heav'n surcharged with potent multitude
Might hap to move new broils: be this or aught
Than this more secret now designed, I haste
To know, and this once known, shall soon return,
And bring ye to the place where thou and Death   840
Shall dwell at ease, and up and down unseen
Wing silently the buxom air, embalmed
With odors; there ye shall be fed and filled
Immeasurably, all things shall be your prey."
He ceased, for both seemed highly pleased, and Death   845

---

813. *dint*: blow; stroke of thunder.
815. *lore*: lesson.
825. *pretences*: claims.
826ff. A parody of Christ's *errand* on earth, where his *sole* self-sacrifice was made *for all* men, where his career ending on the cross was a *lonely* one, and where he promised men that on his return to heaven he would prepare a *place* for those who believed in him.
833. *purlieus*: environs.
836. *surcharged*: overstocked.
842. *buxom*: pliable. See V.270n. *embalmed*: made fragrant and soothing, as with a balm.

Grinned horrible a ghastly smile, to hear
His famine should be filled, and blessed his maw
Destined to that good hour: no less rejoiced
His mother bad, and thus bespake her sire.
    "The key of this infernal pit by due,   850
And by command of heav'n's all-powerful King
I keep, by him forbidden to unlock
These adamantine gates; against all force
Death ready stands to interpose his dart,
Fearless to be o'ermatched by living might.   855
But what owe I to his commands above
Who hates me, and hath hither thrust me down
Into this gloom of Tartarus profound,
To sit in hateful office here confined,
Inhabitant of heav'n, and heav'nly-born,   860
Here in perpetual agony and pain,
With terrors and with clamors compassed round
Of mine own brood, that on my bowels feed:
Thou art my father, thou my author, thou
My being gav'st me; whom should I obey   865
But thee, whom follow? Thou wilt bring me soon
To that new world of light and bliss, among
The gods who live at ease, where I shall reign
At thy right hand voluptuous, as beseems
Thy daughter and thy darling, without end."   870
    Thus saying, from her side the fatal key,
Sad instrument of all our woe, she took;
And towards the gate rolling her bestial train,
Forthwith the huge portcullis high up drew,
Which but herself not all the Stygian powers   875
Could once have moved; then in the key-hole turns
Th' intrícate wards, and every bolt and bar
Of massy iron or solid rock with ease
Unfastens: on a sudden open fly
With impetuous recoil and jarring sound   880

847. *famine:* ravenous appetite.
850. *due:* right.
859. *office:* duty.
865. *obey:* L *oboedire, ob* toward + *oedire* (akin to *audire* to hear). This, the first occurrence of
    a word and idea central to the plot, is a clue to the meaning of *obedience,* i.e., an attitude and
    behavior of a creature toward its creator, of children to parents. See *CD,* p. 414, and cf. other
    uses of *obey, obedient,* and *obedience:* III.95, 107, 190, 191, 269; IV.428, 520, 636; V.501,
    514, 522, 537, 551, 806; VI.185, 740, 741, 902; VII.48, 159, 498; VIII.240, 325, 634; IX.368,
    570, 701; X.14, 145; XI.112; XII.126, 397, 403, 408, 561.
868–70. Cf. the Nicene creed: "We believe in . . . one Lord Jesus Christ . . . who . . . sitteth
    on the right hand of the Father, and . . . of whose kingdom there shall be no end."
875. *powers:* army.
877. *wards:* the matching grooves and notches on keys and in locks.
879–82. Cf. *Aen.* 6.573–74: "Then at last, grating on harsh, jarring hinge, the infernal gates
    open."
883. *Erebus:* primeval Darkness, son of Chaos and brother of *Night* (894); hell.

Th' infernal doors, and on their hinges grate
Harsh thunder, that the lowest bottom shook
Of Erebus. She opened, but to shut
Excelled her power; the gates wide open stood,
That with extended wings a bannered host   885
Under spread ensigns marching might pass through
With horse and chariots ranked in loose array;
So wide they stood, and like a furnace mouth
Cast forth redounding smoke and ruddy flame.
Before their eyes in sudden view appear   890
The secrets of the hoary deep, a dark
Illimitable ocean without bound,
Without dimension, where length, breadth, and highth,
And time and place are lost; where eldest Night
And Chaos, ancestors of Nature, hold   895
Eternal anarchy, amidst the noise
Of endless wars, and by confusion stand.
For Hot, Cold, Moist, and Dry, four champions fierce
Strive here for mastery, and to battle bring
Their embryon atoms; they around the flag   900
Of each his faction, in their several clans,
Light-armed or heavy, sharp, smooth, swift or slow,
Swarm populous, unnumbered as the sands
Of Barca or Cyrene's torrid soil,
Levied to side with warring winds, and poise   905
Their lighter wings. To whom these most adhere,
He rules a moment; Chaos umpire sits,
And by decision more embroils the fray
By which he reigns: next him high arbiter
Chance governs all. Into this wild abyss,   910
The womb of Nature and perhaps her grave,
Of neither sea, nor shore, nor air, nor fire,

885–87. Cf. *Il.* 9.383–84: "Thebes of the hundred gates, whence sally forth two hundred warriors through each with horses and chariots . . ."
889. *redounding*: surging.
890f. Cf. *Met.* 1.5–20: "Before the sea was, and the land, and the sky that hangs over all, the face of Nature showed alike in her whole round, which state have men called chaos: a rough, unordered mass of things, nothing at all save lifeless bulk and warring seeds of ill-matched elements heaped in one. No sun yet shone forth upon the world, nor did the waxing moon renew her slender horns; not yet did the earth hang poised by her own weight in the circumambient air, nor had the ocean stretched her arms along the far reaches of the lands. And, though there was both land and sea and air, no one could tread that land, or swim that sea; and the air was dark. No form of things remained the same; all objects were at odds, for within one body cold things strove with hot, and moist with dry, soft things with hard, things having weight with weightless things."
891. *hoary deep*: greyish white ocean. Cf. the description of the wake of the leviathan in Job 41.32: "one would think the deep to be hoary" or (*NEB*) "like white hair."
898–906. In the simile, countless atoms are enlisted to serve the four warring elements of fire, earth, water, and air, just as countless particles of sand are enlisted by the warring winds of the desert to serve them by lending weight (*poise*) or force to the warring winds. *Barca, Cyrene*: cities in North Africa. *embryon*: undeveloped.
912. Not the four elements, but what they came from.

But all these in their pregnant causes mixed
Confus'dly, and which thus must ever fight,
Unless th' Almighty Maker them ordain   915
His dark materials to create more worlds,
Into this wild abyss the wary Fiend
Stood on the brink of hell and looked a while,
Pondering his voyage; for no narrow frith
He had to cross. Nor was his ear less pealed   920
With noises loud and ruinous (to compare
Great things with small) than when Bellona storms,
With all her battering engines bent to raze
Some capital city; or less than if this frame
Of heav'n were falling, and these elements   925
In mutiny had from her axle torn
The steadfast earth. At last his sail-broad vans
He spreads for flight, and in the surging smoke
Uplifted spurns the ground, thence many a league
As in a cloudy chair ascending rides   930
Audacious, but that seat soon failing, meets
A vast vacuity: all unawares
Flutt'ring his pennons vain plumb down he drops
Ten thousand fathom deep, and to this hour
Down had been falling, had not by ill chance   935
The strong rebuff of some tumultuous cloud
Instinct with fire and niter hurried him
As many miles aloft: that fury stayed,
Quenced in a boggy Syrtis, neither sea,
Nor good dry land: nigh foundered on he fares,   940
Treading the crude consistence, half on foot,
Half flying; behoves him now both oar and sail.
As when a gryphon through the wilderness
With wingèd course o'er hill or moory dale,
Pursues the Arimaspian, who by stealth   945
Had from his wakeful custody purloined

---

919. *frith:* firth, an estuary, where the meeting of a river current and an ocean tide makes the waters turbulent and dangerous (cf. *boiling gulf,* 1027). Chaos was like a firth, but not narrow.
920. *pealed:* assailed, dinned.
922. *Bellona:* goddess of war.
924. *frame:* structure, fabric; also order, plan, scheme, system. A common synonym for universe.
927. *vans:* (L *vannus* fan for winnowing grain) fans. The sails of windmills were called "vans" or "vanes."
933. *Flutt'ring his pennons vain:* flapping his useless wings.
936. *rebuff:* (It. *ri + buffo* puff) counter blast. *tumultuous:* (L *tumere* to swell) exploding.
937. *instinct with:* impelled by. *fire:* sulphur, which is mixed with saltpeter to make gunpowder. Lava was also called "fire"; and the "fire" of thunder and lightning was considered sulphurous. Milton's imagery is both volcanic and meteorological.
939. The Syrtes were tidal marshes on the shore of North Africa.
943–47. According to a legend told by Herodotus, one-eyed creatures called Arimaspi stole gold guarded by griffons, who were half eagle and half lion.

The guarded gold: so eagerly the Fiend
O'er bog or steep, through strait, rough, dense, or rare,
With head, hands, wings, or feet pursues his way,
And swims or sinks, or wades, or creeps, or flies: 950
At length a universal hubbub wild
Of stunning sounds and voices all confused
Borne through the hollow dark assaults his ear
With loudest vehemence: thither he plies,
Undaunted to meet there whatever Power   955
Or Spirit of the nethermost abyss
Might in that noise reside, of whom to ask
Which way the nearest coast of darkness lies
Bordering on light; when straight behold the throne
Of Chaos, and his dark pavilion spread   960
Wide on the wasteful deep; with him enthroned
Sat sable-vested Night, eldest of things,
The consort of his reign; and by them stood
Orcus and Ades, and the dreaded name
Of Demogorgon; Rumor next and Chance,   965
And Tumult and Confusion all embroiled,
And Discord with a thousand various mouths.
    T' whom Satan turning boldly, thus. "Ye Powers
And Spirits of this nethermost abyss,
Chaos and ancient Night, I come no spy,   970
With purpose to explore or to disturb
The secrets of your realm, but by constraint
Wand'ring this darksome desert, as my way
Lies through your spacious empire up to light,
Alone, and without guide, half lost, I seek   975
What readiest path leads where your gloomy bounds
Confine with heav'n; or if some other place
From your dominion won, th' Ethereal King
Possesses lately, thihter to arrive
I travel this profound; direct my course;   980
Directed, no mean recompense it brings
To your behoof, if I that region lost,
All usurpation thence expelled, reduce
To her original darkness and your sway
(Which is my present journey) and once more   985
Erect the standard there of ancient Night;
Yours be th' advantage all, mine the revenge."

961. *wasteful deep*: chaos, the ultimate wasteland.
964. *Orcus*: another name for *Ades* (Hades) or Pluto, king of hell.
965. *Demogorgon*. Not a god of classical mythology. Milton elsewhere identified him with
  Chaos.
977. *Confine with*: border on.
980. *profound*: L *pro* prior to + *fundus* bottom.
982. *behoof*: advantage.

Thus Satan; and him thus the anarch old
With falt'ring speech and visage incomposed
Answered. "I know thee, stranger, who thou art,   990
That mighty leading angel, who of late
Made head against heav'n's King, though overthrown.
I saw and heard, for such a numerous host
Fled not in silence through the frighted deep
With ruin upon ruin, rout on rout,   995
Confusion worse confounded; and heav'n gates
Poured out by millions her victorious bands
Pursuing. I upon my frontiers here
Keep residence; if all I can will serve,
That little which is left so to defend,   1000
Encroached on still through our intestine broils
Weak'ning the scepter of old Night: first hell
Your dungeon stretching far and wide beneath;
Now lately heaven and earth, another world
Hung o'er my realm, linked in a golden chain   1005
To that side heav'n from whence your legions fell:
If that way be your walk, you have not far;
So much the nearer danger; go and speed;
Havoc and spoil and ruin are my gain."
    He ceased; and Satan stayed not to reply,   1010
But glad that now his sea should find a shore,
With fresh alacrity and force renewed
Springs upward like a pyramid of fire
Into the wild expanse, and through the shock
Of fighting elements, on all sides round   1015
Environed wins his way; harder beset
And more endangered, than when Argo passed
Through Bosporus betwixt the justling rocks:
Or when Ulysses on the larboard shunned
Charybdis, and by th' other whirlpool steered.   1020
So he with difficulty and labor hard
Moved on, with difficulty and labor he;

988. *anarch*. The "ruler" of an anarchy ("no ruler") must be a nonruler.
989. *incomposed*: disordered, disturbed.
990. A man possessed of the spirit of an unclean devil addressed Christ in the same words: "I
    know thee who thou art" (Mark 1.24).
1001. *still*: constantly. *intestine broils*: civil wars.
1004. *heaven*: the universe around the earth.
1005. *golden chain*: cf. *Il.* 8.18–27: "Fasten ye a rope of gold from heaven, and all ye gods lay
    hold thereof and all goddesses. . . ."
1008. *speed*: good luck.
1009. *Havoc*: destruction. *spoil*: plunder. *ruin*: what remains after destruction.
1013. *pyramid of fire*: perhaps what is now called a sun pillar, a column of light extending up
    and down from the sun caused by the reflection of light on ice particles in the air.
1018–20. See II.648–66n. *Justling rocks*: mythical floating rocks able to crush ships trying to sail
    between them, and famous for failing to stop the Argonauts on their way through the straits
    at the north end of the Bosporus in quest of the Golden Fleece.
1019–20. Cf. *Od.* 12.234ff. and *Aen.* 3.420ff.

But he once passed, soon after when man fell,
Strange alteration! Sin and Death amain
Following his track, such was the will of Heav'n,   1025
Paved after him a broad and beaten way
Over the dark abyss, whose boiling gulf
Tamely endured a bridge of wondrous length
From hell continued reaching th' utmost orb
Of this frail world; by which the Spirits perverse   1030
With easy intercourse pass to and fro
To tempt or punish mortals, except whom
God and good angels guard by special grace.
But now at last the sacred influence
Of light appears, and from the walls of heav'n   1035
Shoots far into the bosom of dim Night
A glimmering dawn; here Nature first begins
Her farthest verge, and Chaos to retire
As from her outmost works a broken foe
With tumult less and with less hostile din,   1040
That Satan with less toil, and now with ease
Wafts on the calmer wave by dubious light
And like a weather-beaten vessel holds
Gladly the port, though shrouds and tackle torn;
Or in the emptier waste, resembling air   1045
Weighs his spread wings, at leisure to behold
Far off th' empyreal heav'n, extended wide
In circuit, undetermined square or round,
With opal tow'rs and battlements adorned
Of living sapphire, once his native seat;   1050
And fast by hanging in a golden chain

1032–33. *tempt:* L *temptare* to feel, try, tempt; akin to L *tendere* to stretch. For Milton's definition of temptation, see *CD* I.viii. Cf. other uses of *tempt* and *temptation* in *PL*: IV.65; V.846; VI.908; VIII.643; IX.281, 296, 299, 328, 364, 531, 736; X.14. See "Angels," pp. 466–68.
1033. Cf. *CD*, pp. 411–13.
1034. *influence:* (L *influere* to flow into) an astrological term for the effective virtue, power, force (an "etherial fluid") emitted by the stars and the heavens, and acting upon the earth and its creatures; here, a kind of metaphor, since the *sacred* light naturalizes chaos.
1036. *bosom:* (root meaning, "the space embraced by two arms") womb, stomach: here, the interior.
1037. *Nature:* order; the antithesis of Chaos.
1039–40. A military simile. *works:* fortifications.
1043. *holds:* makes for.
1046. *Weighs:* balances (like the arms of a pair of scales), keeps steady.
1047. *empyreal heav'n:* as distinct from the heavens of the universe. See I.117n.
1048. *undetermined:* not authoritatively decided, undeterminable; or (because of its size) beyond Satan's power to tell.
1050. *living:* in its native state, not cut or hewn. Cf. Exod. 20.25. *sapphire.* Cf. Rev. 21.19.
1051. *golden chain.* In a note to his translation of one of Milton's academic exercises (*Prolusion II*), Merritt Y. Hughes says: "Homer's story (*Il.* 8.18–29) of the challenge of Zeus to the other gods to drag him from heaven by a golden chain, and of his boast that he would be able to lift them all up to heaven with it, passed through many allegorical interpretations, from that of Plato's *Theaetetus*, 153c, to Bacon's in *The Advancement of Learning* I.i.3: 'The highest link of nature's chain must needs be tied to the foot of Jupiter's chain.' " The passage in Milton's

This pendent world, in bigness as a star
Of smallest magnitude close by the moon.
Thither full fraught with mischievous revenge,
Accursed, and in a curséd hour, he hies.   1055

Book III

The Argument

God sitting on his throne sees Satan flying towards this world, then newly created; shows him to the Son who sat at his right hand; foretells the success of Satan in perverting mankind; clears his own justice and wisdom from all imputation, having created man free and able enough to have withstood his tempter; yet declares his purpose of grace towards him, in regard he fell not of his own malice, as did Satan, but by him seduced. The Son of God renders praises to his Father for the manifestation of his gracious purpose towards man; but God again declares, that grace cannot be extended towards man without the satisfaction of divine justice; man hath offended the majesty of God by aspiring to Godhead, and therefore with all his progeny devoted to death must die, unless someone can be found sufficient to answer for his offense, and undergo his punishment. The Son of God freely offers himself a ransom for man: the Father accepts him, ordains his incarnation, pronounces his exaltation above all names in heaven and earth; commands all the angels to adore him; they obey, and hymning to their harps in full choir, celebrate the Father and the Son. Meanwhile Satan alights upon the bare convex of this world's outermost orb; where wandering he first finds a place since called the Limbo of Vanity; what persons and things fly up thither; thence comes to the gate of heaven, described ascending by stairs, and the waters above the firmament that flow about it: his passage thence to the orb of the sun; he finds there Uriel the regent of that orb, but first changes himself into the shape of a meaner angel; and pretending a zealous desire to behold the new creation and man whom God had placed there, inquires of him the place of his habitation, and is directed; alights first on Mount Niphates.

---

exercise reads: "and that universal interaction of all things, that lovely concord among them, which Pythagoras poetically symbolized as harmony, was splendidly and aptly represented by Homer's figure of the golden chain which Jove suspended from heaven" (trans. Hughes). See "Scale of Nature," pp. 464–66.
1052. *pendent world*: the universe.

Hail holy Light, offspring of Heav'n first-born,
Or of th' Eternal coeternal beam
May I express thee unblamed? Since God is light,
And never but in unapproachèd light
Dwelt from eternity, dwelt then in thee,   5
Bright effluence of bright essence increate.
Or hear'st thou rather pure ethereal stream,
Whose fountain who shall tell? Before the sun,
Before the heavens thou wert, and at the voice
Of God, as with a mantle didst invest   10
The rising world of waters dark and deep,
Won from the void and formless infinite.
Thee I revisit now with bolder wing,
Escaped the Stygian pool, though long detained
In that obscure sojourn, while in my flight   15
Through utter and through middle darkness borne
With other notes than to th' Orphéan lyre
I sung of Chaos and eternal Night,
Taught by the Heav'nly Muse to venture down
The dark descent, and up to reascend,   20
Though hard and rare: thee I revisit safe,
And feel thy sovran vital lamp; but thou
Revisit'st not these eyes, that roll in vain
To find thy piercing ray, and find no dawn;
So thick a drop serene hath quenched their orbs,   25
Or dim suffusion veiled. Yet not the more

III.1–55. To move from hell to heaven is to move from darkness to light, and Milton marks this change by a second invocation, this one to holy Light, God himself, who is light and dwells in fire, flame, dazzling brightness. Milton's speculations include common theological questions: If God is light and God is eternal, isn't light also without beginning? But God's first words in Gen. 1 are, "Let there be light." Perhaps God was not creating light but only calling upon light to *invest/ The rising world*, the heaven and earth he had just begun to create, cf. Gen. 1.1–3, p. 429. The poet's invocation is not, however, a theological or a scientific discussion. *Light* may carry suggestions of God, Christ ("I am the light of the world"), wisdom, and inspiration of the Holy Spirit, at the same time that it means the physical light by which men see nature—if they are not, like John Milton, totally blind. The invocation is a hymn and a prayer, uttered by Milton, the bard, the *vates*, the seer, the prophetic maker of this poem, who, like Homer, could see only with his memory and his inward eye.
1. *first-born*. In an oration written as an undergraduate (*Prolusion I*) Milton argued that "Day is more ancient than Night; that this world, recently emerged from Chaos, was illuminated by diffused light before Night had begun her alternations."
3. *God is light*. Cf. 1 John 1.5: "This then is the message which we have heard of him, and declare unto you, that God is light, and in him is no darkness at all." *express*: describe. *unblamed*: without being guilty of improper speculation.
4–5. Cf. 1 Tim. 6.16: "[God] only hath immortality, dwelling in the light which no man can approach unto. . . ."
6. *effluence*: L *ex* out + *fluere* to flow. *increate*: uncreated.
10. *invest*: (L *in* + *vestis* garment) envelop. Cf. Ps. 104.1–2 "O Lord my God . . . who coverest thyself with light as with a garment."
16. The *utter* (outer, beyond limits) *darkness* is hell; the *middle*, chaos.
17. *Orphean*. In Greek myth Orpheus, whose music could spellbind wild beasts, descended into hell in a vain effort to charm Pluto and Persephone by song into letting him regain his wife Eurydice. Milton's *notes* are epic, whereas those of Orpheus's hymn "To Night" were lyric.
25. *drop serene*: gutta serena, the medical term for Milton's blindness.
26. *dim suffusion*: suffusio nigra, medical term for a cataract.

Cease I to wander where the Muses haunt
Clear spring, or shady grove, or sunny hill,
Smit with the love of sacred song; but chief
Thee Sion and the flow'ry brooks beneath   30
That wash thy hallowed feet, and warbling flow,
Nightly I visit: nor sometimes forget
Those other two equaled with me in fate,
So were I equaled with them in renown,
Blind Thamyris and blind Maeonides,   35
And Tiresias and Phineus prophets old.
Then feed on thoughts, that voluntary move
Harmonious numbers; as the wakeful bird
Sings darkling, and in shadiest covert hid
Tunes her nocturnal note. Thus with the year   40
Seasons return, but not to me returns
Day, or the sweet approach of ev'n or morn,
Or sight of vernal bloom, or summer's rose,
Or flocks, or herds, or human face divine;
But cloud instead, and ever-during dark   45
Surrounds me, from the cheerful ways of men
Cut off, and for the book of knowledge fair
Presented with a universal blank
Of nature's works to me expunged and razed,
And wisdom at one entrance quite shut out.   50

26–32. "He rendered his studies and various works more easy and pleasant by alloting them their several portions of the day. Of these the time friendly to the Muses fell to his poetry; and he, waking early (as is the use of temperate men), had commonly a good stack of verses ready against his amanuensis came; which if it happened to be later than ordinary, he would complain that 'he wanted to be milked.' The evenings he likewise spent in reading some choice poets, by way of refreshment after the day's toil, and to store his fancy against morning. Besides his ordinary lectures [i.e., readings] out of the Bible and the best commentators on the week day, that was his sole subject on Sunday." From the anonymous *Life of Milton*. In his essay *Of Education* Milton recommended that the students in his ideal boarding school occupy themselves between dinner and bedtime with "the easy grounds of religion and the story of scriptures."
29–32. I.e., the poetry of the Bible, which Milton read in Hebrew, as well as in Latin and English translations. Here he refers chiefly to "those frequent songs [i.e., odes and hymns] throughout the law and prophets [which are] beyond all [pagan examples], not in their divine argument alone, but in the very critical art of composition, [and which] may be easily made appear over all the kinds of lyric poesy to be incomparable." *The Reason of Church Government*, p. 358. *Sion . . . brooks*. Cf. I.10–11. *nightly*: in the night. Cf. *darkling* at 39.
35–36. *Thamyris*: a blind poet alluded to in *Il.* 2.594–600. *Maeonides*: Homer. *Tiresias* was the blind old man in *Oedipus* and *Antigone* whose prophecies proved to be true. *Phineus*: another mythical blind prophet.
37–38. "The thoughts, as if by their own power, produce the lines of poetry." In an early work (*An Apology for Smectymnuus*), speaking of his own experience in writing prose, Milton gave a similar description of the "voluntary" nature of composition: "For me, readers, although I cannot say that I am utterly untrained in those rules which best rhetoricians have given, or unacquainted with those examples which the prime authors of eloquence have written in any learned tongue; yet true eloquence I find to be none, but the serious and hearty love of truth: and that whose mind soever is fully possessed with a fervent desire to know good things, and with the dearest charity to infuse the knowledge of them into others, when such a man would speak, his words (by what I can express), like so many nimble and airy servitors, trip about him at command, and in well-ordered files, as he would wish, fall aptly into their own places."
38. *numbers*: verses. *wakeful bird*: nightingale.
39. *darkling*: in the dark.

So much the rather thou celestial Light
Shine inward, and the mind through all her powers
Irradiate, there plant eyes, all mist from thence
Purge and disperse, that I may see and tell
Of things invisible to mortal sight.   55
   Now had the Almighty Father from above,
From the pure empyrean where he sits
High throned above all highth, bent down his eye,
His own works and their works at once to view:
Above him all the sanctities of heaven   60
Stood thick as stars, and from his sight received
Beatitude past utterance; on his right
The radiant image of his glory sat,
His only Son; on earth he first beheld
Our two first parents, yet the only two   65
Of mankind, in the happy garden placed,
Reaping immortal fruits of joy and love,
Uninterrupted joy, unrivaled love
In blissful solitude; he then surveyed
Hell and the gulf between, and Satan there   70
Coasting the wall of heav'n on this side Night
In the dun air sublime, and ready now
To stoop with wearied wings, and willing feet
On the bare outside of this world, that seemed
Firm land embosomed without firmament,   75
Uncertain which, in ocean or in air.
Him God beholding from his prospect high,
Wherein past, present, future he beholds,
Thus to his only Son foreseeing spake.
   "Only begotten Son, seest thou what rage   80
Transports our Adversary, whom no bounds
Prescribed, no bars of hell, nor all the chains
Heaped on him there, nor yet the main abyss
Wide interrupt can hold; so bent he seems
On desperate revenge, that shall redound   85
Upon his own rebellious head. And now
Through all restraint broke loose he wings his way
Not far off heav'n, in the precincts of light,

57. *pure empyrean:* (Gk *pyr* fire) region of pure light.
60. *sanctities:* angels.
71. *Coasting:* sailing along the shore of.
72. *dun:* dusky. *sublime:* above.
73. *stoop:* descend; (of a heavenly body) to begin to descend; (of a bird of prey) to swoop down on.
74. *world:* the sphere that enclosed all the smaller spheres constituting the universe.
75. *firmament:* the atmosphere, which exists only *within* the universe.
81. The God of the OT could be derisive, and Milton's natural ironic bent led easily to the pun on *Transports,* meaning "enraptures" as well as "carries across."
83. *main:* vast, as in "the ocean main," or (VII.279) *main ocean.*
84. *interrupt:* (a past participle) forming a *wide interval* (between hell and the world).

Directly towards the new-created world,
And man there placed, with purpose to assay   90
If him by force he can destroy, or worse,
By some false guile pervert; and shall pervert;
For man will hearken to his glozing lies,
And easily transgress the sole command,
Sole pledge of his obedience: so will fall   95
He and his faithless progeny: whose fault?
Whose but his own? Ingrate, he had of me
All he could have; I made him just and right,
Sufficient to have stood, though free to fall.
Such I created all th' ethereal Powers   100
And Spirits, both them who stood and them who failed;
Freely they stood who stood, and fell who fell.
Not free, what proof could they have giv'n sincere
Of true allegiance, constant faith or love,
Where only what they needs must do, appeared,   105
Not what they would? What praise could they receive?
What pleasure I from such obedience paid,
When will and reason (reason also is choice)
Useless and vain, of freedom both despoiled,
Made passive both, had served necessity,   110
Not me. They therefore as to right belonged,
So were created, nor can justly accuse
Their Maker, or their making, or their fate,
As if predestination overruled
Their will, disposed by absolute decree   115
Or high foreknowledge; they themselves decreed
Their own revolt, not I: if I foreknew,
Foreknowledge had no influence on their fault,
Which had no less proved certain unforeknown.
So without least impulse or shadow of fate,   120
Or aught by me immutably foreseen,
They trespass, authors to themselves in all
Both what they judge and what they choose; for so
I formed them free, and free they must remain,
Till they enthrall themselves: I else must change   125

92–134. See "God," pp. 468–69, "Reason," p. 464, "Freedom," p. 469, and *CD*, pp. 404–5.
Cf. VIII.325 ff.
93. *glozing*: flattering.
95. *sole pledge*. The only token, sign, proof, evidence of Adam's obedience was his not eating
the fruit. His only "act" of obedience was not eating—as God's only law, only command, was
not to eat. Milton uses *pledge* elsewhere in the sense of "child," a token of its parents' love.
Adam's abstaining was a child of his obedience. In *CD*, p. 414, Milton called the Tree "a
pledge, as it were, and memorial of obedience"—here the word means a concrete "outward
sign." Similarly Samson's hair was a *pledge*, as was his not cutting it.
108. *reason*: the power of judging rightly, of distinguishing true from false and right from wrong.
See *CD*, pp. 402–3 and 414–15, and 418–20. Cf. other related uses of the word: V.102, 106,
487; VI.41, 42, 125, 126; VIII.554, 591; IX.352, 360, 654, 1130; XII.84, 86, 89, 92, 98.
117. *if*: granted that.

Their nature, and revoke the high decree
Unchangeable, eternal, which ordained
Their freedom, they themselves ordained their fall.
The first sort by their own suggestion fell,
Self-tempted, self-depraved: man falls deceived   130
By the other first: man therefore shall find grace,
The other none: in mercy and justice both,
Through heav'n and earth, so shall my glory excel,
But mercy first and last shall brightest shine."
 Thus while God spake, ambrosial fragrance filled   135
All heav'n, and in the blessèd Spirits elect
Sense of new joy ineffable diffused:
Beyond compare the Son of God was seen
Most glorious, in him all his Father shone
Substantially expressed, and in his face   140
Divine compassion visibly appeared,
Love without end, and without measure grace,
Which uttering thus he to his Father spake.
 "O Father, gracious was that word which closed
Thy sovran sentence, that man should find grace;   145
For which both heav'n and earth shall high extol
Thy praises, with th' innumerable sound
Of hymns and sacred songs, wherewith thy throne
Encompassed shall resound thee ever blessed.
For should man finally be lost, should man   150
Thy creature late so loved, thy youngest son
Fall circumvented thus by fraud, though joined
With his own folly? That be from thee far,
That far be from thee, Father, who art judge
Of all things made, and judgest only right.   155
Or shall the Adversary thus obtain
His end, and frustrate thine, shall he fulfill
His malice, and thy goodness bring to naught,
Or proud return though to his heavier doom,
Yet with revenge accomplished, and to hell   160
Draw after him the whole race of mankind,
By him corrupted? Or wilt thou thyself
Abolish thy creation, and unmake,

---

129. *The first sort:* the fallen angels. *suggestion:* temptation.
136. *Spirits elect:* the angels who did not revolt. See "Angels," pp. 466–68.
140. *Substantially:* in essence. But the term had a special meaning in theological discussions about the nature of the Trinity, the subtleties of which Milton avoided in *PL*.
142. *grace.* See "The Fortunate Fall," pp. 470–71.
153. See the words Abraham used in pleading with the Lord, Gen. 18.25: "That be far from thee to do after this manner, to slay the righteous with the wicked: and that the righteous should be as the wicked, that be far from thee: Shall not the Judge of all the earth do right?"
156. *Adversary:* meaning of the Hebrew word *Satan.*
159. *doom:* condemnation.

For him, what for thy glory thou hast made?
So should thy goodness and thy greatness both   165
Be questioned and blasphemed without defense."
     To whom the great Creator thus replied.
"O Son, in whom my soul hath chief delight,
Son of my bosom, Son who art alone
My Word, my wisdom, and effectual might,   170
All hast thou spoken as my thoughts are, all
As my eternal purpose hath decreed:
Man shall not quite be lost, but saved who will,
Yet not of will in him, but grace in me
Freely vouchsafed; once more I will renew   175
His lapsèd powers, though forfeit and enthralled
By sin to foul exorbitant desires;
Upheld by me, yet once more he shall stand
On even ground against his mortal foe,
By me upheld, that he may know how frail   180
His fall'n condition is, and to me owe
All his deliv'rance, and to none but me.
Some I have chosen of peculiar grace
Elect above the rest; so is my will:
The rest shall hear me call, and oft be warned   185
Their sinful state, and to appease betimes
Th' incensèd Deity, while offered grace
Invites; for I will clear their senses dark,
What may suffice, and soften stony hearts
To pray, repent, and bring obedience due.   190
To prayer, repentance, and obedience due,
Though but endeavored with sincere intent,
Mine ear shall not be slow, mine eye not shut.
And I will place within them as a guide
My umpire conscience, whom if they will hear,   195

168–70. Cf. *Aen.* 1.664: "Son, who art alone my strength, my mighty power—O son," etc.
169. *Son of my bosom.* Cf. John 1.18: "the only begotten Son, which is in the bosom of the Father. . . ."
170. *My Word.* Cf. *CD*, pp. 407–8. *my wisdom:* 1 Cor. 1.24: "Christ the power of God, and the wisdom of God."
180–81. Cf. Ps. 39.4: "Lord, make me to know mine end, and the measure of my days, what it is; that I may know how frail I am."
184. *Elect.* Milton rejected the Calvinist doctrine that God had from the beginning predestined the damnation or salvation of each individual soul. Rather, he thought that only the general reward of salvation to all who "believed" was predestined: no soul was damned before it was, so to speak, born. But Milton agreed with St. Augustine that for reasons not revealed to men certain human beings and all unfallen angels were elected in that they were predestined to be exemplarily holy. These were the *blessed Spirits elect* (136) and the sons of Adam here referred to as *of peculiar* [i.e., special or individual] *grace*—that is, holy men, or saints. But at line 330 *saints* means the elect of both sorts—those who were elected from the beginning and those who by their own choice contributed to their own salvation. Cf. *CD*, pp. 406–7: "God . . . has elected whoever believes and continues in the faith."
189. Cf. Ezek. 11.19: "I will take the stony heart out of their flesh, and will give them an heart of flesh."
195. *conscience.* See *CD*, pp. 401–2; also "Reason," p. 464, and cf. other uses of the word: IV.23; X.842, 849; XII.297, 522, 529.

Light after light well used they shall attain,
And to the end persisting, safe arrive.
This my long sufferance and my day of grace
They who neglect and scorn, shall never taste;
But hard be hardened, blind be blinded more,   200
That they may stumble on, and deeper fall;
And none but such from mercy I exclude.
But yet all is not done; man disobeying,
Disloyal breaks his fealty, and sins
Against the high supremacy of Heav'n,   205
Affecting Godhead, and so losing all,
To expiate his treason hath naught left,
But to destruction sacred and devote,
He with his whole posterity must die,
Die he or justice must; unless for him   210
Some other able, and as willing, pay
The rigid satisfaction, death for death.
Say heav'nly Powers, where shall we find such love,
Which of ye will be mortal to redeem
Man's mortal crime, and just th' unjust to save,   215
Dwells in all heaven charity so dear?"
   He asked, but all the heav'nly choir stood mute,
And silence was in heav'n; on man's behalf
Patron or intercessor none appeared,
Much less that durst upon his own head draw   220
The deadly forfeiture, and ransom set.
And now without redemption all mankind
Must have been lost, adjudged to death and hell
By doom severe, had not the Son of God,
In whom the fullness dwells of love divine,   225
His dearest mediation thus renewed.
   "Father, thy word is passed, man shall find grace;
And shall grace not find means, that finds her way,

200. See *CD*, I.viii.
203–16. See "The Fortunate Fall," pp. 470–71.
206. *Affecting:* aspiring to.
208. *sacred and devote:* synonyms for *consecrated*, meaning "set apart for some holy purpose,"
    such as sacrifice.
215. Cf. 1 Pet. 3.18: "For Christ also hath once suffered for sins, the just for the unjust, that
    he might bring us to God."
216. *charity:* LL *caritas* Christian love.
217–18. Cf. Rev. 8.1: "And when he had opened the seventh seal, there was silence in heaven
    about the space of half an hour."
219. *Patron:* an advocate, such as a patron saint. Cf. 1 John 2.1: "My little children, these things
    write I unto you, that ye sin not. And if any man sin, we have an advocate with the Father,
    Jesus Christ the righteous."
222. *redemption:* L *redimere*, to buy back.
224. *doom:* judgment.
225. Cf. Col. 2.9: "In him dwelleth all the fulness of the Godhead bodily."
227. *passed:* pledged.

The speediest of thy wingèd messengers,
To visit all thy creatures, and to all   230
Comes unprevented, unimplored, unsought,
Happy for man, so coming; he her aid
Can never seek, once dead in sins and lost;
Atonement for himself or offering meet,
Indebted and undone, hath none to bring: 235
Behold me then, me for him, life for life
I offer, on me let thine anger fall;
Account me man; I for his sake will leave
Thy bosom, and this glory next to thee
Freely put off, and for him lastly die   240
Well pleased, on me let Death wreck all his rage;
Under his gloomy power I shall not long
Lie vanquished; thou hast giv'n me to possess
Life in myself forever, by thee I live,
Though now to Death I yield, and am his due   245
All that of me can die, yet that debt paid,
Thou wilt not leave me in the loathsome grave
His prey, nor suffer my unspotted soul
Forever with corruption there to dwell;
But I shall rise victorious, and subdue   250
My vanquisher, spoiled of his vaunted spoil;
Death his death's wound shall then receive, and stoop
Inglorious, of his mortal sting disarmed.
I through the ample air in triumph high
Shall lead hell captive maugre hell, and show   255
The powers of darkness bound. Thou at the sight
Pleased, out of heaven shalt look down and smile,
While by thee raised I ruin all my foes,

231. *unprevented:* unanticipated.
233. Cf. Eph. 2.4–5: "But God, who is rich in mercy, for his great love wherewith he loved us, even when we were dead in sins, hath quickened us together with Christ (by grace ye are saved)."
234. *meet:* appropriate.
243–44. Cf. John 5.26 "For as the Father hath life in himself; so hath he given to the Son to have life in himself."
247–49. Cf. Ps. 16.10: "For thou wilt not leave my soul in hell; neither wilt thou suffer thine Holy One to see corruption."
250–59. Cf. 1 Cor. 15.26, 51–55: "The last enemy that shall be destroyed is death. . . . Behold, I shew you a mystery; We shall not all sleep, but we shall all be changed, In a moment, in the twinkling of an eye, at the last trump: for the trumpet shall sound, and the dead shall be raised incorruptible, and we shall be changed. For this corruptible must put on incorruption, and this mortal must put on immortality. So when this corruptible shall have put on incorruption, and this mortal shall have put on immortality, then shall be brought to pass the saying that is written, Death is swallowed up in victory. O death, where is thy sting? O grave, where is thy victory?" Col. 2.15: "And having spoiled principalities and powers, he made a shew of them openly, triumphing over them in it."
254–65. Having predicted his triumphant resurrection after the crucifixion (250–53), Christ skips forward to the time of the Last Judgment, at the end of his one thousand years' reign on earth (the Millennium).
255. Cf. Eph. 4.8: "When he ascended up on high, he led captivity captive." *maugre:* in spite of.
258. *ruin:* L *ruere* hurl to the ground.

Death last, and with his carcass glut the grave:
Then with the multitude of my redeemed   260
Shall enter heaven long absent, and return,
Father, to see thy face, wherein no cloud
Of anger shall remain, but peace assured,
And reconcilement; wrath shall be no more
Thenceforth, but in thy presence joy entire."   265
    His words here ended, but his meek aspéct
Silent yet spake, and breathed immortal love
To mortal men, above which only shone
Filial obedience: as a sacrifice
Glad to be offered, he attends the will   270
Of his great Father. Admiration seized
All heav'n, what this might mean, and wither tend
Wond'ring; but soon th' Almighty thus replied:
    "O thou in heav'n and earth the only peace
Found out for mankind under wrath, O thou   275
My sole complacence! well thou know'st how dear
To me are all my works, nor man the least
Though last created, that for him I spare
Thee from my bosom and right hand, to save,
By losing thee a while, the whole race lost.   280
Thou therefore whom thou only canst redeem,
Their nature also to thy nature join;
And be thy self man among men on earth,
Made flesh, when time shall be, of virgin seed,
By wondrous birth: be thou in Adam's room   285
The head of all mankind, though Adam's son.
As in him perish all men, so in thee
As from a second root shall be restored,
As many as are restored, without thee none.
His crime makes guilty all his sons; thy merit   290
Imputed shall absolve them who renounce

270. *attends*: awaits.
271. *Admiration*: astonishment.
276. *complacence*: source of pleasure.
285–86. Cf. 1 Cor. 11.3, p. 458: "The head of every man is Christ." *room*: place. *Adam's son*: Jesus, son of man.
287. Cf. 1 Cor. 15.22, p. 459: "As in Adam all die, even so in Christ shall all be made alive." See "The Fortunate Fall," pp. 470–71.
288. Cf. Rev. 22.16: "I am the root and the offspring of David."
290–94. Cf. Rom. 5.15–19 [NEB]: "But God's act of grace is out of all proportion to Adam's wrongdoing. For if the wrongdoing of that one man brought death upon so many, its effect is vastly exceeded by the grace of God and the gift that came to so many by the grace of the one man, Jesus Christ. And again, the gift of God is not to be compared in its effect with that one man's sin; for the judicial action, following upon the one offence, issued in a verdict of condemnation, but the act of grace, following upon so many misdeeds, issued in a verdict of acquittal. For if by the wrongdoing of that one man death established its reign, through a single sinner, much more shall those who receive in far greater measure God's grace, and his gift of righteousness, live and reign through the one man, Jesus Christ." *Imputed*: credited by transferal (to *them who* etc.).

Their own both righteous and unrighteous deeds,
And live in thee transplanted, and from thee
Receive new life. So man, as is most just,
Shall satisfy for man, be judged and die,   295
And dying rise, and rising with him raise
His brethren, ransomed with his own dear life.
So heav'nly love shall outdo hellish hate,
Giving to death, and dying to redeem,
So dearly to redeem what hellish hate   300
So easily destroyed, and still destroys
In those who, when they may, accept not grace.
Nor shalt thou by descending to assume
Man's nature, lessen or degrade thine own.
Because thou hast, though throned in highest bliss   305
Equal to God, and equally enjoying
God-like fruition, quitted all to save
A world from utter loss, and hast been found
By merit more than birthright Son of God,
Found worthiest to be so by being good,   310
Far more than great or high; because in thee
Love hath abounded more than glory abounds,
Therefore thy humiliation shall exalt
With thee thy manhood also to this throne;
Here shalt thou sit incarnate, here shalt reign   315
Both God and man, Son both of God and man,
Anointed universal King; all power
I give thee, reign forever, and assume
Thy merits; under thee as Head Supreme
Thrones, Princedoms, Powers, Dominions I reduce: 320
All knees to thee shall bow, of them that bide
In heaven, or earth, or under earth in hell;
When thou attended gloriously from heav'n
Shalt in the sky appear, and from thee send
The summoning Archangels to proclaim   325

297. *ransomed.* Cf. Matt. 20.28: "Even as the Son of man came not to be ministered unto, but
to minister, and to give his life a ransom for many."
307. *fruition:* pleasure of possession. *quitted:* given up.
317. *Anointed:* meaning of the Hebrew word *mashiah.* Cf. Matt. 28.18: "And Jesus came and
spake unto them, saying, All power is given unto me in heaven and in earth."
320. *Princedoms:* Principalities. See "Angels," pp. 466–68. *reduce:* bring back, restore.
321–22. Cf. Phil. 2.10: "That at the name of Jesus every knee should bow, of things in heaven,
and things in earth, and things under the earth."
323–41. Milton's description of the Last Judgment echoes several biblical accounts, including
the prophecies of Christ himself: Matt. 24.30–31: "And then shall appear the sign of the Son
of man in heaven: and then shall all the tribes of the earth mourn, and they shall see the Son
of man coming in the clouds of heaven with power and great glory. And he shall send his
angels with a great sound of a trumpet, and they shall gather together his elect from the four
winds, from one end of heaven to the other." Matt. 25.31–32 "When the Son of man shall
come in his glory, and all the holy angels with him, then shall he sit upon the throne of his
glory: And before him shall be gathered all nations: and he shall separate them one from
another, as a shepherd divideth his sheep from the goats." For descriptions by others, see 2

Thy dread tribunal: forthwith from all winds
The living, and forthwith the cited dead
Of all past ages to the general doom
Shall hasten, such a peal shall rouse their sleep.
Then all thy saints assembled, thou shalt judge   330
Bad men and angels, they arraigned shall sink
Beneath thy sentence; hell, her numbers full,
Thenceforth shall be forever shut. Meanwhile
The world shall burn, and from her ashes spring
New heav'n and earth, wherein the just shall dwell,   335
And after all their tribulations long
See golden days, fruitful of golden deeds,
With joy and love triumphing, and fair truth.
Then thou thy regal scepter shalt lay by,
For regal scepter then no more shall need,   340
God shall be all in all. But all ye gods,
Adore him, who to compass all this dies,
Adore the Son, and honor him as me."
　　No sooner had th' Almighty ceased, but all
The multitude of angels with a shout   345
Loud as from numbers without number, sweet
As from blest voices, uttering joy, heav'n rung
With jubilee, and loud hosannas filled
Th' eternal regions: lowly reverent
Towards either throne they bow, and to the ground   350
With solemn adoration down they cast
Their crowns inwove with amarant and gold,
Immortal amarant, a flow'r which once
In Paradise, fast by the Tree of Life
Began to bloom, but soon for man's offense   355
To heav'n removed where first it grew, there grows,
And flow'rs aloft shading the fount of life,
And where the river of bliss through midst of heav'n
Rolls o'er Elysian flow'rs her amber stream;
With these that never fade the Spirits elect   360

Pet. 3.12–13: ". . . the day of God, wherein the heavens being on fire shall be dissolved, and the elements shall melt with fervent heat[.] Nevertheless we, according to his promise, look for new heavens and a new earth, wherein dwelleth righteousness." Cf. also Rev. 21.1, and 1 Cor. 15.28, and see CD I.XXXIII. *cited:* summoned to appear before a court. *general doom:* universal judgment. *saints:* the elect, mentioned in Matt. 24.31, above. *gods:* angels.
347. *rung:* made ring.
348. *jubilee:* (a Hebrew word for a ram's horn) the joyful noise of celebration. *hosannas:* a Hebrew word from Ps. 118.25 meaning "pray, save [us]!" used liturgically in prayers for deliverance and in praise of God.
349–71. For the source of some of the details in this passage see Rev. 4.4–10, and 21.11. Cf. also Rev. 22.1–2: "And he shewed me a pure river of water of life, clear as crystal, proceeding out of the throne of God and of the Lamb. In the midst of the street of it . . . was there the tree of life . . . and the leaves of the tree were for the healing of the nations."
352. *amarant:* amaranth (Gk *amarantos* unwithering), an imaginary, immortal flower, as well as a real, purple one. Cf. 1 Pet. 5.4: "Ye shall receive a crown of glory that fadeth not away."
359. *Elysian:* like those of Elysium, heaven in Gk mythology. *amber:* clear, pure.

Bind their resplendent locks inwreathed with beams,
Now in loose garlands thick thrown off, the bright
Pavement that like a sea of jasper shone
Impurpled with celestial roses smiled.
Then crowned again their golden harps they took,   365
Harps ever tuned, that glittering by their side
Like quivers hung, and with preamble sweet
Of charming symphony they introduce
Their sacred song, and waken raptures high;
No voice exempt, no voice but well could join   370
Melodious part, such concord is in heav'n.
   Thee Father first they sung omnipotent,
Immutable, immortal, infinite,
Eternal King; thee Author of all being,
Fountain of light, thyself invisible   375
Amidst the glorious brightness where thou sitt'st
Throned inaccessible, but when thou shad'st
The full blaze of thy beams, and through a cloud
Drawn round about thee like a radiant shrine,
Dark with excessive bright thy skirts appear,   380
Yet dazzle heav'n, that brightest Seraphim
Approach not, but with both wings veil their eyes.
Thee next they sang of all creation first,
Begotten Son, Divine Similitude,
In whose conspicuous count'nance, without cloud   385
Made visible, th' Almighty Father shines,
Whom else no creature can behold; on thee
Impressed th' effulgence of his glory abides,
Transfused on thee his ample spirit rests.
He heav'n of heavens and all the Powers therein   390
By thee created, and by thee threw down
Th' aspiring Dominations: thou that day
Thy Father's dreadful thunder didst not spare,
Nor stop thy flaming chariot wheels, that shook
Heav'n's everlasting frame, while o'er the necks   395
Thou drov'st of warring angels disarrayed.

---

370. *exempt*: excluded from participation.
372–82. Cf. Exod. 24.16–17, p. 438, and Isa. 6.1–2, p. 442. Also 1 Tim. 6.15–16: ". . . the King of kings, and Lord of lords; Who only hath immortality, dwelling in the light which no man can approach unto; whom no man hath seen, nor can see. . . ."
377. *but*: except.
383. *of all creation first*. See 170n, and *CD*, p. 408. Milton believed that the orthodox Trinitarian doctrine of the co-eternity of the Father and Son could not be supported by the Scriptures, which in several places refer to Christ as the first-born of God.
384. *Begotten Son*. Cf. John 3.16: "For God so loved the world, that he gave his only begotten son."
385–87. Cf. John 1.18 [NEB]: "No one has ever seen God; but God's only Son, he who is nearest to the Father's heart, he has made him known." John 14.9: "He that hath seen me hath seen the Father."
392. *Dominations*: See "Angels," pp. 466–68.

Back from pursuit thy Powers with loud acclaim
Thee only extolled, Son of thy Father's might,
To execute fierce vengeance on his foes,
Not so on man; him through their malice fall'n,   400
Father of mercy and grace, thou didst not doom
So strictly, but much more to pity incline:
No sooner did thy dear and only Son
Perceive thee purposed not to doom frail man
So strictly, but much more to pity inclined,   405
He to appease thy wrath, and end the strife
Of mercy and justice in thy face discerned,
Regardless of the bliss wherein he sat
Second to thee, offered himself to die
For man's offense. O unexampled love,   410
Love nowhere to be found less than divine!
Hail Son of God, Saviour of men, thy name
Shall be the copious matter of my song
Henceforth, and never shall my harp thy praise
Forget, nor from thy Father's praise disjoin.   415
  Thus they in heav'n, above the starry sphere,
Their happy hours in joy and hymning spent.
Meanwhile upon the firm opacous globe
Of this round world, whose first convex divides
The luminous inferior orbs, enclosed   420
From Chaos and th' inroad of Darkness old,
Satan alighted walks: a globe far off
It seemed, now seems a boundless continent
Dark, waste, and wild, under the frown of Night
Starless exposed, and ever-threatening storms   425
Of chaos blust'ring round, inclement sky;
Save on that side which from the wall of heav'n
Though distant far some small reflection gains
Of glimmering air less vexed with temptest loud:
Here walked the Fiend at large in spacious field.   430
As when a vulture on Imaus bred,
Whose snowy ridge the roving Tartar bounds,
Dislodging from a region scarce of prey
To gorge the flesh of lambs or yeanling kids
On hills where flocks are fed, flies toward the springs   435

401. *doom:* pronounce judgment.
403–10. I.e.: No sooner did . . . [than] He, to appease. . . .
416–30. See "The Universe," pp. 461–63.
429. *vexed:* L *vexare* to shake.
431–39. *Imaus:* a range of mountains running roughly NE from Afghanistan to the Arctic Ocean
    and separating Tartary (roughly Sibera) from Mongolia and Gobi desert. *Sericana:* a region in
    NW China. Satan's flight from hell to Paradise is like a flight from a most barbarous and
    physically rugged country to Eden-like Kashmir, where the *Hydaspes* (modern Jhelum) River
    rises. Folklore had it that vultures could smell their prey clear across a continent.
434. *yeanling:* newborn.

Of Ganges or Hydaspes, Indian streams;
But in his way lights on the barren plains
Of Sericana, where Chineses drive
With sails and wind their cany wagons light:
So on this windy sea of land, the Fiend　　　　　　　440
Walked up and down alone bent on his prey,
Alone, for other creature in this place
Living or lifeless to be found was none,
None yet, but store hereafter from the earth
Up hither like aërial vapors flew　　　　　　　445
Of all things transitory and vain, when sin
With vanity had filled the works of men:
Both all things vain, and all who in vain things
Built their fond hopes of glory or lasting fame,
Or happiness in this or th' other life;　　　　　　　450
All who have their reward on earth, the fruits
Of painful superstition and blind zeal,
Naught seeking but the praise of men, here find
Fit retribution, empty as their deeds;
All th' unaccomplished works of nature's hand,　　　　　　　455
Abortive, monstrous, or unkindly mixed,
Dissolved on earth, fleet hither, and in vain,
Till final dissolution, wander here,
Not in the neighboring moon, as some have dreamed;
Those argent fields more likely habitants,　　　　　　　460
Translated saints, or middle Spirits hold
Betwixt th' angelical and human kind:
Hither of ill-joined sons and daughters born
First from the ancient world those giants came
With many a vain exploit, though then renowned:　　　　　　　465
The builders next of Babel on the plain
Of Sennaär, and still with vain design
New Babels, had they wherewithal, would build:
Others came single; he who to be deemed
A god, leaped fondly into Etna flames,　　　　　　　470
Empedocles, and he who to enjoy

440–41. Cf. Job 1.7: "And the Lord said unto Satan, Whence comest thou? Then Satan answered the Lord, and said, From going to and fro in the earth, and from walking up and down in it."
444. *store*: plenty.
449. *fond*: foolish.
452. *painful*: painstaking.
455–57. *unaccomplished*: incomplete, imperfect. *Abortive*: prematurely born. *monstrous*: L *monstrum*, evil omen, prodigy; abnormal. *unkindly*: (OE *gecynde* nature) unnaturally. *mixed*: conceived by sexual intercourse. *fleet*: OE *fleotan* to float or drift (as refuse floated on the Fleet river, in London).
461. *Translated saints*: holy men whom God removed from earth before they died.
463–65. Cf. Gen. 6.
467. *Sennaär*: Shinar, in Babylonia. See Gen. 11, p. 433, and XII.38–62 for the story of the Tower of Babel.
471. *Empedocles*: a philosopher who secretly threw himself into Etna hoping that by not leaving a trace he would be thought to have been a god. The volcano belched out the metal soles of his shoes and his folly was thereby discovered.

Plato's Elysium, leaped into the sea,
Cleombrotus, and many more too long,
Embryos and idiots, eremites and friars
White, black, and gray, with all their trumpery.   475
Here pilgrims roam, that strayed so far to seek
In Golgotha him dead, who lives in heav'n;
And they who to be sure of paradise
Dying put on the weeds of Dominic,
Or in Franciscan think to pass disguised;   480
They pass the planets seven, and pass the fixed,
And that crystálline sphere whose balance weighs
The trepidation talked, and that first moved;
And now Saint Peter at heav'n's wicket seems
To wait them with his keys, and now at foot   485
Of heav'n's ascent they lift their feet, when lo
A violent crosswind from either coast
Blows them transverse ten thousand leagues awry
Into the devious air, then might ye see
Cowls, hoods and habits with their wearers tossed   490
And fluttered into rags; then relics, beads,
Indulgences, dispenses, pardons, bulls,
The sport of winds: all these upwhirled aloft
Fly o'er the backside of the world far off
Into a limbo large and broad, since called   495
The Paradise of Fools, to few unknown
Long after, now unpeopled, and untrod;
All this dark globe the Fiend found as he passed,
And long he wandered, till at last a gleam
Of dawning light turned thitherward in haste   500
His traveled steps; far distant he descries
Ascending by degrees magnificent

473. *Cleombrotus:* a youth so enamored by Plato's description of the life beyond that he committed suicide.
474. *eremites:* hermits.
475. *White, black, and gray:* the Carmelite, Dominican, and Franciscan orders.
477. *Golgotha:* where Christ was crucified. Cf. Luke 24.5–6: "Why seek ye the living among the dead? He is not here, but is risen."
479. *weeds:* garments.
481–83. See "The Universe," pp. 461–63.
485. Cf. Matt. 16.19: "And I [Jesus] will give unto thee [Peter] the keys of the kingdom of heaven."
489. *devious:* erratic.
490. *Cowls, hoods, habits:* the dress of monks.
491. *relics:* holy objects associated with a saint, assumed by some Catholics to have miraculous powers. *beads* (ME *bede* prayer) as in a rosary.
492. *Indulgences, dispenses, pardons:* various ecclesiastical pardons for sin, which, like Papal bulls, Protestants believed to be worthless. *bulls:* Papal decrees.
494. *backside:* underside, rump.
495. *limbo:* (ML, ablative of *limbus* border) a region, according to Catholic doctrine, bordering on hell, where dwelt the souls of good people who died before the Christian era, as well as those of unbaptized infants. Milton rejects this notion and invents another limbo.
501. *traveled:* (OF *travaillier* to travail, toil) weary.
502. *degrees:* steps.

Up to the wall of heaven a structure high,
At top whereof, but far more rich appeared
The work as of a kingly palace gate   505
With frontispiece of diamond and gold
Embellished; thick with sparkling orient gems
The portal shone, inimitable on earth.
By model, or by shading pencil drawn.
The stairs were such as whereon Jacob saw   510
Angels ascending and descending, bands
Of guardians bright, when he from Esau fled
To Padan-Aram in the field of Luz,
Dreaming by night under the open sky,
And waking cried, "This is the gate of heav'n."   515
Each stair mysteriously was meant, nor stood
There always, but drawn up to heav'n sometimes
Viewless, and underneath a bright sea flowed
Of jasper, or of liquid pearl, whereon
Who after came from earth, sailing arrived,   520
Wafted by angels, or flew o'er the lake
Rapt in a chariot drawn by fiery steeds.
The stairs were then let down, whether to dare
The Fiend by easy ascent, or aggravate
His sad exclusion from the doors of bliss.   525
Direct against which opened from beneath,
Just o'er the blissful seat of Paradise,
A passage down to th' earth, a passage wide,
Wider by far than that of aftertimes
Over Mount Zion, and, though that were large,   530
Over the Promised Land to God so dear,
By which, to visit oft those happy tribes,
On high behests his angels to and fro
Passed frequent, and his eye with choice regard

507. *orient:* lustrous, like the most lustrous of pearls, those from the east.
508. *The portal shone.* Cf. Rev. 21.21.
510–15. Cf. Gen. 27.41–28.17. En route to Syria (*Aram*), Jacob stopped for the night in a place
   called *Luz,* which after his dream he renamed Bethel. "He dreamed, and behold a ladder set
   up on the earth, and the top of it reached to heaven: and behold the angels of God ascending
   and descending on it. And, behold, the Lord stood above it, and said, I am the Lord God of
   Abraham thy father, and the God of Isaac: the land whereon thou liest, to thee I will give it,
   and to thy seed; . . . And Jacob awaked out of his sleep, and he said, Surely the Lord is in
   this place; and I knew it not. And he was afraid, and said, How dreadful is this place! this is
   none other but the house of God, and this is the gate of heaven."
516. *mysteriously.* A mystery is a meaning available only to the initiated.
518. *a bright sea.* See "The Universe," pp. 461–63.
520–22. In one of Christ's parables (Luke 16.19–22), when the beggar Lazarus died, he was
   "carried by the angels" into heaven. Cf. 2 Kings 2.11: "As [Elijah and Elisha] . . . talked . .
   . there appeared a chariot of fire, and horses of fire, and parted them both asunder; and Elijah
   went up by a whirlwind into heaven."
526–27. The axis of the earth is here conceived as parallel to the floor of heaven.
534. *choice regard:* discriminative look.

From Paneas the fount of Jordan's flood   535
To Beërsaba, where the Holy Land
Borders on Egypt and the Arabian shore;
So wide the op'ning seemed, where bounds were set
To darkness, such as bound the ocean wave.
Satan from hence now on the lower stair   540
That scaled by steps of gold to heaven gate
Looks down with wonder at the sudden view
Of all this world at once. As when a scout
Through dark and desert ways with peril gone
All night; at last by break of cheerful dawn   545
Obtains the brow of some high-climbing hill,
Which to his eye discovers unaware
The goodly prospect of some foreign land
First seen, or some renowned metropolis
With glistering spires and pinnacles adorned,   550
Which now the rising sun gilds with his beams.
Such wonder seized, though after heaven seen,
The Spirit malign, but much more envy seized
At sight of all this world beheld so fair.
Round he surveys, and well might, where he stood   555
So high above the circling canopy
Of night's extended shade; from eastern point
Of Libra to the fleecy star that bears
Andromeda far off Atlantic seas
Beyond th' horizon; then from pole to pole   560
He views in breadth, and without longer pause
Down right into the world's first region throws
His flight precipitant, and winds with ease
Through the pure marble air his oblique way
Amongst innumerable stars, that shone   565
Stars distant, but nigh hand seemed other worlds,
Or other worlds they seemed, or happy isles,
Like those Hesperian gardens famed of old,

535. *Paneas:* a later name for Dan, the northernmost city of Palestine as well as for the mountain near which a spring (*fount*) served as one of the sources of the *Jordan River* (*flood*).
536. *Beërsaba:* Beersheba, southernmost city of Palestine.
546. *Obtains:* gains.
556. *circling canopy.* The earth was between Satan and the sun; therefore Satan looked directly down on the conical shadow presumed to be cast by the earth. It was midnight in Eden, as Fowler points out.
558. *fleecy star:* the constellation of Aries, the Ram; in the Zodiac, the sign opposite Libra.
559. *Andromeda:* a constellation near that of Aries.
562. *first region:* the part of the universe between the outer shell and the sphere of the moon. See "The Universe," pp. 461–63.
563–64. *precipitant:* falling headlong, descending vertically. *oblique:* inclined; devious.
564. *marble:* Gk *marmareos* sparkling, gleaming.
566. *other worlds.* The possibility of other inhabited worlds in the universe was recognized by the ancients and was much discussed in Milton's time.
567. See II.410n.
568. *Hesperian gardens:* another classical mythological version of paradise. Here Jupiter placed the daughters of Hesperus to guard a tree on which hung three golden apples.

Fortunate fields, and groves and flow'ry vales,
Thrice happy isles, but who dwelt happy there   570
He stayed not to inquire: above them all
The golden sun in splendor likest heaven
Allured his eye: thither his course he bends
Through the calm firmament; but up or down
By center, or eccentric, hard to tell,   575
Or longitude, where the great luminary
Aloof the vulgar constellations thick,
That from his lordly eye keep distance due,
Dispenses light from far; they as they move
Their starry dance in numbers that compute   580
Days, months, and years, towards his all-cheering lamp
Turn swift their various motions, or are turned
By his magnetic beam, that gently warms
The universe, and to each inward part
With gentle penetration, though unseen,   585
Shoots invisible virtue even to the deep:
So wondrously was set his station bright.
There lands the Fiend, a spot like which perhaps
Astronomer in the sun's lucent orb
Through his glazed optic tube yet never saw.   590
The place he found beyond expression bright,
Compared with aught on earth, metal or stone;
Not all parts like, but all alike informed
With radiant light, as glowing iron with fire;
If metal, part seemed gold, part silver clear;   595
If stone, carbuncle most or chrysolite,
Ruby or topaz, to the twelve that shone
In Aaron's breastplate, and a stone besides
Imagined rather oft than elsewhere seen,

---

575. *hard to tell*. I.e., it is hard for the poet to describe Satan's navigation in his three-dimensional flight; much would depend on the observer's position.
580. *Their starry dance*. In Plato's *Timaeus* the stars are said to dance as a chorus and thus to mark out the divisions of time. *numbers that compute*: rhythms that count out.
582–83. *turned/By his magnetic beam*. Kepler's theory that the planets are moved round the sun by the power of the sun's magnetism had been published in 1609.
586. *virtue*: power, influence.
588–90. Galileo first telescopically observed sunspots in 1609.
591–612. The brightness of the sun is compared with the brightest, most sought after metals (*silver* and *gold*) and precious stones (*carbuncle, chrysolite, ruby, topaz*) because these metals and stones were believed by the alchemists to receive their power to shine from the sun; indeed, the stones were believed to shine in the dark. The hypothetical *philosophers'* (i.e., scientists') *stone*, which if it could be found would turn base metals into gold, was also thought to be a product of the sun. In its powdered form (literal meaning of *elixir*) the stone would, like colloidal gold (*potable gold*), be medicinal, prolonging life. In Exod. 28.15–20 Aaron's *breastplate* is described as decorated with twelve different gems, of which Milton lists the first four. Lines 602–5 describe the efforts of alchemists to imitate the processes of the sun, who was *archchemic* because he was the supreme chemist. To *bind Volatile Hermes* was to remove the "air" from a compound of mercury, which could be extracted from primal matter, i.e., old *Proteus*, who took many forms. *humor*: moisture.

That stone, or like to that which here below   600
Philosophers in vain so long have sought,
In vain, though by their powerful art they bind
Volátile Hermes, and call up unbound
In various shapes old Proteus from the sea,
Drained through a limbec to his native form.   605
What wonder then if fields and regions here
Breathe forth elixir pure, and rivers run
Potable gold, when with one virtuous touch
Th' arch-chemic sun so far from us remote
Produces with terrestrial humor mixed   610
Here in the dark so many precious things
Of color glorious and effect so rare?
Here matter new to gaze the Devil met
Undazzled, far and wide his eye commands,
For sight no obstacle found here, nor shade,   615
But all sunshine, as when his beams at noon
Culminate from th' equator, as they now
Shot upward still direct, whence no way round
Shadow from body opaque can fall, and the air,
Nowhere so clear, sharpened his visual ray   620
To objects distant far, whereby he soon
Saw within ken a glorious angel stand,
The same whom John saw also in the sun:
His back was turned, but not his brightness hid;
Of beaming sunny rays, a golden tiar   625
Circled his head, nor less his locks behind
Illustrious on his shoulders fledge with wings
Lay waving round; on some great charge employed
He seemed, or fixed in cogitation deep.
Glad was the Spirit impure; as now in hope   630
To find who might direct his wand'ring flight
To Paradise the happy seat of man,
His journey's end and our beginning woe.
But first he casts to change his proper shape,
Which else might work him danger or delay: 635
And now a stripling Cherub he appears,
Not of the prime, yet such as in his face
Youth smiled celestial, and to every limb
Suitable grace diffused, so well he feigned;

605. *limbec:* alembic; any device for refining or transmuting as if by distillation.
609. *arch-chemic:* chief alchemist.
617. *Culminate:* reach their zenith. Before the Fall (and consequent tipping of the earth's axis)
    the sun at noon, on the equator, never cast a shadow.
623. *whom John saw.* Cf. Rev. 19.17: "I saw an angel standing in the sun."
625. *tiar:* tiara, crown, halo.
627. *Illustrious:* (L *lustrare* to purify, make bright) shining.
634. *casts:* considers how; contrives; determines.

Under a coronet his flowing hair   640
In curls on either cheek played, wings he wore
Of many a colored plume sprinkled with gold,
His habit fit for speed succinct, and held
Before his decent steps a silver wand.
He drew not nigh unheard; the angel bright,   645
Ere he drew nigh, his radiant visage turned,
Admonished by his ear, and straight was known
Th' Archangel Uriel, one of the sev'n
Who in God's presence, nearest to his throne
Stand ready at command, and are his eyes   650
That run through all the heav'ns, or down to th' earth
Bear his swift errands over moist and dry,
O'er sea and land: him Satan thus accosts.
     "Uriel, for thou of those sev'n Spirits that stand
In sight of God's high throne, gloriously bright,   655
The first art wont his great authentic will
Interpreter through highest heav'n to bring,
Where all his sons thy embassy attend;
And here art likeliest by supreme decree
Like honor to obtain, and as his eye   660
To visit oft this new creation round;
Unspeakable desire to see, and know
All these his wondrous works, but chiefly man,
His chief delight and favor, him for whom
All these his works so wondrous he ordained,   665
Hath brought me from the choirs of Cherubim
Alone thus wand'ring. Brightest Seraph tell
In which of all these shining orbs hath man
His fixèd seat, or fixèd seat hath none,
But all these shining orbs his choice to dwell;   670
That I may find him, and with secret gaze,
Or open admiration him behold
On whom the great Creator hath bestowed
Worlds, and on whom hath all these graces poured;
That both in him and all things, as is meet,   675
The Universal Maker we may praise;
Who justly hath driv'n out his rebel foes
To deepest hell, and to repair that loss
Created this new happy race of men
To serve him better: wise are all his ways."   680
     So spake the false dissembler unperceived;
For neither man nor angel can discern

643. *succinct*: (L *sub* under + *cingere* to tuck) close-fitting.
644. *decent*: graceful.
648. *Uriel*. See "Angels," pp. 466–68.

Hypocrisy, the only evil that walks
Invisible, except to God alone,
By his permissive will, through heav'n and earth: 685
And oft though wisdom wake, suspicion sleeps
At wisdom's gate, and to simplicity
Resigns her charge, while goodness thinks no ill
Where no ill seems: which now for once beguiled
Uriel, though regent of the sun, and held   690
The sharpest-sighted Spirit of all in heav'n;
Who to the fraudulent impostor foul
In his uprightness answer thus returned.
"Fair angel, thy desire which tends to know
The works of God, thereby to glorify   695
The great Work-maister, leads to no excess
That reaches blame, but rather merits praise
The more it seems excess, that led thee hither
From thy empyreal mansion thus alone,
To witness with thine eyes what some perhaps   700
Contented with report hear only in heav'n:
For wonderful indeed are all his works,
Pleasant to know, and worthiest to be all
Had in remembrance always with delight;
But what created mind can comprehend   705
Their number, or the wisdom infinite
That brought them forth, but hid their causes deep.
I saw when at his word the formless mass,
This world's material mold, came to a heap:
Confusion heard his voice, and wild uproar   710
Stood ruled, stood vast infinitude confined;
Till at his second bidding darkness fled,
Light shone, and order from disorder sprung:
Swift to their several quarters hasted then
The cumbrous elements, earth, flood, air, fire,   715

694–701. See "Knowledge," p. 470.
702–4. Cf. Ps. 111.2–4: "The works of the Lord are great, sought out of all them that have
pleasure therein. . . . He hath made his wonderful works to be remembered."
706–7. Cf. Prov. 3.19: "The Lord by wisdom hath founded the earth." Prov. 8.1–27: "Doth not
wisdom cry? and understanding put forth her voice? . . . She crieth at the gates, at the entry
of the city. . . . Unto you, O men, I call. . . . The Lord possessed me in the beginning of
his way, before his works of old. I was set up from everlasting, from the beginning, or ever the
earth was. When there were no depths, I was brought forth; when there were no fountains
abounding with water. Before the mountains were settled, before the hills was I brought forth.
. . . When he prepared the heavens, I was there: when he set a compass upon the face of the
depth. . . ."
708–21. Cf. *Met.* 1.5f.
709. *material mold*: (OE *molde* earth, ground, soil) here, the constituent matter of the universe.
715–21. See "The Universe," pp. 461–63. *This ethereal quintessence.* The sun, on which the
angels are standing, and other heavenly bodies were supposed to be composed of a fifth element,
ether, not the same as air.

And this ethereal quíntessence of heav'n
Flew upward, spirited with various forms,
That rolled orbicular, and turned to stars
Numberless, as thou seest, and how they move;
Each had his place appointed, each his course,   720
The rest in circuit walls this universe.
Look downward on that globe whose hither side
With light from hence, though but reflected, shines;
That place is earth the seat of man, that light
His day, which else as th' other hemisphere   725
Night would invade, but there the neighboring moon
(So call that opposite fair star) her aid
Timely interposes, and her monthly round
Still ending, still renewing through mid-heav'n,
With borrowed light her countenance triform   730
Hence fills and empties to enlighten th' earth,
And in her pale dominion checks the night.
That spot to which I point is Paradise,
Adam's abode, those lofty shades his bow'r.
Thy way thou canst not miss, me mine requires."   735
    Thus said, he turned, and Satan bowing low,
As to superior Spirits is wont in heav'n,
Where honor due and reverence none neglects,
Took leave, and toward the coast of earth beneath,
Down from th' ecliptic, sped with hoped success,   740
Throws his steep flight in many an airy wheel,
Nor stayed, till on Niphates' top he lights.

Book IV

The Argument

Satan now in prospect of Eden, and nigh the place where he must
now attempt the bold enterprise which he undertook alone against God
and man, falls into many doubts with himself, and many passions, fear,
envy, and despair; but at length confirms himself in evil, journeys on
to Paradise, whose outward prospect and situation is described, overleaps
the bounds, sits in the shape of a cormorant on the Tree of Life, as
highest in the Garden to look about him. The Garden described; Satan's
first sight of Adam and Eve; his wonder at their excellent form and happy
state, but with resolution to work their fall; overhears their discourse,

---

717. *spirited with various forms:* presided over, inhabited by, spirits or souls of various forms, as
   in Plato's *Timaeus.*
730. *triform:* cf. *Met.* 7.177: "if only the three-formed goddess will help me and grant her present
   aid in this great deed which I dare attempt."
740. *ecliptic:* the path of the sun.
742. *Niphates:* a mountain in Assyria, to the north of Eden.

thence gathers that the Tree of Knowledge was forbidden them to eat of, under penalty of death; and thereon intends to found his temptation, by seducing them to transgress: then leaves them a while, to know further of their state by some other means. Meanwhile Uriel descending on a sunbeam warns Gabriel, who had in charge the gate of Paradise, that some evil Spirit had escaped the deep, and passed at noon by his sphere in the shape of a good angel down to Paradise, discovered after by his furious gestures in the mount. Gabriel promises to find him ere morning. Night coming on, Adam and Eve discourse of going to their rest: their bower described; their evening worship. Gabriel drawing forth his bands of nightwatch to walk the round of Paradise, appoints two strong angels to Adam's bower, lest the evil Spirit should be there doing some harm to Adam or Eve sleeping; there they find him at the ear of Eve, tempting her in a dream, and bring him, though unwilling, to Gabriel; by whom questioned, he scornfully answers, prepares resistance, but hindered by a sign from heaven, flies out of Paradise.

O for that warning voice, which he who saw
Th' Apocalypse, heard cry in heaven aloud,
Then when the Dragon, put to second rout,
Came furious down to be revenged on men,
"Woe to the inhabitants on earth!" that now,   5
While time was, our first parents had been warned
The coming of their secret foe, and scaped
Haply so scaped his mortal snare; for now
Satan, now first inflamed with rage, came down,
The tempter ere th' accuser of mankind,   10
To wreck on innocent frail man his loss
Of that first battle, and his flight to hell:
Yet not rejoicing in his speed, though bold,
Far off and fearless, nor with cause to boast,
Begins his dire attempt, which nigh the birth   15
Now rolling, boils in his tumultuous breast,
And like a devilish engine back recoils
Upon himself; horror and doubt distract
His troubled thoughts, and from the bottom stir
The hell within him, for within him hell   20
He brings, and round about him, nor from hell
One step no more than from himself can fly
By change of place: now conscience wakes despair
That slumbered, wakes the bitter memory

IV.1–5. Cf. Rev. 12.7–12.
10. *accuser*: betrayer.
11. *wreck*: avenge.
17. *engine*: L *ingenium*, the faculty of invention; here an engine of war, the canon, invented by Satan (see VI.470).
18. *distract*: L *distrahere*, to draw asunder; agitate.

Of what he was, what is, and what must be 25
Worse; of worse deeds worse sufferings must ensue.
Sometimes towards Eden which now in his view
Lay pleasant, his grieved look he fixes sad,
Sometimes towards heav'n and the full-blazing sun,
Which now sat high in his meridian tow'r: 30
Then much revolving, thus in sighs began.
　"O thou that with surpassing glory crowned,
Look'st from thy sole dominion like the god
Of this new world; at whose sight all the stars
Hide their diminished heads; to thee I call, 35
But with no friendly voice, and add thy name
O sun, to tell thee how I hate thy beams
That bring to my remembrance from what state
I fell, how glorious once above thy sphere;
Till pride and worse ambition threw me down 40
Warring in heav'n against heav'n's matchless King:
Ah wherefore! he deserved no such return
From me, whom he created what I was
In that bright eminence, and with his good
Upbraided none; nor was his service hard. 45
What could be less than to afford him praise,
The easiest recompense, and pay him thanks,
How due! yet all his good proved ill in me,
And wrought but malice; lifted up so high
I sdained subjection, and thought one step higher 50
Would set me highest, and in a moment quit
The debt immense of endless gratitude,
So burthensome still paying, still to owe;
Forgetful what from him I still received,
And understood not that a grateful mind 55
By owing owes not, but still pays, at once
Indebted and discharged; what burden then?

31. *revolving:* meditating.
32–41. Milton's nephew Edward Phillips, in his *Life of Milton*, said he saw these lines "several years before the poem was begun." They were, he said, to be the opening lines of a tragedy.
35. *diminished:* reduced in authority or dignity.
37. Cf. John 3.20, p. 456: "For every one that doeth evil hateth the light, neither cometh to the light, lest his deeds should be reproved."
38–39. Cf. Rev. 2.5 "Remember therefore from whence thou art fallen . . ."
43–45. Cf. Ezek. 28.15–17: "Thou wast perfect in thy ways from the day that thou wast created, till iniquity was found in thee. . . . Thine heart was lifted up because of thy beauty, thou hast corrupted thy wisdom by reason of thy brightness: I will cast thee to the ground, I will lay thee before kings, that they may behold thee." James 1.5: "If any of you lack wisdom [to resist temptation], let him ask of God, that giveth to all men liberally, and upbraideth not; and it shall be given him."
50. *sdained:* disdained.
51. *quit:* pay.
53. *still:* always.
56. *owing:* both owing a debt and owning (admitting) a debt. The old form of the past tense of *owe* was *ought. Owe* comes from ME *owen*, to have, to own, to have (to do), hence, to owe.

O had his powerful destiny ordained
Me some inferior angel, I had stood
Then happy; no unbounded hope had raised   60
Ambition. Yet why not? some other Power
As great might have aspired, and me though mean
Drawn to his part; but other Powers as great
Fell not, but stand unshaken, from within
Or from without, to all temptations armed.   65
Hadst thou the same free will and power to stand?
Thou hadst: whom hast thou then or what to accuse,
But heav'n's free love dealt equally to all?
Be then his love accursed, since love or hate,
To me alike, it deals eternal woe.   70
Nay cursed be thou; since against his thy will
Chose freely what it now so justly rues.
Me miserable! which way shall I fly
Infinite wrath, and infinite despair?
Which way I fly is hell; myself am hell;   75
And in the lowest deep a lower deep
Still threat'ning to devour me opens wide,
To which the hell I suffer seems a heav'n.
O then at last relent: is there no place
Left for repentance, none for pardon left?   80
None left but by submission; and that word
Disdain forbids me, and my dread of shame
Among the Spirits beneath, whom I seduced
With other promises and other vaunts
Than to submit, boasting I could subdue   85
Th' Omnipotent. Ay me, they little know
How dearly I abide that boast so vain,
Under what torments inwardly I groan:
While they adore me on the throne of hell,
With diadem and scepter high advanced   90
The lower still I fall, only supreme
In misery; such joy ambition finds.
But say I could repent and could obtain
By act of grace my former state; how soon
Would highth recall high thoughts, how soon unsay   95
What feigned submission swore: ease would recant
Vows made in pain, as violent and void.
For never can true reconcilement grow
Where wounds of deadly hate have pierced so deep:

79–80. Cf. Heb. 12.17 "For ye know how that afterward, when he [Esau] would have inherited
the blessing, he was rejected: for he found no place of repentance, though he sought it carefully
with tears."
87. *abide*: (n the sixteenth and seventeeth centuries erroneously used for *abye*) pay the penalty
for, atone for, suffer for, endure.
94. *act of grace*: suspension of sentence.

Which would but lead me to a worse relapse,   100
And heavier fall: so should I purchase dear
Short intermission bought with double smart.
This knows my punisher; therefore as far
From granting he, as I from begging peace:
All hope excluded thus, behold instead   105
Of us outcast, exiled, his new delight,
Mankind created, and for him this world.
So farewell hope, and with hope farewell fear,
Farewell remorse: all good to me is lost;
Evil be thou my good; by thee at least   110
Divided empire with heav'n's King I hold
By thee, and more than half perhaps will reign;
As man ere long, and this new world shall know."
    Thus while he spake, each passion dimmed his face
Thrice changed with pale, ire, envy and despair,   115
Which marred his borowed visage, and betrayed
Him counterfeit, if any eye beheld.
For heav'nly minds from such distempers foul
Are ever clear. Whereof he soon aware,
Each perturbation smoothed with outward calm,   120
Artificer of fraud; and was the first
That practiced falsehood under saintly show,
Deep malice to conceal, couched with revenge:
Yet not enough had practiced to deceive
Uriel once warned; whose eye pursued him down   125
The way he went, and on th' Assyrian mount
Saw him disfigured, more than could befall
Spirit of happy sort: his gestures fierce
He marked and mad demeanor, then alone,
As he supposed, all unobserved, unseen.   130
So on he fares, and to the border comes
Of Eden, where delicious Paradise,
Now nearer, crowns with her enclosure green,
As with a rural mound the champaign head
Of a steep wilderness, whose hairy sides   135

---

109. *remorse:* L *remordere* to bite again.
110. Cf. Isa. 5.20 "Woe unto them that call evil good, and good evil; that put darkness for light, and light for darkness; that put bitter for sweet, and sweet for bitter!"
115. *changed with pale:* paled (from cherubic red).
118. *distempers:* disorders of body or mind from improper mixture of the humors. See "Physiology and Psychology," pp. 463–64.
123. *couched:* which lay hidden.
126. *Assyrian mount:* Mount Niphates (III.742).
131–71. See "Paradise," pp. 472–73, and VIII.302ff.
132. *Eden:* (a Hebrew word meaning "delight" or "place of pleasure") the region in which Paradise was located. *delicious:* L *deliciae,* delight. *Paradise: paradeisos,* the Gk form of an Oriental word (Sanscrit *paradesa;* Arabic *firdaus;* Hebrew *pardes*) meaning "park" or "pleasure ground."
134. *rural:* as in open fields. *mound:* hedge or other fence bounding a field or garden; a hedgerow.

With thicket overgrown, grotesque and wild,
Access denied; and overhead up grew
Insuperable highth of loftiest shade,
Cedar, and pine, and fir, and branching palm,
A sylvan scene, and as the ranks ascend   140
Shade above shade, a woody theater
Of stateliest view. Yet higher than their tops
The verdurous wall of Paradise up sprung:
Which to our general sire gave prospect large
Into his nether empire neighboring round.   145
And higher than that wall a circling row
Of goodliest trees loaden with fairest fruit,
Blossoms and fruits at once of golden hue
Appeared, with gay enameled colors mixed:
On which the sun more glad impressed his beams   150
Than in fair evening cloud, or humid bow,
When God hath show'red the earth; so lovely seemed
That landscape: and of pure now purer air
Meets his approach, and to the heart inspires
Vernal delight and joy, able to drive   155
All sadness but despair: now gentle gales
Fanning their odoriferous wings dispense
Native perfumes, and whisper whence they stole
Those balmy spoils. As when to them who sail
Beyond the Cape of Hope, and now are past   160
Mozambic, off at sea northeast winds blow
Sabean odors from the spicy shore
Of Araby the Blest, with such delay
Well pleased they slack their course, and many a league
Cheered with the graceful smell old Ocean smiles.   165
So entertained those odorous sweets the Fiend
Who came their bane, though with them better pleased
Than Asmodeus with the fishy fume,
That drove him, though enamored, from the spouse
Of Tobit's son, and with a vengeance sent   170

---

136. *grotesque:* in Milton's time a relatively new word, used in various ways. Milton meant "characterized by interwoven, tangled vines and branches, as in painted and carved decoration." *Bosky* was a synonym.
144. *general:* L *genus* race.
149. *enameled:* bright.
155. *drive:* force to flee.
157. *odoriferous:* L *odorifer* bearing fragrance.
161. *Mozambic:* the channel between Madagascar and the SE coast of Africa—a trade route.
162. *Sabean:* of Sheba, an ancient country in south west Arabia, or *Araby the Blest* (modern Yemen).
166–71. According to the Apocryphal Book of Tobit, an evil spirit, Ashmodeus (Satan?) killed on their wedding nights the seven men who, in succession, had been married to Sarah. But the eighth, Tobias, was advised by the angel Raphael to burn the heart and liver of a fish in the bridal chamber, and the odor drove the daemon lover all the way to Egypt. Raphael thus saved Tobias and his wife from the designs of Satan, though he failed to save Adam and Eve. Cf. Asmadai, VI.365.

From Media post to Egypt, there fast bound.
   Now to th'ascent of that steep savage hill
Satan had journeyed on, pensive and slow;
But further way found none, so thick entwined,
As one continued brake, the undergrowth   175
Of shrubs and tangling bushes had perplexed
All path of man or beast that passed that way:
One gate there only was, and that looked east
On th' other side: which when th' arch-felon saw
Due entrance he disdained, and in contempt,   180
At one slight bound high overleaped all bound
Of hill or highest wall, and sheer within
Lights on his feet. As when a prowling wolf,
Whom hunger drives to seek new haunt for prey,
Watching where shepherds pen their flocks at eve   185
In hurdled cotes amid the field secure,
Leaps o'er the fence with ease into the fold:
Or as a thief bent to unhoard the cash
Of some rich burgher, whose substantial doors,
Cross-barred and bolted fast, fear no assault,   190
In at the window climbs, or o'er the tiles;
So clomb this first grand thief into God's fold:
So since into his church lewd hirelings climb.
Thence up he flew, and on the Tree of Life,
The middle tree and highest there that grew,   195
Sat like a cormorant; yet not true life
Thereby regained, but sat devising death
To them who lived; nor on the virtue thought
Of that life-giving plant, but only used
For prospect, what well used had been the pledge   200
Of immortality. So little knows
Any, but God alone, to value right
The good before him, but perverts best things
To worst abuse, or to their meanest use.
Beneath him with new wonder now he views   205
To all delight of human sense exposed

172. *savage*: L *silvaticus* woody, wild.
176. *perplexed*: L *plectare* to plait or braid.
183–93. Cf. John 10.1–11: "Verily, verily, I say unto you, He that entereth not by the door into
   the sheepfold, but climbeth up some other way, the same is a thief and a robber. . . . The
   thief cometh not, but for to steal, and to kill, and to destroy: I [Christ] am come that they
   might have life, and that they might have it more abundantly. I am the good shepherd." Cf.
   Aen. 9.59–64.
186. *hurdled*: formed by hurdles, sectional fencing made of plaited branches. *cotes*: folds. *secure*:
   (L *sine* without + *cura* care) free from anxiety.
192. *grand thief*: "thief of thieves" (as in "King of kings"); cf. I.29n.
193. *lewd*: ME *lewd*, lay, ignorant, vile, OE *lǣwede* laical. *hirelings*: those who work only for
   money—here, paid clergymen, in contrast to unpaid ministers in some of the Puritan sects.
   Cf. John 10.11–12: "The good shepherd giveth his life for the sheep. But he that is an hireling,
   and not the shepherd, whose own the sheep are not, seeth the wolf coming . . . and fleeth."
194. *Tree of Life*. See Gen. 2.9, p. 431.

In narrow room nature's whole wealth, yea more,
A heav'n on earth: for blissful Paradise
Of God the garden was, by him in the east
Of Eden planted; Eden stretched her line   210
From Auran eastward to the royal tow'rs
Of great Seleucia, built by Grecian kings,
Or where the sons of Eden long before
Dwelt in Telassar: in this pleasant soil
His far more pleasant garden God ordained;   215
Out of the fertile ground he caused to grow
All trees of noblest kind for sight, smell, taste;
And all amid them stood the Tree of Life,
High eminent, blooming ambrosial fruit
Of vegetable gold; and next to life   220
Our death the Tree of Knowledge grew fast by,
Knowledge of good bought dear by knowing ill.
Southward through Eden went a river large,
Nor changed his course, but through the shaggy hill
Passed underneath engulfed, for God had thrown   225
That mountain as his garden mold high raised
Upon the rapid current, which through veins
Of porous earth with kindly thirst up drawn,
Rose a fresh fountain, and with many a rill
Watered the garden; thence united fell   230
Down the steep glade, and met the nether flood,
Which from his darksome passage now appears,
And now divided into four main streams,
Runs diverse, wand'ring many a famous realm
And country whereof here needs no account,   235
But rather to tell how, if art could tell,
How from that sapphire fount the crispèd brooks,
Rolling on orient pearl and sands of gold,
With mazy error under pendent shades
Ran nectar, visiting each plant, and fed   240
Flow'rs worthy of Paradise which not nice art

211. *Auran:* probably the province of Hauran on the eastern border of Israel, and the Harran
    that God told Abram to leave in favor of Canaan.
212. *Seleucia:* a city on the Tigris river, built by one of Alexander's generals, near modern
    Baghdad.
214. *Telassar:* a city in Eden.
219. *blooming:* bearing. *ambrosial:* See II.245n; here the primary meaning may be "giving
    immortality"—Fowler cites Gen. 3.22, p. 432, where God fears lest Adam "put forth his hand,
    and take also of the tree of life, and eat, and live for ever."
220. *vegetable:* living, growing, like a plant.
222. See selection from *Areopagitica*, p. 384, and *CD*, p. 414.
226. *mold:* earth good for gardening, rich and crumbly.
228. *kindly:* (OE *cynd* nature) natural.
237. *sapphire fount:* natural spring whose water, reflecting the sky, was the color of sapphire.
    crispèd: L *crispus*, curly.
238. *orient:* shining, pearl-like.
239. *error:* (L *errare* to go astray) wandering.

In beds and curious knots, but nature boon
Poured forth profuse on hill and dale and plain,
Both where the morning sun first warmly smote
The open field, and where the unpierced shade   245
Embrowned the noontide bow'rs: thus was this place,
A happy rural seat of various view;
Groves whose rich trees wept odorous gums and balm,
Others whose fruit burnished with golden rind
Hung amiable, Hesperian fables true,   250
If true, here only, and of delicious taste:
Betwixt them lawns, or level downs, and flocks
Grazing the tender herb, were interposed,
Or palmy hillock, or the flow'ry lap
Of some irriguous valley spread her store,   255
Flow'rs of all hue, and without thorn the rose:
Another side, umbrageous grots and caves
Of cool recess, o'er which the mantling vine
Lays forth her purple grape, and gently creeps
Luxuriant; meanwhile murmuring waters fall   260
Down the slope hills, dispersed, or in a lake,
That to the fringèd bank with myrtle crowned,
Her crystal mirror holds, unite their streams.
The birds their choir apply; airs, vernal airs,
Breathing the smell of field and grove, attune   265
The trembling leaves, while universal Pan

242. *curious:* (L *cura* care) carefully, neatly, or exquisitely made. *knots:* patterned flower beds. *boon:* bounteous, opposite of *nice* (241).
246. *Embrowned:* darkened.
247. *seat:* (as in "country-seat," estate) residence. *of various view:* with a variety of prospects.
250. *amiable:* lovely. *Hesperian fables.* See III.568n.
252. *lawns:* pastures. *downs:* (OE *dun*) here tracts of open upland.
255. *irriguous:* well-watered.
257. *umbrageous:* shady.
258–63. Fowler's note is illuminating: "That the *myrtle* is intended as Venus' tree is made clear by the immediately succeeding image of the mirror, another of her iconographical attributes. . . . Venus is present not only in her capacity as goddess of gardens, but also as the form-giver, presiding over the generative cycle unfolded in the Graces and the Hours. Paradises were commonly portrayed as gardens of Venus; see, e.g., Spenser, *Faerie Queene* III.vi and IV.x. The vine at 258–60 falls in with the same complex of associations; see Ovid, *Ars amatoria* i.244 (*Venus in vinis, ignis in igne fuit*). . . . [The ancients believed] that wine contains *pneuma,* the stuff of life."
264. *apply:* devote their energies to. *airs:* both breezes and melodies.
266–75. *Pan.* Though Pan probably got his name from the Gk word for shepherd, Milton may here allude to the notion that the name came from the Gk word for "all"—hence *universal Pan.* Fowler notes that Renaissance mythographers interpreted Pan "as a symbol of 'universal nature.' " *Knit:* clasping hands. *Graces:* (L *gratus* beloved) the sister goddesses Euphrosyne (mirth), Aglaia (splendor), and Thalia (bloom), who danced attendance on (*Led on*) Venus. *Hours:* (Gk *hōra* season) goddesses of the seasons. Before the Fall there was only one season —eternal spring. Cf. Milton's *Comus* 983–85. "Along the crisped shades and bow'rs/ Revels the spruce and jocund Spring,/ The Graces and the rosy-bosom'd Hours." *Enna:* a grove of eternal spring in Sicily. *Proserpine:* daughter of the goddess of agriculture, *Ceres. Dis:* Pluto, god of the underworld, who abducted Proserpine. Zeus agreed to free Proserpine if she had not eaten anything while in Hades, but she [cf. Eve] had eaten a pomegranate [cf. apple], and for that was allowed only six months a year on earth. *Daphne:* a famous grove on the *Orontes*

Knit with the Graces and the Hours in dance
Led on th' eternal spring. Not that fair field
Of Enna, where Proserpine gathering flow'rs
Herself a fairer flow'r by gloomy Dis   270
Was gathered, which cost Ceres all that pain
To seek her through the world; nor that sweet grove
Of Daphne by Orontes, and th' inspired
Castalian spring, might with this Paradise
Of Eden strive; nor that Nyseian isle   275
Girt with the river Triton, where old Cham,
Whom Gentiles Ammon call and Libyan Jove,
Hid Amalthea and her florid son
Young Bacchus from his stepdame Rhea's eye;
Nor where Abassin kings their issue guard,   280
Mount Amara, though this by some supposed
True Paradise under the Ethiop line
By Nilus' head, enclosed with shining rock,
A whole day's journey high, but wide remote
From this Assyrian garden, where the Fiend   285
Saw undelighted all delight, all kind
Of living creatures new to sight and strange:
Two of far nobler shape erect and tall,
God-like erect, with native honor clad
In naked majesty seemed lords of all,   290
And worthy seemed, for in their looks divine
The image of their glorious Maker shone,
Truth, wisdom, sanctitude severe and pure,
Severe but in true filial freedom placed;
Whence true authority in men; though both   295
Not equal, as their sex not equal seemed;
For contemplation he and valor formed,
For softness she and sweet attractive grace,
He for God only, she for God in him:
His fair large front and eye sublime declared   300
Absolute rule; and hyacinthine locks

R. near Antioch, sacred to Apollo, consecrated to voluptuousness and luxury, and (according to Fowler) containing "an Apolline oracle (hence *inspired*) and a stream named after the famous *Castalian spring* of Parnassus."

275–79. According to one ancient historian, *Ammon* (the name of the Jove worshipped in N. Africa), king of Libya and husband of *Rhea*, hid *Bacchus*, his son by the nymph *Amalthea*, on the fabulously beautiful island *Nysa* (whence the name *Dionysus*). *Ammon* (or *Hammon*) was thought in Milton's time to have been Noah's son Ham (or *Cham*). *florid*: (L *floridus* blooming), healthy, beautiful, rosy-complexioned.

280–84. *Abassin*: Abyssinian. *Ethiop line*: the equator. *Nilus' head*: head of the Nile.

288–89. Cf. *Met.* 1.84–86: "And, though all other animals are prone, and fix their gaze upon the earth, he gave to man a noble face and bade him stand erect and turn his eyes to heaven."

300. *large front*: broad forehead. *sublime*: noble.

301–11. Cf. 1 Cor. 11.7–15: "For a man indeed ought not to cover his head, forasmuch as he is the image and glory of God: but the woman is the glory of the man. For the man is not of the woman; but the woman of the man. . . . Judge in yourselves: is it comely that a woman pray unto God uncovered? Doth not even nature . . . teach you, that, if a man have long

Round from his parted forelock manly hung
Clust'ring, but not beneath his shoulders broad:
She as a veil down to the slender waist
Her unadorned golden tresses wore   305
Disheveled, but in wanton ringlets waved
As the vine curls her tendrils, which implied
Subjection, but required with gentle sway,
And by her yielded, by him best received,
Yielded with coy submission, modest pride,   310
And sweet reluctant amorous delay.
Nor those mysterious parts were then concealed,
Then was not guilty shame, dishonest shame
Of nature's works, honor dishonorable,
Sin-bred, how have ye troubled all mankind   315
With shows instead, mere shows of seeming pure,
And banished from man's life his happiest life,
Simplicity and spotless innocence.
So passed they naked on, nor shunned the sight
Of God or angel, for they thought no ill: 320
So hand in hand they passed, the loveliest pair
That ever since in love's embraces met,
Adam the goodliest man of men since born
His sons, the fairest of her daughters Eve.
Under a tuft of shade that on a green   325
Stood whispering soft, by a fresh fountain side
They sat them down, and after no more toil
Of their sweet gard'ning labor than sufficed
To recommend cool Zephyr, and made ease
More easy, wholesome thirst and appetite   330
More grateful, to their supper fruits they fell,
Nectarine fruits which the compliant boughs
Yielded them, sidelong as they sat recline
On the soft downy bank damasked with flow'rs:
The savory pulp they chew, and in the rind   335
Still as they thirsted scoop the brimming stream;
Nor gentle purpose, nor endearing smiles
Wanted, nor youthful dalliance as beseems

---

hair, it is a shame unto him? But if a woman have long hair, it is a glory to her: for her hair
is given her for a covering." *hyacinthine:* curled in the form of hyacinth petals—as in some
classical sculpture; an epithet from Homer. *Disheveled:* let down. *wanton:* luxuriant, unres-
trained. *required:* asked for by right of authority (sway). *sway:* controlling influence. *coy:* (L
quietus quiet) modest. *reluctant:* L *reluctare* to struggle against.
312. *mysterious.* Cf. 743, and see 750n.
313. *dishonest:* unchaste.
329. *recommend:* make attractive. *Zephyr:* west wind, the wind of spring and fecundity.
330. *easy:* comfortable.
332. *Nectarine:* Gk *nektar,* the drink of the gods. *compliant:* L *plicare* to bend.
334. *damasked:* ornamental in variegated patterns.
337. *gentle:* OF *gentil* well-born, polite, refined. *purpose:* conversation.
338. *Wanted:* were lacking. *dalliance:* amorous play.

Fair couple, linked in happy nuptial league,
Alone as they. About them frisking played   340
All beasts of th' earth, since wild, and of all chase
In wood or wilderness, forest or den;
Sporting the lion ramped, and in his paw
Dandled the kid; bears, tigers, ounces, pards
Gamboled before them; th' unwieldy elephant   345
To make them mirth used all his might, and wreathed
His lithe proboscis; close the serpent sly
Insinuating, wove with Gordian twine
His braided train, and of his fatal guile
Gave proof unheeded; others on the grass   350
Couched, and now filled with pasture gazing sat,
Or bedward ruminating: for the sun
Declined was hasting now with prone career
To th' Ocean Isles, and in th' ascending scale
Of heav'n the stars that usher evening rose: 355
When Satan still in gaze, as first he stood,
Scarce thus at length failed speech recovered sad.
    "O hell! what do mine eyes with grief behold,
Into our room of bliss thus high advanced
Creatures of other mold, earth-born perhaps,   360
Not Spirits, yet to heav'nly Spirits bright
Little inferior; whom my thoughts pursue
With wonder, and could love, so lively shines
In them divine resemblance, and such grace
The hand that formed them on their shape hath poured.   365
Ah gentle pair, ye little think how nigh
Your change approaches, when all these delights
Will vanish and deliver ye to woe,
More woe, the more your taste is now of joy;
Happy, but for so happy ill secured   370
Long to continue, and this high seat your heav'n
Ill fenced for Heav'n to keep out such a foe

---

341. *chase:* literally, a tract of unenclosed land used as a game preserve; here, a place where animals live.
343. *ramped:* stood rampant—on his hind legs.
344. *ounces:* lynxes. *pards:* leopards.
348. *Insinuating:* (L *insinuare* to bend, curve) worming his way. *Gordian twine:* a twining, twisting motion as intricate and subtle as the Gordian knot.
352. *ruminating:* chewing the cud.
353. *prone:* L *pronus* sinking; also, flying swiftly. *career:* swift course.
354. *Ocean Isles:* the Azores. *scale:* ladder, staircase; but Fowler notes that in the zodiac the *stars that usher evening* "rise in Libra, the Scales, the portion of the sky . . . opposite" Aries, where the sun is setting.
359. *room:* place (left vacant by our fall).
361–62. Cf. Ps. 8.5: "For thou hast made him a little lower than the angels, and hast crowned him with glory and honor."
370. *for so happy:* for people so happy as you.

As now is entered; yet no purposed foe
To you whom I could pity thus forlorn
Though I unpitied: league with you I seek,   375
And mutual amity so strait, so close,
That I with you must dwell, or you with me
Henceforth; my dwelling haply may not please
Like this fair Paradise, your sense, yet such
Accept your Maker's work; he gave it me,   380
Which I as freely give; hell shall unfold,
To entertain you two, her widest gates,
And send forth all her kings; there will be room,
Not like these narrow limits, to receive
Your numerous offspring; if no better place,   385
Thank him who puts me loath to this revenge
On you who wrong me not for him who wronged.
And should I at your harmless innocence
Melt, as I do, yet public reason just,
Honor and empire with revenge enlarged,   390
By conquering this new world, compels me now
To do what else though damned I should abhor."
    So spake the Fiend, and with necessity,
The tyrant's plea, excused his devilish deeds.
Then from his lofty stand on that hgh tree   395
Down he alights among the sportful herd
Of those four-footed kinds, himself now one,
Now other, as their shape served best his end
Nearer to view his prey, and unespied
To mark what of their state he more might learn   400
By word or action marked: about them round
A lion now he stalks with fiery glare,
Then as a tiger, who by chance hath spied
In some purlieu two gentle fawns at play,
Straight couches close, then rising changes oft   405
His couchant watch, as one who chose his ground
Whence rushing he might surest seize them both
Gripped in each paw: when Adam first of men
To first of women Eve thus moving speech
Turned him all ear to hear new utterance flow.   410

376. *strait:* L *strictus* drawn together.
381–83. Cf. Matt. 10.8: "Heal the sick, cleanse the lepers, raise the dead, cast out the devils:
    freely ye have received, freely give." Isa. 14.9, p. 444: "Hell from beneath is moved for thee
    to meet thee at thy coming: it stirreth up the dead for thee, even all the chief ones of the earth;
    it hath raised up from their thrones all the kings of the nations."
386. *puts:* OE *putian* to push, thrust.
387. *for:* in place of.
402. Cf. 1 Pet. 5.8: "Be sober, be vigilant; because your adversary the devil, as a roaring lion,
    walketh about, seeking whom he may devour."
404. *purlieu:* outskirts of a forest.
408–10. A difficult passage. Perhaps "new utterance" means a kind of speech new to Satan, and
    him refers to Satan.

"Sole partner and sole part of all these joys,
Dearer thyself than all; needs must the Power
That made us, and for us this ample world
Be infinitely good, and of his good
As liberal and free as infinite,   415
That raised us from the dust and placed us here
In all this happiness, who at his hand
Have nothing merited, nor can perform
Aught whereof he hath need, he who requires
From us no other service than to keep   420
This one, this easy charge, of all the trees
In Paradise that bear delicious fruit
So various, not to taste that only Tree
Of Knowledge, planted by the Tree of Life,
So near grows death to life, whate'er death is,   425
Some dreadful thing no doubt; for well thou know'st
God hath pronounced it death to taste that Tree,
The only sign of our obedience left
Among so many signs of power and rule
Conferred upon us, and dominion giv'n   430
Over all other creatures that possess
Earth, air, and sea. Then let us not think hard
One easy prohibition, who enjoy
Free leave so large to all things else, and choice
Unlimited of manifold delights: 435
But let us ever praise him, and extol
His bounty, following our delightful task
To prune these growing plants, and tend these flow'rs,
Which were it toilsome, yet with thee were sweet."
    To whom thus Eve replied. "O thou for whom   440
And from whom I was formed flesh of thy flesh,
And without whom am to no end, my guide
And head, what thou hast said is just and right.
For we to him indeed all praises owe,
And daily thanks, I chiefly who enjoy   445
So far the happier lot, enjoying thee
Preeminent by so much odds, while thou
Like consort to thyself canst nowhere find.

411. I.e.: Only partner in and a unique part of . . .
418–19. Cf. Acts 17.24–25: "God that made the world and all things therein . . . [is not]
    worshipped with men's hands, as though he needed any thing, seeing he giveth to all life, and
    breath, and all things."
433. *easy*: not oppressive.
440. *Eve*. Cf. Gen. 3.20: "And Adam called his wife's name Eve; because she was the mother
    of all living." The root of the Hebrew word means "to live."
441. Cf. Gen. 2.23, p. 431.
443. Cf. 1 Cor. 11.3, p. 458: "The head of every man is Christ; and the head of the woman is
    the man; and the head of Christ is God."
447. *so much odds*: such a great amount in excess.

That day I oft remember, when from sleep
I first awaked, and found myself reposed   450
Under a shade on flowers, much wond'ring where
And what I was, whence thither brought, and how.
Not distant far from thence a murmuring sound
Of waters issued from a cave and spread
Into a liquid plain, then stood unmoved   455
Pure as th' expanse of heav'n; I thither went
With unexperienced thought, and laid me down
On the green bank, to look into the clear
Smooth lake, that to me seemed another sky.
As I bent down to look, just opposite,   460
A shape within the wat'ry gleam appeared
Bending to look on me, I started back,
It started back, but pleased I soon returned,
Pleased it returned as soon with answering looks
Of sympathy and love; there I had fixed   465
Mine eyes till now, and pined with vain desire,
Had not a voice thus warned me, 'What thou seest,
What there thou seest fair creature is thyself,
With thee it came and goes: but follow me,
And I will bring thee where no shadow stays   470
Thy coming, and thy soft embraces, he
Whose image thou art, him thou shalt enjoy
Inseparably thine, to him shalt bear
Multitudes like thyself, and thence be called
Mother of human race:' what could I do,   475
But follow straight, invisibly thus led?
Till I espied thee, fair indeed and tall,
Under a platan, yet methought less fair,
Less winning soft, less amiably mild,
Than that smooth wat'ry image; back I turned,   480
Thou following cried'st aloud, 'Return fair Eve,
Whom fli'st thou? Whom thou fli'st, of him thou art,
His flesh, his bone; to give thee being I lent
Out of my side to thee, nearest my heart
Substantial life, to have thee by my side   485
Henceforth an individual solace dear;

450. *reposed*: reclining, resting.
460f. As Narcicuss. Cf. *Met.* 3.415ff.: "While he seeks to slake his thirst another thirst springs
up, and while he drinks he is smitten by the sight of the beautiful form he sees. He loves an
unsubstantial hope and thinks that substance which is only shadow. . . . O fondly foolish boy,
why vainly seek to clasp a fleeting image? What you seek is nowhere; but turn yourself away,
and the object of your love will be no more. That which you behold is but the shadow of a
reflected form and has no substance of its own. With you it comes, with you it stays, and it
will go with you—if you can go."
470. *stays*: awaits.
476. *straight*: at once.
478. *platan*: plane tree.
486. *individual*: inseparable.

Part of my soul I seek thee, and thee claim
My other half': with that thy gentle hand
Seized mine, I yielded, and from that time see
How beauty is excelled by manly grace   490
And wisdom, which alone is truly fair."
   So spake our general mother, and with eyes
Of conjugal attraction unreproved,
And meek surrender, half embracing leaned
On our first father, half her swelling breast   495
Naked met his under the flowing gold
Of her loose tresses hid: he in delight
Both of her beauty and submissive charms
Smiled with superior love, as Jupiter
On Juno smiles, when he impregns the clouds   500
That shed May flowers; and pressed her matron lip
With kisses pure: aside the Devil turned
For envy, yet with jealous leer malign
Eyed them askance, and to himself thus plained.
   "Sight hateful, sight tormenting! thus these two   505
Imparadised in one another's arms
The happier Eden, shall enjoy their fill
Of bliss on bliss, while I to hell am thrust,
Where neither joy nor love, but fierce desire,
Among our other torments not the least,   510
Still unfulfilled with pain of longing pines;
Yet let me not forget what I have gained
From their own mouths; all is not theirs it seems:
One fatal tree there stands of Knowledge called,
Forbidden them to taste: Knowledge forbidden?   515
Suspicious, reasonless. Why should their Lord
Envy them that? Can it be sin to know,
Can it be death? And do they only stand
By ignorance, is that their happy state,
The proof of their obedience and their faith?   520
O fair foundation laid whereon to build
Their ruin! Hence I will excite their minds
With more desire to know, and to reject
Envious commands, invented with design

492. *general.* Cf. *our general sire,* 144.
493. *unreproved:* unreprovable.
499–501. Cf. *Il.* 14.346–51: "and the son of Kronos clasped his consort in his arms. And beneath
   them the divine earth sent forth fresh new grass, and dewy lotus, and crocus, and hyacinth,
   thick and soft, that raised them aloft from the ground. Therein they lay, and were clad on
   with a fair golden cloud, whence fell drops of glittering dew."
500. *impregns:* impregnates.
501. *matron:* here an adjective; wifely.
503. *jealous:* lustful; covetous.
511. *Still:* always. *pines:* is consumed (the metaphor of Tantalus).
517. *Envy:* begrudge.

To keep them low whom knowledge might exalt   525
Equal with gods; aspiring to be such,
They taste and die: what likelier can ensue?
But first with narrow search I must walk round
This garden, and no corner leave unspied;
A chance but chance may lead where I may meet   530
Some wand'ring Spirit of heav'n, by fountain side,
Or in thick shade retired, from him to draw
What further would be learnt. Live while ye may,
Yet happy pair; enjoy, till I return,
Short pleasures, for long woes are to succeed."   535
  So saying, his proud step he scornful turned,
But with sly circumspection, and began
Through wood, through waste, o'er hill, o'er dale his roam.
Meanwhile in utmost longitude, where heav'n
With earth and ocean meets, the setting sun   540
Slowly descended, and with right aspéct
Against the eastern gate of Paradise
Leveled his evening rays: it was a rock
Of alablaster, piled up to the clouds,
Conspicuous far, winding with one ascent   545
Accessible from earth, one entrance high;
The rest was craggy cliff, that overhung
Still as it rose, impossible to climb.
Betwixt these rocky pillars Gabriel sat
Chief of th' angelic guards, awaiting night;   550
About him exercised heroic games
Th' unarmèd youth of heav'n, but nigh at hand
Celestial armory, shields, helms, and spears
Hung high with diamond flaming, and with gold.
Thither came Uriel, gliding through the even   555
On a sunbeam, swift as a shooting star
In autumn thwarts the night, when vapors fired
Impress the air, and shows the mariner
From what point of his compass to beware
Impetuous winds: he thus began in haste.   560
  "Gabriel, to thee thy course by lot hath giv'n
Charge and strict watch that to this happy place
No evil thing approach or enter in;
This day at highth of noon came to my sphere

530. *A chance but chance:* there is a chance that luck. . . .
541–43. The rays of the setting sun struck the inside of the eastern gate at an almost ninety-
    degree angle.
544. *alablaster:* alabaster; a white, translucent marble, veined with colors.
549. *Gabriel.* See "Angels," pp. 466–68.
557. *thwarts:* passes across.
558. *Impress:* exert pressure upon.

A Spirit, zealous, as he seemed, to know   565
More of th' Almighty's works, and chiefly man
God's latest image: I described his way
Bent all on speed, and marked his airy gait;
But in the mount that lies from Eden north,
Where he first lighted, soon discerned his looks   570
Alien from heav'n, with passions foul obscured:
Mine eye pursued him still, but under shade
Lost sight of him; one of the banished crew
I fear, hath ventured from the deep, to raise
New troubles; him thy care must be to find."   575
   To whom the wingèd warrior thus returned:
"Uriel, no wonder if thy perfect sight,
Amid the sun's bright circle where thou sitt'st,
See far and wide: in at this gate none pass
The vigilance here placed, but such as come   580
Well known from heav'n; and since meridian hour
No creature thence: if Spirit of other sort,
So minded, have o'erleaped these earthy bounds
On purpose, hard thou know'st it to exclude
Spiritual substance with corporeal bar.   585
But if within the circuit of these walks,
In whatsoever shape he lurk, of whom
Thou tell'st, by morrow dawning I shall know."
   So promised he, and Uriel to his charge
Returned on that bright beam, whose point now raised   590
Bore him slope downward to the sun now fall'n
Beneath th' Azorès; whether the prime orb,
Incredible how swift, had thither rolled
Diurnal, or this less volúble earth
By shorter flight to th' east, had left him there   595
Arraying with reflected purple and gold
The clouds that on his western throne attend:
Now came still evening on, and twilight gray
Had in her sober livery all things clad;
Silence accompanied, for beast and bird,   600
They to their grassy couch, these to their nests
Were slunk, all but the wakeful nightingale;
She all night long her amorous descant sung;

567. *described:* descried, observed. *way:* course.
568. *gait:* variation of *gate* path (archaic).
572. *shade:* trees forming shade.
592. *prime orb: primum mobile;* see "The Universe," pp. 461–63.
592–97. Whether the sun revolves about the earth (as according to Ptolemy) or the earth revolves about the sun (as according to Copernicus) is an open question in *PL.* Cf. VIII.25–38.
594. *Diurnal:* daily. *voluble:* able to move quickly.
603. *descant:* a strain of melody, sung by a soprano voice.

Silence was pleased: now glowed the firmament
With living sapphires: Hesperus that led   605
The starry host, rode brightest, till the moon
Rising in clouded majesty, at length
Apparent queen unveiled her peerless light,
And o'er the dark her silver mantle threw.
    When Adam thus to Eve: "Fair consort, th' hour   610
Of night, and all things now retired to rest
Mind us of like repose, since God hath set
Labor and rest, as day and night to men
Successive, and the timely dew of sleep
Now falling with soft slumbrous weight inclines   615
Our eyelids; other creatures all day long
Rove idle unemployed, and less need rest;
Man hath his daily work of body or mind
Appointed, which declares his dignity,
And the regard of Heav'n on all his ways;   620
While other animals unactive range,
And of their doings God takes no account.
To morrow ere fresh morning streak the east
With first approach of light, we must be ris'n,
And at our pleasant labor, to reform   625
Yon flow'ry arbors, yonder alleys green,
Our walk at noon, with branches overgrown,
That mock our scant manuring, and require
More hands than ours to lop their wanton growth:
Those blossoms also, and those dropping gums,   630
That lie bestrown unsightly and unsmooth,
Ask riddance, if we mean to tread with ease;
Meanwhile, as nature wills, night bids us rest."
    To whom thus Eve with perfect beauty adorned.
"My author and disposer, what thou bidd'st   635
Unargued I obey; so God ordains,
God is thy law, thou mine: to know no more
Is woman's happiest knowledge and her praise.
With thee conversing I forget all time,
All seasons and their change, all please alike.   640
Sweet is the breath of morn, her rising sweet,
With charm of earliest birds; pleasant the sun
When first on this delightful land he spreads
His orient beams, on herb, tree, fruit, and flow'r,
Glist'ring with dew; fragrant the fertile earth   645

605. *Hesperus:* the Evening Star.
628. *manuring:* OF *manouvrer* to cultivate by manual (L *manus* hand) labor.
635. *disposer:* regulator, manager, employer.
640. *seasons:* times, occasions.
642. *charm:* (OE *cirman* to cry out, make a noise, esp. as of birds) "the blended singing or noise
  of many birds" *OED*.

After soft showers; and sweet the coming on
Of grateful evening mild, then silent night
With this her solemn bird and this fair moon,
And these the gems of heav'n, her starry train:
But neither breath of morn when she ascends   650
With charm of earliest birds, nor rising sun
On this delightful land, nor herb, fruit, flow'r,
Glist'ring with dew, nor fragrance after showers,
Nor grateful evening mild, nor silent night
With this her solemn bird, nor walk by moon,   655
Or glittering starlight without thee is sweet.
But wherefore all night long shine these, for whom
This glorious sight, when sleep hath shut all eyes?"
    To whom our general ancestor replied.
"Daughter of God and man, accomplished Eve,   660
Those have their course to finish, round the earth,
By morrow evening, and from land to land
In order, though to nations yet unborn,
Minist'ring light prepared, they set and rise;
Lest total darkness should by night regain   665
Her old possession, and extinguish life
In nature and all things, which these soft fires
Not only enlighten, but with kindly heat
Of various influence foment and warm,
Temper or nourish, or in part shed down   670
Their stellar virtue on all kinds that grow
On earth, made hereby apter to receive
Perfection from the sun's more potent ray.
These then, though unbeheld in deep of night,
Shine not in vain, nor think, though men were none,   675
That heav'n would want spectators, God want praise;
Millions of spiritual creatures walk the earth
Unseen, both when we wake, and when we sleep:
All these with ceaseless praise his works behold
Both day and night: how often from the steep   680
Of echoing hill or thicket have we heard
Celestial voices to the midnight air,
Sole, or responsive each to other's note
Singing their great Creator: oft in bands
While they keep watch, or nightly rounding walk,   685

648. *solemn:* inspiring awe, devotion, or reverence.
660. *accomplished:* "complete, perfect; esp. in acquirements, or as a result of training," *OED*.
664. *prepared.* Cf. Ps. 74.16: "The day is thine, the night also is thine: thou hast prepared the light and the sun."
667. *soft:* agreeable.
668. *kindly.* Kind originally meant "natural" and "innate"; later, "benevolent."
669. *influence:* (l. *in* + *fluere* flow) originally an astrological term for the flowing of "ethereal fluid" from stars to earth. *foment:* to stimulate by application of warm liquid.

With heav'nly touch of instrumental sounds
In full harmonic number joined, their songs
Divide the night, and lift our thoughts to heaven."
   Thus talking hand in hand alone they passed
On to their blissful bower; it was a place   690
Chos'n by the sovran Planter, when he framed
All things to man's delightful use; the roof
Of thickest covert was inwoven shade
Laurel and myrtle, and what higher grew
Of firm and fragrant leaf; on either side   695
Acanthus, and each odorous bushy shrub
Fenced up the verdant wall; each beauteous flow'r,
Iris all hues, roses, and jessamine
Reared high their flourished heads between, and wrought
Mosaic; underfoot the violet,   700
Crocus, and hyacinth with rich inlay
Broidered the ground, more colored than with stone
Of costliest emblem: other creature here
Beast, bird, insect, or worm durst enter none;
Such was their awe of man. In shadier bower   705
More sacred and sequestered, though but feigned,
Pan or Silvanus never slept, nor nymph,
Nor Faunus haunted. Here in close recess
With flowers, garlands, and sweet-smelling herbs
Espousèd Eve decked first her nuptial bed,   710
And heav'nly choirs the hymenean sung,
What day the genial angel to our sire
Brought her in naked beauty more adorned,
More lovely than Pandora, whom the gods
Endowed with all their gifts, and O too like   715
In sad event, when to the unwiser son
Of Japhet brought by Hermes, she ensnared
Mankind with her fair looks, to be avenged

688. *divide*. The L military phrase *dividere noctem* meant to mark the watches of the night, but
   as Fowler notes, "perhaps there is also a play on the musical sense of *divide* (OED 11 a,
   perform with 'divisions'—florid melodic passages or descants)."
691. *framed*: fashioned.
699. *flourished*: L *flos, floris* flower.
700. Cf. 499–501n.
703. *emblem*: mosaic.
704. *worm*: a class including snakes.
706. *feigned*: existing in fiction.
707–8. *Pan, Silvanus*, and *Faunus* were fauns associated with sacred, sequestered, rural places
   and with generation. *close*: secluded.
711. *hymenean*: wedding hymn; *Hymen*, god of marriage.
712. *genial*: L *genialis*, from *gignere* to beget.
714–19. After Prometheus, the wise son of Iapetus (identified by Christian mythologists with
   Iapet, i.e., *Japhet*, son of Noah) had stolen fire from heaven, angry *Jove* avenged himself on
   all mankind by means of *Pandora*, whom Prometheus' brother fell in love with and married.
   To marriage Pandora brought a treasure chest that, when her unwary husband opened it, turned
   out to hold all the evils and woes that have since afflicted mankind. *authentic*: Gk *authentēs*
   one who does anything with his own hand. *event*: outcome.

On him who had stole Jove's authentic fire.
　　Thus at their shady lodge arrived, both stood,　　　720
Both turned, and under open sky adored
The God that made both sky, air, earth and heav'n
Which they beheld, the moon's resplendent globe
And starry pole: "Thou also mad'st the night,
Maker Omnipotent, and thou the day,　　　725
Which we in our appointed work employed
Have finished happy in our mutual help
And mutual love, the crown of all our bliss
Ordained by thee, and this delicious place
For us too large, where thy abundance wants　　　730
Partakers, and uncropped falls to the ground.
But thou hast promised from us two a race
To fill the earth, who shall with us extol
Thy goodness infinite, both when we wake,
And when we seek, as now, thy gift of sleep."　　　735
　　This said unanimous, and other rites
Observing none, but adoration pure
Which God likes best, into their inmost bow'r
Handed they went; and eased the putting off
These troublesome disguises which we wear,　　　740
Straight side by side were laid, nor turned I ween
Adam from his fair spouse, nor Eve the rites
Mysterious of connubial love refused:
Whatever hypocrites austerely talk
Of purity and place and innocence,　　　745
Defaming as impure what God declares
Pure, and commands to some, leaves free to all.
Our Maker bids increase, who bids abstain
But our destroyer, foe to God and man?
Hailed wedded Love, mysterious law, true source　　　750
Of human offspring, sole propriety
In Paradise of all things common else.
By thee adulterous lust was driv'n from men

724. *pole:* sky.
739. *Handed:* hand in hand.
742. *rites:* those things that are proper for, or incumbent on, one to do.
743. *Mysterious:* beyond explanation.
744–48. Cf. 1 Tim. 4.1–3: "Now the Spirit speaketh expressly, that in the latter times some shall depart from the faith, giving heed to seducing spirits, and doctrines of devils; Speaking lies in hypocrisy; having their conscience seared with a hot iron; Forbidding to marry, and commanding to abstain from meats, which God hath created to be received with thanksgiving of them which believe and know the truth."
747. Cf. 1 Cor. 7.1–2: "It is good for a man not to touch a woman. Nevertheless, to avoid fornication, let every man have his own wife."
748. *bids increase:* cf. Gen. 1.28.
750. Cf. Eph. 5.31–32: "For this cause shall a man leave his father and mother, and shall be joined unto his wife, and they two shall be one flesh. This is a great mystery: but I speak concerning Christ and the church."
751. *propriety:* (OF *proprieté*, L *proprius* one's own) private property.

Among the bestial herds to range, by thee
Founded in reason, loyal, just, and pure,   755
Relations dear, and all the charities
Of father, son, and brother first were known.
Far be it, that I should write thee sin or blame,
Or think thee unbefitting holiest place,
Perpetual fountain of domestic sweets,   760
Whose bed is undefiled and chaste pronounced,
Present, or past, as saints and patriarchs used.
Here Love his golden shafts employs, here lights
His constant lamp, and waves his purple wings,
Reigns here and revels; not in the bought smile   765
Of harlots, loveless, joyless, unendeared,
Casual fruition, nor in court amours,
Mixed dance, or wanton masque, or midnight ball,
Or serenate, which the starved lover sings
To his proud fair, best quitted with disdain.   770
These lulled by nightingales embracing slept,
And on their naked limbs the flow'ry roof
Show'red roses, which the morn repaired. Sleep on,
Blest pair; and O yet happiest if ye seek
No happier state, and know to know no more.   775
    Now had night measured with her shadowy cone
Half way up hill this vast sublunar vault,
And from their ivory port the Cherubim
Forth issuing at th' accustomed hour stood armed
To their night-watches in warlike parade,   780
When Gabriel to his next in power thus spake.
    "Uzziel, half these draw off, and coast the south
With strictest watch; these other wheel the north,
Our circuit meets full west." As flame they part
Half wheeling to the shield, half to the spear.   785
From these, two strong and subtle Spirits he called
That near him stood, and gave them thus in charge.
    "Ithuriel and Zephon, with winged speed
Search through this garden, leave unsearched no nook,

756. *charities*: loves.
761. Cf. Heb. 13.4: "Marriage is honourable in all, and the bed undefiled: but whoremongers and adulterers God will judge."
763. *Love*: Eros or Cupid, whose gold-tipped arrows inspired love—his lead-tipped, hate.
768. *masque*: masquerade.
769. *serenate*: Italian form of *serenade*.
773. *repaired*: restored by replacing.
774–75. See "Knowledge," p. 470.
776–77. The imagined conical shadow cast by the earth in the light of the sun has moved halfway up to its zenith; it is 9 P.M., the end of the first three-hour watch.
782. *coast*: follow the coastline of.
782, 788. See "Angels," pp. 466–68.
783. *wheel*: (military term) turn to.
785. *shield*: left. *spear*: right.

But chiefly where those two fair creatures lodge,   790
Now laid perhaps asleep secure of harm.
This evening from the sun's decline arrived
Who tells of some infernal Spirit seen
Hitherward bent (who could have thought?) escaped
The bars of hell, on errand bad no doubt: 795
Such where ye find, seize fast, and hither bring."
    So saying, on he led his radiant files,
Dazzling the moon; these to the bower direct
In search of whom they sought: him there they found
Squat like a toad, close at the ear of Eve;   800
Assaying by his devilish art to reach
The organs of her fancy, and with them forge
Illusions as he list, phantasms and dreams;
Or if, inspiring venom, he might taint
Th' animal spirits that from pure blood arise   805
Like gentle breaths from rivers pure, thence raise
At least distempered, discontented thoughts,
Vain hopes, vain aims, inordinate desires
Blown up with high conceits engend'ring pride.
Him thus intent Ithuriel with his spear   810
Touched lightly; for no falsehood can endure
Touch of celestial temper, but returns
Of force to its own likeness: up he starts
Discovered and surprised. As when a spark
Lights on a heap of nitrous powder, laid   815
Fit for the tun some magazine to store
Against a rumored war, the smutty grain
With sudden blaze diffused, inflames the air:
So started up in his own shape the Fiend.
Back stepped those two fair angels half amazed   820
So sudden to behold the grisly king;
Yet thus, unmoved with fear, accost him soon.
    "Which of those rebel Spirits adjudged to hell
Com'st thou, escaped thy prison; and transformed,
Why sat'st thou like an enemy in wait   825
Here watching at the head of these that sleep?"
    "Know ye not then" said Satan, filled with scorn,
"Know ye not me? Ye knew me once no mate
For you, there sitting where ye durst not soar;

791. *secure of*: unconcerned about.
793. *Who*: one who. *infernal*: L *infernus* that lies beneath.
804. *inspiring*: L *in* + *spirare* to breathe.
805. *animal spirits*. See "Physiology and Psychology," pp. 463–64.
807. *distempered*: unbalanced; disordered.
809. *conceits*: ideas.
812. *celestial temper*: anything, like the spear, made (tempered) in heaven.
816. I.e.: Ready to be put in barrels to supply an ammunition dump.
817. *Against*: in anticipation of. *smutty grain*: seed-shaped particles that blacken the touch.

Not to know me argue yourselves unknown,   830
The lowest of your throng; or if ye know,
Why ask ye, and superfluous begin
Your message, like to end as much in vain?"
To whom thus Zephon, answering scorn with scorn.
"Think not, revolted Spirit, thy shape the same,   835
Or undiminished brightness, to be known
As when thou stood'st in heav'n upright and pure;
That glory then, when thou no more wast good,
Departed from thee, and thou resembl'st now
Thy sin and place of doom obscure and foul.   840
But come, for thou, be sure, shalt give account
To him who sent us, whose charge is to keep
This place inviolable, and these from harm."
   So spake the Cherub, and his grave rebuke
Severe in youthful beauty, added grace   845
Invincible: abashed the Devil stood,
And felt how awful goodness is, and saw
Virtue in her shape how lovely, saw, and pined
His loss; but chiefly to find here observed
His luster visibly impaired; yet seemed   850
Undaunted. "If I must contend," said he,
"Best with the best, the sender not the sent,
Or all at once; more glory will be won,
Or less be lost." "Thy fear," said Zephon bold,
"Will save us trial what the least can do   855
Single against thee wicked, and thence weak."
   The Fiend replied not, overcome with rage;
But like a proud steed reined, went haughty on,
Champing his iron curb: to strive or fly
He held it vain; awe from above had quelled   860
His heart, not else dismayed. Now drew they nigh
The western point, where those half-rounding guards
Just met, and closing stood in squadron joined
Awaiting next command. To whom their chief
Gabriel from the front thus called aloud.   865
   "O friends, I hear the tread of nimble feet
Hasting this way, and now by glimpse discern
Ithuriel and Zephon through the shade,
And with them comes a third of regal port,
But faded splendor wan; who by his gait   870
And fierce demeanor seems the Prince of Hell,
Not likely to part hence without contést;

830. *argues:* proves.
840. *obscure:* (L *obscurus* covered) dark.
848. *pined:* suffered for.
868. *shade:* shade trees.
870. *wan:* dark, faint, sickly.

Stand firm, for in his look defiance lours."
He scarce had ended, when those two approached
And brief related whom they brought, where found, 875
How busied, in what form and posture couched.
To whom with stern regard thus Gabriel spake.
"Why hast thou, Satan, broke the bounds prescribed
To thy transgressions, and disturbed the charge
Of others, who approve not to transgress 880
By thy example, but have power and right
To question thy bold entrance on this place;
Employed it seems to violate sleep, and those
Whose dwelling God hath planted here in bliss?"
To whom thus Satan, with contemptuous brow. 885
"Gabriel, thou hadst in heav'n th' esteem of wise,
And such I held thee; but this question asked
Puts me in doubt. Lives there who loves his pain?
Who would not, finding way, break loose from hell,
Though thither doomed? Thou wouldst thyself, no doubt, 890
And boldly venture to whatever place
Farthest from pain, where thou mightst hope to change
Torment with ease, and soonest recompense
Dole with delight, which in this place I sought;
To thee no reason; who know'st only good, 895
But evil hast not tried: and wilt object
His will who bound us? Let him surer bar
His iron gates, if he intends our stay
In that dark durance: thus much what was asked.
The rest is true, they found me where they say; 900
But that implies not violence or harm."
Thus he in scorn. The warlike angel moved,
Disdainfully half smiling thus replied.
"O loss of one in heav'n to judge of wise,
Since Satan fell, whom folly overthrew, 905
And now returns him from his prison scaped,
Gravely in doubt whether to hold them wise
Or not, who ask what boldness brought him hither
Unlicensed from his bounds in hell prescribed;
So wise he judges it to fly from pain 910
However, and to scape his punishment.
So judge thou still, presumptuous, till the wrath,
Which thou incurr'st by flying, meet thy flight
Sevenfold, and scourge that wisdom back to hell,

879. *the charge Of:* those under the protection of.
886. *esteem of:* reputation of being.
894. *Dole:* L *dolor* pain, distress, grief, sorrow.
896. *wilt object:* wilt thou produce as an argument (against my escape).
899. *durance:* confinement.
911. *However:* howsoever.

Which taught thee yet no better, that no pain   915
Can equal anger infinite provoked.
But wherefore thou alone? Wherefore with thee
Came not all hell broke loose? Is pain to them
Less pain, less to be fled, or thou than they
Less hardy to endure? Courageous chief,   920
The first in flight from pain, hadst thou alleged
To thy deserted host this cause of flight,
Thou surely hadst not come sole fugitive."
    To which the Fiend thus answered frowning stern.
"Not that I less endure, or shrink from pain,   925
Insulting angel, well thou know'st I stood
Thy fiercest, when in battle to thy aid
The blasting volleyed thunder made all speed
And seconded thy else not dreaded spear.
But still thy words at random, as before,   930
Argue thy inexperience what behoves
From hard assays and ill successes past
A faithful leader, not to hazard all
Through ways of danger by himself untried.
I therefore, I alone first undertook   935
To wing the desolate abyss, and spy
This new-created world, whereof in hell
Fame is not silent, here in hope to find
Better abode, and my afflicted powers
To settle here on earth, or in mid-air;   940
Though for possession put to try once more
What thou and thy gay legions dare against;
Whose easier business were to serve their Lord
High up in heav'n, with songs to hymn his throne,
And practiced distances to cringe, not fight."   945
    To whom the warrior angel soon replied.
"To say and straight unsay, pretending first
Wise to fly pain, professing next the spy,
Argues no leader, but a liar traced,
Satan, and couldst thou faithful add? O name,   950
O sacred name of faithfulness profaned!
Faithful to whom? To thy rebellious crew?
Army of fiends, fit body to fit head;
Was this your discipline and faith engaged,

926. *stood:* withstood.
932. *From:* after. *assays:* attempts; or (military) attacks. *successes:* outcomes.
938. *Fame:* rumor.
939. *afflicted:* (L *affligere* to throw down) downcast, depressed. *powers:* army.
940. *mid-air.* See "The Universe," pp. 461–63.
941. *put:* forced. *try:* test.
942. *gay:* in dress and behavior like courtiers.
945. *distances:* attitudes of deference. *cringe:* bow or kneel in humility or fear.
949. *traced:* found out.

Your military obedience, to dissolve   955
Allegiance to th' acknowledged Power Supreme?
And thou sly hypocrite, who now wouldst seem
Patron of liberty, who more than thou
Once fawned, and cringed, and serviley adored
Heav'n's awful Monarch? Wherefore but in hope   960
To dispossess him, and thyself to reign?
But mark what I areed thee now, avaunt;
Fly thither whence thou fledd'st: if from this hour
Within these hallowed limits thou appear,
Back to th' infernal pit I drag thee chained,   965
And seal thee so, as henceforth not to scorn
The facile gates of hell too slightly barred."
     So threatened he, but Satan to no threats
Gave heed, but waxing more in rage replied.
     "Then when I am thy captive talk of chains,   970
Proud limitary Cherub, but ere then
Far heavier load thyself expect to feel
From my prevailing arm, though heaven's King
Ride on thy wings, and thou with thy compeers,
Used to the yoke, draw'st his triumphant wheels   975
In progress through the road of heav'n star-paved "
     While thus he spake, th' angelic squadron bright
Turned fiery red, sharp'ning in moonèd horns
Their phalanx, and began to hem him round
With ported spears, as thick as when a field   980
Of Ceres ripe for harvest waving bends
Her bearded grove of ears, which way the wind
Sways them; the careful ploughman doubting stands
Lest on the threshing-floor his hopeful sheaves
Prove chaff. On th' other side Satan alarmed   985
Collecting all his might dilated stood,
Like Teneriffe or Atlas unremoved:
His stature reached the sky, and on his crest
Sat Horror plumed; nor wanted in his grasp
What seemed both spear and shield: now dreadful deeds   990

962. *areed*: advise.
966. Cf. Rev. 20.3.
967. *facile*: easily moved.
971. *limitary*: frontier guard; also, one of limited authority.
974. Cf. Ps. 18.10: "And he rode upon a cherub, and did fly: yea, he did fly upon the wings of the wind."
978. *mooned horns*: a crescent-shaped military formation.
980. *ported*: held slantwise, in front.
980ff. Cf. *Il.* 2.147–48: "and even as when the west wind cometh to stir a deep cornfield with violent blast, and the ears bow down. . . ."
981. *Ceres*: Roman goddess of grain; here the grain itself.
983. *careful*: anxious.
987. *Teneriffe* is a mountain in the Canary Islands; *Atlas*, in Morocco. *unremoved*: unremovable.
990–1004. Cf. *Il.* 22.209 and *Aen.* 12.725–27.

Might have ensued, nor only Paradise
In this commotion, but the starry cope
Of heav'n perhaps, or all the elements
At least had gone to wrack, disturbed and torn
With violence of this conflict, and not soon   995
Th' Eternal to prevent such horrid fray
Hung forth in heav'n his golden scales, yet seen
Betwixt Astraea and the Scorpion sign,
Wherein all things created first he weighed,
The pendulous round earth with balanced air   1000
In counterpoise, now ponders all events,
Battles and realms: in these he put two weights
The sequel each of parting and of fight;
The latter quick up flew, and kicked the beam;
Which Gabriel spying, thus bespake the Fiend.   1005
    "Satan, I know thy strength, and thou know'st mine,
Neither our own but giv'n; what folly then
To boast what arms can do, since thine no more
Than Heav'n permits, nor mine, though doubled now
To trample thee as mire: for proof look up,   1010
And read thy lot in yon celestial sign
Where thou art weighed, and shown how light, how weak,
If thou resist." The Fiend looked up and knew
His mounted scale aloft: nor more; but fled
Murmuring, and with him fled the shades of night.   1015

Book V

The Argument

Morning approached, Eve relates to Adam her troublesome dream;
he likes it not, yet comforts her: they come forth to their day labors:
their morning hymn at the door of their bower. God to render man
inexcusable sends Raphael to admonish him of his obedience, of his

992. *cope:* vaultlike canopy.
997–1013. In the classical epic simile that Milton here imitates, the gods weigh the fates of
    opposing heroes before battle (Hector and Achilles in the *Iliad*, Turnus and Aeneas in the
    Aeneid), but Milton adds to this conventional meaning (i.e., the fate of Satan) God's *pondering*,
    or weighing the consequences (*sequel*) of allowing Satan and Gabriel to fight and the conse-
    quences of preventing the fight. The second "weighed" more—was more desirable. Milton
    also enriched the conventional figure by identifying the scales with Libra, the sign in the
    Zodiac, and by alluding to Biblical metaphors of weighing: Isa. 40.12: "Who hath measured
    the waters in the hollow of his hand, and meted out heaven with the span, and comprehended
    the dust of the earth in a measure, and weighed the mountains in scales, and the hills in a
    balance?" 1 Sam. 2.3: "Talk no more so exceeding proudly; let not arrogancy come out of
    your mouth: for the Lord is a God of knowledge, and by him actions are weighed." Dan. 5.27:
    "Tekel; Thou art weighed in the balances, and art found wanting."
V. *Argument. admonish:* (L *admonere* to remind) warn. *avail:* profit. *message:* a messenger's
    errand.

free estate, of his enemy near at hand; who he is, and why his enemy, and whatever else may avail Adam to know. Raphael comes down to Paradise, his appearance described, his coming discerned by Adam afar off sitting at the door of his bower; he goes out to meet him, brings him to his lodge, entertains him with the choicest fruits of Paradise got together by Eve; their discourse at table: Raphael performs his message, minds Adam of his state and of his enemy; relates at Adam's request who that enemy is, and how he came to be so, beginning from his first revolt in heaven, and the occasion thereof; how he drew his legions after him to the parts of the north, and there incited them to rebel with him, persuading all but only Abdiel a Seraph, who in argument dissuades and opposes him, then forsakes him.

Now Morn her rosy steps in th' eastern clime
Advancing, sowed the earth with orient pearl,
When Adam waked, so customed, for his sleep
Was aery light, from pure digestion bred,
And temperate vapors bland, which th' only sound   5
Of leaves and fuming rills, Aurora's fan,
Lightly dispersed, and the shrill matin song
Of birds on every bough; so much the more
His wonder was to find unawakened Eve
With tresses discomposed, and glowing cheek,   10
As through unquiet rest: he on his side
Leaning half-raised, with looks of cordial love
Hung over her enamored, and beheld
Beauty, which whether waking or asleep,
Shot forth peculiar graces; then with voice   15
Mild, as when Zephyrus on Flora breathes,

1–8. The imagery in this fine passage is complex. Sleep was suposed to be induced by vapors generated in the stomach, according to the same physiology expressed in the lines about Satan's hope that by breathing poison into Eve's ear he might "taint / The animal spirits that from pure blood arise / Like gentle breaths from rivers pure" (IV.804–6). Adam's sleep was *aery light* because the elements in his vapors were mixed in perfect proportion (*temperate*)—and because Satan had not poisoned them. These sleep-producing vapors were *dispersed* by the *sound* of *leaves, rills,* and bird *songs*. But associated with all three were vapors of various sorts that acted upon the vapors of sleep: there was the morning breeze that rustled the leaves; there was the mist rising from the stream; and there were, in a pun, the "airs, vernal airs" (cf. IV.264) of the bird songs. Dawn, *Morn, Aurora* is personified first by her *rosy steps* and her *sowing the earth with orient pearl*, and then by her *fan* (the trees), and finally by the mist, which is her veil. For if we remember that Milton later (IX.425) described Eve as "Veiled in a cloud of fragrance," we may realize that *fume* here has the then common meaning of fragrant exhalation or incense, and that the fragrant cloud of fresh, rural morning mist was the goddess's veil. The harmony of rustling leaves, singing birds, and rippling brooks was a literary cliché, as Fowler points out in his note to IV.263–66. But Milton's synesthetic association, here and elsewhere, of the sounds, fragrances, and other nonvisual sensations of morning came from deep within his own experience. According to Milton's history of man the first line of the first love lyric ever sung was Eve's "Sweet is the breath of morn, her rising sweet" (IV.641).
12. *cordial*: (L *cordis* heart) reviving.
15. *peculiar*: (L *peculium* private property) its own.
16. *Zephyrus*: the western wind. *Flora*: goddess of flowers.

Her hand soft touching, whispered thus. "Awake
My fairest, my espoused, my latest found,
Heav'n's last best gift, my ever new delight,
Awake, the morning shines, and the fresh field   20
Calls us, we lose the prime, to mark how spring
Our tended plants, how blows the citron grove,
What drops the myrrh, and what the balmy reed,
How nature paints her colors, how the bee
Sits on the bloom extracting liquid sweet."   25
    Such whispering waked her, but with startled eye
On Adam, whom embracing, thus she spake.
    "O sole in whom my thoughts find all repose,
My glory, my perfection, glad I see
Thy face, and morn returned, for I this night,   30
Such night till this I never passed, have dreamed,
If dreamed, not as I oft am wont, of thee,
Works of day past, or morrow's next design,
But of offense and trouble, which my mind
Knew never till this irksome night; methought   35
Close at mine ear one called me forth to walk
With gentle voice, I thought it thine; it said,
'Why sleep'st thou Eve? now is the pleasant time,
The cool, the silent, save where silence yields
To the night-warbling bird, that now awake   40
Tunes sweetest his love-labored song; now reigns
Full-orbed the moon, and with more pleasing light
Shadowy sets off the face of things; in vain,
If none regard; heav'n wakes with all his eyes,
Whom to behold but thee, nature's desire,   45
In whose sight all things joy, with ravishment
Attracted by thy beauty still to gaze.'
I rose as at thy call, but found thee not;
To find thee I directed then my walk;
And on, me thought, alone I passed through ways   50
That brought me on a sudden to the tree
Of interdicted knowledge: fair it seemed,
Much fairer to my fancy than by day:
And as I wond'ring looked, beside it stood
One shaped and winged like one of those from heav'n   55
By us oft seen; his dewy locks distilled
Ambrosia; on that tree he also gazed;

17–25. Cf. Song Sol. 2.10: "My beloved spake, and said unto me / Rise up, my love, my fair
  one, and come away."
21. *prime:* the first hour of the day.
22. *blows:* blossoms.
23. *myrrh* and balm are odoriferous resins.
34. *offense:* L *offendere* to stumble, commit a fault.
57. *Ambrosia:* heavenly fragrance.

And 'O fair plant,' said he, 'with fruit surcharged,
Deigns none to ease thy load and taste thy sweet,
Nor god, nor man; is knowledge so despised?   60
Or envy, or what reserve forbids to taste?
Forbid who will, none shall from me withhold
Longer thy offered good, why else set here?'
This said he paused not, but with vent'rous arm
He plucked, he tasted; me damp horror chilled   65
At such bold words vouched with a deed so bold:
But he thus overjoyed, 'O fruit divine,
Sweet of thyself, but much more sweet thus cropped,
Forbidden here, it seems, as only fit
For gods, yet able to make gods of men: 70
And why not gods of men, since good, the more
Communicated, more abundant grows,
The author not impaired, but honored more?
Here, happy creature, fair angelic Eve,
Partake thou also; happy though thou art,   75
Happier thou may'st be, worthier canst not be:
Taste this, and be henceforth among the gods
Thyself a goddess, not to earth confined,
But sometimes in the air, as we, sometimes
Ascend to heav'n, by merit thine, and see   80
What life the gods live there, and such live thou.'
So saying, he drew nigh, and to me held,
Even to my mouth of that same fruit held part
Which he had plucked; the pleasant savory smell
So quickened appetite, that I, me thought,   85
Could not but taste. Forthwith up to the clouds
With him I flew, and underneath beheld
The earth outstretched immense, a prospect wide
And various: wond'ring at my flight and change
To this high exaltation; suddenly   90
My guide was gone, and I, methought, sunk down,
And fell asleep; but O how glad I waked
To find this but a dream!" Thus Eve her night
Related, and thus Adam answered sad.
    "Best image of myself and dearer half,   95
The trouble of thy thoughts this night in sleep
Affects me equally; nor can I like
This uncouth dream, of evil sprung I fear;
Yet evil whence? in thee can harbor none,

60. *god:* angel.
61. I.e.: Whose envy or what restriction forbids your being tasted?
73. *impaired:* (L *pejorare* to make worse) injured, diminished.
94. *sad:* soberly.
98. *uncouth:* strange; unpleasant, improper.

Created pure. But know that in the soul 100
Are many lesser faculties that serve
Reason as chief; among these fancy next
Her office holds; of all external things,
Which the five watchful senses represent,
She forms imaginations, aery shapes, 105
Which reason joining or disjoining, frames
All what we affirm or what deny, and call
Our knowledge or opinion; then retires
Into her private cell when nature rests.
Oft in her absence mimic fancy wakes 110
To imitate her; but misjoining shapes,
Wild work produces oft, and most in dreams,
Ill matching words and deeds long past or late.
Some such resemblances methinks I find
Of our last evening's talk, in this thy dream, 115
But with addition strange; yet be not sad.
Evil into the mind of god or man
May come and go, so unapproved, and leave
No spot or blame behind: which gives me hope
That what in sleep thou didst abhor to dream, 120
Waking thou never wilt consent to do.
Be not disheartened then, nor cloud those looks
That wont to be more cheerful and serene
Than when fair morning first smiles on the world,
And let us to our fresh employments rise 125
Among the groves, the fountains, and the flow'rs
That open now their choicest bosomed smells
Reserved from night, and kept for thee in store."
    So cheered he his fair spouse, and she was cheered,
But silently a gentle tear let fall 130
From either eye, and wiped them with her hair;
Two other precious drops that ready stood,
Each in their crystal sluice, he ere they fell
Kissed as the gracious signs of sweet remorse
And pious awe, that feared to have offended. 135
    So all was cleared, and to the field they haste.

100–113. Fowler quotes Burton, *Anatomy of Melancholy* (1621) I.1.2.vii: "Phantasy, or imagination . . . is an inner sense which doth more fully examine the species perceived by common sense, of things present or absent. . . . In time of sleep this faculty is free, and many times conceives strange, stupend, absurd shapes. . . . In men it is subject and governed by reason, or at least should be." See "Physiology and Psychology," pp. 463–64.
104. *represent*: present to the mind.
105. *imagination*: images.
117. *god*: angel.
118. *so unapproved*: so long as it is (1) not approved or (2) not experienced or put to proof.
125. *fresh*: refreshing.
127. *bosomed*: enclosed.
135. *pious*: L *pius*, dutiful; devoted, as becoming to a spouse. *awe*: veneration.

But first from under shady arborous roof,
Soon as they forth were come to open sight
Of day-spring, and the sun, who scarce up risen
With wheels yet hov'ring o'er the ocean brim,   140
Shot parallel to the earth his dewy ray,
Discovering in wide landscape all the east
Of Paradise and Eden's happy plains,
Lowly they bowed adoring, and began
Their orisons, each morning duly paid   145
In various style, for neither various style
Nor holy rapture wanted they to praise
Their Maker, in fit strains pronounced or sung
Unmeditated, such prompt eloquence
Flowed from their lips, in prose or numerous verse,   150
More tuneable than needed lute or harp
To add more sweetness, and they thus began.
    "These are thy glorious works, Parent of good,
Almighty, thine this universal frame,
Thus wondrous fair; thyself how wondrous then!   155
Unspeakable, who sitt'st above these heavens,
To us invisible or dimly seen
In these thy lowest works, yet these declare
Thy goodness beyond thought, and power divine:
Speak ye who best can tell, ye sons of light,   160
Angels, for ye behold him, and with songs
And choral symphonies, day without night,
Circle his throne rejoicing, ye in heav'n,
On earth join all ye creatures to extol
Him first, him last, him midst, and without end.   165
Fairest of stars, last in the train of night,
If better thou belong not to the dawn,
Sure pledge of day, that crown'st the smiling morn
With thy bright circlet, praise him in thy sphere
While day arises, that sweet hour of prime.   170
Thou sun, of this great world both eye and soul,
Acknowledge him thy greater, sound his praise
In thy eternal course, both when thou climb'st,
And when high noon hast gained, and when thou fall'st.

145. *orisons*: prayers.
146. *In various style*: in a variety of styles, or forms—informal, impromptu.
147. *holy rapture*: religious ecstasy.
151. *numerous verse*: metrical (but not rhymed) verse.
153–208. Cf. Ps. 104, pp. 439–41, and 148, pp. 441–42.
165. Cf. Rev. 22.13: "I am Alpha and Omega, the beginning and the end, the first and the last."
166. *Fairest of stars*: Venus, the morning star and the evening star.

Moon, that now meet'st the orient sun, now fli'st   175
With the fixed stars, fixed in their orb that flies,
And ye five other wand'ring fires that move
In mystic dance not without song, resound
His praise, who out of darkness called up light.
Air, and ye elements the eldest birth   180
Of nature's womb, that in quaternion run
Perpetual circle, multiform, and mix
And nourish all things, let your ceaseless change
Vary to our great Maker still new praise.
Ye mists and exhalations that now rise   185
From hill or steaming lake, dusky or gray,
Till the sun paint your fleecy skirts with gold,
In honor to the world's great Author rise,
Whether to deck with clouds the uncolored sky,
Or wet the thirsty earth with falling showers,   190
Rising or falling still advance his praise.
His praise ye winds, that from four quarters blow,
Breathe soft or loud; and wave your tops, ye pines,
With every plant, in sign of worship wave.
Fountains and ye, that warble, as ye flow,   195
Melodious murmurs, warbling tune his praise.
Join voices all ye living souls: ye birds,
That singing up to heaven gate ascend,
Bear on your wings and in your notes his praise;
Ye that in waters glide, and ye that walk   200
The earth, and stately tread, or lowly creep;
Witness if I be silent, morn or even,
To hill, or valley, fountain, or fresh shade
Made vocal by my song, and taught his praise.
Hail universal Lord, be bounteous still   205
To give us only good; and if the night
Have gathered aught of evil or concealed,
Disperse it, as now light dispels the dark."
    So prayed they innocent, and to their thoughts
Firm peace recovered soon and wonted calm.   210
On to their morning's rural work they haste
Among sweet dews and flow'rs; where any row

176. *their orb*: the sphere of the fixed stars, which if it turned about the earth would do so at
    incredible speed.
177. Since Venus has already been mentioned, Fowler suggests Milton may be counting earth.
    The planets (Gk *planētēs* wandering), unlike the fixed stars, change their relative positions.
178. *not without song*. From Pythagoras, Plato took the notion that on the sphere of each of the
    planets there was a siren who sang a note which in combination with the notes sung by the
    others produced a harmony of the spheres inaudible to impure, mortal man.
180. *eldest*. Earth, water, and fire (light) were the first "elements" mentioned in Genesis.
181. *quaternion*: a fourfold changing relationship; i.e., one produces another, or one feeds on
    another, or two or more combine in various ways, then disintegrate. Cf. 415–17.
205. *still*: always.

Of fruit trees over-woody reached too far
Their pampered boughs, and needed hands to check
Fruitless embraces: or they led the vine   215
To wed her elm; she spoused about him twines
Her marriageable arms, and with her brings
Her dow'r th' adopted clusters, to adorn
His barren leaves. Them thus employed beheld
With pity heav'n's high King, and to him called   220
Raphael, the sociable Spirit, that deigned
To travel with Tobias, and secured
His marriage with the seven-times-wedded maid.
    "Raphael," said he, "thou hear'st what stir on earth
Satan from hell scaped through the darksome gulf   225
Hath raised in Paradise, and how disturbed
This night the human pair, how he designs
In them at once to ruin all mankind.
Go therefore, half this day as friend with friend
Converse with Adam, in what bow'r or shade   230
Thou find'st him from the heat of noon retired,
To respite his day-labor with repast,
Or with repose; and such discourse bring on,
As may advise him of his happy state,
Happiness in his power left free to will,   235
Left to his own free will, his will though free,
Yet mutable; whence warn him to beware
He swerve not too secure: tell him withal
His danger, and from whom, what enemy
Late fall'n himself from heav'n, is plotting now   240
The fall of others from like state of bliss;
By violence, no, for that shall be withstood,
But by deceit and lies; this let him know,
Lest wilfully transgressing he pretend
Surprisal, unadmonished, unforewarned."   245
    So spake th' Eternal Father, and fulfilled
All justice: nor delayed the wingèd saint
After his charge received; but from among
Thousand celestial ardors, where he stood
Veiled with his gorgeous wings, up springing light   250
Flew through the midst of heav'n; th' angelic choirs
On each hand parting, to his speed gave way
Through all th' empyreal road; till at the gate
Of heav'n arrived, the gate self-opened wide

221. *Raphael.* See "Angels," pp. 466–68.
222. *Tobias.* Cf. IV.166–71n.
229. Cf. Exod. 33.11: "And the Lord spake unto Moses face to face, as a man speaketh unto
    his friend."
247. *saint:* angel (as the word is used in the Bible).
249. *ardors:* (L *ardere* to burn) bright or effulgent spirits. The Hebrew *saraph* means "to burn."

On golden hinges turning, as by work   255
Divine the sovran Architect had framed.
From hence, no cloud, or, to obstruct his sight,
Star interposed, however small he sees,
Not unconform to other shining globes,
Earth and the gard'n of God, with cedars crowned   260
Above all hills. As when by night the glass
Of Galileo, less assured, observes
Imagined lands and regions in the moon:
Or pilot from amidst the Cyclades
Delos or Samos first appearing kens   265
A cloudy spot. Down thither prone in flight
He speeds, and through the vast ethereal sky
Sails between worlds and worlds, with steady wing
Now on the polar wings, then with quick fan
Winnows the buxom air; till within soar   270
Of tow'ring eagles, to all the fowls he seems
A phoenix, gazed by all, as that sole bird
When to enshrine his relics in the sun's
Bright temple, to Egyptian Thebes he flies.
At once on th' eastern cliff of Paradise   275
He lights, and to his proper shape returns
A Seraph winged; six wings he wore, to shade
His lineaments divine; the pair that clad
Each shoulder broad, came mantling o'er his breast
With regal ornament; the middle pair   280
Girt like a starry zone his waist, and round
Skirted his loins and thighs with downy gold
And colors dipped in heav'n; the third his feet
Shadowed from either heel with feathered mail
Sky-tinctured grain. Like Maia's son he stood,   285
And shook his plumes, that heav'nly fragrance filled
The circuit wide. Straight knew him all the bands
Of angels under watch; and to his state,

255. *work*: works, mechanism.
261–63. Cf. I.288–91n.
264–65. *Delos*, one of the islands forming the *Cyclades*, was the birthplace of Apollo and Diana.
    On *Samos*, another island in the Aegean, Juno was born and was married to Jupiter.
266. *prone*: L *pronus* bent forward.
269. *fan*: L *vannus* fan, fan for winnowing.
270. *buxom*: ME *buxum* pliable, from OE *būgan* to bend.
272–74. *phoenix*: the mythical, unique bird who every five hundred years, after it had burned
    itself up and had been reborn from its own ashes, flew the ashes to a shrine in Heliopolis, the
    city of the sun, which Milton refers to as *Egyptian Thebes*. Christians saw it as a symbol of
    immortality.
277–85. Cf. Isa. 6.2, p. 442. Bush notes that the feathers of the phoenix were traditionally purple,
    gold, and blue. *lineaments*: parts of the body. *zone*: L *zona* belt. *mail*: armor made of pieces
    of metal arranged like fish scales. *grain*: color. *Maia's son*: Mercury, messenger of the gods,
    who also had wings on his heels.
288. *state*: status.

And to his message high in honor rise;
For on some message high they guessed him bound.   290
Their glittering tents he passed, and now is come
Into the blissful field, through groves of myrrh,
And flow'ring odors, cassia, nard, and balm;
A wilderness of sweets; for nature here
Wantoned as in her prime, and played at will   295
Her virgin fancies, pouring forth more sweet,
Wild above rule or art; enormous bliss.
Him through the spicy forest onward come
Adam discerned, as in the door he sat
Of his cool bow'r, while now the mounted sun   300
Shot down direct his fervid rays, to warm
Earth's inmost womb, more warmth than Adam needs;
And Eve within, due at her hour prepared
For dinner savory fruits, of taste to please
True appetite, and not disrelish thirst   305
Of nectarous draughts between, from milky stream,
Berry or grape: to whom thus Adam called.
    "Haste hither Eve, and worth thy sight behold
Eastward among those trees, what glorious shape
Comes this way moving; seems another morn   310
Ris'n on mid-noon; some great behest from Heav'n
To us perhaps he brings, and will vouchsafe
This day to be our guest. But go with speed,
And what thy stores contain, bring forth and pour
Abundance, fit to honor and receive   315
Our heav'nly stranger; well we may afford
Our givers their own gifts, and large bestow
From large bestowed, where nature multiplies
Her fertile growth, and by disburd'ning grows
More fruitful, which instructs us not to spare."   320
    To whom thus Eve. "Adam, earth's hallowed mold,
Of God inspired, small store will serve, where store,

289. *message*: mission.
293. *odors*: substances (bark, roots, or gums) that emit spicy fragrances. *cassia*: cinnamon.
   nard: spikenard. *balm*: balsam. All were used to make perfumed ointments associated with
   religious rituals, and are mentioned in the Bible. Cf. the phoenix in *Met.* 15.398–400:
   "and when he has covered this over with cassia-bark and light spikes of nard, broken cin-
   namon and yellow myrrh, he takes his place upon it and so ends his life among the
   odours."
295. *played*: acted out.
297. *enormous*: L *e* out + *norma* rule.
299. Cf. Gen. 18.1: "And the Lord appeared unto him [Abraham] in the plains of Mamre: and
   he sat in the tent door in the heat of the day."
303. *due*: duly, fittingly.
306. *milky*: pleasant and nourishing.
317. *large*: liberally.
322. *small store*: few stored foods. *store*: a great quantity.

All seasons, ripe for use hangs on the stalk;
Save what by frugal storing firmness gains
To nourish, and superfluous moist consumes: 325
But I will haste and from each bough and brake,
Each plant and juiciest gourd will pluck such choice
To entertain our angel guest, as he
Beholding shall confess that here on earth
God hath dispensed his bounties as in heav'n."   330
    So saying, with dispatchful looks in haste
She turns, on hospitable thoughts intent
What choice to chose for delicacy best,
What order, so contrived as not to mix
Tastes, not well joined, inelegant, but bring   335
Taste after taste upheld with kindliest change,
Bestirs her then, and from each tender stalk
Whatever earth all-bearing mother yields
In India east or west, or middle shore
In Pontus or the Punic coast, or where   340
Alcinous reigned, fruit of all kinds, in coat,
Rough, or smooth-rined, or bearded husk, or shell
She gathers, tribute large, and on the board
Heaps with unsparing hand; for drink the grape
She crushes, inoffensive must, and meaths   345
From many a berry, and from sweet kernels pressed
She tempers dulcet creams, nor these to hold
Wants her fit vessels pure, then strews the ground
With rose and odors from the shrub unfumed.
Meanwhile our primitive great sire, to meet   350
His godlike guest, walks forth, without more train
Accompanied than with his own complete
Perfections, in himself was all his state,
More solemn than the tedious pomp that waits
On princes, when their rich retínue long   355
Of horses led, and grooms besmeared with gold
Dazzles the crowd, and sets them all agape.
Nearer his presence Adam though not awed,
Yet with submiss approach and reverence meek,
As to a superior nature, bowing low,   360

324. *frugal:* L *frugalis* virtuous, *frugal,* from *frux* fruit.
336. *upheld:* maintained, provided with sustenance. *kindliest:* most natural.
339. *middle shore:* between East and West Indies.
340. *Pontus:* south shore of the Black Sea. *Punic:* Tunisian.
341. *Alcinous:* a king whose everbearing gardens are described in the *Odyssey.*
345. *must:* unfermented fruit juice. *meaths:* meads, drinks sweetened with honey.
347. *tempers:* blends.
349. *rose and odors:* roses and other fragrant substances; cf. 22–23n, and 293n. *unfumed:* not
    artificially vaporized, as in burning incense.
353. *state:* air of dignity and authority.
354. *solemn:* awe-inspiring, ceremonial.

   Thus said. "Native of heav'n, for other place
None can than heav'n such glorious shape contain;
Since by descending from the thrones above,
Those happy places thou hast deigned a while
To want, and honor these, vouchsafe with us   365
Two only, who yet by sovran gift possess
This spacious ground, in yonder shady bow'r
To rest, and what the garden choicest bears
To sit and taste, till this meridian heat
Be over, and the sun more cool decline."   370
   Whom thus the angelic Virtue answered mild.
"Adam, I therefore came, nor art thou such
Created, or such place hast here to dwell,
As may not oft invite, though Spirits of heav'n
To visit thee; lead on then where thy bow'r   375
O'ershades; for these mid-hours, till evening rise
I have at will." So to the sylvan lodge
They came, that like Pomona's arbor smiled
With flow'rets decked and fragrant smells; but Eve
Undecked, save with herself more lovely fair   380
Than wood-nymph, or the fairest goddess feigned
Of three that in Mount Ida naked strove,
Stood to entertain her guest from heav'n; no veil
She needed, virtue-proof, no thought infirm
Altered her cheek. On whom the angel "Hail"   385
Bestowed, the holy salutation used
Long after to blest Mary, second Eve.
   "Hail mother of mankind, whose fruitful womb
Shall fill the world more numerous with thy sons
Than with these various fruits the trees of God   390
Have heaped this table." Raised of grassy turf
Their table was, and mossy seats had round,
And on her ample square from side to side
All autumn piled, though spring and autumn here
Danced hand in hand. A while discourse they hold;   395
No fear lest dinner cool; when thus began
Our author. "Heav'nly stranger, please to taste
These bounties which our Nourisher, from whom
All perfect good unmeasured out, descends,

---

365. *want:* be without.
378. *Pomona:* (L *pomum* fruit; later, an apple) a wood nymph, goddess of fruit trees.
379. *decked:* D *dekken* to cover.
381–82. *feigned:* (L *fingere* to invent) imagined, i.e., by the maker of the myth about the judgment of Paris, who awarded the apple of strife to Venus rather than to Juno or Minerva, in a famous beauty contest that led to the rape of Helen and the fall of Troy (the subject of the *Iliad*). Fowler notes that in pictorial representations of the judgment wingfooted Mercury is often one of the figures.
384. *infirm:* weak, irresolute.
385–87. Cf. Luke 1.28–31, p. 455.

To us for food and for delight hath caused   400
The earth to yield; unsavory food perhaps
To spiritual natures; only this I know,
That one Celestial Father gives to all."
   To whom the angel. "Therefore what he gives
(Whose praise be ever sung) to man in part   405
Spiritual, may of purest Spirits be found
No ingrateful food: and food alike those pure
Intelligential substances require
As doth your rational; and both contain
Within them every lower faculty   410
Of sense, whereby they hear, see, smell, touch, taste,
Tasting concoct, digest, assimilate,
And corporeal to incorporeal turn.
For know, whatever was created, needs
To be sustained and fed; of elements   415
The grosser feeds the purer, earth the sea,
Earth and the sea feed air, the air those fires
Ethereal, and as lowest first the moon;
Whence in her visage round those spots, unpurged
Vapors not yet into her substance turned.   420
Nor doth the moon no nourishment exhale
From her moist continent to higher orbs.
The sun that light imparts to all, receives
From all his alimental recompense
In humid exhalations, and at even   425
Sups with the ocean: though in heav'n the trees
Of life ambrosial fruitage bear, and vines
Yield nectar, though from off the boughs each morn
We brush mellifluous dews, and find the ground
Covered with pearly grain; yet God hath here   430
Varied his bounty so with new delights,
As may compare with heaven; and to taste
Think not I shall be nice." So down they sat,
And to their viands fell, nor seemingly
The angel, nor in mist, the common gloss   435
Of theologians, but with keen dispatch
Of real hunger, and concoctive heat

404–33. See CD, pp. 409–11, and "Angels," pp. 466–68.
412. *concoct*: L *concoquere* to cook together, disgust.
419. *unpurged*: still containing grosser elements from earth.
424. *alimental*: L *alere* to nourish.
427. *ambrosial*. See II.245n; cf. III.135 and V.57.
429. *mellifluous*: L *mellis* honey + *fluere* to flow.
430. *pearly grain*. Fowler notes that manna is called "the corn of heaven" and "angel's food" in Ps. 78.24–25, and described as "a small round thing, as small as the hoar frost on the ground" in Exod. 16.14.
433. *nice*: fastidious.
434. *nor seemingly*: not just seemed to.
435. *gloss*: explanation.
437. *concoctive heat*: digestive energy.

To transubstantiate; what redounds, transpires
Through Spirits with ease; nor wonder; if by fire
Of sooty coal the empiric alchemist   440
Can turn, or holds it possible to turn
Metals of drossiest ore to perfect gold
As from the mine. Meanwhile at table Eve
Ministered naked, and their flowing cups
With pleasant liquors crowned. O innocence   445
Deserving Paradise! if ever, then,
Then had the Sons of God excuse to have been
Enamored at that sight; but in those hearts
Love unlibidinous reigned, nor jealousy
Was understood, the injured lover's hell.   450
    Thus when with meats and drinks they had sufficed,
Not burdened nature, sudden mind arose
In Adam, not to let th' occasion pass
Given him by this great conference to know
Of things above his world, and of their being   455
Who dwell in heav'n, whose excellence he saw
Transcend his own so far, whose radiant forms
Divine effulgence, whose high power so far
Exceeded human, and his wary speech
Thus to th' empyreal minister he framed.   460
    "Inhabitant with God, now know I well
Thy favor, in this honor done to man,
Under whose lowly roof thou hast vouchsafed
To enter, and these earthly fruits to taste,
Food not of angels, yet accepted so,   465
As that more willingly thou couldst not seem
At heav'n's high feasts to have fed: yet what compare?"
    To whom the wingèd Hierarch replied.
"O Adam, one Almighty is, from whom
All things proceed, and up to him return,   470
If not depraved from good, created all
Such to perfection, one first matter all,

438. *transubstantiate:* change into another substance. *redounds:* is not digested. *transpires:* passes
    out as vapor through pores, evaporates.
440. *empiric:* working by trial and error, not by theory.
445. *crowned:* filled to overflowing.
446–48. Cf. Gen. 6.1–4.
458. *effulgence:* (L *effulgare* to shine forth) the diffusing of intense light. As in *radiant* in the
    line above, the word emphasizes the energy and dynamism of heavenly beauty.
468. *Hierarch:* member of the hierarchy of angels (see "Angels," pp. 466–68), or one of the
    angelic leaders; from Gk *hieros* sacred + *archos* leader, ruler.
469–90. See *CD*, pp. 409–11, and "The Scale of Nature," pp. 464–66. *consummate:* (L *con-
    summare* to sum up, finish) perfect. *scale:* L *scala* staircase, ladder. *vital spirits.* In Milton's
    physiology spirits were conceived of as liquids produced by the heart and essential to life.
    Animal spirits, also a fluid, produced in the brain, fed the nervous system (sensation, thought,
    and action). *Reason.* See "Reason," p. 464. *discursive:* (like *discourse,* L *discurrere* to run to
    and fro) deliberative. *intuitive:* L *intueri* to look upon) knowing directly, without reasoning.

Endued with various forms, various degrees
Of substance, and in things that live, of life;
But more refined, more spiritous, and pure,   475
As nearer to him placed or nearer tending
Each in their several active spheres assigned,
Till body up to spirit work, in bounds
Proportioned to each kind. So from the root
Springs lighter the green stalk, from thence the leaves   480
More airy, last the bright consummate flow'r
Spirits odórous breathes: flow'rs and their fruit
Man's nourishment, by gradual scale sublimed
To vital spirits aspire, to animal,
To intellectual, give both life and sense,   485
Fancy and understanding, whence the soul
Reason receives, and reason is her being,
Discursive, or intuitive; discourse
Is oftest yours, the latter most is ours,
Differing but in degree, of kind the same.   490
Wonder not then, what God for you saw good
If I refuse not, but convert, as you,
To proper substance; time may come when men
With angels may participate, and find
No inconvenient diet, nor too light fare: 495
And from these corporal nutriments perhaps
Your bodies may at last turn all to spirit,
Improved by tract of time, and winged ascend
Ethereal, as we, or may at choice
Here or in heav'nly paradises dwell;   500
If ye be found obedient, and retain
Unalterably firm his love entire
Whose progeny you are. Meanwhile enjoy
Your fill what happiness this happy state
Can comprehend, incapable of more."   505
     To whom the patriarch of mankind replied.
"O favorable Spirit, propitious guest,
Well hast thou taught the way that might direct
Our knowledge, and the scale of nature set
From center to circumference, whereon   510
In contemplation of created things
By steps we may ascend to God. But say,
What meant that caution joined, 'If ye be found
Obedient'? Can we want obedience then

---

483. *sublimed:* changed from a solid to a gas without becoming a liquid. L *sublimare*, to raise.
484–85. *vital spirits:* fluids in the blood that sustain life; *animal spirits:* fluids that regulate
    sensation and motion (Fowler).
488. *discourse:* reasoning.
493. *proper substance:* substance suitable to me.
509–12. See "The Scale of Nature," pp. 464–66.

To him, or possibly his love desert   515
Who formed us from the dust, and placed us here
Full to the utmost measure of what bliss
Human desires can seek or apprehend?"
    To whom the angel. "Son of heav'n and earth,
Attend: that thou art happy, owe to God;   520
That thou continu'st such, owe to thyself,
That is, to thy obedience; therein stand.
This was that caution giv'n thee; be advised.
God made thee perfect, not immutable;
And good he made thee, but to persevere   525
He left it in thy power, ordained thy will
By nature free, not overruled by fate
Inextricable, or strict necessity;
Our voluntary service he requires,
Not our necessitated, such with him   530
Finds no acceptance, nor can find, for how
Can hearts, not free, be tried whether they serve
Willing or no, who will but what they must
By destiny, and can no other choose?
Myself and all th' angelic host that stand   535
In sight of God enthroned, our happy state
Hold, as you yours, while our obedience holds;
On other surety none; freely we serve,
Because we freely love, as in our will
To love or not; in this we stand or fall.   540
And some are fall'n, to disobedience fall'n,
And so from heav'n to deepest hell; O fall
From what high state of bliss into what woe!"
    To whom our great progenitor. "Thy words
Attentive, and with more delighted ear,   545
Divine instructor, I have heard, than when
Cherubic songs by night from neighboring hills
Aerial music send: nor knew I not
To be both will and deed created free;
Yet that we never shall forget to love   550
Our Maker, and obey him whose command
Single, is yet so just, my constant thoughts
Assured me, and still assure: though what thou tell'st
Hath passed in heav'n, some doubt within me move,
But more desire to hear, if thou consent,   555
The full relation, which must needs be strange,
Worthy of sacred silence to be heard;
And we have yet large day, for scarce the sun
Hath finished half his journey, and scarce begins

521. *owe*: attribute.

His other half in the great zone of heav'n."   560
    Thus Adam made request, and Raphael
After short pause assenting, thus began.
    "High matter thou enjoin'st me. O prime of men,
Sad task and hard, for how shall I relate
To human sense th' invisible exploits   565
Of warring Spirits; how without remorse
The ruin of so many glorious once
And perfect while they stood; how last unfold
The secrets of another world, perhaps
Not lawful to reveal? Yet for thy good   570
This is dispensed, and what surmounts the reach
Of human sense, I shall delineate so,
By lik'ning spiritual to corporal forms,
As may express them best, though what if earth
Be but the shadow of heav'n, and things therein   575
Each to other like, more than on earth is thought?
    "As yet this world was not, and Chaos wild
Reigned where these heav'ns now roll, where earth now rests
Upon her center poised, when on a day
(For time, though in eternity, applied   580
To motion, measures all things durable
By present, past, and future) on such day
As heav'n's great year brings forth, th' empyreal host
Of angels by imperial summons called,
Innumerable before th' Almighty's throne   585

564–76. Milton himself faced two of the three difficulties referred to by this angel, who was, in a way, the first epic poet: how to describe events in heaven to human beings, whose experience is limited to earth, and how to tell the story of Satan's fall without arousing sympathy in his audience or, perhaps, in himself. As for the third, since he was unable to reveal what God had not chosen to reveal to men in the Bible, he could not unlawfully reveal anything. But by means of Raphael's speech to Adam, Milton was about to give an imagined elaboration of a story that was only hinted at, or given in barest outline, in the Bible, and Milton's justification for doing so, as well as his method of presentation, is essentially that of Raphael and all other poets, who believe that truth may be revealed by metaphor and fiction. So, to the spare biblical account of Adam's life Milton added this imagined account of Raphael's visit, as well as the details of Raphael's own account of the revolt in heaven and the creation of the universe, and thus made Raphael's "poem" part of his own larger poem. Milton's task was harder than Raphael's, who had only to find the language to express the facts, whereas Milton had also to do what Aristotle said was the poet's essential task—that is, to invent the plot (or at least the episodes). The Platonic notion that all earthly things are imitations (shadows) of heavenly ideas or realities had been the basis of the chief apology for poetry from Aristotle on down: poetry tells a truth beyond that of history—or history is itself the vehicle of a metaphysical metaphor. Theologians had relied on a similar assumption in their theories about typology and "accommodation" and the meaning of myth. See "Truth and Poetry," pp. 473–74.
578–79. earth . . . poised: cf. Met. 1.12–13: "not yet did the earth hang poised by her own weight in the circumambient air. . . ."
580–82. time and motion. See CD, pp. 410–11.
583. heav'n's great year. The point in time when, according to a myth of Plato, a celestial cycle is completed and all stars and planets are back in the same position as they were at the beginning of the cycle. Fowler notes that the range of allusion may include the myth that the great year also marked the end of a cycle of uniformity and the beginning of one of dissimilarity or disintegration. So the great year here may mark the beginning of the period that would end only with the mllennium.

Forthwith from all the ends of heav'n appeared
Under their hierarchs in orders bright.
Ten thousand thousand ensigns high advanced,
Standards, and gonfalons 'twixt van and rear
Stream in the air, and for distinction serve   590
Of hierarchies, of orders, and degrees;
Or in their glittering tissues bear emblazed
Holy memorials, acts of zeal and love
Recorded eminent. Thus when in orbs
Of circuit inexpressible they stood,   595
Orb within orb, the Father Infinite,
By whom in bliss embosomed sat the Son,
Amidst as from a flaming mount, whose top
Brightness had made invisible, thus spake.
   " 'Hear all ye angels, progeny of Light,   600
Thrones, Dominations, Princedoms, Virtues, Powers,
Hear my decree, which unrevoked shall stand.
This day I have begot whom I declare
My only Son, and on this holy hill
Him have anointed, whom ye now behold   605
At my right hand; your head I him appoint;
And by my Self have sworn to him shall bow
All knees in heav'n, and shall confess him Lord:
Under his great vicegerent reign abide
United as one individual soul   610
Forever happy: him who disobeys
Me disobeys, breaks union, and that day
Cast out from God and blessèd vision, falls
Into utter darkness, deep engulfed, his place
Ordained without redemption, without end.'   615
   "So spake th' Omnipotent, and with his words
All seemed well pleased, all seemed, but were not all.
That day, as other solemn days, they spent
In song and dance about the sacred hill,
Mystical dance, which yonder starry sphere   620
Of planets and of fixed in all her wheels
Resembles nearest, mazes intricate,
Eccentric, intervolved, yet regular
Then most, when most irregular they seem:

589. *gonfalons:* flags of princes or states, fastened to crosspieces or frames.
591. *degrees.* Though there was no rank in Paradise (see IX.883), the angelic society was highly
    hierarchical. See CD I.XXXIII, and lines 707, 750, 792, 838; VIII.176.
593. Unlike the military blazonry of the fallen angels in I.539, as Fowler notes.
595. *circuit:* circumference.
610. *individual:* indivisible.
614. *utter.* Cf. I.72n.
618. *solemn days:* holy days.

And in their motions harmony divine   625
So smooths her charming tones, that God's own ear
Listens delighted. Evening now approached
(For we have also our evening and our morn,
We ours for change delectable, not need)
Forthwith from dance to sweet repast they turn   630
Desirous; all in circles as they stood,
Tables are set, and on a sudden piled
With angels' food, and rubied nectar flows
In pearl, in diamond, and massy gold,
Fruit of delicious vines, the growth of heav'n.   635
Of flow'rs reposed, and with fresh flow'rets crowned,
They eat, they drink, and in communion sweet
Quaff immortality and joy, secure
Of surfeit where full measure only bounds
Excess, before th' all-bounteous King, who show'red   640
With copious hand, rejoicing in their joy.
Now when ambrosial night with clouds exhaled
From that high mount of God, whence light and shade
Spring both, the face of brightest heav'n had changed
To grateful twilight (for night comes not there   645
In darker veil) and roseate dews disposed
All but the unsleeping eyes of God to rest,
Wide over all the plain, and wider far
Than all this globous earth in plain outspread,
(Such are the courts of God) th' angelic throng   650
Dispersed in bands and files their camp extend
By living streams among the trees of life,
Pavilions numberless, and sudden reared,
Celestial tabernacles, where they slept
Fanned with cool winds, save those who in their course   655
Melodious hymns about the sovran throne
Alternate all night long: but not so waked
Satan, so call him now, his former name
Is heard no more in heav'n; he of the first,

625-26. The movements of the angels in their dance, like those of the planets in the Pythagorean theory of music of the spheres (see 178n), produced harmony. Fowler notes that "the intervals between the planetary spheres were analysed as musical proportions by astronomers as late as Kepler." *charming*: enchanting, spellbinding.
637-40. Cf. Ps. 36.8-9: "They shall be abundantly satisfied with the fatness of thy house; and thou shalt make them drink of the river of thy pleasures. For with thee is the fountain of life: in thy light shall we see light."
645-46. Cf. Rev. 21.25: "And the gates of it shall not be shut at all by day: for there shall be no night there."
647. Cf. Ps. 121.4: "Behold, he that keepeth Israel shall neither slumber nor sleep."
651. *files*: detachments.
652. Cf. Rev. 22.1-2: "And he shewed me a pure river of water of life, clear as crystal, proceeding out of the throne of God and of the Lamb. In the midst of the street of it, and on either side of the river, was there the tree of life."

If not the first Archangel, great in power,   660
In favor and pre-eminence, yet fraught
With envy against the Son of God, that day
Honored by his great Father, and proclaimed
Messiah King anointed, could not bear
Through pride that sight, and thought himself impaired.   665
Deep malice thence conceiving and disdain,
Soon as midnight brought on the dusky hour
Friendliest to sleep and silence, he resolved
With all his legions to dislodge, and leave
Unworshiped, unobeyed the throne supreme   670
Contemptuous, and his next subordinate
Awak'ning, thus to him in secret spake.
" 'Sleep'st thou companion dear, what sleep can close
Thy eyelids? and remember'st what decree
Of yesterday, so late hath passed the lips   675
Of heav'n's Almighty. Thou to me thy thoughts
Wast wont, I mine to thee was wont to impart;
Both waking we were one; how then can now
Thy sleep dissent? New laws thou seest imposed;
New laws from him who reigns, new minds may raise   680
In us who serve, new counsels, to debate
What doubtful may ensue, more in this place
To utter is not safe. Assemble thou
Of all those myriads which we lead the chief;
Tell them that by command, ere yet dim night   685
Her shadowy cloud withdraws, I am to haste,
And all who under me their banners wave,
Homeward with flying march where we possess
The quarters of the north, there to prepare
Fit entertainment to receive our King   690
The great Messiah, and his new commands,
Who speedily through all the hierarchies
Intends to pass triumphant, and give laws.'
"So spake the false Archangel, and infused
Bad influence into th' unwary breast   695
Of his associate; he together calls,
Or several one by one, the regent powers,
Under him regent, tells, as he was taught,

664. *Messiah*: the Gk form of the Hebrew *mashiah* anointed.
665. *impaired*. See 73n.
669. *dislodge*: (military term) leave camp.
673. Cf. *Il.* 2.23–25: "Sleepest thou, son of wise Atreus tamer of horses! To sleep all night through beseemeth not one that is a counsellor, to whom peoples are entrusted and so many cares belong." And *Aen.* 4.560–61: "Goddess-born, when such hazard threatens, canst thou still slumber, and seest thou not the perils that from henceforth hem thee in, madman!"
689. Cf. Isa. 14.13, p. 444.

That the Most High commanding, now ere night,
Now ere dim night had disencumbered heav'n,   700
The great hierarchal standard was to move;
Tells the suggested cause, and casts between
Ambiguous words and jealousies, to sound
Or taint integrity; but all obeyed
The wonted signal, and superior voice   705
Of their great potentate; for great indeed
His name, and high was his degree in heav'n;
His count'nance, as the morning star that guides
The starry flock, allured them, and with lies
Drew after him the third part of heav'n's host: 710
Meanwhile th' Eternal eye, whose sight discerns
Abstrusest thoughts, from forth his holy mount
And from within the golden lamps that burn
Nightly before him, saw without their light
Rebellion rising, saw in whom, how spread   715
Among the sons of morn, what multitudes
Were banded to oppose his high decree;
And smiling to his only Son thus said.
   " 'Son, thou in whom my glory I behold
In full resplendence, heir of all my might,   720
Nearly it now concerns us to be sure
Of our omnipotence, and with what arms
We mean to hold what anciently we claim
Of deity or empire, such a foe
Is rising, who intends to erect his throne   725
Equal to ours, throughout the spacious north;
Nor so content, hath in his thought to try
In battle, what our power is, or our right.
Let us advise, and to this hazard draw
With speed what force is left, and all employ   730
In our defense, lest unawares we lose
This our high place, our sanctuary, our hill.'
   "To whom the Son with calm aspect and clear
Lightning divine, ineffable, serene,
Made answer. 'Mighty Father, thou thy foes   735
Justly hast in derision, and secure
Laugh'st at their vain designs and tumults vain,

---

700. *dim night:* the agency that produces night; cf. 642–45. *disencumbered:* (LL *in* + *combrus*
   barricade) i.e., removed the clouds (cf. 642) that barricaded the "sky" of heaven.
702. *suggested:* (L *sub* under + *gerere* to put) insinuating or prompting to evil. *casts:* contrives,
   schemes.
703. *jealousies:* fears, suspicions, resentments. *sound:* measure.
708. Cf. Isa. 14.12, p. 444.
734. *Lightning.* In his vision Daniel saw a man whose face was "as the appearance of lightning,
   and his eyes as lamps of fire" (Dan. 10.6).
736. Cf. Ps. 59.8: "But thou, O Lord, shalt laugh at them; thou shalt have all the heathen in
   derision."

Matter to me of glory, whom their hate
Illustrates, when they see all regal power
Giv'n me to quell their pride, and in event   740
Know whether I be dextrous to subdue
Thy rebels, or be found the worst in heav'n.'
    "So spake the Son, but Satan with his powers
Far was advanced on wingèd speed, an host
Innumerable as the stars of night,   745
Or stars of morning, dewdrops, which the sun
Impearls on every leaf and every flower.
Regions they passed, the mighty regencies
Of Seraphim and Potentates and Thrones
In their triple degrees, regions to which   750
All thy dominion, Adam, is no more
Than what this garden is to all the earth,
And all the sea, from one entire globose
Stretched into longitude; which having passed
At length into the limits of the north   755
They came, and Satan to his royal seat
High on a hill, far blazing, as a mount
Raised on a mount, with pyramids and tow'rs
From diamond quarries hewn, and rocks of gold,
The palace of great Lucifer, (so call   760
That structure in the dialect of men
Interpreted) which not long after, he
Affecting all equality with God,
In imitation of that mount whereon
Messiah was declared in sight of heav'n,   765
The Mountain of the Congregation called;
For thither he assembled all his train,
Pretending so commanded to consult
About the great reception of their King,
Thither to come, and with calumnious art   770
Of counterfeited truth thus held their ears.
    " 'Thrones, Dominations, Princedoms, Virtues, Powers,
If these magnific titles yet remain
Not merely titular, since by decree
Another now hath to himself engrossed   775

739. *Illustrates:* illuminates, makes illustrious or luminous.
740. *event:* L *e* out + *venire* to come.
741. *dextrous:* L *dexter* on the right hand. A pun.
743. *powers:* armies.
750. *triple degrees.* See "Angels," pp. 466–68.
753. *globose:* globe.
754. *Stretched into longitude.* spread out flat.
755. *limits:* regions.
763. *Affecting:* aspiring to, assuming, arrogating.
764–65. Cf. 603.
766. See 689n.

All power, and us eclipsed under the name
Of King anointed, for whom all this haste
Of midnight march, and hurried meeting here,
This only to consult how we may best
With what may be devised of honors new   780
Receive him coming to receive from us
Knee-tribute yet unpaid, prostration vile,
Too much to one, but double how endured,
To one and to his image now proclaimed?
But what if better counsels might erect   785
Our minds and teach us to cast off this yoke?
Will ye submit your necks, and choose to bend
The supple knee? Ye will not, if I trust
To now ye right, or if ye know yourselves
Natives and sons of heav'n possessed before   790
By none, and if not equal all, yet free,
Equally free; for orders and degrees
Jar not with liberty, but well consist.
Who can in reason then or right assume
Monarchy over such as live by right   795
His equals, if in power and splendor less,
In freedom equal? or can introduce
Law and edíct on us, who without law
Err not, much less for this to be our Lord,
And look for adoration to th' abuse   800
Of those imperial titles which assert
Our being ordained to govern, not to serve?'
    "Thus far his bold discourse without control
Had audience, when among the Seraphim
Abdiel, than whom none with more zeal adored   805
The Deity, and divine commands obeyed,
Stood up, and in a flame of zeal severe
The current of his fury thus opposed.
    " 'O argument blasphémous, false and proud!
Words which no ear ever to hear in heav'n   810
Expected, least of all from thee, ingrate,
In place thyself so high above thy peers.
Canst thou with impious obloquy condemn
The just decree of God, pronounced and sworn,
That to his only Son by right endued   815
With regal scepter, every soul in heav'n

777. *King anointed.* Cf. 664n.
790. *possessed:* (modifies *heav'n*) owned, claimed.
805. *Abdiel.* See "Angels," pp. 466–68.
813. *impious:* disloyal. *obloquy:* (L *ob* against + *loqui* to speak) calumny.
816–18. Cf. Phil. 2.10–11: "At the name of Jesus every knee should bow, of things in heaven,
    and things in earth, and things under the earth; And . . . every tongue should confess that
    Jesus Christ is Lord."

Shall bend the knee, and in that honor due
Confess him rightful King? Unjust thou says't,
Flatly unjust, to bind with laws the free,
And equal over equals to let reign,   820
One over all with unsucceeded power.
Shalt thou give law to God, shalt thou dispute
With him the points of liberty, who made
Thee what thou art, and formed the pow'rs of heav'n
Such as he pleased, and circumscribed their being?   825
Yet by experience taught we know how good,
And of our good, and of our dignity
How provident he is, how far from thought
To make us less, bent rather to exalt
Our happy state under one head more near   830
United. But to grant it thee unjust,
That equal over equals monarch reign:
Thyself though great and glorious dost thou count,
Or all angelic nature joined in one,
Equal to him begotten Son, by whom   835
As by his Word the mighty Father made
All things, ev'n thee, and all the Spirits of heav'n
By him created in their bright degrees,
Crowned them with glory, and to their glory named
Thrones, Dominations, Princedoms, Virtues, Powers,   840
Essential Powers, nor by his reign obscured,
But more illustrious made, since he the head
One of our number thus reduced becomes,
His laws our laws, all honor to him done
Returns our own. Cease then this impious rage,   845
And tempt not these; but hasten to appease
Th' incensèd Father and th' incensèd Son,
While pardon may be found in time besought.'

821. *unsucceeded*: without successor.
822–25. Cf. Rom. 9.20: "Nay but, O man, who art thou that repliest against God? Shall the
  thing formed say to him that formed it, Why hast thou made me thus?"
827. *dignity*: high status.
828. *provident*: careful in preparing for future exigencies.
831–45. The awkward and precipitous syntax of Abdiel's speech reflects his unartful zeal. The
  argument goes like this: "Granted that it would be unjust for an equal to reign as monarch
  over his equals; but do you, though great and powerful—though, indeed, a complete and
  perfect angel—do you count yourself equal to Christ, by whom God made all things (including
  you) by whom God created all the angels in their bright degrees, crowned them with glory,
  and named them to their glory Thrones, Dominations, etc., and by putting Christ above them
  as ruler did not obscure that glory, but rather made it more glorious since in taking this
  assignment as head of us he becomes one of us [as Jesus was later to become man], his laws
  become our laws, and all honor done to him is done to all of us." *the Word*. See III.170n.
  Cf. Col. 1.16–18: "For by him [Christ] were all things created, that are in heaven, and that
  are in earth, visible and invisible, whether they be thrones, or dominions, or principalities, or
  powers: all things were created by him, and for him: And he is before all things, and by him
  all things consist. And he is the head of the body, the church." *bright*: illustrious, glorious.

"So spake the fervent angel, but his zeal
None seconded, as out of season judged,   850
Or singular and rash, whereat rejoiced
Th' Apostate, and more haughty thus replied.
'That we were formed then say'st thou? and the work
Of secondary hands, by task transferred
From Father to his Son? Strange point and new!   855
Doctrine which we would know whence learnt: who saw
When this creation was? Remember'st thou
Thy making, while the Maker gave thee being?
We know no time when we were not as now;
Know none before us, self-begot, self-raised   860
By our own quick'ning power, when fatal course
Had circled his full orb, the birth mature
Of this our native heav'n, ethereal sons.
Our pussiance is our own, our own right hand
Shall teach us highest deeds, by proof to try   865
Who is our equal: then thou shalt behold
Whether by supplication we intend
Address, and to begirt th' Almighty throne
Beseeching or besieging. This report,
These tidings carry to th' anointed King;   870
And fly, ere evil intercept thy flight.'
    "He said, and as the sound of waters deep
Hoarse murmur echoed to his words applause
Through the infinite host, nor less for that
The flaming Seraph fearless, though alone   875
Encompassed round with foes, thus answered bold.
    " 'O alienate from God, O Spirit accurst,
Forsaken of all good; I see thy fall
Determined, and thy hapless crew involved
In this perfidious fraud, contagion spread   880
Both of thy crime and punishment: henceforth
No more be troubled how to quit the yoke
Of God's Messiah; those indulgent laws
Will not be now vouchsafed, other decrees
Against thee are gone forth without recall;   885
That golden scepter which thou didst reject
Is now an iron rod to bruise and break
Thy disobedience. Well thou didst advise,

---

861. *fatal course:* the course of fate.
864–65. Cf. Ps. 45.4: "And in thy majesty ride prosperously because of truth and meekness and
    righteousness; and thy right hand shall teach thee terrible things."
872. Cf. Rev. 19.6 "And I heard as it were the voice of a great multitude, and as the voice of
    many waters, and as the voice of mighty thunderings, saying, Alleluia: for the Lord God
    omnipotent reigneth."
882–83. Cf. Matt. 11.30: "For my [Christ's] yoke is easy, and my burden is light."

Yet not for thy advice or threats I fly
These wicked tents devoted, lest the wrath   890
Impendent, raging into sudden flame
Distinguish not: for soon expect to feel
His thunder on thy head, devouring fire.
Then who created thee lamenting learn,
When who can uncreate thee thou shalt know.'   895
    "So spake the Seraph Abdiel faithful found,
Among the faithless, faithful only he;
Among innumerable false, unmoved,
Unshaken, unseduced, unterrified
His loyalty he kept, his love, his zeal;   900
Nor number, nor example with him wrought
To swerve from truth, or change his constant mind
Though single. From amidst them forth he passed,
Long way through hostile scorn, which he sustained
Superior, nor of violence feared aught;   905
And with retorted scorn his back he turned
On those proud tow'rs to swift destruction doomed."

Book VI

The Argument

Raphael continues to relate how Michael and Gabriel were sent forth
to battle against Satan and his angels. The first fight described: Satan
and his powers retire under night: he calls a council, invents devilish
engines, which in the second day's fight put Michael and his angels to
some disorder; but they at length pulling up mountains overwhelmed
both the force and machines of Satan: yet the tumult not so ending,
God on the third day sends Messiah his Son, for whom he had reserved
the glory of that victory: he in the power of his Father coming to the
place, and causing all his legions to stand still on either side, with
his chariot and thunder driving into the midst of his enemies, pursues
them unable to resist towards the wall of heaven; which opening, they
leap down with horror and confusion into the place of punishment
prepared for them in the deep: Messiah returns with triumph to his
Father.

890. Cf. Num. 16.26: "And he spake unto the congregation, saying, Depart, I pray you, from
the tents of these wicked men, and touch nothing of theirs, lest ye be consumed in all their
sins." Ps. 84.10: "For a day in thy courts is better than a thousand. I had rather be a doorkeeper
in the house of my God, than to dwell in the tents of wickedness." *devoted:* doomed.
906. *retorted:* (L *re* back + *torquere* to turn, twist) retaliated.
907. Cf. 2 Pet. 2.1: "But there were false prophets also among the people, even as there shall
be false teachers among you, who privily shall bring in damnable heresies, even denying the
Lord that bought them, and bring upon themselves swift destruction."

"All night the dreadless angel unpursued
Through heav'n's wide champaign held his way, till Morn,
Waked by the circling Hours, with rosy hand
Unbarred the gates of light. There is a cave
Within the mount of God, fast by his throne,   5
Where light and darkness in perpetual round
Lodge and dislodge by turns, which makes through heav'n
Grateful vicissitude, like day and night;
Light issues forth, and at the other door
Obsequious darkness enters, till her hour   10
To veil the heav'n, though darkness there might well
Seem twilight here; and now went forth the Morn
Such as in highest heav'n, arrayed in gold
Empyreal; from before her vanished night,
Shot through with orient beams: when all the plain   15
Covered with thick embattled squadrons bright,
Chariots and flaming arms, and fiery steeds
Reflecting blaze on blaze, first met his view:
War he perceived, war in procinct, and found
Already known what he for news had thought   20
To have reported: gladly then he mixed
Among those friendly Powers who him received
With joy and acclamations loud, that one
That of so many myriads fall'n, yet one
Returned not lost: on to the sacred hill   25
They led him high applauded, and present
Before the seat supreme; from whence a voice
From midst a golden cloud thus mild was heard.
   " 'Servant of God, well done, well hast thou fought
The better fight, who single hast maintained   30
Against revolted multitudes the cause
Of truth, in word mightier than they in arms;
And for the testimony of truth hast borne
Universal reproach, far worse to bear
Than violence: for this was all thy care   35
To stand approved in sight of God, though worlds
Judged thee perverse: the easier conquest now
Remains thee, aided by this host of friends,

VI.3. *Hours:* four beautiful daughters of Jove, goddesses of the seasons and guards of the gates
   of heaven.
8. *vicissitude:* (L *vicissim* in turn, *vicis* change, alternation) alternating succession of contrasting
   things.
10. *Obsequious:* (L *ob* toward + *sequi* to follow) compliant.
14. *Empyreal:* (GK *pyr* fire) heavenly.
16. *embattled:* in battle array.
19. *in procinct:* prepared.
29. *Servant of God:* the literal meaning of the Hebrew word *abdiel*. Cf. Matt. 25.21: "His lord
   said unto him, Well done, thou good and faithful servant." 2 Tim. 4.7: "I have fought a good
   fight, I have finished my course, I have kept the faith."
33–34. Cf. Ps. 69.7: "Because for thy sake I have borne reproach."
36. Cf. 2 Tim. 2.15: "Study to show thyself approved unto God."

Back on thy foes more glorious to return
Than scorned thou didst depart, and to subdue   40
By force, who reason for their law refuse,
Right reason for their law, and for their King
Messiah, who by right of merit reigns.
Go Michael of celestial armies prince,
And thou in military prowess next   45
Gabriel, lead forth to battle these my sons
Invincible, lead forth my armèd saints
By thousands and by millions ranged for fight;
Equal in number to that godless crew
Rebellious, them with fire and hostile arms   50
Fearless assault, and to the brow of heav'n
Pursuing drive them out from God and bliss,
Into their place of punishment, the gulf
Of Tartarus, which ready opens wide
His fiery chaos to receive their fall.'   55
   "So spake the Sovran Voice, and clouds began
To darken all the hill, and smoke to roll
In dusky wreaths reluctant flames, the sign
Of wrath awaked: nor with less dread the loud
Ethereal trumpet from on high gan blow: 60
At which command the powers militant,
That stood for heav'n, in mighty quadrate joined
Of union irresistible, moved on
In silence their bright legions, to the sound
Of instrumental harmony that breathed   65
Heroic ardor to advent'rous deeds
Under their godlike leaders, in the cause
Of God and his Messiah. On they move
Indissolubly firm; nor obvious hill,
Nor strait'ning vale, nor wood, nor stream divides   70
Their perfect ranks; for high above the ground
Their march was, and the passive air upbore
Their nimble tread; as when the total kind
Of birds in orderly array on wing
Came summoned over Eden to receive   75
Their names of thee; so over many a tract
Of heav'n they marched, and many a province wide
Tenfold the length of this terrene: at last

42. *Right reason.* See "Reason," p. 464.
44ff. For the biblical authority for the war in heaven see Isa. 14.1–21, pp. 443–45, Rev. 12.4–
    9, p. 460, and CD, pp. 412–13.
44–46. See "Angels," pp. 466–68.
47. *saints:* angels.
56–59. Cf. Exod. 19.16, 18, p. 136.
58. *reluctant:* L *re* back + *luctari* to struggle.
62. *quadrate:* a square military formation in close order.
69. *obvious:* standing in the way of.
78. *terrene:* (an adjective used as a noun) terrain.

Far in th' horizon to the north appeared
From skirt to skirt a fiery region, stretched   80
In battailous aspéct, and nearer view
Bristled with upright beams innumerable
Of rigid spears, and helmets thronged, and shields
Various, with boastful argument portrayed,
The banded powers of Satan hasting on   85
With furious expedition; for they weened
That selfsame day by fight, or by surprise
To win the mount of God, and on his throne
To set the envier of his state, the proud
Aspirer, but their thoughts proved fond and vain   90
In the mid-way: though strange to us it seemed
At first, that angel should with angel war,
And in fierce hosting meet, who wont to meet
So oft in festivals of joy and love
Unanimous, as sons of one great Sire   95
Hymning th' Eternal Father: but the shout
Of battle now began, and rushing sound
Of onset ended soon each milder thought.
High in the midst exalted as a god
Th' Apostate in his sun-bright chariot sat   100
Idol of majesty divine, enclosed
With flaming Cherubim, and golden shields;
Then lighted from his gorgeous throne, for now
'Twixt host and host but narrow space was left,
A dreadful interval, and front to front   105
Presented stood in terrible array
Of hideous length: before the cloudy van,
On the rough edge of battle ere it joined,
Satan with vast and haughty strides advanced,
Came tow'ring, armed in adamant and gold;   110
Abdiel that sight endured not, where he stood
Among the mightiest, bent on highest deeds,
And thus his own undaunted heart explores.
    " 'O heav'n! that such resemblance of the Highest
Should yet remain, where faith and realty   115
Remain not; wherefore should not strength and might
There fail where virtue fails, or weakest prove

81. *battailous:* warlike.
83–84. On the shields were drawn heraldic emblems with their mottoes.
86. *furious:* (L *furia* rage) rushing. *expedition:* speed.
90. *fond* (ME *fon* fool) foolish. *vain:* L *vanus* empty.
93. *hosting:* hostile encounter.
100. *Apostate:* Gk *apo* out from, against + *stēnai* to stand.
110. See I.48n.
115. *realty:* sincerity.

Where boldest; though to sight unconquerable?
His puissance, trusting in th' Almighty's aid,
I mean to try, whose reason I have tried   120
Unsound and false; nor is it aught but just,
That he who in debate of truth hath won,
Should win in arms, in both disputes alike
Victor; though brutish that contést and foul,
When reason hath to deal with force, yet so   125
Most reason is that reason overcome.'
   "So pondering, and from his armèd peers
Forth stepping opposite, half-way he met
His daring foe, at this prevention more
Incensed, and thus securely him defied.   130
   " 'Proud, art thou met? Thy hope was to have reached
The highth of thy aspiring unopposed,
The throne of God unguarded, and his side
Abandoned at the terror of thy power
Or potent tongue; fool, not to think how vain   135
Against the Omnipotent to rise in arms;
Who out of smallest things could without end
Have raised incessant armies to defeat
Thy folly, or with solitary hand
Reaching beyond all limit at one blow   140
Unaided could have finished thee, and whelmed
Thy legions under darkness; but thou seest
All are not of thy train; there be who faith
Prefer, and piety to God, though then
To thee not visible, when I alone   145
Seemed in thy world erroneous to dissent
From all: my sect thou seest, now learn too late
How few sometimes may know, when thousands err.'
   "Whom the grand Foe with scornful eye askance
Thus answered. 'Ill for thee, but in wished hour   150
Of my revenge, first sought for thou return'st
From flight, seditious angel, to receive
Thy merited reward, the first assay
Of this right hand provoked, since first that tongue
Inspired with contradiction durst oppose   155
A third part of the gods, in synod met
Their deities to assert, who while they feel
Vigor divine within them, can allow

120. *tried*: (Of *trier* to sift, cull, pick out) proved.
129. *prevention*: the act of forestalling.
130. *securely*: confidently.
144. *piety*: devotion.
147. *sect*: kind (of person).
156. *third*. See II.692n.

Omnipotence to none. But well thou com'st
Before thy fellows, ambitious to win   160
From me some plume, that thy success may show
Destruction to the rest: this pause between
(Unanswered lest thou boast) to let thee know;
At first I thought that liberty and heav'n
To heav'nly souls had been all one; but now   165
I see that most through sloth had rather serve,
Minist'ring Spirits, trained up in feast and song;
Such hast thou armed, the minstrelsy of heav'n,
Servility with freedom to contend,
As both their deeds compared this day shall prove.'   170
   "To whom in brief thus Abdiel stern replied.
'Apostate, still thou err'st, nor end wilt find
Of erring, from the path of truth remote:
Unjustly thou deprav'st it with the name
Of servitude to serve whom God ordains,   175
Or nature; God and nature bid the same,
When he who rules is worthiest, and excels
Them whom he governs. This is servitude,
To serve th' unwise, or him who hath rebelled
Against his worthier, as thine now serve thee,   180
Thyself not free, but to thyself enthralled;
Yet lewdly dar'st our minist'ring upbraid.
Reign thou in hell thy kingdom, let me serve
In heav'n God ever blest, and his divine
Behests obey, worthiest to be obeyed;   185
Yet chains in hell, not realms expect: meanwhile
From me returned, as erst thou saidst, from flight,
This greeting on thy impious crest receive.'
   "So saying, a noble stroke he lifted high,
Which hung not, but so swift with tempest fell   190
On the proud crest of Satan, that no sight,
Nor motion of swift thought, less could his shield
Such ruin intercept: ten paces huge
He back recoiled; the tenth on bended knee
His massy spear upstayed; as if on earth   195
Winds under ground or waters forcing way
Sidelong, had pushed a mountain from his seat

161. *thy success:* the outcome of your action.
163. I.e.: Lest thou boast that I did not answer your argument.
174. *deprav'st:* malignest.
176. See "Reason," p. 464.
182. *lewdly:* ignorantly and basely.
193. *ruin:* L *ruere* to fall.

Half sunk with all his pines. Amazement seized
The rebel Thrones, but greater rage to see
Thus foiled their mightiest: ours joy filled, and shout,   200
Presage of victory and fierce desire
Of battle: whereat Michaël bid sound
Th' Archangel trumpet; through the vast of heav'n
It sounded, and the faithful armies rung
Hosanna to the Highest: nor stood at gaze   205
The adverse legions, nor less hideous joined
The horrid shock: now storming fury rose,
And clamor such as heard in heav'n till now
Was never, arms on armor clashing brayed
Horrible discord, and the madding wheels   210
Of brazen chariots raged; dire was the noise
Of conflict; overhead the dismal hiss
Of fiery darts in flaming volleys flew,
And flying vaulted either host with fire.
So under fiery cope together rushed   215
Both battles main, with ruinous assault
And inextinguishable rage; all heav'n
Resounded, and had earth been then, all earth
Had to her center shook. What wonder? when
Millions of fierce encount'ring angels fought   220
On either side, the least of whom could wield
These elements, and arm him with the force
Of all their regions: how much more of power
Army against army numberless to raise
Dreadful combustion warring, and disturb,   225
Though not destroy, their happy native seat;
Had not th' Eternal King Omnipotent
From his stronghold of heav'n high overruled
And limited their might; though numbered such
As each divided legion might have seemed   230
A numerous host, in strength each armèd hand
A legion; led in fight, yet leader seemed
Each warrior single as in chief, expert
When to advance, or stand, or turn the sway
Of battle, open when, and when to close   235

198–202. *Amazement* and *rage seized* the rebellious angels; *joy* and *shout*(ing) and *desire* filled
ours. Fowler notes: "The *shout* is *Presage* of the final *victory* over Satan; when 'The Lord
himself shall descend from heaven with a shout, with the voice of the archangel, and with the
trump of God: and the dead in Christ shall rise' (I Thess. 4.16)."
199. Here as elsewhere, Milton uses the name of one of the angelic orders to mean all angels.
205. *Hosanna.* Seee III.348.
212. *dismal:* (L *dies mali,* evil days) sinister, dreadful.
216. *battles main:* (military term) the principal, central body of an army (as distinguished from
the van, rear, and wings) in full array. See 654n.
223. *their regions:* the regions of the four *elements* of the earth. Cf. *quarters* in III.714, and see
"The Universe," pp. 461–63.
225. *combustion:* violent commotion.

The ridges of grim war; no thought of flight, ·
None of retreat, no unbecoming deed
That argued fear; each on himself relied,
As only in his arm the moment lay
Of victory; deeds of eternal fame   240
Were done, but infinite: for wide was spread
That war and various; sometimes on firm ground
A standing fight, then soaring on main wing
Tormented all the air; all air seemed then
Conflicting fire: long time in even scale   245
The battle hung; till Satan, who that day
Prodigious power had shown, and met in arms
No equal, ranging through the dire attack
Of fighting Seraphim confused, at length
Saw where the sword of Michael smote, and felled   250
Squadrons at once; with huge two-handed sway
Brandished aloft the horrid edge came down
Wide-wasting; such destruction to withstand
He hasted, and opposed the rocky orb
Of tenfold adamant, his ample shield   255
A vast circumference: at his approach
The great Archangel from his warlike toil
Surceased, and glad as hoping here to end
Intestine war in heav'n, the Arch-Foe subdued
Or captive dragged in chains, with hostile frown   260
And visage all inflamed first thus began.
    " 'Author of evil, unknown till thy revolt,
Unnamed in heav'n, now plenteous, as thou seest
These acts of hateful strife, hateful to all,
Though heaviest by just measure on thyself   265
And thy adherents: how hast thou disturbed
Heav'n's blessèd peace, and into nature brought
Misery, uncreated till the crime
Of thy rebellion! how hast thou instilled
Thy malice into thousands, once upright   270
And faithful, now proved false! But think not here
To trouble holy rest; heav'n casts thee out
From all her confines. Heav'n the seat of bliss
Brooks not the works of violence and war.
Hence then, and evil go with thee along   275
Thy offspring, to the place of evil, hell,

236. *ridges:* ranks.
239. *moment:* the force or weight that will tip the scales.
243. *main:* powerful.
244. *Tormented:* agitated, stirred up.
254. *rocky:* made of rock, i.e., adamant, diamond.
259. *Intestine war:* civil war.
267. *nature.* Cf. 176. In the form of God or order nature existed from the beginning—even
    before the creation of the universe.

Thou and thy wicked crew; there mingle broils,
Ere this avenging sword begin thy doom,
Or some more sudden vengeance winged from God
Precipitate thee with augmented pain.'   280
    "So spake the Prince of Angels; to whom thus
The Adversary. 'Nor think thou with wind
Of airy threats to awe whom yet with deeds
Thou canst not. Hast thou turned the least of these
To flight, or if to fall, but that they rise   285
Unvanquished, easier to transact with me
That thou shouldst hope, imperious, and with threats
To chase me hence? Err not that so shall end
The strife which thou call'st evil, but we style
The strife of glory: which we mean to win,   290
Or turn this heav'n itself into the hell
Thou fablest, here however to dwell free,
If not to reign: meanwhile thy utmost force,
And join him named Almighty to thy aid,
I fly not, but have sought thee far and nigh.'   295
    "They ended parle, and both addressed for fight
Unspeakable; for who, though with the tongue
Of angels, can relate, or to what things
Liken on earth conspicuous, that may lift
Human imagination to such highth   300
Of godlike power: for likest gods they seemed,
Stood they or moved, in stature, motion, arms
Fit to decide the empire of great heav'n.
Now waved their fiery swords, and in the air
Made horrid circles; two broad suns their shields   305
Blazed opposite, while expectation stood
In horror; from each hand with speed retired
Where erst was thickest fight, th' angelic throng,
And left large field, unsafe within the wind
Of such commotion, such as to set forth   310
Great things by small, if nature's concord broke,
Among the constellations war were sprung,
Two planets rushing from aspéct malign

---

277. *mingle:* concoct. *broils:* (Fr *brouiller* to disorder) quarrels.
284–88. I.e.: Hast thou turned the weakest of my host to flight, made any fall who have not
    risen again, that thou shouldst hope it would be easier to negotiate with me imperiously and
    to chase me hence with threats?
288. *Err not:* Do not make the mistake of believing.
296. *parle:* parley. *addressed:* (OF *a* + *drecier* to straighten, arrange) prepared.
299. *conspicuous:* L *conspicere* to get sight of, perceive.
302. *Stood they or moved:* standing or moving.
310–13. I.e.: Such commotion as if (*to set forth . . . small*), nature's concord having been broken,
    war were to spring up among the constellations [and] two diametrically opposed planets should
    combat, etc. *aspéct malign.* Astrologists believe that when two planets are diametrically opposed
    in the heavens (in *malign aspect*), their conflicting rays are harmful to people.

Of fiercest opposition in mid sky,
Should combat, and their jarring spheres confound.   315
Together both with next to almighty arm,
Uplifted imminent one stroke they aimed
That might determine, and not need repeat,
As not of power, at once; nor odds appeared
In might or swift prevention; but the sword   320
Of Michael from the armory of God
Was giv'n him tempered so, that neither keen
Nor solid might resist that edge: it met
The sword of Satan with steep force to smite
Descending, and in half cut sheer, nor stayed,   325
But with swift wheel reverse, deep ent'ring shared
All his right side; then Satan first knew pain,
And writhed him to and fro convolved; so sore
The griding sword with discontinuous wound
Passed through him, but th' ethereal substance closed   330
Not long divisible, and from the gash
A stream of nectarous humor issuing flowed
Sanguine, such as celestial Spirits may bleed,
And all his armor stained erewhile so bright.
Forthwith on all sides to his aid was run   335
By angels many and strong, who interposed
Defense, while others bore him on their shields
Back to his chariot, where it stood retired
From off the files of war; there they him laid
Gnashing for anguish and despite and shame   340
To find himself not matchless, and his pride
Humbled by such rebuke, so far beneath
His confidence to equal God in power.
Yet soon he healed; for Spirits that live throughout
Vital in every part, not as frail man   345
In entrails, heart or head, liver or reins,
Cannot but by annihilating die;
Nor in their liquid texture mortal wound
Receive, no more than can the fluid air:

---

315. *confound:* (L *confundere* to pour together) destroy.
317. *imminent:* L *imminere,* to project, threaten.
318. *determine:* (L *de* + *terminare* to limit) to bring to an end. *repeat:* repetition.
319. *As not of power.* I.e.: since they would not have the power (to repeat the blow). *odds:* inequality.
320. *prevention:* power to forestall, to strike the first blow.
321. Cf. Jer. 50.25: "The Lord hath opened his armoury, and hath brought forth the weapons of his indignation."
326. *shared:* OE *sceran* to shear.
328. *convolved* L *con* together + *volvere* to roll. *sore:* painfully.
329. *griding:* (ME *gird* to strike, to smite) piercing through so as to cause intense, rasping pain. *discontinous:* gaping.
335–36. *to his aid was run / By angels:* (L syntax. Cf. II.213 and IX.253) angels ran aid to him.
344–53. See "Angels," pp. 466–68.

All heart they live, all head, all eye, all ear,   350
All intellect, all sense, and as they please,
They limb themselves, and color, shape, or size
Assume, as likes them best, condense or rare.
    "Meanwhile in other parts like deeds deserved
Memorial, where the might of Gabriel fought,   355
And with fierce ensigns pierced the deep array
Of Moloch furious king, who him defied,
And at his chariot wheels to drag him bound
Threatened, nor from the Holy One of heav'n
Refrained his tongue blasphémous; but anon   360
Down clov'n to the waist, with shattered arms
And uncouth pain fled bellowing. On each wing
Uriel and Raphael his vaunting foe,
Though huge, and in a rock of diamond armed,
Vanquished Adramelech, and Asmadai,   365
Two potent Thrones, that to be less than gods
Disdained, but meaner thoughts learned in their flight,
Mangled with ghastly wounds through plate and mail.
Nor stood unmindful Abdiel to annoy
The atheist crew, but with redoubled blow   370
Ariel and Arioch, and the violence
Of Ramiel scorched and blasted overthrew.
I might relate of thousands, and their names
Eternize here on earth; but those elect
Angels contented with their fame in heav'n   375
Seek not the praise of men: the other sort
In might though wondrous and in acts of war,
Nor of renown less eager, yet by doom
Cancelled from heav'n and sacred memory,
Nameless in dark oblivion let them dwell.   380
For strength from truth divided and from just,
Illaudable, naught merits but dispraise
And ignominy, yet to glory aspires
Vainglorious, and through infamy seeks fame:
Therefore eternal silence be their doom.   385
    "And now their mightiest quelled, the battle swerved,
With many an inroad gored; deformèd rout
Entered, and foul disorder; all the ground
With shivered armor strown, and on a heap

---

353. *condense or rare:* solid or vaporous.
356. *array:* troops in formation.
359–60. Cf. 2 Kings 19.22: "Whom hast thou reproached and blasphemed? and against whom
    hast thou exalted thy voice, and lifted up thine eyes on high? even against the Holy One of
    Israel."
362. *uncouth:* (hitherto) unknown.
365, 371–72. See "Angels," pp. 466–68.
369. *annoy:* molest.
370. *atheist:* godless.

Chariot and charioteer lay overturned   390
And fiery foaming steeds; what stood, recoiled
O'erwearied, through the faint Satanic host
Defensive scarce, or with pale fear surprised,
Then first with fear surprised and sense of pain
Fled ignominious, to such evil brought   395
By sin of disobedience, till that hour
Not liable to fear or flight or pain.
Far otherwise th' inviolable saints
In cubic phalanx firm advanced entire,
Invulnerable, impenetrably armed: 400
Such high advantages their innocence
Gave them above their foes, not to have sinned,
Not to have disobeyed; in fight they stood
Unwearied, unobnoxious to be pained
By wound, though from their place by violence moved.   405
    "Now night her course began, and over heav'n
Inducing darkness, grateful truce imposed,
And silence on the odious din of war:
Under her cloudy covert both retired,
Victor and vanquished: on the foughten field   410
Michaël and his angels prevalent
Encamping, placed in guard their watches round,
Cherubic waving fires: on th' other part
Satan with his rebellious disappeared,
Far in the dark dislodged, and void of rest,   415
His potentates to council called by night;
And in the midst thus undismayed began.
    " 'O now in danger tried, now known in arms
Not to be overpowered, companions dear,
Found worthy not of liberty alone,   420
Too mean pretense, but what we more affect,
Honor, dominion, glory, and renown,
Who have sustained one day in doubtful fight,
(And if one day, why not eternal days?)
What heaven's Lord had powerfullest to send   425
Against us from about his throne, and judged
Sufficient to subdue us to his will,
But proves not so: then fallible, it seems,
Of future we may deem him, though till now

---

393. *Defensive scarce:* scarcely defending themselves. *surprised:* (L *super* over + *prendere* to take) overcome, seized unexpectedly.
404. *unobnoxious:* (L *ob* open to + *noxa* harm) not liable.
411. *prevalent:* victorious.
415. *dislodged:* (military term) shifted his quarters.
421. *mean:* low. *pretense:* aim. *affect:* aspire to.
423. *doubtful:* indecisive.
429. *Of future:* in the future.

Omniscient thought. True is, less firmly armed,   430
Some disadvantage we endured and pain,
Till now not known, but known as soon contemned,
Since now we find this our empyreal form
Incapable of mortal injury
Imperishable, and though pierced with wound,   435
Soon closing, and by native vigor healed.
Of evil then so small as easy think
The remedy; perhaps more valid arms,
Weapons more violent, when next we meet,
May serve to better us, and worse our foes,   440
Or equal what between us made the odds,
In nature none: if other hidden cause
Left them superior, while we can preserve
Unhurt our minds, and understanding sound,
Due search and consultation will disclose.'   445
    "He sat; and in th' assembly next upstood
Nisroch, of Principalities the prime;
As one he stood escaped from cruel fight,
Sore toiled, his riven arms to havoc hewn,
And cloudy in aspéct thus answering spake.   450
'Deliverer from new lords, leader to free
Enjoyment of our right as gods; yet hard
For gods, and too unequal work we find
Against unequal arms to fight in pain,
Against unpained, impassive; from which evil   455
Ruin must needs ensue; for what avails
Valor or strength, though matchless, quelled with pain
Which all subdues, and makes remiss the hands
Of mightiest. Sense of pleasure we may well
Spare out of life perhaps, and not repine,   460
But live content, which is the calmest life:
But pain is perfect misery, the worst
Of evils, and excessive, overturns
All patience. He who therefore can invent
With what more forcible we may offend   465
Our yet unwounded enemies, or arm
Ourselves with like defense, to me deserves
No less than for deliverance what we owe.'

432. *known as soon contemned:* despised as soon as known.
438. *valid:* L *validus* strong.
439. *violent:* powerful.
447. *Nisroch.* See "Angels," pp. 466–68.
449. *to havoc hewn:* cut to pieces.
455. *impassive:* (L *passus,* from *pati* to suffer) insensitive.
458. *remiss:* L *remissum* relaxed.
465. *offend:* (L *offendere* to strike against) attack.
468. *I.e.:* No less than what we owe [Satan] for [our] deliverance.

"Whereto with look composèd Satan replied.
'Not uninvented that, which thou aright   470
Believ'st so main to our success, I bring;
Which of us who beholds the bright surfáce
Of this ethereous mold whereon we stand,
This continent of spacious heav'n, adorned
With plant, fruit, flow'r ambrosial, gems and gold,   475
Whose eye so superfically surveys
These things, as not to mind from whence they grow
Deep under ground, materials dark and crude,
Of spiritous and fiery spume, till touched
With heav'n's ray, and tempered they shoot forth   480
So beauteous, op'ning to the ambient light.
These in their dark nativity the deep
Shall yield us, pregnant with infernal flame,
Which into hollow engines long and round
Thick-rammed, at th' other bore with touch of fire   485
Dilated and infuriate shall send forth
From far with thund'ring noise among our foes
Such implements of mischief as shall dash
To pieces, and o'erwhelm whatever stands
Adverse, that they shall fear we have disarmed   490
The thunderer of his only dreaded bolt.
Nor long shall be our labor, yet ere dawn,
Effect shall end our wish. Meanwhile revive;
Abandon fear; to strength and counsel joined
Think nothing hard, much less to be despaired.'   495
He ended, and his words their drooping cheer
Enlightened, and their languished hope revived.
Th' invention all admired, and each, how he
To be th' inventor missed, so easy it seemed
Once found, which yet unfound most would have thought   500
Impossible: yet haply of thy race
In future days, if malice should abound,
Some one intent on mischief, or inspired
With dev'lish machination might devise
Like instrument to plague the sons of men   505
For sin, on war and mutual slaughter bent.

471. *main*: essential.
479. *spume*. See 512n.
481. *ambient*: circumfused, enveloping.
483. *infernal*: L *infernus* that which lies beneath.
485. *Thick*: compactly. *other bore*: the touchhole, drilled into the barrel of a cannon, into which
    fine powder was poured to serve as a fuse for the charge.
494. *counsel*: judgment, wisdom, prudence.
496. *cheer*: (OF *chiere*, *chere*, face) state of mind.
498. *admired*: wondered at.
501. *haply*: by chance.

Forthwith from council to the work they flew,
None arguing stood, innumerable hands
Were ready, in a moment up they turned
Wide the celestial soil, and saw beneath   510
Th' originals of nature in their crude
Conception; sulphurous and nitrous foam
They found, they mingled, and with subtle art,
Concocted and adusted they reduced
To blackest grain, and into store conveyed: 515
Part hidden veins digged up (nor hath this earth
Entrails unlike) of mineral and stone,
Whereof to found their engines and their balls
Of missive ruin; part incentive reed
Provide, pernicious with one touch to fire.   520
So all ere day-spring, under conscious night
Secret they finished, and in order set,
With silent circumspection unespied.
Now when fair morn orient in heav'n appeared
Up rose the victor angels, and to arms   525
The matin trumpet sung: in arms they stood
Of golden panoply, refulgent host,
Soon banded; others from the dawning hills
Looked round, and scouts each coast light-armèd scour,
Each quarter, to descry the distant foe,   530
Where lodged, or whither fled, or if for fight,
In motion or in alt: him soon they met
Under spread ensigns moving nigh, in slow
But firm battalion; back with speediest sail
Zophiel, of Cherubim the swiftest wing,   535
Came flying, and in mid-air aloud thus cried.
    " 'Arm, warriors, arm for fight, the foe at hand,
Whom fled we thought, will save us long pursuit
This day, fear not his flight; so thick a cloud
He comes, and settled in his face I see   540
Sad resolution and secure: let each
His adamantine coat gird well, and each
Fit well his helm, gripe fast his orbèd shield,

512. *foam:* like *spume* (479), a word for the chemical compound called a "salt." Potassium nitrate and sulphur are components of gunpowder.
514. *concocted:* refined by mixing and cooking. *adusted:* dried by heating.
515. *grain:* granules.
518. *found:* (L *fundere* to pour) to form or cast, as in a foundry.
519. *missive:* capable of being projected. *incentive:* kindling (a pun involving *incendiary*, L *incendium* a fire, and *incentive*, L *incinere* to strike up a tune, from *in* + *canere* to sing). *incentive reed:* both matchstick and musical instrument.
520. *pernicious:* (L *pernix* nimble) quick; and (L *per* + *nex* violent death) destructive.
521. *conscious:* guiltily aware (of what they were doing).
532. *alt:* halt.
535. *Zophiel:* See "Angels," pp. 466–68.
541. *Sad:* firm. *secure:* confident.

Borne ev'n or high, for this day will pour down,
If I conjecture aught, no drizzling shower,   545
But rattling storm of arrows barbed with fire.'
So warned he them aware themselves, and soon
In order, quit of all impediment;
Instant without disturb they took alarm,
And onward move embattled; when behold   550
Not distant far with heavy pace with foe
Approaching gross and huge; in hollow cube
Training his devilish enginry, impaled
On every side with shadowing squadrons deep,
To hide the fraud. At interview both stood   555
A while, but suddenly at head appeared
Satan: and thus was heard commanding loud.
    " 'Vanguard, to right and left the front unfold;
That all may see who hate us, how we seek
Peace and composure, and with open breast   560
Stand ready to receive them, if they like
Our overture, and turn not back perverse;
But that I doubt, however witness heaven,
Heav'n witness thou anon, while we discharge
Freely our part: ye who appointed stand   565
Do as you have in charge, and briefly touch
What we propound, and loud that all may hear.'
    "So scoffing in ambiguous words, he scarce
Had ended; when to right and left the front
Divided, and to either flank retired.   570
Which to our eyes discovered new and strange,
A triple-mounted row of pillars laid
On wheels (for like to pillars most they seemed
Or hollowed bodies made of oak or fir
With branches lopped, in wood or mountain felled)   575
Brass, iron, stony mold, had not their mouths
With hideous orifice gaped on us wide,
Portending hollow truce; at each behind

544. *ev'n:* straight out in front of the body.
547–48. *aware themselves:* already wary, cautious of danger. *Aware* and *warn* both come from
OE *wær* wary. *and soon* [they were] *In order:* battle order. *quit:* free. *impediment:* equipment
not needed in battle.
549. I.e.: Instantly without disorder they obeyed the call to arms.
550. *embattled:* in battle formation.
552. *gross:* compact. Cf. II.570.
553. *Training:* (OF *traîner* to draw) pulling. *impaled:* fenced in.
555. *At interview:* in view of one another.
560. *composure:* agreement. *breast:* front ranks; also heart.
562. *overture:* (L *apertura* opening, hole) offer to negotiate; opening of the ranks concealing the
cannon—or the muzzle of the cannon.
564. *discharge:* another pun.
566–67. *charge, touch, propound, loud:* all puns.
572. *triple-mounted:* in three rows. Cf. 605 and 650.
576. *mold:* matter.

A Seraph stood, and in his hand a reed
Stood waving tipped with fire; while we suspense,　　　580
Collected stood within our thoughts amused,
Not long, for sudden all at once their reeds
Put forth, and to a narrow vent applied
With nicest touch. Immediate in a flame,
But soon obscured with smoke, all heav'n appeared,　　　585
From those deep-throated engines belched, whose roar
Emboweled with outrageous noise the air,
And all her entrails tore, disgorging foul
Their devilish glut, chained thunderbolts and hail
Of iron globes, which on the victor host　　　590
Leveled, with such impetuous fury smote,
That whom they hit, none on their feet might stand,
Though standing else as rocks, but down they fell
By thousands, Angel on Archangel rolled,
The sooner for their arms; unarmed they might　　　595
Have easily as Spirits evaded swift
By quick contraction or remove; but now
Foul dissipation followed and forced rout;
Nor served it to relax their serried files.
What should they do? If on they rushed, repulse　　　600
Repeated, and indecent overthrow
Doubled, would render them yet more despised,
And to their foes a laughter; for in view
Stood ranked of Seraphim another row
In posture to displode their second tire　　　605
Of thunder: back defeated to return
They worse abhorred. Satan beheld their plight,
And to his mates thus in derision called.
　　" 'O friends, why come not on these victors proud?
Erewhile they fierce were coming, and when we,　　　610
To entertain them fair with open front
And breast, (what could we more?) propounded terms
Of composition, straight they changed their minds,
Flew off, and into strange vagaries fell,
As they would dance, yet for a dance they seemed　　　615

580. *suspense:* undecided where to turn.
581. *amused:* preoccupied; or (in the military snese) with attention diverted from the enemy's intention.
587. *Emboweled:* disemboweled.
598. *Foul dissipation:* dishonorable rout.
599. *served it:* did it do any good. *relax:* loosen up, make less compact. *serried files:* rows pressed together in close order.
601. *indecent.* Like *foul* in 598, *indecent* implies obscene, offensive to good taste, not to be looked at, not to be countenanced; hence, disgraceful.
605. *displode:* explode. *tire:* volley.
611–19. *front* (face), *breast* (heart), *propounded, composition, Flew off, result* (L *re* back + *saltare* to leap): all puns.
614. *vagaries:* eccentric motions.

Somewhat extravagant and wild, perhaps
For joy of offering peace: but I suppose
If our proposals once again were heard
We should compel them to a quick result.'
    "To whom thus Belial in like gamesome mood.   620
'Leader, the terms we sent were terms of weight,
Of hard contents, and full of force urged home,
Such as we might perceive amused them all,
And stumbled many: who receives them right,
Had need from head to foot well understand;   625
Not understood, this gift they have besides,
They show us when our foes walk not upright."
    "So they among themselves in pleasant vein
Stood scoffing, highthened in their thoughts beyond
All doubt of victory, Eternal Might   630
To match with their inventions they presumed
So easy, and of his thunder made a scorn,
And all his host derided, while they stood
A while in trouble; but they stood not long,
Rage prompted them at length, and found them arms   635
Against such hellish mischief fit to oppose.
Forthwith (behold the excellence, the power,
Which God hath in his mighty angels placed)
Their arms away they threw, and to the hills
(For earth hath this variety from heav'n   640
Of pleasure situate in hill and dale)
Light as the lightning glimpse they ran, they flew,
From their foundations loos'ning to and fro
They plucked the seated hills with all their load,
Rocks, waters, woods, and by the shaggy tops   645
Uplifting bore them in their hands: amaze,
Be sure, and terror seized the rebel host,
When coming towards them so dread they saw
The bottom of the mountains upward turned,
Till on those cursèd engines' triple-row   650
They saw them whelmed, and all their confidence
Under the weight of mountains buried deep,
Themselves invaded next, and on their heads
Main promontories flung, which in the air

---

623. *amused:* held their attention; bewildered them (pun). Cf. 581.
624. *stumbled:* perplexed (pun).
625. *understand.* Another pun.
633. *they:* the rebels' enemies.
653. *invaded:* attacked.
654. *Main:* (OE *magan* to be able) (when used of an army) numerous and fully equipped; (of things) great in bulk or strength; (of earth or rock) forming the principal or entire mass; as in "with might and main." *promontories:* L *promunturium* a mountain ridge, a headland.

Came shadowing, and oppressed whole legions armed,   655
Their armor helped their harm, crushed in and bruised
Into their substance pent, which wrought them pain
Implacable, and many a dolorous groan,
Long struggling underneath, ere they could wind
Out of such prison, though Spirits of purest light,   660
Purest at first, now gross by sinning grown.
The rest in imitation to like arms
Betook them, and the neighboring hills uptore;
So hills amid the air encountered hills
Hurled to and fro with jaculation dire,   665
That underground they fought in dismal shade;
Infernal noise; war seemed a civil game
To this uproar; horrid confusion heaped
Upon confusion rose: and now all heav'n
Had gone to wrack, with ruin overspread,   670
Had not th' Almighty Father where he sits
Shrined in his sanctuary of heav'n secure,
Consulting on the sum of things, foreseen
This tumult, and permitted all, advised:
That his great purpose he might so fulfill,   675
To honor his anointed Son avenged
Upon his enemies, and to declare
All power on him transferred: whence to his Son
Th' assessor of his throne he thus began.
    " 'Effulgence of my glory, Son beloved,   680
Son in whose face invisible is beheld
Visibly, what by Deity I am,
And in whose hand what by decree I do,
Second Omnipotence, two days are passed,
Two days, as we compute the days of heav'n,   685
Since Michael and his powers wents forth to tame
These disobedient; sore hath been their fight,
As likeliest was, when two such foes met armed;
For to themselves I left them, and thou know'st,
Equal in their creation they were formed,   690
Save what sin hath impaired, which yet hath wrought
Insensibly, for I suspend their doom;
Whence in perpetual fight they needs must last

---

665. *jaculation:* L *jacere* to throw; *jaculum* a dart.
673. *Consulting on:* considering. *the sum of things.* Fowler notes that the phrase is a translation of L *summa rerum,* "highest public interest," and that by *sum* Milton may intend the meaning of "goal."
674. *advised:* advisedly, having advised himself. L *ad* toward + *visum,* from *videre* to see. Milton plays a variation on *foreseen* in the line above, and *providence,* which is his theme.
679. *assessor:* (L *assessor,* one who sits beside) associate.
681–82. Cf. Col. 1.15: "Who is the image of the invisible God . . ."
692. *Insensibly:* imperceptibly.

Endless, and no solution will be found:
War wearied hath performed what war can do,   695
And to disordered rage let loose the reins,
With mountains as with weapons armed, which makes
Wild work in heav'n, and dangerous to the main.
Two days are therefore passed, the third is thine;
For thee I have ordained it, and thus far   700
Have suffered, that the glory may be thine
Of ending this great war, since none but thou
Can end it. Into thee such virtue and grace
Immense I have transfused, that all may know
In heav'n and hell thy power above compare,   705
And this perverse commotion governed thus,
To manifest thee worthiest to be Heir
Of all things, to be Heir and to be King
By sacred unction, thy deservèd right.
Go then thou mightiest in thy Father's might,   710
Ascend my chariot, guide the rapid wheels
That shake heav'n's basis, bring forth all my war,
My bow and thunder, my almighty arms
Gird on, and sword upon thy puissant thigh;
Pursue these sons of darkness, drive them out   715
From all heav'n's bounds into the utter deep:
There let them learn, as likes them, to despise
God and Messiah his anointed King.'
    "He said, and on his Son with rays direct
Shone full, he all his Father full expressed   720
Ineffably into his face received,
And thus the Filial Godhead answering spake:
    " 'O Father, O Supreme of heav'nly Thrones,
First, highest, holiest, best, thou always seek'st
To glorify thy Son, I always thee,   725
As is most just; this I my glory account,
My exaltation, and my whole delight,

---

695. *War wearied:* war, itself worn out.
698. *main:* i.e., "continent" of heaven.
699. *therefore:* in that way. *the third is thine.* Fowler notes that "Typologically, the reference would be to Christ's rising on the third day . . . : Messiah's defeat of Satan here foreshadows the later victory of the resurrection." See XII.232–33n.
701. *suffered:* permitted.
712. *war:* instrument of war.
714. Cf. Ps. 45.3: "Gird thy sword upon thy thigh, O most mighty, with thy glory and thy majesty."
716. *utter:* outer.
720–21. Cf. 2 Cor. 4.6: "For God, who commanded the light to shine out of darkness, hath shined in our hearts, to give the light of the knowledge of the glory of God in the face of Jesus Christ." *ineffably:* unutterably.
725. Cf. John 17.1: "These words spake Jesus, and lifted up his eyes to heaven, and said, Father, the hour is come; glorify thy Son, that thy Son also may glorify thee."

That thou in me well pleased, declar'st thy will
Fulfilled, which to fulfill is all my bliss.
Scepter and power, thy giving, I assume,   730
And gladlier shall resign, when in the end
Thou shalt be all in all, and I in thee
For ever, and in me all whom thou lov'st:
But whom thou hat'st, I hate, and can put on
Thy terrors, as I put thy mildness on,   735
Image of thee in all things; and shall soon,
Armed with thy might, rid heav'n of these rebelled,
To their prepared ill mansion driven down
To chains of darkness, and th' undying worm,
That from thy just obedience could revolt,   740
Whom to obey is happiness entire.
Then shall thy saints unmixed, and from th' impure
Far separate, circling thy holy mount
Unfeignèd hallelujahs to thee sing,
Hymns of high praise, and I among them chief.'   745
So said, he o'er his scepter bowing, rose
From the right hand of Glory where he sat,
And the third sacred morn began to shine
Dawning through heav'n: forth rushed with whirlwind sound
The chariot of Paternal Deity,   750
Flashing thick flames, wheel within wheel undrawn,
Itself instinct with spirit, but convoyed
By four Cherubic shapes, four faces each
Had wondrous, as with stars their bodies all
And wings were set with eyes, with eyes the wheels   755
Of beryl, and careering fires between;
Over their heads a crystal firmament,
Whereon a sapphire throne, inlaid with pure

728. Cf. Matt. 3.17: "And lo a voice from heaven, saying, This is my beloved Son, in whom I
   am well pleased."
731–32. Cf. 1 Cor. 15.24, 28: "Then cometh the end when he shall have delivered up the
   kingdom to God, even the Father; when he shall have put down all rule and all authority and
   power. . . . And when all things shall be subdued unto him, then shall the Son also himself
   be subject unto him that put all things under him, that God may be all in all."
734. Cf. Ps. 139.21: "Do not I hate them, O Lord, that hate thee? and am not I grieved with
   those that rise up against thee?"
738. Cf. John 14.2: "In my Father's house are many mansions: if it were not so, I [Christ] would
   have told you. I go to prepare a place for you." ill: evil, painful, unwholesome. mansion: (L
   manere to dwell) abode.
739. Cf. 2 Pet. 2.4: ". . . God spared not the angels that sinned, but cast them down to hell,
   and delivered them into chains of darkness, to be reserved unto judgement." Jude 6: "And the
   angels which kept not the first estate, but left their own habitation, he hath reserved in everlasting
   chains under darkness unto the judgement of the great day." Isa. 66.24: "And they shall go
   forth, and look upon the carcases of the men that have transgressed against me: for their worm
   shall not die, neither shall their fire be quenched; and they shall be an abhorring unto all
   flesh." Mark 9.44: "Where their worm dieth not, and the fire is not quenched."
749–59. See Ezek. 1.
752. instinct with: (L in + stinguere to prick, to stick) impelled by.
755. Cf. Ezek. 10.12: "And their whole body and their backs, and their hands, and their wings,
   and the wheels, were full of eyes round about, even the wheels that they four had."

Amber, and colors of the show'ry arch.
He in celestial panoply all armed   760
Of radiant Urim, work divinely wrought,
Ascended, at his right hand Victory
Sat eagle-winged, beside him hung his bow
And quiver with three-bolted thunder stored,
And from about him fierce effusion rolled   765
Of smoke and bickering flame, and sparkles dire;
Attended with ten thousand thousand saints,
He onward came, far off his coming shone,
And twenty thousand (I their number heard)
Chariots of God, half on each hand were seen: 770
He on the wings of Cherub rode sublime
On the crystálline sky, in sapphire throned,
Illustrious far and wide, but by his own
First seen: them unexpected joy surprised,
When the great ensign of Messiah blazed   775
Aloft by angels borne, his sign in heav'n:
Under whose conduct Michael soon reduced
His army, circumfused on either wing,
Under their Head embodied all in one.
Before him Power Divine his way prepared;   780
At his command the uprooted hills retired
Each to his place, they heard his voice and went
Obsequious, heav'n his wonted face renewed,
And with fresh flow'rets hill and valley smiled.
This saw his hapless foes but stood obdured,   785
And to rebellious fight rallied their powers
Insensate, hope conceiving from despair.
In heav'nly Spirits could such perverseness dwell?

759. *show'ry arch*: rainbow.
761. *Urim*. When God instructed Moses to make his brother Aaron a priest, he gave instructions about the holy garments Aaron was to wear. These included a "breastplate of judgement," into which was to be put "Urim and Thummin" (Exod. 28.30). *Urim* would seem to be a symbol, or a jewel or jewels. Fowler notes that "many alchemical theorists" thought *Urim* was the philosopher's stone. Cf. III.596–605.
763. *eagle-winged*. The eagle was the symbol of Jupiter, the hurler of thunderbolts.
766. *bickering*: flickering.
767. Cf. Rev. 5.11: "And I beheld, and I heard the voice of many angels round the throne and the beasts and the elders: and the number of them was ten thousand times ten thousand, and thousands of thousands."
769–70. Cf. Ps. 68.17: "The chariots of God are twenty thousand, even thousands of angels: the Lord is among them, as in Sinai, in the holy place."
771. Cf. Sam. 22.11: "And he rode upon a cherub, and did fly: and he was seen upon the wings of the wind." *sublime*: raised up.
773. *Illustrious*: luminous.
776. Cf. Matt. 24.30: "And then shall appear the sign of the Son of man in heaven: and then shall all the tribes of the earth . . . see the Son of man coming in the clouds of heaven with power and great glory."
777. *reduced*: L *re* back + *ducere* to lead.
778. *circumfused*: (L *circum* around + *fundere* to pour) dispersed.
785. *obdured*: hardened. Cf. III.200n.
788. Cf. *Aen.* 1.11: "Can resentment so fierce dwell in heavenly breasts?"

But to convince the proud what signs avail,
Or wonders move th' obdúrate to relent?   790
They hardened more by what might most reclaim,
Grieving to see his glory, at the sight
Took envy, and aspiring to his highth,
Stood re-embattled fierce, by force or fraud
Weening to prosper, and at length prevail   795
Against God and Messiah, or to fall
In universal ruin last, and now
To final battle drew; disdaining flight,
Or faint retreat; when the great Son of God
To all his host on either hand thus spake.   800
    " 'Stand still in bright array ye saints, here stand
Ye angels armed, this day from battle rest;
Faithful hath been your warfare, and of God
Accepted, fearless in his righteous cause,
And as ye have received, so have ye done   805
Invincibly; but of this cursèd crew
The punishment to other hand belongs,
Vengenace is his, or whose he sole appoints;
Number to this day's work is not ordained
Nor multitude, stand only and behold   810
God's indignation on these godless poured
By me, not you but me they have despised,
Yet envied; against me is all their rage,
Because the Father, t' whom in heav'n supreme
Kingdom and power and glory appertains,   815
Hath honored me according to his will.
Therefore to me their doom he hath assigned;
That they may have their wish, to try with me
In battle which the stronger proves, they all,
Or I alone against them, since by strength   820
They measure all, of other excellence
Not emulous, nor care who them excels;
Nor other strife with them do I vouchsafe.'
    "So spake the Son, and into terror changed
His count'nance too severe to be beheld   825
And full of wrath bent on his enemies.
At once the Four spread out their starry wings
With dreadful shade contiguous, and the orbs
Of his fierce chariot rolled, as with the sound

---

791. *what might most reclaim*. I.e., the sight of Christ.
801. Cf. Exod. 14.13, p. 434.
808. Cf. Rom. 12.19: "Dearly beloved, avenge not yourselves, but rather give place unto wrath:
    for it is written, Vengeance is mine; I will repay, saith the Lord."
823. *voutsafe*: vouchsafe, grant.
827. *the Four*: Ezekiel's *four Cherubic shapes* of line 753.

Of torrent floods, or of a numerous host.   830
He on his impious foes right onward drove,
Gloomy as night; under his burning wheels
The steadfast empyrean shook throughout,
All but the throne itself of God. Full soon
Among them he arrived; in his right hand   835
Grasping ten thousand thunders, which he sent
Before him, such as in their souls infixed
Plagues; they astonished all resistance lost,
All courage; down their idle weapons dropped;
O'er shields and helms, and helmèd heads he rode   840
Of Thrones and mighty Seraphim prostráte,
That wished the mountains now might be again
Thrown on them as a shelter from his ire.
Nor less on either side tempestuous fell
His arrows, from the fourfold-visaged Four,   845
Distinct with eyes, and from the living wheels,
Distinct alike with multitude of eyes;
One spirit in them ruled, and every eye
Glared lightning, and shot forth pernicious fire
Among th' accursed, that withered all their strength,   850
And of their wonted vigor left them drained,
Exhausted, spiritless, afflicted, fall'n.
Yet half his strength he put not forth, but checked
His thunder in mid-volley, for he meant
Not to destroy, but root them out of heav'n: 855
The overthrown he raised, and as a herd
Of goats or timorous flock together thronged
Drove them before him thunderstruck, pursued
With terrors and with furies to the bounds
And crystal wall of heav'n, which op'ning wide,   860
Rolled inward, and a spacious gap disclosed
Into the wasteful deep; the monstrous sight
Strook them with horror backward, but far worse

833. Cf. 2 Sam. 22.8: "Then the earth shook and trembled; the foundations of heaven moved
    and shook, because he was wroth."
836–38. Cf. Ps. 18.13–14: "The Lord also thundered in the heavens, and the Highest gave his
    voice; hail stones and coals of fire. Yea, he sent out his arrows, and scattered them; and he
    shot out lightnings, and discomfited them." *thunders*: thunderbolts, i.e., flashes of lightning.
838. *Plagues*: L *plaga* a blow. *astonished*: (L ex out + *tonare* to thunder) struck with fear.
842–43. Cf. Hos. 10.8: "The high places also of Aven, the sin of Israel, shall be destroyed:
    . . . and they shall say to the mountains, Cover us; and to the hills, Fall on us."
846. *Distinct*: decorated.
849. *pernicious*: deadly. Cf. 520.
857. *goats*. Cf. Matt. 25.31–41: "When the Son of man shall come in his glory . . . then shall
    he sit upon the throne of his glory: and before him shall be gathered all nations: and he shall
    separate them one from another, as a shepherd divideth his sheep from the goats: and he shall
    set the sheep on his right hand, but the goats on the left. . . . Then shall he say also unto
    them on the left hand, Depart from me, ye cursed, into everlasting fire, prepared for the devil
    and his angels."
862. *wasteful*: full of emptiness. *monstrous*: unnatural.

Urged them behind; headlong themselves they threw
Down from the verge of heav'n, eternal wrath 865
Burnt after them to the bottomless pit.
"Hell heard th' unsufferable noise, hell saw
Heav'n ruining from heav'n, and would have fled
Affrighted; but strict fate had cast too deep
Her dark foundations, and too fast had bound. 870
Nine days they fell; confounded Chaos roared,
And felt tenfold confusion in their fall
Through his wild anarchy, so huge a rout
Encumbered him with ruin: hell at last
Yawning received them whole, and on them closed, 875
Hell their fit habitation fraught with fire
Unquenchable, the house of woe and pain.
Disburdened heav'n rejoiced, and soon repaired
Her mural breach, returning whence it rolled.
Sole victor from th' expulsion of his foes 880
Messiah his triumphal chariot turned:
To meet him all his saints, who silent stood
Eye-witnesses of his almighty acts,
With jubilee advanced; and as they went,
Shaded with branching palm, each order bright 885
Sung triumph, and him sung victorious King,
Son, Heir, and Lord, to him dominion giv'n,
Worthiest to reign: he celebrated rode
Triumphant through mid-heav'n, into the courts
And temple of his mighty Father throned 890
On high: who into glory him received,
Where now he sits at the right hand of bliss.
"Thus measuring things in heav'n by things on earth
At thy request, and that thou may'st beware
By what is past, to thee I have revealed 895
What might have else to human race been hid;
The discord which befell, and war in heav'n
Among th' angelic powers, and the deep fall
Of those too high aspiring, who rebelled
With Satan, he who envies now thy state, 900
Who now is plotting how he may seduce
Thee also from obedience, that with him

868. *ruining*: (L *ruina* a falling) tumbling down.
871. *confounded* (L *con* together + *fundere*, *fusum*, to pour) confused.
874–75. Cf. Isa. 5.14: "Therefore hell hath enlarged herself, and opened her mouth without measure: and their glory, and their multitude, and their pomp, and he that rejoiceth, shall descend into it."
884. *jubilee*: joyful shouting.
892. Cf. Heb. 1.3: "Who [Christ, after his crucifixion and resurrection] being the brightness of his [God's] glory, and the express image of his person, and upholding all things by the word of his power, when he had by himself purged our sins, sat down on the right hand of the majesty on high. . . ."

Bereaved of happiness thou may'st partake
His punishment, eternal misery;
Which would be all his solace and revenge,   905
As a despite done against the Most High,
Thee once to gain companion of his woe.
But listen not to his temptations, warn
Thy weaker; let it profit thee to have heard
By terrible example the reward   910
Of disobedience; firm they might have stood,
Yet fell; remember, and fear to transgress."

Book VII

The Argument

Raphael at the request of Adam relates how and wherefore this world
was first created; that God, after the expelling of Satan and his angels
out of heaven, declared his pleasure to create another world and other
creatures to dwell therein; sends his Son with glory and attendance of
angels to perform the work of creation in six days: the angels celebrate
with hymns the performance thereof, and his reascension into heaven.

Descend from heav'n Urania, by that name
If rightly thou art called, whose voice divine
Following, above th' Olympian hill I soar,
Above the flight of Pegasean wing.
The meaning, not the name I call: for thou   5
Nor of the muses nine, nor on the top

909. *Thy weaker:* Cf. 1 Pet. 3.7: "Likewise, ye husbands, dwell with them according to knowledge, giving honour unto the wife, as unto the weaker vessel, and as being heirs together of the grace of life; that your prayers be not hindered."

VII.1. *Urania:* (Gk *Ourania* the heavenly one) the Muse of astronomy.

2–3. Cf. I.14–15. In Greek mythology, Mount Olympus was the dwelling place of the gods, and *Pegasus* was a winged horse, representing poetic inspiration, who dwelt in the heavens. See 17–20n, below.

5–12. Cf. the speech of Wisdom in Prov. 8.22–30, where she says "The Lord possessed me in the beginning of his way [NEB: "created me the beginning of his works"], before his works of old. I was set up from everlasting, from the beginning, or ever the earth was. When there were no depths, I was brought forth; when there were no fountains abounding with water. Before the mountains were settled, before the hills was I brought forth: While as yet he had not made the earth, nor the fields, nor the highest part of the dust of the world. When he prepared the heavens, I was there: when he set a compass upon the face of the depth: When he established the clouds above: when he strengthened the fountains of the deep: When he gave to the sea his decree, that the waters should not pass his commandment: when he appointed the foundations of the earth: Then I was by him, as one brought up with him: and I was daily his delight, rejoicing always before him." Since Christ in the form of the Logos, or Word, was the only other agency or power said to have been present with God at the Creation, Wisdom's sibling would seem to be Christ. But Milton clearly does not pray for Christ's assistance. His Muse defies personification or deification; she is, we must think, the holy spirit that inspired Moses and other religious poets and prophets in the Judeo-Christian tradition. Nor may we doubt that Milton believed literally in her being or powers of performance. Milton called her Urania for want of a more appropriate or lovelier word.

Of old Olympus dwell'st, but heav'nly born,
Before the hills appeared, or fountain flowed,
Thou with eternal Wisdom didst converse,
Wisdom thy sister, and with her didst play   10
In presence of th' Almighty Father, pleased
With thy celestial song. Up led by thee
Into the heav'n of heav'ns I have presumed,
An earthly guest, and drawn empyreal air,
Thy temp'ring; with like safety guided down   15
Return me to my native element:
Lest from this flying steed unreined (as once
Bellerophon, though from a lower clime)
Dismounted, on th' Aleian field I fall
Erroneous there to wander and forlorn.   20
Half yet remains unsung, but narrower bound
Within the visible diurnal sphere;
Standing on earth, not rapt above the pole,
More safe I sing with mortal voice, unchanged
To hoarse or mute, though fall'n on evil days,   25
On evil days though fall'n, and evil tongues;
In darkness, and with dangers compassed round,
And solitude; yet not alone, while thou
Visit'st my slumbers nightly, or when morn
Purples the east: still govern thou my song,   30
Urania, and fit audience find, though few.
But drive far off the barbarous dissonance
Of Bacchus and his revelers, the race
Of that wild rout that tore the Thracian bard
In Rhodope, where woods and rocks had ears   35

9. *converse:* (L *con* with + *vertere* to turn about; *conversaria* to live, keep company with) associate,
live.
15. *Thy temp'ring:* made suitable (for a mortal) by thee. The "air" of the empyrean was ethereal,
not like the air of the earth's four elements. See "The Universe," pp. 461–63.
16. *native element:* the earth.
17–20. Pegasus *unreined* may be too dangerous a vehicle for any human being, but in the case
of *Bellerophon,* Jupiter made Pegasus throw his rider. Milton alludes to *Bellerophon's* pre-
sumption in trying to gain forbidden knowledge as well as to the consequences, one of which,
Hughes notes, was said to have been blindness. *Aleian:* (Gk wandering) the field on which
Bellerophon fell, and was doomed to wander the rest of his life. *Erroneous:* wandering. Cf. *Il.*
6.200–202: "But when even Bellerophon came to be hated of all the gods, then wandered he
alone in the Aleian plain, devouring his own soul, and avoiding the paths of men."
22. *diurnal sphere:* the universe, which is *diurnal* because from earth it all seems to revolve
daily.
23. *rapt:* transported. *pole:* zenith of the universe; i.e., above the universe.
25–28. If Milton here refers to his personal life right after the Restoration, when he went into
hiding for fear of arrest, *hoarse or mute* may mean the rejected options of speaking out polem-
ically or not speaking at all. He has chosen to continue to "speak" as a poet, and now to speak
more safely of earthly things, not heavenly.
32–38. In Greek mythology, the music of Orpheus, the *Thracian bard,* son of the Muse Calliope,
charmed even the *woods* and *rocks,* but he and his mother were unable to prevent his being
murdered by a *wild rout* of Bacchanalian *revelers,* who threw his dismembered body in the
Hebrus river, which rises in the *Rhodope* mountains, sacred to Bacchus. The *barbarous dis-
sonance* is, perhaps, that of Restoration society.

To rapture, till the savage clamor drowned
Both harp and voice; nor could the Muse defend
Her son. So fail not thou, who thee implores:
For thou art heav'nly, she an empty dream.
  Say goddess, what ensued when Raphael,   40
The affable Archangel, had forewarned
Adam by dire example to beware
Apostasy, by what befell in heaven
To those apostates, lest the like befall
In Paradise to Adam or his race,   45
Charged not to touch the interdicted tree,
If they transgress, and slight that sole command,
So easily obeyed amid the choice
Of all tastes else to please their appetite,
Though wand'ring. He with his consorted Eve   50
The story heard attentive, and was filled
With admiration, and deep muse to hear
Of things so high and strange, things to their thought
So unimaginable as hate in heav'n,
And war so near the peace of God in bliss   55
With such confusion: but the evil soon
Driv'n back redounded as a flood on those
From whom it sprung, impossible to mix
With blessedness. Whence Adam soon repealed
The doubts that in his heart arose: and now   60
Led on, yet sinless, with desire to know
What nearer might concern him, how this world
Of heav'n and earth conspicuous first began,
When, and whereof created, for what cause,
What within Eden or without was done   65
Before his memory, as one whose drouth
Yet scarce allayed still eyes the current stream,
Whose liquid murmur heard new thirst excites,
Proceeded thus to ask his heav'nly guest.
  "Great things, and full of wonder in our ears,   70
Far differing from this world, thou hast revealed
Divine interpreter, by favor sent
Down from the empyrean to forewarn
Us timely of what might else have been our loss,
Unknown, which human knowledge could not reach: 75

43. *Apostasy:* (Gk *apo* away from + *stēnai* to stand) defection.
46. *touch.* Cf. Gen. 3.2,3, p. 432.
50. *consorted:* (L *con* with, together + *sors* lot, fate, share) wedded.
52. *admiration:* wonder, astonishment. *muse:* meditation.
57. *redounded:* L *re* back + *undare* to rise in waves.
59. *repealed:* gave up.
63. *conspicuous:* visible.
67. *current:* flowing.

For which to the Infinitely Good we owe
Immortal thanks, and his admonishment
Receive with solemn purpose to observe
Immutably his sovran will, the end
Of what we are. But since thou hast vouchsafed   80
Gently for our instruction to impart
Things above earthly thought, which yet concerned
Our knowing, as to Highest Wisdom seemed,
Deign to descend now lower, and relate
What may no less perhaps avail us known,   85
How first began this heav'n which we behold
Distant so high, with moving fires adorned
Innumerable, and this which yields or fills
All space, the ambient air wide interfused
Embracing round this florid earth, what cause   90
Moved the Creator in his holy rest
Through all eternity so late to build
In chaos, and the work begun, how soon
Absolved, if unforbid thou may'st unfold
What we, not to explore the secrets ask   95
Of his eternal empire, but the more
To magnify his works, the more we know.
And the great light of day yet wants to run
Much of his race though steep, suspense in heav'n
Held by thy voice, thy potent voice he hears,   100
And longer will delay to hear thee tell
His generation, and the rising birth
Of nature from the unapparent deep:
Or if the star of evening and the moon
Haste to thy audience, night with her will bring   105
Silence, and sleep list'ning to thee will watch,
Or we can bid his absence, till thy song
End, and dismiss thee ere the morning shine."
     Thus Adam his illustrious guest besought:
And thus the godlike angel answered mild.   110
"This also thy request with caution asked
Obtain: though to recount almighty works
What words or tongue of Seraph can suffice,
Or heart of man suffice to comprehend?
Yet what thou canst attain, which best may serve   115

79. *end:* purpose (i.e., to observe . . . his will).
90. *florid:* L *flos, floris* flower.
94. *Absolved:* finished.
97. Cf. Job 36.24: "Remember that thou magnify his work, which men behold."
99. *suspense:* attentive; also, hanging.
102. *His generation:* the creation of him.
103. *unapparent deep:* chaos, invisible because without form.
106. *watch:* stay awake.

To glorify the Maker, and infer
Thee also happier, shall not be withheld
Thy hearing, such commission from above
I have received, to answer thy desire
Of knowledge within bounds; beyond abstain   120
To ask, nor let thine own inventions hope
Things not revealed, which th' invisible King,
Only omniscient, hath suppressed in night,
To none communicable in earth or heaven:
Enough is left besides to search and know.   125
But knowledge is as food, and needs no less
Her temperance over appetite, to know
In measure what the mind may well contain,
Oppresses else with surfeit, and soon turns
Wisdom to folly, as nourishment to wind.   130
    "Know then, that after Lucifer from heav'n
(So call him, brighter once amidst the host
Of angels, than that star the stars among)
Fell with his flaming legions through the deep
Into his place, and the great Son returned   135
Victorious with his saints, th' Omnipotent
Eternal Father from his throne beheld
Their multitude, and to his Son thus spake.
    " 'At least our envious foe hath failed, who thought
All like himself rebellious, by whose aid   140
This inaccessible high strength, the seat
Of Deity supreme, us dispossessed,
He trusted to have seized, and into fraud
Drew many, whom their place knows here no more;
Yet far the greater part have kept, I see,   145
Their station, heav'n yet populous retains
Number sufficient to possess her realms
Though wide, and this high temple to frequent
With ministeries due and solemn rites:
But lest his heart exalt him in the harm   150
Already done, to have dispeopled heav'n,
My damage fondly deemed, I can repair
That detriment, if such it be to lose

---

116. *infer:* (L *inferre* to bring about) make.
121. *inventions:* powers of discovery, as well as discoveries. Eccles. 7.29: "God hath made man upright; but they have sought out many inventions [i.e., subtleties, falsehoods]."
122–23. Cf. 1 Tim. 1.17: ". . . the King eternal, immortal, invisible, the only wise God. . . ."
139. *At least:* a misprint for "at last"?
142. *us dispossessed:* we having been dispossessed.
143. *fraud:* deception, error.
144. Cf. Job 7.10: "He shall return no more to his house, neither shall his place know him any more."
152. *fondly:* foolishly.

Self-lost, and in a moment will create
Another world, out of one man a race   155
Of men innumerable, there to dwell,
Not here, till by degrees of merit raised
They open to themselves at length the way
Up hither, under long obedience tried,
And earth be changed to heav'n, and heav'n to earth,   160
One kingdom, joy and union without end.
Meanwhile inhabit lax, ye Powers of heav'n;
And thou my Word, begotten Son, by thee
This I perform, speak thou, and be it done:
My overshadowing Spirit and might with thee   165
I send along, ride forth, and bid the deep
Within appointed bounds be heav'n and earth,
Boundless the deep, because I am who fill
Infinitude, nor vacuous the space.
Though I uncircumscribed myself retire,   170
And put not forth my goodness, which is free
To act or not, necessity and chance
Approach not me, and what I will is fate.'
    "So spake th' Almighty, and to what he spake
His Word, the Filial Godhead, gave effect.   175
Immediate are the acts of God, more swift
Than time or motion, but to human ears
Cannot without process of speech be told,
So told as earthly notion can receive.
Great triumph and rejoicing was in heav'n   180
When such was heard declared the Almighty's will;
Glory they sung to the Most High, good will
To future men, and in their dwellings peace:
Glory to him whose just avenging ire
Had driven out th' ungodly from his sight   185
And th' habitations of the just; to him

154–61. Cf. St. Augustine, *City of God* XXII.i (trans. Marcus Dods): "[God] at the same time foresaw what good He Himself would bring out of the evil, and how from this mortal race, deservedly and justly condemned, He would by this grace collect, as now He does, a people so numerous, that He thus fills up and repairs the blank made by the fallen angels, and that thus that . . . heavenly city is not defrauded of the full number of its citizens, but perhaps may even rejoice in a still more overflowing population."
162. *inhabit lax*: dwell loose, i.e., spread out and fill the vacancies left by the fallen angels.
163. Cf. III.170n. and John 1.1–4, p. 456.
165. Cf. Luke 1.35, p. 455. "And the angel answered and said unto her, The Holy Ghost shall come upon thee, and the power of the Highest shall overshadow thee: therefore also that holy thing which shall be born of thee shall be called the Son of God."
168–73. If God fills *infinitude*, the universe could not have been created out of nothing. And even if God had *retired* from Chaos, or was not making his influence felt there, that did not mean that *fate* or *chance* ruled there. Nor was God forced by necessity to make the universe. Creation was an act of his free will. See *CD*, pp. 401–2 and 409.
179. *notion*: intellect.
182–83. Cf. Luke 2.13–14: "And suddenly there was with the angel a multitude of the heavenly host praising God, and saying, 'Glory to God in the highest, and on earth peace, good will toward men.' "

Glory and praise, whose wisdom had ordained
Good out of evil to create, instead
Of Spirits malign a better race to bring
Into their vacant room, and thence diffuse   190
His good to worlds and ages infinite.
So sang the hierarchies: meanwhile the Son
On his great expedition now appeared,
Girt with omnipotence, with radiance crowned
Of majesty divine, sapience and love   195
Immense, and all his Father in him shone.
About his chariot numberless were poured
Cherub and Seraph, Potentates and Thrones,
And Virtues, winged Spirits, and chariots winged,
From the armory of God, where stand of old   200
Myriads between two brazen mountains lodged
Against a solemn day, harnessed at hand,
Celestial equipage; and now came forth
Spontaneous, for within them spirit lived,
Attendant on their Lord: heav'n opened wide   205
Her ever-during gates, harmonious sound
On golden hinges moving, to let forth
The King of Glory in his powerful Word
And Spirit coming to create new worlds.
On heav'nly ground they stood, and from the shore   210
They viewed the vast immeasurable abyss
Outrageous as a sea, dark, wasteful, wild,
Up from the bottom turned by furious winds
And surging waves, as mountains to assault
Heav'n's highth, and with the center mix the pole.   215
    " 'Silence, ye troubled waves, and thou deep, peace,'
Said then th' Omnific Word, 'your discord end:'
    "Nor stayed, but on the wings of Cherubim
Uplifted, in paternal glory rode
Far into chaos, and the world unborn;   220
For chaos heard his voice: him all his train
Followed in bright procession to behold
Creation, and the wonders of his might.
Then stayed the fervid wheels, and in his hand

194. Cf. Ps. 18.39: "For thou hast girded me with strength unto the battle."
201. Cf. Zech. 6.1: "And I turned, and lifted up mine eyes, and looked, and, behold, there
   came four chariots out from between two mountains; and the mountains were mountains of
   brass."
202. *Against:* in preparation for. *solemn:* appointed, festive, holy, important.
204. Cf. Ezek. 1.20, p. 449.
206–8. *during:* lasting. Cf. Ps. 24.9: "Lift up your heads, O ye gates; even lift them up, ye
   everlasting doors; and the King of glory shall come in."
212. *Outrageous:* violent.
216. Cf. Mark 4.39: "And he arose, and rebuked the wind, and said unto the sea, Peace, be
   still. And the wind ceased, and there was a great calm."
217. *Omnific:* all-creating.
224. *fervid:* burning.

He took the golden compasses, prepared   225
In God's eternal store, to circumscribe
This universe, and all created things:
One foot he centered, and the other turned
Round through the vast profundity obscure,
And said, 'Thus far extend, thus far thy bounds,   230
This be thy just circumference, O world.'
Thus God the heav'n created, thus the earth,
Matter unformed and void: darkness profound
Covered th' abyss: but on the wat'ry calm
His brooding wings the Spirit of God outspread,   235
And vital virtue infused, and vital warmth
Throughout the fluid mass, but downward purged
The black tartareous cold infernal dregs
Adverse to life. then founded, then conglobed
Like things to like, the rest to several place   240
Disparted, and between spun out the air,
And earth self-balanced on her center hung.
    " 'Let there be light,' said God, and forthwith light
Ethereal, first of things, quintessence pure
Sprung from the deep, and from her native east   245
To journey through the airy gloom began,
Sphered in a radiant cloud, for yet the sun
Was not; she in a cloudy tabernacle
Sojourned the while. God saw the light was good;
And light from darkness by the hemisphere   250
Divided: light the day, and darkness night
He named. Thus was the first day ev'n and morn:
Nor passed uncelebrated, nor unsung
By the celestial choirs, when orient light
Exhaling first from darkness they beheld;   255
Birthday of heav'n and earth; with joy and shout
The hollow universal orb they filled,
And touched their golden harps, and hymning praised

225. Cf. Prov. 8.27.
232. From here on the account of creation follows that in Genesis; pp. 429–31.
233. *profound*: L *pro* out of + *fundus* bottom.
235. *brooding wings*. The Hebrew word translated in the King James version as "moved" also
    means "brood" or "hover." Cf. I.20–22 and note.
236. *virtue*: power.
238. *tartareous*: pertaining to Tartarus, in Greek myth the *infernal* region below Hades. The
    dregs are stuff other than the elements that constitute the universe.
239. *founded*: (L *fundere* to pour, melt, fuse) mixed together. *conglobed*: rolled into a ball.
242. Cf. Job 26.7: "He stretcheth out the north over the empty place, and hangeth the earth
    upon nothing."
244. *quintessence*: the fifth element, of which heavenly things are made. See "The Universe,"
    pp. 461–63.
248. Cf. Ps. 19.4: "Their line is gone out through all the earth, and their words to the end of
    the world. In them hath he set a tabernacle for the sun."
252. *ev'n and morn*: night and day, or one twenty-four-hour period measured, as the Jews measure,
    from sundown to sundown. Cf. Gen. 1.5, p. 352.

God and his works, Creator him they sung,
Both when first evening was, and when first morn.   260
    "Again, God said, 'Let there be firmament
Amid the waters, and let it divide
The waters from the waters': and God made
The firmament, expanse of liquid, pure,
Transparent, elemental air, diffused   265
In circuit to the uttermost convex
Of this great round: partition firm and sure,
The waters underneath from those above
Dividing: for as earth, so he the world
Built on circumfluous waters calm, in wide   270
Crystálline ocean, and the loud misrule
Of Chaos far removed, lest fierce extremes
Contiguous might distemper the whole frame:
And heav'n he named the firmament: so ev'n
And morning chorus sung the second day.   275
    "The earth was formed, but in the womb as yet
Of waters, embryon immature involved,
Appeared not: over all the face of earth
Main ocean flowed, not idle, but with warm
Prolific humor soft'ning all her globe,   280
Fermented the great mother to conceive,
Satiate with genial moisture, when God said,
'Be gathered now ye waters under heav'n
Into one place, and let dry land appear.'
Immediately the mountains huge appear   285
Emergent, and their broad bare backs upheave
Into the clouds, their tops ascend the sky:
So high as heaved the tumid hills, so low
Down sunk a hollow bottom broad and deep,
Capacious bed of waters: thither they   290
Hasted with glad precipitance, uprolled
As drops on dust conglobing from the dry;
Part rise in crystal wall, or ridge direct,

261. *firmament.* See "The Universe," pp. 461–63.
264. *liquid:* clear, transparent, bright.
267. *this great round:* the universe.
269–70. Cf. Ps. 24.2: "For he [the Lord] hath founded it [the world] upon the seas, and established it upon the floods.
270. *circumfluous waters.* Cf. 236–42n above.
271. *Crystalline ocean:* not the crystalline sphere. See "The Universe," pp. 461–63.
273. *distemper:* disturb the order and mixture of the elements. *frame.* See II.924n.
274. *heav'n:* the sky.
277. *involved:* enfolded.
278f. Cf. *Met.* 1.416f.
279. *Main:* (as in "mainland," or "the ocean main") of great expanse.
280. *humor:* moisture.
282. *genial:* (L *genialis,* from *gignere* to beget) generative; cf. *Prolific humor* two lines above.
288. *tumid:* swollen.
290–306. Cf. Ps. 104, pp. 439–41.

For haste; such flight the great command impressed
On the swift floods: as armies at the call   295
Of trumpet (for of armies thou hast heard)
Troop to their standard, so the wat'ry throng,
Wave rolling after wave, where way they found,
If steep, with torrent rapture, if through plain,
Soft-ebbing; nor withstood them rock or hill,   300
But they, or under ground, or circuit wide
With serpent error wand'ring, found their way,
And on the washy ooze deep channels wore;
Easy, ere God had bid the ground be dry,
All but within those banks, where rivers now   305
Stream, and perpetual draw their humid train.
The dry land, earth, and the great receptacle
Of congregated waters he called seas:
And saw that it was good, and said, 'Let th' earth
Put forth the verdant grass, herb yielding seed,   310
And fruit-tree yielding fruit after her kind;
Whose seed is in herself upon the earth.'
He scarce had said, when the bare earth, till then
Desert and bare, unsightly, unadorned,
Brought forth the tender grass, whose verdure clad   315
Her universal face with pleasant green,
Then herbs of every leaf, that sudden flow'red
Op'ning their various colors, and made gay
Her bosom smelling sweet: and these scarce blown,
Forth flourished thick the clust'ring vine, forth crept   320
The swelling gourd, up stood the corny reed
Embattled in her field: add the humble shrub,
And bush with frizzled hair implicit: last
Rose as in dance the stately trees, and spread
Their branches hung with copious fruit; or gemmed   325
Their blossoms: with high woods the hills were crowned,
With tufts the valleys and each fountain side,
With borders long the rivers. That earth now
Seemed like to heav'n, a seat where gods might dwell,
Or wander with delight, and love to haunt   330
Her sacred shades: though God had yet not rained
Upon the earth, and man to till the ground
None was, but from the earth a dewy mist

299. *rapture:* L *rapere* to sweep away.
302. Cf. *mazy error*, IV.239.
303. *washy ooze:* mud like that of a wash, or land alternately covered and exposed by the movement
of the sea.
319. *blown:* blossomed.
321. *corny:* (L *cornus* horn) hard as horn. *reed:* cane, bamboo.
322. *humble* (L *humus* ground) low-growing.
323. *implicit:* (L *implicare* to infold) tangled.
325. *gemmed:* L *gemmare* to put forth buds.

Went up and watered all the ground, and each
Plant of the field, which ere it was in the earth   335
God made, and every herb, before it grew
On the green stem; God saw that it was good:
So ev'n and morn recorded the third day.
    "Again th' Almighty spake: 'Let there be lights
High in th' expanse of heaven to divide   340
The day from night; and let them be for signs,
For seasons, and for days, and circling years,
And let them be for lights as I ordain
Their office in the firmament of heav'n
To give light on the earth'; and it was so.   345
And God made two great lights, great for their use
To man, the greater to have rule by day,
The less by night altern: and made the stars,
And set them in the firmament of heav'n
To illuminate the earth, and rule the day   350
In their vicissitude, and rule the night,
And light from darkness to divide. God saw,
Surveying his great work, that it was good:
For of celestial bodies first the sun
A mighty sphere he framed, unlightsome first,   355
Though of ethereal mold: then formed the moon
Globose, and every magnitude of stars,
And sowed with stars the heav'n thick as a field:
Of light by far the greater part he took,
Transplanted from her cloudy shrine, and placed   360
In the sun's orb, made porous to receive
And drink the liquid light, firm to retain
Her gathered beams, great palace now of light.
Hither as to their fountain other stars
Repairing, in their golden urns draw light,   365
And hence the morning planet gilds her horns;
By tincture or reflection they augment
Their small peculiar, though from human sight
So far remote, with dimunition seen.
First in his east the glorious lamp was seen,   370
Regent of day, and all th' horizon round
Invested with bright rays, jocund to run

338. *recorded:* bore witness to.
351. *vicissitude:* regular alternation.
356. *mold:* stuff.
360. *cloudy shrine.* Cf. 248.
366. Through his telescope Galileo had discovered that Venus has phases, like the moon. In
    her first quarter her image was crescent-shaped.
367. *tincture:* absorption, as in dyeing.
368. *peculiar:* (L *peculium* private property) own (light).
371. *horizon:* rim of the image of the sun.

His longitude through heav'n's high road: the gray
Dawn, and the Pleiades before him danced
Shedding sweet influence: less bright the moon,   375
But opposite in leveled west was set
His mirror, with full face borrowing her light
From him, for other light she needed none
In that aspéct, and still that distance keeps
Till night, then in the east her turn she shines,   380
Revolved on heav'n's great axle, and her reign
With thousand lesser lights dividual holds,
With thousand thousand stars, that then appeared
Spangling the hemisphere: then first adorned
With their bright luminaries that set and rose,   385
Glad evening and glad morn crowned the fourth day.
   And God said, 'Let the waters generate
Reptile with spawn abundant, living soul:
And let fowl fly above the earth, with wings
Displayed on the op'n firmament of heav'n.'   390
And God created the great whales, and each
Soul living, each that crept, which plenteously
The waters generated by their kinds,
And every bird of wing after his kind;
And saw that it was good, and blessed them, saying,   395
'Be fruitful, multiply, and in the seas
And lakes and running streams the waters fill;
And let the fowl be multiplied on the earth.'
Forthwith the sounds and seas, each creek and bay
With fry innumerable swarm, and shoals   400
Of fish that with their fins and shining scales
Glide under the green wave, in sculls that oft
Bank the mid-sea: part single or with mate
Graze the seaweed their pasture, and through groves
Of coral stray, or sporting with quick glance   405
Show to the sun their waved coats dropped with gold,
Or in their pearly shells at ease, attend
Moist nutriment, or under rocks their food

373. *longitude*: distance from east to west.
374. Cf. Job 38.31: "Canst thou bind the sweet influences of Pleiades, or loose the bands of Orion?"
379. *In that aspect*: i.e., when full.
382. *dividual*: divided.
386. *Glad*: (OE *glæd* bright, glad) bright, gay, beautiful.
388. *Reptile*: (L *repere* to creep) snakes, lizards, etc.
390. *Displayed* (L *displicare* to unfold) spread out.
400. *shoals*. Like "schools" and perhaps *sculls*, two lines below, *shoals* is related to OE *scolu*, *sceolu*, a crowd.
403. *bank*: form a bank of, make a wave in.
406. *dropped*: flecked.
407. *attend*: (L *attendere* to stretch) await or watch for.

In jointed armor watch: on smooth the seal,
And bended dolphins play: part huge of bulk   410
Wallowing unwieldy, enormous in their gait
Tempest the ocean: there leviathan
Hugest of living creatures, on the deep
Stretched like a promontory sleeps or swims,
And seems a moving land, and at his gills   415
Draws in, and at his trunk spouts out a sea.
Meanwhile the tepid caves, and fens and shores
Their brood as numerous hatch, from th' egg that soon
Bursting with kindly rupture forth disclosed
Their callow young, but feathered soon and fledge   420
They summed their pens, and soaring th' air sublime
With clang despised the ground, under a cloud
In prospect; there the eagle and the stork
On cliffs and cedar tops their eyries build:
Part loosely wing the region, part more wise   425
In common, ranged in figure wedge their way,
Intelligent of seasons, and set forth
Their aery caravan high over seas
Flying, and over lands with mutual wing
Easing their flight; so steers the prudent crane   430
Her annual voyage, borne on winds; the air
Floats, as they pass, fanned with unnumbered plumes:
From branch to branch the smaller birds with song
Solaced the woods, and spread their painted wings
Till ev'n, nor then the solemn nightingale   435
Ceased warbling, but all night tuned her soft lays:
Others on silver lakes and rivers bathed
Their downy breast; the swan, with archèd neck
Between her white wings mantling proudly, rows
Her state with oary feet: yet oft they quit   440
The dank, and rising on stiff pennons, tow'r

412. *leviathan*. Cf. I.200–8n.
419. *kindly*: natural.
420. *callow*: without feathers. *fledge*: fit to fly.
421. *summed their pens*: brought their feathers to full growth.
422–23. *clang*: cry, like that of cranes or geese. *despised*: literally, looked down upon (*the ground*, which seemed [*In prospect*] to be *under a cloud* of birds).
425. *loosely*: separately. *region*: the middle air; see 442 and note. See "The Universe," pp. 461–63.
426. *In common*: in a convoy.
429–30. Ancient lore was that cranes rested in flight by placing their necks on the backs of birds in front of them. But Fowler notes St. Basil's belief that storks in flight "used their wings to support [those of] their ancient parents."
432. *Floats*: moves in waves.
434. *painted*: colored.
439. I.e.: proudly mantling herself between her white wings, or wearing her wings like a cloak. Cf. V.279.
440. *state*: a person of high rank: i.e., she rows her ladyship, as lords and ladies were rowed on the Thames.
441. *dank*: pond, lake, pool. *tow'r*: to fly high into.

The mid-aerial sky: others on ground
Walked firm; the crested cock whose clarion sounds
The silent hours, and th' other whose gay train
Adorns him, colored with the florid hue   445
Of rainbows and starry eyes. The waters thus
With fish replenished, and the air with fowl,
Evening and morn solemnized the fifth day.
    "The sixth, and the creation last arose
With evening harps and matin, when God said,   450
'Let th' earth bring forth soul living in her kind,
Cattle and creeping things, and beast of the earth,
Each in their kind.' The earth obeyed, and straight
Op'ning her fertile womb teemed at a birth
Innumerous living creatures, perfect forms,   455
Limbed and full grown: out of the ground up rose
As from his lair the wild beast where he wons
In forest wild, in thicket, brake, or den;
Among the trees in pairs they rose, they walked:
The cattle in the fields and meadows green: 460
Those rare and solitary, these in flocks
Pasturing at once, and in broad herds upsprung.
The grassy clods now calved, now half appeared
The tawny lion, pawing to get free
His hinder parts, then springs as broke from bonds,   465
And rampant shakes his brinded mane; the ounce,
The libbard, and the tiger, as the mole
Rising, the crumbled earth above them threw
In hillocks; the swift stag from under ground
Bore up his branching head: scarce from his mold   470
Behemoth biggest born of earth upheaved
His vastness: fleeced the flocks and bleating rose,
As plants: ambiguous between sea and land
The river-horse and scaly crocodile.
At once came forth whatever creeps the ground,   475
Insect or worm; those waved their limber fans

---

442. *mid-aerial sky*: mid-air, the region of clouds and cold. Cf. *two black clouds . . . encounter*
    in mid-air, II.714–18.
444. *th' other*: the peacock.
447. *replenished*: (L *plenus* full) fully supplied, perfected, stocked. Cf. VIII.371n.
450. *matin*: morning.
454. *teemed*: bore, brought forth.
457. *wons*: dwells.
461. *rare*: dispersed.
466. *brinded*: brindled.
467. *libbard*: leopard.
471. *Behemoth*: the name given by the translator of the King James version to the dragon-crocodile-
    hippopotamuslike amphibian described in Job 40.15–41.34, and also called leviathan. Com-
    mentators had identified the beast as an elephant, and as Fowler notes, line 474 suggests that
    Milton here was thinking of a land animal.
474. *river-horse*: Gk. *hippos* horse; *potamos* river.
476. *worm*: any animal that worms its way.

For wings, and smallest lineaments exact
In all the liveries decked of summer's pride
With spots of gold and purple, azure and green:
These as a line their long dimension drew,   480
Streaking the ground with sinuous trace; not all
Minims of nature; some of serpent kind
Wondrous in length and corpulence involved
Their snaky folds, and added wings. First crept
The parsimonious emmet, provident   485
Of future, in small room large heart enclosed,
Pattern of just equality perhaps
Hereafter, joined in her popular tribes
Of commonalty: swarming next appeared
The female bee that feeds her husband drone   490
Deliciously, and builds her waxen cells
With honey stored: the rest are numberless,
And thou their natures know'st, and gav'st them names,
Needless to thee repeated; nor unknown
The serpent subtlest beast of all the field,   495
Of huge extent sometimes, with brazen eyes
And hairy mane terrific, though to thee.
Not noxious, but obedient at thy call.
Now heav'n in all her glory shone, and rolled
Her motions, as the great First Mover's hand   500
First wheeled their course; earth in her rich attire
Consummate lovely smiled; air, water, earth,
By fowl, fish, beast, was flown, was swum, was walked
Frequent; and of the sixth day yet remained;
There wanted yet the master work, the end   505
Of all yet done; a creature who not prone
And brute as other creatures, but endued
With sanctity of reason, might erect
His stature, and upright with front serene

478. *pride:* glory.
482. *Minims:* smallest animals.
483. *corpulence:* bulk. *involved:* coiled.
484. Cf. Isa. 30.6: ". . . the land of trouble and anguish, from whence come the young and old
   lion, the viper and fiery flying serpent."
485. *parsimonious:* (L *parcere to spare*) thrifty. *emmet:* ant.
486. *large heart:* great wisdom. See I.437–46n.
488–89. I.e., united in self-governing groups of common people.
502. *Consummate.* See V.481n.
504. *Frequent:* (L *frequens* crowded) in throngs.
505–16. The syntax of this sentence is elliptical: There wanted yet . . . a creature who . . . might
   erect . . . and . . . govern . . . and from these virtues might be sufficiently magnanimous to
   correspond with heaven yet sufficiently grateful to acknowledge whence his good descends and
   (consequently?), with his heart . . . directed in devotion thither (i.e., whence his good descends),
   to adore, etc. *end:* purpose. *sanctity:* the virtue or blessing of holiness which sets the sanctified
   apart. *front:* face. *Magnanimous:* great-souled, noble, high-minded, self-respecting. *correspond:*
   confer, consult, converse. The notion that man's erect stance is a sign of his superiority over
   all other animals is ancient.

Govern the rest, self-knowing, and from thence   510
Magnanimous to correspond with heav'n,
But grateful to acknowledge whence his good
Descends, thither with heart and voice and eyes
Directed in devotion, to adore
And worship God supreme, who made him chief   515
Of all his works: therefore th' Omnipotent
Eternal Father (for where is not he
Present) thus to his Son audibly spake.
  " 'Let us make now man in our image, man
In our similitude, and let them rule   520
Over the fish and fowl of sea and air,
Beast of the field, and over all the earth,
And every creeping thing that creeps the ground.'
This said, he formed thee, Adam, thee O man
Dust of the ground, and in thy nostrils breathed   525
The breath of life; in his own image he
Created thee, in the image of God
Express, and thou becam'st a living soul.
Male he created thee, but thy consórt
Female for race; then blessed mankind, and said,   530
'Be fruitful, multiply, and fill the earth,
Subdue it, and throughout dominion hold
Over fish of the sea, and fowl of the air,
And every living thing that moves on the earth.'
Wherever thus created, for no place   535
Is yet distinct by name, thence, as thou know'st
He brought thee into this delicious grove,
This garden, planted with the trees of God,
Delectable both to behold and taste;
And freely all their pleasant fruit for food   540
Gave thee, all sorts are here that all th' earth yields,
Variety without end; but of the tree
Which tasted works knowledge of good and evil,
Thou may'st not; in the day thou eat'st, thou di'st;
Death is the penalty imposed, beware,   545
And govern well thy appetite, lest Sin
Surprise thee, and her black attendant Death.
Here finished he, and all that he had made
Viewed, and behold all was entirely good;
So ev'n and morn accomplished the sixth day: 550
Yet not till the Creator from his work
Desisting, though unwearied, up returned
Up to the heav'n of heav'ns his high abode,

528. *Express*: exact. Cf. Heb. 1.1–3: "God . . . hath . . . spoken to us by his Son, Who being
    . . . the express image of his person, etc."
537. *delicious*. See IV.132n.

Thence to behold his new-created world
Th' addition of his empire, how it showed   555
In prospct from his throne, how good, how fair,
Answering his great idea. Up he rode
Followed with acclamation and the sound
Symphonious of ten thousand harps that tuned
Angelic harmonies: the earth, the air   560
Resounded (thou remember'st, for thou heard'st),
The heav'ns and all the constellations rung,
The planets in their stations list'ning stood,
While the bright pomp ascended jubilant.
'Open, ye everlasting gates,' they sung,   565
'Open, ye heav'ns, your living doors; let in
The great Creator from his work returned
Magnificent, his six days' work, a world;
Open, and henceforth oft; for God will deign
To visit oft the dwellings of just men   570
Delighted, and with frequent intercourse
Thither will send his wingèd messengers
On errands of supernal grace.' So sung
The glorious train ascending: he through heav'n,
That opened wide her blazing portals, led   575
To God's eternal house direct the way,
A broad and ample road, whose dust is gold
And pavement stars, as stars to thee appear,
Seen in the Galaxy, that Milky Way
Which nightly as a circling zone thou seest   580
Powdered with stars. And now on earth the seventh
Evening arose in Eden, for the sun
Was set, and twilight from the east came on,
Forerunning night; when at the holy mount
Of heav'n's high-seated top, th' imperial throne   585
Of Godhead, fixed forever firm and sure,
The Filial Power arrived, and sat him down
With his great Father, for he also went
Invisible, yet stayed (such privilege
Hath Omnipresence) and the work ordained,   590
Author and end of all things, and from work
Now resting, blessed and hallowed the sev'nth day,

557. *idea*: (Gk *idein* to see) eternal archetype or pattern, as in Plato; image or concept (in the mind of God).
559. *Symphonious*: harmonious.
564. *pomp*: procession. *jubilant*: (L *jubilum* a wild cry, shout) making a joyful noise.
565–66. Cf. 206–8n.
575. *blazing*: effulgent, radiant.
580. *zone*: belt.
588–90. *he*: the Father. *went Invisible*. Cf. 165 and 196. *ordained*: ordered, enacted.

As resting on that day from all his work,
But not in silence holy kept; the harp
Had work and rested not, the solemn pipe,   595
And dulcimer, all organs of sweet stop,
All sounds on fret by string or golden wire
Tempered soft tunings, intermixed with voice
Choral or unison: of incense clouds
Fuming from golden censers hid the mount.   600
Creation and the six day's acts they sung:
'Great are thy works, Jehovah, infinite
Thy power; what thought can measure thee or tongue
Relate thee; greater now in thy return
Than from the giant angels; thee that day   605
Thy thunders magnified; but to create
Is greater than created to destroy.
Who can impair thee, mighty king, or bound
Thy empire? Easily the proud attempt
Of Spirits apostate and their counsels vain   610
Thou hast repelled, while impiously they thought
Thee to diminish, and from thee withdraw
The number of thy worshipers. Who seeks
To lessen thee, against his purpose serves
To manifest the more thy might: his evil   615
Thou usest, and from thence creat'st more good.
Witness this new-made world, another heav'n
From heaven gate not far, founded in view
On the clear hyaline, the glassy sea;
Of amplitude almost immense, with stars   620
Numerous, and every star perhaps a world
Of destined habitation; but thou know'st
Their seasons: among these the seat of men,
Earth with her nether ocean circumfused,
Their pleasant dwelling-place. Thrice happy men,   625
And sons of men, whom God hath thus advanced,

596. *dulcimer.* Fowler notes that "the dulcimer is here not the stringed instrument usually called by that name, but the Hebrew 'bagpipe' (Gk *symphonia*)." *organs:* wind instruments.
598. *Tempered:* brought into harmony. *tunings:* musical sounds.
599–600. Cf. Rev. 8.3. "And another angel came and stood at the altar, having a golden censer; and there was given unto him much incense, that he should offer it with the prayers of all saints upon the golden altar which was before the throne."
599. *Choral:* in parts.
608. *impair:* (LL *impejorare* to make worse) diminish, lessen.
619. See "The Universe," pp. 461–63. *hyaline.* From the word for glass used in the Greek of Rev. 4.6.
620. *immense:* (L *im* not + *mensus* measured) immeasurable.
621–22. See III.566n.
623. *seasons.* As in Acts 1.6–7: "They asked of [Christ] . . . wilt thou at this time restore again the kingdom of Israel? And he said . . . it is not for you to know the times or the seasons, which the Father hath put in his own power."
624. *nether ocean:* the waters below the firmament. Cf. 261–73.

Created in his image, there to dwell
And worship him, and in reward to rule
Over his works, on earth, in sea, or air,
And multiply a race of worshipers   630
Holy and just: thrice happy if they know
Their happiness, and persevere upright.'
    "So sung they, and the empyrean rung,
With hallelujahs: thus was Sabbath kept.
And thy request think now fulfilled, that asked   635
How first this world and face of things began,
And what before thy memory was done
From the beginning, that posterity
Informed by thee might know; if else thou seek'st
Aught, not surpassing human measure, say."   640

Book VIII

The Argument

Adam inquires concerning celestial motions, is doubtfully answered,
and exhorted to search rather things more worthy of knowledge: Adam
assents, and still desirous to detain Raphael, relates to him what he
remembered since his own creation, his placing in Paradise, his talk
with God concerning solitude and fit society, his first meeting and
nuptials with Eve, his discourse with the angel thereupon; who after
admonitions repeated departs.

The angel ended, and in Adam's ear
So charming left his voice, that he a while
Thought him still speaking, still stood fixed to hear;
Then as new-waked thus gratefully replied.
"What thanks sufficient, or what recompense   5
Equal have I to render thee, divine
Historian, who thus largely hast allayed
The thirst I had of knowledge, and vouchsafed
This friendly condescension to relate
Things else by me unsearchable, now heard   10

632. *persevere.* In theology perseverance means "continuance in a state of grace until it is suc-
    ceeded by a state of glory."
634. *hallelujahs.* See II.243n.
VIII.1–4. When he divided Book VII of the first, ten-book edition into Books VII and VIII of
    the present, twelve-book edition, Milton replaced a line reading "To whom thus Adam gratefully
    replied" with these introductory lines.
2. *charming:* (L *canere* to sing, as in English *chant*) spell-binding.

With wonder, but delight, and, as is due,
With glory attribúted to the high
Creator; something yet of doubt remains,
Which only thy solution can resolve.
When I behold this goodly frame, this world   15
Of heav'n and earth consisting, and compute
Their magnitudes, this earth a spot, a grain,
An atom, with the firmament compared
And all her numbered stars, that seem to roll
Spaces incomprehensible (for such   20
Their distance argues and their swift return
Diurnal) merely to officiate light
Round this opacous earth, this punctual spot,
One day and night; in all their vast survey
Useless besides; reasoning I oft admire,   25
How nature wise and frugal could commit
Such disproportions, with superfluous hand
So many nobler bodies to create,
Greater so manifold, to this one use,
For aught appears, and on their orbs impose   30
Such restless revolution day by day
Repeated, while the sedentary earth,
That better might with far less compass move,
Served by more noble than herself, attains
Her end without least motion, and receives,   35
As tribute such a sumless journey brought
Of incorporeal speed, her warmth and light;
Speed, to describe whose swiftness number fails."
    So spake our sire, and by his count'nance seemed
Ent'ring on studious thoughts abstruse, which Eve   40
Perceiving where she sat retired in sight,
With lowliness majestic from her seat,
And grace that won who saw to wish her stay,
Rose, and went forth among her fruits and flow'rs,
To visit how they prospered, bud and bloom,   45
Her nursery; they at her coming sprung

11. *but.* This conjunction suggests that *wonder* implies some puzzlement or effort to understand.
14. *solution:* (L *solvere* to loosen) explanation.
15. *frame.* See II.924n.
16. *compute:* (L *com* + *putare* to reckon, think). take account of, consider.
19. *numbered:* numerous.
22. *officiate:* supply.
23. *opacous:* L *opacus* shady, dark. *punctual:* (L *punctus* point) as small as a point.
25. *admire:* wonder.
29. *Greater so manifold:* so many times greater.
30. *For aught appears:* as far as can be seen.
36. *sumless journey:* immeasurable distance.
45. *visit:* (L *videre* to see) to go to see.
46. *Her nursery:* the objects of her nursing.

And touched by her fair tendance gladlier grew.
Yet went she not as not with such discourse
Delighted, or not capable her ear
Of what was high: such pleasure she reserved,   50
Adam relating, she sole auditress;
Her husband the relater she preferred
Before the angel, and of him to ask
Chose rather; he, she knew would intermix
Grateful digressions, and solve high dispute   55
With conjugal caresses, from his lip
Not words alone pleased her. O when meet now
Such pairs, in love and mutual honor joined?
With goddess-like demeanor forth she went;
Not unattended, for on her as queen   60
A pomp of winning Graces waited still,
And from about her shot darts of desire
Into all eyes to wish her still in sight.
And Raphael now to Adam's doubt proposed
Benevolent and facile thus replied.   65
     "To ask or search I blame thee not, for heav'n
Is as the book of God before thee set,
Wherein to read his wondrous works, and learn
His seasons, hours, or days, or months, or years:
This to attain, whether heav'n move or earth,   70
Imports not, if thou reckon right; the rest
From man or angel the great Architect
Did wisely to conceal, and not divulge
His secrets to be scanned by them who ought
Rather admire; or if they list to try   75
Conjecture, he his fabric of the heav'ns
Hath left to their disputes, perhaps to move
His laughter at their quaint opinions wide
Hereafter, when they come to model heav'n
And calculate the stars, how they will wield   80
The mighty frame, how build, unbuild, contrive
To save appearances, how gird the sphere
With centric and eccentric scribbled o'er,
Cycle and epicycle, orb in orb:

55. *high dispute*: profound debate.
61. *pomp*. See V.353n. *Graces*. See IV.267n.
65. *facile*: easy and mild in manner.
74. *scanned*: judged critically.
75. *admire*: marvel.
76. *fabric*: structural plan, design.
78. *wide*: as in "wide of the mark."
80. *calculate*: arrange, design; or, anticipate movements mathematically. *wield*: manage, deal with.
81–82. *contrive / To save appearances*: try to find explanations for the apparent inadequacies of their hypotheses.
83–84. Both Ptolemaic and Copernican astronomies restorted to complicated theories to explain variations (apparent irregularities) in the motions of the planets.

Already by thy reasoning this I guess,   85
Who art to lead thy offspring, and supposest
That bodies bright and greater should not serve
The less not bright, nor heav'n such journeys run,
Earth sitting still, when she alone receives
The benefit: consider first, that great   90
Or bright infers not excellence: the earth
Though, in comparison of heav'n, so small,
Nor glistering, may of solid good contain
More plenty than the sun that barren shines,
Whose virtue on itself works no effect,   95
But in the fruitful earth; there first received
His beams, unactive else, their vigor find.
Yet not to earth are those bright luminaries
Officious, but to thee earth's habitant.
And for the heav'n's wide circuit, let it speak   100
The Maker's high magnificence, who built
So spacious, and his line stretched out so far;
That man may know he dwells not in his own;
An edifice too large for him to fill,
Lodged in a small partition, and the rest   105
Ordained for uses to his Lord best known.
The swiftness of those circles áttribute,
Though numberless, to his omnipotence,
That to corporeal substances could add
Speed almost spiritual; me thou think'st not slow,   110
Who since the morning hour set out from heav'n
Where God resides, and ere mid-day arrived
In Eden, distance inexpressible
By numbers that have name. But this I urge,
Admitting motion in the heav'ns, to show   115
Invalid that which thee to doubt it moved;
Not that I so affirm, though so it seem
To thee who hast thy dwelling here on earth.
God to remove his ways from human sense,
Placed heav'n from earth so far, that earthly sight,   120
If it presume, might err in things too high,

91. *infers:* implies, brings about.
96–97. The sun's beams perform no function until the earth has *received* them.
99. *Officious.* Cf. *officiate,* line 22.
100. *speak:* bespeak.
102. Cf. Job 38.5: "Who hath laid the measures thereof, if thou knowest? or who hath stretched the line upon it?"
107. *attribute:* pay tribute.
108. *numberless.* Probably modifies swiftness, as Fowler notes. Cf. 36n.
110. *Speed almost spiritual:* almost the speed of thought. Cf. *incorporeal speed,* line 37.
115–18. Raphael carefully does not grant Adam's assumption that because the planets seem to revolve about the earth, they in fact do.

And no advantage gain. What if the sun
Be center to the world, and other stars
By his attractive virtue and their own
Incited, dance about him various rounds?   125
Their wand'ring course now high, now low, then hid,
Progressive, retrograde, or standing still,
In six thou seest, and what if sev'nth to these
The planet earth, so steadfast though she seem,
Insensibly three difference motions move?   130
Which else to several spheres thou must ascribe,
Moved contrary with thwart obliquities,
Or save the sun his labor, and that swift
Nocturnal and diurnal rhomb supposed,
Invisible else above all stars, the wheel   135
Of day and night; which needs not thy belief,
If earth industrious of herself fetch day
Traveling east, and with her part averse
From the sun's beam meet night, her other part
Still luminous by his ray. What if that light   140
Sent from her through the wide transpicuous air,
To the terrestrial moon be as a star
Enlight'ning her by day, as she by night
This earth? Reciprocal, if land be there,
Fields and inhabitants: her spots thou seest   145
As clouds, and clouds may rain, and rain produce
Fruits in her softened soil, for some to eat
Allotted there; and other suns perhaps
With their attendant moons thou wilt descry
Communicating male and female light,   150

122–40. For background, see "The Universe," pp. 461–63. Raphael simply raises the possibility
that what appears to Adam as movements in the heavens are largely the result of movements
of the earth as it spins on its axis and, like the "other" planets, orbits the sun. Such an hypothesis
should relieve Adam of his doubts about the "disproportions" (line 27) he had found in nature's
design, for it would (1) place the tiny earth elsewhere than the center of the universe, (2)
eliminate the need to imagine the speed (*labor,* line 133) of the sun in his daily orbit of the
earth, and (3) dispense with the *supposed* device of the *primum mobile* (*that swift nocturnal
and diurnal rhomb*), which was, after all, *invisible.* Milton, we may assume, was here more
interested in the nature of scientific speculation and the limits of knowledge than in the details
of the contemporary scientific debate, which would not, in any event, have been relevant to
a dialogue between an angel and prelapsarian man, whose world, incidentally, moved differently
from that of postlapsarian man. Newton was about twenty when Milton wrote these lines, but
Kepler had already suggested that the *attractive virtue* (power) of the sun moved the planets.
See III. 582–83n. *rounds:* circular dances. *wand'ring.* The Greek word *planētēs* means wanderer.
Progressive: moving in the direction of the general planetary course; *retrograde* is the opposite.
three motions. About the third, editors disagree. Adam could not have observed precession of
the equinoxes (a phenomenon with a cycle of nearly 26,000 years) because before the Fall
there were no equinoxes by which to measure precession—the earth's axis then being perpen-
dicular to the plane of its orbit. Fowler, citing J. L. E. Dreyer, *A History of Astronomy from
Thales to Kepler* (1953), p. 328, notes that Copernicus's third motion was not the tilt of the
earth's axis (which causes the semiannual equinoxes) but an incorrectly hypothecated swivel
of the axis that would account for a phenomenon which Adam might have observed (inac-
curately, as it turned out): "that the axis of the earth . . . always points to the same spot in the
celestial sphere." *rhomb:* (Gk *rombos* a top, spinning motion, magic wheel) the *primum mobile.*

Which two great sexes animate the world,
Stored in each orb perhaps with some that live.
For such vast room in nature unpossessed
By living soul, desert and desolate,
Only to shine, yet scarce to cóntribute   155
Each orb a glimpse of light, conveyed so far
Down to this habitable, which returns
Light back to them, is obvious to dispute.
But whether thus these things, or whether not,
Whether the sun predominant in heav'n   160
Rise on the earth, or earth rise on the sun,
He from the east his flaming road begin,
Or she from west her silent course advance
With inoffensive pace that spinning sleeps
On her soft axle, while she paces ev'n,   165
And bears thee soft with the smooth air along,
Solicit not thy thoughts with matters hid,
Leave them to God above, him serve and fear;
Of other creatures, as him pleases best,
Wherever placed, let him dispose: joy thou   170
In what he gives to thee, this Paradise
And thy fair Eve, heav'n is for thee too high
To know what passes there; be lowly wise:
Think only what concerns thee and thy being;
Dream not of other worlds, what creatures there   175
Live, in what state, condition, or degree,
Contented that thus far hath been revealed
Not of earth only but of highest heav'n."
    To whom thus Adam cleared of doubt, replied.
"How fully hast thou satisfied me, pure   180
Intelligence of heav'n, angel serene,
And freed from intricacies, taught to live
The easiest way, nor with perplexing thoughts
To interrupt the sweet of life, from which
God hath bid dwell far off all anxious cares,   185
And not molest us, unless we ourselves
Seek them with wand'ring thoughts, and notions vain.
But apt the mind or fancy is to rove
Unchecked, and of her roving is no end;
Till warned, or by experience taught, she learn,   190
That not to know at large of things remote
From use, obscure and subtle, but to know
That which before us lies in daily life,

153–58. I.e.: For whether such vast room in nature is unpossessed . . . is open to question.
164. *inoffensive*: (L *offendare* to strike against, stumble, injure; Engl. *to offend* to stumble) without
    stumbling.
167. *Solicit*: disturb.
181. *Intelligence*: intelligent or rational being, spirit. *serene*: pure, clear, bright, calm, steady.

Is the prime wisdom; what is more, is fume,
Or emptiness, or fond impertinence,   195
And renders us in things that most concern
Unpracticed, unprepared, and still to seek.
Therefore from this high pitch let us descend
A lower flight, and speak of things at hand
Useful, whence haply mention may arise   200
Of something not unseasonable to ask
By sufferance, and thy wonted favor deigned.
Thee I have heard relating what was done
Ere my remembrance: now hear me relate
My story, which perhaps thou hast not heard;   205
And day is yet not spent; till then thou seest
How subtly to detain thee I devise,
Inviting thee to hear while I relate,
Fond, were it not in hope of thy reply:
For while I sit with thee, I seem in heav'n,   210
And sweeter thy discourse is to my ear
Than fruits of palm-tree pleasantest to thirst
And hunger both, from labor, at the hour
Of sweet repast; they satiate, and soon fill,
Though pleasant, but thy words with grace divine   215
Imbued, bring to their sweetness no satiety."
    To whom thus Raphael answered heav'nly meek.
"Nor are thy lips ungraceful, sire of men,
Nor tongue ineloquent; for God on thee
Abundantly his gifts hath also poured   220
Inward and outward both, his image fair:
Speaking or mute all comeliness and grace
Attends thee, and each word, each motion forms.
Nor less think we in heav'n of thee on earth
Than of our fellow-servant, and inquire   225
Gladly intot he ways of God with man:
For God we see hath honored thee, and set
On man his equal love: say therefore on;
For I that day was absent, as befell,
Bound on a voyage uncouth and obscure,   230
Far on excursion toward the gates of hell;
Squared in full legion (such command we had)
To see that none thence issued forth a spy,
Or enemy, while God was in his work,

---

194. *fume*: vapor; somethng unsubstantial; something that "goes to the head" and clouds the
    reason.
195. *fond impertinence*: foolish irrelevance.
197. *still to seek*: always lacking.
198. *pitch*: summit.
218. Cf. Ps. 45.2: "Grace is poured into thy lips: therefore God hath blessed thee for ever."
230. *uncouth*: strange.

Lest he incensed at such eruption bold,   235
Destruction with creation might have mixed.
Not that they durst without his leave attempt,
But us he sends upon his high behests
For state, as sovran King, and to inure
Our prompt obedience. Fast we found, fast shut   240
The dismal gates, and barricadoed strong;
But long ere our approaching heard within
Noise, other than the sound of dance or song,
Torment, and loud lament, and furious rage.
Glad we returned up to the coasts of light   245
Ere Sabbath evening: so we had in charge.
But thy relation now; for I attend,
Pleased with thy words no less than thou with mine."
    So spake the godlike Power, and thus our sire.
"For man to tell how human life began   250
Is hard; for who himself beginning knew?
Desire with thee still longer to converse
Induced me. As new-waked from soundest sleep
Soft on the flow'ry herb I found me laid
In balmy sweat, which with his beams the sun   255
Soon dried, and on the reeking moisture fed.
Straight toward heav'n my wond'ring eyes I turned,
And gazed a while the ample sky, till raised
By quick instinctive motion up I sprung,
As thitherward endeavoring, and upright   260
Stood on my feet; about me round I saw
Hill, dale, and shady woods, and sunny plains,
And liquid lapse of murmuring streams; by these,
Creatures that lived, and moved, and walked, or flew,
Birds on the branches warbling; all things smiled,   265
With fragrance and with joy my heart o'erflowed.
Myself I then perused, and limb by limb
Surveyed, and sometimes went, and sometimes ran
With supple joints, as lively vigor led:
But who I was, or where, or from what cause,   270
Knew not; to speak I tried, and forthwith spake,
My tongue obeyed and readily could name
Whate'er I saw. 'Thou sun,' said I, 'fair light,
And thou enlightened earth, so fresh and gay,
Ye hills and dales, ye rivers, woods, and plains,   275
And ye that live and move, fair creatures, tell,
Tell, if ye saw, how came I thus, how here?

239. *For state:* as expressions of his power and glory. *inure:* strengthen by exercise.
246. *Sabbath evening:* eve of the Seventh Day.
256. *reeking moisture:* vapor.
263. *lapse:* (L *labi* to slip, slide) flow.
268. *went:* walked.

Not of myself; by some great Maker then,
In goodness and in power preeminent;
Tell me, how may I know him, how adore,   280
From whom I have that thus I move and live,
And feel that I am happier than I know.'
While thus I called, and strayed I knew not wither,
From where I first drew air, and first beheld
This happy light, when answer none returned,   285
On a green shady bank profuse of flow'rs
Pensive I sat me down; there gentle sleep
First found me, and with soft oppression seized
My drowsèd sense, untroubled, though I thought
I then was passing to my former state   290
Insensible, and forthwith to dissolve:
When suddenly stood at my head a dream,
Whose inward apparition gently moved
My fancy to believe I yet had being,
And lived: one came, methought, of shape divine,   295
And said, 'Thy mansion wants thee, Adam, rise,
First man, of men innumerable ordained
First father, called by thee I come thy guide
To the garden of bliss, thy seat prepared.'
So saying, by the hand he took me raised,   300
And over fields and waters, as in air
Smooth sliding without step, last led me up
A woody mountain; whose high top was plain,
A circuit wide, enclosed, with goodliest trees
Planted, with walks, and bowers, that what I saw   305
Of earth before scarce pleasant seemed. Each tree
Load'n with fairest fruit, that hung to the eye
Tempting, stirred in me sudden appetite
To pluck and eat; whereat I waked, and found
Before mine eyes all real, as the dream   310
Had lively shadowed: here had new begun
My wand'ring, had not he who was my guide
Up hither, from among the trees appeared,
Presence Divine. Rejoicing, but with awe
In adoration at his feet I fell   315
Submiss: he reared me, and 'Whom thou sought'st I am,'
Said mildly, 'Author of all this thou seest
Above, or round about thee or beneath.
This paradise I give thee, count it thine

281. Cf. Acts 17.28: [St. Paul preaching in Athens said] "For in him we live, and move, and
    have our being; as certain also of your own poets have said, For we are also his offspring."
296. *mansion:* dwelling place. *wants:* lacks.
299. *seat:* residence.
311. *lively:* vividly.
316. *Submiss:* submissive.

To till and keep, and of the fruit to eat: 320
Of every tree that in the garden grows
Eat freely with glad heart; fear here no dearth:
But of the tree whose operation brings
Knowledge of good and ill, which I have set
The pledge of thy obedience and thy faith,   325
Amid the garden by the Tree of Life,
Remember what I warn thee, shun to taste,
And shun the bitter consequence: for know,
The day thou eat'st thereof, my sole command
Transgressed, inevitably thou shalt die;   330
From that day mortal, and this happy state
Shalt lose, expelled from hence into a world
Of woe and sorrow.' Sternly he pronounced
The rigid interdiction, which resounds
Yet dreadful in mine ear, though in my choice   335
Not to incur; but soon his clear aspéct
Returned and gracious purpose thus renewed.
'Not only these fair bounds, but all the earth
To thee and to thy race I give; as lords
Possess it, and all things that therein live,   340
Or live in sea, or air, beast, fish, and fowl.
In sign whereof each bird and beast behold
After their kinds; I bring them to receive
From thee their names, and pay thee fealty
With low subjection; understand the same   345
Of fish within their wat'ry residence,
Not hither summoned, since they cannot change
Their element to draw the thinner air.'
As thus he spake, each bird and beast behold
Approaching two and two, these cow'ring low   350
With blandishment, each bird stooped on his wing.
I named them, as they passed, and understood
Their nature, with such knowledge God endued
My sudden apprehension: but in these
I found not what methought I wanted still;   355

320. *keep*: care for.
323. *operation*: (L *operari* to work) action.
325. *pledge*. See III.95 and note; also IV.428.
329–31. Milton followed the language of Gen.: "in the day that thou eatest thereof thou shalt surely die." But since Adam did not die on that day, Milton followed the commentators who interpreted *die* to mean *From that day mortal*, i.e., subject to death. See *CD*, p. 418.
335–36. I.e.: Though it is within my power to choose not to incur this doom.
337. *purpose*: speech.
343–44. See *CD*, pp. 409–10.
350. *cow'ring*: stooping.
351. *blandishment*: flattering gesture. *stooped*: (a participle, like *cow'ring*) swooped down, like a bird of prey (a term from falconry). But Milton is thinking of another term from falconry, cowering, which meant, "The quivering of young hawks, who shake their wings, in sign of obedience to the old ones."

And to the heav'nly Vision thus presumed.
  " 'O by what name, for thou above all these,
Above mankind, or aught than mankind higher,
Surpassest far my naming, how may I
Adore thee, Author of this universe,   360
And all this good to man, for whose well-being
So amply, and with hands so liberal
Thou hast provided all things: but with me
I see not who partakes. In solitude
What happiness, who can enjoy alone,   365
Or all enjoying, what contentment find?'
Thus I presumptuous; and the Vision bright,
As with a smile more brightened, thus replied.
  " 'What call'st thou solitude? Is not the earth
With various living creatures, and the air   370
Replenished, and all these at thy command
To come and play before thee? Know'st thou not
Their language and their ways? They also know,
And reason not contemptibly; with these
Find pastime, and bear rule; thy realm is large.'   375
So spake the Universal Lord, and seemed
So ordering. I with leave of speech implored,
And humble deprecation thus replied.
  " 'Let not my words offend thee, Heav'nly Power,
My Maker, be propitious while I speak.   380
Hast thou not made me here thy substitute,
And these inferior far beneath me set?
Among unequals what society
Can sort, what harmony or true delight?
Which must be mutual, in proportion due   385
Giv'n and received; but in disparity
The one intense, the other still remiss
Cannot well suit with either, but soon prove
Tedious alike: of fellowship I speak
Such as I seek, fit to participate   390
All rational delight, wherein the brute
Cannot be human consort; they rejoice
Each with their kind, lion with lioness;
So fitly them in pairs thou hast combined;
Much less can bird with beast, or fish with fowl   395
So well converse, nor with the ox the ape;

371. *Replenished:* fully stocked.
373. *know:* have knowledge and understanding.
384. *sort:* consort, meet as equals.
387. *intense:* (L *intendere* to stretch out) high-strung in a musical sense; therefore of one pitch
(high). *remiss:* (L *remittere* to send back, relax) low strung, of low pitch.
390. *participate:* partake of.
396. *converse:* L *conversari* to keep company with.

Worse then can man with beast, and least of all.'
"Whereto th' Almighty answered, not displeased.
'A nice and subtle happiness I see
Thou to thyself proposest, in the choice   400
Of thy associates, Adam, and wilt taste
No pleasure, though in pleasure, solitary.
What think'st thou then of me, and this my state,
Seem I to thee sufficiently possessed
Of happiness, or not? who am alone   405
From all eternity, for none I know
Second to me or like, equal much less.
How have I then with whom to hold converse
Save with the creatures which I made, and those
To me inferior, infinite descents   410
Beneath what other creatures are to thee?'
"He ceased, I lowly answered. 'To attain
The highth and depth of thy eternal ways
All human thoughts come short, Supreme of things;
Thou in thyself art perfect, and in thee   415
Is no deficience found; not so is man,
But in degree, the cause of his desire
By conversation with his like to help,
Or solace his defects. No need that thou
Shouldst propagate, already infinite;   420
And through all numbers absolute, though One;
But man by number is to manifest
His single imperfection, and beget
Like of his like, his image multiplied,
In unity defective, which requires   425
Collateral love, and dearest amity.
Thou in thy secrecy although alone,
Best with thyself accompanied, seek'st not
Social communication, yet so pleased,
Canst raise thy creature to what highth thou wilt   430
Of union or communion, deified;
I by conversing cannot these erect
From prone, nor in their ways complacence find.'
Thus I emboldened spake, and freedom used
Permissive, and acceptance found, which gained   435

399. *nice*: discriminating.
416-26. Compared with God, a human being is imperfect because in its unity, or singleness, it
does not contain all—is not divinely infinite and self-sufficient. It seeks to remedy (*help*, as in
"help meet") or compensate for (*solace*) this imperfection by companionship with another
human being. A human being's desire to procreate or multiply itself is a sign of the same
imperfection—a lack of God's self-contained infinity of numbers. Singleness (unity) in God is
perfection; in human beings it is an imperfection. *absolute*: complete, perfect. *Collateral*: (L
latus side) side by side; mutual, equal.
431. Fowler notes that "it is difficult not to see [in *union or communion*] references to mystical
union and Holy Communion" (i.e., "identity" and "fellowship").
433. *complacence*: pleasure, delight.
435. *Permissive*: permitted (modifies *freedom*).

This answer from the gracious Voice Divine.
    " 'Thus far to try thee, Adam, I was pleased,
And find thee knowing not of beasts alone,
Which thou hast rightly named, but of thyself,
Expressing well the spirit within thee free,   440
My image, not imparted to the brute,
Whose fellowship therefore unmeet for thee
Good reason was thou freely shouldst dislike,
And be so minded still; I, ere thou spak'st,
Knew it not good for man to be alone,   445
And no such company as then thou saw'st
Intended thee, for trial only brought,
To see how thou couldst judge of fit and meet:
What next I bring shall please thee, be assured,
Thy likeness, thy fit help, thy other self,   450
Thy wish, exactly to thy heart's desire.'
    "He ended, or I heard no more, for now
My earthly by his heav'nly overpowered,
Which it had long stood under, strained to the highth
In that celestial colloquy sublime,   455
As with an object that excels the sense,
Dazzled and spent, sunk down, and sought repair
Of sleep, which instantly fell on me, called
By nature as in aid, and closed mine eyes.
Mine eyes he closed, but open left the cell   460
Of fancy my internal sight, by which
Abstract as in a trance methought I saw,
Though sleeping, where I lay, and saw the shape
Still glorious before whom awake I stood;
Who stooping opened my left side, and took   465
From thence a rib, with cordial spirits warm,
And life-blood streaming fresh; wide was the wound,
But suddenly with flesh filled up and healed:
The rib he formed and fashioned with his hands;
Under his forming hands a creature grew,   470
Man-like, but different sex, so lovely fair,
That what seemed fair in all the world, seemed now
Mean, or in her summed up, in her contained
And in her looks, which from that time infused
Sweetness into my heart, unfelt before,   475
And into all things from her air inspired
The spirit of love and amorous delight.

450. *fit help*: help meet, as in Gen., "I will make him an help meet."
462. *Abstract*: (L *ab* from + *trahere* to draw) mentally withdrawn.
466. *cordial*: (L *cor* heart) vital.
476–77. *air*: breath, as well as looks. *inspired*: breathed into, as well as prompted. *spirit*: breath, as well as life.

She disappeared, and left me dark, I waked
To find her, or for ever to deplore
Her loss, and other pleasures all abjure: 480
When out of hope, behold her, not far off,
Such as I saw her in my dream, adorned
With what all earth or heaven could bestow
To make her amiable: on she came,
Led by her heav'nly Maker, though unseen,   485
And guided by his voice, nor uniformed
Of nuptial sanctity and marriage rites:
Grace was in all her steps, heav'n in her eye,
In every gesture dignity and love.
I overjoyed could not forbear aloud.   490
    " 'This turn hath made amends; thou hast fulfilled
Thy words, Creator bounteous and benign,
Giver of all things fair, but fairest this
Of all thy gifts, nor enviest. I now see
Bone of my bone, flesh of my flesh, my self   495
Before me; woman is her name, of man
Extracted; for this cause he shall forgo
Father and mother, and to his wife adhere;
And they shall be one flesh, one heart, one soul.'
    "She heard me thus, and though divinely brought,   500
Yet innocence and virgin modesty,
Her virtue and the conscience of her worth,
That would be wooed, and not unsought be won,
Not obvious, not obtrusive, but retired,
The more desirable, or to say all,   505
Nature herself, though pure of sinful thought,
Wrought in her so, that seeing me, she turned;
I followed her, she what was honor knew,
And with obsequious majesty approved
My pleaded reason. To the nuptial bow'r   510
I led her blushing like the morn: all heav'n,
And happy constellations on that hour
Shed their selectest influence; the earth
Gave sign of gratulation, and each hill;
Joyous the birds; fresh gales and gentle airs   515

---

484. *amiable*: lovable.
494. *nor enviest*: nor dost thou begrudge me it.
495. Cf. Gen. 2.23–24, p. 431.
496–97. *woman is her name* . . . : The Hebrew word for *woman* is *'isshah*; for man, *'ish*.
502. *conscience*: consciousness.
504. *obvious*: L *obvius* easy of access, outgoing.
508. Cf. Heb. 13.4: "Marriage is honourable in all, and the bed undefiled; but whoremongers and adulterers God will judge."
509. *obsequious*: compliant, devoted.
514. *gratulation*: rejoicing.

Whispered it to the woods, and from their wings
Flung rose, flung odors from the spicy shrub,
Disporting, till the amorous bird of night
Sung spousal, and bid haste the evening star
On his hill top, to light the bridal lamp.   520
Thus I have told thee all my state, and brought
My story to the sum of earthly bliss
Which I enjoy, and must confess to find
In all things else delight indeed, but such
As used or not, works in the mind no change,   525
Nor vehement desire, these delicacies
I mean of taste, sight, smell, herbs, fruits, and flow'rs,
Walks, and the melody of birds; but here
Far otherwise, transported I behold,
Transported touch; here passion first I felt,   530
Commotion strange, in all enjoyments else
Superior and unmoved, here only weak
Against the charm of beauty's powerful glance.
Or nature failed in me, and left some part
Not proof enough such object to sustain,   535
Or from my side subducting, took perhaps
More than enough; at least on her bestowed
Too much of ornament, in outward show
Elaborate, of inward less exact.
For well I understand in the prime end   540
Of nature her th' inferior, in the mind
And inward faculties, which most excel,
In outward also her resembling less
His image who made both, and less expressing
The character of that dominion giv'n   545
O'er other creatures; yet when I approach
Her loveliness, so absolute she seems
And in herself complete, so well to know
Her own, that what she wills to do or say,
Seems wisest, virtuousest, discreetst, best;   550
All higher knowledge in her presence falls
Degraded, wisdom in discourse with her
Loses discount'nanced, and like folly shows;
Authority and reason on her wait,

517. *rose . . . odors.* Cf. V.293n and 349.
518. *Disporting:* frolicking.
519. *evening star:* Venus.
526. *vehement:* L *vehe* lacking + *mens* mind. Cf. use of *vehemence* in Argument to IX.
531. *Commotion:* mental agitation.
535. *proof:* resistant. *sustain:* withstand.
539. *Elaborate:* highly finished, worked out in detail. *exact:* (L *exigere* to demand, to weigh
     accurately, to bring to perfection) perfect, finished, highly wrought, elaborate, well-designed.
547. *absolute.* Cf. 421 and note.
553. *discount'nanced:* disconcerted, made to lose its self-confidence, abashed.

As one intended first, not after made   555
Occasionally; and to consúmmate all,
Greatness of mind and nobleness their seat
Build in her loveliest, and create an awe
About her, as a guard angelic placed."
To whom the angel with contracted brow.   560
    "Accuse not nature, she hath done her part;
Do thou but thine, and be not diffident
Of wisdom, she deserts thee not, if thou
Dismiss not her, when most thou need'st her nigh,
By áttributing overmuch to things   565
Less excellent, as thou thyself perceiv'st.
For what admir'st thou, what transports thee so,
An outside? Fair no doubt, and worthy well
Thy cherishing, thy honoring, and thy love,
Not thy subjection: weigh with her thyself;   570
Then value: ofttimes nothing profits more
Than self-esteem, grounded on just and right
Well managed; of that skill the more thou know'st,
The more she will acknowledge thee her head,
And to realities yield all her shows: 575
Made so adorn for thy delight the more,
So awful, that with honor thou may'st love
Thy mate, who sees when thou art seen least wise.
But if the sense of touch whereby mankind
Is propagated seem such dear delight   580
Beyond all other, think the same vouchsafed
To cattle and each beast; which would not be
To them made common and divulged, if aught
Therein enjoyed were worthy to subdue
The soul of man, or passion in him move.   585
What higher in her society thou find'st
Attractive, human, rational, love still;
In loving thou dost well, in passion not,
Wherein true love consists not; love refines
The thoughts, and heart enlarges, hath his seat   590
In reason, and is judicious, is the scale
By which to heav'nly love thou may'st ascend,

556. *Occasionally*: incidentally.
557. *greatness of mind*: magnanimity. Cf. VII.511, and Introduction, p. xii.
562. *diffident*: (L *dis* + *fidere* to trust) distrustful.
573. *skill*: understanding; reason for doing something.
574. Cf. 1 Cor. 11.31: "The head of every man is Christ; and the head of the woman is the man; and the head of Christ is God."
577. *awful*: awe-inspiring.
590. *heart enlarges*: makes the intellect capacious; cf. VII.486 and I.437–46n.
591. *scale*: ladder.

Not sunk in carnal pleasure, for which cause
Among the beasts no mate for thee was found."
    To whom thus half abashed Adam replied.   595
"Neither her outside formed so fair, nor aught
In procreation common to all kinds
(Though higher of the genial bed by far,
And with mysterious reverence I deem)
So much delights me, as those graceful acts,   600
Those thousand decencies that daily flow
From all her words and actions, mixed with love
And sweet compliance, which declare unfeigned
Union of mind, or in us both one soul;
Harmony to behold in wedded pair   605
More grateful than harmonious sound to the ear.
Yet these subject not; I to thee disclose
What inward thence I feel, not therefore foiled,
Who meet with various objects, from the sense
Variously representing; yet still free   610
Approve the best, and follow what I approve.
To love thou blam'st me not, for love thou say'st
Leads up to heav'n, is both the way and guide;
Bear with me then, if lawful what I ask;
Love not the heav'nly Spirits, and how their love   615
Express they, by looks only, or do they mix
Irradiance, virtual or immediate touch?"
    To whom the angel with a smile that glowed
Celestial rosy red, love's proper hue,
Answered. "Let it suffice thee that thou know'st   620
Us happy, and without love no happiness.
Whatever pure thou in the body enjoy'st
(And pure thou wert created) we enjoy
In eminence, and obstacle find none
Of membrane, joint, or limb, exclusive bars: 625
Easier than air with air, if Spirits embrace,
Total they mix, union of pure with pure
Desiring; nor restrained conveyance need
As flesh to mix with flesh, or soul with soul.

595. Cf. *discount'nanced*, 553 and note.
598. *genial*: of or pertaining to marriage or generation. Cf. VII.282.
599. *mysterious*. See IV.750n.
601. *decencies*: fitting, becoming, or appropriate acts.
608. *therefore foiled*: thereby defiled, dishonored (by *these*, in line above). Cf. Mark 7.18: "And
    [Christ] saith unto them . . . Do you not perceive, that whatsoever thing from without entereth
    into the man, it cannot defile him."
609–11. *Who . . . the best*. "Who by means of my senses experience various things variously
    represented."
616–17. Expression of love *by looks* would be virtually the same as *touch*; *immediate*, or real,
    touch would produce an interpenetration of emitted radiances of light, spirit, intelligence.
620ff. See "Angels," pp. 466–68.
628. *conveyance*: mode of expression.

But I can now no more; the parting sun   630
Beyond the earth's green cape and verdant isles
Hesperian sets, my signal to depart.
Be strong, live happy, and love, but first of all
Him whom to love is to obey, and keep
His great command; take heed lest passion sway   635
Thy judgment to do aught, which else free will
Would not admit; thine and of all thy sons
The weal or woe in thee is placed; beware.
I in thy perserving shall rejoice,
And all the blest: stand fast; to stand or fall   640
Free in thine own arbitrament it lies.
Perfect within, no outward aid require;
And all temptation to transgress repel."
    So saying, he arose; whom Adam thus
Followed with benediction. "Since to part,   645
Go heavenly guest, ethereal messenger,
Sent from whose sovran goodness I adore.
Gentle to me and affable hath been
Thy condescension, and shall be honored ever
With grateful memory: thou to mankind   650
Be good and friendly still, and oft return."
    So parted they, the angel up to heav'n
From the thick shade, and Adam to his bow'r.

Book IX

The Argument

Satan having compassed the earth, with meditated guile returns as a
mist by night into Paradise, enters into the serpent sleeping. Adam and
Eve in the morning go forth to their labors, which Eve proposes to divide
in several places, each laboring apart: Adam consents not, alleging the
danger, lest that enemy, of whom they were forewarned, should attempt
her found alone: Eve loath to be thought not circumspect or firm enough,
urges her going apart, the rather desirous to make trial of her strength;
Adam at last yields: the Serpent finds her alone; his subtle approach,
first gazing, then speaking, with much flattery extolling Eve above all
other creatures. Eve wondering to hear the Serpent speak, asks how he
attained to human speech and such understanding not till now; the

630–32. *Hesperian* means "western," but Raphael alludes to the gardens of Hesperus, thought
to be, like the Isles of the Blest, in the eastern Atlantic (cf. III.568)—perhaps the Azores or,
as here, the Cape Verde Islands.
634–35. Cf. 1 John 5.3: "For this is the love of God, that we keep his commandments."
639. *persevering*. See VII.632n.
641. *arbitrament*: power to decide.
642. *require*: request.

Serpent answers, that by tasting of a certain tree in the garden he attained both to speech and reason, till then void of both: Eve requires him to bring her to that tree, and finds it to be the Tree of Knowledge forbidden: the Serpent now grown bolder, with many wiles and arguments induces her at length to eat; she pleased with the taste deliberates a while whether to impart thereof to Adam or not, at last brings him of the fruit, relates what persuaded her to eat thereof: Adam at first amazed, but perceiving her lost, resolves through vehemence of love to perish with her; and extenuating the trespass, eats also of the fruit: the effects thereof in them both; they seek to cover their nakedness; then fall to variance and accusation of one another.

No more of talk where God or angel guest
With man, as with his friend, familiar used
To sit indulgent, and with him partake
Rural repast, permitting him the while
Venal discourse unblamed: I now must change   5
Those notes to tragic; foul distrust, and breach
Disloyal on the part of man, revolt,
And disobedience: on the part of heav'n
Now alienated, distance and distaste,
Anger and just rebuke, and judgment giv'n,   10
That brought into this world a world of woe,
Sin and her shadow Death, and misery
Death's harbinger: sad task, yet argument
Not less but more heroic than the wrath
Of stern Achilles on his foe pursued   15
Thrice fugitive about Troy wall; or rage
Of Turnus for Lavinia disespoused,
Or Neptune's ire or Juno's, that so long
Perplexed the Greek and Cytherea's son;
If answerable style I can obtain   20
Of my celestial patroness, who deigns
Her nightly visitation unimplored,
And dictates to me slumb'ring, or inspires
Easy my unpremeditated verse:
Since first this subject for heroic song   25
Pleased me long choosing, and beginning late;

IX.3. *indulgent:* L *indulgere* to grant as a favor. *partake:* share.
5. *Venial:* (L *venia* grace, favor) pardonable.
6. *breach:* disagreement, quarrel; breaking of a law, duty, or promise.
14–19. The themes of the *Il.*, the *Aen.*, and the *Od. heroic:* appropriate to heroes, as well as to epic poetry; cf. *heroic song* (25) and *heroic name* (40). *his foe:* Hector. *Lavinia* was betrothed to *Turnus* but given in marriage by her father to Aeneas. *Neptune* made life hard for (*perplexed*) Odysseus (*the Greek*); and *Juno* for Aeneas, son of Venus (*Cytherea*). Man's odyssey would be more heroic than that of Odysseus or Aeneas.
20. *answerable:* capable of meeting requirements; corresponding, suitable.
21. *patroness:* Urania. See VII.1.
23–24. Cf. III.37ff. and n.

Not sedulous by nature to indite
Wars, hitherto the only argument
Heroic deemed, chief mastery to dissect
With long and tedious havoc fabled knights   30
In battles feigned; the better fortitude
Of patience and heroic martyrdom
Unsung; or to describe races and games,
Or tilting furniture, emblazoned shields,
Impresses quaint, caparisons and steeds;   35
Bases and tinsel trappings, gorgeous knights
At joust and tournament; then marshaled feast
Served up in hall with sewers, and seneschals;
The skill of artifice or office mean,
Not that which justly gives heroic name   40
To person or to poem. Me of these
Nor skilled nor studious, higher argument
Remains, sufficient of itself to raise
That name, unless an age too late, or cold
Climate, or years damp my intended wing   45
Depressed, and much they may, if all be mine,
Not hers who brings it nightly to my ear.
  The sun was sunk, and after him the star
Of Hesperus, whose office is to bring
Twilight upon the earth, short arbiter   50
'Twixt day and night, and now from end to end
Night's hemisphere had veiled the horizon round:
When Satan who late fled before the threats
Of Gabriel out of Eden, now improved
In meditated fraud and malice, bent   55
On mans destruction, maugre what might hap
Of heavier on himself, fearless returned.
By night he fled, and at midnight returned
From compassing the earth, cautious of day,
Since Uriel regent of the sun descried   60
His entrance, and forewarned the Cherubim

28. *argument*: subject; narrative.
29. *maistry*: mastery, skill.
31. *feigned*: represented in fiction.
34–38. Milton alludes to medieval romances such as Malory's *Morte d'Arthur* and such Renaissance epics as those of Tasso and Spenser. *tilting furniture*: equipment for jousting. *Impresses quaint*: skillfully wrought coats of arms. *caparisons*: rich trappings for horses. *Bases*: mantles worn from waist to knee by knights on horseback. The *seneschal*, the majordomo, arranged the banquets at which *sewers* seated the guests, tasted the wine, and served the food.
44–45. Milton wonders whether (1) society has not lost its taste for true Christian heroism or for epic poems, or (2) the climate (Gk *klima* inclination, latitude) of England is not inimical to the production of works of genius, or (3) he is himself not too old for such an undertaking. *damp*: depress, check. *wing*. Cf. I.14–15; III.13; VII.3–4.
54. *improved*: increased.
56. *maugre*: in spite of.
59. Cf. Job 1.7: "And the Lord said unto Satan, Whence comes thou? Then Satan answered the Lord, and said, From going to and fro in the earth, and from walking up and down in it."

That kept their watch; thence full of anguish driv'n,
The space of seven continued nights he rode
With darkness, thrice the equinoctial line
He circled, four times crossed the car of Night   65
From pole to pole, traversing each colure;
On the eighth returned, and on the coast averse
From entrance on Cherubic watch, by stealth
Found unsuspected way. There was a place,
Now not, though sin, not time, first wrought the change,   70
Where Tigris at the foot of Paradise
Into a gulf shot under ground, till part
Rose up a fountain by the Tree of Life;
In with the river sunk, and with it rose
Satan involved in rising mist, then sought   75
Where to lie hid; sea he had searched and land
From Eden over Pontus, and the pool
Maeotis, up beyond the river Ob;
Downward as far antarctic; and in length
West from Orontes to the ocean barred   80
At Darien, thence to the land where flows
Ganges and Indus: thus the orb he roamed
With narrow search; and with inspection deep
Considered every creature, which of all
Most opportune might serve his wiles, and found   85
The serpent subtlest beast of all the field.
Him after long debate, irresolute
Of thoughts revolved, his final sentence chose
Fit vessel, fittest imp of fraud, in whom
To enter, and his dark suggestions hide   90
From sharpest sight: for in the wily snake,
Whatever sleights none would suspicious mark,
As from his wit and native subtlety
Proceeding, which in other beasts observed
Doubt might beget of diabolic pow'r   95
Active within beyond the sense of brute.

63–66. Before the earth was tilted on its axis at the time of the Fall, there were no *colures*, the two circles that run perpendicular to the circle of the earth's annual orbit around the sun and that intersect that circle at the two points of the equinoxes and the two points of the solstices. Whatever his reason for referring to them, Milton intended to picture Satan keeping the earth between him and the sun, first by following the equator for three days and then (for four) so timing his transpolar flights as to achieve the same effect. *equinoctial line*: in the Ptolemaic system of astronomy the circle of the sun around the earth, in the same plane, before the Fall, with that of the earth's equator.
77–81. *Pontus*: the Black Sea. *Maeotis*: the Sea of Azov in Russia. *Ob*: in Siberia, runs into the Arctic Ocean. *Orontes*: a river in N. Syria. *Darien*: the Isthmus of Panama.
87–88. *irresolute / Of thoughts revolved*: undecided after meditating. *sentence*: judgment.
89. *imp*: offshoot; child.
90. *suggestions*: temptations.
92. *sleights*: deceitful artifices.
95. *Doubt*: suspicion.

Thus he resolved, but first from inward grief
His bursting passion into plaints thus poured:
   "O earth, how like to heav'n, if not preferred
More justly, seat worthier of gods, as built   100
With second thoughts, reforming what was old!
For what God after better worse would build?
Terrestrial heav'n, danced round by other heav'ns
That shine, yet bear their bright officious lamps,
Light above light, for thee alone, as seems,   105
In thee concentring all their precious beams
Of sacred influence: as God in heav'n
Is center, yet extends to all, so thou
Centring receiv'st from all those orbs; in thee,
Not in themselves, all their known virtue appears   110
Productive in herb, plant, and nobler birth
Of creatures animate with gradual life
Of growth, sense, reason, all summed up in man.
With what delight could I have walked thee round,
If I could joy in aught, sweet interchange   115
Of hill and valley, rivers, woods and plains,
Now land, now sea, and shores with forest crowned,
Rocks, dens, and caves; but I in none of these
Find place or refuge; and the more I see
Pleasures about me, so much more I feel   120
Torment within me, as from the hateful siege
Of contraries; all good to me becomes
Bane, and in heav'n much worse would be my state.
But neither here seek I, no nor in heav'n
To dwell, unless by mastering heav'n's Supreme;   125
Nor hope to be myself less miserable
By what I seek, but others to make such
As I, though thereby worse to me redound:
For only in destroying I find ease
To my relentless thoughts; and him destroyed,   130
Or won to what may work his utter loss,
For whom all this was made, all this will soon
Follow, as to him linked in weal or woe:
In woe then; that destruction wide may range:
To me shall be the glory sole among   135
The infernal Powers, in one day to have marred
What he Almighty styled, six nights and days
Continued making, and who knows how long

103–7. Satan joins Eve (IV.657) and Adam (VIII.15ff) in this observation. *danced*. Cf. III.580n;
   V.178, 620–27; VII.374; VIII.125. *officious*: helpful, ministering.
112–13. *gradual*: progressive, from, as Fowler notes, vegetable (*growth*) to animal (*sense*) to
   rational (*reason*) souls. Cf. V.469–90; and see "Physiology and Psychology," pp. 463–64.
121. The pain (*Torment*) within Satan is in conflict with, is besieged by, *pleasures* from without.
   siege: persistent attack; also, seat, throne.
123. *Bane*: poison; cause of ruin or woe. Cf. I.692.

Before had been contriving, though perhaps
Not longer than since I in one night freed   140
From servitude inglorious well-nigh half
Th' angelic name, and thinner left the throng
Of his adorers: he to be avenged,
And to repair his numbers thus impaired,
Whether such virtue spent of old now failed   145
More angels to create, if they at least
Are his created, or to spite us more,
Determined to advance into our room
A creature formed of earth, and him endow,
Exalted from so base original,   150
With heav'nly spoils, our spoils: what he decreed
He effected; man he made, and for him built
Magnificent this world, and earth his seat,
Him lord pronounced, and, O indignity!
Subjected to his service angel wings,   155
And flaming ministers to watch and tend
Their earthy charge: of these the vigilance
I dread, and to elude, thus wrapped in mist
Of midnight vapor glide obscure, and pry
In every bush and brake, where hap may find   160
The serpent sleeping, in whose mazy folds
To hide me, and the dark intent I bring.
O foul descent! that I who erst contended
With gods to sit the highest, am now constrained
Into a beast, and mixed with bestial slime,   165
This essence to incarnate and imbrute,
That to the highth of deity aspired;
But what will not ambition and revenge
Descend to? Who aspires must down as low
As high he soared, obnoxious first or last   170
To basest things. Revenge, at first though sweet,
Bitter ere long back on itself recoils;
Let it; I reck not, so it light well aimed,
Since higher I fall short, on him who next
Provokes my envy, this new favorite   175
Of Heav'n, this man of clay, son of despite,
Whom us the more to spite his Maker raised
From dust: spite then with spite is best repaid."
     So saying, through each thicket dank or dry,

145. *virtue:* power.
150. *base original:* common origin (i.e., *earth*).
155–57. Cf. Ps. 104.4, p. 439: "Who maketh his angels spirits; his ministers a flaming fire." Ps.
     91.11: "For he shall give his angels charge over thee, to keep thee in all thy ways."
160. *hap:* luck.
170. *obnoxious:* (L *ob* facing + *noxa* harm) vulnerable; (with *to*) dependent on, subject to the
     power of.
173. *reck:* care.

Like a black mist low creeping, he held on   180
His midnight search, where soonest he might find
The serpent: him fast sleeping soon he found
In labyrinth of many a round self-rolled,
His head the midst, well stored with subtle wiles:
Not yet in horrid shade or dismal den,   185
Nor nocent yet, but on the grassy herb
Fearless unfeared he slept: in at his mouth
The Devil entered, and his brutal sense,
In heart or head, possessing soon inspired
With act intelligential; but his sleep   190
Disturbed not, waiting close th' approach of morn.
Now whenas sacred light began to dawn
In Eden on the humid flow'rs, that breathed
Their morning incense, when all things that breathe,
From th' earth's great altar send up silent praise   195
To the Creator, and his nostrils fill
With grateful smell, forth came the human pair
And joined their vocal worship to the choir
Of creatures wanting voice; that done, partake
The season, prime for sweetest scents and airs: 200
Then commune how that day they best may ply
Their growing work; for much their work outgrew
The hands' dispatch of two gard'ning so wide.
And Eve first to her husband thus began.
   "Adam, well may we labor still to dress   205
This garden, still to tend plant, herb and flow'r,
Our pleasant task enjoined, but till more hands
Aid us, the work under our labor grows,
Luxurious by restraint; what we by day
Lop overgrown, or prune, or prop, or bind,   210
One night or two with wanton growth derides,
Tending to wild. Thou therefore now advise
Or hear what to my mind first thoughts present,
Let us divide our labors, thou where choice
Leads thee, or where most needs, whether to wind   215
The woodbine round this arbor, or direct
The clasping ivy where to climb, while I

186. *nocent:* harmful; guilty of crime.
191. *close:* hidden.
192. *whenas:* when. *sacred light.* Cf. III.1–6; IX.107.
196–97. Cf. Gen. 8.21: "And [after the Flood] the Lord smelled a sweet savour; and the Lord said in his heart, I will not again curse the ground any more for man's sake." *grateful:* gratifying, pleasant.
198. *choir:* Gk *chorus* dance, company of dancers.
199–200. *wanting:* lacking. *partake / The season.* Bush suggests "enjoy the morning." *prime:* the best. But the word also means the first hour of the day, and a set time for morning prayers.
201. *ply:* apply [themselves] to.
209. *luxurious:* luxuriant.

In yonder spring of roses intermixed
With myrtle, find what to redress till noon:
For while so near each other thus all day   220
Our task we choose, what wonder if so near
Looks intervene and smiles, or object new
Casual discourse draw on, which intermits
Our day's work brought to little, though begun
Early, and th' hour of supper comes unearned."   225
     To whom mild answer Adam thus returned.
"Sole Eve, associate sole, to me beyond
Compare above all living creatures dear,
Well hast thou motioned, well thy thoughts employed
How we might best fulfill the work which here   230
God hath assigned us, nor of me shalt pass
Unpraised: for nothing lovelier can be found
In woman, than to study household good,
And good works in her husband to promote.
Yet not so strictly hath our Lord imposed   235
Labor, as to debar us when we need
Refreshment, whether food, or talk between,
Food of the mind, or this sweet intercourse
Of looks and smiles, for smiles from reason flow,
To brute denied, and are of love the food,   240
Love not the lowest end of human life.
For not to irksome toil, but to delight
He made us, and delight to reason joined.
These paths and bowers doubt not but our joint hands
Will keep from wilderness with ease, as wide   245
As we need walk, till younger hands ere long
Assist us: but if much convérse perhaps
Thee satiate, to short absence I could yield.
For solitude sometimes is best society,
And short retirement urges sweet return.   250
But other doubt possesses me, lest harm
Befall thee severed from me; for thou know'st
What hath been warned us, what malicious foe
Envying our happiness, and of his own
Despairing, seeks to work us woe and shame   255
By sly assault; and somewhere nigh at hand
Watches, no doubt, with greedy hope to find
His wish and best advantage, us asunder,
Hopeless to circumvent us joined, where each
To other speedy aid might lend at need;   260

218. *spring*: thicket.
219. *redress*: set upright again.
229. *motioned*: proposed.
232–34. For the biblical authority for Milton's ideas of the mutual duties of husband and wife
     see CD II.XV.

Whether his first design be to withdraw
Our fealty from God, or to disturb
Conjugal love, than which perhaps no bliss
Enjoyed by us excites his envy more;
Or this, or worse, leave not the faithful side   265
That gave thee being, still shades thee and protects.
The wife, where danger or dishonor lurks,
Safest and seemliest by her husband stays,
Who guards her, or with her the worst endures."
    To whom the virgin majesty of Eve,   270
As one who loves, and some unkindness meets,
With sweet austere composure thus replied.
    "Offspring of heav'n and earth, and all earth's lord,
That such an enemy we have, who seeks
Our ruin, both by thee informed I learn,   275
And from the parting angel overheard
As in a shady nook I stood behind,
Just then returned at shut of evening flow'rs.
But that thou shouldst my firmness therefore doubt
To God or thee, because we have a foe   280
May tempt it, I expected not to hear.
His violence thou fear'st not, being such,
As we, not capable of death or pain,
Can either not receive, or can repel.
His fraud is then thy fear, which plain infers   285
Thy equal fear that my firm faith and love
Can by his fraud be shaken or seduced,
Thoughts, which how found they harbor in thy breast,
Adam, misthought of her to thee so dear?"
    To whom with healing words Adam replied.   290
"Daughter of God and man, immortal Eve,
For such thou art, from sin and blame entire:
Not diffident of thee do I dissuade
Thy absence from my sight, but to avoid
Th' attempt itself, intended by our foe.   295
For he who tempts, though in vain, at least asperses
The tempted with dishonor foul, supposed
Not incorruptible of faith, not proof
Against temptation: thou thyself with scorn
And anger wouldst resent the offered wrong,   300

265. *Or this:* whether (his *design,* 261) be this.
270. *virgin majesty:* maidenly dignity.
272. *austere:* (Gk *austēros* making the tongue dry and rough) uniting astringency with sourness; stern
292. *entire:* (L *integer* untouched) free.
293. *diffident:* (L *dis* + *fidere* to trust) distrustful.
296–99. I.e.: Who tempts another, even unsuccessfully, dishonors him by implying that the tempted is capable of being tempted. Cf. 327–33. *asperses:* (L *ad* + *spargere* to scatter) bespatters. *faith:* loyalty.

Though ineffectual found; misdeem not then,
If such affront I labor to avert
From thee alone, which on us both at once
The enemy, though bold, will hardly dare,
Or daring, first on me th' assault shall light.   305
Nor thou his malice and false guile contemn;
Subtle he needs must be, who could seduce
Angels, nor think superfluous others' aid.
I from the influence of thy looks receive
Access in every virtue, in thy sight   310
More wise, more watchful, stronger, if need were
Of outward strength; while shame, thou looking on,
Shame to be overcome or overreached
Would utmost vigor raise, and raised unite.
Why shouldst not thou like sense within thee feel   315
When I am present, and thy trial choose
With me, best witness of thy virtue tried."
　So spake domestic Adam in his care
And matrimonial love; but Eve, who thought
Less attribúted to her faith sincere,   320
Thus her reply with accent sweet renewed.
　"If this be our condition, thus to dwell
In narrow circuit straitened by a foe,
Subtle or violent, we not endued
Single with like defense, wherever met,   325
How are we happy, still in fear of harm?
But harm precedes not sin: only our foe
Tempting affronts us with his foul esteem
Of our integrity: his foul esteem
Sticks no dishonor on our front, but turns   330
Foul on himself; then wherefore shunned or feared
By us? who rather double honor gain
From his surmise proved false, find peace within,
Favor from Heav'n, our witness from th' event.
And what is faith, love, virtue unassayed   335
Alone, without exterior help sustained?
Let us not then suspect our happy state
Left so imperfect by the Maker wise,
As not secure to single or combined.
Frail is our happiness, if this be so,   340

306. *contemn:* view with contempt.
310. *Access:* increase.
320. *sincere:* whole, unadulterated.
323. *straitened:* confined.
327–28. I.e.: In tempting us our foe only confronts (also insults) us. . . .
330. *front:* countenance.
334. *event:* (L *e* out + *venire* to come) outcome.
335–36. Cf. *Areopagitica,* pp. 384–85.
339. I.e.: As not to be safe for us, whether alone or together.

And Eden were no Eden thus exposed."
   To whom thus Adam fervently replied.
"O woman, best are all things as the will
Of God ordained them, his creating hand
Nothing imperfect or deficient left   345
Of all that he created, much less man,
Or aught that might his happy state secure,
Secure from outward force; within himself
The danger lies, yet lies within his power:
Against his will he can receive no harm.   350
But God left free the will, for what obeys
Reason, is free, and reason he made right,
But bid her well beware, and still erect,
Lest by some fair appearing good surprised
She dictate false, and misinform the will   355
To do what God expressly hath forbid.
Not then mistrust, but tender love enjoins,
That I should mind thee oft, and mind thou me.
Firm we subsist, yet possible to swerve,
Since reason not impossibly may meet   360
Some specious object by the foe suborned,
And fall into deception unaware,
Not keeping strictest watch, as she was warned.
Seek not temptation then, which to avoid
Were better, and most likely if from me   365
Thou sever not: trial will come unsought.
Wouldst thou approve thy constancy, approve
First thy obedience; th' other who can know,
Not seeing thee attempted, who attest?
But if thou think, trial unsought may find   370
Us both securer than thus warned thou seem'st,
Go; for thy stay, not free, absents thee more;
Go in thy native innocence, rely
On what thou hast of virtue, summon all,
For God towards thee hath done his part, do thine."   375
   So spake the patriarch of mankind, but Eve
Persisted, yet submiss, though last, replied.
   "With thy permission then, and thus forewarned
Chiefly by what thy own last reasoning words
Touched only, that our trial, when least sought,   380

341. *Eden.* See IV.132n.
352. See "Reason," p. 464.
353. I.e.: But he bid reason to be very careful and always alert.
358. *mind:* remind.
361. *suborned:* (L *sub* secretly + *ornare* to equip) secretly procured or enlisted to commit a
    crime.
367. *approve:* prove.
371. *securer:* more careless, less on guard. Cf. 380–81.
377. *submiss:* submissive.

May find us both perhaps far less prepared,
The willinger I go, nor much expect
A foe so proud will first the weaker seek;
So bent, the more shall shame him his repulse."
Thus saying, from her husband's hand her hand   385
Soft she withdrew, and like a wood-nymph light
Oread or Dryad, or of Delia's train,
Betook her to the groves, but Delia's self
In gait surpassed and goddess-like deport,
Though not as she with bow and quiver armed,   390
But with such gardening tools as art yet rude,
Guiltless of fire had formed, or angels brought.
To Pales, or Pomona, thus adorned,
Likest she seemed, Pomona when she fled
Vertumnus, or to Ceres in her prime,   395
Yet virgin of Proserpina from Jove.
Her long with ardent look his eye pursued
Delighted, but desiring more her stay.
Oft he to her his charge of quick return
Repeated, she to him as oft engaged   400
To be returned by noon amid the bow'r,
And all things in best order to invite
Noontide repast, or afternoon's repose.
O much deceived, much failing, hapless Eve,
Of thy presumed return! event perverse!   405
Thou never from that hour in Paradise
Found'st either sweet repast, or sound repose;
Such ambush hid among sweet flow'rs and shades
Waited with hellish rancor imminent
To intercept thy way, or send thee back   410
Despoiled of innocence, of faith, of bliss.
For now, and since first break of dawn the Fiend,
Mere serpent in appearance, forth was come,
And on his quest, where likeliest he might find

386. *light*: light-footed. Cf. 452.
387. *Oread*: a mountain nymph. *Dryad*: a wood nymph. *Delia*: Diana, goddess of the wood, who hunted with a *train* of nymphs.
389. *deport*: bearing.
392. *Guiltless of fire*. In pastoral Paradise there was no need for swords or ploughshares—hence no need for metal, smelting, or fire. Milton may allude to the guilt of Prometheus, who stole fire from heaven, according to a Greek myth that accounted for the introduction of evil into the world.
393–96. *Pales* was a goddess of animal husbandry; *Pomona*, of horticulture; *Ceres*, of agriculture (esp. of grain crops). *Vertumnus* wooed Pomona in many disguises before she accepted him. *Jove* made Ceres pregnant with *Proserpina*.
404. *failing*: mistaking, erring, at fault. *hapless*: unlucky.
405. *event*: outcome. *perverse*: (L *perversus* turned the wrong way) adverse, unpropitious, turned from right to wrong. Cf. I.164.
409. *imminent*: intent.
413. *Mere*: pure, nothing more or less than.

The only two of mankind, but in them   415
The whole included race, his purposed prey.
In bow'r and field he sought, where any tuft
Of grove or garden-plot more pleasant lay,
Their tendance or plantation for delight,
By fountain or by shady rivulet   420
He sought them both, but wished his hap might find
Eve separate, he wished, but not with hope
Of what so seldom chanced, when to his wish,
Beyond his hope, Eve separate he spies,
Veiled in a cloud of fragrance, where she stood,   425
Half spied, so thick the roses bushing round
About her glowed, oft stooping to support
Each flow'r of slender stalk, whose head though gay
Carnation, purple, azure, or specked with gold,
Hung drooping unsustained, them she upstays   430
Gently with myrtle band, mindless the while,
Herself, though fairest unsupported flow'r,
From her best prop so far, and storm so nigh.
Nearer he drew, and many a walk traversed
Of stateliest covert, cedar, pine, or palm,   435
Then voluble and bold, now hid, now seen
Among thick-woven arborets and flow'rs
Embordered on each bank, the hand of Eve:
Spot more delicious than those gardens feigned
Or of revived Adonis, or renowned   440
Alcinous, host of old Laertes' son,
Or that, not mystic, where the sapient king
Held dalliance with his fair Egyptian spouse.
Much he the place admired, the person more.
As one who long in populous city pent,   445
Where houses thick and sewers annoy the air,
Forth issuing on a summer's morn to breathe

419. I.e.: Which they had cultivated or planted for their pleasure.
431. *mindless the while*: not mindful for the moment (that she was so far . . .). *myrtle band*: ties
of myrtle vine.
436. *voluble*: undulating; moving easily or quickly.
437. *arborets*: groves, arbors.
438. *hand*: handiwork.
439–43. After his death, the beautiful youth *Adonis*, at the pleading of enamored Aphrodite,
was *revived* by Zeus. The gardens of Adonis were beds of beautiful, rapidly withering plants
set around images of him by worshiping maidens. See I.446–57n. Odysseus (*Laertes' son*) was
entertained in the gardens of *Alcinous*. Unlike these mythological (*mystic*) gardens was the real,
or historical, garden where Solomon (*the sapient king*) entertained his bride, a Pharaoh's
daughter. It was thought to be the garden alluded to in the Song Sol. *sapient*: L *sapere* to taste,
be wise. Fowler calls it a "heavily thematic word" in *PL* and refers to *sapience* in line 1018,
where *taste* and *savor* (L *sapere*) are part of the context.
446. *annoy*: (etymologically related to noisome) make offensive to the smell (though the OED
does not list that meaning).

Among the pleasant villages and farms
Adjoined, from each thing met conceives delight,
The smell of grain, or tedded grass, or kine,   450
Or dairy, each rural sight, each rural sound;
If chance with nymph-like step fair virgin pass,
What pleasing seemed, for her now pleases more,
She most, and in her look sums all delight.
Such pleasure took the Serpent to behold   455
This flow'ry plat, the sweet recess of Eve
Thus early, thus alone; her heav'nly form
Angelic, but more soft, and feminine,
Her graceful innocence, her every air
Of gesture or least action overawed   460
His malice, and with rapine sweet bereaved
His fierceness of the fierce intent it brought:
That space the Evil One abstracted stood
From his own evil, and for the time remained
Stupidly good, of enmity disarmed,   465
Of guile, of hate, of envy, of revenge;
But the hot hell that always in him burns,
Though in mid-heav'n, soon ended his delight,
And tortures him now more, the more he sees
Of pleasure not for him ordained: then soon   470
Fierce hate he recollects, and all his thoughts
Of mischief, gratulating, thus excites.
    "Thoughts, whither have ye led me, with what sweet
Compulsion thus transported to forget
What hither brought us, hate, not love, nor hope   475
Of Paradise for hell, hope here to taste
Of pleasure, but all pleasure to destroy,
Save what is in destroying, other joy
To me is lost. Then let me not let pass
Occasion which now smiles, behold alone   480
The woman, opportune to all attempts,
Her husband, for I view far round, not nigh,
Whose higher intellectual more I shun,
And strength, of courage haughty, and of limb
Heroic built, though of terrestrial mold,   485

450. *tedded grass:* hay spread out to dry. *kine:* cattle.
453. *for:* because of.
456. *plat:* plot. *recess:* retreat.
459. *air:* manner.
461. *rapine:* like *rapture,* L *rapere* to seize and carry off.
463. *abstracted:* mentally withdrawn.
465. *stupidly good:* good because stupified, or impotent.
472–73. I.e.: And thus calls out (*excites*) all his thoughts of mischief. *gratulating:* rejoicing.
481. *opportune to:* (L *ob* facing + *portus* port, harbor) ready for, open to, liable to.
484. *courage:* mind, spirit, disposition. *haughty:* noble, exalted.
485. *of terrestrial mold:* made of earthly material.

Foe not informidable, exempt from wound,
I not; so much hath hell debased, and pain
Enfeebled me, to what I was in heav'n.
She fair, divinely fair, fit love for gods,
Not terrible, though terror be in love   490
And beauty, not approached by stronger hate,
Hate stronger, under show of love well feigned,
The way which to her ruin now I tend."
    So spake the Enemy of mankind, enclosed
In serpent, inmate bad, and toward Eve   495
Addressed his way, not with indented wave,
Prone on the ground, as since, but on his rear,
Circular base of rising folds, that tow'red
Fold above fold a surging maze, his head
Crested aloft, and carbuncle his eyes;   500
With burnished neck of verdant gold, erect
Amidst his circling spires, that on the grass
Floated redundant: pleasing was his shape,
And lovely, never since of serpent kind
Lovelier, not those that in Illyria changed   505
Hermione and Cadmus, or the god
In Epidaurus; nor to which transformed
Ammonian Jove, or Capitoline was seen,
He with Olympias, this with her who bore
Scipio, the highth of Rome. With tract oblique   510
At first, as one who sought accéss, but feared
To interrupt, sidelong he works his way.
As when a ship by skilful steersman wrought
Nigh river's mouth or foreland, where the wind
Veers oft, as oft so steers, and shifts her sail;   515
So varied he, and of his tortuous train
Curled many a wanton wreath in sight of Eve,

486–87. Cf. 283 and VI.327.
490. *terrible:* terrifying.
491. *not:* unless.
496. *indented:* zigzag.
497–503. Cf. *Aen.* 5.84–89: "So had he spoken, when from the foot of the shrine a slippery
serpent trailed seven huge coils, fold upon fold seven times, peacefully circling the mound and
gliding among the altars; his back chequered with blue spots, and his scales ablaze with the
sheen of dappled gold, even as in the clouds the rainbow darts a thousand shifting tints athwart
the sun."
500. *carbuncle:* red.
502. *spires:* coils.
503. *redundant:* (L *re* back + *undare* to rise in waves) undulating; overflowing.
504–10. *Cadmus,* founder of Thebes, thinking himself cursed for slaying a serpent, asked to be
changed into a snake; then his wife, *Hermione,* made and was granted the same wish. Aes-
culapius, the god of healing, was brought to Rome, from *Epidaurus,* in Greece, in the form
of a snake, to rid the city of a plague. The *Jove* worshipped in Libya and called Ammon (cf.
IV.277n) made love to *Olympias* (mother of Alexander the Great) in the form of a snake.
Capitoline Jove (worshipped in Rome), similarly disguised, sired *Scipio* Africanus. *tract:* course,
route.
513–15. Cf. *opportune,* 481 and n.
517. *wanton:* unruly, gay, luxuriant, provocative.

To lure her eye; she busied heard the sound
Of rustling leaves, but minded not, as used
To such disport before her through the field, 520
From every beast, more duteous at her call,
Than at Circean call the herd disguised.
He bolder now, uncalled before her stood;
But as in gaze admiring: oft he bowed
His turret crest, and sleek enameled neck, 525
Fawning, and licked the ground whereon she trod.
His gentle dumb expression turned at length
The eye of Eve to mark his play; he glad
Of her attention gained, with serpent tongue
Organic, or impulse of vocal air, 530
His fraudulent temptation thus began.
  "Wonder not, sovran mistress, if perhaps
Thou canst, who art sole wonder, much less arm
Thy looks, the heav'n of mildness, with disdain,
Displeased that I approach thee thus, and gaze 535
Insatiate, I thus single, nor have feared
Thy awful brow, more awful thus retired.
Fairest resemblance of thy Maker fair,
Thee all things living gaze on, all things thine
By gift, and thy celestial beauty adore 540
With ravishment beheld, there best beheld
Where universally admired; but here
In this enclosure wild, these beasts among,
Beholders rude, and shallow to discern
Half what in thee is fair, one man except, 545
Who sees thee? (and what is one?) who shouldst be seen
A goddess among gods, adored and served
By angels numberless, thy daily train."
  So glozed the Tempter, and his proem tuned;
Into the heart of Eve his words made way, 550
Though at the voice much marveling; at length
Not unamazed she thus in answer spake.
"What may this mean? Language of man pronounced
By tongue of brute, and human sense expressed?
The first at least of these I thought denied 555
To beasts, whom God on their creation-day
Created mute to all articulate sound;
The latter I demur, for in their looks
Much reason, and in their actions oft appears.
Thee, serpent, subtlest beast of all the field 560

522. Circe cast spells over men and changed them into various kinds of animals.
825. *enameled:* of various colors.
530. *Organic:* instrumental, used as a tool. *impulse:* surge.
549. *glozed:* flattered. *proem:* prelude.
558. *demur:* (L *demorari* to linger, to delay) hesitate about, take exception to.

I knew, but not with human voice endued;
Redouble then this miracle, and say,
How cam'st thou speakable of mute, and how
To me so friendly grown above the rest
Of brutal kind, that daily are in sight?   565
Say, for such wonder claims attention due."
    To whom the guileful Tempter thus replied.
"Empress of this fair world, resplendent Eve,
Easy to me it is to tell thee all
What thou command'st, and right thou shouldst be obeyed: 570
I was at first as other beasts that graze
The trodden herb, of abject thoughts and low,
As was my food, nor aught but food discerned
Or sex, and apprehended nothing high:
Till on a day roving the field, I chanced   575
A goodly tree far distant to behold
Loaden with fruit of fairest colors mixed,
Ruddy and gold: I nearer drew to gaze;
When from the boughs a savory odor blown,
Grateful to appetite, more pleased my sense   580
Than smell of sweetest fennel, or the teats
Of ewe or goat dropping with milk at ev'n,
Unsucked of lamb or kid, that tend their play.
To satisfy the sharp desire I had
Of tasting those fair apples, I resolved   585
Not to defer; hunger and thirst at once,
Powerful persuaders, quickened at the scent
Of that alluring fruit, urged me so keen.
About the mossy trunk I wound me soon,
For high from ground the branches would require   590
Thy utmost reach or Adam's: round the tree
All other beasts that saw, with like desire
Longing and envying stood, but could not reach.
Amid the tree now got, where plenty hung
Tempting so nigh, to pluck and eat my fill   595
I spared not, for such pleasure till that hour
At feed or fountain never had I found.
Sated at length, ere long I might perceive
Strange alteration in me, to degree
Of reason in my inward powers, and speech   600
Wanted not long, though to this shape retained.
Thenceforth to speculations high or deep
I turned my thoughts, and with capacious mind

572. *abject*: mean-spirited, servile.
579. *savory*. See 442n and 1018–19n. *Savor* (L *sapere* to taste, to have good taste) meant both
    "physical taste" and "intellectual discernment."
581–82. According to Pliny *fennel* aids snakes in shedding their skin and sharpens their eyesight.
    More recent folklore held that snakes sucked the *teats* of sheep.

Considered all things visible in heav'n,
Or earth, or middle, all things fair and good;   605
But all that fair and good in thy divine
Semblance, and in thy beauty's heav'nly ray
United I beheld; no fair to thine
Equivalent or second, which compelled
Me thus, though importune perhaps, to come   610
And gaze, and worship thee of right declared
Sovran of creatures, universal dame."
      So talked the spirited sly snake; and Eve
Yet more amazed unwary thus replied.
      "Serpent, thy overpraising leaves in doubt   615
The virtue of that fruit, in thee first proved:
But say, where grows the tree, from hence how far?
For many are the trees of God that grow
In Paradise, and various, yet unknown
To us, in such abundance lies our choice,   620
As leaves a greater store of fruit untouched,
Still hanging incorruptible, till men
Grow up to their provision, and more hands
Help to disburden nature of her bearth."
      To whom the wily adder, blithe and glad.   625
"Empress, the way is ready, and not long,
Beyond a row of myrtles, on a flat,
Fast by a fountain, one small thicket past
Of blowing myrrh and balm; if thou accept
My conduct, I can bring thee thither soon."   630
      "Lead then," said Eve. He leading swiftly rolled
In tangles, and made intricate seem straight,
To mischief swift. Hope elevates, and joy
Brightens his crest, as when a wand'ring fire,
Compact of unctuous vapor, which the night   635
Condenses, and the cold environs round,
Kindled through agitation to a flame,
Which oft, they say, some evil spirit attends,

605. *middle:* the regions between.
608. *fair:* beauty.
610. *importune:* inopportunely.
612. *universal dame:* mistress of the universe.
613. *spirited:* inspired by (and possessed by) the spirit Satan.
616. *virtue:* power. *proved:* tested.
623. *Grow up to their provision:* increase to a number where the demand equals the supply
    (which has been provided by the providence of God).
624. *bearth:* (Milton's apparently deliberate spelling) what she bears.
629. *blowing myrrh and balm:* blossoming trees that exude the aromatic gums called myrrh and
    balm (or balsam) frequently mentioned in the Bible.
634. *wand'ring fire: ignis fatuus,* or will-o'-the-wisp.
635. *Compact:* composed. *unctuous:* oily.

Hovering and blazing with delusive light,
Misleads th' amazed night-wanderer from his way   640
To bogs and mires, and oft through pond or pool,
There swallowed up and lost, from succor far.
So glistered the dire snake, and into fraud
Led Eve our credulous mother, to the tree
Of prohibition, root of all our woe;   645
Which when she saw, thus to her guide she spake.
   "Serpent, we might have spared our coming hither,
Fruitless to me, though fruit be here to excess,
The credit of whose virtue rest with thee,
Wondrous indeed, if cause of such effects.   650
But of this tree we may not taste nor touch;
God so commanded, and left that command
Sole daughter of his voice; the rest, we live
Law to ourselves, our reason is our law."
   To whom the Tempter guilefully replied.   655
"Indeed? hath God then said that of the fruit
Of all these garden trees ye shall not eat,
Yet lords declared of all in earth or air?"
   To whom thus Eve yet sinless. "Of the fruit
Of each tree in the garden we may eat,   660
But of the fruit of this fair tree amidst
The garden, God hath said, 'Ye shall not eat
Thereof, nor shall ye touch it, lest ye die.' "
   She scarce had said, though brief, when now more bold
The Tempter, but with show of zeal and love   665
To man, and indignation at his wrong,
New part puts on, and as to passion moved,
Fluctuates disturbed, yet comely, and in act
Raised, as of some great matter to begin.
As when of old some orator renowned   670
In Athens or free Rome, where eloquence

---

640. *amazed*: perplexed, as in a maze. Cf. Eve's amazement, line 614.
649. I.e.: Let the belief in (or reason for believing in, or the custody of) whose powers remain
   with thee.
653. *Sole daughter of his voice*: God's only commandment. In Hebrew *Bath Kol*, "daughter of
   a voice," means a voice from heaven.
654. Cf. Rom. 2.14: "For when the Gentiles, which have not the law, do by nature the things
   contained in the law, these, having not the law, are a law unto themselves."
667. *New part puts on*. Satan's rhetorical task has changed because the argument has changed:
   now the topic is philosophical, religious, and political, and his speech will be like one of those
   great, ancient deliberative (or political) orations advising the audience on the best course of
   action. In his new role he will urge man to exercise his "right to know."
668. *Fluctuates*: (L *fluctuare* to undulate) Milton may ironically glance at Satan's snakelike
   motion, but the primary senses of the word are to pace back and forth and to express vacillation
   of mental attitude. *disturbed*: disordered, discomposed. *act*: in Latin rhetoric *actio* meant the
   exterior air or bearing of an orator.
669. *Raised*: drawn up to full dignity.

Flourished, since mute, to some great cause addressed,
Stood in himself collected, while each part,
Motion, each act won audience ere the tongue,
Sometimes in highth began, as no delay   675
Of preface brooking through his zeal of right.
So standing, moving, or to highth upgrown
The Tempter all impassioned thus began.
    "O sacred, wise, and wisdom-giving plant,
Mother of science, now I feel thy power   680
Within me clear, not only to discern
Things in their causes, but to trace the ways
Of highest agents, deemed however wise.
Queen of this universe, do not believe
Those rigid threats of death; ye shall not die: 685
How should ye? By the fruit? It gives you life
To knowledge. By the Threat'ner? Look on me,
Me who have touched and tasted, yet both live,
And life more perfect have attained than fate
Meant me, by vent'ring higher than my lot.   690
Shall that be shut to man, which to the beast
Is open? Or will God incense his ire
For such a petty trespass, and not praise
Rather your dauntless virtue, whom the pain
Of death denounced, whatever thing death be,   695
Deterred not from achieving what might lead
To happier life, knowledge of good and evil;
Of good, how just? Of evil, if what is evil
Be real, why not known, since easier shunned?
God therefore cannot hurt ye, and be just;   700
Not just, not God; not feared then, nor obeyed:
Your fear itself of death removes the fear.
Why then was this forbid? Why but to awe,
Why but to keep ye low and ignorant,
His worshipers; he knows that in the day   705

---

672. *to some great cause addressed*: prepared to speak on some great question of debate or case before a court.
673–74. *Stood in himself collected.* Cf. *in act Raised* (668). *each part, Motion, each act*: never satisfactorily explained (why each?). Thinking of accounts of classical orators as versatile actors able to move their audiences simply by pantomine, Milton may see the silent serpent Satan *fluctuating* (668) in role, gesture, and physical bearing or attitude. *audience*: attention.
675. *in highth*: in the kind of impassioned style orators usually do not work up to until well into their oration.
677. *standing, moving.* Cf. 673, 674, and VI.301–3. *to highth upgrown.* Cf. *in act Raised* (668), *act* (674), and *highth* (675).
680. *science*: knowledge.
687. *To*: in addition to.
692. *incense*: L *incendere* to set on fire.
694–95. *virtue*: courage, manliness; but perhaps also, goodness. *the pain / Of death denounced*: the announcement of the punishment of death.

Ye eat thereof, your eyes that seem so clear,
Yet are but dim, shall perfectly be then
Opened and cleared, and ye shall be as gods,
Knowing both good and evil as they know.
That ye should be as gods, since I as man,   710
Internal man, is but proportion meet,
I of brute human, ye of human gods.
So ye shall die perhaps, by putting off
Human, to put on gods, death to be wished,
Though threatened, which no worse than this can bring.   715
And what are gods that man may not become
As they, participating godlike food?
The gods are first, and that advantage use
On our belief, that all from them proceeds;
I question it, for this fair earth I see,   720
Warmed by the sun, producing every kind,
Them nothing: if they all things, who enclosed
Knowledge of good and evil in this tree,
That whoso eats thereof, forthwith attains
Wisdom without their leave? And wherein lies   725
Th' offense, that man should thus attain to know?
What can your knowledge hurt him, or this tree
Impart against his will if all be his?
Or is it envy, and can envy dwell
In heav'nly breasts? These, these and many more   730
Causes import your need of this fair fruit.
Goddess humane, reach then, and freely taste."
    He ended, and his words replete with guile
Into her heart too easy entrance won:
Fixed on the fruit she gazed, which to behold   735
Might tempt alone, and in her ears the sound
Yet rung of his persuasive words, impregned
With reason, to her seeming, and with truth;
Meanwhile the hour of noon drew on, and waked
An eager appetite, raised by the smell   740
So savory of that fruit, which with desire,
Inclinable now grown to touch or taste,
Solicited her longing eye; yet first
Pausing a while, thus to herself she mused:
    "Great are thy virtues, doubtless, best of fruits,   745

711. *Internal man.* Cf. *my inward powers* (600).
713–14. An ironic parody of phrases used to describe the process of salvation; cf. 1 Cor. 15.53: "For this corruptible must put on incorruption, and this mortal must put on immortality."
717. *participating*: sharing, partaking of.
722. I.e.: If they [produced] all things.
731. *Causes*: reasons. *import*: indicate, prove.
732. *humane*: a common spelling for *human* in the seventeenth century, but in the only other instances of this spelling in Milton's poetry the word means kind, gentle, or gracious.
741. *savory.* See 579n.
745. *virtues*: powers.

Though kept from man, and worthy to be admired,
Whose taste, too long forborne, at first assay
Gave elocution to the mute, and taught
The tongue not made for speech to speak thy praise:
Thy praise he also who forbids thy use,   750
Conceals not from us, naming thee the Tree
Of Knowledge, knowledge both of good and evil;
Forbids us then to taste, but his forbidding
Commends thee more, while it infers the good
By thee communicated, and our want: 755
For good unknown, sure is not had, or had
And yet unknown, is as not had at all.
In plain then, what forbids he but to know,
Forbids us good, forbids us to be wise?
Such prohibitions bind not. But if death   760
Bind us with after-bands, what profits then
Our inward freedom? In the day we eat
Of this fair fruit, our doom is, we shall die.
How dies the serpent? He hath eat'n and lives,
And knows, and speaks, and reasons, and discerns,   765
Irrational till then. For us alone
Was death invented? Or to us denied
This intellectual food, for beasts reserved?
For beasts it seems: yet that one beast which first
Hath tasted, envies not, but brings with joy   770
The good befall'n him, author unsuspect,
Friendly to man, far from deceit or guile.
What fear I then, rather what know to fear
Under this ignorance of good and evil,
Of God or death, of law or penalty?   775
Here grows the cure of all, this fruit divine,
Fair to the eye, inviting to the taste,
Of virtue to make wise: what hinders then
To reach, and feed at once both body and mind?"
    So saying, her rash hand in evil hour   780
Forth reaching to the fruit, she plucked, she ate:
Earth felt the wound, and nature from her seat
Sighing through all her works gave signs of woe,
That all was lost. Back to the thicket slunk
The guilty serpent, and well might, for Eve   785

754. *infers:* implies.
755. *want:* lack.
758. *In plain:* plainly.
763. *doom:* irrevocable destiny.
770. *envies:* begrudges.
771. *author:* authority, informant. *unsuspect:* beyond suspicion.
782. *her seat:* where she holds court.
782–84. Cf. *Aen.* 4.166–70: "Primal Earth and nuptial Juno give the sign; fires flashed in Heaven,
   the witness to their bridal, and on the mountain-top screamed the nymphs. That day was the
   first of death, that first the cause of woe."

Intent now wholly on her taste, naught else
Regarded, such delight till then, as seemed,
In fruit she never tasted, whether true
Or fancied so, through expectation high
Of knowledge, nor was Godhead from her thought.   790
Greedily she engorged without restraint,
And knew not eating death: satiate at length,
And hightened as with wine, jocund and boon,
Thus to herself she pleasingly began.
    "O sovran, virtuous, precious of all trees   795
In Paradise, of operation blest
To sapience, hitherto obscured, infamed,
And thy fair fruit let hang, as to no end
Created; but henceforth my early care,
Not without song, each morning, and due praise   800
Shall tend thee, and the fertile burden ease
Of thy full branches offered free to all;
Till dieted by thee I grow mature
In knowledge, as the gods who all things know;
Though others envy what they cannot give;   805
For had the gift been theirs, it had not here
Thus grown. Experience, next to thee I owe,
Best guide; not following thee, I had remained
In ignorance, thou open'st wisdom's way,
And giv'st accéss, though secret she retire.   810
And I perhaps am secret; Heav'n is high,
High and remote to see from thence distinct
Each thing on earth; and other care perhaps
May have diverted from continual watch
Our great Forbidder, safe with all his spies   815
About him. But to Adam in what sort
Shall I appear? shall I to him make known
As yet my change, and give him to partake
Full happiness with me, or rather not,
But keep the odds of knowledge in my power   820
Without copartner? so to add what wants
In female sex, the more to draw his love,
And render me more equal, and perhaps,
A thing not undesirable, sometime
Superior; for inferior who is free?   825
This may be well: but what if God have seen,

792. *knew not* [that she was] *eating.*
793. *jocund and boon:* merry and (in a jovial bacchanalian sense) jolly, convivial.
795. *virtuous, precious:* most powerful and valuable.
796–97. *of operation blest / To:* endowed with the power to give. *sapience:* wisdom. Cf. *science* (knowledge) in 680 and 442n. *obscured:* imperfectly understood. *infamed:* defamed.
805. I.e.: Though they [the gods] begrudge to others what they have no power to give.
811. *secret:* hidden, unseen.
816. *sort:* manner.
820. *odds:* advantage.

And death ensue? Then I shall be no more,
And Adam wedded to another Eve,
Shall live with her enjoying, I extinct;
A death to think. Confirmed then I resolve,   830
Adam shall share with me in bliss or woe:
So dear I love him, that with him all deaths
I could endure, without him live no life."
    So saying, from the tree her step she turned,
But first low reverence done, as to the power   835
That dwelt within, whose presence had infused
Into the plant sciential sap, derived
From nectar, drink of gods. Adam the while
Waiting desirous her return, had wove
Of choicest flow'rs a garland to adorn   840
Her tresses, and her rural labors crown,
As reapers oft are wont their harvest queen.
Great joy he promised to his thoughts, and new
Solace in her return, so long delayed;
Yet oft his heart, divine of something ill,   845
Misgave him; he the falt'ring measure felt;
And forth to meet her went, the way she took
That morn when first they parted; by the Tree
Of Knowledge he must pass; there he her met,
Scarce from the tree returning; in her hand   850
A bough of fairest fruit that downy smiled,
New gathered, and ambrosial smell diffused.
To him she hasted, in her face excuse
Came prologue, and apology to prompt,
Which with bland words at will she thus addressed.   855
    "Hast thou not wondered, Adam, at my stay?
Thee I have missed, and thought it long, deprived
Thy presence, agony of love till now
Not felt, nor shall be twice, for never more
Mean I to try, what rash untried I sought,   860
The pain of absence from thy sight. But strange
Hath been the cause, and wonderful to hear:
This tree is not as we are told, a tree
Of danger tasted, nor to evil unknown
Op'ning the way, but of divine effect   865
To open eyes, and make them gods who taste;
And hath been tasted such: the serpent wise,

---

837. *sciential:* knowledge-producing.
845. *divine of:* divining.
846. *falt'ring measure:* irregular [heart] beat.
853–55. I.e.: Excuse came like the prologue in a play, and apology served as a prompter, as Eve
    recited her speech of self-defense, which she dressed, or adorned, in the following way with
    soothing words chosen without regard to anything but her own purpose.
860–85. In reading this passage remember that *try, taste, test,* and *tempt* can be synonymous.

Or not restrained as we, or not obeying,
Hath eaten of the fruit, and is become,
Not dead, as we are threatened, but thenceforth   870
Endued with human voice and human sense,
Reasoning to admiration, and with me
Persuasively hath so prevailed, that I
Have also tasted, and have also found
Th' effects to correspond, opener mine eyes,   875
Dim erst, dilated spirits, ampler heart,
And growing up to godhead; which for thee
Chiefly I sought, without thee can despise.
For bliss, as thou hast part, to me is bliss,
Tedious, unshared with thee, and odious soon.   880
Thou therefore also taste, that equal lot
May join us, equal joy, as equal love;
Lest thou not tasting, different degree
Disjoin us, and I then too late renounce
Deity for thee, when fate will not permit."   885
      Thus Eve with count'nance blithe her story told;
But in her cheek distemper flushing glowed.
On th' other side, Adam, soon as he heard
The fatal trespass done by Eve, amazed,
Astonied stood and blank, while horror chill   890
Ran through his veins, and all his joints relaxed;
From his slack hand the garland wreathed for Eve
Down dropped, and all the faded roses shed:
Speechless he stood and pale, till thus at length
First to himself he inward silence broke.   895
      "O fairest of creation, last and best
Of all God's works, creature in whom excelled
Whatever can to sight or thought be formed,
Holy, divine, good, amiable, or sweet!
How art thou lost, how on a sudden lost,   900
Defaced, deflow'red, and now to death devote?
Rather how hast thou yielded to transgress
The strict forbiddance, how to violate
The sacred fruit forbidd'n! some cursèd fraud
Of enemy hath beguiled thee, yet unknown,   905
And me with thee hath ruined, for with thee
Certain my resolution is to die;

872. *to admiration:* so as to cause wonder and delight.
881. *equal lot.* Cf. *consort,* 954n.
887. *distemper:* physical disorder; intoxication.
889. *amazed:* stupefied; confused; terror-stricken.
890. *Astonied:* (L *ex + tonare* to thunder) stunned. *blank:* pale, confounded.
901. *devote:* devoted, doomed.
904. *sacred:* consecrated, set apart.
906–7. I.e.: My resolution to die with thee is fixed, unalterable. Cf. *fixed,* 952.

How can I live without thee, how forgo
Thy sweet converse and love so dearly joined,
To live again in these wild woods forlorn?   910
Should God create another Eve, and I
Another rib afford, yet loss of thee
Would never from my heart; no no, I feel
The link of nature draw me: flesh of flesh,
Bone of my bone thou art, and from thy state   915
Mine never shall be parted, bliss or woe."
    So having said, as one from sad dismay
Recomforted, and after thoughts disturbed
Submitting to what seemed remédiless,
Thus in calm mood his words to Eve he turned.   920
    "Bold deed thou hast presumed, advent'rous Eve,
And peril great provoked, who thus hast dared
Had it been only coveting to eye
That sacred fruit, sacred to abstinence,
Much more to taste it under ban to touch.   925
But past who can recall, or done undo?
Not God omnipotent, nor fate; yet so
Perhaps thou shalt not die, perhaps the fact
Is not so heinous now, foretasted fruit,
Profaned first by the serpent, by him first   930
Made common and unhallowed ere our taste;
Nor yet on him found deadly, he yet lives,
Lives, as thou saidst, and gains to live as man
Higher degree of life, inducement strong
To us, as likely tasting to attain   935
Proportional ascent, which cannot be
But to be gods, or angels demi-gods.
Nor can I think that God, Creator wise,
Though threat'ning, will in earnest so destroy
Us his prime creatures, dignified so high,   940
Set over all his works, which in our fall,
For us created, needs with us must fail,
Dependent made; so God shall uncreate,
Be frustrate, do, undo, and labor lose,
Not well conceived of God, who though his power   945
Creation could repeat, yet would be loath
Us to abolish, lest the Adversary
Triumph and say; 'Fickle their state whom God
Most favors, who can please him long? Me first

914–15. *flesh of flesh,* / *Bone of my bone.* Cf. Gen. 2.23–24, p. 431.
925. *touch.* Cf. VII.46 and IX.651 and 663, where the command not to touch the fruit (Gen.
    3.2, 3, p. 432) is alluded to. Adam says it was dangerous even to look at the fruit and certainly
    more dangerous to eat what they had been told not even to touch.
928. *fact:* crime, deed.
944. *frustrate:* frustrated, defined by "do, undo."

He ruined, now mankind; whom will he next?'   950
Matter of scorn, not to be given the Foe.
However I with thee have fixed my lot,
Certain to undergo like doom; if death
Consort with thee, death is to me as life;
So forcible within my heart I feel   955
The bond of nature draw me to my own,
My own in thee, for what thou art is mine;
Our state cannot be severed, we are one,
One flesh; to lose thee were to lose myself."
    So Adam, and thus Eve to him replied.   960
"O glorious trial of exceeding love,
Illustrious evidence, example high!
Engaging me to emulate, but short
Of thy perfection, how shall I attain,
Adam, from whose dear side I boast me sprung,   965
And gladly of our union hear thee speak,
One heart, one soul in both; whereof good proof
This day affords, declaring thee resolved,
Rather than death or aught than death more dread
Shall separate us, linked in love so dear,   970
To undergo with me one guilt, one crime,
If any be, of tasting this fair fruit,
Whose virtue, for of good still good proceeds,
Direct, or by occasion hath presented
This happy trial of thy love, which else   975
So eminently never had been known.
Were it I thought death menaced would ensue
This my attempt, I would sustain alone
The worst, and not persuade thee, rather die
Deserted, than oblige thee with a fact   980
Pernicious to thy peace, chiefly assured
Remarkably so late of thy so true,
So faithful love unequaled; but I feel
Far otherwise th' event, not death, but life
Augmented, opened eyes, new hopes, new joys,   985
Taste so divine, that what of sweet before

953. *Certain*: resolved. Cf. 907. *doom*: sentence of punishment.
954. *Consort*: keep company, associate. Since the noun *consort* (L *con* with + *sortis* lot, fate; *consors* partner, fellow, one having a common lot or fate with another) is used several times in reference to Eve's married relationship with Adam, Milton's choice of the verb here, in the context of *lot* and *like doom* barely avoids the suggestion that Adam would be jealous of death, as Eve earlier feared that Adam would find a second Eve.
974. *Direct, or by occasion*: as the real, fundamental cause, or as the immediate, circumstantial cause.
977. *menaced*: threatened.
980. *obliged*: (L *obligare* to bind one in a criminal plot) make guilty, liable to penalty. *fact*: deed, crime.
981–82. I.e.: Particularly since I have so recently been notably assured of, etc.
984. *event*: consequence.

Hath touched my sense, flat seems to this, and harsh.
Of my experience, Adam, freely taste,
And fear of death deliver to the winds."
   So saying, she embraced him, and for joy   990
Tenderly wept, much won that he his love
Had so ennobled, as of choice to incur
Divine displeasure for her sake, or death.
In recompense (for such compliance bad
Such recompense best merits) from the bough   995
She gave him of that fair enticing fruit
With liberal hand: he scrupled not to eat
Against his better knowledge, not deceived,
But fondly overcome with female charm.
Earth trembled from her entrails, as again   1000
In pangs, and nature gave a second groan;
Sky loured, and muttering thunder, some sad drops
Wept at completing of the mortal sin
Original; while Adam took no thought,
Eating his fill, nor Eve to iterate   1005
Her former trespass feared, the more to soothe
Him with her loved society, that now
As with new wine intoxicated both
They swim in mirth, and fancy that they feel
Divinity within them breeding wings   1010
Wherewith to scorn the earth: but that false fruit
Far other operation first displayed,
Carnal desire inflaming, he on Eve
Began to cast lascivious eyes, she him
As wantonly repaid; in lust they burn: 1015
Till Adam thus 'gan Eve to dalliance move.
   "Eve, now I see thou art exact of taste,
And elegant, of sapience no small part,
Since to each meaning savor we apply,
And palate call judicious; I the praise   1020
Yield thee, so well this day thou hast purveyed.
Much pleasure we have lost, while we abstained

998–99. Cf. 1 Tim. 2.14: "And Adam was not deceived, but the woman being deceived was in the transgression." Cf. St. Augustine, *The City of God*, XIV.xi (trans. Marcus Dods): "We cannot believe that Adam was deceived, and supposed the devil's word to be truth, and therefore transgressed God's law, but that he by the drawings of kindred yielded to the woman, the husband to the wife, the one human being to the only other human being." *fondly*: foolishly.
1003–4. *mortal sin / Original*. Cf. CD, p. 417.
1005. *iterate*: repeat.
1012. *operation*. Cf. VIII.323n.
1017. *exact*: L *exigere* to demand.
1018–19. *elegant*: L *eligere* to select. *sapience*: L *sapere*, to taste, have sense, know. Adam says that we use the word savor to mean both the ability to taste or enjoy (*taste*) and the ability to know or discriminate (*sapience*). Cf. 442, 579, 741.
1021. *purveyed*: provided.

From this delightful fruit, nor known till now
True relish, tasting; if such pleasure be
In things to us forbidden, it might be wished,   1025
For this one tree had been forbidden ten.
But come, so well refreshed, now let us play,
As meet is, after such delicious fare;
For never did thy beauty since the day
I saw thee first and wedded thee, adorned   1030
With all perfections, so inflame my sense
With ardor to enjoy thee, fairer now
Than ever, bounty of this virtuous tree."
    So said he, and forbore not glance or toy
Of amorous intent, well understood   1035
Of Eve, whose eye darted contagious fire.
Her hand he seized, and to a shady bank,
Thick overhead with verdant roof embow'red
He led her nothing loath; flow'rs were the couch,
Pansies, and violets, and asphodel,   1040
And hyacinth, earth's freshest softest lap.
There they their fill of love and love's disport
Took largely, of their mutual guilt the seal,
The solace of their sin, till dewy sleep
Oppressed them, wearied with their amorous play.   1045
Soon as the force of that fallacious fruit,
That with exhilarating vapor bland
About their spirits had played, and inmost powers
Made err, was now exhaled, and grosser sleep
Bred of unkindly fumes, with conscious dreams   1050
Encumbered, now had left them, up they rose
As from unrest, and each the other viewing,
Soon found their eyes how opened, and their minds
How darkened; innocence, that as a veil
Had shadowed them from knowing ill, was gone,   1055
Just confidence, and native righteousness,
And honor from about them, naked left
To guilty shame: he covered, but his robe

1027–28. Cf. Exod. 32.6: "And they rose up early on the morrow, and offered burnt offerings, and brought peace offerings; and the people sat down to eat and drink, and rose up to play." 1 Cor. 10.7: "Neither be ye idolaters, as were some of them; as it is written, The people sat down to eat and drink, and rose up to play. Neither let us commit fornication, as some of them committed. . . ." *meet:* appropriate.
1034. *toy:* caress.
1042–44. *fill of love . . . took . . . solace:* In Prov. 71.18 a harlot says, "Come, let us take our fill of love until the morning: let us solace ourselves with loves."
1047. *bland:* flattering, seductive, sensuously pleasing.
1050. *unkindly:* unnatural. *fumes:* noxious exhalations rising to the brain from the stomach. *conscious:* self-knowing, guilty.
1051. *Encumbered:* oppressed.
1054–58. Cf. *CD*, p. 419.
1058. *he covered:* i.e., shame covered them.

Uncovered more. So rose the Danite strong
Hercúlean Samson from the harlot-lap   1060
Of Philistéan Dálilah, and waked
Shorn of his strength, they destitute and bare
Of all their virtue: silent, and in face
Confounded long they sat, as strucken mute,
Till Adam, though not less than Eve abashed,   1065
At length gave utterance to these words constrained.
    "O Eve, in evil hour thou didst give ear
To that false worm, of whomsoever taught
To counterfeit man's voice, true in our fall,
False in our promised rising; since our eyes   1070
Opened we find indeed, and find we know
Both good and evil, good lost and evil got,
Bad fruit of knowledge, if this be to know,
Which leaves us naked thus, of honor void,
Of innocence, of faith, of purity,   1075
Our wonted ornaments now soiled and stained,
And in our faces evident the signs
Of foul concupiscence; whence evil store;
Even shame, the last of evils; of the first
Be sure then. How shall I behold the face   1080
Henceforth of God or angel, erst with joy
And rapture so oft beheld? Those heav'nly shapes
Will dazzle now this earthly, with their blaze
Insufferably bright. O might I here
In solitude live savage, in some glade   1085
Obscured, where highest woods impenetrable
To star or sunlight, spread their umbrage broad,
And brown as evening: cover me ye pines,
Ye cedars, with innumerable boughs
Hide me, where I may never see them more.   1090
But let us now, as in bad plight, devise
What best may for the present serve to hide
The parts of each from other, that seem most
To shame obnoxious, and unseemliest seen,

1059–62. *Samson* (of the tribe of Dan) told *Dalilah* (of the Philistines, enemies of Israel) that his strength was due to his not cutting his hair. She sheared it off while he slept, and he was no longer strong as Hercules. See Judg. 16.
1063–64. *in face / Confounded*: with an expression of dismay, confusion, shame. Cf. *confound* in II.382.
1066. *constrained*: strained, forced, unnatural.
1078. *evil store*: an abundance of evil.
1079. *the last . . . the first*: perhaps: "Be sure that if the signs of shame are evident in our faces, signs of the evils that caused it are also evident."
1080–84. Cf. VII.506–11, where Adam was promised the privilege to *correspond with Heaven*.
1088. *brown*: dark.
1090. Cf. Rev. 6.16: "And said to the mountains and rocks, Fall on us, and hide us from the face of him that sitteth on the throne, and from the wrath of the Lamb."
1094. *obnoxious*: exposed, subject.

Some tree whose broad smooth leaves together sewed,   1095
And girded on our loins, may cover round
Those middle parts, that this newcomer, shame,
There sit not, and reproach us as unclean."
    So counseled he, and both together went
Into the thickest wood, there soon they chose   1100
The figtree, not that kind for fruit renowned,
But such as at this day to Indians known
In Malabar or Deccan spreads her arms
Branching so broad and long, that in the ground
The bended twigs take root, and daughters grow   1105
About the mother tree, a pillared shade
High overarched, and echoing walks between;
There oft the Indian herdsman shunning heat
Shelters in cool, and tends his pasturing herds
At loopholes cut through thickest shade: those leaves   1110
They gathered, broad as Amazonian targe,
And with what skill they had, together sewed,
To gird their waist, vain covering if to hide
Their guilt and dreaded shame; O how unlike
To that first naked glory. Such of late   1115
Columbus found th' American so girt
With feathered cincture, naked else and wild,
Among the trees on isles and woody shores.
Thus fenced, and as they thought, their shame in part
Covered, but not at rest or ease of mind,   1120
They sat them down to weep, nor only tears
Rained at their eyes, but high winds worse within
Began to rise, high passions, anger, hate,
Mistrust, suspicion, discord, and shook sore
Their inward state of mind, calm region once   1125
And full of peace, now tossed and turbulent:
For understanding ruled not, and the will
Heard not her lore, both in subjection now
To sensual appetite, who from beneath
Usurping over sovran reason claimed   1130
Superior sway: from thus distempered breast,
Adam, estranged in look and altered style,
Speech intermitted thus to Eve renewed.

1101–10. Milton's description follows in detail that of the "arched Indian Figtree" in Gerard's
  Herball (1597) and others. Milton did not know that the banyan, which fits the description in
  other respects, has small leaves. *Malabar or Deccan*. In India.
1111. *Amazonian targe*: the shields of Amazons.
1117. *cincture*: belt.
1121. Cf. Ps. 137.1: "By the rivers of Babylon, there we [the Israelites in exile] sat down, yea,
  we wept, when we remembered Zion."
1127–31. See "Physiology and Psychology," pp. 463–64.
1132. *estranged*: unlike himself.

"Would thou hadst hearkened to my words, and stayed
With me, as I besought thee, when that strange   1135
Desire of wand'ring this unhappy morn,
I know not whence possessed thee; we had then
Remained still happy, not as now, despoiled
Of all our good, shamed, naked, miserable.
Let none henceforth seek needless cause to approve   1140
The faith they owe; when earnestly they seek
Such proof, conclude, they then begin to fail."
    To whom soon moved with touch of blame thus Eve.
"What words have passed thy lips, Adam severe,
Imput'st thou that to my default, or will   1145
Of wand'ring, as thou call'st it, which who knows
But might as ill have happened thou being by,
Or to thyself perhaps: hadst thou been there,
Or here th' attempt, thou couldst not have discerned
Fraud in the serpent, speaking as he spake;   1150
No ground of enmity between us known,
Why he should mean me ill, or seek to harm.
Was I to have never parted from thy side?
As good have grown there still a lifeless rib.
Being as I am, why didst not thou the head   1155
Command me absolutely not to go,
Going into such danger as thou saidst?
Too facile then thou didst not much gainsay,
Nay didst permit, approve, and fair dismiss.
Hadst thou been firm and fixed in thy dissent,   1160
Neither had I transgressed, nor thou with me."
    To whom then first incensed Adam replied.
"Is this the love, is this the recompense
Of mine to thee, ingrateful Eve, expressed
Immutable when thou wert lost, not I,   1165
Who might have lived and joyed immortal bliss,
Yet willingly chose rather death with thee:
And am I now upbraided, as the cause
Of thy transgressing? not enough severe,
It seems, in thy restraint: what could I more?   1170
I warned thee, I admonished thee, foretold
The danger, and the lurking enemy
That lay in wait; beyond this had been force,
And force upon free will hath here no place.

1140. *approve*: prove.
1141. *owe*: own.
1155. *head*. Cf. 1 Cor. 11.3: "the head of the woman is the man."
1158. *facile*: easily persuaded; mild mannered.
1164–65. *expressed / Immutable*: demonstrated to be unchangeable.

But confidence then bore thee on, secure   1175
Either to meet no danger, or to find
Matter of glorious trial; and perhaps
I also erred in overmuch admiring
What seemed in thee so perfect, that I thought
No evil durst attempt thee, but I rue   1180
That error now, which is become my crime,
And thou th' accuser. Thus it shall befall
Him who to worth in women overtrusting
Lets her will rule; restraint she will not brook,
And left to herself, if evil thence ensue,   1185
She first his weak indulgence will accuse."
    Thus they in mutual accusation spent
The fruitless hours, but neither self-condemning,
And of their vain contést appeared no end.

Book X

The Argument

Man's transgression known, the guardian angels forsake Paradise, and
return up to heaven to approve their vigilance, and are approved, God
declaring that the entrance of Satan could not be by them prevented.
He sends his Son to judge the transgressors, who descends and gives
sentence accordingly; then in pity clothes them both, and reascends.
Sin and Death, sitting till then at the gates of hell, by wondrous sympathy
feeling the success of Satan in this new world, and the sin by man there
committed, resolve to sit no longer confined in hell, but to follow Satan
their sire up to the place of man: to make the way easier from hell to
this world to and fro, they pave a broad highway or bridge over chaos,
according to the track that Satan first made; then preparing for earth,
they meet him proud of his success returning to hell; their mutual
gratulation. Satan arrives at Pandemonium, in full assembly relates with
boasting his success against man; instead of applause is entertained with
a general hiss by all his audience, transformed with himself also suddenly
into serpents, according to his doom given in Paradise; then deluded
with a show of the Forbidden Tree springing up before them, they
greedily reaching to take of the fruit, chew dust and bitter ashes. The
proceedings of Sin and Death; God foretells the final victory of his Son
over them, and the renewing of all things; but for the present commands
his angels to make several alterations in the heavens and elements. Adam

1175. *secure*: sure, self-assured.
1177. *Matter of*: occasion for.

more and more perceiving his fallen condition, heavily bewails, rejects
the condolement of Eve; she persists and at length appeases him: then
to evade the curse likely to fall on their offspring, proposes to Adam
violent ways which he approves not, but conceiving better hope, puts
her in mind of the late promise made them, that her seed should be
revenged on the Serpent, and exhorts her with him to seek peace of the
offended Deity, by repentance and supplication.

Meanwhile the heinous and despiteful act
Of Satan done in Paradise, and how
He in the serpent had perverted Eve,
Her husband she, to taste the fatal fruit,
Was known in heav'n; for what can scape the eye   5
Of God all-seeing, or deceive his heart
Omniscient, who in all things wise and just,
Hindered not Satan to attempt the mind
Of man, with strength entire, and free will armed,
Complete to have discovered and repulsed   10
Whatever wiles of foe or seeming friend.
For still they knew, and ought to have still remembered
The high injunction not to taste that fruit,
Whoever tempted; which they not obeying,
Incurred, what could they less, the penalty,   15
And manifold in sin, deserved to fall.
Up into heav'n from Paradise in haste
Th' angelic guards ascended, mute and sad
For man, for of his state by this they knew,
Much wond'ring how the subtle Fiend had stol'n   20
Entrance unseen. Soon as th' unwelcome news
From earth arrived at heaven gate, displeased
All were who heard, dim sadness did not spare
That time celestial visages, yet mixed
With pity, violated not their bliss.   25
About the new-arrived, in multitudes
Th' ethereal people ran, to hear and know
How all befell: they towards the throne supreme
Accountable made haste to make appear
With righteous plea, their utmost vigilance,   30
And easily approved: when the Most High
Eternal Father from his secret cloud,
Amidst in thunder uttered thus his voice.

X. 10. *Complete:* perfectly equipped.
16. *manifold in sin.* See CD, p. 416.
22–25. *displeased . . . bliss:* "all who heard were displeased, and on that occasion dim sadness
   crossed their faces; but since the sadness was mixed with pity it could not be said to have
   affected their perpetual bliss."
28–31. *they . . . approved:* "knowing that they were liable to be called to account, they hastened
   toward the throne, in order to make evident that they had watched with the utmost care; and
   they vindicated their conduct" (E. M. W. Tillyard).

"Assembled Angels, and ye Powers returned
From unsuccessful charge, be not dismayed,   35
Nor troubled at these tidings from the earth,
Which your sincerest care could not prevent,
Foretold so lately what would come to pass,
When first this tempter crossed the gulf from hell.
I told ye then he should prevail and speed   40
On his bad errand, man should be seduced
And flattered out of all, believing lies
Against his Maker; no decree of mine
Concurring to necessitate his fall,
Or touch with lightest moment of impulse   45
His free will, to her own inclining left
In even scale. But fall'n he is, and now
What rests, but that the mortal sentence pass
On his transgression, death denounced that day,
Which he presumes already vain and void,   50
Because not yet inflicted, as he feared,
By some immediate stroke; but soon shall find
Forbearance no acquittance ere day end.
Justice shall not return as bounty scorned.
But whom send I to judge them? Whom but thee   55
Vicegerent Son, to thee I have transferred
All judgment, whether in heav'n, or earth, or hell.
Easy it may be seen that I intend
Mercy colleague with justice, sending thee
Man's friend, his mediator, his designed   60
Both ransom and redeemer voluntary,
And destined man himself to judge man fall'n."
   So spake the Father, and unfolding bright
Toward the right hand his glory, on the Son
Blazed forth unclouded deity; he full   65
Resplendent all his Father manifest
Expressed, and thus divinely answered mild.
   "Father Eternal, thine is to decree,
Mine both in heav'n and earth to do thy will
Supreme, that thou in me thy Son beloved   70
May'st ever rest well pleased. I go to judge
On earth these thy transgressors; but thou know'st,
Whoever judged, the worst on me must light,

40. *speed:* succeed.
45. *moment:* the smallest weight that will tip a balance (scale).
53. *Forbearance is no acquittance.* A proverbial expression meaning that just because you have
   not been punished (or presented with a bill) don't think you're off the hook.
54. A hard line, which seems to mean, "They will not be able to reject my justice as they scorned
   my generosity."
55–57. Cf. John 5.22: "For the Father judgeth no man, but hath committed all judgment unto
   the Son."

When time shall be, for so I undertook
Before thee; and not repenting, this obtain   75
Of right, that I may mitigate their doom
On me derived, yet I shall temper so
Justice with mercy, as may illustrate most
Them fully satisfied, and thee appease.
Attendance none shall need, nor train, where none   80
Are to behold the judgment, but the judged,
Those two; the third best absent is condemned,
Convict by flight, and rebel to all law:
Conviction to the serpent none belongs."
    Thus saying, from his radiant seat he rose   85
Of high collateral glory: him thrones and powers,
princedoms, and dominations ministrant
Accompanied to heaven gate, from whence
Eden and all the coast in prospect lay.
Down he descended straight; the speed of gods   90
Time counts not, though with swiftest minutes winged.
Now was the sun in western cadence low
From noon, and gentle airs due at their hour
To fan the earth now waked, and usher in
The evening cool, when he from wrath more cool   95
Came the mild judge and intercessor both
To sentence man: the voice of God they heard
Now walking in the garden, by soft winds
Brought to their ears, while day declined; they heard,
And from his presence hid themselves among   100
The thickest trees, both man and wife, till God
Approaching, thus to Adam called aloud.
    "Where art thou Adam, wont with joy to meet
My coming seen far off? I miss thee here,
Not pleased, thus entertained with solitude,   105
Where obvious duty erewhile appeared unsought:
Or come I less conspicuous, or what change
Absents thee, or what chance detains? Come forth."
He came, and with him Eve, more loth, though first
To offend, discount'nanced both, and discomposed;   110
Love was not in their looks, either to God

77. *derived:* diverted.
78. *illustrate most:* best show.
80. *train:* attendants.
83. *Convict:* convicted.
84. The serpent has no right to trial by law.
86. *collateral:* placed side by side.
89. *coast:* (L *costa* side) surrounding territory.
92. *cadence:* L *cadere* to fall.
101. God: Christ.
106. *obvious duty:* your social obligation to greet me (L *obvius* in the way, so as to meet, meeting; affable, courteous).

Or to each other, but apparent guilt,
And shame, and perturbation, and despair,
Anger, and obstinacy, and hate, and guile.
Whence Adam falt'ring long, thus answered brief.   115
    "I heard thee in the garden, and of thy voice
Afraid, being naked, hid myself." To whom
The gracious Judge without revile replied.
    "My voice thou oft hast heard, and hast not feared,
But still rejoiced, how is it now become   120
So dreadful to thee? That thou art naked, who
Hath told thee? Hast thou eaten of the tree
Whereof I gave thee charge thou shouldst not eat?"
    To whom thus Adam sore beset replied.
"O heav'n! in evil strait this day I stand   125
Before my Judge, either to undergo
Myself the total crime, or to accuse
My other self, the partner of my life;
Whose failing, while her faith to me remains,
I should conceal, and not expose to blame   130
By my complaint; but strict necessity
Subdues me, and calamitous constraint,
Lest on my head both sin and punishment,
However insupportable, be all
Devolved; though should I hold my peace, yet thou   135
Wouldst easily detect what I conceal.
This woman whom thou mad'st to be my help,
And gav'st me as thy perfect gift, so good,
So fit, so acceptable, so divine,
That from her hand I could suspect no ill,   140
And what she did, whatever in itself,
Her doing seemed to justify the deed;
She gave me of the tree, and I did eat."
    To whom the Sovran Presence thus replied.
"Was she thy God, that her thou didst obey   145
Before his voice, or was she made thy guide,
Superior, or but equal, that to her
Thou didst resign thy manhood, and the place
Wherein God set thee above her made of thee,
And for thee, whose perfection far excelled   150
Hers in all real dignity: adorned
She was indeed, and lovely to attract
Thy love, not thy subjection, and her gifts
Were such as under government well seemed,

112. *apparent:* easily seen.
118. *revile:* reviling, abusive attack.
131. *necessity.* Cf. IV.393.
135. *Devolved:* passed down.
149–50. Cf. 1 Cor. 11.8–9: "For the man is not of the woman; but the woman of the man.
    Neither was the man created for the woman; but the woman for the man."

Unseemly to bear rule, which was thy part   155
And person, hadst thou known thyself aright."
   So having said, he thus to Eve in few:
"Say woman, what is this which thou hast done?"
   To whom sad Eve with shame nigh overwhelmed,
Confessing soon, yet not before her judge   160
Bold or loquacious, thus abashed replied.
   "The serpent me beguiled and I did eat."
   Which when the Lord God heard, without delay
To judgment he proceeded on th' accused
Serpent though brute, unable to transfer   165
The guilt on him who made him instrument
Of mischief, and polluted from the end
Of his creation; justly then accursed,
As vitiated in nature: more to know
Concerned not man (since he no further knew)   170
Nor altered his offense; yet God at last
To Satan first in sin his doom applied,
Though in mysterious terms, judged as then best:
And on the serpent thus his curse let fall.
   "Because thou hast done this, thou art accursed   175
Above all cattle, each beast of the field;
Upon thy belly groveling thou shalt go,
And dust shalt eat all the days of thy life.
Between thee and the woman I will put
Enmity, and between thine and her seed;   180
Her seed shall bruise thy head, thou bruise his heel."
   So spake this oracle, then verified
When Jesus son of Mary second Eve,
Saw Satan fall like lightning down from heav'n,
Prince of the air; then rising from his grave   185
Spoiled principalities and powers, triumphed
In open show, and with ascension bright
Captivity led captive through the air,
The realm itself of Satan long usurped,
Whom he shall tread at last under our feet;   190

155–56. *part / And person:* role and character (persona as in L *persona* mask).
167. *end:* purpose.
173. *mysterious:* having a hidden meaning.
175–81. Cf. Gen. 3.14–15, p. 432.
184. Cf. Luke 10.17–18: "And the seventy returned again with joy, saying, Lord, even the devils are subject unto us through thy name. And he said unto them, I beheld Satan as lightning fall from heaven."
185–90. Cf. Eph. 2.2: "Wherein in time past ye walked according to the course of this world, according to the prince of the power of the air, the spirit that now worketh in the children of disobedience." Col. 2.15: "And having spoiled principalities and powers, he made a shew of them openly, triumphing over them in it." Ps. 68.18: "Thou hast ascended on high, thou hast led captivity captive: thou hast received gifts for men; yea, for the rebellious also, that the Lord God might dwell among them." Rom. 16.20: "And the God of peace shall bruise Satan under your feet shortly. The grace of our Lord Jesus Christ be with you. Amen."

Ev'n he who now foretold his fatal bruise,
And to the woman thus his sentence turned.
    "Thy sorrow I will greatly multiply
By thy conception; children thou shalt bring
In sorrow forth, and to thy husband's will   195
Thine shall submit, he over thee shall rule."
    On Adam last thus judgment he pronounced.
"Because thou hast hearkened to the voice of thy wife,
And eaten of the tree concering which
I charged thee, saying: Thou shalt not eat thereof,   200
Cursed is the ground for thy sake, thou in sorrow
Shalt eat thereof all the days of thy life;
Thorns also and thistles it shall bring thee forth
Unbid, and thou shalt eat th' herb of the field,
In the sweat of thy face shalt thou eat bread,   205
Till thou return unto the ground, for thou
Out of the ground wast taken: know thy birth,
For dust thou art, and shalt to dust return."
    So judged he man, both judge and savior sent,
And th' instant stroke of death denounced that day   210
Removed far off; then pitying how they stood
Before him naked to the air, that now
Must suffer change, disdained not to begin
Thenceforth the form of servant to assume,
As when he washed his servants' feet, so now   215
As father of his family he clad
Their nakedness with skins of beasts, or slain,
Or as the snake with youthful coat repaid;
And thought not much to clothe his enemies:
Nor he their outward only with the skins   220
Of beasts, but inward nakedness, much more
Opprobrious, with his robe of righteousness,
Arraying covered from his Father's sight.
To him with swift ascent he up returned,
Into his blissful bosom reassumed   225
In glory as of old, to him appeased
All, though all-knowing, what had passed with man
Recounted, mixing intercession sweet.

210. *denounced:* proclaimed, gave warning of.
213–17. Cf. Phil. 2.7: "But [Christ] made himself of no reputation, and took upon him the form
of a servant, and was made in the likeness of men." John 13.5: "After that he poureth water
into a basin, and began to wash the disciples' feet, and to wipe them with the towel wherewith
he was girded."
217–18. *or slain,* / *Or:* either of beasts slain for their hides or of others, like the snake, that shed
their skins.
219. *thought not much:* thought it not too much.
222. Cf. Isa. 61.10: "I will greatly rejoice in the Lord, my soul shall be joyful in my God; for
he hath clothed me with the garments of salvation, he hath covered me with the robe of
righteousness, as a bridegroom decketh himself with ornaments, and as a bride adorneth herself
with her jewels."

Meanwhile ere thus was sinned and judged on earth,
Within the gates of hell sat Sin and Death,   230
In counterview within the gates, that now
Stood open wide, belching outrageous flame
Far into chaos, since the fiend passed through,
Sin opening, who thus now to Death began.
"O son, why sit we here each other viewing   235
Idly, while Satan our great author thrives
In other worlds, and happier seat provides
For us his offspring dear? It cannot be,
But that success attends him; if mishap,
Ere this he had returned, with fury driv'n   240
By his avengers, since no place like this
Can fit his punishment, or their revenge.
Methinks I feel new strength within me rise,
Wings growing, and dominion giv'n me large
Beyond this deep; whatever draws me on,   245
Or sympathy, or some connatural force
Powerful at greatest distance to unite
With secret amity things of like kind
By secretest conveyance. Thou my shade
Inseparable must with me along: 250
For Death from Sin no power can separate.
But lest the difficulty of passing back
Stay his return perhaps over this gulf
Impassable, impervious, let us try
Advent'rous work, yet to thy power and mine   255
Not unagreeable, to found a path
Over this main from hell to that new world
Where Satan now prevails, a monument
Of merit high to all th' infernal host,
Easing their passage hence, for intercourse,   260
Or transmigration, as their lot shall lead.
Nor can I miss the way, so strongly drawn
By this new-felt attraction and instinct."
    Whom thus the meager shadow answered soon.

232. *outrageous:* unrestrained, fierce.
235. Cf. 2 Kings 7.3: "And there were four leprous men at the entering in of the gate: and they
said one to another, Why sit we here until we die?" Matt. 20.6: "And about the eleventh hour
he went out, and found others standing idle, and saith unto them, Why stand ye here all the
day idle?"
236. *author:* father. Cf. II.864.
241. *like this.* Modifies *fit.*
246. *sympathy:* an attraction between opposite (or complementary) natures or between similar
natures. *connatural:* innate.
249. *conveyance:* communication.
254. *impervious:* (L *im* not + *per* through + *via* way) affording no passage.
256. *found:* establish, lay the foundation for.
260–61. *intercourse, / Or transmigration:* going back and forth, or emigrating to earth.
264. *meager:* having no or little flesh.

"Go whither fate and inclination strong   265
Leads thee, I shall not lag behind, nor err
The way, thou leading, such a scent I draw
Of carnage, prey innumerable, and taste
The savor of death from all things there that live:
Nor shall I to the work thou enterprisest   270
Be wanting, but afford thee equal aid."
   So saying, with delight he snuffed the smell
Of mortal change on earth. As when a flock
Of ravenous fowl, though many a league remote,
Against the day of battle, to a field,   275
Where armies lie encamped, come flying, lured
With scent of living carcasses designed
For death, the following day, in bloody fight.
So scented the grim feature, and upturned
His nostril wide into the murky air,   280
Sagacious of his quarry from so far.
Then both from out hell gates into the waste
Wide anarchy of chaos damp and dark
Flew diverse, and with power (their power was great)
Hovering upon the water, what they met   285
Solid or slimy, as in raging sea
Tossed up and down, together crowded drove
From each side shoaling towards the mouth of hell.
As when two polar winds blowing adverse
Upon the Cronian Sea, together drive   290
Mountains of ice, that stop th' imagined way
Beyond Petsora eastward, to the rich
Cathaian coast. The aggregated soil
Death with his mace petrific, cold and dry,
As with a trident smote, and fixed as firm   295
As Delos floating once; the rest his look

277. *designed:* marked out.
279. *feature:* (l. *facere* to make) a creature, sometimes used as a term of contempt.
281. *Sagacious:* keen in sense perception, especially in scenting.
284. *diverse:* in different directions.
285–304. The engineers, Sin and Death, first built a *mole* (300), or *gathered beach* (299), extending like a pier or breakwater from the mouth of hell out into the *waters* (285) of chaos. on this they built the first pier of the bridge, which Milton describes (313) as a *ridge* (i.e., a long reef) *of pendent* (i.e., supported by arches) *rock.* The other end of the bridge was fastened by *pins* and *chains* to the outer shell of the universe (302–3, 318). Later (415) Milton called the whole thing a *causey,* a word sometimes used to refer to both a bridge and its causewaylike approaches.
288. *shoaling:* forming a shoal.
290–93. A sea passage in the Arctic Ocean (*Cronian Sea*) between a bay in Siberia (Pechora) and the north China (*Cathay*) coast was only an *imagined* (by Hudson) *way* because it was blocked by ice.
293–98. Death's *mace* petrified the *cold and dry* elements of the collected matter and made the other (hot and liquid) elements into a kind of mortar, using asphalt and the magic power of his look, which, like that of Medusa, a Gorgon, turned what was looked at into stone. Neptune was said to have *fixed* the *floating* island of *Delos* (in the Aegean) by a stroke of his *trident.*

Bound with Gorgonian rigor not to move,
And with asphaltic slime; broad as the gate,
Deep to the roots of hell the gathered beach
They fastened, and the mole immense wrought on   300
Over the foaming deep high-arched, a bridge
Of length prodigious joining to the wall
Immovable of this now fenceless world
Forfeit to Death; from hence a passage broad,
Smooth, easy, inoffensive down to hell.   305
So, if great things to small may be compared,
Xerxes, the liberty of Greece to yoke,
From Susa his Memnonian palace high
Came to the sea, and over Hellespont
Bridging his way, Europe with Asia joined,   310
And scourged with many a stroke th' indignant waves.
Now had they brought the work by wondrous art
Pontifical, a ridge of pendent rock
Over the vexed abyss, following the track
Of Satan, to the selfsame place where he   315
First lighted from his wing, and landed safe
From out of chaos to the outside bare
Of this round world: with pins of adamant
And chains they made all fast, too fast they made
And durable; and now in little space   320
The confines met of empyrean heav'n
And of this world, and on the left hand hell
With long reach interposed; three sev'ral ways
In sight, to each of these three places led.
And now their way to earth they had descried,   325
To Paradise first tending, when behold
Satan in likeness of an angel bright
Betwixt the Centaur and the Scorpion steering
His zenith, while the sun in Aries rose:

303. *fenceless:* defenseless.
305. *inoffensive:* free from obstacles.
306–11. *Xerxes,* the powerful Persian king who invaded *Greece* in 480 B.C., ordered that the sea
be whipped for having destroyed the bridge of boats he built over the *Hellespont. Susa,* the
winter residence of Xerxes, was founded by the son of Memnon.
313. *Pontifical.* L *pontifex* was thought to have come from *pons, pontis* bridge + *facere* to make,
and Milton could not resist making a punning allusion to the papacy or any episcopacy—or
the chance to reinforce the pun by the word *rock* and its allusion to the doctrine that Peter (L
petrus rock) was the first pope: "Thou art Peter, and upon this rock I will build my church";
Matt. 16.18.
314. *vexed:* (L *vexare* to shake, agitate) stormy.
320–24. See "The Universe," pp. 461–63.
322. Cf. Matt. 25.33: "And he shall set the sheep on his right hand, but the goats on the left."
328–29. Fowler notes: "The . . . reason for steering *betwixt the Centaur* (Sagittarius) *and the
Scorpion* is . . . that the only constellation noticeably spread over these two signs is Anguis [L
for snake], the serpent held by Ophiuchus [Gk for serpent-bearer]. . . . Anguis has its head in
Libra, and extends through Scorpio into Sagittarius. Accordingly Satan enters the world in
Libra [III.551–61], but leaves it between Scorpio and Sagittarius."

Disguised he came, but those his children dear   330
Their parent soon discerned, though in disguise.
He, after Eve seduced, unminded slunk
Into the wood fast by, and changing shape
To observe the sequel, saw his guileful act
By Eve, though all unweeting, seconded   335
Upon her husband, saw their shame that sought
Vain covertures; but when he saw descend
The Son of God to judge them, terrified
He fled, not hoping to escape, but shun
The present, fearing guilty what his wrath   340
Might suddenly inflict; that past, returned
By night, and list'ning where the hapless pair
Sat in their sad discourse, and various plaint,
Thence gathered his own doom, which understood
Not instant, but of future time. With joy   345
And tidings fraught, to hell he now returned,
And at the brink of chaos, near the foot
Of this new wondrous pontifice, unhoped
Met who to meet him came, his offspring dear.
Great joy was at their meeting, and at sight   350
Of that stupendious bridge his joy increased.
Long he admiring stood, till Sin, his fair
Enchanting daughter, thus the silence broke.
    "O Parent, these are thy magnific deeds,
Thy trophies, which thou view'st as not thine own,   355
Thou art their author and prime architect:
For I no sooner in my heart divined,
My heart, which by a secret harmony
Still moves with thine, joined in connection sweet,
That thou on earth hadst prospered, which thy looks   360
Now also evidence, but straight I felt
Though distant from thee worlds between, yet felt
That I must after thee with this thy son;
Such fatal consequence unites us three:
Hell could no longer hold us in her bounds,   365
Nor this unvoyageable gulf obscure
Detain from following thy illustrious track.
Thou hast achieved our liberty, confined
Within hell gates till now, thou us empow'red
To fortify thus far, and overlay   370
With this portentous bridge the dark abyss.

332. *after Eve seduced:* Eve having been seduced. *unminded:* unnoticed.
334. *sequel:* consequence.
335. *unweeting:* unaware.
364. *consequence:* connection of cause to effect.
370. *fortify:* build "what amounts to a military road" (Hughes).

Thine now is all this world, thy virtue hath won
What thy hands builded not, thy wisdom gained
With odds what war hath lost, and fully avenged
Our foil in heav'n; here thou shalt monarch reign,   375
There didst not; there let him still victor sway,
As battle hath adjudged, from this new world
Retiring, by his own doom alienated,
And henceforth monarchy with thee divide
Of all things parted by th' empyreal bounds,   380
His quadrature, from thy orbicular world,
Or try thee now more dangerous to his throne."
   Whom thus the Prince of Darkness answered glad.
"Fair daughter, and thou son and grandchild both,
High proof ye now have giv'n to be the race   385
Of Satan (for I glory in the name,
Antagonist of heav'n's Almighty King)
Amply have merited of me, of all
Th' infernal empire, that so near heav'n's door
Triumphal with triumphal act have met,   390
Mine with this glorious work, and made one realm
Hell and this world, one realm, one continent
Of easy thoroughfare. Therefore while I
Descend through darkness, on your road with ease
To my associate powers, them to acquaint   395
With these successes, and with them rejoice,
You two this way, among those numerous orbs
All yours, right down to Paradise descend;
There dwell and reign in bliss, thence on the earth
Dominion exercise and in the air,   400
Chiefly on man, sole lord of all declared,
Him first make sure your thrall, and lastly kill.
My substitutes I send ye, and create
Plenipotent on earth, of matchless might
Issuing from me: on your joint vigor now   405
My hold of this new kingdom all depends,
Through Sin to Death exposed by my exploit.
If your joint power prevail, th' affairs of hell
No detriment need fear, go and be strong."
   So saying he dismissed them, they with speed   410
Their course through thickest constellations held
Spreading their bane; the blasted stars looked wan,

---

372. *virtue:* power, courage.
373–75. I.e.: thy wisdom regained all that was lost—and then some. *foil:* defeat.
381. Cf. Rev. 21.16: "And the city [of God] lieth four-square, and the length is as large as the breadth."
382. *try:* discover from experience.
403–4. *create / Plenipotent:* give [them] full power.
412. *bane:* poison, death, ruin, woe. *blasted:* injured, or ruined, as by a harmful wind. *wan:* dark, dusky.

And planets, planet-strook, real eclipse
Then suffered. Th' other way Satan went down
The causey to hell gate; on either side   415
Disparted chaos over-built exclaimed,
And with rebounding surge the bars assailed,
That scorned his indignation: through the gate,
Wide open and unguarded, Satan passed,
And all about found desolate; for those   420
Appointed to sit there, had left their charge,
Flown to the upper world; the rest were all
Far to the inland retired, about the walls
Of Pandemonium, city and proud seat
Of Lucifer, so by allusion called,   425
Of that bright star to Satan paragoned.
There kept their watch the legions, while the grand
In council sat, solicitous what chance
Might intercept their emperor sent, so he
Departing gave command, and they observed.   430
As when the Tartar from his Russian foe
By Astracan over the snowy plains
Retires, or Bactrian Sophi from the horns
Of Turkish crescent, leaves all waste beyond
The realm of Aladule, in his retreat   435
To Tauris or Casbeen: so these the late
Heav'n-banished host, left desert utmost hell
Many a dark league, reduced in careful watch
Round their metropolis, and now expecting
Each hour their great adventurer from the search   440

413. *planet-strook*: injured by the astrological influence of a planet. Planets in *eclipse* seem to lose their light; here they really did so.
415. *causey*: causeway.
425. *Lucifer*: the morning star. Commentators had taken "Lucifer" in Isa. 14.12 (see I.84n) to mean Satan. Cf. V.708–10. *allusion*: metaphor.
426. *paragoned*: compared.
427. *the grand*: the great consulting *peers* of 456. See I.794ff.
431–36. *Astracan* was a region west of the Caspian Sea inhabited by Tatars but conquered by Russia in the sixteenth century. In his *Brief History of Moscovia* Milton described its chief city (modern Astrakhan) as "situate in an island [at the mouth of the Volga River] . . . walled with earth, but the castle with earth and timber; the houses . . . poor and simple; the ground utterly barren, and without wood: they live there on fish . . . which hanging up to dry in the streets and houses brings swarms of flies, and infection to the air, and oft great pestilence. This island . . . is the Russian limit toward the Caspian, which he keeps with a strong garrison [against the Turks to the south and the Tartars beyond the steppes (*snowy plains*) to the east]." Milton remembered a particular siege of the city of seventy thousand "Turkes and Tartars," which was raised "by reason of the winter approached" and because the Russians sent a relief expedition. The other retreating pagan army in this simile was Persian. *Aladule*, a region now divided between Turkey and Iran, once called Armenia, was the farthest western reach of the Persian empire. From this wild and mountainous country Anadule, a Persian king (*Bactrian Sophi*), was forced to retreat eastward from the Turks, first to Tabriz (*Tauris*) and later to Kazvin (*Casbeen*). The simile emphasizes the physical hardships of life in such rugged, uncivilized outposts, as well as the religion of the infidel Tatars, Turks, and Persians.
438. *reduced*: drawn together.

Of foreign worlds: he through the midst unmarked,
In show plebeian angel militant
Of lowest order, passed; and from the door
Of that Plutonian hall, invisible
Ascended his high throne, which under state   445
Of richest texture spread, at th' upper end
Was placed in regal luster. Down a while
He sat, and round about him saw unseen:
At last as from a cloud his fulgent head
And shape star-bright appeared, or brighter, clad   450
With what permissive glory since his fall
Was left him, or false glitter: all amazed
At that so sudden blaze the Stygian throng
Bent their aspéct, and whom they wished beheld,
Their mighty chief returned: loud was th' acclaim: 455
Forth rushed in haste the great consulting peers,
Raised from their dark divan, and with like joy
Congratulant approached him, who with hand
Silence, and with these words attention won.
     "Thrones, dominations, princedoms, virtues, powers,   460
For in possession such, not only of right,
I call ye and declare ye now, returned
Successful beyond hope, to lead ye forth
Triumphant out of this infernal pit
Abominable, accurst, the house of woe,   465
And dungeon of our tyrant: now possess,
As lords, a spacious world, to our native heaven
Little inerfior, by my adventure hard
With peril great achieved. Long were to tell
What I have done, what suffered, with what pain   470
Voyaged th' unreal, vast, unbounded deep
Of horrible confusion, over which
By Sin and Death a broad way now is paved
To expedite your glorious march; but I
Toiled out my uncouth passage, forced to ride   475
Th' untractable abyss, plunged in the womb
Of unoriginal Night and Chaos wild,
That jealous of their secrets fiercely opposed
My journey strange, with clamorous uproar
Protesting fate supreme; thence how I found   480

445. *state:* canopy.
451. *permissive:* permitted.
457. *Raised:* adjourned. *divan:* (A Persian word) council of state.
461. The titles are no longer only claims to heavenly ranks now that the fallen angels possess
     the earth.
471. *unreal.* According to Plato, only ideas (that is, forms) are real; chaos was "without form."
475. *uncouth:* unfamiliar.
477. *unoriginal:* having no origin or beginning.
480. *Protesting:* calling as a witness, appealing to.

The new-created world, which fame in heav'n
Long had foretold, a fabric wonderful
Of absolute perfection, therein man
Placed in a paradise, by our exile
Made happy: him by fraud I have seduced   485
From his creator, and the more to increase
Your wonder, with an apple; he thereat
Offended, worth your laughter, hath giv'n up
Both his beloved man and all his world,
To Sin and Death a prey, and so to us,   490
Without our hazard, labor, or alarm,
To range in, and to dwell, and over man
To rule, as over all he should have ruled.
True is, me also he hath judged, or rather
Me not, but the brute serpent in whose shape   495
Man I deceived; that which to me belongs,
Is enmity, which he will put between
Me and mankind; I am to bruise his heel;
His seed, when is not set, shall bruise my head:
A world who would not purchase with a bruise,   500
Or much more grievous pain? Ye have th' account
Of my performance: what remains, ye gods,
But up and enter now into full bliss."
    So having said, a while he stood, expecting
Their universál shout and high applause   505
To fill his ear, when contrary he hears
On all sides, from innumerable tongues
A dismal universal hiss, the sound
Of public scorn; he wondered, but not long
Had leisure, wond'ring at himself now more;   510
His visage drawn he felt to sharp and spare,
His arms clung to his ribs, his legs entwining
Each other, till supplanted down he fell
A monstrous serpent on his belly prone,
Reluctant, but in vain, a greater power   515
Now ruled him, punished in the shape he sinned,
According to his doom: he would have spoke,
But hiss for hiss returned with forkèd tongue
To forkèd tongue, for now were all transformed
Alike, to serpents all as acacessóies   520
To his bold riot: dreadful was the din

508. *dismal* (L *dies mali* evil days) sinister, dreadful.
512. *clung*: (participle) stuck fast.
513. *supplanted*: (L *supplantare* to overthrow by tripping up, from *sub* under + *planta* sole of
    the foot) tripped up; made to fall (as Satan supplanted Eve).
515. *Reluctant*: L *re* + *luctare* to struggle.

Of hissing through the hall, thick swarming now
With complicated monsters, head and tail,
Scorpion and asp, and amphisbaena dire,
Cerastes horned, hydrus, and ellops drear,   525
And dipsas (not so thick swarmed once the soil
Bedropped with blood of Gorgon, or the isle
Ophiusa) but still greatest he the midst,
Now dragon grown, larger than whom the sun
Engendered in the Pythian vale on slime,   530
Huge Python, and his power no less he seemed
Above the rest still to retain; they all
Him followed issuing forth to th' open field,
Where all yet left of that revolted rout
Heav'n-fall'n, in station stood or just array,   535
Sublime with expectation when to see
In triumph issuing forth their glorious chief;
They saw, but other sight instead, a crowd
Of ugly serpents; horror on them fell,
And horrid sympathy; for what they saw,   540
They felt themselves now changing; down their arms,
Down fell both spear and shield, down they as fast,
And the dire hiss renewed, and the dire form
Catched by contagion, like in punishment,
As in their crime. Thus was th' applause they meant,   545
Turned to exploding hiss, triumph to shame
Cast on themselves from their own mouths. There stood
A grove hard by, sprung up with this their change,
His will who reigns above, to aggravate
Their penance, laden with fair fruit, like that   550
Which grew in Paradise, the bait of Eve

523. *complicated:* (L *cum* together + *plicare* to fold) tangled.
524–32. *Scorpion:* an arachnid with a venomous sting at the tip of its tail. *asp:* a small viper of Egypt. *Cerastes:* a kind of asp with horny processes over each eye. The *hydrus* (a sea-snake), *ellops,* and *dipsas* (whose bite was supposed to produce mortal thirst) were fabulous serpents, as was the *amphisbaena,* which had a head at each end. *Gorgon:* Medusa, the drops of blood from whose severed head turned into snakes. *Ophiusa:* (Gk "island of serpents") modern Formentara, off the E coast of Spain. *Python:* a fabulous serpent who guarded a shrine at Delphi which Apollo appropriated after slaying the serpent. Apollo was considered a type of Christ.
535. *in station:* at [their] stations. *just array:* close, or full, formation.
536. *Sublime:* raised up.
546. *exploding:* L *explodere* to drive out a player by clapping, from *ex* out + *plaudere, plodere* to clap. *Applause* is derived from *ad* toward + *plaudere.*
547–72. The biblical passages on which this episode is grounded are Deut. 32.32–33: "For their vine is of the vine of Sodom, and of the fields of Gomorrah: their grapes are grapes of gall, their clusters are bitter: Their wine is the poison of dragons, and the cruel venom of asps," and Gen. 19.24: "Then the Lord rained upon Sodom and upon Gomorrah brimstone and fire from the Lord out of heaven." But Milton got the idea for the ironic apples from the well-known Jewish historian Josephus, who claimed such fruit grew by the Dead Sea (*bituminous lake,* cf. I.411), and from the myth of Tantalus, whose punishment consisted of enduring a thirst that he could not quench because when he stooped to drink the stream receded and when he reached for luscious fruit it too eluded him. The trees are an ironic metamorphosis of the Tree of Knowledge, and the image of the snakes in the tree may have come, as Fowler points out, from a late Latin poet's account of "a dreadful grove hung with Jupiter's spoils" from the war against the Giants, one of whom was Ophion (581), which means "serpent." *Megaera:* one of the mythical snaky-haired Erinys, or avenging spirits. *gust:* (L *gustus* taste) relish, gusto. *drugged:* nauseated. *triumphed:* triumphed over.

Used by the Tempter: on that prospect strange
Their earnest eyes they fixed, imagining
For one forbidden tree a multitude
Now ris'n, to work them further woe or shame;   555
Yet parched with scalding thirst and hunger fierce,
Though to delude them sent, could not abstain,
But on they rolled in heaps, and up the trees
Climbing, sat thicker than the snaky locks
That curled Megaera: greedily they plucked   560
The fruitage fair to sight, like that which grew
Near that bituminous lake where Sodom flamed;
This more delusive, not the touch, but taste
Deceived; they fondly thinking to allay
Their appetite with gust, instead of fruit   565
Chewed bitter ashes, which th' offended taste
With spattering noise rejected: oft they assayed,
Hunger and thirst constraining, drugged as oft,
With hatefulest disrelish writhed their jaws
With soot and cinders filled; so oft they fell   570
Into the same illusion, not as man
Whom they triumphed once lapsed. Thus were they plagued
And worn with famine, long and ceaseless hiss,
Till their lost shape, permitted, they resumed,
Yearly enjoined, some say, to undergo   575
This annual humbling certain numbered days,
To dash their pride, and joy for man seduced.
However some tradition they dispersed
Among the heathen of their purchase got,
And fabled how the serpent, whom they called   580
Ophion with Eurynome, the wide-
Encroaching Eve perhaps, had first the rule
Of high Olympus, thence by Saturn driv'n
And Ops, ere yet Dictaean Jove was born.
Meanwhile in Paradise the hellish pair   585
Too soon arrived, Sin there in power before, .

572–84. The fallen angels were *permitted* by God to resume their original *shape* except during
the annual repetition of the ironic serpentine metamorphosis. Among the heathen whom they
later seduced they spread (*dispersed*) the story (*tradition*) that Satan and Eve were the original
rulers of heaven. Milton followed a common Christian interpretation of the myth in identifying
Ophion as Satan, but he seems to have invented the suggestion that *Eurynome* could have
been falsely interpreted as Eve because the Gk word *Eurynome* could mean wide-encroaching
and could be an epithet for Eve. *Saturn* and Rhea (*Ops*) overthrew (in this version of the story)
Ophion and *Eurynome*, but they were in turn overthrown by Jupiter (*Jove*, who lived on the
mountain Dicte) whom Christians interpreted as God. *purchase:* prey.
585–90. *Sin* (586) and *Death* (588) are in syntactical apposition with *hellish pair*. Before the Fall
sin was present in Paradise only potentially (*in power*), but *once* it had become *actual* in the
act of Adam and Eve, it could be said to be totally (*in body* as well as spirit) in Paradise. The
word play in *dwell Habitual habitant* is enriched by the derivation of *habit*, L *habere* to have,
possess.

Once actual, now in body, and to dwell
Habitual habitant; behind her Death
Close following pace for pace, not mounted yet
On his pale horse: to whom Sin thus began.   590
    "Second of Satan sprung, all-conquering Death,
What think'st thou of our empire now, though earned
With travail difficult, not better far
Than still at hell's dark threshold to have sat watch,
Unnamed, undreaded, and thyself half-starved?"   595
    Whom thus the Sin-born monster answered soon.
"To me, who with eternal famine pine,
Alike is hell, or Paradise, or heaven,
There best, where most with ravin I may meet;
Which here, though plenteous, all too little seems   600
To stuff this maw, this vast unhidebound corpse."
    To whom th' incestuous mother thus replied.
"Thou therefore on these herbs, and fruits, and flow'rs
Feed first, on each beast next, and fish, and fowl,
No homely morsels, and whatever thing   605
Thy scythe of Time mows down, devour unspared,
Till I in man residing through the race,
His thoughts, his looks, words, actions all infect,
And season him thy last and sweetest prey."
    This said, they both betook them several ways,   610
Both to destroy, or unimmortal make
All kinds, and for destruction to mature
Sooner or later; which th' Almighty seeing,
From his transcendent seat the saints among,
To those bright orders uttered thus his voice.   615
    "See with what heat these dogs of hell advance
To waste and havoc yonder world, which I
So fair and good created, and had still
Kept in that state, had not the folly of man
Let in these wasteful furies, who impute   620
Folly to me, so doth the prince of hell
And his adherents, that with so much ease
I suffer them to enter and possess
A place so heav'nly, and conniving seem
To gratify my scornful enemies,   625
That laugh, as if transported with some fit
Of passion, I to them had quitted all,

590. Cf. Rev. 6.8.
599. *ravin*: prey.
601. *unhidebound*: literally not bound by its hide, which is infinitely expansible.
617. *havoc*: plunder.
624. *conniving*: (L *coniveo*, to let a crime go unnoticed) lying low.
626–27. *as if . . . passion*. Modifies *I*. *quitted*: surrendered.

At random yielded up to their misrule;
And know not that I called and drew them thither
My hell-hounds, to lick up the draff and filth   630
Which man's polluting sin with taint hath shed
On what was pure, till crammed and gorged, nigh burst
With sucked and glutted offal, at one sling
Of thy victorious arm, well-pleasing Son,
Both Sin, and Death, and yawning grave at last   635
Through chaos hurled, obstruct the mouth of hell
For ever, and seal up his ravenous jaws.
Then heav'n and earth renewed shall be made pure
To sanctity that shall receive no stain:
Till then the curse pronounced on both precedes."   640
    He ended, and the heav'nly audience loud
Sung halleluiah, as the sound of seas,
Through multitude that sung: "Just are thy ways,
Righteous are thy decrees on all thy works;
Who can extenuate thee? Next, to the Son,   645
Destined restorer of mankind, by whom
New heav'n and earth shall to the ages rise,
Or down from heav'n descend." Such was their song,
While the Creator calling forth by name
His mighty angels gave them several charge,   650
As sorted best with present things. The sun
Had first his precept so to move, so shine,
As might affect the earth with cold and heat
Scarce tolerable, and from the north to call
Decrepit winter, from the south to bring   655
Solstitial summer's heat. To the blank moon
Her office they prescribed, to th' other five
Their planetary motions and aspécts
In sextile, square, and trine, and opposite,

630. *draff*: refuse, swill.
633. Cf. 1 Sam. 25.29: ". . . the souls of thine enemies, them shall he sling out, as out of the middle of a sling."
640. *precedes*: has precedence.
641–43. Cf. Rev. 19.6: "And I heard as it were the voice of a great multitude, and as the voice of many waters, and as the voice of many thunderings, saying, Alleluia: for the Lord God omnipotent reigneth."
643–44. Cf. Rev. 15.3: "And they sing the song of Moses the servant of God, and the song of the Lamb, saying, Great and marvellous are thy works, Lord God Almighty; just and true are thy ways, thou King of saints." Rev. 16.7: "And I heard another out of the altar say, Even so, Lord God Almighty, true and righteous are thy judgments."
645. *extenuate*: disparage.
647. *ages*: the Millennium.
647–48. Cf. Rev. 21.1–2.
651. *sorted . . . with*: suited.
656. *blank*: white, pale.
657–706. See "The Universe," pp. 461–63.
659. *sextile, square, trine,* and *opposite* are astrological terms describing the relative positions of planets as angles of 60, 90, 120, and 180 degrees.

Of noxious efficacy, and when to join   660
In synod unbenign, and taught the fixed
Their influence malignant when to show'r,
Which of them rising with the sun, or falling,
Should prove tempestuous: to the winds they set
Their corners, when with bluster to confound   665
Sea, air, and shore, the thunder when to roll
With terror through the dark aerial hall.
Some say he bid his angels turn askance
The poles of earth twice ten degrees and more
From the sun's axle; they with labor pushed   670
Oblique the centric globe: some say the sun
Was bid turn reins from th' equinoctial road
Like distant breadth to Taurus with the sev'n
Atlantic Sisters, and the Spartan Twins
Up to the Tropic Crab; thence down amain   675
By Leo and the Virgin and the Scales,
As deep as Capricorn, to bring in change
Of seasons to each clime; else had the spring
Perpetual smiled on earth with vernant flow'rs,
Equal in days and nights, except to those   680
Beyond the polar circles; to them day
Had unbenighted shone, while the low sun
To recompense his distance, in their sight
Had rounded still th' horizon, and not known
Or east or west, which had forbid the snow   685
From cold Estotiland, and south as far
Beneath Magellan. At that tasted fruit
The sun, as from Thyestean banquet, turned
His course intended; else how had the world
Inhabited, though sinless, more than now,   690
Avoided pinching cold and scorching heat?
These changes in the heav'ns, though slow, produced
Like change on sea and land, sideral blast,
Vapor, and mist, and exhalation hot,

661. *synod:* conjunction. *fixed:* fixed stars.
673–77. All but *Atlantic Sisters* (the Pleiades) are constellations in the zodiac.
679. *vernant:* vernal.
684. *still:* always.
686. *Estotiland:* fabulous island near the NE coast of N. America; perhaps the NE coast of Labrador.
687. *Magellan:* the region of the Straits of Magellan.
688–89. When Atreus invited his brother Thyestes to a banquet where he served the flesh of Thyestes' son, the sun to avoid the sight changed his course.
693. *sideral blast:* blight or ruin caused by the malign influence of the stars. See *bane* in 412 and n.

Corrupt and pestilent: now from the north   695
Of Norumbega, and the Samoed shore
Bursting their brazen dungeon, armed with ice
And snow and hail and stormy gust and flaw,
Boreas and Caecias and Argestes loud
And Thrascias rend the woods and seas upturn;   700
With adverse blast upturns them from the south
Notus and Afer black with thund'rous clouds
From Serraliona; thwart of these as fierce
Forth rush the Levant and the ponent winds
Eurus and Zephyr with their lateral noise,   705
Sirocco and Libecchio. Thus began
Outrage from lifeless things; but Discord first
Daughter of Sin, among th' irrational,
Death introduced through fierce antipathy:
Beast now with beast gan war, and fowl with fowl,   710
And fish with fish; to graze the herb all leaving,
Devour'd each other; nor stood much in awe
Of man, but fled him, or with count'nance grim
Glared on him passing: these were from without
The growing miseries, which Adam saw   715
Already in part, though hid in gloomiest shade,
To sorrow abandoned, but worse felt within,
And in a troubled sea of passion tossed,
Thus to disburden sought with sad complaint.
    "O miserable of happy! Is this the end   720
Of this new glorious world, and me so late
The glory of that glory, who now become
Accurst of blessèd, hide me from the face
Of God, whom to behold was then my highth
Of happiness: yet well, if here would end   725
The misery, I deserved if, and would bear
My own deservings; but this will not serve;
All that I eat or drink, or shall beget,
Is propagated curse. O voice once heard
Delightfully, 'Increase and multiply,'   730
Now death to hear! For what can I increase
Or multiply, but curses on my head?
Who of all ages to succeed, but feeling
The evil on him brought by me, will curse
My head, 'Ill fare our ancestor impure,   735
For this we may thank Adam'; but his thanks

695–706. *Norumbega*: northeastern North America, including New England. *Samoed*: Siberian *brazen dungeon*: the cave in which Aeolus imprisoned the winds. *flaw*: squall. *Boreas, Caecius, Argestes, Thrascias*: winds that blow from the N, NE, and NW. *Notus, Afer*: winds that blow from the S and SW (Africa). *Serraliona*: Sierra Leone, on the W coast of Africa. *thwart*: diagonally. *Levant*: from the east. *ponent*: from the west. *Eurus*: the east wind. *Zephyr*: the west wind. *Sirocco, Libecchio*: winds from the SE and SW.

Shall be the execration; so besides
Mine own that bide upon me, all from me
Shall with a fierce reflux on me redound,
On me as on their natural center light   740
Heavy, though in their place. O fleeting joys
Of Paradise, dear bought with lasting woes!
Did I request thee, Maker, from my clay
To mold me man, did I solicit thee
From darkness to promote me, or here place   745
In this delicious garden? As my will
Concurred not to my being, it were but right
And equal to reduce me to my dust,
Desirous to resign, and render back
All I received, unable to perform   750
Thy terms too hard, by which I was to hold
The good I sought not. To the loss of that,
Sufficient penalty, why hast thou added
The sense of endless woes? Inexplicable
Thy justice seems; yet to say truth, too late   755
I thus contest; then should have been refused
Those terms whatever, when they were proposed:
Thou didst accept them; wilt thou enjoy the good,
Then cavil the conditions? And though God
Made thee without thy leave, what if thy son   760
Prove disobedient, and reproved, retort,
'Wherefore didst thou beget me? I sought it not:'
Wouldst thou admit for his contempt of thee
That proud excuse? Yet him not thy election,
But natural necessity begot.   765
God made thee of choice his own, and of his own
To serve him, thy reward was of his grace,
Thy punishment then justly is at his will.
Be it so, for I submit, his doom is fair,
That dust I am, and shall to dust return: 770
O welcome hour whenever! Why delays
His hand to execute what his decree
Fixed on this day? Why do I overlive,
Why am I mocked with death, and lengthened out
To deathless pain? How gladly would I meet   775
Mortality my sentence, and be earth

740. *On me . . . light:* fall upon me, be my lot.
741. *Heavy, though in their place.* Having found *their natural center* (740), the curses should,
by Adam's law of gravitation, be weightless.
743–44. Cf. Isa. 45.9: "Woe unto him that striveth with his Maker! Let the potsherd strive with
the potsherds of the earth. Shall the clay say to him that fashioneth it, What makest thou? or
thy work, He hath no hands?"
748. *equal:* fair, just.
762. Cf. Isa. 45.10: "Woe unto him that saith unto his father, What begettest thou? or to the
woman, What hast thou brought forth?"
764. *election:* choice.

Insensible, how glad would lay me down
As in my mother's lap! There I should rest
And sleep secure; his dreadful voice no more
Would thunder in my ears, no fear of worse   780
To me and to my offspring would torment me
With cruel expectation. Yet one doubt
Pursues me still, lest all I cannot die,
Lest that pure breath of life, the spirit of man
Which God inspired, cannot together perish   785
With this corporeal clod; then in the grave,
Or in some other dismal place, who knows
But I shall die a living death? O thought
Horrid, if true! Yet why? It was but breath
Of life that sinned; what dies but what had life   790
And sin? The body properly hath neither.
All of me then shall die: let this appease
The doubt, since human reach no further knows.
For though the Lord of all be infinite,
Is his wrath also? Be it, man is not so,   795
But mortal doomed. How can he exercise
Wrath without end on man whom death must end?
Can he make deathless death? That were to make
Strange contradiction, which to God himself
Impossible is held, as argument   800
Of weakness, not of power. Will he draw out,
For anger's sake, finite to infinite
In punished man, to satisfy his rigor
Satisfied never; that were to extend
His sentence beyond dust and nature's law,   805
By which all causes else according still
To the reception of their matter act,
Not to th' extent of their own sphere. But say
That death be not one stroke, as I supposed,
Bereaving sense, but endless misery   810
From this day onward, which I feel begun
Both in me, and without me, and so last
To perpetuity; ay me, that fear
Comes thund'ring back with dreadful revolution
On my defenseless head; both Death and I   815
Am found eternal, and incorporate both,
Nor I on my part single, in me all

778. *mother's lap*: cf. *Met.* 1.393: "our great mother is the earth."
782–93. Milton believed that the soul dies with the body. *all I*: all of me.
801–8. Adam argues that *finite* (802) *matter* (807) cannot suffer *infinite* punishment because according to *nature's law* the efficacy of all *causes* (forces) is limited by the nature of the things they act upon. The notion is as old as Aristotle.
810. *Bereaving*: taking away. *endless misery*. Cf. *CD* I.XXXIII.
814. *revolution*: recurrence.
816. *incorporate*: united in one body.

Posterity stands cursed: fair patrimony
That I must leave ye, sons; O were I able
To waste it all myself, and leave ye none!   820
So disinherited how would ye bless
Me now your curse! Ah, why should all mankind
For one man's fault thus guiltless be condemned,
If guiltless? But from me what can proceed,
But all corrupt, both mind and will depraved,   825
Not to do only, but to will the same
With me? How can they then acquitted stand
In sight of God? Him after all disputes
Forced I absolve: all my evasions vain
And reasonings, though through mazes, lead me still   830
But to my own conviction: first and last
On me, me only, as the source and spring
Of all corruption, all the blame lights due;
So might the wrath. Fond wish! Couldst thou support
That burden heavier than the earth to bear,   835
Than all the world much heavier, though divided
With that bad woman? Thus what thou desir'st,
And what thou fear'st, alike destroys all hope
Of refuge, and concludes thee miserable
Beyond all past example and future,   840
To Satan only like both crime and doom.
O conscience, into what abyss of fears
And horrors hast thou driv'n me; out of which
I find no way, from deep to deeper plunged!"
    Thus Adam to himself lamented loud   845
Through the still night, not now, as ere man fell,
Wholesome and cool, and mild, but with black air
Accompanied, with damps and dreadful gloom,
Which to his evil conscience represented
All things with double terror: on the ground   850
Outstretched he lay, on the cold ground, and oft
Cursed his creation, Death as oft accused
Of tardy execution, since denounced
The day of his offense. "Why comes not Death,"
Said he, "with one thrice-ácceptáble stroke   855
To end me? Shall Truth fail to keep her word,
Justice divine not hasten to be just?
But Death comes not at call, Justice divine
Mends not her slowest pace for prayers or cries.

---

825. *mind and will depraved*. Cf. CD, p. 417.
828–34. Cf. CD, I.xix, where Milton says that "conviction of sin" is the first of four steps towards
    regeneration of a sinner. *Fond*: foolish.
848. *damps*: noxious vapors.
853. *since denounced*: inasmuch as it was announced as coming on the day of the crime. Cf.
    962.

O woods, O fountains, hillocks, dales and bow'rs,   860
With other echo late I taught your shades
To answer, and resound far other song."
Whom thus afflicted when sad Eve beheld,
Desolate where she sat, approaching nigh,
Soft words to his fierce passion she assayed: 865
But her with stern regard he thus repelled.
    "Out of my sight, thou serpent, that name best
Befits thee with him leagued, thyself as false
And hateful; nothing wants, but that thy shape,
Like his, and color serpentine may show   870
Thy inward fraud, to warn all creatures from thee
Henceforth; lest that too heav'nly form, pretended
To hellish falsehood, snare them. But for thee
I had persisted happy, had not thy pride
And wand'ring vanity, when least was safe,   875
Rejected my forewarning, and disdained
Not to be trusted, longing to be seen
Though by the Devil himself, him overweening
To overreach, but with the serpent meeting
Fooled and beguiled, by him thou, I by thee,   880
To trust thee from my side, imagined wise,
Constant, mature, proof against all assaults,
And understood not all was but a show
Rather than solid virtue, all but a rib
Crooked by nature, bent, as now appears,   885
More to the part sinister from me drawn,
Well if thrown out, as supernumerary
To my just number found. O why did God,
Creator wise, that peopled highest heav'n
With Spirits masculine, create at last   890
This novelty on earth, this fair defect
Of nature, and not fill the world at once
With men as angels without feminine,
Or find some other way to generate
Mankind? This mischief had not then befall'n,   895

867. *thou serpent.* Bush notes that "In patristic etymologizing, 'Heva,' Eve's name aspirated, meant 'serpent.' "
872–73. *pretended* / To: (L *prae* before + *tendere* stretch) held before, as a disguise.
878. *overweening:* overconfident. *him overweening* / To *overreach:* i.e., being overconfident that you could get the better of him.
884–88. One sign of Adam's fallen condition is this expression of misogyny. It is a composite of myths well known in Milton's time: that woman was morally crooked because the rib she was made of was defective; that the rib was taken from Adam's left side (the Bible does not specify), not because that was nearest Adam's heart, but because the left, or *sinister,* side is the evil side; and that Adam originally had thirteen ribs on his left side, so that the removal of one left him perfect.
891–92. *defect* / Of *nature.* Fowler notes that "Aristotle had said . . . that the female is a defective male."

And more that shall befall, innumerable
Disturbances on earth through female snares,
And strait conjunction with this sex: for either
He never shall find out fit mate, but such
As some misfortune brings him, or mistake,   900
Or whom he wishes most shall seldom gain
Through her perverseness, but shall see her gained
By a far worse, or if she love, withheld
By parents, or his happiest choice too late
Shall meet, already linked and wedlock-bound   905
To a fell adversary, his hate or shame:
Which infinite calamity shall cause
To human life, and household peace confound."
    He added not, and from her turned, but Eve
Not so repulsed, with tears that ceased not flowing,   910
And tresses all disordered, at his feet
Fell humble, and embracing them, besought
His peace, and thus proceeded in her plaint.
    "For sake me not thus, Adam, witness Heav'n
What love sincere, and reverence in my heart   915
I bear thee, and unweeting have offended,
Unhappily deceived; thy suppliant
I beg, and clasp thy knees; bereave me not,
Whereon I live, thy gentle looks, thy aid,
Thy counsel in this uttermost distress,   920
My only strength and stay: forlorn of thee,
Whither shall I betake me, where subsist?
While yet we live, scarce one short hour perhaps,
Between us two let there be peace, both joining,
As joined in injuries, one enmity   925
Against a foe by doom express assigned us,
That cruel serpent: on me exercise not
Thy hatred for this misery befall'n,
On me already lost, me than thyself
More miserable; both have sinned, but thou   930
Against God only, I against God and thee,
And to the place of judgment will return,
There with my cries importune Heaven, that all
The sentence from thy head removed may light
On me, sole cause to thee of all this woe,   935
Me me only just object of his ire."
    She ended weeping, and her lowly plight,
Immovable till peace obtained from fault

898. *strait:* close; also, distressful.
906. *fell:* cruel, terrible.
926. *doom express:* explicit judgment. *assigned* modifies *enmity.*
931. Cf. Ps. 51.4: "Against thee, thee only, have I sinned, and done this evil in thy sight: that
    thou mightest be justified when thou speakest, and be clear when thou judgest."
938. *Immovable:* (modifies *plight*) unalterable.

Acknowledged and deplored, in Adam wrought
Commiseration; soon his heart relented   940
Towards her, his life so late and sole delight,
Now at his feet submissive in distress,
Creature so fair his reconcilement seeking,
His counsel whom she had displeased, his aid;
As one disarmed, his anger all he lost,   945
And thus with peaceful words upraised her soon.
  "Unwary, and too desirous, as before,
So now of what thou know'st not, who desir'st
The punishment all on thyself; alas,
Bear thine own first, ill able to sustain   950
His full wrath those thou feel'st as yet least part,
And my displeasure bear'st so ill. If prayers
Could alter high decrees, I to that place
Would speed before thee, and be louder heard,
That on my head all might be visited,   955
Thy frailty and infirmer sex forgiv'n,
To me committed and by me exposed.
But rise, let us no more contend, nor blame
Each other, blamed enough elsewhere, but strive
In offices of love, how we may light'n   960
Ech other's burden in our share of woe;
Since this day's death denounced, if aught I see,
Will prove no sudden, but a slow-paced evil,
A long day's dying to augment our pain,
And to our seed (O hapless seed!) derived."   965
  To whom thus Eve, recovering heart, replied.
"Adam, by sad experiment I know
How little weight my words with thee can find,
Found so erroneous, thence by just event
Found so unfortunate; nevertheless,   970
Restored by thee, vile as I am, to place
Of new acceptance, hopeful to regain
Thy love, the sole contentment of my heart
Living or dying, from thee I will not hide
What thoughts in my unquiet breast are ris'n,   975
Tending to some relief of our extremes,
Or end, though sharp and sad, yet tolerable,
As in our evils, and of easier choice.
If care of our descent perplex us most,

959. *elsewhere:* i.e., in heaven, or "the place of judgment" (932).
960. *offices:* services, attentions.
961. Cf. Gal. 6.2: "Bear ye one another's burdens, and so fulfil the law of Christ."
965. *derived:* passed on. Cf. 77n.
969. *event:* consequence.
978. *As in our evils:* considering our afflictions.
979. I.e.: If concern for our descendants most disturbs us.

Which must be born to certain woe, devoured   980
By Death at last, and miserable it is
To be to others cause of misery,
Our own begotten, and of our loins to bring
Into this cursèd world a woeful race,
That after wretched life must be at last   985
Food for so foul a monster, in thy power
It lies, yet ere conception to prevent
The race unblest, to being yet unbegot.
Childless thou art, childless remain; so Death
Shall be deceived his glut, and with us two   990
Be forced to satisfy his rav'nous maw.
But if thou judge it hard and difficult,
Conversing, looking, loving, to abstain
From love's due rites, nuptial embraces sweet,
And with desire to languish without hope,   995
Before the present object languishing
With like desire, which would be misery
And torment less than none of what we dread,
Then both ourselves and seed at once to free
From what we fear for both, let us make short,   1000
Let us seek Death, or he not found, supply
With our own hands his office on ourselves;
Why stand we longer shivering under fears,
That show no end but death, and have the power,
Of many ways to die the shortest choosing,   1005
Destruction with destruction to destroy."
     She ended here, or vehement despair
Broke off the rest; so much of death her thoughts
Had entertained, as dyed her cheeks with pale.
But Adam with such counsel nothing swayed,   1010
To better hopes his more attentive mind
Laboring had raised, and thus to Eve replied.
     "Eve thy contempt of life and pleasure seems
To argue in thee something more sublime
And excellent than what thy mind contemns;   1015
But self-destruction therefore sought, refutes
That excellence thought in thee, and implies,
Not thy contempt, but anguish and regret
For loss of life and pleasure overloved.
Or if thou covet death, as utmost end   1020
Of misery, so thinking to evade
The penalty pronounced, doubt not but God

987. *prevent*: to keep from existing.
990. *deceived*: cheated out of.
996. *object*: Eve.
1007. *vehement*: intense, powerful.

Hath wiselier armed his vengeful ire than so
To be forestalled; much more I fear lest death
So snatched will not exempt us from the pain   1025
We are by doom to pay: rather such acts
Of contumácy will provoke the Highest
To make death in us live: then let us seek
Some safer resolution, which methinks
I have in view, calling to mind with heed   1030
Part of our sentence, that thy seed shall bruise
The serpent's head; piteous amends, unless
Be meant, whom I conjecture, our grand foe
Satan, who in the serpent hath contrived
Against us this deceit: to crush his head   1035
Would be revenge indeed; which will be lost
By death brought on ourselves, or childless days
Resolved, as thou proposest; so our foe
Shall scape his punishment ordained, and we
Instead shall double ours upon our heads.   1040
No more be mentioned then of violence
Against ourselves, and wilful barrenness,
That cuts us off from hope, and savors only
Rancor and pride, impatience and despite,
Reluctance against God and his just yoke   1045
Laid on our necks. Remember with what mild
And gracious temper he both heard and judged
Without wrath or reviling; we expected
Immediate dissolution, which we thought
Was meant by death that day, when lo, to thee   1050
Pains only in child-bearing were foretold,
And bringing forth, soon recompensed with joy,
Fruit of thy womb: on me the curse aslope
Glanced on the ground, with labor I must earn
My bread; what harm? Idleness had been worse;   1055
My labor will sustain me; and lest cold
Or heat should injure us, his timely care
Hath unbesought provided, and his hands
Clothed us unworthy, pitying while he judged;
How much more, if we pray him, will his ear   1060

1031–32. Cf. 175–81n.
1045. *Reluctance:* L *re* + *luctari* to struggle.
1050–52. Cf. John 16.19–21: "Now Jesus [speaking to his disciples about his Second Coming]
. . . said unto them, Do ye enquire among yourselves of what I said, A little while, and ye
shall not see me: and again, a little while, and ye shall see me? Verily, verily, I say unto you,
That ye shall . . . be sorrowful: but your sorrow shall be turned into joy. A woman when she
is in travail hath sorrow, because her hour is come: but as soon as she is delivered of the child,
she remembereth no more the anguish, for joy that a man is born into the world."
1053. *Fruit of thy womb.* Cf. Luke 1.41–42: "And it came to pass, that, when Elizabeth [the
mother of John the Baptist] heard the salutation of Mary, the babe leaped in her womb; and
Elizabeth was filled with the Holy Ghost: And she spake out with a loud voice, and said,
Blessed art thou among women, and blessed is the fruit of thy womb."

Be open, and his heart to pity incline,
And teach us further by what means to shun
Th' inclement seasons, rain, ice, hail and snow,
Which now the sky with various face begins
To show us in this mountain, while the winds   1065
Blow moist and keen, shattering the graceful locks
Of these fair spreading trees; which bids us seek
Some better shroud, some better warmth to cherish
Our limbs benumbed, ere this diurnal star
Leave cold the night, how we his gathered beams   1070
Reflected, may with matter sere foment,
Or by collision of two bodies grind
The air attrite to fire, as late the clouds
Justling or pushed with winds rude in their shock
Tine the slant lightning, whose thwart flame driv'n down   1075
Kindles the gummy bark of fir or pine,
And sends a comfortable heat from far,
Which might supply the sun: such fire to use,
And what may else be remedy or cure
To evils which our own misdeeds have wrought,   1080
He will instruct us praying, and of grace
Beseeching him, so as we need not fear
To pass commodiously this life, sustained
By him with many comforts, till we end
In dust, our final rest and native home.   1085
What better can we do, than to the place
Repairing where he judged us, prostrate fall
Before him reverent, and there confess
Humbly our faults, and pardon beg, with tears
Watering the ground, and with our sighs the air   1090
Frequenting, sent from hearts contrite, in sign
Of sorrow unfeigned, and humiliation meek.
Undoubtedly he will relent and turn
From his displeasure; in whose look serene,
When angry most he seemed and most severe,   1095
What else but favor, grace, and mercy shone?"
    So spake our father penitent, nor Eve
Felt less remorse: they forthwith to the place
Repairing where he judged them prostrate fell
Before him reverent, and both confessed   1100

1066. *shattering:* scattering.
1067–73. "Which bids us seek . . . how we may with kindling nurse to life (or activity) focused
    and reflected sunbeams [as with some natural equivalent of a burning glass], or how by striking
    together two bodies we may turn air to fire by the heat of friction." *shroud:* shelter. *foment:*
    nourish. *attrite:* L *ad* + *terere* to rub.
1075. *Tine:* kindle. *thwart:* slanting.
1078. *supply:* take the place of.
1083. *commodiously:* conveniently.
1091. *Frequenting:* (L *frequens* crowded), filling.

Humbly their faults, and pardon begged, with tears
Watering the ground, and with their sighs the air
Frequenting, sent from hearts contrite, in sign
Of sorrow unfeigned, and humiliation meek.

Book XI

The Argument

The Son of God presents to his Father the prayers of our first parents
now repenting, and intercedes for them: God accepts them, but declares
that they must no longer abide in Paradise; sends Michael with a band
of Cherubim to dispossess them; but first to reveal to Adam future things:
Michael's coming down. Adam shows to Eve certain ominous signs; he
discerns Michael's approach, goes out to meet him: the angel denounces
their departure. Eve's lamentation. Adam pleads, but submits: the angel
leads him up to a high hill, sets before him in vision what shall happen
till the Flood.

Thus they in lowliest plight repentant stood
Praying, for from the mercy-seat above
Prevenient grace descending had removed
The stony from their hearts, and made new flesh
Regenerate grow instead, that sighs now breathed   5
Unutterable, which the spirit of prayer
Inspired, and winged for heav'n with speedier flight
Than loudest oratory: yet their port
Not of mean suitors, nor important less
Seemed their petition, than when th' ancient pair   10
In fables old, less ancient yet than these,
Deucalion and chaste Pyrrha to restore
The race of mankind drowned, before the shrine
Of Themis stood devout. To heav'n their prayers

XI.1. *stood*: remained.
2. *mercy-seat*: the golden cover of the Ark of the Covenant, which stood in the Holy of Holies
of the Tabernacle of the Israelites. On it was sprinkled the blood of sacrificed animals on the
day of the atonement. See I.383–87n, and XII.249–56. Here, a metaphor for the place of
expiation in heaven.
3. *Prevenient grace*: the grace of God acting before man wills to turn from sin or ask forgiveness.
4. *stony*. Cf. Ezek. 11.19: "I will take the stony heart out of their flesh, and will give them an
heart of flesh."
5–7. Cf. Rom. 8.26: "Likewise the Spirit also helpeth our infirmities: for we know not what we
should pray for as we ought: but the Spirit itself maketh intercession for us with groanings
which cannot be uttered."
8–9. *port . . . important*. The root meaning of the L *portare*, "to bear or carry" informs the word
play. The bearing, carriage, style of the prayers was dignified, and what they carried was of
great import, significance, consequence.
10–14. In classical myth *Deucalion* (like Noah) and *Pyrrha*, his wife, the sole survivors of a
universal flood, sought guidance from the oracle of *Themis*, goddess of justice. Cf. *Met*. 1.318f.

Flew up, nor missed the way, by envious winds   15
Blown vagabond or frustrate: in they passed
Dimensionless through heav'nly doors; then clad
With incense, where the golden altar fumed,
By their great Intercessor, came in sight
Before the Father's throne: them the glad Son   20
Presenting, thus to intercede began.
    "See Father, what first-fruits on earth are sprung
From thy implanted grace in man, these sighs
And prayers, which in this golden censer, mixed
With incense, I thy priest before thee bring,   25
Fruits of more pleasing savor from thy seed
Sown with contrition in his heart, than those
Which his own hand manuring all the trees
Of Paradise could have produced, ere fall'n
From innocence. Now therefore bend thine ear   30
To supplication, hear his sighs though mute;
Unskilful with what words to pray, let me
Interpret for him, me his advocate
And propitiation, all his works on me
Good or not good ingraft, my merit those   35
Shall perfect, and for these my death shall pay.
Accept me, and in me from these receive
The smell of peace toward mankind, let him live
Before thee reconciled, at least his days
Numbered, though sad, till death, his doom (which I   40
To mitigate thus plead, not to reverse)
To better life shall yield him, where with me
All my redeemed may dwell in joy and bliss,
Made one with me as I with thee am one."
    To whom the father, without cloud, serene.   45
"All thy request for man, accepted Son,
Obtain, all thy request was my decree:

16. *frustrate:* prevented from reaching its goal.
17–25. Cf. Rev. 8.3–4: "And another angel came and stood at the altar, having a golden censer; and there was given unto him much incense, that he should offer it with the prayers of all saints upon the golden altar which was before the throne. And the smoke of the incense, which came with the prayers of the saints, ascended up before God out of the angel's hand."
20. *glad:* pleased; full of brightness or beauty (as in "the glad sun," IV.150).
22. *first-fruits:* an offering to God. Cf. Cain's offering, XI.435.
28. *manuring:* (OF *manouvrer,* from L *manu operari* to work by hand) cultivating.
32–36. Cf. 1 John 2.1–2: "And if any man sin, we have an advocate with the Father, Jesus Christ the righteous: And he is the propititation for our sins."
44. Cf. John 17.11: "And now I am no more in the world, but these are in the world, and I come to thee. Holy Father, keep through thine own name those whom thou hast given me, that they may be one, as we are." John 17.21–23: "That they all may be one; as thou, Father, art in me, and I in thee, that they also may be one in us: that the world may believe that thou hast sent me. And the glory which thou gavest me I have given them; that they may be one, even as we are one: I in them, and thou in me, that they may be made perfect in one; and that the world may know that thou hast sent me, and hast loved them, as thou hast loved me."
45. *without cloud.* See III.378–79.

But longer in that Paradise to dwell,
The law I gave to nature him forbids:
Those pure immortal elements that know   50
No gross, no unharmonious mixture foul,
Eject him tainted now, and purge him off
As a distemper, gross to air as gross,
And mortal food, as may dispose him best
For dissolution wrought by sin, that first   55
Distempered all things, and of incorrupt
Corrupted. I at first with two fair gifts
Created him endowed, with happiness
And immortality: that fondly lost,
This other served but to eternize woe;   60
Till I provided death; so death becomes
His final remedy, and after life
Tried in sharp tribulation, and refined
By faith and faithful works, to second life,
Waked in the renovation of the just,   65
Resigns him up with heav'n and earth renewed.
But let us call to synod all the blest
Through heav'n's wide bounds; from them I will not hide
My judgments, how with mankind I proceed,
As how with peccant angels late they saw;   70
And in their state, though firm, stood more confirmed."
    He ended, and the Son gave signal high
To the bright minister that watched, he blew
His trumpet, heard in Oreb since perhaps
When God descended, and perhaps once more   75
To sound at general doom. Th' angelic blast
Filled all the regions: from their blissful bow'rs
Of amarantine shade, fountain or spring,
By the waters of life, where'er they sat

50–57. Paradise is a perfect ecological system immune to entropy. When man introduces disorder (*distemper, unharmonious mixture foul* and *gross*), which is the same thing as impurity, the system (*Those pure immortal elements*, in perfect temper, i.e., mixture, balance), *ejects* the *gross, distempered* part, i.e., *man*, purging him off into the imperfect ecological system east of Eden, of postlapsarian history. There *corrupted* man would live in air less pure than that of Paradise, eat impure mortal food, and become a part of the processes of *dissolution* instigated by his original distempering, disordering, imbalancing sin. The central metaphor depends on the theory of humors; see "Physiology and Psychology," pp. 463–64. The syntax of the passage would be clearer if in line 53 there were no comma after *distemper*, a comma after the first *gross*, and no comma after the second *gross*. Cf. 284–85.
59. *fondly*: foolishly.
64. *faithful works*. Cf. CD I.XXII.
74. *Oreb*. See I.6n.
75. *general doom*: the Last Judgment. Cf. Matt. 24.31: "And he shall send his angels with a great sound of a trumpet, and they shall gather together his elect from the four winds, from one end of heaven to the other." 1 Cor. 15.52: "In a moment, in the twinkling of an eye, at the last trump: for the trumpet shall sound, and the dead shall be raised incorruptible, and we shall be changed."
77. *regions*: the lower, middle and upper air. See I.10–15n.
78. *amarantine*. See III.352n.

In fellowships of joy, the sons of light   80
Hasted, resorting to the summons high,
And took their seats; till from his throne supreme
Th' Almighty thus pronounced his sovran will.
    "O sons, like one of us man is become
To know both good and evil, since his taste   85
Of that defended fruit; but let him boast
His knowledge of good lost, and evil got,
Happier, had it sufficed him to have known
Good by itself, and evil not at all.
He sorrows now, repents, and prays contrite,   90
My motions in him; longer than they move,
His heart I know, how variable and vain
Self-left. Lest therefore his now bolder hand
Reach also of the Tree of Life, and eat,
And live forever, dream at least to live   95
Forever, to remove him I decree,
And send him from the garden forth to till
The ground whence he was taken, fitter soil.
    "Michael, this my behest have thou in charge,
Take to thee from among the Cherubim   100
Thy choice of flaming warriors, lest the Fiend
Or in behalf of man, or to invade
Vacant possession some new trouble raise:
Haste thee, and from the Paradise of God
Without remorse drive out the sinful pair,   105
From hallowed ground th' unholy, and denounce
To them and to their progeny from thence
Perpetual banishment. Yet lest they faint
At the sad sentence rigorously urged,
For I behold them softened and with tears   110
Bewailing their excess, all terror hide.
If patiently thy bidding they obey,
Dismiss them not disconsolate; reveal
To Adam what shall come in future days,
As I shall thee enlighten, intermix   115
My cov'nant in the woman's seed renewed;
So send them forth, though sorrowing, yet in peace:

---

86. *defended:* forbidden.
91–93. I.e.: I know how variable and vain his heart will be when, after I cease sending my
    impulses, he is left to himself. *motions:* impulses. See *Prevenient grace,* line 3.
102. *in behalf of:* with regard to.
105. *remorse:* pity.
106. *denounce:* deliver a judgment of punishment.
108. *faint:* lose courage.
109. *urged:* carried out.
111. *excess:* transgression, enormity.
116. *Covenant.* See "Covenant," pp. 469–70, and CD, pp. 422–23.

And on the east side of the garden place,
Where entrance up from Eden easiest climbs,
Cherubic watch, and of a sword the flame   120
Wide-waving, all approach far off to fright,
And guard all passage to the Tree of life:
Lest Paradise a receptácle prove
To spirits foul, and all my trees their prey,
With whose stol'n fruit man once more to delude."   125
    He ceased; and th' archangelic power prepared
For swift descent, with him the cohort bright
Of watchful Cherubim; four faces each
Had, like a double Janus, all their shape
Spangled with eyes more numerous than those   130
Of Argus, and more wakeful than to drowse,
Charmed with Arcadian pipe, the pastoral reed
Of Hermes, or his opiate rod. Meanwhile
To resalute the world with sacred light
Leucóthea waked, and with fres dews embalmed   135
The earth, when Adam and first matron Eve
Had ended now their orisons, and found
Strength added from above, new hope to spring
Out of despair, joy, but with fear yet linked;
Which thus to Eve his welcome words renewed.   140
    "Eve, easily may faith admit, that all
The good which we enjoy, from heav'n descends;
But that form us aught should ascend to heav'n
So prevalent as to concern the mind
Of God high-blest, or to incline his will,   145
Hard to belief may seem; yet this will prayer,
Or one short sigh of human breath, upborne
Ev'n to the seat of God. For since I sought
By prayer th' offended Deity to appease,
Kneeled and before him humbled all my heart,   150
Methought I saw him placable and mild,
Bending his ear; persuasion in me grew
That I was heard with favor; peace returned
Home to my breast, and to my memory
His promise, that thy seed shall bruise our foe;   155
Which then not minded in dismay, yet now
Assures me that the bitterness of death

128–33. Cf. Ezek. 1.18, p. 448. *Janus:* a Roman god with two faces looking in opposite directions.
   Jealous Juno set *Argus*, with his hundred eyes, to watch Io, Jove's mistress, but *Hermes* with
   music and stories put Argus asleep. *opiate god:* Hermes's sleep-producing caduceus. Cf. *Met.*
   1.716.
135. *Leucothea:* goddess of the dawn.
144. *prevalent:* able to prevail.
157. Cf. 1 Sam. 15.32–33 [*NEB*]: "Then Samuel said, 'Bring Agag king of the Amalekites.' So
   Agag came to him with faltering steps and said, 'Surely the bitterness of death has passed.'
   Samuel said, 'Your sword has made women childless, and your mother of all women shall be
   childless too.' Then Samuel hewed Agag in pieces before the Lord at Gilgal."

Is past, and we shall live. Whence Hail to thee,
Eve rightly called, mother of all mankind,
Mother of all things living, since by thee   160
Man is to live, and all things live for man."
    To whom thus Eve with sad demeanor meek.
"Ill-worthy I such title should belong
To me transgressor, who for thee ordained
A help, became thy snare; to me reproach   165
Rather belongs, distrust and all dispraise:
But infinite in pardon was my Judge,
That I who first brought death on all, am graced
The source of life; next favorable thou,
Who highly thus to entitle me vouchsaf'st,   170
Far other name deserving. But the field
To labor calls us now with sweat imposed,
Though after sleepless night; for see the morn,
All unconcerned with our unrest, begins
Her rosy progress smiling; let us forth,   175
I never from thy side henceforth to stray,
Where'er our day's work lies, though now enjoined
Laborious, till day droop; while here we dwell,
What can be toilsome in these pleasant walks?
Here let us live, though in fall'n state, content."   180
    So spake, so wished much-humbled Eve, but fate
Subscribed not; nature first gave signs, impressed
On bird, beast, air, air suddenly eclipsed
After short blush of morn; nigh in her sight
The bird of Jove, stooped from his airy tow'r,   185
Two birds of gayest plume before him drove:
Down from a hill the beast that reigns in woods,
First hunter then, pursued a gentle brace,
Goodliest of all the forest, hart and hind;
Direct to th' eastern gate was bent their flight.   190
Adam observed, and with his eye the chase
Pursuing, not unmoved to Eve thus spake.
    "O Eve, some further change awaits us nigh,
Which heaven by these mute signs in nature shows
Forerunners of his purpose, or to warn   195
Us haply too secure of our discharge

159. *rightly called, mother:* (cf. Gen. 3.20) because *Hava*, the Hebrew word from which *Eve* was derived, came from *hai*, meaning 'to live.'
180. Cf. Phil. 4.11: "Not that I speak in respect of want: for I have learned, in whatsoever state I am, therewith to be content."
182. *signs:* omens.
183. *eclipsed:* darkened.
185. *bird of Jove:* eagle. *stooped:* swooped. *tow'r:* soaring.
187. *beast that reigns:* lion.
196. *secure:* sure.

From penalty, because from death released
Some days; how long, and what till then our life,
Who knows, or more than this, that we are dust,
And thither must return and be no more.   200
Why else this double object in our sight
Of flight pursued in th' air and o'er the ground
One way the selfsame hour? Why in the east
Darkness ere day's mid-course, and morning light
More orient in yon western cloud that draws   205
O'er the blue firmament a radiant white,
And slow descends, with something heav'nly fraught."
    He erred not, for by this the heav'nly bands
Down from a sky of jasper lighted now
In Paradise, and on a hill made alt,   210
A glorious apparition, had not doubt
And carnal fear that day dimmed Adam's eye.
Not that more glorious, when the angels met
Jacob in Mahanaim, where he saw
The field pavilioned with his guardians bright;   215
Nor that which on the flaming mount appeared
In Dothan, covered with a camp of fire,
Against the Syrian king, who to surprise
One man, assassin-like had levied war,
War unproclaimed. The princely Hierarch   220
In their bright stand, there left his powers to seize
Possession of the garden; he alone,
To find where Adam sheltered, took his way,
Not unperceived of Adam, who to Eve,
While the great visitant approached, thus spake.   225
    "Eve, now expect great tidings, which perhaps
Of us will soon determine, or impose
New laws to be observed; for I descry
From yonder blazing cloud that veils the hill
One of the heav'nly host, and by his gait   230
None of the meanest, some great Potentate
Or of the Thrones above, such majesty
Invests him coming; yet not terrible,

205. *orient:* bright, shining.
209. *jasper.* Cf. Rev. 4.3.
210. *made alt:* (military term) came to a halt.
213–15. Cf. Gen. 32.1–2: "And Jacob went on his way, and the angels of God met him. And when Jacob saw them, he said, "This is God's host: and he called the name of that place Mahanaim."
216–20. The king of Syria, warring on Israel, sent a detachment to Dothan (where Elisha, the prophet, was miraculously publishing the war plans of the king) with orders to kill Elisha. But the Lord saved his prophet by surrounding him with "horses and chariots of fire." 2 Kings 6.8ff.
220. *Hierarch:* Michael.
221. *bright stand:* shining formation, or station. *powers:* army, host.
227. *determine:* make an end.

That I should fear, nor sociably mild,
As Raphael, that I should much confide,   235
But solemn and sublime, whom not to offend,
With reverence I must meet, and thou retire."
He ended; and th' Archangel soon drew nigh,
Not in his shape celestial, but as man
Clad to meet man; over his lucid arms   240
A military vest of purple flowed
Livelier than Meliboean, or the grain
Of Sarra, worn by kings and heroes old
In time of truce; Iris had dipped the woof;
His starry helm unbuckled showed him prime   245
In manhood where youth ended; by his side
As in a glistering zodiac hung the sword,
Satan's dire dread, and in his hand the spear.
Adam bowed low, he kingly from his state
Inclined not, but his coming thus declared.   250
   "Adam, Heav'n's high behest no preface needs:
Sufficient that thy prayers are heard, and Death,
Then due by sentence when thou didst transgress,
Defeated of his seizure many days
Giv'n thee of grace, wherein thou may'st repent,   255
And one bad act with many deeds well done
May'st cover: well may then thy Lord appeased
Redeem thee quite from Death's rapacious claim;
But longer in this Paradise to dwell
Permits not; to remove thee I am come,   260
And send thee from the garden forth to till
The ground whence thou wast taken, fitter soil."
   He added not, for Adam at the news
Heart-strook with chilling gripe of sorrow stood,
That all his senses bound; Eve, who unseen   265
Yet all had heard, with audible lament
Discovered soon the place of her retire.
   "O unexpected stroke, worse than of Death!
Must I thus leave thee Paradise? thus leave
Thee native soil, these happy walks and shades,   270
Fit haunt of gods? where I had hope to spend,
Quiet though sad, the respite of that day
That must be mortal to us both. O flow'rs,

240. *lucid*: shining.
242–43. Meliboea and Tyre (*Sarra*) were famous for their purple dye (*grain*).
244. *Iris*: goddess of the rainbow.
247. *zodiac*: girdle.
249. *state*: dignified standing.
254. *Defeated of his seizure*: (legal language) deprived of his possession.
267. *Discovered*: revealed.
272. *respite*: period of postponement.

That never will in other climate grow,
My early visitation, and my last   275
At ev'n, which I bred up with tender hand
From the first op'ning bud, and gave ye names,
Who now shall rear ye to the sun, or rank
Your tribes, and water from th' ambrosial fount?
Thee lastly nuptial bower, by me adorned   280
With what to sight or smell was sweet; from thee
How shall I part, and whither wander down
Into a lower world, to this obscure
And wild, how shall we breathe in other air
Less pure, accustomed to immortal fruits?"   285
    Whom thus the Angel interrupted mild.
"Lament not Eve, but patiently resign
What justly thou hast lost; nor set thy heart,
Thus over-fond, on that which is not thine;
Thy going is not lonely, with thee goes   290
Thy husband, him to follow thou art bound;
Where he abides, think there thy native soil."
    Adam by this from the cold sudden damp
Recovering, and his scattered spirits returned,
To Michael thus his humble words addressed.   295
    "Celestial, whether among the Thrones, or named
Of them the highest, for such of shape may seem
Prince above princes, gently hast thou told
Thy message, which might else in telling wound,
And in performing end us; what besides   300
Of sorrow and dejection and despair
Our frailty can sustain, thy tidings bring,
Departure from this happy place, our sweet
Recess, and only consolation left
Familiar to our eyes, all places else   305
Inhospitable appear and desolate,
Nor knowing us nor known: and if by prayer
Incessant I could hope to change the will
Of him who all things can, I would not cease
To weary him with my assiduous cries: 310
But prayer against his absolute decree
No more avails than breath against the wind,
Blown stifling back on him that breathes it forth:
Therefore to his great bidding I submit.
This most afflicts me, that departing hence,   315
As from his face I shall be hid, deprived

283. *to this*: compared with this.
293. *damp*: dejection.
309. *can*: is able to do, has knowledge of.
316. Cf. Gen. 4.14 "Behold, thou hast driven me out this day from the face of the earth; and
from thy face shall I be hid; and I shall be a fugitive and a vagabond in the earth; and it shall

His blessed count'nance; here I could frequent,
With worship, place by place where he vouchsafed
Presence Divine, and to my sons relate:
'On this mount he appeared, under this tree   320
Stood visible, among these pines his voice
I heard, here with him at this fountain talked:'
So many grateful altars I would rear
Of grassy turf, and pile up every stone
Of luster from the brook, in memory,   325
Or monument to ages, and thereon
Offer sweet-smelling gums and fruits and flow'rs:
In yonder nether world where shall I seek
His bright appearances, or footstep trace?
For though I fled him angry, yet recalled   330
To life prolonged and promised race, I now
Gladly behold though but his utmost skirts
Of glory, and far off his steps adore."
    To whom thus Michael with regard benign.
"Adam, thou know'st heav'n his, and all the earth,   335
Not this rock only; his omnipresence fills
Land, sea, and air, and every kind that lives,
Fomented by his virtual power and warmed:
All th' earth he gave thee to possess and rule,
No despicable gift; surmise not then   340
His presence to these narrow bounds confined
Of Paradise or Eden: this had been
Perhaps thy capital seat, from whence had spread
All generations, and had hither come
From all the ends of th' earth, to celebrate   345
And reverence thee their great progenitor.
But this preeminence thou hast lost, brought down
To dwell on even ground now with thy sons:
Yet doubt not but in valley and in plain
God is as here, and will be found alike   350
Present, and of his presence many a sign

---

come to pass, that every one that findeth me shall slay me." Ps. 27.9: "Hide not thy face far from me; put not thy servant away in anger: thou hast been my help; leave me not, neither forsake me, O God of my salvation."
332. *skirts:* outermost edges; but cf. III.380, where Milton's use may derive from a Hebrew word (in Isa. 6.1) meaning "the skirt of his robe" and implying God's glory. Cf. Exod. 33.23 and [NEB] Job 26.14
335–38. Cf. Ps. 139.7–12: "Whither shall I go from thy spirit? or whither shall I flee from thy presence? If I ascend up into heaven, thou art there: if I make my bed in hell, behold, thou art there. If I take the wings of the morning, and dwell in the uttermost parts of the seas; Even there shall thy hand lead me, and thy right hand shall hold me. If I say, Surely the darkness shall cover me; even the night shall be light about me. Yea, the darkness hideth not from thee; but the night shineth as the day: the darkness and the light are both alike to thee." Jer. 23.24: "Can any hide himself in secret places that I shall not see him? saith the Lord. Do not I fill heaven and earth? saith the Lord." *Fomented:* nursed to life, nurtured. *virtual:* (L *virtus* strength) efficacious.

Still following thee, still compassing thee round
With goodness and paternal love, his face
Express, and of his steps the track divine.
Which that thou may'st believe, and be confirmed,   355
Ere thou from hence depart, know I am sent
To show thee what shall come in future days
To thee and to thy offspring; good with bad
Expect to hear, supernal grace contending
With sinfulness of men; thereby to learn   360
True patience, and to temper joy with fear
And pious sorrow, equally inured
By moderation either state to bare,
Prosperous or adverse: so shalt thou lead
Safest thy life, and best prepared endure   365
Thy mortal passage when it comes. Ascend
This hill; let Eve (for I have drenched her eyes)
Here sleep below while thou to foresight wak'st,
As once thou slept'st while she to life was formed."
   To whom thus Adam gratefully replied.   370
"Ascend, I follow thee, safe guide, the path
Thou lead'st me, and to the hand of Heav'n submit,
However chast'ning, to the evil turn
My obvious breast, arming to overcome
By suffering, and earn rest from labor won,   375
If so I may attain." So both ascend
In the visions of God: it was a hill
Of Paradise the highest, from whose top
The hemisphere of earth in clearest ken
Stretched out to amplest reach of prospect lay.   380
Not higher that hill nor wider looking round,
Whereon for different cause the Tempter set
Our second Adam in the wilderness,
To show him all earth's kingdoms and their glory.
His eye might there command wherever stood   385
City of old or modern fame, the seat
Of mightiest empire, from the destined walls

362. *pious sorrow:* L *pius,* dutiful; pity consistent with proper religious attitudes.
367. *drenched.* Cf. II.73 *the sleepy drench / Of that forgetful lake.*
374. *obvious:* exposed.
377. Cf. Ezek. 40.2: "In the visions of God brought he me into the land of Israel, and set me upon a very high mountain . . ."
379. *ken:* view.
381–84. In the temptations of Christ, which Milton recounted in *PR,* the devil took Christ "up into an exceeding high mountain and [showed] him all the kingdoms of the world, and the glory of them" (Matt. 4.8), and offered Christ "all these things" if Christ would "fall down and worship" him.
387–96. These *destined* (yet to come) cities were great capitals: *Cambalu* (Peking) of Cathay, a vaguely defined region in N China ruled by such khans as Genghis and Kubla; *Samarkand,* on the Oxus River, of the SW part of Tatary (now SW Russia), ruled by another khan, Tamburlaine (*Temir*); *Paquin* (Peking) of China (Milton's contemporaries were not sure whether Cambalu and Paquin were the same city); *Agra* and *Lahore* of the *mogul* empire in India; *Echatan* (modern Hamadan) and *Hispahan* (modern Isfahan), of Persia (Iran); *Bizance* (Byzantium—modern Istanbul) of the Turkish empire, ruled by *sultans,* who came from

Of Cambalu, seat of Cathaian Can,
And Samarkand by Oxus, Temir's throne,
To Paquin of Sinaean kings, and thence   390
To Agra and Lahore of Great Mogul
Down to the golden Chersonese, or where
The Persian in Ecbatan sat, or since
In Hispahan, or where the Russian Czar
In Moscow, or the Sultan in Bizance,   395
Turkéstan-born; nor could his eye not ken
Th' empire of Negus to his utmost port
Ercoco and the less marítime kings
Mombaza, and Quiloa, and Melind,
And Sofala thought Ophir, to the realm   400
Of Congo, and Angola farthest south;
Or thence from Niger flood to Atlas mount
The kingdoms of Almansor, Fez and Sus,
Marocco and Algiers, and Tremisen;
On Europe thence, and where Rome was to sway   405
The world: in spirit perhaps he also saw
Rich Mexico the seat of Motezume,
And Cusco in Peru, the richer seat
Of Atabalipa, and yet unspoiled
Guiana, whose great city Geryon's sons   410
Call El Dorado: but to nobler sights
Michael from Adam's eyes the film removed
Which that false fruit that promised clearer sight
Had bred; then purged with euphrasy and rue
The visual nerve, for he had much to see;   415

Turkestan (a region now divided among Russia, China, and Afghanistan). *the golden Chersonese:* the Malay Peninsula, thought by some to be *Ophir,* the country from which Solomon got the gold for his temple. Other places had been suggested, among them *Sofala* (400).

397–404. On the African continent: the *empire* of the King (*Negus*) is Abyssinia; *Ercoco* (modern Arkiko) is on the Red Sea; *Mombaza* (modern Mombasa), *Melind* (modern Malindi), *Quiloa* (modern Kilwa) and *Sofala* are on the east coast; the S part of the W coast in Milton's time was called *Angola;* the territory between the *Niger* River and the *Atlas* Mountains (in N Morocco and Algeria), are the *kingdoms of Almansor* (a tenth-century Mohammedan prince), i.e., the province of *Sus* (Tunis)and the cities of *Fez* and *Tremisen* (modern Tiemecen), which Milton thought of as capitals of small nations.

400. *Ophir.* Cf. 1 Kings 9.28: "And they came to Ophir, and fetched from thence gold, four hundred and twenty talents, and brought it to king Solomon." 1 Kings 10.11: "And the navy also of Hiram, that brought gold from Ophir, brought in from Ophir great plenty of almug trees, and precious stones."

406–11. *in spirit.* No matter how high the mount in Paradise, Adam could not see the other side of the sphere. Atahualpa (*Atabalipa*) was the Inca emperor defeated by Pizarro. *Guiana* was a region containing modern Surinam, Guyana, and French Guiana, part of Venezuela and part of Brazil; its capital, Manoa, was supposed by the Spanish (*Geryon's sons*) to be the residence of *El Dorado,* the Gilded King. *yet unspoiled:* in Milton's time, not yet plundered by the Spanish (unlike Mexico and Persia).

414. *euphrasy:* the herb "eyebright," like *rue* (another herb) believed to improve vision. Fowler notes that *euphrasy* comes from Gk *euphrasia* cheerfulness and that the word, like *rue,* may

And from the well of life three drops instilled.
So deep the power of these ingredients pierced,
Ev'n to the inmost seat of mental sight,
That Adam now enforced to close his eyes,
Sunk down and all his spirits became entranced: 420
But him the gentle angel by the hand
Soon raised, and his attention thus recalled.
   "Adam, now ope thine eyes, and first behold
Th' effects which thy original crime hath wrought
In some to spring from thee, who never touched   425
Th' excepted tree, nor with the snake conspired,
Nor sinned thy sin, yet from that sin derive
Corruption to bring forth more violent deeds."
   His eyes he opened, and beheld a field,
Part arable and tilth, whereon were sheaves   430
New-reaped, the other part sheep-walks and folds;
I' th' midst an altar as the landmark stood
Rustic, of grassy sord; thither anon
A sweaty reaper from his tillage brought
First-fruits, the green ear, and the yellow sheaf,   435
Unculled, as came to hand; a shepherd next
More meek came with the firstlings of his flock
Choicest and best; then sacrificing, laid
The inwards and their fat, with incense strewed,
On the cleft wood, and all due rites performed.   440
His off'ring soon propitious fire from heav'n
Consumed with nimble glance, and grateful steam;
The other's not, for his was not sincere;
Whereat he inly raged, and as they talked,
Smote him into the midriff with a stone   445
That beat out life; he fell, and deadly pale
Groaned out his soul with gushing blood effused.
Much at that sight was Adam in his heart
Dismayed, and thus in haste to th' angel cried.
   "O teacher, some great mischief hath befall'n   450
To that meek man, who well had sacrificed;
Is piety thus and pure devotion paid?"
   T' whom Michael thus, he also moved, replied.

---

be a pun—that euphrasy and rue as joy and sorrow are "correlates of the 'joy' and 'pious sorrow'
that Michael told Adam to temper, at 361ff."
416. Cf. Ps. 36.9: "For with thee is the fountain of life: in thy light shall we see light."
429–60. Cf. Gen. 4.1–16.
430. *tilth*: cultivated land.
432. *landmark*: boundary-marker.
433. *sord*: sward, turf.
435. *First-fruits*. Cf. 22.
436. *Unculled*: unselected; not, like Abel's the *choicest and best* (438).
439. *inwards*: innards.
441. *propitious*: indicative of God's favor.
442. *nimble glance*: quick flash.

"These two are brethren, Adam, and to come
Out of thy loins; th' unjust the just hath slain,   455
For envy that his brother's offering found
From Heav'n acceptance; but the bloody fact
Will be avenged, and th' other's faith approved
Lose no reward, thou here thou see him die,
Rolling in dust and gore." To which our sire.   460
    "Alas, both for the deed and for the cause!
But have I now seen death? Is this the way
I must return to native dust? O sight
Of terror, foul and ugly to behold,
Horrid to think, how horrible to feel!"   465
    To whom thus Michaël. "Death thou hast seen
In his first shape on man; but many shapes
Of Death, and many are the ways that lead
To his grim cave, all dismal; yet to sense
More terrible at th' entrance than within.   470
Some, as thou saw'st, by violent stroke shall die,
By fire, flood, famine; by intemperance more
In meats and drinks, which on the earth shall bring
Diseases dire, of which a monstrous crew
Before thee shall appear; that thou may'st know   475
What misery th' inabstinence of Eve
Shall bring on men." Immediately a place
Before his eyes appeared, sad, noisome, dark,
A lazar-house it seemed, wherein were laid
Numbers of all diseased, all maladies   480
Of ghastly spasm, or racking torture, qualms
Of heart-sick agony, all feverous kinds,
Convulsions, epilepsies, fierce catarrhs,
Intestine stone and ulcer, colic pangs,
Demoniac frenzy, moping melancholy   485
And moon-struck madness, pining atrophy,
Marasmus, and wide-wasting pestilence,
Dropsies, and asthmas, and joint-racking rheums.
Dire was the tossing, deep the groans, Despair
Tended the sick busiest from couch to couch;   490
And over them triumphant Death his dart
Shook, but delayed to strike, though oft invoked
With vows, as their chief good, and final hope.

457. *fact*: crime. Cf. IX.928.
458–59. Cf. Heb. 11.4: "By faith Abel offered unto God a more excellent sacrifice than Cain,
by which he obtained witness that he was righteous, God testifying of his gifts: and by it he
being dead yet speaketh."
478. *sad*: lamentable.
479. *lazar-house*: hospital.
485–87. These lines were not in the first ed. *pining atrophy, Marasmus*: all three words mean
"wasting away."

Sight so deform what heart of rock could long
Dry-eyed behold? Adam could not, but wept,   495
Though not of woman born; compassion quelled
His best of man, and gave him up to tears
A space, till firmer thoughts restrained excess,
And scarce recovering words his plaint renewed.
    "O miserable mankind, to what fall   500
Degraded, to what wretched state reserved!
Better end here unborn. Why is life giv'n
To be thus wrested from us? Rather why
Obtruded on us thus? who if we knew
What we receive, would either not accept   505
Life offered, or soon beg to lay it down,
Glad to be so dismissed in peace. Can thus
Th' image of God in man created once
So goodly and erect, though faulty since,
To such unsightly sufferings be debased   510
Under inhuman pains? Why should not man,
Retaining still divine similitude
In part, from such deformities be free,
And for his Maker's image sake exempt?"
    "Their Maker's image," answered Michael, "then   515
Forsook them, when themselves they vilified
To serve ungoverned appetite, and took
His image whom they served, a brutish vice,
Inductive mainly to the sin of Eve.
Therefore so abject is their punishment,   520
Disfiguring not God's likeness, but their own,
Or if his likeness, by themselves defaced
While they pervert pure nature's healthful rules
To loathsome sickness, worthily, since they
God's image did not reverence in themselves."   525
    "I yield it just," said Adam, "and submit.
But is there yet no other way, besides
These painful passages, how we may come
To death, and mix with our connatural dust?"
    "There is,' said Michael, "if thou well observe   530
The rule of not too much, by temperance taught
In what thou eat'st and drink'st, seeking from thence
Due nourishment, not gluttonous delight,
Till many years over thy head return:
So may'st thou live, till like ripe fruit thou drop   535
Into thy mother's lap, or be with ease

---

497. *best of man*: manliness, courage.
516. *vilified*: lowered.
519. *Inductive*: conducive.
524. *worthily*: deservedly.

Gathered, not harshly plucked, for death mature:
This is old age; but then thou must outlive
Thy youth, thy strength, thy beauty, which will change
To withered weak and gray; thy senses then   540
Obtuse, all taste of pleasure must forgo,
To what thou hast, and for the air of youth
Hopeful and cheerful, in thy blood will reign
A melancholy damp of cold and dry
To weigh thy spirits down, and last consume   545
The balm of life." To whom our ancestor.
    "Henceforth I fly not death, nor would prolong
Life much, bent rather how I may be quit
Fairest and easiest of this cumbrous charge,
Which I must keep till my appointed day   550
Of rend'ring up, and patiently attend
My dissolution.' Michaël replied.
    "Nor love thy life, nor hate; but what thou liv'st
Live well, how long or short permit to Heav'n:
And now prepare thee for another sight."   555
    He looked and saw a spacious plain, whereon
Were tents of various hue; by some were herds
Of cattle grazing: others, whence the sound
Of instruments that made melodious chime
Was heard, of harp and organ; and who moved   560
Their stops and chords was seen: his volant touch
Instinct through all proportions low and high
Fled and pursued transverse the resonant fugue.
In other part stood one who at the forge
Laboring, two massy clods of iron and brass   565
Had melted (whether found where casual fire
Had wasted woods on mountain or in vale,
Down to the veins of earth, thence gliding hot
To some cave's mouth, or whether washed by stream
From underground) the liquid ore he drained   570
Into fit molds prepared; from which he formed
First his own tools; then, what might else be wrought

544. *damp*: vapor; depression or dejection; but Milton suggests "humor," since in the theory of the humors melancholy was supposed to be *cold* (of the earth) and *dry* (of the air).
546. *balm*: balsam, "preservative essence, conceived by Paracelsus to exist in all organic bodies" OED.
551. *attend*: await.
556–73. Cf. Gen. 4.20–22.
561–63. Milton describes the fugue and the playing of a fugue. *volant*: (L *volare* to fly) nimble. *touch*: skill in or style of playing an instrument. *Instinct*: instinctive, innate, untutored. *proportions*: (technical musical term) here, ratios of pitches; perhaps, scales. *Fled and pursued*: descriptive of both the player's hands and of the music. In a fugue (L *fugere* to flee) one variation of the theme seems to chase another. *transverse*: across either scales, or keyboard or strings. *resonant*: literally re-sounding, since in a fugue the same notes or theme(s) are, in a way, repeated.
566. *casual*: L *casus* fall, chance. *fire*: lightning.

Fusile or grav'n in metal. After these,
But on the hither side a different sort
From the high neighboring hills, which was their seat,   575
Down to the plain descended: by their guise
Just men they seemed, and all their study bent
To worship God aright, and know his works
Not hid, nor those things last which might preserve
Freedom and peace to men: they on the plain   580
Long had not walked, when from the tents behold
A bevy of fair women, richly gay
In gems and wanton dress; to the harp they sung
Soft amorous ditties, and in dance came on:
The men though grave, eyed them, and let their eyes   585
Rove without rein, till in the amorous net
Fast caught, they liked, and each his liking chose;
And now of love they treat till th' evening star
Love's harbinger appeared; then all in heat
They light the nuptial torch, and bid invoke   590
Hymen, then first to marriage rites invoked;
With feast and music all the tents resound.
Such happy interview and fair event
Of love and youth not lost, songs, garlands, flow'rs,
And charming symphonies attached the heart   595
Of Adam, soon inclined to admit delight,
The bent of nature; which he thus expressed.
    "True opener of mine eyes, prime angel blest,
Much better seems this vision, and more hope
Of peaceful days portends, than those two past;   600
Those were of hate and death, or pain much worse,
Here nature seems fulfilled in all her ends."
    To whom thus Michael. "Judge not what is best
By pleasure, though to nature seeming meet,
Created, as thou art, to nobler end   605
Holy and pure, conformity divine.
Those tents thou saw'st so pleasant, were the tents
Of wickedness, wherein shall dwell his race
Who slew his brother; studious they appear
Of arts that polish life, inventors rare,   610

573. *Fusile or grav'n:* cast or sculptured.
573–74. Turning from the descendants of Cain, Milton speaks of those of Seth, Adam's third
    son, who lived in the hills bordering Cain's plain, east of Eden, opposite the hill of Paradise.
580. Here Milton begins the story of the *Giants of mighty bone* (642) based on Gen. 6.1–4.
    Milton implies that the heroic race was the offspring of the descendants of Seth ("sons of God")
    and the descendants of Cain ("daughters of men").
588. *evening star:* Venus.
591. *Hymen:* god of marriage.
595. *symphonies:* concerted or harmonious music. *attached:* seized.
596. *soon:* easily.
607–8. Cf. Ps. 84.10: "For a day in thy courts is better than a thousand. I had rather be a
    doorkeeper in the house of my God, than to dwell in the tents of wickedness."

Unmindful of their Maker, though his spirit
Taught them, but they his gifts acknowledged none.
Yet they a beauteous offspring shall beget;
For that fair female troop thou saw'st, that seemed
Of goddesses, so blithe, so smooth, so gay,   615
Yet empty of all good wherein consists
Woman's domestic honor and chief praise;
Bred only and completed to the taste
Of lustful appetence, to sing, to dance,
To dress, and troll the tongue, and roll the eye.   620
To these that sober race of men, whose lives
Religious titled them the Sons of God,
Shall yield up all their virtue, all their fame
Ignobly, to the trains and to the smiles
Of these fair atheists, and now swim in joy,   625
(Erelong to swim at large) and laugh; for which
The world erelong a world of tears must weep."
    To whom thus Adam of short joy bereft.
"O pity and shame, that they who to live well
Entered so fair, should turn aside to tread   630
Paths indirect, or in the mid way faint!
But still I see the tenor of man's woe
Holds on the same, from woman to begin."
    "From man's effeminate slackness it begins,"
Said th' angel, "who should better hold his place   635
By wisdom, and superior gifts received.
But now prepare thee for another scene."
    He looked and saw wide territory spread
Before him, towns, and rural works between,
Cities of men with lofty gates and tow'rs,   640
Concourse in arms, fierce faces threat'ning war,
Giants of mighty bone, and bold emprise;
Part wield their arms, part curb the foaming steed,
Single or in array of battle ranged
Both horse and foot, nor idly must'ring stood;   645
One way a band select from forage drives
A herd of beeves, fair oxen and fair kine

---

618. *completed*: equipped.
619. *appetence*: craving.
620. *troll*: roll, wag.
624. *trains*: guile, wiles, trickery.
638–73. Cf. similar scenes depicted on the shields of Achilles (*Il.* 18.478–608) and Aeneas (*Aen.* 8.626–728).
641. *Concourse*: (L *concurrere* to run together) encounter.
642. *emprise*: chivalric adventure.
646–55. Cf. *Il.* 18.527ff.: "Then the others when they beheld these ran upon them and quickly cut off the herds of oxen and fair flocks of white sheep, and slew the shepherds withal. But the besiegers, as they sat before the speechplaces and heard much din among the oxen, mounted forthwith behind their high-stepping horses, and came up with speed. Then they arrayed their battle and fought beside the river banks, and smote one another with bronze-shod spears."

From a fat meadow ground; or fleecy flock,
Ewes and their bleating lambs over the plain,
Their booty; scarce with life the shepherds fly,   650
But call in aid, which makes a bloody fray;
With cruel tournament the squadrons join;
Where cattle pastured late, now scattered lies
With carcasses and arms th' ensanguined field
Deserted: others to a city strong   655
Lay siege, encamped; by battery, scale, and mine,
Assaulting; others from the wall defend
With dart and jav'lin, stones and sulphurous fire;
On each hand slaughter and gigantic deeds.
In other part the sceptered heralds call   660
To council in the city gates: anon
Gray-headed men and grave, with warriors mixed,
Assemble, and harangues are heard, but soon
In factious opposition, till at last
Of middle age one rising, eminent   665
In wise deport, spake much of right and wrong,
Of justice, of religion, truth and peace,
And judgment from above: him old and young
Exploded, and had seized with violent hands,
Had not a cloud descending snatched him thence   670
Unseen amid the throng: so violence
Proceeded, and oppression, and sword-law
Through all the plain, and refuge none was found.
Adam was all in tears, and to his guide
Lamenting turned full sad; "O what are these,   675
Death's ministers, not men, who thus deal death
Inhumanly to men, and multiply
Ten-thousandfold the sin of him who slew
His brother; for of whom such massacre
Make they but of their brethren, men of men?   680
But who was that just man, whom had not Heav'n
Rescued, had in his righteousness been lost?"
    To whom thus Michael. "These are the product
Of those ill-mated marriages thou saw'st:
Where good with bad were matched, who of themselves   685
Abhor to join; and by imprudence mixed,
Produce prodigious births of body or mind.
Such were these giants, men of high renown;
For in those days might only shall be admired,
And valor and heroic virtue called;   690

656. I.e.: By battering, scaling, and tunneling under (the walls).
665. *one:* Enoch, who "walked with God: and he was not; for God took him" (Gen. 5.24). See
    700–9n.
669. *Exploded.* See X.546n.

To overcome in battle, and subdue
Nations, and bring home spoils with infinite
Manslaughter, shall be held the highest pitch
Of human glory, and for glory done
Of triumph, to be styled great conquerors,   695
Patrons of mankind, gods, and sons of gods,
Destroyers rightlier called and plagues of men.
Thus fame shall be achieved, renown on earth,
And what most merits fame in silence hid.
But he the sev'nth from thee, whom thou beheld'st   700
The only righteous in a world perverse,
And therefore hated, therefore so beset
With foes for daring single to be just,
And utter odious truth, that God would come
To judge them with his saints: him the Most High   705
Rapt in a balmy cloud with wingèd steeds
Did, as thou saw'st, receive, to walk with God
High in salvation and the climes of bliss,
Exempt from death; to show thee what reward
Awaits the good, the rest what punishment;   710
Which now direct thine eyes and soon behold."
    He looked, and saw the face of things quite changed;
The brazen throat of war had ceased to roar,
All now was turned to jollity and game,
To luxury and riot, feast and dance,   715
Marrying or prostituting, as befell,
Rape or adultery, where passing fair
Allured them; thence from cups to civil broils.
At length a reverend sire among them came,
And of their doings great dislike declared,   720
And testified against their ways; he oft
Frequented their assemblies, whereso met,
Triumphs or festivals, and to them preached

700–9. Cf. Jude 14–15: "And Enoch also, the seventh from Adam, prophesied of these, saying,
Behold, the Lord cometh with ten thousands of his saints, to execute judgment upon all, and
to convince all that are ungodly among them of all their ungodly deeds which they have ungodly
committed, and of all their hard speeches which ungodly sinners have spoken against him."
Heb. 11.5: "By faith Enoch was translated that he should not see death; and was not found,
because God had translated him: for before his translation he had this testimony, that he pleased
God."
715. *luxury*: (L *luxus* excess) lust.
717. *passing fair*. Fowler notes a possible pun: "surpassing beauties" and "women passing by."
719. *a reverend sire*: Noah. Cf. Gen. 6–9. Christian interpretations appear in the NT; cf. 1 Pet.
3.19–21 [NEB]: "In the body [Christ] was put to death; in the spirit he was brought to life.
And in the spirit he went and made his proclamation to the imprisoned spirits. They had
refused obedience long ago, while God waited patiently in the days of Noah and the building
of the ark, and in the ark a few persons, eight in all, were brought to safety through the water.
This water prefigured the water of baptism through which you are now brought to safety." Cf.
Heb. 11.7: "By faith Noah, being warned of God of things not seen as yet, moved with fear,
prepared an ark to the saving of his house; by which he condemned the world, and became
heir of the righteousness which is by faith."
723. *Triumphs*: pageants.

Conversion and repentance, as to souls
In prison under judgments imminent: 725
But all in vain: which when he saw, he ceased
Contending, and removed his tents far off;
Then from the mountain hewing timber tall,
Began to build a vessel of huge bulk,
Measured by cubit, length, and breadth, and highth,   730
Smeared round with pitch, and in the side a door
Contrived, and of provisions laid in large
For man and beast: when lo a wonder strange!
Of every beast, and bird, and insect small
Came sevens and pairs, and entered in, as taught   735
Their order: last the sire and his three sons
With their four wives; and God made fast the door.
Meanwhile the southwind rose, and with black wings
Wide hovering, all the clouds together drove
From under heav'n; the hills to their supply   740
Vapor, and exhalation dusk and moist,
Sent up amain; and now the thickened sky
Like a dark ceiling stood; down rushed the rain
Impetuous, and continued till the earth
No more was seen; the floating vessel swum   745
Uplifted; and secure with beakèd prow
Rode tilting o'er the waves, all dwellings else
Flood overwhelmed, and them with all their pomp
Deep under water rolled; sea covered sea,
Sea without shore; and in their palaces   750
Where luxury late reigned, sea-monsters whelped
And stabled; of mankind, so numerous late,
All left, in one small bottom swum embarked.
How didst thou grieve then, Adam, to behold
The end of all thy offspring, end so sad,   755
Depopulation; thee another flood,
Of tears and sorrow a flood thee also drowned,
And sunk thee as thy sons; till gently reared
By th' angel, on thy feet thou stood'st at last,
Though comfortless, as when a father mourns   760
His children, all in view destroyed at once;
And scarce to th' angel utter'dst thus thy plaint.
    "O visions ill foreseen! Better had I
Lived ignorant of future, so had borne
My part of evil only, each day's lot   765

---

750. *Sea without shore*: cf. *Met.* 1.291–92: "And now the sea and land have no distinction. All
    is sea, but a sea without shore."
753. *swum*: floated.
765–66. Cf. Matt. 6.34: "Take therefore no thought for the morrow: for the morrow shall take
    thought for the things of itself. Sufficient unto the day is the evil thereof."

Enough to bear; those now, that were dispensed
The burd'n of many ages, on me light
At once, by my foreknowledge gaining birth
Abortive, to torment me ere their being,
With thought that they must be. Let no man seek   770
Henceforth to be foretold what shall befall
Him or his children, evil he may be sure,
Which neither his foreknowing can prevent,
And he the future evil shall no less
In apprehension than in substance feel   775
Grievous to bear: but that care now is past,
Man is not whom to warn: those few escaped
Famine and anguish will at last consume
Wand'ring that wat'ry desert: I had hope
When violence was ceased, and war on earth,   780
All would have then gone well, peace would have crowned
With length of happy days the race of man;
But I was far deceived; for now I see
Peace to corrupt no less than war to waste.
How comes it thus? unfold, celestial guide,   785
And whether here the race of man will end."
   To whom thus Michael. "Those whom last thou saw'st
In triumph and luxurious wealth, are they
First seen in acts of prowess eminent
And great exploits, but of true virtue void;   790
Who having spilt much blood, and done much waste
Subduing nations, and achieved thereby
Fame in the world, high titles, and rich prey,
Shall change their course to pleasure, ease, and sloth,
Surfeit, and lust, till wantonness and pride   795
Raise out of friendship hostile deeds in peace.
The conquered also, and enslaved by war
Shall with their freedom lost all virtue lose
And fear of God, from whom their piety feigned
In sharp contést of battle found no aid   800
Against invaders; therefore cooled in zeal
Thenceforth shall practice how to live secure,
Worldly or dissolute, on what their lords
Shall leave them to enjoy; for th' earth shall bear
More than enough, that temperance may be tried: 805
So all shall turn degenerate, all depraved,
Justice and temperance, truth and faith forgot;
One man except, the only son of light
In a dark age, against example good,
Against allurement, custom, and a world   810

810–11. *a world* / *Offended*: a displeased, unfriendly world.

Offended; fearless of reproach and scorn,
Or violence, he of their wicked ways
Shall them admonish, and before them set
The paths of righteousness, how much more safe,
And full of peace, denouncing wrath to come   815
On their impenitence; and shall return
Of them derided, but of God observed
The one just man alive; by his command
Shall build a wondrous ark, as thou beheld'st,
To save himself and household from amidst   820
A world devote to universal wrack.
No sooner he with them of man and beast
Select for life shall in the ark be lodged,
And sheltered round, but all the cataracts
Of heav'n set open on the earth shall pour   825
Rain day and night, all fountains of the deep
Broke up, shall heave the ocean to usurp
Beyond all bounds, till inundation rise
Above the highest hills: then shall this mount
Of Paradise by might of waves be moved   830
Out of his place, pushed by the hornèd flood,
With all his verdure spoiled, and trees adrift
Down the great river to the op'ning gulf,
And there take root an island salt and bare,
The haunt of seals and orcs, and sea-mews' clang.   835
To teach thee that God áttributes to place
No sanctity, if none be thither brought
By men who there frequent, or therein dwell.
And now what further shall ensue, behold."
    He looked, and saw the ark hull on the flood,   840
Which now abated, for the clouds were fled,
Driv'n by a keen north wind, that blowing dry
Wrinkled the face of deluge, as decayed;
And the clear sun on his wide wat'ry glass
Gazed hot, and of the fresh wave largely drew,   845
As after thirst, which made their flowing shrink
From standing lake to tripping ebb, that stole
With soft foot towards the deep, who now had stopped
His sluices, as the heav'n his windows shut.
The ark no more now floats, but seems on ground   850
Fast on the top of some high mountain fixed.
And now the tops of hills as rocks appear;
With clamor thence the rapid currents drive

815. *denouncing:* proclaiming.
821. *devote:* doomed.
833. I.e.: Down the Euphrates River to the Persian Gulf.
835. *orcs:* whales, or sea monsters. *sea-mews:* gulls. *clang:* shrill scream.
840. *hull:* drift.

Towards the retreating sea their furious tide.
Forthwith from out the ark a raven flies,   855
And after him, the surer messenger,
A dove sent forth once and again to spy
Green tree or ground whereon his foot may light;
The second time returning, in his bill
An olive leaf he brings, pacific sign: 860
Anon dry ground appears, and from his ark
The ancient sire descends with all his train;
Then with uplifted hands, and eyes devout,
Grateful to Heav'n, over his head beholds
A dewy cloud, and in the cloud a bow   865
Conspicuous with three listed colors gay,
Betok'ning peace from God, and cov'nant new.
Whereat the heart of Adam erst so sad
Greatly rejoiced, and thus his joy broke forth.
    "O thou who future things canst represent   870
As present, heav'nly instructor, I revive
At this last sight, assured that man shall live
With all the creatures, and their seed preserve.
Far less I now lament for one whole world
Of wicked sons destroyed, than I rejoice   875
For one man found so perfect and so just,
That God vouchsafes to raise another world
From him, and all his anger to forget.
But say, what mean those colored streaks in heav'n,
Distended as the brow of God appeased,   880
Or serve they as a flow'ry verge to bind
The fluid skirts of that same wat'ry cloud,
Lest it again dissolve and show'r the earth?"
    To whom th' Archangel. "Dextrously thou aim'st;
So willingly doth God remit his ire,   885
Though late repenting him of man depraved,
Grieved at his heart, when looking down he saw
The whole earth filled with violence, and all flesh
Corrupting each their way; yet those removed,
Such grace shall one just man find in his sight,   890
That he relents, not to blot out mankind,
And makes a cov'nant never to destroy
The earth again by flood, nor let the sea
Surpass his bounds, nor rain to drown the world
With man therein or beast; but when he brings   895
Over the earth a cloud, will therein set
His triple-colored bow, whereon to look
And call to mind his cov'nant: day and night,

866. *listed:* striped.

Seed-time and harvest, heat and hoary frost
Shall hold their course, till fire purge all things new,   900
Both heav'n and earth, wherein the just shall dwell."

Book XII

The Argument

The angel Michael continues from the Flood to relate what shall
succeed; then, in the mention of Abraham, comes by degrees to explain,
who that Seed of the Woman shall be, which was promised Adam and
Eve in the Fall; his incarnation, death, resurrection, and ascension; the
state of the church till his second coming. Adam greatly satisfied and
recomforted by these relations and promises descends the hill with Mi-
chael; wakens Eve, who all this while had slept, but with gentle dreams
composed to quietness of mind and submission. Michael in either hand
leads them out of Paradise, the fiery sword waving behind them, and
the Cherubim taking their stations to guard the place.

As one who in his journey bates at noon,
Though bent on speed, so here the Archangel paused
Betwixt the world destroyed and world restored,
If Adam aught perhaps might interpose;
Then with transition sweet new speech resumes.   5
    "Thus thou hast seen one world begin and end;
And man as from a second stock proceed.
Much thou hast yet to see, but I perceive
Thy mortal sight to fail; objects divine
Must needs impair and weary human sense: 10
Henceforth what is to come I will relate,
Thou therefore give due audience, and attend.
This second source of men, while yet but few,
And while the dread of judgment past remains
Fresh in their minds, fearing the Deity,   15
With some regard to what is just and right
Shall lead their lives, and multiply apace,
Laboring the soil, and reaping plenteous crop,
Corn wine and oil; and from the herd or flock,
Oft sacrificing bullock, lamb, or kid,   20
With large wine-offerings poured, and sacred feast,

900. I.e., till the Millennium.
XII.1–5. Milton added these lines when Book X of the 1st ed. was divided to make Books XI
    and XII of the 2nd ed. *bates:* pauses for rest and refreshment. *transition:* (musical term) passing
    from one note or key to another.
7. *second stock:* i.e., from the old root and stump a new branch, which will become a *second*
    tree.

Shall spend their days in joy unblamed, and dwell
Long time in peace by families and tribes
Under paternal rule; till one shall rise
Of proud ambitious heart, who not content   25
With fair equality, fraternal state,
Will arrogate dominion undeserved
Over his brethren, and quite dispossess
Concord and law of nature from the earth;
Hunting (and men not beasts shall be his game)   30
With war and hostile snare such as refuse
Subjection to his empire tyrannous:
A mighty hunter thence he shall be styled
Before the Lord, as in despite of Heav'n,
Or from Heav'n claiming second sovranty;   35
And from rebellion shall derive his name,
Though of rebellion others he accuse.
He with a crew, whom like ambition joins
With him or under him to tyrannize,
Marching from Eden towards the west, shall find   40
The plain, wherein a black bituminous gurge
Boils out from under ground, the mouth of hell;
Of brick, and of that stuff they cast to build
A city and tow'r, whose top may reach to heav'n;
And get themselves a name, lest far dispersed   45
In foreign lands their memory be lost,
Regardless whether good or evil fame.
But God who oft descends to visit men
Unseen, and through their habitations walks
To mark their doings, them beholding soon,   50
Comes down to see their city, ere the tower
Obstruct heav'n tow'rs, and in derision sets
Upon their tongues a various spirit to raze
Quite out their native language, and instead
To sow a jangling noise of words unknown: 55
Forthwith a hideous gabble rises loud
Among the builders; each to other calls

24. *one*: Nimrod. Cf. Gen. 10.8: "And Cush begat Nimrod: he began to be a mighty one in the earth. He was a mighty hunter before the Lord: wherefore it is said, Even as Nimrod the mighty hunter before the Lord. And the beginning of his kingdom was Babel."
33–35. Milton's explanation of the biblical phrase *Before the Lord* is that Nimrod claimed either superiority to God or power next only to God's.
36. Bush notes that "the name *Nimrod* was mistakenly linked with the Hebrew verb meaning 'to rebel.' "
38–62. Cf. Gen. 11.1–9, p. 433, and III.466ff.
41. *gurge*: whirlpool.
43. *cast*: decide.
44. *A city*: Babylon.
52. *in derision*. Cf. Ps. 2.4, p. 439: "He that sitteth in the heavens shall laugh: the Lord shall have them in derision."
53. *various*: divisive.

Not understood, till hoarse, and all in rage,
As mocked they storm; great laughter was in heav'n
And looking down, to see the hubbub strange   60
And hear the din; thus was the building left
Ridiculous, and the work Confusion named."
  Whereto thus Adam fatherly displeased.
"O execrable son so to aspire
Above his brethren, to himself assuming   65
Authority usurped, from God not giv'n:
He gave us only over beast, fish, fowl
Dominion absolute; that right we hold
By his donation; but man over men
He made not lord; such title to himself   70
Reserving, human left from human free.
But this usurper his encroachment proud
Stays not on man; to God his tower intends
Siege and defiance: wretched man! What food
Will he convey up thither to sustain   75
Himself and his rash army, where thin air
Above the clouds will pine his entrails gross,
And famish him of breath, if not of bread?"
  To whom thus Michael. "Justly thou abhorr'st
That son, who on the quiet state of men   80
Such trouble brought, affecting to subdue
Rational liberty; yet know withal,
Since thy original lapse, true liberty
Is lost, which always with right reason dwells
Twinned, and from her hath no dividual being: 85
Reason in man obscured, or not obeyed,
Immediately inordinate desires
And upstart passions catch the government
From reason, and to servitude reduce
Man till then free. Therefore since he permits   90
Within himself unworthy powers to reign
Over free reason, God in judgment just
Subjects him from without to violent lords;
Who oft as undeservedly enthrall

62. *Confusion:* erroneously thought to be the meaning of *Babel.*
67–69. Cf. Gen. 9.2.
77. *pine:* waste away.
81. *affecting:* aspiring.
82–101. *Rational liberty.* Milton begins a discussion of the relationship of right reason and
    Christian doctrine to civil and religious freedom—the idea of protestant Christian liberalism
    that is an important part of the poem's conclusion. Up to this point the words *free, freedom,*
    and *liberty,* in their political senses, have (with one exception) all occurred in speeches of
    Satan or in ironic references to him. Only here at the end does Milton use them unironically.
    Cf. X.307; XI.798; XII.82, 95, 100, 526. But see especially *CD,* paragraph 7 of its Preface,
    p. 400 and p. 425; and "Reason," p. 464, and "Freedom," p. 469. *Right reason* is the instinctive
    power to distinguish between right and wrong—i.e., conscience. Discursive reason is a logical
    skill used to seek or to prove the truth.

His outward freedom: tyranny must be,   95
Though to the tyrant thereby no excuse.
Yet sometimes nations will decline so low
From virtue, which is reason, that no wrong,
But justice, and some fatal curse annexed
Deprives them of their outward liberty,   100
Their inward lost: witness th' irreverent son
Of him who built the ark, who for the shame
Done to his father, heard this heavy curse,
'Servant of servants,' on his vicious race.
Thus will this latter, as the former world,   105
Still tend from bad to worse, till God at last
Wearied with their iniquities, withdraw
His presence from among them, and avert
His holy eyes; resolving from thenceforth
To leave them to their own polluted ways;   110
And one peculiar nation to select
From all the rest, of whom to be invoked,
A nation from one faithful man to spring:
Him on this side Euphrates yet residing,
Bred up in idol-worship; O that men   115
(Canst thou believe?) should be so stupid grown,
While yet the patriarch lived, who scaped the Flood,
As to forsake the living God, and fall
To worship their own work in wood and stone
For gods! Yet him God the Most High vouchsafes   120
To call by vision from his father's house,
His kindred and false gods, into a land
Which he will show him, and from him will raise
A mighty nation, and upon him show'r
His benediction so, that in his seed   125
All nations shall be blest; he straight obeys,
Not knowing to what land, yet firm believes:
I see him, but thou canst not, with what faith
He leaves his gods, his friends, and native soil
Ur of Chaldaea, passing now the ford   130
To Haran, after him a cumbrous train
Of herds and flocks, and numerous servitude;
Not wand'ring poor, but trusting all his wealth
With God, who called him, in a land unknown.
Canaan he now attains, I see his tents   135
Pitched about Sechem, and the neighboring plain

101–4. Cf. Gen. 9.21–25.
111. *peculiar:* particular.
113. *one faithful man:* Abraham, meaning "Father of many nations." Cf. Gen. 11.31–32, p. 433, and 12.1–7, pp. 433–34.
115. Cf. Joshua 24.2.
132. *servitude:* servants.

Of Moreh; there by promise he receives
Gift to his progeny of all that land;
From Hamath northward to the desert south
(Things by their names I call, though yet unnamed)   140
From Hermon east to the great western sea,
Mount Hermon, yonder sea, each place behold
In prospect, as I point them; on the shore
Mount Carmel; here the double-founted stream
Jordan, true limit eastward; but his sons   145
Shall dwell to Senir, that long ridge of hills.
This ponder, that all nations of the earth
Shall in his seed be blessed; by that seed
Is meant thy great Deliverer, who shall bruise
The Serpent's head; whereof to thee anon   150
Plainlier shall be revealed. This patriarch blest,
Whom 'faithful Abraham' due time shall call,
A son, and of his son a grandchild leaves,
Like him in faith, in wisdom, and renown;
The grandchild with twelve sons increased, departs   155
From Canaan, to a land hereafter called
Egypt, divided by the river Nile;
See where it flows, disgorging at seven mouths
Into the sea: to sojourn in that land
He comes invited by a younger son   160
In time of dearth, a son whose worthy deeds
Raise him to be the second in that realm
Of Pharaoh: there he dies, and leaves his race
Growing into a nation, and now grown
Suspected to a sequent king, who seeks   165
To stop their overgrowth, as inmate guests
Too numerous; whence of guests he makes them slaves
Inhospitably, and kills their infant males:
Till by two brethren (those two brethren call
Moses and Aaron) sent from God to claim   170
His people from enthralment, they return
With glory and spoil back to their promised land.
But first the lawless tyrant, who denies

139–41. The Promised Land was bounded on the north by the city of Hamath, on the Orontes
River (in west Syria); on the south by the Wilderness of Zin; on the east by Mount Herman;
and on the west by the Mediterranean Sea.
144. *Mount Carmel*: a mountain range near Haifa, on the Mediterranean shore of Israel. *double-founted*: having two sources, believed to be fountains called Jor and Dan.
152. *'faithful Abraham.'* Cf. Gen. 17.5: "Neither shall thy name any more be called Abram,
but thy name shall be Abraham; for a father of many nations have I made thee." Gal. 3.9:
"So then they which be of faith are blessed with faithful Abraham."
153–64. The *son* was Isaac; the *grandchild*, Jacob, one of whose *twelve sons*, Joseph, *invited*
(160) the Israelites to Egypt. The story is told in Gen. 21–50.
163–311. The story of Moses begins after the death of Joseph. The journey of the Israelites, led
by Moses, from captivity to freedom in the *promised land* (172) begins in Exodus and ends in
the last chapter of Deuteronomy with the death of Moses.
173–93. Cf. Exod. 7–13. *denies*: refuses.

To know their God, or message to regard,
Must be compelled by signs and judgments dire;   175
To blood unshed the rivers must be turned,
Frogs, lice and flies must all his palace fill
With loathed intrusion, and fill all the land;
His cattle must of rot and murrain die,
Botches and blains must all his flesh emboss,   180
And all his people; thunder mixed with hail,
Hail mixed with fire must rend th' Egyptian sky
And wheel on th' earth, devourng where it rolls;
What it devours not, herb, or fruit, or grain,
A darksome cloud of locusts swarming down   185
Must eat, and on the ground leave nothing green:
Darkness must overshadow all his bounds,
Palpable darkness, and blot out three days;
Last with one midnight stroke all the first-born
Of Egypt must lie dead. Thus with ten wounds   190
The river-dragon tamed at length submits
To let his sojourners depart, and oft
Humbles his stubborn heart, but still as ice
More hardened after thaw, till in his rage
Pursuing whom he late dismissed, the sea   195
Swallows him with his host, but them lets pass
As on dry land between two crystal walls,
Awed by the rod of Moses so to stand
Divided, till his rescued gain their shore:
Such wondrous power God to his saint will lend,   200
Though present in his angel, who shall go
Before them in a cloud, and pillar of fire,
By day a cloud, by night a pillar of fire,
To guide them in their journey, and remove
Behind them, while th' obdúrate king pursues: 205
All night he will pursue, but his approach
Darkness defends between till morning watch;
Then through the fiery pillar and the cloud
God looking forth will trouble all his host
And craze their chariot wheels: when by command   210
Moses once more his potent rod extends
Over the sea; the sea his rod obeys;
On their embattled ranks the waves return,

---

180. *Botches:* boils. *blains:* blisters. *emboss:* cover with bosses or studs.
190–91. Cf. Ezek. 29.3: ". . . Pharaoh king of Egypt, the great dragon that lieth in the midst of his rivers . . ."
194–222. Cf. Exod. 13.17–22, and 14.5–31.
207. *defends:* holds off.
210. *craze:* crush, smash.

And overwhelm their war: the race elect
Safe towards Canaan from the shore advance   215
Through the wild desert, not the readiest way,
Lest ent'ring on the Canaanite alarmed
War terrify them inexpert, and fear
Return them back to Egypt, choosing rather
Inglorious life with servitude; for life   220
To noble and ignoble is more sweet
Untrained in arms, where rashness leads not on.
This also shall they gain by their delay
In the wide wilderness, there they shall found
Their government, and their great senate choose   225
Through the twelve tribes, to rule by laws ordained:
God from the mount of Sinai, whose gray top
Shall tremble, he descending, will himself
In thunder lightning and loud trumpet's sound
Ordain them laws; part such as appertain   230
To civil justice, part religious rites
Of sacrifice, informing them, by types
And shadows, of that destined Seed to bruise
The Serpent, by what means he shall achieve
Mankind's deliverance. But the voice of God   235
To mortal ear is dreadful; they beseech
That Moses might report to them his will,
And terror cease; he grants what they besought
Instructed that to God is no access
Without mediator, whose high office now   240
Moses in figure bears, to introduce
One greater, of whose day he shall foretell,
And all the Prophets in their age the times
Of great Messiah shall sing. Thus laws and rites
Established, such delight hath God in men   245
Obedient to his will, that he vouchsafes

214. *war*: army.
217. *alarmed*: prepared to fight (modifies *Canaanite*).
216–69. Cf. Exod., pp. 434–38: 13.17–18, 19.16–25, 20.18–20, 24.1–9, 40.34–38.
225. *senate*. the Seventy Elders. Cf. Num. 11.16–25.
232–33. *types*: (in theology) persons, objects, or events of OT history, prefiguring some persons or things revealed in the new dispensation. *shadows*: types, foreshadowings. In CD Milton refers to Moses as a type of Christ, Noah's ark as a type of baptism before the law, manna as a type of the Lord's Supper, the destruction of Jerusalem as a type of Christ's Second Coming. See CD, p. 426.
240. *mediator*: Moses as mediator is a type of Christ.
241. *in figure*: as a type. See 232–33n.
241–42. Cf. Deut. 18.15–19: "The Lord thy God will raise up unto thee a Prophet from the midst of thee, of thy brethren, like unto me; unto him ye shall hearken; According to all that thou desiredst of the Lord thy God in Horeb in the day of the assembly, saying, Let me not hear again the voice of the Lord my God, neither let me see this great fire any more, that I die not. And the Lord said unto me, They have well spoken that which they have spoken. I will raise them up a Prophet from among their brethren, like unto thee, and will put my words in his mouth; and he shall speak unto them all that I shall command them."

Among them to set up his tabernacle,
The Holy One with mortal men to dwell:
By his prescript a sanctuary is framed
Of cedar, overlaid with gold, therein   250
An ark, and in the ark his testimony,
The records of his cov'nant, over these
A mercy-seat of gold between the wings
Of two bright Cherubim, before him burn
Seven lamps as in a zodiac representing   255
The heav'nly fires; over the tent a cloud
Shall rest by day, a fiery gleam by night,
Save when they journey, and at length they come,
Conducted by his angel to the land
Promised to Abraham and his seed: the rest   260
Were long to tell, how many battles fought,
How many kings destroyed, and kingdoms won,
Or how the sun shall in mid-heav'n stand still
A day entire, and night's due course adjourn,
Man's voice commanding, 'Sun in Gibeon stand,   265
And thou moon in the vale of Aialon,
Till Israel overcome'; so call the third
From Abraham, son of Isaac, and from him
His whole descent, who thus shall Canaan win."
   Here Adam interposed. "O sent from heav'n,   270
Enlight'ner of my darkness, gracious things
Thou hast revealed, those chiefly which concern
Just Abraham and his seed: now first I find
Mine eyes true op'ning, and my heart much eased,
Erewhile perplexed with thoughts what would become   275
Of me and all mankind; but now I see
His day, in whom all nations shall be blest,
Favor unmerited by me, who sought
Forbidden knowledge by forbidden means.
This yet I apprehend not, why to those   280

---

260. Cf. Gen. 22.17–18: "That in blessing, I will bless thee, and in multiplying I will multiply thy seed as the stars of the heaven, and as the sand which is upon the sea shore; and thy seed shall possess the gate of his enemies; And in thy seed shall all the nations of the earth be blessed; because thou hast obeyed my voice." Gen. 26.3: "Sojourn in this land, and I will be with thee, and will bless thee; for unto thee, and unto thy seed, I will give all these countries, and I will perform the oath which I sware unto Abraham thy father."

263–67. Cf. Josh. 10.12–13: "Then spake Joshua to the Lord in the day when the Lord delivered up the Amorites before the children of Israel, and he said in the sight of Israel, Sun, stand thou still upon Gibeon; and thou, Moon, in the valley of Ajalon. And the sun stood still, and the moon stayed, until the people had avenged themselves upon their enemies. Is not this written in the book of Jasher? So the sun stood still in the midst of heaven, and hasted not to go down about a whole day."

267. Cf. Gen. 32.28: "And he said, Thy name shall be called no more Jacob, but Israel: for as a prince hast thou power with God and with men, and hast prevailed."

277. *His day:* the age of Abraham. Adam mistakenly thinks God's covenant with Abraham constitutes a promise of paradise regained. It was to be only a type of Christ's *day*. Cf. John 8.56: "Your father Abraham rejoiced to see my day."

Among whom God will deign to dwell on earth
So many and so various laws are giv'n;
So many laws argue so many sins
Among them; how can God with such reside?"
    To whom thus Michael. "Doubt not but that sin   285
Will reign among them, as of thee begot;
And therefore was law given them to evince
Their natural pravity, by stirring up
Sin against law to fight; that when they see
Law can discover sin, but not remove,   290
Save by those shadowy expiations weak,
The blood of bulls and goats, they may conclude
Some blood more precious must be paid for man,
Just for unjust, that in such righteousness
To them by faith imputed, they may find   295
Justification towards God, and peace
Of conscience, which the law by ceremonies
Cannot appease, nor man the moral part
Perform, and not performing cannot live.
So law appears imperfect, and but giv'n   300
With purpose to resign them in full time
Up to a better cov'nant, disciplined
From shadowy types to truth, from flesh to spirit,
From imposition of strict laws, to free
Acceptance of large grace, from servile fear   305
To filial, works of law to works of faith.
And therefore shall not Moses, though of God
Highly beloved, being but the minister

285–306. *law*: the Mosaic Law, referred to in 226, 230, and 244, i.e., the will of God revealed in Exodus, Leviticus, Numbers, and Deuteronomy, and designed to govern the behavior of man in all aspects of his life, private, civil, and religious. For the Christian view of this law see Rom. 3.19–28 and *CD*, pp. 422–25. *evince*: show. *pravity*: (L *pravus* crooked, bad) moral perversion. *shadowy expiations*: sacrifices that were types of Christ's sacrifice. Cf. Heb. 10.1: "For the law having a shadow of good things to come and not the very image of the things, can never with those sacrifices which they offered year by year continually make the comers thereunto perfect." *shadowy types*. See 232–33n. *works of law*. Cf. Gal. 2.16: "Knowing that man is not justified by the works of the law, but by the faith of Jesus Christ, even we have believed in Jesus Christ, that we might be justified by the faith of Christ, and not by the works of the law: for by the works of the law shall no flesh be justified." *faith*: faith in Christ by which the sinner is justified in the sight of God. Cf. *CD*, I.xx, and other uses of the word in this special sense: 409, 427, 488.
307–14. Cf. Deut. 34.1–6: "And Moses went up from the plains of Moab unto the mountain of Nebo, to the top of Pisgah, that is over against Jericho. And the Lord shewed him all the land of Gilead, unto Dan . . . and all the land of Judah, unto the utmost sea . . . And the Lord said unto him, This is the land which I sware unto Abraham, unto Isaac, and unto Jacob, saying, I will give it unto thy seed: I have caused thee to see it with thine eyes, but thou shalt not go over thither. So Moses the servant of the Lord died there in the land of Moab, according to the word of the Lord. And he buried him in a valley in the land of Moab, over against Beth-peor: but no man knoweth of his sepulchre unto this day." Cf. *CD*, p. 422. *therefore*: i.e., because Moses represents the Old Law, not the New, of which Joshua is the representative. *Joshua*. The Hebrew word *Yēshūa*, meaning "savior," became *Iesous* in Greek, the language of the NT. As Moses's successor, Joshua led the Israelites over Jordan into the Promised Land. His story is told in the book of Joshua. *who*: Christ.

Of law, his people into Canaan lead;
But Joshua whom the Gentiles Jesus call,   310
His name and office bearing, who shall quell
The adversary Serpent, and bring back
Through the world's wilderness long-wandered man
Safe to eternal paradise of rest.
Meanwhile they in their earthly Canaan placed   315
Long time shall dwell and prosper, but when sins
National interrupt their public peace,
Provoking God to raise them enemies:
From whom as oft he saves them penitent
By judges first, then under kings; of whom   320
The second, both for piety renowned
And puissant deeds, a promise shall receive
Irrevocable, that his regal throne
Forever shall endure; the like shall sing
All prophecy, that of the royal stock   325
Of David (so I name this king) shall rise
A Son, the Woman's Seed to thee foretold,
Foretold to Abraham, as in whom shall trust
All nations, and to kings foretold, of kings
The last, for of his reign shall be no end.   330
But first a long succession must ensue,
And his next son for wealth and wisdom famed,
The clouded Ark of God till then in tents
Wand'ring, shall in a glorious temple enshrine.
Such follow him, as shall be registered   335
Part good, part bad, of bad the longer scroll,
Whose foul idolatries and other faults
Heaped to the popular sum, will so incense
God, as to leave them, and expose their land,
Their city, his temple, and his holy ark   340
With all his sacred things, a scorn and prey
To that proud city, whose high walls thou saw'st
Left in confusion, Babylon thence called.
There in captivity he lets them dwell

315–30. This history is told in Judg., Sam., and Kings. *The second:* David, with whom God
made a covenant (*promise*) through the prophet Nathan, in 2 Sam. 7.16: "Thine house and
thy kingdom shall be established for ever before thee: thy throne shall be established for ever."
All prophecy: the books of the Prophets in the OT, esp. Isa., esp. 9.6–7, p. 443. Cf. Dan.
7.13–14: "I saw in the night visions, and, behold, one like the Son of man came with the
clouds of heaven, and came to the Ancient of days, and they brought him near before him.
And there was given him dominion, and glory, and a kingdom, that all people, nations, and
languages, should serve him: his dominion is an everlasting dominion, which shall not pass
away, and his kingdom that which shall not be destroyed."
332. *son:* Solomon, son of David.
334. *temple.* See 1 Kings 6 and 2 Chron. 3–4.
335–47. The Babylonian Captivity (sixth century B.C.) is described in 2 Kings 25, 2 Chron. 36,
and Jer. 39 and 52.
338. I.e.: Added to the human faults of common people.

The space of seventy years, then brings them back,			345
Rememb'ring mercy, and his cov'nant sworn
To David, stablished as the days of Heav'n.
Returned from Babylon by leave of kings
Their lords, whom God disposed, the house of God
They first re-edify, and for a while				350
In mean estate live moderate, till grown
In wealth and multitude, factious they grow;
But first among the priests dissension springs,
Men who attend the altar, and should most
Endeavor peace: their strife pollution brings			355
Upon the temple itself: at last they seize
The scepter, and regard not David's sons,
Then lose it to a stranger, that the true
Anointed King Messiah might be born
Barred of his right; yet at his birth a star			360
Unseen before in heav'n proclaims him come,
And guides the eastern sages, who inquire
His place, to offer incense, myrrh, and gold;
His place of birth a solemn angel tells
To simple shepherds, keeping watch by night;			365
They gladly thither haste, and by a choir
Of squadroned angels hear his carol sung.
A virgin is his mother, but his sire
The Power of the Most High; he shall ascend
The throne hereditary, and bound his reign			370
With earth's wide bounds, his glory with the heav'ns."
	He ceased, discerning Adam with such joy
Surcharged, as had like grief been dewed in tears,
Without the vent of words, which these he breathed.
	"O prophet of glad tidings, finisher			375
Of utmost hope! now clear I understand
What oft my steadiest thoughts have searched in vain,
Why our great expectation should be called
The Seed of Woman: Virgin Mother, hail,
High in the love of Heav'n, yet from my loins			380

348. *kings*: Cyrus the Great, Darius, and Artaxerxes, the Persians under whom Jerusalem was rebuilt, as described in Ezra.
349. *disposed*: made well-disposed.
353–58. As told in the Apocryphal book of 2 Macabees. *sons*: descendants. *a stranger*: Antipater, whom Julius Caesar appointed Procurator of Judea, and whose son Herod the Great ruled at the time of the birth of Christ.
360–71. Cf. Matt. 2 and Luke 2.
364 *solemn*: awe-inspiring.
369. *Power*: the Holy Ghost. Cf. *CD*, pp. 420–21.
370–71. Cf. Ps. 2.8: "Ask of me, and I shall give thee the heathen for thine inheritance, and the uttermost parts of the earth for thy possession." Cf. *CD* I.XXXIII.
375. *finisher*: completer.
379–80. Cf. Luke 1.31–35, pp. 455–56.

Thou shalt proceed, and from thy womb the Son
Of God Most High; so God with man unites.
Needs must the Serpent now his capital bruise
Expect with mortal pain: say where and when
Their fight, what stroke shall bruise the Victor's heel."   385
    To whom thus Michael. "Dream not of their fight,
As of a duel, or the local wounds
Of head or heel: not therefore joins the Son
Manhood to Godhead, with more strength to foil
Thy enemy; nor so is overcome   390
Satan, whose fall from heavn'n, a deadlier bruise,
Disabled not to give thee thy death's wound:
Which he who comes thy Saviour, shall recure,
Not by destroying Satan, but his works
In thee and in thy seed: nor can this be,   395
But by fulfilling that which thou didst want,
Obedience to the law of God, imposed
On penalty of death, and suffering death,
The penalty to thy transgression due,
And due to theirs which out of thine will grow: 400
So only can high justice rest apaid.
The law of God exact he shall fulfill
Both by obedience and by love, though love
Alone fulfill the law; thy punishment
He shall endure by coming in the flesh   405
To a reproachful life and cursèd death,
Proclaiming life to all who shall believe
In his redemption, and that his obedience
Imputed becomes theirs by faith, his merits
To save them, not their own, though legal works.   410
For this he shall live hated, be blasphemed,
Seized on by force, judged, and to death condemned
A shameful and accursed, nailed to the Cross
By his own nation, slain for bringing life;
But to the Cross he nails thy enemies,   415
The law that is against thee, and the sins
Of all mankind, with him there crucified,
Never to hurt them more who rightly trust
In this his satisfaction; so he dies,

383. *capital*: (L *caput* head) involving loss of the head or life. *bruise*: crushing blow.
393. *recure*: heal.
396. *want*: lack.
401. *apaid*: satisfied.
403–4. Cf. Rom. 13.10: "Love worketh no ill to his neighbor: therefore love is the fulfilling of
    the law."
409–10. I.e.: And that his merits have them, not their own obedience to the Old Law.
409. *Imputed*: See III.291n.
415–17. Cf. Col. 2.14: "Blotting out the handwriting of ordinances that was against us, which
    was contrary to us, and took it out of the way, nailing it to his cross."
419. *satisfaction*: payment of a penalty. See "The Fortunate Fall," pp. 470–71.

But soon revives, Death over him no power   420
Shall long usurp; ere the third dawning light
Return, the stars of morn shall see him rise
Out of his grave, fresh as the dawning light,
Thy ransom paid, which man from Death redeems,
His death for man, as many as offered life   425
Neglect not, and the benefit embrace
By faith not void of works: this God-like act
Annuls thy doom, the death thou shouldst have died,
In sin for ever lost from life; this act
Shall bruise the head of Satan, crush his strength   430
Defeating Sin and Death, his two main arms,
And fix far deeper in his head their stings
Than temporal death shall bruise the Victor's heel,
Or theirs whom he redeems, a death like sleep,
A gentle wafting to immortal life.   435
Nor after resurrection shall he stay
Longer on earth than certain times to appear
To his disciples, men who in his life
Still followed him; to them shall leave in charge
To teach all nations what of him they learned   440
And his salvation, them who shall believe
Baptizing in the profluent stream, the sign
Of washing them from guilt of sin to life
Pure, and in mind prepared, if so befall,
For death, like that which the Redeemer died.   445
All nations they shall teach; for from that day
Not only to the sons of Abraham's loins
Salvation shall be preached, but to the sons
Of Abraham's faith wherever through the world;
So in his seed all nations shall be blest.   450
Then to the heav'n of heav'ns he shall ascend
With victory, triumphing through the air
Over his foes and thine; there shall surprise
The Serpent, prince of air, and drag in chains
Through all his realm, and there confounded leave;   455
Then enter into glory, and resume
His seat at God's right hand, exalted high
Above all names in heav'n; and thence shall come,

425–26. I.e.: For as many as accept his offer of life. Neglect: (from L nec not + legere to pick
up) slight, disregard.
442. profluent: flowing.
445–50. Cf. Rom. 4.16; Gal. 3.7–9, 16; Eph. 4.11–12.
454–65. Cf. Rev. 20.
458–65. For Milton's orthodox belief in the Second Coming, the Millennium and Last Judgment,
see CD I.XXXIII. quick: living. The phrase comes from the Apostles' Creed.

When this world's dissolution shall be ripe,
With glory and power to judge both quick and dead,   460
To judge th' unfaithful dead, but to reward
His faithful, and receive them into bliss,
Whether in heav'n or earth, for then the earth
Shall all be paradise, far happier place
Than this of Eden, and far happier days."   465
    So spake th' Archangel Michaël, then paused,
As at the world's great period; and our sire
Replete with joy and wonder thus replied.
    "O goodness infinite, goodness immense!
That all this good of evil shall produce,   470
And evil turn to good; more wonderful
Than that which by creation first brought forth
Light out of darkness! Full of doubt I stand,
Whether I should repent me now of sin
By me done and occasioned, or rejoice   475
Much more, that much more good thereof shall spring,
To God more glory, more good will to men
From God, and over wrath grace shall abound.
But say, if our Deliverer up to heav'n
Must reascend, what will betide the few   480
His faithful, left among th' unfaithful herd,
The enemies of truth; who then shall guide
His people, who defend? Will they not deal
Worse with his followers than with him they dealt?"
    "Be sure they will," said th' angel; "but from heav'n   485
He to his own a Comforter will send,
The promise of the Father, who shall dwell
His Spirit within them, and the law of faith
Working through love, upon their hearts shall write,
To guide them in all truth, and also arm   490
With spiritual armor, able to resist

---

467. *great period:* at the end of the thousand years of the Millennium—end of the world.
469–78. See "The Fortunate Fall," pp. 470–71.
478. Cf. Rom. 5.20: "Moreover the law entered, that the offence might abound. But where sin
    abounded, grace did much more abound."
485–551. Milton's brief history of the Christian church, from the time of the Apostles to the
    Second Coming, contains many echoes from the NT, particularly from the letters of St. Paul
    to members of the earliest "churches," and reflects Milton's protestantism.
486. Cf. John 15.26: [Christ says] "But when the Comforter is come, whom I will send unto
    you from the Father, even the spirit of truth, which proceedeth from the Father, he shall testify
    of me."
489. Cf. Gal. 5.6: "For in Jesus Christ neither circumcision availeth any thing, nor uncircum-
    cision; but faith which worketh by love." Heb. 8.10: "For this is the covenant that I will make
    with the house of Israel after those days, saith the Lord; I will put my laws into their mind,
    and write them in their hearts."
491–92. Cf. Eph. 6.11–16: "Put on the whole armour of God, that ye may be able to stand
    against the wiles of the devil. . . . Above all, taking the shield of faith, wherewith ye shall be
    able to quench all the fiery darts of the wicked."

Satan's assaults, and quench his fiery darts,
What man can do against them, not afraid,
Though to the death, against such cruelties
With inward consolations recompensed,   495
And oft supported so as shall amaze
Their proudest persecutors: for the Spirit
Poured first on his apostles, whom he sends
To evangelize the nations, then on all
Baptized, shall them with wondrous gifts endue   500
To speak all tongues, and do all miracles,
As did their Lord before them. Thus they win
Great numbers of each nation to receive
With joy the tidings brought from heav'n: at length
Their ministry performed, and race well run,   505
Their doctrine and their story written left,
They die; but in their room, as they forewarn,
Wolves shall succeed for teachers, grievous wolves,
Who all the sacred mysteries of heav'n
To their own vile advantages shall turn   510
Of lucre and ambition, and the truth
With superstitions and traditions taint,
Left only in those written records pure,
Though not but by the Spirit understood.
Then shall they seek to avail themselves of names,   515
Places and titles, and with these to join
Secular power, though feigning still to act
By spiritual, to themselves appropriating
The Spirit of God, promised alike and giv'n
To all believers; and from that pretense,   520
Spiritual laws by carnal power shall force
On every conscience; laws which none shall find
Left them enrolled, or what the Spirit within
Shall on the heart engrave. What will they then
But force the Spirit of Grace itself, and bind   525

493. Cf. Ps. 56.11: "In God have I put my trust: I will not be afraid what man can do unto me."
497–502. Cf. Acts 2.4, 43: "And they [the apostles] were all filled with the Holy Ghost, and
began to speak with other tongues [languages] . . . and many wonders and signs were done by
the apostles."
505. Cf. Heb. 12.1: "Wherefore seeing we also are compassed about with so great a cloud of
witnesses, let us lay aside every weight, and the sin which doth so easily beset us, and let us
run with patience the race that is set before us." 1 Cor. 9.24: "Know ye not that they which
run in a race run all, but one receiveth the prize? So run, that ye may obtain."
508. *Wolves:* a common metaphor among Puritans for the corrupt clergy of the established church.
Cf. Acts 20.29: "For I know this, that after my departing shall grievous wolves enter in among
you, not sparing the flock."
515. *names:* honors.
516. *Places:* ranks, offices.
521. *carnal:* secular.
522–24. I.e.: Written in the Bible or, by the Holy Spirit, in the hearts of men.
525–26. Cf. 2 Cor. 3.17: "Now the Lord is that Spirit: and where the Spirit of the Lord is, there
is liberty."

His consort Liberty; what, but unbuild
His living temples, built by faith to stand,
Their own faith not another's: for on earth
Who against faith and conscience can be heard
Infallible? Yet many will presume: 530
Whence heavy persecution shall arise
On all who in the worship persevere
Of Spirit and Truth; the rest, far greater part,
Will deem in outward rites and specious forms
Religion satisfied; Truth shall retire   535
Bestuck with sland'rous darts, and works of faith
Rarely be found: so shall the world go on,
To good malignant, to bad men benign,
Under her own weight groaning, till the day
Appear of respiration to the just,   540
And vengeance to the wicked, at return
Of him so lately promised to thy aid,
The Woman's Seed, obscurely then foretold,
Now amplier known thy Saviour and thy Lord,
Last in the clouds from heav'n to be revealed   545
In glory of the Father, to dissolve
Satan with his perverted world, then raise
From the conflagrant mass, purged and refined,
New heav'ns, new earth, ages of endless date
Founded in righteousness and peace of love,   550
To bring forth fruits joy and eternal bliss."
    He ended; and thus Adam last replied.
"How soon hath thy prediction, seer blest,
Measured this transient world, the race of time,
Till time stand fixed: beyond is all abyss,   555
Eternity, whose end no eye can reach.
Greatly instructed I shall hence depart,
Greatly in peace of thought, and have my fill
Of knowledge, what this vessel can contain;

526–28. Cf. I.17–18, and 1 Cor. 3.17: "If any man defile the temple of God, him shall God
destroy; for the temple of God is holy, which temple ye are."
533. Cf. John 4.23–24: "But the hour cometh, and now is, when the true worshippers shall
worship the Father in spirit and in truth."
539. Cf. Rom. 8.22: "For we know that the whole creation groaneth and travaileth in pain
together until now."
540. *respiration:* rest, respite.
545–47. Cf. Matt. 24.30: "And then shall appear the sign of the Son of man in heaven: and
then shall all the tribes of the earth mourn, and they shall see the Son of man coming in the
clouds of heaven with power and great glory." 2 Thess. 1.7–8: "And to you who are troubled
rest with us, when the Lord Jesus shall be revealed from heaven with his mighty angels. In
flaming fire taking vengeance on them that know not God, and that obey not the gospel of
our Lord Jesus Christ."
546. *dissolve:* melt by heat, as in smelting.
549–51. Cf. Rev. 21.
555. Cf. Rev. 10.5–6: "And the angel which I saw stand upon the sea . . . sware . . . that there
should be time no longer."

Beyond which was my folly to aspire.   560
Henceforth I learn, that to obey is best,
And love with fear the only God, to walk
As in his presence, ever to observe
His providence, and on him sole depend,
Merciful over all his works, with good   565
Still overcoming evil, and by small
Accomplishing great things, by things deemed weak
Subverting worldly strong, and worldly wise
By simply meek; that suffering for truth's sake
Is fortitude to highest victory,   570
And to the faithful death the gate of life;
Taught this by his example whom I now
Acknowledge my Redeemer ever blest."
    To whom thus also th' angel last replied:
"This having learnt, thou hast attained the sum   575
Of wisdom; hope no higher, though all the stars
Thou knew'st by name, and all th' ethereal powers,
All secrets of the deep, all nature's works,
Or works of God in heav'n, air, earth, or sea,
And all the riches of this world enjoy'dst,   580
And all the rule, one empire; only add
Deeds to thy knowledge answerable, add faith,
Add virtue, patience, temperance, add love,
By name to come called charity, the soul
Of all the rest: then wilt thou not be loath   585
To leave this Paradise, but shalt possess
A paradise within thee, happier far.
Let us descend now therefore from this top
Of speculation; for the hour precise
Exacts our parting hence; and see the guards,   590
By me encamped on yonder hill, expect
Their motion, at whose front a flaming sword,
In signal of remove, waves fiercely round;
We may no longer stay: go, waken Eve;
Her also I with gentle dreams have calmed   595
Portending good, and all her spirits composed
To meek submission: thou at season fit

565–68. Cf. Ps. 145.9: "The Lord is good to all: and his tender mercies are over all his works."
Rom. 12.21: "Be not overcome of evil, but overcome evil with good," 1. Cor. 1.27: "But God
hath chosen the foolish things of the world to confound the wise; and God hath chosen the
weak things of the world to confound the things which are mighty." Rev. 2.10: "Fear none of
those things which thou shalt suffer; behold, the devil shall cast some of you into prison, that
ye may be tried; and ye shall have tribulation ten days: be thou faithful unto death, and I will
give thee a crown of life."
581–84. Cf. 2 Pet. 1.5–7: "And besides this, giving all diligence, add to your faith virtue; and
to virtue knowledge; And to knowledge temperance; and to temperance patience; and to patience
godliness; And to godliness brotherly kindness; and to brotherly kindness charity."
591–92. *expect / Their motion*: (military) await their marching orders.
593. *remove*. (military) departure.

Let her with thee partake what thou hast heard,
Chiefly what may concern her faith to know,
The great deliverance by her seed to come   600
(For by the Woman's Seed) on all mankind.
That ye may live, which will be many days,
Both in one faith unanimous though sad,
With cause for evils past, yet much more cheered
With meditation on the happy end."   605
   He ended, and they both descend the hill;
Descended, Adam to the bow'r where Eve
Lay sleeping ran before, but found her waked;
And thus with words not sad she him received.
   "Whence thou return'st, and whither went'st, I know;   610
For God is also in sleep, and dreams advise,
Which he hath sent propitious, some great good
Presaging, since with sorrow and heart's distress
Wearied I fell asleep: but now lead on;
In me is no delay; with thee to go,   615
Is to stay here; without thee here to stay,
Is to go hence unwilling; thou to me
Art all things under heav'n, all places thou,
Who for my wilful crime art banished hence.
This further consolation yet secure   620
I carry hence; though all by me is lost,
Such favor I unworthy am vouchsafed,
By me the Promised Seed shall all restore."
   So spake our mother Eve, and Adam heard
Well pleased, but answered not; for now too nigh   625
Th' Archangel stood, and from the other hill
To their fixed station, all in bright array
The Cherubim descended; on the ground
Gliding metéorous, as evening mist
Ris'n from a river o'er the marish glides,   630
And gathers ground fast at the laborer's heel
Homeward returning. High in front advanced,
The brandished sword of God before them blazed
Fierce as a comet; which with torrid heat,

615–19. Cf. Ruth 1.16: "And Ruth said, Intreat me not to leave thee, or to return from following
after thee: for whither thou goest, I will go; and where thou lodgest, I will lodge: thy people
shall be my people, and thy God my God." And cf. Eve's song of love to Adam before the
Fall, IV.641ff.
629. *meteorous*: phosphorescent.
630. *marish*: marsh.
631–32. Cf. Gen. 3.19: "In the sweat of thy face shalt thou eat bread, till thou return unto the
ground; for out of it wast thou taken: for dust thou art, and unto dust shalt thou return." Gen.
3.23: "Therefore the Lord God sent him forth from the garden of Eden, to till the ground
from whence he was taken."
633. Cf. Gen. 3.24: "So he drove out the man; and he placed at the east of the garden of Eden
Cherubims, and a flaming sword which turned every way, to keep the way of the tree of life."

And vapor as the Libyan air adust,   635
Began to parch that temperate clime; whereat
In either hand the hast'ning angel caught
Our ling'ring parents, and to th' eastern gate
Led them direct, and down the cliff as fast
To the subjected plain; then disappeared.   640
They looking back, all th' eastern side beheld
Of Paradise, so late their happy seat,
Waved over by that flaming brand, the gate
With dreadful faces thronged and fiery arms:
Some natural tears they dropped, but wiped them soon;   645
The world was all before them, where to choose
Their place of rest, and Providence their guide:
They hand in hand with wand'ring steps and slow,
Through Eden took their solitary way.

635. *vapor:* smoke. *adust:* parched.
637–38. Cf. Gen. 19.15–16: "And when the morning arose, then the angels hastened Lot, saying, Arise, take thy wife, and thy two daughters, which are here; lest thou be consumed in the iniquity of the city. And while he lingered, the men laid hold upon his hand, and upon the hand of his wife, and upon the hand of his two daughters; the Lord being merciful unto him; and they brought him forth, and set him without the city."
640. *subjected:* lying below.
648. *hand in hand.* Cf. IV.321, 488–89, 689, 739; VIII.510–11; IX.385, 1037.

A Note on the Text

The three authoritative texts of *Paradise Lost* are the manuscript of Book I, in the Morgan Library, in New York; the first edition, published in ten books, in 1667; and the second edition, in twelve books, in 1674. Though blind and dependent on the eyes of several copyists, Milton was remarkably successful in supervising the work of his printers, and as a result the text of the poem presents relatively few problems. Spelling and punctuation were not then as standardized as they are now. Manuscripts in Milton's own hand show that he was not consistent in his spelling; and authors in his time were generally in these matters at the mercy of the whims of copyists and printers. In spelling Milton seems to have preferred forms that most clearly indicated his pronunciation of the word: he preferred *hunderd* to *hundred*. In punctuation, his aim was not to supply visual aids to his syntax, but to indicate the length of pauses between words or groups of words. A colon marked a pause shorter than that of a period and longer than that of a semicolon. Milton put commas where we would omit them, and omitted them where modern usage requires them. Readers should pause slightly where he puts them, and pause more briefly where the syntax, or modern usage, would seem to call for a comma. The capitalization and italicizing in the original texts reflect the tendency of the time to capitalize many nouns and some adjectives, and to set proper nouns in italic type.

In the second edition, on which my text is based, the opening lines look something like this:

> Of Mans First Disobedience, and the Fruit
> Of that Forbidden Tree, whose mortal tast
> Brought Death into the World, and all our woe,
> With loss of *Eden*, till one greater Man
> Restore us, and regain the blissful Seat,
> Sing Heav'nly Muse, that on the secret top
> Of *Oreb*, or of *Sinai*, didst inspire
> That Shepherd, who first taught the chosen Seed,
> In the Beginning how the Heav'ns and Earth
> Rose out of *Chaos*: or if *Sion* Hill
> Delight thee more, and *Siloa's* Brook that flow'd
> Fast by the Oracle of God; I thence
> Invoke thy aid to my adventrous Song,
> . . . .

In order to present a text as free as possible from meaningless distractions, I have normalized the spelling and capitalization and changed all italics to Roman. I have retained two of Milton's eccentric spellings: *sovran* for *sovereign*, because Milton always used the word where only two syllables were called for; and *highth* for *height*, because only that form appears in the text, and Milton may have preferred the sound of it to that of *height* (i.e., hīt). In normalizing the use of capitals, I have had to be somewhat arbitrary. Wherever Milton seems clearly to have intended a personification I have capitalized the word: *chaos, night,* and *nature,* for example, are therefore sometimes capitalized, sometimes not. I have distinguished the word *Spirit* when used to refer to an angel. In synonyms and epithets for God and Satan I have retained the capitals except where the speaker might not have been so proper. I have used quotation marks to set off all direct address.

With a few exceptions, noted below, I have followed the lead of several recent editors in retaining the punctuation of the original editions. The initial difficulties presented by Milton's punctuation disappear after a little practice in reading; and the advantages of being guided by it are considerable. *Paradise Lost must* be read aloud, or at least clearly heard in the mind, and in general the punctuation helps one discover the complicated rhythms that distinguish the sound of the poem and emphasize its meanings. Though some of the marks must be assumed to be errors of the copyist or printer, my principle has been to change a mark only when the original pointing seemed both to be clearly erroneous and to make the meaning of the line unnecessarily obscure.

In the following list of my emendations, the second of the two versions is that of the 1674 edition:

I.716	grav'n;] grav'n,	VI.847	eyes;] eyes,
II.282	where] were	VII.17	unreined] unrein'd,
II.444	escape?] escape.	VII.21	unsung,] unsung
II.688	replied:] reply'd,	VII.321	swelling] smelling
II.798	list,] list	VII.418	th' egg] the Egg
II.980	profound;] profound,	VII.451	soul] Foul
III.276	dear] dear,	VII.561	Resounded] Resounded,
III.475	black,] black		heard'st),] heardst)
III.507	Embellished;]	VII.588	Father,] Father(
	Imbellisht,	VII.601	sung.] sung,
III.645	unheard;] unheard,	VIII.16	compute] compute,
IV.131	comes] comes,	VIII.25	besides;] besides,
IV.345	them;] them,	VIII.71	right;] right,
IV.751	propriety] propriety,	VIII.194	wisdom;] Wisdom,
IV.773	on,] on	VIII.369	solitude?] solitude,
IV.824	prison;] prison,	VIII.372	thee?] thee,
IV.934	untried.] untri'd,	VIIII.373	ways?] wayes,
V.182	multiform,] multiform;	IX.133	woe:] woe,
V.197	souls:] Souls,	IX.199	voice;] voice,
V.587	bright.] bright	IX.211	derides,] derides
V.811	ingrate,] ingrate	IX.687	knowledge:] knowledge?
VI.14	Empyreal;] Empyreal,		Threat'ner?]
VI.185	obeyed;] obey'd,		Threatner,
VI.200	mightiest:] mightiest,	IX.849	pass;] pass,
VI.203	heav'n] Heaven	IX.944	lose] loose
VI.251	once;] once,	IX.953	doom;] doom,
VI.269	rebellion!] Rebellion?	IX.1001	groan;] groan,
VI.???	false!] false.	IX.1002	loured,] lowr'd
VI.338	chariot,] Chariot;	IX.1058	Shame:] shame
VI.565	part:] part;	IX.1059	more.] more,

VI.594	rolled,] Rowl'd;	X. The	Death,] death
VI.595	arms] Arms,	Argu-	
VI.624	many:] many,	ment,	
VI.772	throned,] Thron'd.	1.6	
VI.774	seen:] seen,	X.755	late] late,
X. The	condition,] condition	X.778	lap!] lap?
Argu-		X.801	he] he,
ment,			
1.24		X.841	like,] like
X.83	law:] Law	XI.80	joy,] joy:
X.95	cool,] coole	XI.91	him;] him,
X.99	declined;] declin'd,	XI.319	relate:] relate;
X.207	taken:] taken,	XI.472	famine;] famine,
X.285	waters,] Waters;	XI.736	sire] sire,
X.436	Casbeen:] *Casbeen*.	XI.787	¶] no ¶

BIOGRAPHICAL,
HISTORICAL, AND
LITERARY BACKGROUNDS

ISABEL RIVERS

[Political and Religious Issues in the Time of Milton]†

England in the Early 17th Century

The population of England in Milton's youth was roughly 4½ million, mostly living in the country; that of London was about 300,000. Contemporaries sometimes divided the population into the 'three estates' of clergy, nobility, and commons. The commons included both what we would call the middle class, the gentry, the various professions, merchants, and yeomen (prosporous farmers); and artisans and agricultural labourers—the 'meaner sort'. This last group, who formed the bulk of the population, had no say in the government of the country; when contemporaries talked about the people they rarely meant to include these. The attitude to the poor was theoretically paternalistic; they were supposed to be provided for, but in practice lived appallingly hard lives.

The central government was in two parts: the executive comprised the king and his privy council, and the legislative the king in parliament (consisting of lords and commons). Only men of a certain property had the right to elect members of parliament. Local government was in the hands of the gentry, who as justices of the peace, aided by the parish officers, kept the countryside in order. The great gulf between rich and poor was controlled by an authoritarian system. A prosperous Londoner like Milton might remain ignorant of how most of his countrymen lived.

Nevertheless in comparison with European countries, which were constantly engaged in religious wars, England in the early part of the century could seem to contemporaries, and to those who looked back in nostalgia after the experience of the civil war, a haven of peace and prosperity.

❊   ❊   ❊

The Civil War: A Summary of the Issues 1640–9

There is perpetual disagreement among historians as to what exactly the civil war was about. This is partly because some of the issues only emerged during the course of events, and people took a long time to recognize them. The opponents of Charles I in the early 1640s did not foresee the outcome; no one set out with a programme to abolish the monarchy and establish a commonwealth; there was no long-term so-

† From "Milton's Life and Times: Aids to Study," *John Milton: Introductions*, ed. John Broadbent (Cambridge, 1973) 33, 41–43, 46–48, 50–52, 55. Reprinted with the permission of Cambridge University Press.

lution for the problems of the church. Individuals fought the king for a variety of reasons. However we can distinguish three main areas of conflict—political, religious, social. Nineteenth-century historians (such as Macaulay and Gardiner) concentrated on the first two; partly as a reaction, 20th-century historians (such as Tawney, Trevor-Roper and Hill) have concentrated on the last. There was similar disagreement among contemporaries about the causes of the conflict (though the social division was not clearly observed until the end of the first civil war). The religious conflict is summarized in the section on church reform below. Milton was not interested in, and indeed largely ignorant of, the social and economic conflicts of the protagonists, so they are hardly touched on here. This does not mean that the socio-economic issues were unimportant, but this section deals only with the political.

The political conflict was chiefly over the question of sovereignty, over where the power of the state was to reside, though it was not originally seen in these terms. The most widely held political theory was that of the balanced constitution, or mixed monarchy, in which sovereignty was shared between king and parliament, with a balance between 'prerogative' and 'privilege'. At the beginning of the Long Parliament Charles and his advisers were attacked for overstepping the limits of prerogative; appeal was made to the traditional constitution and fundamental laws. Much of this opposition to the crown was conservative. Conversely, as parliament asserted itself Charles counterattacked by accusing parliament (quite accurately) of attempting to encroach on his prerogative.

Constitutional royalism proved an inadequate theory in a period of conflict. On one side it was challenged by the theory of the divine right of kings. Though put forward by James I, that was a minority view held chiefly by high Anglican clergymen. Divine theory did not come into its own until the reign of James II (although one important aspect of it, the idea that the ruler makes law and is not bound by it, is an essential element of the thought of Hobbes, who asserted the need for absolute sovereignty). There was however a widespread emotional reverence for monarchy. On the other side some of the king's opponents began to abandon their appeal to tradition, and switch to revolutionary opinions: that parliament could make law by itself; that government was based on a contract between ruler and ruled, so that the king was answerable to his subjects; and that rights were more important than custom.

The conflict was originally between two parties, king and parliament; in the course of the first civil war (1642–6) the army became a third party. The Presbyterians in parliament had limited objectives and wanted reconciliation with the king. The army Independents under Cromwell wanted religious toleration and more extreme constitutional changes, though still under monarchy. Only a minority group like the Diggers wanted social equality, though the army, particularly after it had been new-modelled, was regarded as a social threat and a haven for upstarts. The Levellers, army radicals opposed by Cromwell, wanted the abolition of the monarchy, an extension of the franchise, and other political reforms. The king tried to play the rival groups against each other; then he allied with the Scots. Cromwell ceased to trust him, and after the royalist defeat in the second civil war (1648) the king's execution became inevitable.

Whereas a majority of the people may have supported the Long Parliament's initial reforms, the victors of the second civil war and the establishers of the commonwealth were a tiny minority. This paradox, the fact that their appeal to a theory of popular sovereignty was combined with dependence on army support for survival, was to plague the attempts of the Cromwellians for the next ten years to arrive as a satisfactory constitutional settlement.

※　　※　　※

Milton and Church Reform 1641–4, 1659

The difficulties of the Anglican church dated from the Reformation, but they came to a head in the 1630s with the activities of Archbishop Laud. There were three main parties in the church at this time: the high Anglicans (or Laudians), moderate Anglicans, and Puritans (or Presbyterians). Outside the Anglican church were the Catholics, the Independents, and various sects.

The Puritans opposed the Laudians in two ways: they wanted to purify the church government and ritual on the model of the continental Protestant churches (this included abolishing the bishops and substituting presbyters); and they were opposed to the spread of Arminianism (belief in free will) among the high Anglicans, because it conflicted with their Calvinist belief in predestination.

Laud was anxious to enforce his own view of church discipline, which included a strong emphasis on ceremonial and the idea of 'the beauty of holiness'. To his antagonists this was popery. In addition to this doctrinal and ecclesiastical opposition, there was much secular, political hostility to the bishops' interference in state affairs (Laud was virtually prime minister). Laud attempted to silence Puritan opposition by strict censorship of press and pulpit. Many Puritans were driven out of the church into separatism, and there were large migrations to the Netherlands and America. Perhaps the majority would have been content with moderate church reform and moderate limitations on the power of bishops, but Laud's extremism made this impossible. The Long Parliament struck back at him; amid a barrage of pamphleteering and petitioning the bishops were removed from power; eventually Laud was executed and episcopacy (the rule of bishops in the church) abolished.

The Westminster Assembly (consisting mostly of Presbyterians) was set up to decide the question of church government and doctrine. It proved impossible to do this to everyone's satisfaction. The Presbyterians wanted to imitate the Scottish model; this would have meant a theocratic system tolerating no dissent. There was strong opposition from the Independents and the smaller sects over the issue of toleration; for these groups, Presbyterianism rapidly replaced episcopacy as the enemy: 'New presbyter is but old priest writ large', said Milton *On the new forcers of conscience*. Some were in favor of complete disestablishment of the church from the state and toleration for private conscience (though few were prepared to tolerate Catholics).

After the second civil war (1648) the Presbyterians moved into opposition; they were appalled at the execution of the king. The establishment of the commonwealth did not settle the church problem, however. Cromwell at first favoured disestablishment, and under the commonwealth and protectorate there was in practice a good deal of toleration for those groups that were not considered politically subversive. But the Church of England continued to muddle along, controlled by various committees; its position was not resolved until its drastic reconstitution at the Restoration.

Milton was the grandson of a Catholic and the son of an Anglican; though he was destined for the church, Laud's disciplinary measures made him a Puritan. In 1640 he was Presbyterian in his sympathies. When a group of Presbyterian ministers writing under the name of Smectymnuus (made up from their initials) engaged in pamphlet warfare with Bishop Hall, Milton came to their help in five pamphlets published in 1641–2: *Of reformation touching church discipline in England*, *Of prelatical episcopacy*, *Animadversions upon the remonstrant's defence against Smectymnuus*, *The reason of church government urged against prelaty* (the first to which he put his name), and *An apology against a pamphlet called 'A modest confutation'*. Relying on scripture and trying to discredit his opponents' use of early church history, Milton urged the abolition of bishops and the substitution of presbyters; he argued that until this was done the Reformation in England would not be complete. He put forward his view of the true minister, and prayed passionately for a reformed England. But though he was defending the official Presbyterian position, his future break with Presbyterianism was implied in his hostility not simply to bishops but to all hired priests.

The break came (though Milton never officially acknowledged it) as a result of attacks on his divorce pamphlets. Parliament's printing ordinance seemed a revival of Laudian censorship, and Milton immediately joined the toleration controversy. Religious liberty now became his overriding interest. In *Areopagitica* (1644) he argued that the licensing of the press inhibits the spread of Christian truth; the proliferation of sects, which the Presbyterians regarded with horror, seemed to Milton a sign of health, an essential means of testing truth. He moved into attack on the Presbyterian clergy for their support of the king; they are savagely lashed in the *The tenure of kings* and in the posthumously published *Character of the Long Parliament.*

Milton lost all interest in external church reform in the 1650s and hoped instead for complete disestablishment: he envisaged ministers being elected and voluntarily supported by their congregations. At first he pinned his hopes on Cromwell, who made no move in this direction; in *A treatise of civil power in ecclesiastical causes* and *Considerations touching the likeliest means to remove hirelings out of the church* (1659) he addressed his plea for toleration and disestablishment to Richard Cromwell's parliament and the Rump. The far more important religious work of these years was the formulation of his own system of theology in *Christian doctrine.*

*   *   *

Milton as a Public Servant 1649–60

The execution of Charles I was among other things a great tactical error. Charles' conduct at his trial and the patent illegality of the proceedings did much to restore his popularity. From now on his victors had to face their lack of constitutional status; the fact that they had no positive programme did not help. Cromwell's essential problem was the narrowness of his support. With each more conservative step that he took he broke with important groups, first with the political radicals, the Levellers, then with the republicans, then with religous radicals like the fifth monarchists. Because he depended on army support he could not accept the crown and thus satisfy the constitutionalists. He could not govern effectively either with or without a parliament. Cromwell was a man of action and not a theorist; he relied on his strong religious sense to guide him. His great interest was not in political reform but in religious liberty. He regarded himself as God's instrument, and was fond of referring to the English as the apple of God's eye. His strength held the government together; at his death there was confusion. The army and the civilians were unable to agree; there was a widespread desire for settled forms of government which the revolutionaries could not satisfy.

After three years spent on private study Milton returned to public controversy in 1649 with an attack on the royalist-Presbyterian alliance, and a defence of the right to execute tyrants, in *The tenure of kings and magistrates.* He argued that the ruler derives his power from the people by contract, and they have the right to revoke power if it is abused. Grateful for this unsolicited testimonial, the council of state hired Milton as secretary for foreign tongues, a post which combined letter-writing with propaganda and censorship (an ironical position for the author of *Areopagitica*). Much of his time was spent in the daily routine of a civil servant; his more glamorous work was to defend the regime from its critics. Immediately after Charles' death a book called *Eikon basilike* (the king's image) began to circulate. Based on Charles' notes (expanded by Gauden his chaplain, though this was not known at the time), it fed the new cult of Charles the martyr. Milton answered it, not very effectively, in *Eikonoklastes* (image-breaker). But there was a new opponent to face. The French scholar Claude de Saumaise (Salmasius) was commissioned by Charles II to attack the commonwealth in *Defensio regia pro Carolo I* (royal defence). Salmasius was ignorant of consitutional monarchy and asserted that the king was above the law, but he made telling attacks on the illegality of the commonwealth, its reliance on military force, and its lack of popular support. Milton answered in *Defensio pro populo anglicano* (1st defence of the English people). He wriggled out of the problem by defining the people as the enlightened part of the nation. The *2nd defence* was written in answer to Pierre du Moulin's *Regii sanguinis clamor* (cry of the king's blood) published anonymously. Milton became embroiled in controversy with Alexander More whom he thought to be the author of the *Clamor*, and the tedious *3rd defence* consists largely of personal abuse.

In the *1st defence* Milton was defending the Rump; the *2nd defence* was written under the protectorate. Milton's argument shifts from concern with the people to the idea of virtuous leadership. Cromwell is exhorted to become the ideal leader, but Milton devotes a good deal of space to praising his opponents; he is clearly uncertain about the tendencies of the protectorate government. After Cromwell's death Milton turned against the idea of a single ruler; his answer to the confusion of the pre-Restoration period was a proposal in *The ready and easy way to establish a free commonwealth* for the Rump to perpetuate itself as a permanent grand council, a kind of dictatorship by enlightened aristocracy. It was already out of date when it was published.

Milton's political views run through changes that are common with revolutionaries. It is possible to be cynical about them. He seems to have seized on political theories that were appropriate to the problem in hand without really thinking them through. He adapted his ideas to suit the political situation. But this is not altogether a fault. The doctrinaire republicans who opposed Cromwell were unrealistic and incapable of forming a government themselves. Milton was not really interested in abstract political theory; he was antipathetic to authority and ancient forms, whether in church or state. The good old cause for him was a political system guided by a virtuous elite who would allow religious freedom to the individual conscience. But he came to feel that only a virtuous nation would know how to use such liberty; the Restoration was a just punishment on a people who had abused their opportunity.

* * *

Milton at the Restoration 1660–74

Charles II came back in 1660 on a surge of royalist feeling, promising indemnity for past actions and religious toleration for the future, but the country was soon to be disillusioned. Charles' government was incompetent and extravagant, and the contrast with Cromwell was striking; whereas Cromwell had tried to make England godly and powerful, Charles' main concern was to keep his throne safe and to avoid parliamentary interference. The hope of religious toleration was soon squashed by a series of repressive acts of parliament which divided the Church of England rigidly from the nonconformists; the nonconformists, or dissenters, included many Presbyterians who had welcomed the Restoration, but they became subject to various penalties and disadvantages as second-class citizens. Charles' own attempts to secure toleration for Catholics (and hence for Protestant nonconformists) were prevented by anti-Catholic feeling which was largely political.

Two of Milton's anti-monarchical tracts were condemned at the Restoration, but apart from a short spell in prison (illegal, as he had not been named as excluded from the Act of Indemnity) he escaped further punishment. Since Milton was the most vehement defender of regicide there is a question as to why he escaped. One answer is that he was not important enough; another, more likely, is that powerful friends interceded. The Restoration meant the destruction of Milton's hopes for the political and religious reformation of England. He lost his position and his wealth; he retired to private life and to poetry. He returned only once to public controversy with a blast against Catholicism in *Of true religion* 1673; the last years of his life were spent on his major poems, and then, as he acquired a public, on revising and publishing his early works. But though his years of public service might have seemed wasted, his political disappointment was of crucial importance for the writing of his great poems, and for his understanding of such ideas as servitude, liberty, and paradise.

DAVID MASSON

[A Brief Life of Milton]†

John Milton was born in Bread Street, Cheapside, London, on the 9th of December 1608. His father, known as "Mr. John Milton of Bread

† From *The Encyclopaedia Britannica*, 9th ed., 1888. Masson's *Life of John Milton: Narrated in Connection with the Political, Ecclesiastical, and Literary History of His Time*, 7 vols. (London, 1859–94), is certainly the most monumental of all biographies of the poet. Scholars have since discovered additional facts; critics have interpreted Milton's works in many ways; and biographers have written variously about Milton's life and work. But no biographer or critic has seen and presented Milton in his full historical context better than Masson. He was ideally

Street, Scrivener," was himself an interesting man. He was a native of Oxfordshire, having been born there in or about 1563, the son of a Richard Milton, yeoman of Stanton-St-John's, of whom there are traces as one of the sturdiest adherents to the old Roman Catholic religion that had been left in his district. The son, however, had turned Protestant, and, having been cast off on that account, had come to London in [about 1583 and had become an apprentice to a scrivener.

By 1590 he was active in the business,] but not till February 1600, when he was about thirty-seven, did he enter the profession as a qualified member of the Scriveners' Company. It was then that he set up his "house and shop" in Bread Street, and began, like other scriveners, his lawyerly business of drawing up wills, marriage-settlements, [deeds, mortgages, and] such related business as that of receiving money from clients for investment and lending it out to the best advantage.

It was at the same time that he married Sarah Jeffrey, one of the two orphan daughters of a Paul Jeffrey, of St Swithin's, London, "citizen and merchant-taylor," originally from Essex, who had died before 1583. At the date of her marriage she was about twenty-eight years old. Her widowed mother, Mrs Ellen Jeffrey, came to reside in the house in Bread Street, and died there in February 1610–11.

Before this death of the maternal grandmother, three children had been born to the scrivener and his wife, of whom only two survived,— the future poet, and an elder sister, called Anne. Of three more children, born subsequently, only one survived—Christopher, the youngest of the family, born December 3, 1615.

The first sixteen years of Milton's life, coinciding exactly with the last sixteen of the reign of James I, [were lived in the house on Bread Street, in a neighborhood in Old London "wholly inhabited by rich merchants."] His father, while prospering in business, continued to be known as a man of "ingenious" tastes,[1] and even acquired some distinction in the London musical world of that time by his occasional contributions to important musical publications. Music was thus a part of the poet's domestic education from his infancy. Whatever else could be added was added without stint. Again and again Milton speaks with gratitude and affection of the ungrudging pains bestowed by his father on his early education. "Both at the grammar school and also under other masters at home," according to the son, "he caused me to be instructed daily."

---

prepared, in 1883, to write a short biography for the *Encyclopedia*. Since Masson, all the chief sources of specifically biographical information have been collected in three books: Helen Darbishire's *Early Lives of Milton* (London, 1932); John Diekhoff's *Milton on Himself: Milton's Utterances upon Himself and His Works* (1939; London, 1965); and J. Milton French's *Life Records of John Milton*, 5 vols. (New Brunswick, N.J., 1949–58). The definitive biography is William Riley Parker's *Milton: A Biography*, 2 vols. (Oxford, 1968). See the bibliography at the end of this volume for other good, shorter biographies.

I have slightly and silently abridged Masson's text and have bracketed my summaries and revisions.

1. Tastes of the well-bred, or well-educated.

In 1618 Milton's domestic tutor was Thomas Young, a Scotsman from Perthshire, and graduate of the university of St Andrews, afterwards a man of no small distinction among the English Puritan clergy, but then only curate or assistant to some parish clergyman in or near London, and eking out his livelihood by private teaching. Young's tutorship lasted till 1620, when he was drawn abroad by an offer of the pastorship or chaplaincy to the congregation of English merchants in Hamburg. Already, however, his tutorship had been only supplementary to the education which the boy was receiving by daily attendance at St Paul's School, [a few minutes' walk from home]. The headmaster of the school was Mr Alexander Gill, an elderly Oxford divine, of high reputation for scholarship and teaching ability. Under him, as usher or second master, was his son, Alexander Gill the younger, also an Oxford graduate of scholarly reputation, but of blustering character. Milton's acquaintanceship with this younger Gill, begun at St Paul's school, led to subsequent friendship and correspondence. Far more affectionate and intimate was the friendship formed by Milton at St Paul's with a certain young Charles Diodati, his schoolfellow there, the son of a naturalized Italian physician, Dr Theodore Diodati, who had settled in London in good medical practice, and was much respected, both on his own account, and as being the brother of the famous Protestant divine, Jean or Giovanni Diodati of Geneva. Young Diodati, who was destined for his father's profession, left the school for Oxford University early in 1623; but Milton remained till the end of 1624. A family incident of that year was the marriage of his elder sister, Anne, with Edward Phillips, a clerk in the Government office called the Crown Office in Chancery. Milton had then all but completed his sixteenth year, and was as scholarly, as accomplished, and as handsome a youth as St Paul's school had sent forth. We learn from himself that his exercises "in English or other tongue, prosing or versing, but chiefly this latter," had begun to attract attention even in his boyhood. This implies that he must have had a stock of attempts in English and Latin by him of earlier date than 1624. Of these the only specimens that now remain are his paraphrases of Psalms 114[2] and 136.

On February 12, 1625, Milton, at the age of sixteen years and two months, was entered as a student of Christ's College, Cambridge, in the grade of a "Lesser Pensioner."[3] His matriculation entry in the books of the university is two months later, April 9, 1625. Between these two dates James I. had died, and had been succeeded by Charles I.

Cambridge University was then in the full flush of its prosperity on that old system of university education which combined Latin and Greek studies with plentiful drill and disputation in the scholastic logic and

2. See p. 350, below.
3. For his £50-a-year fee, middle-class Milton had fewer privileges than did "greater pensioners." A skilled worker earned about £50 a year.

philosophy, but with little of physical science, and next to no mathematics. There were sixteen colleges in all, dividing among them a total of about 2900 members of the university. Christ's College, to which Milton belonged, ranked about third in the university in respect of numbers, counting about 265 members on its books. At least three students who entered Christ's after Milton, but during his residence, deserve mention. One was Edward King, a youth of Irish birth and high Irish connexions, who entered in 1626, at the age of fourteen; another was John Cleveland, afterwards known as royalist and satirist, who entered in 1627; and the third was Henry More, subsequently famous as the Cambridge's Platonist, who entered in 1631, just before Milton left. Milton's own brother, Christopher, joined him in the college in February 1631, at the age of fifteen.

Milton's academic course lasted seven years and five months, or from February 1625 to July 1632, bringing him from his seventeenth year to his twenty-fourth. The first four years were his time of undergraduateship. It was in the second of these, the year 1626, that there occurred that quarrel between him and his tutor, Mr Chappell, which Dr Johnson,[4] making the most of a lax tradition from Aubrey,[5] magnified into the supposition that Milton may have been one of the last students in either of the English universities that suffered the indignity of corporal punishment. The legend deserves no credit; but it is certain that Milton, on account of some disagreement with Chappell, leading to the interference of Dr Bainbrigge, left college for a time, and that, when he did return, it was under an arrangement which, while securing that he should not lose a term by his absence, transferred him from the tutorship of Chappell to that of Mr Nathaniel Tovey, another of the fellows of Christ's. From a reference to the matter in the first of Milton's Latin elegies[6] one infers that the cause of the quarrel was some outbreak of self-assertion on Milton's part. We learn indeed, from words of his own elsewhere, that it was not only Chappell and Bainbrigge that he had offended by his independent demeanor, but that, for the first two or three years of his undergraduateship, he was generally unpopular, for the same reason, among the younger men of his college. They had nicknamed him "The Lady," a nickname which the students of the other colleges took up, converting it into "The Lady of Christ's"; and, though the allusion was chiefly to the peculiar grace of his personal appearance, it conveyed also a sneer at what the rougher men thought his unusual prudishness, the haughty fastidiousness of his tastes and morals. Quite as distant as the information that he was for a while

4. Samuel Johnson, "Life of Milton," in his *Lives of the English Poets* (1779).
5. John Aubrey, "Minutes of the Life of Mr. John Milton," in Darbishire, *Early Lives*, pp. 1–15.
6. "To Charles Diodati" (1626).

unpopular with the majority of his fellow-students are the proofs that they all came round him at last with respect and deference. The change had certainly occurred before January 1629, when, at the age of twenty, he took his B.A. degree. By that time his intellectual pre-eminence in his college, and indeed among his coevals in the whole university, had once come to be acknowledged. His reputation for scholarship and literary genius, extraordinary even then, was more than confirmed during the remaining three years and a half of his residence in Cambridge. A fellowship in Christ's which fell vacant in 1630 would undoubtedly have been his had the election to such posts depended then absolutely on merit. As it was, the fellowship was conferred, by royal favor and mandate, on Edward King, his junior in college standing by sixteen months. In July 1632 Milton completed his career at the university by taking his M.A. degree. His signature in the University Register stands at the head of the list of those who graduated as masters that year from Christ's. Anthony Wood's[7] summary of the facts of his university career as a whole is that he "performed the collegiate and academical exercises to the admiration of all, and was esteemed to be a virtuous and sober person, yet not to be ignorant of his own parts." The statement is in perfect accordance with Milton's own account. He speaks of "a certain niceness of nature, an honest haughtiness, and self-esteem of what I was or what I might be," as one of his earliest characteristics; and, though intimating that, even while actually a student at Cambridge, he had "never greatly admired" the system of the place, he leaves us in no doubt as to the quite exceptional applause with which he had gone through all the prescribed work. To the regular Latin and Greek of the university he had added, he tells us, French, Italian, and Hebrew. He had also learnt fencing and other gentlemanly exercises of the time, and was an expert swordsman.

Of Milton's skill at Cambridge in what Wood calls "the collegiate and academical exercises" specimens remain in his "*Prolusiones Quædam Oratoriæ*." They consist of seven rhetorical Latin essays, generally in a whimsical vein, delivered by him, in his undergraduateship or during his subsequent bachelorship in arts, either in the hall of Christ's College or in the public University School.[8] Relics of Milton's Cambridge period are also four of his Latin "Familiar Epistles";[9] but more important are the poetical remains. These include the greater number of his preserved Latin poems as well as the magnificent Christmas ode "On the Morning of Christ's Nativity" (1629), [the exquisite companion

---

7. Anthony Wood, "Life of Milton," in his *Fasti Oxonienses* (1691–92), in Darbishire, *Early Lives*, pp. 35–48.
8. A lecture room open to all members of the university. Milton's early dedication to poetry and his ambition to be England's epic poet are set forth in the lines "At a Vacation Exercise" (see pp. 351–52, below).
9. Published in 1674, the last year of Milton's life.

pieces "L'Allegro" and "Il Penseroso," and the] sonnet "On arriving at the Age of twenty-three,"[1] dating itself certainly in December 1631.

Just before Milton quitted Cambridge, his father, then verging on his seventieth year, had practically retired from his Bread Street business, leaving the active management of it to a partner, named Thomas Bower, a former apprentice of his, and had gone to spend his declining years [first in the hamlet of Hammersmith, on the Thames, about six miles west of his house on Bread Street, and then, two years later, to the village of Horton, not far from Windsor. In these two places Milton resided with his father and mother] for the next six years,—from July 1632 to April 1638.

Although, when he had gone to Cambridge, it had been with the intention of becoming a clergyman, that intention had been abandoed. His reasons were that "tyranny had invaded the church," and that, finding he could not honestly subscribe the oaths and obligations required, he "thought it better to preserve a blameless silence before the sacred office of speaking begun with servitude and forswearing." In other words, he was disgusted with the system of high prelacy[2] which Laud, who had been bishop of London and minister paramount in ecclesiastical matters since 1628, was establishing and maintaining in the Church of England. "Church-outed by the prelates," as he emphatically expresses it, he seems to have thought for a time of the law. From that too he recoiled; and, leaving the legal profession for his brother Christopher, he had decided that the only life possible for himself was one of leisurely independence, dedicated wholly to scholarship and literature. His compunctions on this subject, expressed already in his sonnet on arriving at his twenty-third year, are expressed more at length in an English letter sent by him, shortly after the date of that sonnet, and with a copy of the sonnet included, to some friend who had been remonstrating with him on his "belatedness" and his persistence in a life of mere dream and study. There were gentle remonstrances also from his excellent father. Between such a father and such a son, however, the conclusion was easy. What it was may be learnt from Milton's fine Latin poem "Ad Patrem." There, in the midst of an enthusiastic recitation of all that his father had done for him hitherto, it is intimated that the agreement between them on their one little matter of difference was already complete, and that, as the son was bent on a private life of literature and poetry, it had been decided that he should have his own way, and should in fact, so long as he chose, be the master of his father's means and the chief person in the Horton household. For the six years from 1632 this, accordingly, was Milton's position. In perfect leisure, and in a pleasant

1. See Sonnet 7, p. 352, below.
2. The *system of high prelacy* refers to episcopacy, or governance by a self-perpetuating hierarchy of prelates, or high-ranking clergymen, such as bishops. This system had considerable power over the private lives of all Englishmen. See *presbyters*, in n. 9, p. 326, below. The Church of England was episcopal, as the church of Scotland was presbyterian.

rural retirement with Windsor at the distance of an easy walk, and London only about 17 miles off, he went through, he tells us, a systematic course of reading in the Greek and Latin classics, varied by mathematics, music, and the kind of physical science we should now call cosmography.

It is an interesting fact that Milton's very first public appearance in the world of English authorship was in so honorable a place as the second folio edition of *Shakespeare* in 1632. His enthusiastic eulogy on Shakespeare, written in 1630, was one of three anonymous pieces prefixed to that second folio, along with reprints of the commendatory verses that had appeared in the first folio, one of them Ben Jonson's immortal tribute to Shakespeare's memory. Among the poems actually written by Milton at Horton the first, in all probability, after the Latin hexameters "*Ad Patrem*," was the fragment called *Arcades*. It was part of a pastoral masque got up by the young people of the noble family of Egerton in honor of their venerable relative the countess-dowager of Derby, and performed before that lady at her mansion of Harefield, near Uxbridge, about 10 miles from Horton. That Milton contributed the words for the entertainment was, almost certainly, owing to his friendship with Henry Lawes, one of the chief court musicians of that time, whose known connexion with the Egerton family points him out as the probable manager of the Harefield masque. Next in order among the compositions at Horton may be mentioned the three short pieces, "At a Solemn Music," "On Time," and "Upon the Circumcision"; after which comes *Comus*, the largest and most important of all Milton's minor poems. The name by which that beautiful drama is now universally known was not given to it by Milton himself. He entitled it, more simply and vaguely, "A Masque presented at Ludlow Castle, 1634, before the Earl of Bridgewater, Lord President of Wales." The existence of this poem is certainly due to Milton's intimacy with Lawes. The earl of Bridgewater, the head of the Egerton family, had been appointed to the high office of the presidency or viceroyalty of Wales, the official seat of which was Ludlow in Shropshire; it had been determined that among the festivities on his assumption of the office there should be a great masque in the hall of Ludlow Castle, with Lawes for the stage manager and one of the actors; Milton had been applied to by Lawes for the poetry; and, actually, on Michaelmas night, September 29, 1634, the drama furnished by Milton was performed in Ludlow Castle before a great assemblage of the nobility and gentry of the Welsh principality, Lawes taking the part of "the attendant spirit," while the parts of "first brother," "second brother," and "the lady" were taken by the earl's three youngest children, Viscount Brackley, Mr Thomas Egerton, and Lady Alice Egerton.

In May, 1636, a troublesome lawsuit against his now aged and infirm father was instituted by a certain Sir Thomas Cotton, baronet, nephew and executor of a deceased John Cotton, Esq., accusing the elder Milton and his partner Bower, or both, of having, in their capacity as scriveners, misappropriated divers large sums of money that had been entrusted to them by the deceased Cotton to be let out at interest.

The lawsuit was still in progress when, on the 3rd of April 1637, Milton's mother died, at the age of about sixty-five. A flat blue stone, with a brief inscription, visible on the chancel-pavement of Horton church, still marks the place of her burial. Milton's testimony to her character is that she was a "person of purest reputation, particularly known for her charities through the neighborhood." The year 1637 was otherwise eventful in his biography. It was in that year that his *Comus*, after lying in manuscript for more than two years, was published by itself, in the form of a small quarto of thirty-five pages. The author's name was withheld, and the entire responsibility of the publication was assumed by Henry Lawes. Milton seems to hve been in London when the little volume appeared. He was a good deal in London, at all events, during the summer and autumn months immediately following his mother's death. The plague, which had been on one of its periodical visits of ravage through England since early in the preceding year, was then especially severe in the Horton neighborhood, while London was comparatively free. It was probably in London that Milton heard of the death of young Edward King of Christ's College, whom he had left as one of the most popular of the fellows of the college, and one of the clerical hopes of the university. King had sailed from Chester for a vacation visit to his relatives in Ireland, when, on the 10th of August, the ship, in perfectly calm water, struck on a rock and went down, he and nearly all the other passengers going down with her. There is no mention of the sad accident in two otherwise very interesting Latin *Familiar Epistles* of Milton, of September 1637, both addressed to his medical friend Charles Diodati, and both dated from London; but how deeply the death of King had affected him appears from his occupation shortly afterwards.

In November 1637, and probably at Horton, whence the plague had by that time vanished, he wrote his matchless pastoral monody of "Lycidas." It was his contribution to a collection of obituary verses, Greek, Latin, and English, which King's numerous friends, at Cambridge and elsewhere, were getting up in lamentation for his sad fate. The collection did not appear till early in 1638, when it was published in two parts, with black-bordered title-pages, from the Cambridge University press, one consisting of twenty-three Latin and Greek pieces, the other of thirteen English pieces, the last of which was Milton's monody, signed only with his initials "J. M." It was therefore early in 1638, when Milton was in his thirtieth year, that copies of his "Lycidas" may have been in circulation among those who had already become acquainted with his *Comus*.

Milton was then on the wing for a foreign tour. He had long set his heart on a visit to Italy, and circumstances now favored his wish. His younger brother, Christopher, though but twenty-two years of age, and just about to be called to the bar of the Inner Temple, had married; and the young couple had gone to reside at Horton to keep the old man company. And the vexatious Cotton lawsuit, after hanging on for nearly two years, was at an end, as far as the elder Milton was concerned, with the most absolute and honorable vindication of his character for probity, though with some continuation of the case against his partner, Bower.[3] Before the end of April 1638 John was on his way across the Channel, taking one English man-servant with him. At the time of his departure the last great news in England was that of the National Scottish Covenant, or solemn oath and band of all ranks and classes of the Scottish people to stand by each other to the death in resisting the ecclesiastical innovations which Laud and Charles had been forcing upon Scotland. To Charles the news of this "damnable Covenant," as he called it, was enraging beyond measure; but to the mass of the English Puritans it was far from unwelcome, promising, as it seemed to do, for England herself, the subversion at last of that system of "Thorough," or despotic government by the king and his ministers without parliaments, under which the country had been groaning since the contemptuous dissolution of Charles's third parliament ten years before.

Through Paris, where Milton made but a short stay, receiving polite attention from the English ambassador, Lord Scudamore, and having the honor of an introduction to the famous Hugo Grotius,[4] then ambassador for Sweden at the French court, he moved on rapidly to Italy, by way of Nice. After visiting Genoa, Leghorn, and Pisa, he arrived at Florence, August 1638. Enchanted by the city and its society, he remained there two months, frequenting the chief academies or literary clubs, and even taking part in their proceedings. It was in the neighborhood of Florence also that he "found and visited" the great Galileo, then old and blind, and still nominally a prisoner to the Inquisition for his astronomical heresy. From Florence, by Siena, Milton went to Rome.

3. "The Cotton lawsuit was dropped on 1 February 1638, and Milton senior was awarded 20 shillings for his expenses. On the same day a loan of £150 was made to Sir John Cope of Hanwell, Oxfordshire, who gave a bond of £300 as security. This was made payable to John Milton junior, who would receive £12 each year in interest so long as the debt remained unpaid. The scrivener decided, moreover, to sell his valuable property south of Covent Garden, property held in both his name and John's. . . . The continental journey would cost in the neighborhood of £300. . . . Henry Lawes managed the business of getting a passport, sending Milton a letter under the hand and seal of Theophilus Howard, Earl of Suffolk, Lord Warden of the Cinque Ports" (Parker 1. 167–68.)
4. It is hard to think of anyone, other than Galileo, whom Milton would have been so pleased to meet as Hugo Grotius, one of the most distinguished scholars alive, who had written Latin elegies at the age of eight and entered Leiden University at the age of eleven. By the time he was eighteen (1601) he had published a volume of Latin poetry and a Latin tragedy, Adamus Exul (Adam in Exile), which Milton had read. By the time Milton met him, Grotius had written De Jure Belli et Pacis, the first great work on international law, and had spent three years in prison for his public opposition to the Calvinist belief in predestination.

He reached the Eternal City some time in October, and spent about another two months there, not only going about among the ruins and antiquities and visiting the galleries, but mixing also, as he had done in Florence, with the learned society of the academies. There is record of his having dined once, in company with several other Englishmen, at the hospitable table of the English Jesuit College. The most picturesque incident, however, of his stay in Rome was his presence at a great musical entertainment in the palace of Cardinal Francesco Barberini. Here he had the honor of a specially kind reception by the cardinal himself.

Late in November he left Rome for Naples. Here also he was fortunate. The great man of the place was the now very aged Giovanni Battista Manso, marquis of Villa, the friend and biographer of the great Tasso.[5] By a happy accident Milton obtained an introduction to Manso, and nothing could exceed the courtesy of the attentions paid by the aged marquis to the young English stranger. He had hardly been in Naples a month, however, when there came news from England which not only stopped an intention he had formed of extending his tour to Sicily and thence into Greece, but urged his immediate return home. "The sad news of civil war in England," he says, "called me back; for I considered it base that, while my fellow-countrymen were fighting at home for liberty, I should be travelling abroad for intellectual culture." In December 1638, therefore, he set his face northwards again.

His return journey, however, probably because he learnt that the news he had first received was exaggerated or premature, was broken into stages. He spent a second two months in Rome, ascertained to have been January and February 1638–39; during which two months, as he tells us, he was in some danger from the papal police, because the English Jesuits in Rome had taken offence at his habit of free speech, wherever he went, on the subject of religion. Though he did not alter his demeanor in the least in this particular, nothing happened; and from Rome he got safely to Florence, welcomed back heartily by his Florentine friends, and renewing his meetings with them privately and in their academies. His second visit to Florence, including an excursion to Lucca, extended over two months; and not till April 1639 did he take his leave, and proceed, by Bologna and Ferrara, to Venice. About a month was given to Venice; and thence, having shipped for England the books he had collected in Italy, he went on, by Verona and Milan, over the Alps, to Geneva. In this Protestant city he spent a week or two in June, forming interesting acquaintanceships there too, and having daily conversations with the great Protestant theologian Dr Jean Diodati, the uncle of his friend Charles Diodati. From Geneva he returned to Paris, and so to England. He was home again in August 1639, having been absent in all fifteen or sixteen months.

5. Torquato Tasso, the greatest Italian poet of the late Renaissance (d. 1595), wrote the epic poem *Gerusalemme Liberata* (Jerusalem Liberated).

Milton's Continental tour, and especially the Italian portion of it, remained one of the chief pleasures of his memory through all his subsequent life. One sad and marring memory did mingle itself with all that was otherwise so delightful in his Italian reminiscences. His bosom friend and companion from boyhood, the half-Italian Charles Diodati, who had been to him as Jonathan to David, and into whose ear he had hoped to pour the whole narrative of what he had seen and done abroad, had died during his absence. He had died, in Blackfriars, London, in August 1638, not four months after Milton had gone away on his tour. The intelligence had not reached Milton till some months afterwards, probably not till his second stay in Florence; and, though he must have learnt some of the particulars from the youth's uncle in Geneva, he did not know them fully till his return to England. How profoundly they affected him appears from his *Epitaphium Damonis*, then written in memory of his dead friend. The importance of this poem in Milton's biograhy cannot be overrated. It is perhaps the noblest of all his Latin poems; and, though in the form of a pastoral, and even of a pastoral of the most artificial sort, it is unmistakably an outburst of the most passionate personal grief.

That Milton, now in his thirty-first year, had been girding himself for some greater achievement in poetry than any he had yet attempted, *Comus* not excepted, we should have known otherwise. What we should not have known, but for ann incidental passage in the *Epitaphium Damonis*, is that, at the time of his return from Italy, he had chosen a subject for such a high literary effort of a new Miltonic sort. The passage is one in which, after referring to the hopes of Diodati's medical career as so suddenly cut short by his death, Milton speaks of himself as the survivor and of his own projects in *his* profession of literature.[6] In translation, it may run thus:—

"I have a theme of the Trojans cruising our southern headlands
  Shaping to song, and the realm of Imogen, daughter of Pandras,
  Brennus and Arvirach, dukes, and Bren's bold brother, Belinus;
  Then the Armorican settlers under the laws of the Britons,
  Ay, and the womb of Igraine fatally pregnant with Arthur,
  Uther's son, whom he got disguised in Gorlois' likeness,
  All by Merlin's craft. O then if life shall be spared me,
  Thou shalt be hung, my pipe,[7] far off on some dying old pine-tree.
  Much-forgotten of me; or else your Latin music
  Changed for the British war-screech! What then? For one to
    do all things,

6. Ten years earlier, at the age of nineteen, in a college performance, "At a Vacation Exercise in the College," as he identified it, Milton had included some verses in which he told his fellow students of his commitment to his native language and of one of the uses he hoped to put it to—a poem as ambitious in subject as the great epics of Homer. The lines are reprinted on pp. 351–52, below.
7. Shepherd's flute, implying his career as a pastoral, or lyric, poet.

One to hope all things, fits not! Prize sufficiently ample
Mine, and distinction great (unheard-of ever thereafter
Though I should be and inglorious all through the world of the
    stranger),
If but the yellow-haired Ouse shall read me, the drinker of Alan,
Humber, which whirls as it flows, and Trent's whole valley of
    orchards,
Thames, my own Thames, above all, and Tamar's western waters,
Tawny with ores, and where the white waves swinge the far
    Orkneys."

Interpreted prosaically, this means that Milton was meditating an epic of which King Arthur was to be the central figure, but which should include somehow the whole cycle of British and Arthurian legend, and that not only was this epic to be in English, but he had resolved that all his poetry for the future should be in the same tongue.

Not long after Milton's return the house at Horton ceased to be the family home. Christopher Milton and his wife went to reside at Reading, taking the old gentleman with them, while Milton himself preferred London. He had first taken lodgings in St Bride's Churchyard, at the foot of Fleet Street; but, after a while, probably early in 1640, he removed to a "pretty garden house" of his own, at the end of an entry, in the part of Aldersgate Street which lies immediately on the city side of what is now Maidenhead Court.[8] His sister, whose first husband had died in 1631, had married a Mr Thomas Agar, his successor in the Crown Office; and it was arranged that her two sons by her first husband should be educated by their uncle. John Phillips, the younger of them, only nine years old, had boarded with him in the St Bride's Churchyard lodgings; and, after the removal to Aldersgate Street, the other brother, Edward Phillips, only a year older, became his boarder also. Gradually a few other boys, the sons of well-to-do personal friends, joined the two Phillipses, whether as boarders or for daily lessons, so that the house in Aldersgate Street became a small private school.

What meanwhile of the great Arthurian epic? That project, we find, had been given up, and Milton's mind was roving among many other subjects, and balancing their capabilities. How he wavered between Biblical subjects and heroic subjects from British history, and how many of each kind suggested themselves to him, one learns from a list in his own handwriting among the Milton MSS. at Cambridge. It contains jottings of no fewer than fifty-three subjects from the Old Testament, eight from the Gospels, thirty-three from British and English history before the Conquest, and five from Scottish history. It is curious that all or most of them are headed or described as subjects for "tragedies," as if the epic form had now been abandoned for the dramatic. It is more

8. In the Barbican of modern London.

interesting still to observe which of the subjects fascinated Milton most. Though several of them are sketched pretty fully, not one is sketched at such length and so particularly as *Paradise Lost*. It is the first subject on the list, and there are four separate drafts of a possible tragedy under that title, two of them merely enumerating the *dramatis personæ*, but the last two indicating the plot and the division into acts. Thus, in 1640, twenty-seven years before *Paradise Lost* was given to the world, he had put down the name on paper, and had committed himself to the theme.

To these poetic dreamings and schemings there was to be a long interruption. The Scottish National Covenant had led to extraordinary results. Not only were Charles and Laud checkmated in their design of converting the mild Episcopal system which King James had established in Scotland into a high Laudian prelacy; but, in a General Assembly held at Glasgow in the end of 1638, Episcopacy had been utterly abolished in Scotland, and the old Presbyterian system of Knox and Melville revived. To avenge this, and restore the Scottish bishops, Charles had marched to the Border with an English army; but, met there by the Covenanting army under General Alexander Leslie, he had not deemed it prudent to risk a battle, and had yielded to a negotiation conceding to the Scots all their demands. This "First Bishops' War," as it came to be called, was begun and concluded while Milton was abroad. About the time of his return, however, Charles had again broken with the Scots. Milton had been watching the course of affairs since then with close and eager interest. He had seen and partaken in the sympathetic stir in favor of the Scots which ran through the popular and Puritan mind of England. He had welcomed the practical proof of this sympathy given in that English parliament of April 1640, called "The Short Parliament," which Charles, in his straits for supplies against the Scots, had reluctantly summoned at last, but was obliged to dismiss as unmanageable. Charles had, nevertheless, with money raised somehow, entered on the "Second Bishops' War." This time the result was momentous indeed.

The Scots, not waiting to be attacked in their own country, took the aggressive, and invaded England. In August 1640, after one small engagement with a portion of Charles's army, they were in possession of Newcastle and of all the northern English counties. The English then had their opportunity. A treaty with the Scots was begun, which the English Puritans, who regarded their presence in England as the very blessing they had been praying for, were in no haste to finish; and, on the 3rd of November 1640, there met that parliament which was to be famous in English history, and in the history of the world, as "The Long Parliament."

Of the first proceedings of this parliament, including the trial and execution of Strafford, the impeachment and imprisonment of Laud and others, and the break-down of the system of Thorough by miscellaneous reforms and by guarantees for parliamentary liberty, Milton was only a spectator. It was when the church question emerged distinctly as the question paramount, and there had arisen divisions on that question among those who had been practically unanimous in matters of civil reform, that he plunged in as an active adviser. There were three parties on the church question. There was a high-church party, contending for Episcopacy by divine right, and for the maintenance of English Episcopacy very much as it was; there was a middle party, defending Episcopacy on grounds of usage and expediency, but desiring to see the powers of bishops greatly curtailed, and a limited Episcopacy, with councils of presbyters[9] round each bishop, substituted for the existing high Episcopacy; and there was the root-and-branch party, as it called itself, desiring the entire abolition of Episcopacy and the reconstruction of the English Church on something like the Scottish Presbyterian model. Since the opening of the parliament there had been a storm of pamphlets crossing one another in the air from these three parties.

The chief manifesto of the high-church party was a pamphlet by Joseph Hall, bishop of Exeter, entitled *Humble Remonstrance to the High Court of Parliament.* In answer to Hall, and in representation of the views of the root-and-branch party, there had stepped forth, in March 1640–41, five leading Puritan parish ministers, the initials of whose names, clubbed together on the title-page of their joint production, made the uncouth word "Smectymnuus." These were Stephen Marshall, Edmund Calamy, Thomas Young, Matthew Newcomen, and William Spurstow. The Thomas Young whose name comes in the middle was no other than the Scottish Thomas Young who had been Milton's domestic preceptor in Bread Street. Having returned from Hamburg in 1628, he had been appointed to the vicarage of Stowmarket in Suffolk, in which living he had remained ever since, with the reputation of being one of the most solid and learned Puritans among the English parish clergy. The famous Smectymnuan pamphlet in reply to Hall was mainly Young's. What is more interesting is that his old pupil Milton was secretly in partnership with him and his brother-Smectymnuans.

Milton's hand is discernible in a portion of the original Smectymnuan pamphlet; and he continued to aid the Smectymnuans in their subsequent rejoinders to Hall's defences of himself. It was more in Milton's way, however, to appear in print independently; and in May 1641, while the controversy between Hall and the Smectymnuans was going on, he put forth a pamphlet of his own. It was entitled *Of Reformation touching Church Discipline in England and the Causes that have hitherto hindered it*, and consisted of a review of English ecclesiastical history, with an

---

9. *Presbyters* are elders; in the early Christian church, they were teachers or officers. In the Reformed church, which consisted simply of its members, all were equal under Christ, its head. They were elected—unlike the pope, cardinals, bishops, and priests of the Catholic church, who were appointed by the hierarchy, or the "Episcopacy."

appeal to his countrymen to resume that course of reformation which he considered to have been prematurely stopped in the preceding century, and to sweep away the last relics of papacy and prelacy.[1] Among all the root-and-branch pamphlets of the time it stood out, and stands out still, as the most thorough-going and tremendous. It was followed by four others in rapid succession,—to wit, *Of Prelatical Episcopacy and whether it may be deduced from the Apostolical Times* (June 1641), *Animadversions upon the Remonstrant's Defence against Smectymnuus* (July 1641), *The Reason of Church Government urged against Prelaty* (February 1641–42), *Apology against a Pamphlet called a Modest Confutation of the Animadversions, &c.* (March 1642). The first of these was directed chiefly against that middle party which advocated a limited Episcopacy, with especial reply to the arguments of Archbishop Ussher, as the chief exponent of the views of that party. Two of the others, as the titles imply, belong to the Smectymnuan series, and were castigations of Bishop Hall. The greatest of the four, and the most important of all Milton's anti-Episcopal pamphlets after the first, is that entitled *The Reason of Church Government*.[2] It is there that Milton takes his readers into his confidence, speaking at length of himself and his motives in becoming a controversialist. Poetry, he declares, was his real vocation; it was with reluctance that he had resolved to "leave a calm and pleasing solitariness, fed with cheerful and confident thoughts, to embark in a troubled sea of noise and hoarse disputes"; but duty had left him no option. The great poem or poems he had been meditating could wait; and meanwhile, though in prose-polemics he had the use only of his "left hand," that hand should be used with all its might in the cause of his country and of liberty.

The parliament had advanced in the root-and-branch direction so far as to have passed a bill for the exclusion of bishops from the House of Lords, and compelled the king's assent to that bill, when, in August 1642, the further struggle between Charles and his subjects took the form of civil war. All England was then divided into the Royalists, supporting the king, and the Parliamentarians, adhering to that majority of the Commons, with a minority of the Lords, which sat on as the parliament. While the first battles of the civil war were being fought with varying success, this parliament, less impeded than when it had been full, moved on more and more rapidly in the root-and-branch direction, till, by midsummer 1643, the abolition of Episcopacy had been decreed, and the question of the future non-prelatic constitution of the Church of England referred to a synod of divines, to meet at Westminster under parliamentary authority. About the end of May [1642] as his nephew Edward Phillips remembered, Milton had gone away on a country journey, without saying whither or for what purpose;

1. See *Of Reformation*, pp. 353–55, below.
2. See *Reason of Church Government*, pp. 356–61, below.

and, when he had returned, about a month afterwards, it was with a young wife, and with some of her sisters and other relatives in her company. His bride was Mary Powell, the eldest daughter of Richard Powell, Esq., of Forest Hill, near Oxford.[3] She was the third of a family of eleven sons and daughters, of good standing, but in rather embarrassed circumstances, and was seventeen years and four months old, while Milton was in his thirty-[fourth] year. However the marriage came about, it was a most unfortunate event. The Powell family were strongly Royalist, and the girl herself seems to have been frivolous, unsuitable, and stupid. Hardly were the honeymoon festivities over in Aldersgate Street when, her sisters and other relatives having returned to Forest Hill and left her alone with her husband, she pined for home again and begged to be allowed to go back on a visit. Milton consented, on the understanding that the visit was to be a brief one. This seems to have been in July [1642, a month before the beginning of the Civil War]. Soon, however, the intimation from Forest Hill was that he need not look ever to have his wife in his house again. The resolution seems to have been mainly the girl's own, abetted by her mother; but, it is a fair conjecture that the whole of the Powell family had repented of their sudden connexion with so prominent a Parliamentarian and assailant of the Church of England as Milton. While his wife ran away, his old father, who had been residing for three years with his younger and lawyer son at Reading, came to take up his quarters in Aldersgate Street.

Milton's conduct under the insult of his wife's desertion was most characteristic. Always fearless and speculative, he converted his own case into a public protest against the existing law and theory of marriage. This work, *The Doctrine and Discipline of Divorce Restored, to the good of both Sexes*, published in August 1643, without his name, but with no effort at concealment, declared the notion of a sacramental sanctity in the marriage relation to be a clerically invented superstition, and arguing that inherent incompatibility of character, or contrariety of mind, between two married persons, is a perfectly just reason for divorce.[4] There was no reference to his own case, except by implication; but the boldness of the speculation roused attention and sent a shock through London. It was a time when the authors of heresies of this sort, or of any sort, ran considerable risks. The famous Westminster Assembly of Divines, called by the Long Parliament, had met on the appointed day, July 1, 1643; the Scots, in consenting to send an army into England to assist the parliament in their war with the king, had proposed as one of the conditions, their Solemn League and Covenant, binding the two nations to endeavor after a uniformity of religion and of ecclesiastical

---

3. Powell owed Milton's father a semi-annual interest payment of £12, due on June 12, 1642, on a loan of £300 at 8 percent made in 1627. He was deeply in debt. He paid the interest and promised Milton a dowry of £1,000, which was never paid.
4. See pp. 361–77, below.

discipline, with the extirpation of all "heresy, schism, and profaneness," as well as popery and prelacy; the Solemn League and Covenant had been enthusiastically accepted in England, and was being sworn to universally by the Parliamentarians; and one immediate effect was that four eminent Scottish divines and two Scottish lay commissioners were added to the Westminster Assembly and became leaders there. Whether Milton's divorce tract was formally discussed in the Assembly during the first months of its sitting is unknown; but it is certain that the London clergy, including not a few members of the Assembly, were then talking about it privately with anger and execration. That there might be no obstacle to a more public prosecution, Milton threw off the anonymous in a second and much enlarged edition of the tract, in February 1644, dedicated openly to the parliament and the Assembly. Then, for a month or two, during which the gossip about him and his monstrous doctrine was spreading more and more, he turned his attention to other subjects.

Among the questions in agitation in the general ferment of opinion brought about by the civil war was that of a reform of the national system of education and especially of the universities. To this question Milton made a contribution in June 1644, in a small *Tract on Education*, in the form of a letter to Mr Samuel Hartlib, a German then resident in London and interesting himself busily in all philanthropic projects and schemes of social reform.

In the very next month, however, July 1644, he returned to the divorce subject in a pamphlet addressed specially to the clergy and entitled *The Judgment of Martin Bucer concerning Divorce*. The outcry against him then reached its height. He was attacked in pamphlets; he was denounced in pulpits all through London, and more than once in sermons before the two Houses of Parliament by prominent divines of the Westminster Assembly; strenuous efforts were made to bring him within definite parliamentary censure. In the cabal formed against him for this purpose a leading part was played, at the instigation of the clergy, by the Stationers' Company of London. That company, representing the publishers and booksellers of London, had a plea of their own against him, on the ground that his doctrine was not only immoral, but had been put forth in an illegal manner. His first divorce treatise, though published immediately after the "Printing Ordinance" of the parliament of June 14, 1643, requiring all publications to be licensed for press by one of the official censors, and to be registered in the books of the Stationers' Company, had been issued without license and without registration. Complaint to this effect was made against Milton, with some others liable to the same charge of contempt of the printing ordinance, in a petition of the Stationers to the House of Commons in August 1644; and the matter came before committee both in that House and in the Lords. It is to this circumstance that the world owes the most popular and eloquent, if not the greatest, of all Milton's prose-writings, his famous *Areopagitica, a Speech of Mr John Milton for the Liberty of Unlicensed Printing to the Parliament of England.*

It appeared in the end of November 1644, deliberately unlicensed and unregistered, as was proper on such an occasion, and was a remonstrance addressed to the parliament, as if in an oration to them face to face, against their ordinance of June 1643 and the whole system of licensing and censorship of the press. Nobly eulogistic of the parliament in other respects, it denounced their printing ordinance as utterly unworthy of them, and of the new era of English liberties which they were initiating, and called for its repeal.[5] Though that effect did not follow, the pamphlet virtually accomplished its purpose. The licensing system had received its deathblow; and, though the Stationers returned to the charge in another complaint to the House of Lords, Milton's offence against the press ordinance was condoned. He was still assailed in pamphlets, and found himself "in a world of disesteem"; but he lived on through the winter of 1644–45 undisturbed in his house in Aldersgate Street.

In March 1645 he published simultaneously his *Tetrachordon, or Expositions upon the four chief places of Scripture which treat of Marriage,* and his *Colasterion, a Reply to a nameless Answer against the Doctrine and Discipline of Divorce.* In these he replied to his chief recent assailants, lay and clerical, with merciless severity.

It was not merely Milton's intellectual eminence that had saved him from prosecution for his divorce heresy. A new tendency of national opinion on the church question had operated in his favor, and in favor of all forms of free speculation. There had occurred in the Westminster Assembly itself, and more largely throughout the general community, that split of English Puritanism into the two opposed varieties of Presbyterianism on the one hand and Independency or Congregationalism on the other which explains the whole subsequent history of the Puritan revolution. Out of this theoretical discussion as to the constitution of the church there had grown the all-important practical question of toleration. The Presbyterians insisted that the whole population of England should necessarily belong to the one national Presbyterian Church, be compelled to attend its worship, and be subject to its discipline, while the Independents demanded that, if a Presbyterian Church should be set up as the national and state-paid church, there should at least be liberty of dissent from it, and toleration for those that chose to form themselves into separate congregations.

Vehement within the Westminster Assembly itself, the controversy had attained wider dimensions out of doors, and had inwrought itself in a most remarkable manner with the conduct of the war. Orthodox Presbyterian Calvinists were still the majority of the Puritan body; but,

5. See pp. 382–91, below.

in the new atmosphere of liberty, there had sprung up, from secret and long-suppressed seeds in the English mind, a wonderful variety of sects and denominations, mingling other elements with their Calvinism, or hardly Calvinistic at all,—most of them, it is true, fervidly Biblical and Christian after their different sorts, but not a few professing the most coolly inquisitive and sceptical spirit, and pushing their speculations to strange extremes of free-thinking. These sects, growing more and more numerous in the large towns, had become especially powerful in the English Parliamentary army. That army had, in fact, become a marching academy of advanced opinionists and theological debaters.

Now, as all the new Puritan sects, differing however much among themselves, saw their existence and the perpetuity of their tenets threatened by that system of ecclesiastical uniformity which the Presbyterians proposed to establish, they had, one and all, abjured Presbyterianism, and adopted the opposite principle of Independency, with its appended principle of toleration. Hence an extraordinary conflict of policies among those who seemed to be all Parliamentarians, all united in fighting against the king. The auxiliary Scottish army, which had come into England in January 1644, and had helped the English generals to beat the king in the great battle of Marston Moor in July 1644, thought that he had then been almost sufficiently beaten, and that the object of the Solemn League and Covenant would be best attained by bringing him to such terms as should secure an immediate Presbyterian settlement and the suppression of the Independents and sectaries. In this the chief English commanders, such as Essex and Manchester, agreed substantially with the Scots.

Cromwell, on the other hand, who was now the recognized head of the army Independents, did not think that the king had been sufficiently beaten, even for the general purposes of the war, and was resolved that the war should be pushed on to a point at which a Presbyterian settlement should be impossible without guarantees for liberty of conscience and a toleration of non-Presbyterian sects. Through the latter part of 1644, accordingly, Milton had been saved from the penalties which his Presbyterian opponents would have inflicted on him by this general championship of liberty of opinion by Cromwell and the army Independents. Before the middle of 1645 he, with others who were on the black books of the Presbyterians as heretics, was safer still. Though the parliament had voted, in January 1645, that the future national church of England should be on the Presbyterian system, Cromwell and the Independents had taken care to have the question of toleration left open; and, within the next month or two, by Cromwell's exertions, a completely new face was put upon the war by the removal of all the chief officers that had been in command hitherto, and the equipment of the New Model army, with Fairfax as its commander-in-chief and Cromwell himself as lieutenant-general.

The Scots and the stricter English Presbyterians looked on malignantly while this army took the field, calling it an "Army of Sectaries," and almost hoping it would be beaten. On June 14, 1645, however, there was fought the great battle of Naseby, utterly ruining the king at last, and leaving only relics of his forces here and there. Milton's position then may be easily understood. Though his first tendency on the church question had been to some form of a Presbyterian constitution for the church, he had parted utterly now from the Scots and Presbyterians, and become a partisan of Independency, having no dread of "sects and schisms," but regarding them rather as healthy signs in the English body-politic. He was, indeed, himself one of the most noted sectaries of the time, for in the lists of sects drawn out by contemporary Presbyterian writers special mention is made of one small sect who were known as *Miltonists* or *Divorcers*.

So far as Milton was concerned personally, his interest in the divorce speculation came to an end in July or August 1645, when, by friendly interference, a reconciliation was effected between him and his wife. The ruin of the king's cause at Naseby had suggested to the Powells that it might be as well for their daughter to go back to her husband after their two years of separation. It was not, however, in the house in Aldersgate Street that she rejoined him, but in a larger house, which he had taken in the adjacent street called Barbican, for the accommodation of an increasing number of pupils.

The house in Barbican was tenanted by Milton from about August 1645 to September or October 1647. Among his first occupations there must have been the revision of the proof sheets of the first edition of his collected poems. It appeared as a tiny volume, copies of which are now very rare, with the title *Poems of Mr John Milton, both English and Latin, composed at several times.*[6] The title-page gives the date 1645, but January 1646 seems to have been the exact month of the publication. The appearance of the volume indicates that Milton may have been a little tired by this time of his notoriety as a prose-polemic, and desirous of being recognized once more in his original character of literary man and poet.

Some family incidents of importance appertain to this time of residence in Barbican. Oxford having surrendered to Fairfax in June 1646, the whole of the Powell family had to seek refuge in London, and most of them found shelter in Milton's house. His first child, a daughter named Anne, was born there on the 29th of July that year; on the 1st of January 1647 his father-in-law Mr Powell died there, leaving his affairs in confusion; and in the following March his own father died there, at the age of eighty-four, and was buried in the adjacent church

6. According to Parker (2.1210), seventy-four copies now exist in public and institutional libraries.

of St Giles, Cripplegate. For the rest, the two years, in Barbican are nearly blank in Milton's biography.

The great Revolution was still running its course. For a time Charles's surrender of himself in May 1646, to the auxiliary Scottish army rather than to Fairfax and Cromwell, and his residence with that Scottish army at Newcastle in negotiation with the Scots, had given the Presbyterians the advantage; but, after the Scots had evacuated England in January 1647, leaving Charles a captive with his English subjects, and especially after the English army had seized him at Holmby in June 1647 and undertaken the further management of the treaty with him, the advantage was all the other way. It was a satisfaction to Milton, and perhaps still a protection for him, that the "Army of Independents and Sectaries" had come to be really the masters of England.

From Barbican Milton removed, in September or October 1647, to a smaller house in that part of High Holborn which adjoins Lincoln's Inn Fields. His Powell relatives had now left him, and he had reduced the number of his pupils, or perhaps kept only his two nephews. But, though thus more at leisure, he did not yet resume his projected poem, but occupied himself rather with three works of scholarly labor which he had already for some time had on hand. One was the compilation in English of a complete history of England, or rather of Great Britain, from the earliest times; another was the preparation in Latin of a complete system of divinity, drawn directly from the Bible; and the third was the collection of materials for a new Latin dictionary. Milton had always a fondness for such labors of scholarship and compilation. Of a poetical kind there is nothing to record, during his residence in High Holborn, but an experiment in psalm-translation, in the shape of Psalms lxxx.-lxxxviii. done into service-metre in April 1648, and the "Sonnet to Fairfax," written in September of the same year. This last connects him again with the course of public affairs. The king, having escaped from the custody of the army chiefs, and taken refuge in the Isle of Wight, had been committed to closer custody there; all negotiation between him and parliament had been declared at an end; and the result would probably have been his deposition, but for the consequences of a secret treaty he had contrived to make with the Scots. By this treaty the Scots engaged to invade England in the king's behalf, rescue him from the English parliament and army, and restore him to his full royalty, while he engaged in return to ratify the Covenant, the Presbyterian system of church government, and all the other conclusions of the Westminster Assembly, throughout England, and to put down Independency and the sects. Thus, in May 1648, began what is called the Second Civil War, consisting first of new risings of the Royalists in various parts of England, and then of a conjunction of these with a great invasion of England by a Royalist Scottish army, under the command of the duke of Hamilton.

It was all over in August 1648, when the crushing defeat of the Scottish army by Cromwell in the three days' battle of Preston, and the simultaneous suppression of the English Royalist insurrection in the southeast counties by Fairfax's siege and capture of Colchester, left Charles at the mercy of the victors.—Milton's "Sonnet to Fairfax" was a congratulation to that general-in-chief of the parliament on his success at Colchester, and attested the exultation of the writer over the triumph of the Parliamentary cause.[7] His exultation continued through what followed. After one more dying effort of the parliament at negotiation with Charles, the army took the whole business on itself. The king was brought from the Isle of Wight; the parliament, manipulated by the army officers, and purged of all members likely to impede the army's purpose, was converted into an instrument for that purpose; a court of high justice was set up for the trial of Charles; and on January 30, 1649, he was brought to the scaffold in front of Whitehall. By that act England became a republic, governed, without King or House of Lords, by the persevering residue or "Rump" of the recent House of Commons, in conjunction with an executive council of state, composed of forty-one members appointed annually by that House.

The first Englishman of mark out of parliament to attach himself openly to the new republic was John Milton. This he did by the publication of his pamphlet entitled, *Tenure of Kings and Magistrates, proving that it is lawful, and hath been held so in all ages, for any who have the power, to call to account a Tyrant or wicked King, and, after due conviction, to depose and put him to death, if the ordinary Magistrate have neglected to do it.* It was out within a fortnight after the king's death, and was Milton's last performance in the house in High Holborn.

The chiefs of the new republic could not but perceive the importance of securing the services of a man who had so opportunely and so powerfully spoken out in favor of their tremendous act, and who was otherwise so distinguished. In March 1649, accordingly, Milton was offered, and accepted, the secretaryship for foreign tongues to the council of state of the new Commonwealth. The salary was to be £288 a year [equal to about five times the pay of a skilled worker, ten times that of a day laborer]. To be near his new duties in attendance on the council, which held its daily sittings for the first few weeks in Derby House, close to Whitehall, but afterwards regularly in Whitehall itself, he removed at once to temporary lodgings at Charing Cross. In the very first meetings of council which Milton attended he must have made personal acquaintance with President Bradshaw, Fairfax, Cromwell himself, Sir Henry Vane, Whitlocke, Henry Marten, Hasilrig, Sir Gilbert Pickering, and the other chiefs of the council and the Commonwealth, if indeed he had not known some of them before. After a little while, for his

7. See Sonnet 15, p. 391, below.

greater convenience, official apartments were assigned him in Whitehall itself.

At the date of Milton's appointment to the secretaryship he was forty. His special duty was the drafting of such letters as were sent by the council of state, or sometimes by the Rump Parliament, to foreign states and princes, with the examination and translation of letters in reply, and with personal conferences, when necessary, with the agents of foreign powers in London, and with envoys and ambassadors. As Latin was the language employed in the written diplomatic documents, his post came to be known indifferently as the secretaryship for foreign tongues or the Latin secretaryship. In that post, however, his duties, more particularly at first, were very light in comparison with those of his official colleague, Mr Walter Frost, the general secretary. Foreign powers held aloof from the English republic as much as they could; and, while Mr Frost had to be present in every meeting of the council, keeping the minutes, and conducting all the general correspondence, Milton's presence was required only when some piece of foreign business did turn up. Hence, from the first, his employment in very miscellaneous work. Especially, the council looked to him for everything in the nature of literary vigilance and literary help in the interests of the struggling Commonwealth. He was employed in the examination of suspected papers, and in interviews with their authors and printers; and he executed several great literary commissions expressly entrusted to him by the council.

The first of these was his pamphlet entitled *Observtions on Ormond's Articles of Peace with the Irish Rebels*. It was published in May 1649, and was in defence of the republic against a complication of Royalist intrigues and dangers in Ireland. A passage of remarkable interest in it is one of eloquent eulogy on Cromwell. More important still was the *Eikonoklastes* (which may be translated "Image-Smasher"), published by Milton in October 1649, by way of counterblast to the famous *Eikon Basilike* ("Royal Image"), which had been in circulation in thousands of copies since the king's death, and had become a kind of Bible in all Royalist households, on the supposition that it had been written by the royal martyr himself.

A third piece of work was of a more laborious nature. In the end of 1649 there appeared abroad, under the title of *Defensio Regia pro Carolo I.*, a Latin vindication of the memory of Charles, with an attack on the English Commonwealth, intended for circulation on the Continent. As it had been written, at the instance of the exiled royal family, by Salmasius, or Claude de Saumaise, of Leyden, then of enormous celebrity over Europe as the greatest scholar of his age, it was regarded as a serious blow to the infant Commonwealth. To answer it was thought a task worthy of Milton, and he threw his whole strength into the performance through the year 1650, interrupting himself only by a new and enlarged edition of his *Eikonoklastes*. Not till April 1651 did the result appear;

but then the success was prodigious. Milton's Latin *Pro Populo Anglicano Defensio*, as it was called, ran at once over the British Islands and the Continent, rousing acclamation everywhere, and was received by scholars as an annihilation of the great Salmasius.

Through the rest of 1651 the observation was that the two agencies which had co-operated most visibly in raising the reputation of the Commonwealth abroad were Milton's books and Cromwell's battles.— These battles of Cromwell, in the service of the Commonwealth he had founded, had kept him absent from the council of state, of which he was still a member, since shortly after the beginning of Milton's secretaryship. For nearly a year he had been in Ireland, as lord lieutenant, reconquering that country after its long rebellion; and then, for another year, he had been in Scotland, crushing the Royalist commotion there round Charles II, and annexing Scotland to the English republic. The annexation was complete on the 3d of September 1651, when Cromwell, chasing Charles II, and his army out of Scotland, came up with them at Worcester and gained his crowning victory. The Commonwealth then consisted of England, Ireland, and Scotland, and Cromwell was its supreme chief.

Through the eventful year 1651 Milton had added to the other duties of his secretaryship that of Government journalist. Through the whole of that year, if not from an earlier period, he acted as licenser and superintending editor of the *Mercurius Politicus*, a newspaper issued twice a week, of which Mr Marchamont Needham was the working editor and proprietor.

About the end of 1651 Milton left his official rooms in Whitehall for a house he had taken on the edge of St James's Park, in what was then called Petty France, Westminster. The house existed till the other day, but has been pulled down.[8] In Milton's time it was a villa-looking residence, with a garden, in a neighborhood of villas and gardens. He had now more to do in the special work of his office, in consequence of the increase of correspondence with foreign powers. But he had for some time been in ailing health; and a dimness of eyesight which had been growing upon him gradually for ten years had been settling rapidly, since his labor over the answer to Salmasius, into total blindness. Actually, before or about May 1652, when he was but in his forty-fourth year, his blindness was total, and he could go about only with some one to lead him.[9] Hence a rearrangement of his secretarial duties. Such of these duties as he could perform at home, or by occasional visits to the

8. The house was pulled down in 1877 to make way for the Metropolitan Railway, later the Metropolitan Line of the London Underground. Next door lived Lord Scudamore, the English ambassador who, when Milton was in Paris, introduced him to the great Grotius. In the nineteenth century, it was owned by Jeremy Bentham and was lived in by William Hazlitt and by John Stuart Mill (Parker 2.999).

9. See Sonnets 19 and 22, pp. 393–94, below.

Council Office near, he continued to perform; but much of the routine work was done for him by assistants, one of them a well-known German named Weckherlin, under the superintendence of Mr John Thurloe, who had succeeded Mr. Walter Frost in the general secretaryship.

To the interval between May and September 1652, though the exact date is uncertain, we have to refer the death of his only son, who had been born in his official Whitehall apartments in the March of the preceding year, and the death also of his wife, just after she had given birth to his third daughter, Deborah. With the three children thus left him—Anne, but six years old, Mary, not four, and the infant Deborah—the blind widower lived on in his house in Petty France in such desolation as can be imagined. He had recovered sufficiently to resume his secretarial duties; and the total number of his dictated state letters for the single year 1652 is equal to that of all the state letters of his preceding term of secretaryship put together.

On the 20th of April 1653 there was Cromwell's great act of armed interference by which he turned out the small remnant of the Rump Parliament, dismissed their council of state, and assumed the government of England, Ireland, and Scotland into his own hands. For several months, indeed, he acted only as interim dictator, governing by a council of his officers, and waiting for the conclusions of that select body of advisers which he had called together from all parts of the country, and which the Royalists nicknamed "The Barebones Parliament." In December 1653, however, his formal sovereignty began under the name of the Protectorate, passing gradually into more than kingship. This change from government by the Rump and its council to government by a single military Lord Protector and his council was regarded by many as treason to the republican cause, and divided those who had hitherto been the united Commonwealth's men into the "Pure Republicans," represented by such men as Bradshaw and Vane, and the "Oliverians," adhering to the Protector. Milton, whose boundless admiration of Cromwell had shown itself already in his Irish tract of 1649 and in his recent sonnet,[1] was recognized as one of the Oliverians. He remained in Oliver's service and was his Latin secretary through the whole of the Protectorate. For a while, indeed, his Latin letters to foreign states in Cromwell's name were but few,—Mr Thurloe, as general secretary, officiating as Oliver's right-hand man in everything, with a Mr Philip Meadows under him, at a salary of £200 a year, as deputy for the blind Mr Milton in foreign correspondence and translations. The reason for this temporary exemption of Milton from routine duty may have been that he was then engaged on an answer, by commission from the late Government, to an anonymous pamphlet, published at the Hague, with

1. See Sonnet 16, p. 392, below.

the title *Regii Sanguinis Clamor ad Cœlum adversus Parricidas Angli-canos* ("Cry of the Royal Blood to Heaven against the English Parricides").

Salmasius was now dead, and the Commonwealth was too stable to suffer from such attacks; but no Royalist pamphlet had appeared so able or so venomous as this in continuation of the Salmasian controversy. All the rather because it was in the main a libel on Milton himself did a reply from his pen seem necessary. It came out in May 1654, with the title *Joannis Miltoni Angli pro Populo Anglicnao Defensio Secunda* ("Second Defence of John Milton, Englishman, for the People of England"). It is one of the most interesting of all Milton's writings. The author of the libel to which it replied was Dr Peter du Moulin the younger, a naturalized French Presbyterian minister, then moving about in English society, close to Milton; but, as that was a profound secret, and the work was universally attributed on the Continent to an Alexander Morus, a French minister of Scottish descent, then of much oratorical celebrity in Holland—who had certainly managed the printing in consultation with the now deceased Salmasius, and had contributed some portion of the matter,—Milton had made this Morus the responsible person and the one object of his castigations. They were frightful enough. If Salmasius had been slaughtered in the former *Defensio*, Morus was murdered and gashed in this. His moral character was blasted by exposure of his antecendents, and he was blazoned abroad in Europe as a detected clerical blackguard.

The terrific castigation of Morus, however, is but part of the *Defensio Secunda*. It contains passages of singular autobiographical and historical value, and includes laudatory sketches of such eminent Commonwealth's men as Bradshaw, Fairfax, Fleetwood, Lambert, and Overton, together with a long panegyric on Cromwell himself and his career, which remains to this day unapproached for elaboration and grandeur by any estimate of Cromwell from any later pen.

The most active time of his secretaryship for Oliver was from April 1655 onwards. In that month, in the course of a general revision of official salaries under the Protectorate, Milton's salary of £288 a year hitherto was reduced to £200 a year, with a kind of redefinition of his office, recognizing it, we may say, as a Latin secretaryship extraordinary. Mr Phillip Meadows was to continue to do all the ordinary Foreign Office work, under Thurloe's inspection; but Milton was to be called in on special occasions. Hardly was the arrangement made when a signal occasion did occur. In May 1655 all England was horrified by the news of the massacre of the Vaudois Protestants by the troops of Emanuele II, duke of Savoy and prince of Piedmont, in consequence of their disobedience to an edict requiring them either to leave their native valleys or to conform to the Catholic religion. Cromwell and his council took the matter up with all their energy; and the burst of indignant letters on the subject despatched in that month and the next to the duke of Savoy himself, Louis XIV of France, Cardinal Mazarin, the Swiss cantons, the States-General of the United Provinces, and the kings of Sweden and Denmark, were all by Milton. His famous sonnet "On the late Massacre in Piedmont" was his more private expression of feeling on the same occasion.

This sonnet was in circulation, and the case of the Vaudois Protestants was still occupying Cromwell, when, in August 1655, there appeared the last of Milton's great Latin pamphlets. It was his *Pro Se Defensio*, in answer to an elaborate self-defence which Morus had put forth on the Continent since Milton's attack on his character, and it consisted mainly of a re-exposure of that unfortunate clergyman.

Thence, through the rest of Cromwell's Protectorate, Milton's life was of comparatively calm tenor. He was in much better health than usual, bearing his blindness with courage and cheerfulness; he was steadily busy with such more important despatches to foreign powers as the Protector, then in the height of his great foreign policy, and regarded with fear and deference by all European monarchs and states from Gibraltar to the Baltic, chose to confide to him; and his house in Petty France seems to have been, more than at any previous time since the beginning of his blindness, a meeting-place for friends and visitors, and a scene of pleasant hospitalities. The four sonnets now numbered xix.– xxii., one of them to young Mr Lawrence, the son of the president of Cromwell's council, and two of the others to Cyriack Skinner, belong to this time of domestic quiet, as do also no fewer than ten of his Latin *Familiar Epistles*.

His second marriage belongs to the same years, and gleams even yet as the too brief consummation of this happiest time in the blind man's life. The name of his second wife was Katherine Woodcock. He married her on the 12th of November 1656; but, after only fifteen months, he was again a widower, by her death in childbirth in February 1657–58. The child dying with her, only the three daughters by the first marriage remained. The touching sonnet which closes the series of Milton's *Sonnets* is his sacred tribute to the memory of his second marriage and to the virtues of the wife he had so soon lost.[2] Even after that loss we find him still busy for Cromwell. Mr Meadows having been sent off on diplomatic missions, Andrew Marvell had, in September 1657, been brought in, much to Milton's satisfaction, as his assistant or colleague in the Latin secretaryship; but this had by no means relieved him from duty. Some of his greatest despatches for Cromwell, including letters, of the highest importance, to Louis XIV, Mazarin, and Charles Gustavus of Sweden, belong to the year 1658.

One would like to know precisely in what personal relations Milton

2. See Sonnet 23, p. 394, below.

and Cromwell stood to each other. There is, unfortunately, no direct record to show what Cromwell thought of Milton; but there is ample record of what Milton thought of Cromwell. "Our chief of men," he had called Cromwell in his sonnet of May 1652; and the opinion remained unchanged. He thought Cromwell the greatest and best man of his generation, or of many generations; and he regarded Cromwell's assumption of the supreme power, and his retention of that power with a sovereign title, as no real suppression of the republic, but as absolutely necessary for the preservation of the republic, and for the safeguard of the British Islands against a return of the Stuarts. Nevertheless, under this prodigious admiration of Cromwell, there were political doubts and reserves. Milton was so much of a modern radical of the extreme school in his own political views and sympathies that he cannot but have been vexed by the growing conservatism of Cromwell's policy through his Protectorate. To his grand panegyric on Oliver in the *Defensio Secunda* of 1654 he had ventured to append cautions against self-will, over-legislation, and over-policing; and he cannot have thought that Oliver had been immaculate in these respects through the four subsequent years.

The attempt to revive an aristocracy and a House of Lords, on which Cromwell was latterly bent, cannot have been to Milton's taste. Above all, Milton dissented *in toto* from Cromwell's church policy. It was Milton's fixed idea, almost his deepest idea, that there should be no such thing as an Established Church, or state-paid clergy, of any sort or denomination or mixture of denominations, in any nation, and that, as it had been the connexion between church and state, begun by Constantine, that had vitiated Christianity in the world, and kept it vitiated, so Christianity would never flourish as it ought till there had been universal disestablishment and disendowment of the clergy, and the propagation of the gospel were left to the zeal of voluntary pastors, self-supported, or supported modestly by their flocks. He had at one time looked to Cromwell as the likeliest man to carry this great revolution in England. But Cromwell, after much meditation on the subject in 1652 and 1653, had come to the opposite conclusion. The conservation of the Established Church of England, in the form of a broad union of all evangelical denominations of Christians, whether Presbyterians, or Independents, or Baptists, or moderate Old Anglicans, that would accept state-pay with state-control, had been the fundamental notion of his Protectorate, persevered in to the end. This must have been Milton's deepest disappointment with the Oliverian rule.

Cromwell's death on the 3d of September 1658 left the Protectorship to his son Richard. Milton and Marvell continued in their posts, and a number of the Foreign Office letters of the new Protectorate were of Milton's composition. Thinking the time fit, he also put forth, in October 1658, a new edition of his *Defensio Prima*, and, early in 1659, a new English pamphlet, entitled *Treatise of Civil Power in Ecclesiastical Causes*, ventilating those notions of his as to the separation of church and state which he had been obliged of late to keep to himself.

Meanwhile, though all had seemed quiet round Richard at first, the jealousies of the army officers left about him by Oliver, and the conflict of political elements let loose by Oliver's death, were preparing his downfall. In May 1659 Richard's Protectorate was at an end. The country had returned with pleasure to what was called "the good old cause" of pure republicanism; and the government was in the hands of "the Restored Rump," consisting of the reassembled remains of that Rump Parliament which Cromwell had dissolved in 1653. To this change, as inevitable in the circumstances, or even promising, Milton adjusted himself. The last of his known official performances in his Latin secretaryship are two letters in the name of William Lenthall, as the speaker of the restored Rump, one to the king of Sweden and one to the king of Denmark, both dated May 15, 1659. Under the restored Rump, if ever, he seemed to have a chance for his notion of church-disestablishment; and, accordingly, in August 1659, he put forth, with a prefatory address to that body, a large pamphlet entitled *Considerations touching the likeliest means to remove Hirelings out of the Church*. The restored Rump had no time to attend to such matters. They were in struggle for their own existence with the army chiefs; and the British Islands were in that state of hopeless confusion and anarchy which, after passing through a brief phase of attempted military government (October to December 1659), and a second revival of the purely republican or Rump government (December 1659 to February 1659–60), issued in Monk's march from Scotland, assumption of the dictatorship in London, and recall of all the survivors of the original Long Parliament to enlarge the Rump to due dimensions and assist him in further deliberations. Through all this anarchy the Royalist elements had been mustering themselves, and the drift to the restoration of the Stuart dynasty, as the only possible or feasible conclusion, had become apparent.

To prevent that issue, to argue against it and fight against it to the last, was the work to which Milton had then set himself. His disestablishment notion and all his other notions had been thrown aside; the preservation of the republic in any form, and by any compromise of differences within itself, had become his one thought, and the study of practical means to this end his most anxious occupation. In a *Letter to a Friend concerning the Ruptures of the Commonwealth*, written in October 1659, he had propounded a scheme of a kind of dual government for reconciling the army chiefs with the Rump; through the following winter, his anxiety over the signs of the growing enthusiasm throughout the country for the recall of Charles II, had risen to a kind of agony; and early in March 1660 his agony found vent in a pamphlet of the most passionate vehemence entitled *The Ready and Easy Way to*

Establish a Free Commonwealth, and the Excellence thereof compared with the Inconveniences and Dangers of readmitting Kingship in this Nation.[3] An abridgment of the practical substance of this pamphlet was addressed by him to General Monk in a letter entitled *The Present Means and Brief Delineation of a Free Commonwealth.* Milton's proposal was that the central governing apparatus of the British Islands for the future should consist of one indissoluble Grand Council or parliament, which should include all the political chiefs, while there should be a large number of provincial councils or assemblies sitting in the great towns for the management of local and county affairs. The scheme, so far as the public attended to it at all, was received with laughter; the Royalist demonstrations were now fervid and tumultuous; and it remained only for the new and full parliament of two Houses which had been summoned under Monk's auspices, and which is now known as the Convention Parliament, to give effect to Monk's secret determination and the universal popular desire. Not even then would Milton be silent. In *Brief Notes on a late Sermon,* published in April 1660, in reply to a Royalist discourse by a Dr Griffith, he made another protest against the recall of the Stuarts, even hinting that it would be better that Monk should become king himself; and in the same month he sent forth a second edition of his *Ready and Easy Way,* more frantically earnest than even the first, and containing additional passages of the most violent denuciation of the royal family, and of prophecy of the degradation and disaster they would bring back with them. This was the dying effort. On the 25th of April the Convention Parliament met; on the 1st of May they resolved unanimously that the government by King, Lords, and Commons should be restored; and on the 29th of May Charles II. made his triumphal entry into London. The chief republicans had by that time scattered themselves, and Milton was in hiding in an obscure part of the city.

How Milton escaped the scaffold at the Restoration is a mystery now, and was a mystery at the time. Actually, in the terrible course through the two Houses of the Convention Parliament of that Bill of Indemnity by which the fates of the surviving regicides and of so many others of the chief republican culprits were determined, Milson was named for special punishment. It was voted by the Commons that he should be taken into custody by the sergeant-at-arms, for prosecution by the attorney-general on account of his *Eikonoklastes* and *Defensio Prima,* and that all copies of those books should be called in and burnt by the hangman. There was, however, some powerful combination of friendly influences in his favor, with Monk probably abetting. At all events, on the 29th of August 1660, when the Indemnity Bill did come out complete, with the king's assent, granting full pardon to all for their past

---

3. See pp. 395–96, below.

offences, with the exception of about a hundred persons named in the bill itself for various degrees of punishment, thirty-four of them for death and twenty-six for the highest penalty short of death, Milton did not appear as one of the exceptions on any ground or in any of the grades. From that moment, therefore, he could emerge from his hiding, and go about as a free man. Not that he was yet absolutely safe. During the next two or three months London was in excitement over the trials of such of the excepted regicides and others as had not succeeded in escaping abroad, and the hangings and quarterings of ten of them; there were several public burnings by the hangman at the same time of Milton's condemned pamphlets; and the appearance of the blind man himself in the streets, though he was legally free, would have caused him to be mobbed and assaulted. Nay, notwithstanding the Indemnity Bill, he was in some legal danger to as late as December 1660. Though the special prosecution ordered against him by the Commons had been quashed by the subsequent Indemnity Bill, the sergeant-at-arms had taken him into custody.[4] Entries in the Commons journals of December 17 and 19 show that Milton complained of the sergeant-at-arms for demanding exorbitant fees for his release, and that the House arranged the matter.

Milton did not return to Petty France. For the first months after he was free he lived as closely as possible in a house near what is now Red Lion Square, Holborn. Thence he removed, apparently early in 1661, to a house in Jewin Street, in his old Aldersgate-Street and Barbican neighborhood.

In Jewin Street Milton remained for two or three years, or from 1661 to 1664. They were the time of his deepest degradation, that time of which he speaks when he tells us how, by the Divine help, he had been able to persevere undauntedly—

> —"though fallen on evil days,
> On evil days though fallen, and evil tongues,
> In darkness, and with dangers compassed round,
> And solitude."[5]

The "evil days" were those of the Restoration in its first or Clarendonian stage, with its revenges and reactions, its return to high Episopacy and suppression of every form of dissent and sectarianism, its new and shameless royal court, its open proclamation and practice of anti-Puritanism in morals and in literature no less than in politics. For the main part of this world of the Restoration Milton was now nothing more than an infamous outcast, the detestable blind republican and regicide who had, by too great clemency, been left unhanged. The friends that adhered to

---

4. According to Parker (1.575–76) the records show only that "Milton was arrested and imprisoned, probably in November, 1660," and that "in December, 1660, he was granted an official pardon"
5. PL VII.25–28.

him still, and came to see him in Jewin Street, were few in number, and chiefly from the ranks of those nonconforming denominations, Independents, Baptists, or Quakers, who were themselves under similar obloquy. Besides his two nephews, the faithful Andrew Marvell, Cyriack Skinner, and some others of his former admirers, English or foreign, we hear chiefly of a Dr Nathan Paget, who was a physician in the Jewin-Street neighborhood, and of several young men who would drop in upon him by turns, partly to act as his amanuenses, and partly for the benefit of lessons from him—one of them an interesting Quaker youth, named Thomas Ellwood. With all this genuine attachment to him of a select few, Milton could truly enough describe his conditions after the Restoration as one of "solitude."

Nor was this the worst. His three daughters, on whom he ought now to have been able principally to depend, were his most serious domestic trouble. The poor motherless girls, the eldest in her seventeenth year in 1662,[6] the second in her fifteenth, and the youngest in her eleventh, had grown up, in their father's blindness and too great self-absorption, ill-looked-after and but poorly educated; and the result now appeared. They "made nothing of neglecting him"; they rebelled against the drudgery of reading to him or otherwise attending on him; they "did combine together and counsel his maid-servant to cheat him in her marketings"; they actually "had made away some of his books, and would have sold the rest." It was to remedy this horrible state of things that Milton consented to a third marriage. The wife found for him was Elizabeth Minshull, of a good Cheshire family, and a relative of Dr Paget's. They were married on the 24th of February 1663, the wife being then only in her twenty-fifth year, while Milton was in his fifty-fifth. She proved an excellent wife; and the Jewin Street household, though the daughters remained in it, must have been under better management from the time of her entry into it. From that date Milton's circumstances must have been more comfortable, and his thoughts about himself less abject, than they had been through the two proceeding years, though his feeling in the main must have been still that of his own Samson:—

> "Now blind, disheartened, shamed, dishonored, quelled,
> To what can I be useful? wherein serve
> My nation, and the work from heaven imposed!
> But to sit idle on the household hearth,
> A burdenous drone, to visitants a gaze,
> Or pitied object."[7]

That might be the appearance, but it was not the reality. All the while of his seeming degradation he had found some solace in renewed industry of various kinds among his books and tasks of scholarship, and all the

6. Anne, who was crippled, illiterate, perhaps retarded.
7. *Samson Agonistes* 563–68.

while, more particularly, he had been building up his *Paradise Lost*. He had begun the poem in earnest, we are told, in his house in Petty France, in the last year of Cromwell's Protectorate, and then not in the dramatic form contemplated eighteen years before, but deliberately in the epic form. He had made but little way when there came the interruption of the anarchy preceding the Restoration and of the Restoration itself; but the work had been resumed in Jewin Street and prosecuted there steadily, by dictations of twenty or thirty lines at a time to whatever friendly or hired amanuensis chanced to be at hand. Considerable progress had been made in this way before his third marriage; and after that the work proceeded apace, his nephew Edward Phillips, who was then out in the world on his own account, looking in when he could to revise the growing manuscript.

In 1669, or 1670, Milton and his wife moved to a smaller house, with a garden, not far from Jewin Street, but in a more private portion of the same suburb. This, which was to be the last of all Milton's London residences, was in the part of the present Bunhill Row which faces the houses that conceal the London artillery-ground and was then known as "Artillery Walk, leading to Bunhill Fields." Here the poem was certainly finished before July 1665; for, when, in that month, Milton and his family, to avoid the Great Plague of London, then beginning its fearful ravages, went into temporary country-quarters in a cottage in Chalfont St Giles, Buckinghamshire, about 23 miles from London, the finished manuscript was taken with him, in probably more than one copy. This we learn from his young Quaker friend, Thomas Ellwood, who had taken the cottage for him, and who was shown one of the manuscript copies, and allowed to take it away with him for perusal, during Milton's stay at Chalfont. Why the poem was not published immediately after the cessation of the Great Plague, does not distinctly appear, but may be explained partly by the fact that the official licenser hesitated before granting the necessary *imprimatur* to a book by a man of such notorious republican antecedents, and partly by the paralysis of all business in London by the Great Fire of September 1666. It was not till the 27th of April 1667 that Milton concluded an agreement with a publisher for the printing of his epic. By the agreement of that date, still extant, Milton sold to Samuel Simmons, printer, of Aldersgate Street, London, for £5 down, the promise of another £5 after the sale of a first edition of thirteen hundred copies, and the further promise of two additional sums of £5 each after the sale of two or more editions of the same size respectively, all his copyright and commercial interest in *Paradise Lost* for ever. The poem was duly entered by Simmons as ready for publication in the Stationers' Registers on the 20th of the following August; and shortly after that date it was out in London as a neatly printed small quarto, with the title *Paradise Lost: A Poem written in Ten Books: By John Milton*. The publishing price was 3s., equal to about

10s. 6d. now [i.e., in the 1880s]. It is worth noting as an historical coincidence that the poem appeared just at the time of the fall and disgrace of Clarendon.

The effect of the publication of *Paradise Lost* upon Milton's reputation can only be described adequately, as indeed it was consciously described by himself in metaphor, by his own words on Samson's feat of triumph over the Philistines:—

> But he, though blind of sight,
> Despised, and thought extinguished quite,
> With inward eyes illuminated,
> His fiery virtue roused
> From under ashes into sudden flame,
> And as an evening dragon came,
> Assailant on the perched roosts
> And nests in order ranged
> Of tame villatic fowl; but as an eagle
> His cloudless thunder bolted on their heads."

As the poem circulated and found readers, whether in the first copies sent forth by Simmons, or in subsequent copies issued between 1667 and 1669, with varied title-pages, and the latest of them with a prefixed prose "Argument," the astonishment broke out everywhere. "This man cuts us all out, and the ancients too" is the saying attributed to Dryden on the occasion; and it is the more remarkable because the one objection to the poem which at first, we are told, "stumbled many" must have "stumbled" Dryden most of all. Except in the drama, rhyme was then thought essential in anything professing to be a poem; blank verse was hardly regarded as verse at all; Dryden especially had been and was the champion of rhyme, contending for it even in the drama; and yet here was an epic not only written in blank verse, but declaring itself on that account to be "an example set, the first in English, of ancient liberty recovered to heroic poem from the troublesome and modern bondage of riming." That, notwithstanding this obvious blow struck by the poem at Dryden's pet literary theory, he should have welcomed the poem so enthusiastically and proclaimed its merits so emphatically, says much as once for his critical perception and for the generosity of his temper. An opinion proclaimed by the very chief of the Restoration literature could not but prevail among the contemporary scholars; and, though execration of the blind and unhanged regicide had not ceased among the meaner critics, the general vote was that he had nobly redeemed himself. One consequence of his renewed celebrity was that visitors of all ranks again sought him out for the honor of his society and conversation. His obscure house in Artillery Walk, Bunhill, we are told, became an attraction now, "much more than he did desire," for the learned notabilities of his time.

The year 1669, when the first edition of *Paradise Lost* had been completely sold out, and Milton had received his second £5 on account of it may be taken as the time of the perfect recognition of his pre-eminence among the English poets of his generation. He was then sixty years of age; and it is to about that year that the accounts that have come down to us of his personal appearance and habits in his later life principally refer. They describe him as to be seen every other day led about in the streets in the vicinity of his Bunhill residence, a slender figure, of middle stature or a little less, generally dressed in a grey cloak or overcoat, and wearing sometimes a small silver-hilted sword, evidently in feeble health, but still looking younger than he was, with his lightish hair, and his fair, rather than aged or pale, complexion. He would sit in his garden at the door of his house, in warm weather, in the same kind of grey overcoat, "and so, as well as in his room, received the visits of people of distinguished parts, as well as quality." Within doors he was usually dressed in neat black. He was a very early riser, and very regular in the distribution of his day, spending the first part, to his midday dinner, always in his own room, amid his books, with an amanuensis to read for him and write to his dictation. Music was always a chief part of his afternoon and evening relaxation, whether when he was by himself or when friends were with him. His manner with friends and visitors was extremely courteous and affable, with just a shade of stateliness. In free conversation, either at the midday dinner, when a friend or two happened, by rare accident, to be present, or more habitually in the evening and at the light supper which concluded it, he was the life and soul of the company, from his "flow of subject" and his "unaffected cheerfulness and civility," though with a marked tendency to the satirical and sarcastic in his criticisms of men and things. This tendency to the sarcastic was connected by some of those who observed it with a peculiarity of his voice or pronunciation. "He pronounced the letter *r* very hard," Aubrey tells us, adding Dryden's note on the subject: "*litera canina*, the dog-letter, a certain sign of a satirical wit." He was extremely temperate in the use of wine or any strong liquors, at meals and at all other times; and when supper was over, about nine o'clock, "he smoked his pipe and drank a glass of water, and went to bed." He suffered much from gout, the effects of which had become apparent in a stiffening of his hands and finger-joints, and the recurring attacks of which in its acute form were very painful. His favorite poets among the Greeks were Homer and the Tragedians, especially Euripides; among the Latins, Virgil and Ovid; among the English, Spenser and Shakespeare. Among his English contemporaries, he thought most highly of Cowley. He had ceased to attend any church, belonged to no religious communion, and had no religious observances in his family. His reasons for this were a matter for curious surmise among his friends, because of the profoundly religious character of his own mind; but he does not seem ever to have furnished the explanation. The matter became of less interest perhaps after 1669, when his three daughters ceased to reside with him, having been sent out, at considerable expense, "to learn some curious and ingenious sorts of manufacture that are proper for women to learn, particularly embroideries in gold or silver." After that the household in Bunhill consisted only of Milton, his wife, a single maid-servant, and the "man" or amanuensis who came in for the day.

The remaining years of Milton's life, extending through that part of the reign of Charles II which figures in English history under the name of "The Cabal Administration," were by no means unproductive. In 1669 he published, under the title of *Accedence Commenced Grammar*, a small English compendium of Latin grammar that had been lying among his papers. In 1670 there appeared, in a rather handsome form, and with a prefixed portrait of him by Faithorne, done from the life, and the best and most authentic that now exists, his *History of Britain to the Norman Conquest*, being all that he had been able to accomplish of his intended complete history of England. In 1671 there followed his *Paradise Regained* and *Samson Agonistes*, bound together in one small volume, and giving ample proof that his poetic genius had not exhausted itself in the preceding great epic. His only publication in 1672 was a Latin digest of Ramist logic, entitled *Artis Logicæ Plenior Institutio*, of no great value, and doubtless from an old manuscript of his earlier days. In 1673, at a moment when the growing political discontent with the government of Charles II and the conduct of his court had burst forth in the special form of a "No-Popery" agitation and outcry, Milton ventured on the dangerous experiment of one more political pamphlet, in which, under the title *Of True Religion, Heresy, Schism, Toleration, and what best means may be used against the growth of Popery*, he put forth, with a view to popular acceptance, as mild a version as possible of his former principles on the topics discussed. In the same year appeared the second edition of his *Minor Poems*. Thus we reach the year 1674, the last of Milton's life. One incident of that year was the publication of the second edition of *Paradise Lost*, with the poem rearranged as now into twelve books, instead of the original ten. Another was the publication of a small volume containing his Latin *Epistolæ Familiares*, together with the *Prolusiones Oratoriæ* of his student-days at Cambridge,—these last thrown in as a substitute for his Latin state letters in his secretaryship for the Commonwealth and the Protectorate, the printing of which was stopped by order from the Foreign Office. A third publication of the same year, and probably the very last thing dictated by Milton, was a translation of a Latin document from Poland relating to the recent election of the heroic John Sobieski to the throne of that kingdom, with the title *A Declaration or Letters Patents of the Election of this present King of Poland, John the Third*. It seems to have been out in London in August or September 1674. On the 8th of the following

November, being a Sunday, Milton died, in his house in Bunhill, of "gout struck in," or gout-fever, at the age of sixty-five years and eleven months. He was buried, the next Thursday, in the church of St Giles, Cripplegate, beside his father, a considerable concourse attending the funeral.

A Selection of Milton's Prose and Poetry

A Paraphrase on Psalm 114†

When the blest seed of Terah's faithful Son,
After long toil their liberty had won,
And past from Pharian fields to Canaan Land,
Led by the strength of the Almighty's hand,
Jehovah's wonders were in Israel shown,   5
His praise and glory was in Israel known.
That saw the troubled sea, and shivering fled,
And sought to hide his froth-becurled head
Low in the earth, Jordan's clear streams recoil,
As a faint host that hath received the foil.   10
The high, huge-bellied mountains skip like rams
Amongst their ewes, the little hills like lambs.
Why fled the ocean? And why skipt the mountains?
Why turned Jordan toward his crystal fountains?
Shake earth, and at the presence be aghast   15
Of him that ever was, and aye shall last,
That glassy floods from rugged rocks can crush,
And make soft rills from fiery flint-stones gush.

† From Milton's first collection of poems (1645). According to the heading, this paraphrase was "don by the Author at fifteen years old." Here as in all the following selections from Milton's poetry and prose, I have modernized the spelling, punctuation, and use of capital letters and italics.
1. *Terah's faithful son*: Abraham.
3. *Pharian fields*: Egypt. *Canaan Land*: the "Promised Land," i.e., the area in Palestine between the Jordan River and the Mediterranean Sea.
7. *sea*: the Red Sea. Cf. Exod. 14.
10. *foil*: repulse.
14. *fountains*: springs, sources.
17. Cf. Exod. 17.6.

From At a Vacation Exercise in the College, Part Latin, Part English†

The Latin speeches ended, the English thus began.

Hail, native language, that by sinews weak
Didst move my first endeavoring tongue to speak,
And mad'st imperfect words with childish trips,
Half unpronounced, slide through my infant lips,
Driving dumb Silence from the portal door,   5
Where he had mutely sat two years before:
Here I salute thee and thy pardon ask
That now I use thee in my latter task:
Small loss it is that thence can come unto thee;
I know my tongue but little grace can do thee: 10
Thou need'st not be ambitious to be first,
Believe me, I have thither packed the worst:
And, if it happen as I did forecast,
The daintiest dishes shall be served up last.
I pray thee then deny me not thy aid   15
For this same small neglect that I have made,
But haste thee straight to do me once a pleasure,
And from thy wardrobe bring thy chiefest treasure;
Not those new-fangled toys and trimming slight
Which takes our late fantastics with delight,   20
But cull those richest robes and gay'st attire
Which deepest spirits and choicest wits desire.
I have some naked thoughts that rove about
And loudly knock to have their passage out,
And weary of their place do only stay   25
Till thou hast decked them in thy best array;
That so they may without suspect or fears
Fly swiftly to this fair assembly's ears;
Yet I had rather, if I were to choose,
Thy service in some graver subject use,   30
Such as may make thee search thy coffers round,
Before thou clothe my fancy in fit sound:

---

† First published in *Poems, &c. upon Several Occasions* . . . 1673. Text from *The Complete Poetical Works*, ed. Douglas Bush (Boston, 1965). Milton recited these verses at the end of a playful academic oration written in Latin prose and delivered at Cambridge during the summer of 1628, when he was nineteen. He had hitherto written almost all his poetry in Latin, and as Bush notes, Milton here "takes his hearers into his confidence . . . , salutes his native language, avows his distaste for the trifling themes and eccentric style of some student poets, and goes on, in couplets of more smoothness and eloquence, to sketch the 'graver' subjects that attract him—nature and the cosmos and 'kings and queens and heroes old.' "
8. *latter:* later.
18. *wardrobe:* closet or chest for clothes or costumes. The next two lines allude to the very latest poetic styles.

Such where the deep transported mind may soar
Above the wheeling poles, and at heav'n's door
Look in, and see each blissful deity   35
How he before the thunderous throne doth lie,
Listening to what unshorn Apollo sings
To the touch of golden wires, while Hebe brings
Immortal nectar to her kingly sire;
Then passing through the spheres of watchful fire,   40
And misty regions of wide air next under,
And hills of snow and lofts of pilèd thunder,
May tell at length how green-eyed Neptune raves,
In Heav'n's defiance mustering all his waves;
Then sing of secret things that came to pass   45
When beldam Nature in her cradle was;
And last of kings and queens and heroes old,
Such as the wise Demodocus once told
In solemn songs at King Alcinous' feast,
While sad Ulysses' soul and all the rest   50
Are held with his melodious harmony
In willing chains and sweet captivity.

*   *   *

Sonnet 7†

How soon hath Time, the subtle thief of youth,
  Stol'n on his wing my three and twentieth year!
  My hasting days fly on with full career,
  But my late spring no bud or blossom show'th.
Perhaps my semblance might deceive the truth,   5
  That I to manhood am arrived so near,
  And inward ripeness doth much less appear,
  That some more timely-happy spirits endu'th.
Yet be it less or more, or soon or slow,

33. *deep:* high.
37. *unshorn:*the conventional classical epithet for Apollo, who was the god of both the sun and poetry.
38. *Hebe:* daughter of Zeus, and cupbearer to the gods.
40. The poet's soaring imagination may fly down from heaven through the concentric spheres that surround the earth. See "The Universe," pp. 461–63, below.
46. *beldam:* granny.
48. *Demodocus:* the bard whose song of the Trojan War made Odysseus cry (*Od.* 8. 521).
† Written in 1631 or 1632 and published in *Poems* (1645). In the draft of a letter to an unknown friend, in Milton's hand, this sonnet appears as an example of "my nightward thoughts some while since."
3. *full career:* full speed.
5. *semblance:* appearance.
8. *timely-happy:* lucky with respect to time.
9–12. *Yet be it less . . . will of Heaven:* yet whether my maturity is greater or less, comes sooner or later, it will be adequate to whatever challenge time and the will of God leads me to.

It shall be still in strictest measure ev'n   10
To that same lot, however mean or high,
Toward which Time leads me, and the will of Heav'n;
  All is, if I have grace to use it so,
  As ever in my great task-Master's eye.

From Of Reformation in England
and
The Causes that Hitherto Have Hindered It†

In two books.
Written to a Friend.

*   *   *

O, sir, I do now feel myself inwrapped on the sudden into those mazes and labyrinths of dreadful and hideous thoughts, that which way to get out, or which way to end, I know not, unless I turn mine eyes, and with your help lift up my hands to that eternal and propitious throne, where nothing is readier than grace and refuge to the distresses of mortal suppliants: and it were a shame to leave these serious thoughts less piously than the heathen were wont to conclude their graver discourses.

Thou, therefore, that sittest in light and glory unapproachable, parent of angels and men! next, thee I implore, omnipotent King, Redeemer of that lost remnant whose nature thou didst assume, ineffable and everlasting Love! and thou, the third subsistence of divine infinitude, illumining Spirit, the joy and solace of created things! one Tripersonal[1] godhead! look upon this thy poor and almost spent and expiring church, leave her not thus a prey to these importunate wolves, that wait and think long till they devour thy tender flock; these wild boars that have broke into thy vineyard, and left the print of their polluting hoofs on the souls of thy servants. O let them not bring about their damned designs, that stand now at the entrance of the bottomless pit, expecting the watchword to open and let out those dreadful locusts and scorpions, to reinvolve us in that pitchy cloud of infernal darkness, where we shall never more see the sun of thy truth again, never hope for the cheerful

---

10. *Still:* always. *ev'n:* equal.
11. *mean:* lowly.
13–14. *All is . . . task-Master's eye.* Perhaps this means that time is endless, as it is in my master's eye, if I am favored by him to use it as if it were, i.e., be patient. Milton concluded Sonnet 19 (see p. 393 below) with the line "They also serve who only stand and wait." For Milton patience was a heroic virtue, cf. *PL* IX 31–32.
† The concluding paragraphs of Milton's first anti-episcopal tract, published in May 1641. Reprinted from the revised edition of *The Student's Milton,* ed. Frank Allen Patterson (New York, 1933) 468–69. The footnotes are by Don M. Wolfe and William Alfred, in *The Complete Prose Works of John Milton,* vol. 1 (New Haven, 1953) 613–17.
1. Contrary to Milton's position in *PL* and *CD,* in which he is plainly unitarian. In *PL* Milton speaks of Christ as "by merit more than birthright, Son of God" (III.308).

dawn, never more hear the bird of morning sing. Be moved with pity at the afflicted state of this our shaken monarchy, that now lies laboring under her throes, and struggling against the grudges of more dreaded calamities.

O, thou, that, after the impetuous rage of five bloody inundations,[2] and the succeeding sword of intestine war, soaking the land in her own gore, didst pity the sad and ceaseless revolution of our swift and thick-coming sorrows; when we were quite breathless, of thy free grace didst motion peace, and terms of covenant with us; and having first well nigh freed us from antichristian thraldom, didst build up this Britannic empire to a glorious and enviable height, with all her daughter-islands about her; stay us in this felicity, let not the obstinacy of our half-obedience and will-worship bring forth that viper of sedition, that for these fourscore years hath been breeding to eat through the entrails of our peace; but let her cast her abortive spawn without the danger of this travailing and throbbing kingdom: that we may still remember in our solemn thanks-givings, how for us, the northern ocean even to the frozen Thule[3] was scattered with the proud shipwrecks of the Spanish armada, and the very maw of hell ransacked, and made to give up her concealed destruction, ere she could vent it in that horrible and damned blast.

O how much more glorious will those former deliverances appear, when we shall know them not only to have saved us from greatest miseries past, but to have reserved us for greatest happiness to come! Hitherto thou hast but freed us, and that not fully, from the unjust and tyrannous claim of thy foes; now unite us entirely, and appropriate us to thyself, tie us everlastingly in willing homage to the prerogative of thy eternal throne.

And now we know, O thou our most certain hope and defence, that thine enemies have been consulting all the sorceries of the great whore,[4] and have joined their plots with that sad intelligencing tyrant[5] that mischiefs the world with his mines of Ophir[6], and lies thirsting to revenge his naval ruins that have larded our seas: but let them all take counsel together, and let it come to nought; let them decree, and do thou cancel it; let them gather themselves, and be scattered; let them embattle themselves, and be broken; let them embattle, and be broken, for thou art with us.

---

2. Milton here evidently refers to the invasions of the Romans, the Picts and Scots, the Anglo-Saxons, the Danes, and the Normans.
3. Thule is the name given to some land vaguely to the north of Britain by Pytheas, the Greek geographer (whose work we know only through fragments and hearsay). The name came to be applied to such various coasts to the north of Scotland as the Shetlands, Norway, even Iceland, and came, figuratively, to mean the northernmost limit of the world.
4. See Rev. 17.1, 19.2. The Puritans frequently called the Roman Catholic Church the "Whore of Babylon."
5. Philip II of Spain (1556–98), who had sent out workers and informers to combat Protestantism in England and Europe.
6. See 1 Kings 10.11. Ophir was a region rich in gold; Milton's reference is to the South American holdings of the king of Spain.

Then, amidst the hymns and hallelujahs of saints, some one may perhaps be heard offering at high strains in new and lofty measures to sing and celebrate thy divine mercies and marvellous judgments in this land throughout all ages; whereby this great and warlike nation, instructed and inured to the fervent and continual practice of truth and righteousness, and casting far from her the rags of her old vices, may press on hard to that high and happy emulation to be found the soberest, wisest, and most Christian people at that day, when thou, the eternal and shortly expected King, shalt open the clouds[7] to judge the several kingdoms of the world, and distributing national honors and rewards to religious and just commonwealths, shalt put an end to all earthly tyrannies, proclaiming thy universal and mild monarchy through heaven and earth; where they undoubtedly, that by their labors, counsels, and prayers, have been earnest for the common good of religion and their country, shall receive above the inferior orders of the blessed, the regal addition of principalities, legions, and thrones[8] into their glorious titles, and in supereminence of beatific vision, progressing the dateless and irrevoluble circle of eternity, shall clasp inseparable hands with joy and bliss, in overmeasure for ever.

But they contrary, that by the impairing and diminution of the true faith, the distresses and servitude of their country, aspire to high dignity, rule, and promotion here, after a shameful end in this life, (which God grant them,) shall be thrown down eternally into the darkest and deepest gulf of hell, where, under the despiteful control, the trample and spurn of all the other damned, that in the anguish of their torture, shall have no other ease than to exercise a raving and bestial tyranny over them as their slaves and negroes, they shall remain in that plight for ever, the basest, the lower-most, the most dejected, most underfoot, and down-trodden vassals of perdition.

7. See Matt. 24.30 and John 1.51.
8. Principalities and thrones are the names of two of the nine orders of angels. The other seven orders are angels, archangels, virtues, powers, dominations, cherubim, and seraphim. *Legions* is Milton's word for these remaining seven orders.

From The Reason of Church Government
Urged Against Prelaty†

*   *   *

Lastly, I should not choose this manner of writing, wherein knowing myself inferior to myself, led by the genial¹ power of nature to another task, I have the use, as I may account it, but of my left hand. And though I shall be foolish in saying more to this purpose, yet, since it will be such a folly, as wisest men going about to commit, have only confessed and so committed, I may trust with more reason, because with more folly, to have courteous pardon. For although a poet, soaring in the high reason of his fancies,² with his garland and singing robes about him, might, without apology, speak more of himself than I mean to do; yet for me sitting here below in the cool element of prose, a mortal thing among many readers of no empyreal conceit,³ to venture and divulge unusual things of myself, I shall petition to the gentler sort, it may not be envy to me. I must say, therefore, that after I had for my first years, by the ceaseless diligence and care of my father, (whom God recompense!) been exercised to the tongues, and some sciences,⁴ as my age would suffer, by sundry masters and teachers, both at home and at the schools, it was found that whether aught was imposed me by them that had the overlooking, or betaken to of mine own choice in English, or other tongue, prosing or versing, but chiefly this latter, the style, by certain vital signs it had, was likely to live. But much latelier in the private academies of Italy, whether I was favored to resort, perceiving that some trifles which I had in memory, composed at under twenty or thereabout, (for the manner is, that every one must give some proof of his wit and reading there,) met with acceptance above what was looked for; and other things, which I had shifted in scarcity of books and

---

† This selection, from the preface to Book II of Milton's pamphlet *The Reason of Church Government Urged Against Prelaty* (1642), is the most valuable of three autobiographical passages that appear in Milton's prose works: it is the most informative, and it is not, like the other two, written in self-defense (the other two appear in *An Apology Against . . . Smectymnuus* and *The Second Defense of the English People*. *Reason of Church Government*, the fourth of a series of five pamphlets, was the first that carried the name of the author: "By Mr. John Milton." The definitive edition of the work is that of Ralph A. Haug, in *Complete Prose Works of John Milton*, vol. 1 (New Haven, 1953) 736–861.

    In the title, *Reason* means the rationale, or the arguments in favor of. The *church government* Milton argues for is the Presbyterian form, which was more democratic than *Prelaty*, or rule by bishops and the state.

1. Generative.
2. Imagination.
3. Lofty conceptions.
4. What Milton meant by *sciences* is suggested in a sentence in his essay "Of Education": "Having thus passed the principles of arithmetic, geometry, astronomy and geography, with a general compact [summary] of physics [natural things], [the students] may descend in mathematics to the instrumental science of trigonometry, and from thence to fortification, architecture, enginery [machinery] or navigation. And in natural philosophy [science] they may proceed leisurely from the history of meteors, minerals, plants and living creatures, as far as anatomy."

conveniences to patch up amongst them, were received with written encomiums, which the Italian is not forward to bestow on men of this side the Alps; I began thus far to assent both to them and divers of my friends here at home, and not less to an inward prompting which now grew daily upon me, that by labor and intense study, (which I take to be my portion in this life,) joined with the strong propensity of nature, I might perhaps leave something so written to aftertimes, as they should not willingly let it die. These thoughts at once possessed me, and these other; that if I were certain to write as men buy leases, for three lives and downward,[5] there ought no regard be sooner had than to God's glory, by the honor and instruction of my country. For which cause, and not only for that I knew it would be hard to arrive at the second rank among the Latins, I applied myself to that resolution, which Ariosto followed against the persuasions of Bembo,[6] to fix all the industry and art I could unite to the adorning of my native tongue, not to make verbal curiosities the end, (that were a toilsome vanity,) but to be an interpreter and relater of the best and sagest things among mine own citizens throughout this island in the mother dialect. That what the greatest and choicest wits of Athens, Rome, or modern Italy, and those Hebrews of old did for their country, I, in my proportion, with this over and above, of being a Christian, might do for mine; not caring to be once named abroad, though perhaps I could attain to that, but content with these British islands as my world whose fortune hath hitherto been, that if the Athenians, as some say, made their small deeds great and renowned by their eloquent writers, England hath had her noble achievements made small by the unskilful handling of monks and mechanics.[7]

Time serves not now, and perhaps I might seem too profuse to give any certain account of what the mind at home, in the spacious circuits of her musing, hath liberty to propose to herself, though of highest hope and hardest attempting; whether that epic form whereof the two poems of Homer, and those other two of Virgil and Tasso,[8] are a diffuse, and the book of Job a brief model: or whether the rules of Aristotle[9] herein are strictly to be kept, or nature to be followed, which in them that know art, and use judgment, is no transgression, but an enriching of art: and lastly, what king or knight, before the conquest, might be chosen in whom to lay the pattern of a Christian hero. And as Tasso gave to a prince of Italy his choice whether he would command him to write of

---

5. A very long time. A lease for three lives extends to the death of the longest lived of three persons named in the lease.
6. When Pietro Bembo, an Italian Renaissance poet, tried to persuade Ariosto not to write his *Orlando Furioso* in Italian, Ariosto said he would rather be preeminent among Tuscan poets than second or third among the Latin poets.
7. Manual laborers.
8. I.e., the *Il.*, the *Od.*, the *Aen.*, and *Jerusalem Delivered*.
9. Aristotle's *Poetics*, a collection of notes on the art of poetry, mainly of dramatic and epic poems, had become, almost two thousand years after they were written, a handbook for writing and for judging poems.

Godfrey's expedition against the Infidels, or Belisarius against the Goths, or Charlemain against the Lombards;[1] if to the instinct of nature and the emboldening of art aught may be trusted, and that there be nothing adverse in our climate,[2] or the fate of this age, it haply would be no rashness, from an equal diligence and inclination, to present the like offer in our own ancient stories; or whether those dramatic constitutions, wherein Sophocles and Euripides reign, shall be found more doctrinal and exemplary to a nation. The Scripture also affords us a diverse pastoral drama in the Song of Solomon, consisting of two persons, and a double chorus, as Origen[3] rightly judges. And the Apocalypse of St. John[4] is the majestic image of a high and stately tragedy, shutting up and intermingling her solemn scenes and acts with a sevenfold chorus of hallelujahs and harping symphonies: and this my opinion the grave authority of Pareus,[5] commenting that book, is sufficient to confirm. Or if occasion shall lead, to imitate those magnific odes and hymns, wherein Pindarus and Callimachus[6] are in most things worthy; some others in their frame judicious, in their matter most an end faulty. But those frequent songs throughout the law and prophets beyond all these, not in their divine argument alone, but in the very critical art of composition, may be easily made appear over all the kinds of lyric poesy to be incomparable. These abilities, wheresoever they be found, are the inspired gift of God, rarely bestowed, but yet to some (though most abuse) in every nation; and are of power, beside the office of a pulpit, to imbreed and cherish[7] in a great people the seeds of virtue and public civility, to allay the perturbations of the mind, and set the affections in right tune; to celebrate in glorious and lofty hymns the throne and equipage of God's almightiness, and what he works, and what he suffers to be wrought with high providence in his church; to sing the victorious agonies of martyrs and saints, the deeds and triumphs of just and pious nations, doing valiantly through faith against the enemies of Christ; to deplore the general relapses of kingdoms and states from justice and God's true worship. Lastly, whatsoever in religion is holy and sublime, in virtue amiable or grave, whatsoever hath passion or admiration in all the changes of that which is called fortune from without, or the wily subtleties and refluxes of man's thoughts from within; all these things with a solid and treatable smoothness to paint out and describe. Teaching over the whole book of sanctity and virtue, through all the instances of example, with such delight to

1. Tasso chose the first.
2. Milton took seriously the theory that climate affected one's creative powers. Cf. PL IX.45.
3. One of the first great Christian scholars, Origen's knowledge of Greek philosohy and literature enhanced his commentaries on the Bible.
4. The biblical Book of Revelation.
5. The contemporary author of A Commentary on the Revelation.
6. Pindar was the author of great Greek odes, and Callimachus was an Alexandrian scholar famous for his hymns.
7. Foster.

those especially of soft and delicious temper,[8] who will not so much as look upon truth herself, unless they see her elegantly dressed; that whereas the paths of honesty and good life appear now rugged and difficult, though they be indeed easy and pleasant, they will then appear to all men both easy and pleasant, though they were rugged and difficult indeed. And what a benefit this would be to our youth and gentry, may be soon guessed by what we know of the corruption and bane which they suck in daily from the writings and interludes[9] of libidinous and ignorant poetasters, who having scarce ever heard of that which is the main consistence of a true poem, the choice of such persons as they ought to introduce, and what is moral and decent to each one; do for the most part lay up vicious principles in sweet pills to be swallowed down, and make the taste of virtuous documents harsh and sour. But because the spirit of man cannot demean itself lively in this body, without some recreating intermission of labor and serious things, it were happy for the commonwealth, if our magistrates, as in those famous governments of old, would take into their care, not only the deciding of our contentious lawcases and brawls, but the managing of our public sports and festival pastimes; that they might be, not such as were authorized a while since,[1] the provocations of drunkenness and lust, but such as may inure and harden our bodies by martial exercises to all warlike skill and performance; and may civilize, adorn, and make discreet our minds by the learned and affable meeting of frequent academies, and the procurement of wise and artful recitations, sweetened with eloquent and graceful enticements to the love and practice of justice, temperance, and fortitude, instructing and bettering the nation at all opportunities, that the call of wisdom and virtue may be heard everywhere, as Solomon saith: "She crieth without, she uttereth her voice in the streets, in the top of high places, in the chief concourse, and in the openings of the gates." Whether this may not be, not only in pulpits, but after another persuasive method, at set and solemn paneguries,[2] in theatres, porches,[3] or what other place or way may win most upon the people to receive at once both recreation and instruction, let them in authority consult. The thing which I had to say, and those intentions which have lived within me ever since I could conceive myself anything worth to my country, I return to crave excuse that urgent reason hath plucked from me, by an abortive and foredated discovery. And the accomplishment of them lies not but in a power above man's to promise; but that none hath by more studious ways endeavored, and with more unwearied spirit

8. Sensuous temperament.
9. Dramatic performances.
1. In 1633 Charles I, perhaps in order to infuriate the Puritans, issued an order, called the Book of Sports, making games and dancing lawful on Sundays.
2. Public assemblies.
3. Church porches, sometimes used as stages for players, speakers, or preachers.

that none shall, that I dare almost aver of myself, as far as life and free leisure will extend; and that the land had once enfranchised herself from this impertinent[4] yoke of prelaty, under whose inquisitorious and tyrannical duncery no free and splendid wit can flourish. Neither do I think it shame to convenant with any knowing reader, that for some few years yet I may go on trust with him toward the payment of what I am now indebted, as being a work not to be raised from the heat of youth, or the vapors of wine; like that which flows at waste from the pen of some vulgar amorist,[5] or the trencher fury of a rhyming parasite,[6] nor to be obtained by the invocation of dame memory and her siren daughters,[7] but by devout prayer to that eternal Spirit who can enrich with all utterance and knowledge, and sends out his seraphim with the hallowed fire of his altar to touch and purify the lips of whom he pleases: to this must be added industrious and select reading, steady observation, insight into all seemly and generous arts and affairs; till which in some measure be compassed, at mine own peril and cost, I refuse not to sustain this expectation from as many as are not loth to hazard so much credulity upon the best pledges that I can give them. Although it nothing content me to have disclosed thus much beforehand, but that I trust hereby to make it manifest with what small willingness I endure to interrupt the pursuit of no less hopes than these, and leave a calm and pleasing solitariness, fed with cheerful and confident thoughts, to embark in a troubled sea of noises and hoarse disputes, put from beholding the bright countenance of truth in the quiet and still air of delightful studies, to come into the dim reflection of hollow antiquities sold by the seeming bulk, and there be fain to club[8] quotations with men whose learning and belief lies in marginal stuffings, who, when they have, like good sumpters,[9] laid ye down their horse-loads of citations and fathers at your door, with a rhapsody of who and who were bishops here or there, ye may take off their packsaddles, their day's work is done, and episcopacy, as they think, stoutly vindicated. Let any gentle apprehension that can distinguish learned pains from unlearned drudgery imagine what pleasure or profoundness can be in this, or what honor to deal against such adversaries. But were it the meanest under-service, if God by his secretary[1] conscience enjoin it, it were sad for me if I should draw back; for me especially, now when all men offer their aid to help, ease, and lighten the difficult labors of the church, to whose service, by the intentions of my parents and friends, I was destined of a child, and in mine own resolutions: till coming to some maturity of years, and per-

4. Presumptuous.
5. Writer of erotic verse.
6. Poetic frenzy induced by heavy eating and drinking of a rhymster who writes for pay.
7. The goddess Memory was said to be the mother of the Muses, each of whom presided over a different art of science—e.g., dance, history, epic poetry, lyric poetry, etc.
8. Collect.
9. Drivers of packhorses.
1. One entrusted with the secrets or commands of God.

ceiving what tyranny had invaded the church, that he who would take orders must subscribe slave, and take an oath[2] withal, which, unless he took with a conscience that would retch, he must either straight perjure, or split his faith; I thought it better to prefer a blameless silence before the sacred office of speaking, bought and begun with servitude and forswearing. Howsoever, thus church-outed by the prelates, hence may appear the right I have to meddle in these matters, as before the necessity and constraint appeared.

From The Doctrine and Discipline of Divorce Restored to the Good of Both Sexes (1643)[†]

[On July 1, 1643, about ten months after Milton's wife of six weeks had left him to return to her family, the Westminster Assembly of Divines convened for its first meeting. A large group of laymen and clergymen, it had been commissioned by Parliament to reform the Church of England. One month later, an anonymous, forty-eight-page pamphlet was published bearing the following title page:

The Doctrine and Discipline of Divorce:
Restored to the Good of Both Sexes,
From the bondage of Canon Law, and other mistakes,
to Christian freedom, guided by the Rule of Charity.
Wherein also many places of Scripture have
recovered their long-lost meaning.
Seasonable to be now thought on in the
Reformation intended.

* * *

LONDON,
Printed by T.P. and M.S. in Goldsmith's Alley. 1 6 4 3.

Milton offered the Assembly a concrete suggestion: make incompatibility legitimate grounds for divorce. Had he been arguing only for his own freedom, he might just as well have urged the Assembly to make desertion grounds for divorce. But he chose a harder argument because, the tract suggests, he found loveless marriage more unnatural and more painful.

Canon, or ecclesiastical law, which concerns the theory (doctrine) and practice (discipline) of the sacraments, of which marriage was one, had

---

2. The oath of the canons of 1604 included acknowledgment of the king as the "only supreme governor" of the realm, belief that "The Book of Common Prayer, and of ordering of Bishops, Priests, and Deacons" was according to the word of God, and subscription to the 39 Articles.

† With the kind permission of Oxford University Press this stylistically modernized abridgement of the first edition (1643) is taken from the text established by Stephen Orgel and Jonathan Goldberg for their Oxford Authors edition of *John Milton* (Oxford and New York, 1990) 182–226. That edition is the source of the information in some of the following footnotes. Other notes owe something to Lowell W. Coolidge's definitive edition of the second edition (1644) of the tract, in *Complete Prose Works*, vol. 2 (New Haven, 1959) 217–356. The present selection is about one-third the length of the first edition.

developed in the Roman Catholic Church over the centuries. The Church of England had appropriated much of it, and the English Crown and Parliament had enforced the decrees and judgments of the ecclesiastical courts—unlike some other post-Reformation governments that had made marriage a civil matter. So Milton's proposed reform would be a step in the right direction, toward individual freedom (and virtue), as well as toward the separation of church and state.

It has been observed that though Milton proposed his reformation "to the good of both sexes," he nowhere in the argument refers to the possibility of a woman's divorcing a man. Perhaps the explanations of that neglect should include a recognition that Milton was more interested in getting a law changed than in discoursing on marriage in the abstract. He was addressing the Westminster Assembly of Divines and Parliament, exclusively male audiences.

One of the interesting things in the manifesto of the title page is the cocksureness of the author, who claims to have "recovered the long-lost meanings" of "many places of Scripture." Lesser writers could make a persuasive case simply on grounds of reason and the law of nature, but the authority of the Canon Law was based on what the Bible said ("places of Scripture") and on what generations of learned commentators had said the passages meant. What the Bible says seems inconsistent, and the councils and commentators did not all agree. Moses and St. Paul don't sound as if they agreed. Still, Milton thought he could remove the inconsistency by reinterpreting a few of the crucial passages.

His most effective argument with the deeply religious people in his audience was probably his appeal to the notion that Christ had freed his followers from much of the law of the Old Testament, and that people freed from the bondage of the canon law could be "guided by the Rule of Charity." And perhaps he implied that nothing that Paul said about marriage could be inconsistent with what he said about the indispensable virtue of love: "Now abideth faith, hope, charity, these three; but the greatest of these is charity." *Charity*, the Greek-derived word used in the King James Version for *love*, is the last word in Milton's little book, which carried as an epigraph some words of Christ that seemed to say that a good teacher is like a good steward, able to bring forth good things both old and new (from the old Law and the new "Christian" Dispensation).

It was a radical proposal, however, and Milton could hardly have been unprepared for the outrage it elicited, from conservative and liberal alike. Presbyterians, whom he had recently defended with his eloquence, were no less incensed than Anglicans.]

Many men, whether it be their fate or fond[1] opinion, easily persuade themselves, if God would but be pleased a while to withdraw his just punishments from us, and to restrain what power either the devil or any earthly enemy hath to work us woe, that then man's nature would find immediate rest and releasement from all evils. But verily they who think so, if they be such as have a mind large enough to take into their thoughts

---

1. Foolish.

a general survey of human things, would soon prove themselves in that opinion far deceived. For though it were granted us by divine indulgence to be exempt from all that can be harmful to us from without, yet the perverseness of our folly is so bent, that we should never lin[2] hammering out of our own hearts, as it were out of a flint, the seeds and sparkles of new miseries to ourselves, till all were in a blaze again.

*   *   *

What thing more instituted to[3] the solace and delight of man than marriage? And yet the misinterpreting of some scripture, directed mainly against the abusers of the law for divorce given by Moses,[4] hath changed the blessing of matrimony not seldom into a familiar and coinhabiting mischief; at least into a drooping and disconsolate household captivity, without refuge or redemption. So ungoverned and so wild a race doth superstition run us, from one extreme of abused liberty into the other of unmerciful restraint. For although God in the first ordaining of marriage[5] taught us to what end he did it, in words expressly implying the apt and cheerful conversation[6] of man with woman, to comfort and refresh him against the evil of solitary life, not mentioning the purpose of generation till afterwards, as being but a secondary end in dignity, though not in necessity: yet now, if any two be but once handed[7] in the church, and have tasted in any sort of the nuptial bed, let them find themselves never so mistaken in their dispositions through any error, concealment, or misadventure, that through their different tempers,[8] thoughts, and constitutions, they can neither be to one another a remedy against loneliness, nor live in any union or contentment all their days; yet they shall, so they be but found suitably weaponed to the least possibility of sensual enjoyment, be made, spite of antipathy, to fadge[9] together, and combine as they may to their unspeakable wearisomeness, and despair of all sociable delight in the ordinance which God established to that very end. What a calamity is this, and, as the wise man, if he were alive, would sigh out in his own phrase, what a "sore evil is this under the sun!"[1] All which we can refer justly to no other author than the canon law and her adherents, not consulting with charity, the interpreter and guide of our faith, but resting in the mere element[2] of the

2. Cease.
3. Established for.
4. The law is in Deut. 24.1: "When a man hath taken a wife, and married her, and it come to pass that she find no favor in his eyes, because he hath found some uncleanness in her: then let him write her a bill of divorcement, and give it in her hand, and send her out of his house." For the misinterpretation, see p. 373, below.
5. Milton alludes to Gen. 2.18: "And the Lord God said, it is not good that the man should be alone: I will make him an help meet for him"; And Gen. 2.24: "Therefore shall a man leave his father and mother, and shall cleave to his wife: and they shall be one flesh."
6. Intimacy.
7. Pledged to one another.
8. Temperaments.
9. Fit.
1. See 5.13 in Eccles., supposed to have been written by King Solomon, the "wise man."
2. Raw data.

text; doubtless by the policy of the devil to make that gracious ordinance become unsupportable, that what with men not daring to venture upon wedlock, and what with men wearied out of it, all inordinate licence might abound.

It was for many ages that marriage lay in disgrace with most of the ancient doctors, as a work of the flesh, almost a defilement, wholly denied to priests, and the second time dissuaded to all, as he that reads Tertullian or Jerome[3] may see at large. Afterwards it was thought so sacramental[4] that no adultery could dissolve it; yet there remains a burden on it as heavy as the other two were disgraceful or superstitious, and of as much iniquity, crossing a law not only written by Moses, but charactered in us by nature, of more antiquity and deeper ground than marriage itself; which law is to force nothing against the faultless proprieties of nature, yet that this may be colorably done,[5] our Saviour's words touching divorce are, as it were, congealed into a stony rigour, inconsistent both with his doctrine and his office; and that which he preached only to the conscience[6] is by canonical tyranny snatched into the compulsive censure of a judicial court, where laws are imposed even against the venerable and secret power of nature's impression, to love, whatever cause be found to loathe—which is a heinous barbarism both against the honor of marriage, the dignity of man and his soul, the goodness of Christianity, and all the human respects of civility. Notwithstanding that some the wisest and gravest among the Christian emperors, who had about them, to consult with, those of the Fathers then living, who for their learning and holiness of life are still with us in great renown, have made their statutes and edicts concerning this debate far more easy and relenting in many necessary cases, wherein the canon is inflexible. And Hugo Grotius,[7] a man of these times, one of the best learned, seems not obscurely to adhere in his persuasion to the equity of those imperial decrees, in his notes upon the Evangelists, much allaying the outward roughness of the text, which hath for the most part been too immoderately expounded; and excites the diligence of others to inquire further into this question, as containing many points which have not yet been explained. By which, and by mine own apprehension of what public duty each man owes, I conceive myself exhorted among the rest to communicate such thoughts as I have, and offer them now in this general labor of reformation to the candid view both of church and magistrate, especially because I see it the hope of good men that those irregular and unspiritual courts have spun their utmost date in this land, and some better course must now be constituted.

3. *Tertullian* and *Jerome* were two of the early Christian scholars ("ancient doctors") whose writings were influential in the formation of Christian theology.
4. So irreversible, like baptism, extreme unction, and entering holy orders.
5. Made to seem true.
6. Urged, not ordered.
7. See p. 321, n. 4, above.

He therefore that by adventuring shall be so happy as with success to ease and set free the minds of ingenuous and apprehensive[8] men from this needless thraldom; he that can prove it lawful and just to claim the performance of a fit and matchable[9] conversation, no less essential to the prime scope of marriage than the gift of bodily conjunction, or else to have an equal plea of divorce as well as for that corporal deficiency, he that can but lend us the clue that winds out this labyrinth of servitude[1] to such a reasonable and expedient liberty as this, deserves to be reckoned among the public benefactors of civil and humane life above the inventors of wine and oil; for this is a far dearer, far nobler and more desirable cherishing to man's life, unworthily exposed to sadness and mistake, which he shall vindicate.

*　*　*

To remove, therefore, if it be possible, this great and sad oppression, which through the strictness of a literal interpreting hath invaded and disturbed the dearest and most peaceable estate of household society, to the overburdening, if not the overwhelming, of many Christians better worth than to be so deserted of the church's considerate care, this position shall be laid down, first proving, then answering, what may be objected either from Scripture or light of reason:

That indisposition, unfitness, or contrariety of mind arising from a cause in nature unchangeable, hindering and ever likely to hinder the main benefits of conjugal society, which are solace and peace, is a greater reason of divorce than natural frigidity, especially if there be no children and that there be mutual consent.

For all sense and reason and equity reclaims[2] that any law or covenant how solemn or strait soever, either between God and man or man and man, though of God's joining, should bind against a prime and principal scope of its own institution, and of both or either party covenanting;[3] neither can it be of force to engage a blameless creature to his own perpetual sorrow, mistaken for his expected solace, without suffering charity to step in and do a confessed good work of parting those whom nothing holds together but this of God's joining, falsely supposed against the express end of his own ordinance. And what his chief end was of creating woman to be joined with man, his own instituting words declare and are infallible to inform us what is marriage and what is no marriage, unless we can think them set there to no purpose: "It is not good," saith

---

8. Honorable and perceptive.
9. Meet and appropriate to a good "match."
1. Show us a way out of this maze of laws that enslave us, as Ariadne gave Theseus the thread by means of which he could find his way out of the Minotaur's labyrinth.
2. Rejects (the idea).
3. Work against one of the chief aims of the law or covenant and of those who made the covenant.

he, "that man[4] should be alone. I will make him a help meet for him."
From which words so plain, less cannot be concluded, nor is by any
learned interpreter, than that in God's intention a meet and happy
conversation is the chiefest and the noblest end of marriage, for we find
here no expression so necessarily implying carnal knowledge as this
prevention of loneliness to the mind and spirit of man. And indeed it
is a greater blessing from God, more worthy so excellent a creature as
man is, and a higher end to honor and sanctify the league of marriage
whenas the solace and satisfaction of the mind is regarded and provided
for before the sensitive pleasing of the body. And with all generous[5]
persons married thus it is that where the mind and person pleases aptly,
there some unaccomplishment of the body's delight may be better borne
with than when the mind hangs off in an unclosing disproportion,
though the body be as it ought; for there all corporal delight will soon
become unsavoury and contemptible. And the solitariness of man, which
God had namely and principally ordered to prevent by marriage, hath
no remedy, but lies under a worse condition than the loneliest single
life; for in single life the absence and remoteness of a helper might inure
him to expect his own comforts out of himself, or to seek with hope;
but here the continual sight of his deluded thoughts, without cure, must
needs be to him, if especially his complexion[6] incline him to melan-
choly, a daily trouble and pain of loss, in some degree like that which
reprobates[7] feel. Lest therefore so noble a creature as man should be
shut up incurably under a worse evil by an easy mistake in that ordinance
which God gave him to remedy a less evil, reaping to himself sorrow
while he went to rid away solitariness, it cannot avoid to be concluded
that if the woman be naturally so of disposition as will not help to
remove, but help to increase that same God-forbidden loneliness which
will in time draw on with it a general discomfort and dejection of mind
not beseeming either Christian profession or moral conversation, un-
profitable and dangerous to the commonwealth, when the household
estate, out of which must flourish forth the vigor and spirit of all public
enterprises, is so ill-contented and procured at home, and cannot be
supported; such a marriage can be no marriage, whereto the most honest
end is wanting; and the aggrieved person shall do more manly to be
extraordinary and singular in claiming the due right whereof he is frus-
trated than to piece up his lost contentment by visiting the stews, or
stepping to his neighbor's bed, which is the common shift in this mi-
fortune; or else by suffering his useful life to waste away and be lost
under a secret affliction of an unconscionable size to human strength.

How vain, therefore, is it, and how preposterous in the canon law,

4. The King James Version reads "the man."
5. Unselfish.
6. Temperament.
7. People rejected by God.

to have made such careful provision against the impediment of carnal performance, and to have had no care about the unconversing inability of mind so defective to the purest and most sacred end of matrimony, and that the vessel of voluptuous enjoyment must be made good to him that has taken it upon trust, without any caution; whenas the mind, from whence must flow the acts of peace and love—a far more precious mixture than the quintessence of an excrement—though it be found never so deficient and unable[8] to perform the best duty of marriage in a cheerful and agreeable conversation, shall be thought good enough, however flat and melancholious it be, and must serve, though to the eternal disturbance and languishing of him that complains him.[9] Yet wisdom and charity, weighing God's own institution, would think that the pining of a sad spirit wedded to loneliness should deserve to be freed, as well as the impatience of a sensual desire so providently relieved. * * *

But some are ready to object that the disposition ought seriously to be considered before. But let them know again that, for all the wariness [that] can be used, it may yet befall a discreet man to be mistaken in his choice: the soberest and best governed men are least practised in these affairs; and who knows not that the bashful muteness of a virgin may ofttimes hide all the unliveliness and natural sloth which is really unfit for conversation; nor is there that freedom of access granted or presumed as may suffice to a perfect discerning till too late; and where any indisposition is suspected, what more usual than the persuasion of friends that acquaintance, as it increases, will amend all. And lastly, it is not strange though many who have spent their youth chastely are in some things not so quick-sighted while they haste too eagerly to light the nuptial torch; nor is it therefore that for a modest error a man should forfeit so great a happiness, and no charitable means to release him, since they who have lived most loosely, by reason of their bold accustoming, prove most successful in their matches, because their wild affections unsettling at will have been as so many divorces to teach them experience. Whenas the sober man honoring the appearance of modesty, and hoping well of every social virtue under that veil, may easily chance to meet, if not with a body impenetrable, yet often with a mind to all other due conversation inaccessible, and to all the more estimable and superior purposes of matrimony useless and almost lifeless; and what a solace, what a fit help such a consort would be through the whole life of a man, is less pain to conjecture than to have experience.

And that we may further see what a violent cruel thing it is to force the continuing of those together whom God and nature in the gentlest end of marriage never joined, divers evils and extremities that follow upon such a compulsion shall here be set in view. * * *

8. No matter how deficient and unable it may be found.
9. Bewails (his fate).

* * * Lastly, the supreme dictate of charity is hereby many ways neglected and violated; which I shall forthwith address to prove. First, we know St Paul saith, "It is better to marry than to burn.[1] Marriage therefore was given as a remedy of that trouble: but what might this burning mean? Certainly not the mere motion of carnal lust, not the mere goad of a sensitive[2] desire: God does not principally take care for such cattle. What is it then but that desire which God put into Adam in Paradise before he knew the sin of incontinence; that desire which God saw it was not good that man should be left alone to burn in; the desire and longing to put off an unkindly solitariness by uniting another body, but not without a fit soul to his, in the cheerful society of wedlock? Which if it were so needful before the fall, when man was much more perfect in himself, how much more is it needful now against all the sorrows and casualties of this life to have an intimate and speaking help, a ready and reviving associate in marriage? Whereof, who misses by chancing on a mute and spiritless mate remains more alone than before, and in a burning less to be contained than that which is fleshly, and more to be considered, as being more deeply rooted even in the faultless innocence of nature. As for that other burning, which is but as it were the venom of a lusty and over-abounding concoction, strict life and labor, with the abatement of a full diet, may keep that low and obedient enough; but this pure and more inbred desire of joining to itself in conjugal fellowship a fit conversing soul (which desire is properly called love) "is stronger than death", as the spouse of Christ thought; "many waters cannot quench it, neither can the floods drown it."[3] This is that rational burning that marriage is to remedy, not to be allayed with fasting, nor with penance to be subdued, which how can he assuage who by mishap hath met the unmeetest and most unsuitable mind? Who hath the power to struggle with an intelligible[4] flame, not in Paradise to be resisted, become now more ardent by being failed of what in reason it looked for; and even then most unquenched when the importunity of a provender burning[5] is well enough appeased, and yet the soul hath obtained nothing of what it justly desires. Certainly such a one forbidden to divorce is in effect forbidden to marry, and compelled to greater difficulties than in a single life; for if there be not a more human burning which marriage must satisfy, or else may be dissolved, than that of copulation, marriage cannot be honorable for the mere reducing and terminating of lust between two, seeing many beasts in voluntary and chosen couples live together as unadulterously, and are as truly married in that respect. But all ingenuous men will see that the dignity and

---

1. 1 Cor. 7.9.
2. Sensual.
3. Song Sol. 8.6–7. Christian exegetes interpreted this secular love song of the Old Testament as a dialogue of love between Christ and the Church.
4. Mental.
5. Urge to feed.

blessing of marriage is placed rather in the mutual enjoyment of that which the wanting soul needfully seeks, than of that which the plenteous body would jollily give away. Hence it is that Plato[6] in his festival discourse brings in Socrates relating what he feigned to have learned from the prophetess Diotima, how Love was the son of Penury, begot of Plenty in the garden of Jupiter. Which divinely sorts[7] with that which in effect Moses tells us: that Love was the son of Loneliness, begot in Paradise by that sociable and helpful aptitude which God implanted between man and woman toward each other.[8] * * *

Thirdly, yet it is next to be feared, if he must be still bound without reason by a deaf rigor, that when he perceives the just expectance of his mind defeated, he will begin even against law to cast about where he may find his satisfaction more complete, unless he be a thing heroically virtuous; and that are not the common lump of men, for whom chiefly the laws ought to be made; though not to their sins, yet to their unsinning weaknesses—it being above their strength to endure the lonely estate which while they shunned they are fallen into. And yet there follows upon this a worse temptation; for if he be such as hath spent his youth unblamably, and laid up his chiefest earthly comforts in the enjoyment of a contented marriage, nor did neglect that furtherance which was to be obtained therein by constant prayers, when he shall find himself bound fast to an uncomplying discord of nature, or, as it oft happens, to an image of earth and phlegm,[9] with whom he looked to be the copartner of a sweet and gladsome society, and sees withal that his bondage is now inevitable, though he be almost the strongest Christian, he will be ready to despair in virtue, and mutin[1] against divine providence. And this doubtless is the reason of those lapses and that melancholy despair which we see in many wedded persons—though they understand it not, or pretend other causes because they know no remedy—and is of extreme danger; therefore when human frailty surcharged is at such a loss, charity ought to venture much, and use bold physic, lest an overtossed faith endanger to shipwreck.

Fourthly, marriage is a covenant the very being whereof consists not in a forced cohabitation and counterfeit performance of duties, but in unfeigned love and peace. Thence saith Solomon in Ecclesiastes,[2] "Live joyfully with the wife whom thou lovest all thy days, for that is thy portion." How then where we find it impossible to rejoice or to love can we obey this precept? How miserably do we defraud ourselves of that comfortable portion which God gives us by striving vainly to glue an error together which God and nature will not join, adding but more

6. In *Symposium* 203.
7. Is consistent.
8. Gen. 2.18–24.
9. One of the four humors (see p. 463, below). Phlegmatic people were sluggish, cold, dull.
1. Rebel.
2. Eccles. 9.9.

vexation and violence to that blissful society by our importunate super-stition, that will not hearken to St Paul, I Cor. 7, who speaking of marriage and divorce, determines plain enough in general that God therein "hath called us to peace," and not "to bondage." Yea, God himself commands in his law more than once, and by his prophet Malachi,[3] as Calvin and the best translations read, that "he who hates, let him divorce"; that is, he who cannot love or delight.

I cannot therefore be so diffident as not securely to conclude that he who can receive nothing of the most important helps in marriage, being thereby disenabled to return that duty which is his with a clear and hearty countenance, and thus continues to grieve whom he would not, and is no less grieved—that man ought even for love's sake and peace to move divorce upon good and liberal conditions to the divorced. And it is a less breach of wedlock to part with wise and quiet consent betimes than still to soil and profane that mystery of joy and union with a polluting sadness and perpetual distemper, for it is not the outward continuing of marriage that keeps whole that covenant, but whosoever does most according to peace and love, whether in marriage or in divorce, he it is that breaks marriage least, it being so often written that "love only is the fulfilling of every commandment."

Fifthly, as those priests of old were not to be long in sorrow,[4] or if they were, they could not rightly execute their function, so every true Christian in a higher order of priesthood is a person dedicate to joy and peace, offering himself a lively sacrifice of praise and thanksgiving, and there is no Christian duty that is not to be seasoned and set off with cheerfulness; which in a thousand outward and intermitting crosses[5] may yet be done well, as in this vale of tears: but in such a bosom[6] affliction as this, which grinds the very foundations of his inmost nature, when he shall be forced to love against a possibility, and to use dissimulation against his soul in the perpetual and ceaseless duties of a husband, doubtless his whole duty of serving God must needs be blurred and tainted with a sad unpreparedness and dejection of spirit, wherein God has no delight. Who sees not therefore how much more Christianly it would be to break by divorce that which is more broken by undue and forcible keeping, rather that "to cover the altar of the Lord with continual tears, so that he regardeth not the offering any more",[7] rather than that the whole worship of a Christian man's life should languish and fade away beneath the weight of an immeasureable grief and discouragement. And because some think the children of a second matrimony succeeding a divorce would not be a holy seed, why should we not think them more

---

3. Mal. 2.16. The King James Version, however, reads, "For the Lord, the God of Israel, saith that he hateth putting away."
4. The law, in Lev. 21.1–6, was that priests were not to prolong acts of mourning.
5. Trials.
6. Intimate.
7. Mal. 2.13.

holy than the offspring of a former ill-twisted wedlock, begotten only
out of a bestial necessity, without any true love or contentment or joy
to their parents? So that in some sense we may call them the "children
of wrath"[8] and anguish, which will as little conduce to their sanctifying
as if they had been bastards; for nothing more than disturbance of mind
suspends us from approaching to God—such a disturbance especially
as both assaults our faith and trust in God's providence, and ends, if
there be not a miracle of virtue on either side, not only in bitterness
and wrath, the canker of devotion, but in a desperate and vicious care-
lessness when he sees himself, without fault of his, trained[9] by a deceitful
bait into a snare of misery, betrayed by an alluring ordinance and then
made the thrall of heaviness and discomfort by an undivorcing law of
God, as he erroneously thinks, but of man's iniquity, as the truth is; for
that God prefers the free and cheerful worship of a Christian before the
grievous and exacted observance of an unhappy marriage, besides that
the general maxims of religion assure us, will be more manifest by
drawing a parallel argument from the ground of divorcing an idolatress,
which was, lest she should alienate his heart from the true worship of
God: and, what difference is there whether she pervert him to superstition
by enticing sorcery, or disenable him in the whole service of God through
the disturbance of her unhelpful and unfit society, and so drive him at
last through murmuring and despair to thoughts of atheism. Neither
doth it lessen the cause of separating, in that the one willingly allures
him from the faith, the other perhaps unwillingly drives him; for in the
account of God it comes all to one that the wife loses him a servant,
and therefore by all the united force of the Decalogue[1] she ought to be
disbanded[2]—unless we must set marriage above God and charity, which
is a doctrine of devils no less than forbidding to marry.

*   *   *

Seventhly, the canon law and divines[3] consent that if either party be
found contriving against the other's life, they may be severed by divorce,
for a sin against the life of marriage is greater than a sin against the bed:
the one destroys, the other but defiles. The same may be said touching
those persons who, being of a pensive nature and course of life, have
summed up all their solace in that free and lightsome conversation which
God and man intends in marriage; whereof when they see themselves
deprived by meeting an unsociable consort, they ofttimes resent one
another's mistake so deeply that long it is not ere grief end one of them.
When therefore this danger is foreseen, that the life is in peril by living
together, what matter is it whether helpless grief or wilful practice be
the cause? This is certain, that the preservation of life is more worth

8. Eph. 2.3. The phrase means unregenerate, or unsaved people.
9. Lured.
1. The Ten Commandments.
2. Dismissed.
3. The clergy.

than the compulsory keeping of marriage; and it is no less than cruelty to force a man to remain in that state as the solace of his life which he and his friends know will be either the undoing or the disheartening of his life. And what is life without the vigor and spiritful exercise of life? How can it be useful either to private or public employment? Shall it be therefore quite dejected, though never so valuable, and left to molder away in heaviness for the superstitious and impossible performance of an ill-driven bargain? Nothing more inviolable than vows made to God; yet we read in Numbers[4] that if a wife had made such a vow, the mere will and authority of her husband might break it. How much more may he break the error of his own bonds with an unfit and mistaken wife, to the saving of his welfare, his life, yes, his faith and virtue, from the hazard of overstrong temptations! For if man be lord of the sabbath[5] to the curing of a fever, can he be less than lord of marriage in such important causes as these?

* * *

But what are all these reasonings worth, will some reply, whenas the words of Christ[6] are plainly against all divorce, "except in case of fornication"? Let such remember, as a thing not to be denied, that all places of Scripture wherein just reason of doubt arises from the letter are to be expounded by considering upon what occasion everything is set down, and by comparing other texts. The occasion which induced our Saviour to speak of divorce was either to convince[7] the extravagance of the Pharisees in that point, or to give a sharp and vehement answer to a tempting question. And in such cases, that we are not to repose all upon the literal terms of so many words, many instances will teach us, wherein we may plainly discover how Christ meant not to be taken word for word, but, like a wise physician, administering one excess against another, to reduce us to a perfect mean. Where the Pharisees were strict, there Christ seems remiss; where they were too remiss, he saw it needful to seem most severe—in one place he censures an unchaste look to be adultery already committed, another time he passes over actual adultery with less reproof than for an unchaste look, not so heavily condemning secret weakness as open malice. So here he may be justly thought to have given this rigid sentence against divorce, not to cut off all remedy from a good man who finds himself consuming away in a disconsolate and unenjoyed matrimony, but to lay a bridle upon the bold abuses of those overweening rabbis, which he could not more effectually do than

---

4. Num. 6.15.
5. When Jesus cured a man with a withered hand on the Sabbath, knowing that the scribes and the Pharisees would think he was breaking the law, he said, "The Son of man is Lord . . . of the Sabbath" (Luke 6.5–10).
6. "It hath been said, Whosoever shall put away his wife, let him give her a writing of divorcement: but I say unto you, that whosoever shall put away his wife, saving for the cause of fornication, causes her to commit adultery and whosoever shall marry her that is divorced committeth adultery" (Matt. 5.31–32).
7. Confute.

by a countersway of restraint curbing their wild exorbitance almost into the other extreme—as when we bow things the contrary way to make them come to their natural straightness. And that this was the only intention of Christ is most evident, if we attend but to his own words and protestation made in the same sermon, not many verses before he treats of divorcing, that he came not to abrogate from the law "one jot or tittle", and denounces against them that shall so teach.

* * *

Moses, Deut. 24: 1, established a grave and prudent law full of moral equity, full of due consideration towards nature, that cannot be resisted, a law consenting with the laws of wisest men and civilest nations: that when a man hath married a wife, if it come to pass that he cannot love her by reason of some displeasing natural quality or unfitness in her, let him write her a bill of divorce. The intent of which law undoubtedly was this, that if any good and peaceable man should discover some helpless disagreement or dislike either of mind or body whereby he could not cheerfully perform the duty of a husband without perpetual dissembling of offence and disturbance to his spirit, rather than to live uncomfortably and unhappily both to himself and to his wife, rather than to continue undertaking a duty which he could not possibly discharge, he might dismiss her whom he could not tolerably, and so not conscionably, retain. And this law the spirit of God by the mouth of Solomon, Prov. 30: 21, 23, testifies to be a good and a necessary law, by granting it that to "dwell with a hated woman" (for *hated* the Hebrew word signifies) "is a thing that nature cannot endure". What follows then, but that law must remedy what nature cannot undergo?

Now that many licentious and hardhearted men took hold of this law to cloak their bad purposes is nothing strange to believe. And these were they, not for whom Moses made the law, God forbid, but whose hardness of heart taking ill advantage by this law he held it better to suffer as by accident, where it could not be detected, rather than good men should lose their just and lawful privilege of remedy. Christ therefore having to answer these tempting Pharisees, according as his custom was, not meaning to inform their proud ignorance what Moses did in the true intent of the law, which they had ill cited, suppressing the true cause for which Moses gave it, and extending it to every slight matter, tells them their own, what Moses was forced to suffer by their abuse of his law. Which is yet more plain if we mark that our Saviour, in the fifth of Matth., cites not the law of Moses, but the pharisaical tradition falsely grounded upon that law. And in those other places, chapter 19 and Mark 10, the Pharisees cite the law, but conceal the wise and humane reason there expressed; which our Saviour corrects not in them, whose pride deserved not his instruction, only returns them what is proper to them: "Moses for the hardness of your heart suffered you" (that is, such as you) "to put away your wives; and to you he wrote this precept" for that cause which ("to you") must be read with an impression,[8] and understood limitedly of such as covered ill purposes under that law; for it was seasonable that they should hear their own unbounded licence rebuked, but not seasonable for them to hear a good man's requisite liberty explained.

* * * Therefore we must look higher, since Christ himself recalls us to the beginning, and we shall find that the primitive reason of never divorcing was that sacred and not vain promise of God to remedy man's loneliness by "making him a help meet for him," though not now in perfection, as at first, yet still in proportion as things now are. And this is repeated, (verse 20), when all other creatures were fitly associated and brought to Adam, as if the divine power had been in some care and deep thought, because "there was not yet found a help meet for man". And can we so slightly depress[9] the all-wise purpose of a deliberating God, as if his consultation had produced no other good for man but to join him with an accidental companion of propagation, which his sudden[1] word had already made for every beast? Nay, a far less good to man it will be found if she must at all adventures[2] be fastened upon him individually.[3] And therefore even plain sense and equity, and, which is above them both, the all-interpreting voice of charity herself cries loud that this primitive reason, this consulted promise of God "to make a meet help" is the only cause that gives authority to this command of not divorcing to be a command. And it might be further added that if the true definition of a wife were asked in good earnest, this clause of being "a meet help" would show itself so necessary and so essential in that demonstrative argument that it might be logically concluded, therefore she who naturally and perpetually is no meet help can be no wife; which clearly takes away the difficulty of dismissing such a one.

* * *

Lastly, Christ himself[4] tells who should not be put asunder, namely, those whom God hath joined. A plain solution of this great controversy, if men would but use their eyes: for when is it that God may be said to join? When the parties and their friends consent? No, surely; for that may concur to lewdest ends. Or is it when church rites are finished? Neither; for the efficacy of those depends upon the presupposed fitness of either party. Perhaps after carnal knowledge? Least of all; for that may join persons whom neither law nor nature dares join. 'Tis left that only then when the minds are fitly disposed and enabled to maintain a cheerful conversation, to the solace and love of each other, according as God intended and promised in the very first foundation of matrimony, "I

8. Emphasis.
9. Devalue.
1. Unpremeditated.
2. Recklessly.
3. Inseparably.
4. Matt. 19.6: "What therefore God hath joined together, let no man put asunder."

will make him a help-meet for him"; for surely what God intended and promised, that only can be thought to be of his joining, and not the contrary.

* * *

Lastly, all law is for some good that may be frequently attained without the admixture of a worse inconvenience; but the law forbidding divorce never attains to any good end of such prohibition, but rather multiplies evil. If it aim at the establishment of matrimony, we know that cannot thrive under a loathed and forced yoke, but is daily violated; if it seek to prevent the sin of divorcing, that lies not in the law to prevent; for he that would divorce and marry again but for the law, hath in the sight of God done it already. Civil or political sin it never was, neither to Jew nor Gentile, nor by any judicial intendment of Christ, only culpable as it transgresses the allowance of Moses in the inward man, which not any law but conscience only can evince. The law can only look whether it be an injury to the divorced, which in truth it can be none as a mere separation; for if she consent, wherein has the law to right her? or consent not, then is it either just and so deserved, or if unjust, such in all likelihood was the divorcer, and to part from an unjust man is happiness, and no injury to be lamented. But suppose it be an injury, the law is not able to amend it unless she think it other than a miserable redress to return back from whence she was expelled, or but entreated to be gone, or else to live apart still married without marriage, a married widow. Last, if it be to chasten the divorcer, what law punishes a deed which is not moral but natural, a deed which cannot certainly be found to be an injury, or how can it be punished by prohibiting the divorce, but that the innocent must equally partake? So that we see the law can to no rational purpose forbid divorce; it can only take care that the conditions of divorce be not injurious.

But what, shall then the disposal of that power return again to the master of family?[5] Wherefore not, since God there put it, and the presumptuous canon thence bereft it? This only must be provided, that the ancient manner be observed in the presence of the minister and other grave selected elders, who after they shall have admonished and pressed upon him the words of our Savior, and he shall have protested[6] in the faith of the eternal gospel and the hope he has of happy resurrection that otherwise than thus he cannot do, and thinks himself and this his case not contained in that prohibition of divorce which Christ pronounced, the matter not being of malice, but of nature, and so not capable of reconciling; to constrain him further were to unchristian him, to unman him, to throw the mountain of Sinai upon him, with the weight of the whole law to boot, flat against the liberty and essence of

5. Deut 24.1: "When a man hath taken a wife, . . . then let him write her a bill of divorcement. . . ."
6. Solemnly declared.

the gospel; and yet nothing available[7] either to the sanctity of marriage, the good of husband, wife or children, nothing profitable either to church or commonwealth. But this would bring in confusion: be of good cheer, it would not: it wrought so little disorder among the Jews that from Moses till after the captivity not one of the prophets thought it worth rebuking; for that of Malachi[8] well looked into will appear to be not against divorcing, but rather against keeping strange concubines, to the vexation of their Hebrew wives. If, therefore, we Christians may be thought as good and tractable as the Jews were (and certainly the prohibitors of divorce presume us to be better, then less confusion is to be feared for this among us than was among them. If we be worse, or but as bad, which lamentable examples confirm we are, then have we more, or at least as much, need of this permitted law as they to whom God expressly gave it under a harsher covenant. Let not, therefore, the frailty of man go on thus inventing needless troubles to itself, to groan under the false imagination of a strictness never imposed from above enjoining that for duty which is an impossible and vain supererogating. 'Be not righteous overmuch' is the counsel of Ecclesiastes,[9] why shouldest thou destroy thyself? Let us not be thus overcurious to strain at atoms, and yet to stop every vent and cranny of permissive liberty, lest nature, wanting those needful pores and breathing-places which God hath not debarred our weakness, either suddenly break out into some wide rupture of open vice and frantic heresy, or else inwardly fester with repining and blasphemous thoughts under an unreasonable and fruitless rigour of unwarranted law. Against which evils nothing can more beseem the religion of the church or the wisdom of the state than to consider timely and provide. And in so doing let them not doubt but they shall vindicate the misreputed honor of God and his great lawgiver by suffering him to give his own laws according to the condition of man's nature best known to him, without the unsufferable imputation of dispersing legally with many ages of ratified adultery. They shall recover the misattended words of Christ to the sincerity of their true sense from manifold contradictions, and shall open them with the key of charity. Many helpless Christians they shall raise from the depth of sadness and distress, utterly unfitted as they are to serve God or man; many they shall reclaim from obscure and giddy sects, many regain from dissolute and brutish license, many from desperate hardness, if ever that were justly pleaded. They shall set free many daughters of Israel not wanting much of her sad plight whom "Satan had bound eighteen years.[1] Man they shall restore

7. Suitable.
8. Mal. 2.14–16. The Revised Standard Version (1952) reads, "For I hate divorce says the Lord God of Israel." Most translators and commentators, before and since, disagreed with Milton.
9. Eccles. 7.16.
1. See Luke 13.11–16, for the account of Jesus' incurring the indignation of a rabbi for healing a crippled woman on the Sabbath.

to his just dignity and prerogative in nature, preferring the soul's free peace before the promiscuous draining of a carnal rage. Marriage, from a perilous hazard and snare, they shall reduce[2] to be a more certain haven and retirement of happy society, when they shall judge according to God and Moses (and how not then according to Christ?), when they shall judge it more wisdom and goodness to break that covenant seemingly, and keep it really, than by compulsion of law to keep it seemingly, and by compulsion of blameless nature to break it really, at least if it were ever truly joined. The vigor of discipline they may then turn with better success upon the prostitute looseness of the times, when men, finding in themselves the infirmities of former ages, shall not be constrained above the gift of God in them to unprofitable and impossible observances never required from the civilest, the wisest, the holiest nations, whose other excellencies in moral virtue they never yet could equal. Last of all, to those whose mind still is to maintain textual restrictions[3] whereof the bare sound cannot consist sometimes with humanity, much less with charity, I would ever answer by putting them in remembrance of a command above all commands which they seem to have forgot, and who spake it; in comparison whereof, this which they so exalt is but a petty and subordinate precept. "Let them go," therefore, with whom I am loath to couple them, yet they will needs run into the same blindness with the Pharisees; "let them go therefore," and consider well what this lesson means, "I will have mercy and not sacrifice,"[4] for on that "saying all the law and prophets depend"[5] much more the gospel, whose end and excellence is mercy and peace. Or if they cannot learn that, how will they hear this, which yet I shall not doubt to leave with them as a conclusion, that God the Son hath put all other things under his own feet,[6] but his commandments he hath left all under the feet of charity.

From the Second Edition of The Doctrine and Discipline of Divorce (1644)†

[The difference between the first and second editions of *The Doctrine and Discipline of Divorce* is suggested by Milton's revisions in the title page. "Restored from the bondage of canon law, and other mistakes, to Christian freedom, guided by the law of Charity" became "restored . . . to the true

2. Restore.
3. Enforce the letter of the law.
4. Matt. 9.13: "I [Jesus to his critics] will have mercy and not sacrifice: for I am come not to call the righteous, but sinners to repentance."
5. Matt. 22.40.
6. 1 Cor. 15.27: "For he hath put all things under his feet."
† Reprinted with the permission of Macmillan Publishing Company from *John Milton: Complete Poems and Major Prose* by Merritt Y. Hughes. Copyright © 1985, 1957 by Macmillan Publishing Company.

meaning of Scripture in the Law and Gospel compared," thereby calling attention to the author's renewed efforts to resolve the apparent contradictions between what Moses said in the Old Testament and what Jesus said to the Pharisees in the New with regard to divorce. In his much-expanded second edition, Milton "greatly enlarged the function of general ideas: reason, nature, and Christian Liberty" (Ernest Sirluck, *Complete Prose* 2.150). That he was primarily interested in changing the laws concerning divorce, not in just debating the issues, is suggested by his addressing the new edition "To the Parliament of England with the Assembly," and by his pointing out in that address how the issues of domestic freedom were related to those of civil freedom.

An epigraph that did not appear in the first edition also hints at a shift in Milton's aims. Milton had been told that among those who were condemning his *Doctrine* as heresy were Presbyterians whom he had worked with in the pamphlet campaign against the power of the prelacy, and that among these critics some had not even read his work. For their benefit he quoted Prov. 18.13: "He that answereth a matter before he heareth it, it is folly and shame unto him."

Though some who were outraged had not read the tract, there were many who at least had bought it—the first edition seems to have sold out in six months. The new edition was almost twice as long as the first. The first tells us much of Milton's ideas about marriage and perhaps of his private experience; the second shows us more of his rhetorical power and more evidence of his erudition. The introduction to the second edition sets the oratorical style that Milton had practiced during his schooldays and that he would soon turn to again in writing *Areopagitica*.]

TO THE PARLIAMENT OF ENGLAND WITH THE ASSEMBLY.
THE AUTHOR J.M.

If it were seriously asked (and it would be no untimely question, renowned Parliament, select Assembly) who of all teachers and masters that have ever taught hath drawn the most disciples after him, both in religion and in manners, it might be not untruly answered, custom. * * * Error supports custom, custom countenances error; and these two between them would persecute and chase away all truth and solid wisdom out of human life, were it not that God, rather than man, once in many ages calls together the prudent and religious counsels of men deputed to repress the encroachments and to work off the inveterate blots and obscurities wrought upon our minds by the subtle insinuating of error and custom; who, with the numerous and vulgar train of their followers, make it their chief design to envy and cry down the industry of free reasoning, under the terms of humor[1] and innovation; as if the womb of teeming truth were to be closed up if she presume to bring forth aught that sorts not with their unchewed notions and suppositions. Against which notorious injury and abuse of man's free soul to testify

---

1. Peculiarity.

and oppose the utmost that study and true labor can attain, heretofore the incitement of men reputed grave hath led me among others. And now the duty and the right of an instructed Christian calls me through the chance of good or evil report to be the sole advocate of a discountenanced truth: a high enterprise, Lords and Commons, a high enterprise and a hard, and such as every seventh son of a seventh son does not venture on.

Nor have I amidst the clamor of so much envy and impertinence whither to appeal, but to the concourse of so much piety and wisdom here assembled. Bringing in my hands an ancient and most necessary, most charitable and yet most injured, statue of Moses:[2] not repealed ever by him who only had the authority, but thrown side with much inconsiderate neglect under the rubbish of canonical ignorance; as once the whole law was by some such like conveyance in Josiah's time.[3] And he who shall endeavor the amendment of any old neglected grievance in church or state, or in the daily course of life, if he be gifted with abilities of mind that may raise him to so high an undertaking, I grant he hath already much whereof not to repent him. Yet let me aread him not to be the foreman[4] of any misjudged opinion, unless his resolutions be firmly seated in a square and constant mind, not conscious to itself of any deserved blame and regardless of ungrounded suspicions. For this let him be sure, he shall be boarded[5] presently by the ruder sort, but not by discreet and well-nurtured men, with a thousand idle descants[6] and surmises. Who, when they cannot confute the least joint or sinew of any passage in the book, yet God forbid that truth should be truth because they have a boisterous conceit of some pretenses in the writer. But were they not more busy and inquisitive than the apostle[7] commends, they would hear him at least, "rejoicing so the truth be preached, whether of envy or other pretense whatsoever." For truth is as impossible to be soiled by any outward touch as the sunbeam, though this ill hap wait on her nativity, that she never comes into the world but like a bastard, to the ignominy of him that brought her forth; till time, the midwife rather than the mother of truth, have washed and salted the infant, declared her legitimate, and churched the father of his young Minerva from the needless causes of his purgation.[8]

---

2. Deut 24.1, the crucial text: ". . . let him write her a bill of divorcement, etc." Milton pictures himself as pleading the cae of this much-abused law, much as he "asserts [takes the part of] eternal Providence and justifies the ways of God to men" in *PL*.
3. Cf. 2 Kings 22 and 23; and 2 Chron. 34.
4. Spokesman.
5. Accosted.
6. Carping criticisms.
7. Paul, in Phil. 1.18.
8. Minerva was born from the head of Jupiter, hence a brainchild. Among the rites inherited by the Christian church from the Jewish Law, and retained by the Anglican Church, to the unhappiness of the Presbyterians, who thought them too ritualistic, was the "churching" ["purifying" in the Old Law] of mothers after childbirth. Milton's humor here accorded with the oratorical convention calling for an effort to win the sympathy of the audience.

Yourselves can best witness this, worthy patriots, and better will, no doubt, hereafter. For who among ye of the foremost that have travailed in her behalf to the good of church or state, hath not been often traduced to be the agent of his own by-ends, under pretext of reformation? So much the more I shall not be unjust to hope that however infamy or envy may work in other men to do her fretful will against this discourse, yet that the experience of your own uprightness misinterpreted will put ye in mind to give it free audience and generous construction.[9]

* * *

The greatest burden in the world is superstition, not only of ceremonies in the church but of imaginary and scarecrow sins at home. What greater weakening, what more subtle stratagem against our Christian warfare,[1] when besides the gross body of real transgressions to encounter, we shall be terrified by a vain and shadowy menacing of faults that are not? When things indifferent shall be set to overfront[2] us under the banners of sin, what wonder if we be routed, and by this art or our adversary, fall into the subjection of worst and deadliest offenses? The superstition of the papist is, "Touch not, taste not,"[3] when God bids both; and ours is, "Part not, separate not," when God and charity both permits and commands. "Let all your things be done with charity," saith St. Paul; and his master saith, "She is the fulfilling of the law."[4] Yet now a civil, an indifferent, a sometime dissuaded law of marriage, must be forced upon us to fulfil, not only without charity but against her. No place in heaven or earth, except hell, where charity may not enter: yet marriage, the ordinance of our solace and contentment, the remedy of our loneliness, will not admit now either of charity or mercy to come in and mediate or pacify the fierceness of this gentle ordinance, the unremedied loneliness of this remedy. Advise ye well, supreme senate, if charity be thus excluded and expulsed, how ye will defend the untainted honor of your own actions and proceedings.

He who marries, intends as little to conspire his own ruin as he that swears allegiance: and as a whole people is in proportion to an ill government, so is one man to an ill marriage.[5] If they, against any authority, covenant, or statute, may by the sovereign edict of charity save not only their lives but honest liberties from unworthy bondage, as well may he against any private covenant, which he never entered to his mischief, redeem himself from unsupportable disturbances to honest peace and

---

9. This paragraph suggests that Milton had been publicly accused of trying to reform the divorce laws because he himself wanted to get a divorce. No doubt, he tells his audience, you too have had your motives impugned, have been accused of working from a hidden agenda.
1. Apparently an allusion to John Downame's *Christian Warfare* (1604), which contains four chapters on "Satan's Stratagems."
2. Confront.
3. See Col. 2.20–21, where Paul says Christians should not obey the arbitrary teachings of men.
4. See 1 Cor. 16.14 and Rom. 13.10
5. For a discussion of the importance of the idea of this paragraph in the development of Milton's thought, see Sirluck, *Complete Prose* 2. 152–57.

just contentment. And much the rather, for that to resist the highest magistrate through tyrannizing, God never gave us express allowance, only he gave us reason, charity, nature and good example to bear us out; but in this economical[6] misfortune thus to demean ourselves, besides the warrant of those four great directors, which doth as justly belong hither, we have an express law of God, and such a law as whereof our Savior with a solemn threat forbade the abrogating.[7] For no effect of tyranny can sit more heavy on the commonwealth than this household unhappiness on the family. And farewell all hope of true reformation in the state, while such an evil as this lies undiscerned or unregarded in the house: on the redress whereof depends not only the spiritful and orderly life of our grown men, but the willing and careful education of our children.

* * *

It would not be the first or second time since our ancient druids, by whom this island was the cathedral of philosophy to France, left off their pagan rites, that England hath had this honor vouchsafed from heaven, to give out reformation to the world. Who was it but our English Constantine[8] that baptized the Roman empire? Who but the Northumbrian Willibrorde and Winifride of Devon, with their followers, were the first apostles of Germany? Who but Alcium and Wycliffe our countrymen, opened the eyes of Europe, the one in arts, the other in religion? Let not England forget her precedence of teaching nations how to live.

Know, worthies, know and exercise the privilege of your honored country. A greater title I here bring ye than is either in the power or in the policy of Rome to give her monarchs. This glorious act will style ye the defenders of charity.[9] Nor is this yet the highest inscription that will adorn so religious and so holy a defense as this. Behold here the pure and sacred law of God and his yet purer and more sacred name, offering themselves to you, first of all Christian reformers, to be acquitted from the long-suffered ungodly atttibute of patronizing adultery. Defer not to wipe off instantly these imputative blurs and stains cast by rude fancies upon the throne and beauty itself of inviolable holiness, lest some other people more devout and wise than we bereave us this offered immortal glory, our wonted prerogative, of being the first asserters in every great vindication.

For me, as far as my part leads me, I have already my greatest gain, assurance and inward satisfaction to have done in this nothing unworthy of an honest life and studies well employed. * * *

6. Domestic, as distinct from civil.
7. See Matt. 5.19–20.
8. Constantine I, "Constantine the Great," born in what is now Yugoslavia, was crowned emperor in York, where he was living with his father. Milton knew of a legend that Constantine was born in Britain.
9. Of the three Christian virtues, faith, hope, and charity, charity was the greatest. Kings of England were said to be defenders of the faith.

I seek not to seduce the simple and illiterate. My errand is to find out the choicest and the learnedest who have this high gift of wisdom to answer solidly, or to be convinced. I crave if from the piety, the learning, and the prudence which is housed in this place. It might perhaps more fitly have been written in another tongue: and I had done so, but that the esteem I have of my country's judgment, and the love I bear to my native language to serve it first with what I endeavor, made me speak it thus, ere I assay the verdict of outlandish readers. And perhaps also here I might have ended nameless, but that the address of these lines chiefly to the Parliament of England might have seemed ingrateful not to acknowledge by whose religious care, unwearied watchfulness, courageous and heroic resolutions, I enjoy the peace and studious leisure to remain.

The Honorer and Attendant of their
Noble worth and virtues,

JOHN MILTON

From Areopagitica†

[Ten years after he published *Areopagitica*, Milton said he had written it "in order to deliver the press from the restraints with which it was encumbered; [in order] that the power of determining what was true and what was false, what ought to be published and what to be suppressed, might no longer be entrusted to a few illiterate and illiberal [i.e., uneducated] individuals, who refused their sanction to any work which contained views or sentiments at all above the level of the vulgar superstition" (*Second Defense of the English People*, 1654). The restraints that "encumbered" the press were essentially those established by a "licensing order" issued by Parliament in June 1643, largely, it would appear, at the request of the press itself—acting through the Stationers Company, the guild of owners of licensed presses, who were interested in protecting their exclusive rights to publish.

Like most lobbies, it argued for the public good—in this case, the need to suppress "the great late abuses and frequent disorders in printing many false, forged, scandalous, seditious, libelous, and unlicensed books to the great defamation of Religion and government." Others, in and out of Parliament, in those contentious times, were also interested in controlling the press, though their goals were not so clear-cut or unanimous as those of the publishers. The order required that all papers, pamphlets, and books carry the name of the author, the name of the licensed publisher, and an indication

---

† This is not an abridgment of *Areopagitica*, which is a carefully wrought work of art of great integrity about eight times as long as the sum of these excerpts. It is, rather, a selection of passages of particular interest to readers of *Paradise Lost*.

The text is essentially that of Merritt Y. Hughes, *John Milton: Complete Poems and Major Prose* (New York, 1957) 716–49, here reprinted by permission of Macmillan Publishing Company. Many of the notes derive from that edition. The definitive edition of *Areopagitica* is that of Ernest Sirluck, *Complete Prose Works of Milton* (New Haven, 1959) 158–83, 480–570.

that the publication had been licensed by "such person or persons as both, or either" of the houses of Parliament should appoint.

Like the motives of those who urged Parliament to issue the order, Milton's motives in protesting it were mixed. Early in 1644 Parliament was petitioned to enforce the order against, among others, John Milton, author of the *Doctrine and Discipline of Divorce*, the second edition of which had just been published without license. That petition came to nothing, but Milton was becoming notorious as the author of an unlicensed piece of licentiousness, and in August he and his work were cited by the Stationers Company as a flagrant example of the need for stricter enforcement of the order.

The order seemed to Milton, however, to be more than a personal matter. Like laws about divorce, this repressive law was one more reason to worry about the possibility that the Revolution would succeed only in replacing one sort of conservative tyranny with another—the Church of England with a national Presbyterian Church, empowered to encumber the freedom of those who were seeking the truth and publishing their view of it.

Milton was not arguing for the right of anyone to publish with impunity anything at any time. After publication authors might be prosecuted for libel or other "mischief." But, provided they were prepared to suffer the consequences, John Milton and others should not have to obtain anyone's permission to publish what they wished, especially the permission of the kind of people likely to serve as licensers. And when, near the end Milton makes an exception to "popery and open superstition," he does not make an exception to his proposed ban on prepublication censorship. He speaks, rather, of the currently much-discussed need to tolerate differing opinions among members of congregations and to avoid the multiplication of splinter groups, or the founding of new sects. Like all the anti-Presbyterians, the tolerationists, or Independents, he did not advocate toleration of popery within Protestant churches. Since popery does not tolerate toleration, it should not be tolerated. He does not say all writing except popish writing should be unlicensed.

The full title of the work is "Areopagitica; a speech of Mr. John Milton for the liberty of unlicensed printing, to the Parliament of England." Below it on the title page is a quotation (in Greek) from Euripides' *The Suppliants*, and a translation:

This is true liberty when free born men
Having to advise the public may speak free,
Which he who can, and will, deserves high praise,
Who neither can nor will, may hold his peace;
What can be juster in a state than this?]

Areopagitica

* * *

I deny not but that it is of greatest concernment in the church and commonwealth to have a vigilant eye how books demean themselves, as well as men; and thereafter to confine, imprison, and do sharpest justice on them as malefactors; for books are not absolutely dead things, but do contain a potency of life in them to be as active as that soul was whose progeny they are; nay, they do preserve as in a vial the purest efficacy and extraction of that living intellect that bred them. I know they are as lively, and as vigorously productive, as those fabulous dragon's teeth:[1] and being sown up and down may chance to spring up armed men. And yet, on the other hand, unless wariness be used, as good almost kill a man as kill a good book: who kills a man kills a reasonable creature, God's image; but he who destroys a good book kills reason itself, kills the image of God, as it were, in the eye. Many a man lives a burden to the earth; but a good book is the precious lifeblood of a master spirit, embalmed and treasured up on purpose to a life beyond life. Tis true, no age can restore a life, whereof perhaps there is no great loss; and revolutions of ages do not oft recover the loss of a rejected truth, for the want of which whole nations fare the worse. We should be wary, therefore, what persecution we raise against the living labors of public men, how we spill that seasoned life of man preserved and stored up in books; since we see a kind of homicide may be thus committed, sometimes a martyrdom; and if it extend to the whole impression, a kind of massacre, whereof the execution ends not in the slaying of an elemental life, but strikes at that ethereal and fifth essence,[2] the breath of reason itself; slays an immortality rather than a life.

* * *

Good and evil we know in the field of this world grow up together almost inseparably; and the knowledge of good is so involved and interwoven with the knowledge of evil, and in so many cunning resemblances hardly to be discerned, that those confused seeds which were imposed on Psyche[3] as an incessant labor to cull out, and sort asunder, were not more intermixed. It was from out the rind of one apple tasted, that the knowledge of good and evil, as two twins cleaving together, leaped forth into the world. And perhaps this is that doom which Adam fell into of knowing good and evil—that is to say, of knowing good by evil. As therefore the state of man now is; what wisdom can there be to choose, what continence to forbear,[4] without the knowledge of evil? He that can apprehend and consider vice with all her baits and seeming pleasures, and yet abstain, and yet distinguish, and yet prefer that which is truly better, he is the true warfaring Christian. I cannot praise a fugitive and cloistered virtue unexercised and unbreathed,[5] that never sallies out and seeks her adversary, but slinks out of the race, where that immortal garland is to be run for, not without dust and heat. Assuredly we bring not innocence into the world, we bring impurity much rather; that which

---

1. Those sown by the slayer of the dragon.
2. Something not composed of "elements." See "The Universe," pp. 461–63, below.
3. In revenge for stealing the love of Cupid, Venus made Psyche sort out from a huge pile of mixed seed the various kinds.
4. Endure.
5. Not exhausted.

purifies us is trial, and trial is by what is contrary. That virtue therefore which is but a youngling in the contemplation of evil, and knows not the utmost that vice promises to her followers, and rejects it, is but a blank [6] virtue, not a pure; her whiteness is but an excremental[7] whiteness; which was the reason why our sage and serious poet Spenser (whom I dare be known to think a better teacher than Scotus or Aquinas)[8] describing true temperance under the person of Guion, brings him in with his palmer through the cave of Mammon, and the bower of earthly bliss, that he might see and know, and yet abstain.[9]

Since therefore the knowledge and survey of vice is in this world so necessary to the constituting of human virtue, and the scanning of error to the confirmation of truth, how can we more safely, and with less danger, scout into the regions of sin and falsity, than by reading all manner of tractates, and hearing all manner of reason? And this is the benefit which may be had of books promiscuously[1] read.

* * *

Many there be that complain of divine providence for suffering Adam to transgress. Foolish tongues! when God gave him reason, he gave him freedom to choose, for reason is but choosing; he had been else a mere artificial Adam such an Adam as he is in the motions.[2] We ourselves esteem not of that obedience, or love, or gift, which is of force. God therefore left him free, set before him a provoking object, ever almost in his eyes; herein consisted his merit, herein the right of his reward, the praise of his abstinence. Wherefore did he create passions within us, pleasures round about us, but that these rightly tempered are the very ingredients of virtue? They are not skilful considerers of human things who imagine to remove sin by removing the matter of sin; for, besides that it is a huge heap increasing under the very act of diminishing, though some part of it may for a time be withdrawn from some persons, it cannot from all, in such a universl thing as books are; and when this is done, yet the sin remains entire. Though ye take from a covetous man all his treasure, he has yet one jewel left, ye cannot bereave him of his covetousness. Banish all objects of lust, shut up all youth into the severest discipline that can be exercised in any hermitage, ye cannot make them chaste that came not thither so: such great care and wisdom is required to the right managing of this point. Suppose we could expel sin by this means; look how much we thus expel of sin, so much we expel of virtue: for the matter of them both is the same: remove that, and ye remove them both alike. This justifies the high providence of

---

6. Pale, colorless.
7. Superficial.
8. John Duns Scotus and St. Thomas Aquinas, great scholastic philosophers (Christian "doctors," or teachers) of the thirteenth century.
9. Milton misremembered this episode in the *Faerie Queene* (II.viii).
1. At random.
2. Puppet shows.

God, who, though he command us temperance, justice, continence, yet pours out before us, even to a profuseness, all desirable things, and gives us minds that can wander beyond all limit and saitety. Why should we then affect a rigor contrary to the manner of God and of nature, by abridging or scanting those means, which books freely permitted are, both to the trial of virtue and the exercise of truth?

* * *

And lest some should persuade ye, Lords and Commons, that these arguments of learned men's discouragement at this your order are mere flourishes, and not real, I could recount what I have seen and heard in other countries, where this kind of inquisition tyrannizes; when I have sat among their learned men (for that honor I had) and been counted happy to be born in such a place of philosophic freedom as they supposed England was, while themselves did nothing but bemoan the servile condition into which learning amongst them was brought; that this was it which had damped the glory of Italian wits; that nothing had been there written now these many years but flattery and fustian. There it was that I found and visited the famous Galileo, grown old, a prisoner to the Inquisition, for thinking in astronomy otherwise than the Franciscan and Dominican licensers thought. And though I knew that England then was groaning loudest under the prelatical yoke, nevertheless I took it as a pledge of future happiness, that other nations were so persuaded of her liberty.

Yet was it beyond my hope, that those worthies were then breathing in her air, who should be her leaders to such a deliverance, as shall never be forgotten by any revolution of time that this world hath to finish. When that was once begun, it was as little in my fear that what words of complaint I heard among learned men of other parts uttered against the inquisition, the same I should hear, by as learned men at home, uttered in time of parliament against an order of licensing; and that so generally, that when I had disclosed myself a companion of their discontent, I might say, if without envy, that he[3] whom an honest quæstorship had endeared to the Sicilians was not more by them importuned against Verres, than the favorable opinion which I had among many who honor ye, and are known and respected by ye, loaded me with entreaties and persuasions, that I would not despair to lay together that which just reason should bring into my mind, towards the removal of an understood thraldom upon learning.

* * *

Truth indeed came once into the world with her divine Master, and was a perfect shape most glorious to look on; but when he ascended, and his apostles after him were laid asleep, then straight arose a wicked

3. The people of Sicily who were unjustly treated by their Praetor, Verres, did not urge Cicero more urgently to defend their interests than I was urged by many whom you know and respect to write this speech in defense of the freedom of learning.

race of deceivers, who, as that story goes of the Egyptian Typhon with his conspirators, how they dealt with the good Osiris, took the virgin Truth, hewed her lovely form into a thousand pieces, and scattered them to the four winds. From that time ever since, the sad friends of Truth, such as durst appear, imitating the careful search that Isis made for the mangled body of Osiris, went up and down gathering up limb by limb still as they could find them. We have not yet found them all, Lords and Commons, nor ever shall do, till her Master's second coming; he shall bring together every joint and member, and shall mold them into an immortal feature[4] of loveliness and perfection. Suffer not these licensing prohibitions to stand at every place of opportunity, forbidding and disturbing them that continue seeking, that continue to do our obsequies[5] to the torn body of our martyred saint.

We boast our light; but if we look not wisely on the sun itself, it smites us into darkness. Who can discern those planets that are oft combust,[6] and those stars of brightest magnitude that rise and set with the sun, until the opposite motion of their orbs bring them to such a place in the firmament, where they may be seen evening or morning? The light which we have gained was given us, not to be ever staring on, but by it to discover onward things more remote from our knowledge. It is not the unfrocking of a priest, the unmitering of a bishop, and the removing him from off the presbyterian shoulders that will make us a happy nation: no; if other things as great in the church, and in the rule of life both economical[7] and political, be not looked into and reformed, we have looked so long upon the blaze that Zwinglius and Calvin[8] hath beaconed up to us that we are stark blind.

There be who perpetually complain of schisms and sects, and make it such a calamity that any man dissents from their maxims. It is their own pride and ignorance which causes the disturbing, who neither will hear with meekness, nor can convince, yet all must be suppressed which is not found in their syntagma.[9] They are the troublers, they are the dividers of unity, who neglect and permit not others to unite those dissevered pieces which are yet wanting to the body of Truth. To be still searching what we know not by what we know, still closing up truth to truth as we find it (for all her body is homogeneal and proportional), this is the golden rule in theology as well as in arithmetic,[1] and makes up the best harmony in a church; not the forced and outward union of cold and neutral and inwardly divided minds.

4. Shape.
5. Pay our respects.
6. Within eight degrees and thirty minutes of the sun.
7. Domestic.
8. Ulrich Zwingli, in Zurich, and a few years later John Calvin, in Geneva, were influential founders of the protestantism of the Presbyterians.
9. Compilation of beliefs.
1. In the equation a:b = c:d, one can find the value of any of the four unknowns if the values of the other three are known.

Lords and Commons of England! consider what nation it is whereof
ye are, and whereof ye are the governors; a nation not slow and dull,
but of a quick, ingenious, and piercing spirit, acute to invent, subtle
and sinewy to discourse, not beneath the reach of any point the highest
that human capacity can soar to. Therefore the studies of learning in
her deepest sciences have been so ancient and so eminent among us
that writers of good antiquity and ablest judgment have been persuaded
that even the school of Pythagoras, and the Persian wisdom,[2] took be-
ginning from the old philosophy of this island. And that wise and civil
Roman, Julius Agricola, who governed once here for Cæsar, preferred
the natural wits of Britain before the labored studies of the French. Nor
is it for nothing that the grave and frugal Transylvanian sends out yearly
from as far as the mountainous borders of Russia, and beyond the
Hercynian wilderness,[3] not their youth, but their staid men to learn our
language and our theologic arts. Yet that which is above all this, the
favor and the love of Heaven, we have great argument to think in a
peculiar manner propitious and propending[4] towards us. Why else was
this nation chosen before any other, that out of her, as out of Sion,[5]
should be proclaimed and sounded forth the first tidings and trumpet
of reformation to all Europe? And had it not been the obstinate per-
verseness of our prelates against the divine and admirable spirit of Wy-
cliffe,[6] to suppress him as a schismatic and innovator, perhaps neither
the Bohemian Huss and Jerome,[7] no, nor the name of Luther or of
Calvin, had been ever known: the glory of reforming all our neighbors
had been completely ours. But now, as our obdurate clergy have with
violence demeaned the matter, we are become hitherto the latest and
the backwardest scholars, of whom God offered to have made us the
teachers.

Now once again by all concurrence of signs, and by the general instinct
of holy and devout men, as they daily and solemnly express their
thoughts, God is decreeing to begin some new and great period in his
church, even to the reforming of reformation itself. What does he then
but reveal himself to his servants, and as his manner is, first to his
Englishmen? I say, as his manner is, first to us, though we mark not
the method of his counsels, and are unworthy. Behold now this vast
city, a city of refuge, the mansion house of liberty, encompassed and

2. Though unlike and unrelated, both the Pythagorean school and the Persian wisdom were
essentially mystical.
3. Transylvania enjoyed religious freedom at this time, and the Reformed church was strong.
"Mountainous borders" of Russia may refer to the Carpathian Mountains, which separated
Transylvania from Moldavia, which borderd on Russia, and the "Hercynian wilderness" may
refer to the Transylvanian Alps, Transylvania's southern border. Both ranges were densely
forested.
4. Favorably inclined toward.
5. Mount Zion in Jerusalem, meaning Jerusalem as the birthplace of Christianity.
6. John Wycliffe (1320?–84), and English forerunner of protestantism.
7. Jerome of Prague (d. 1416). He and John Huss (d. 1415) were early Czech reformers, both
influenced by the writings of Wycliffe.

surrounded with his protection; the shop of war hath not there more anvils and hammers waking, to fashion out the plates[8] and instruments of armed justice in defense of beleaguered Truth, than there be pens and heads there sitting by their studious lamps, musing, searching, revolving new notions and ideas wherewith to present, as with their homage and their fealty, the approaching reformation; others as fast reading, trying all things, assenting to the force of reason and convincement.

* * *

What could a man require more from a nation so pliant and so prone to seek after knowledge? What wants there to such a towardly and pregnant soul but wise and faithful laborers, to make a knowing people, a nation of prophets, of sages, and of worthies? We reckon more than five months yet to harvest; there need not be five weeks had we but eyes to lift up the fields are white already.[9] Where there is much desire to learn, there of necessity will be much arguing, much writing, many opinions; for opinion in good men is but knowledge in the making. Under these fantastic terrors of sect and schism, we wrong the earnest and zealous thirst after knowledge and understanding which God hath stirred up in this city.

* * *

* * * It is a lively and cheerful presage of our happy success and victory. For as in a body, when the blood is fresh, the spirits pure and vigorous, not only to vital, but to rational faculties, and those in the acutest and the pertest operations of wit and subtlety, it argues in what good plight and constitution the body is; so when the cheerfulness of the people is so sprightly up, as that it has not only wherewith to guard well its own freedom and safety, but to spare, and to bestow upon the solidest and sublimest points of controversy and new invention, it betokens us not degenerated nor drooping to a fatal decay, but casting off the old and wrinkled skin of corruption to outlive these pangs and wax young again, entering the glorious ways of truth and prosperous virtue, destined to become great and honorable in these latter ages. Methinks I see in my mind a noble and puissant nation rousing herself like a strong man after sleep, and shaking her invincible locks. Methinks I see her as an eagle muing[1] her mighty youth, and kindling her undazzled eyes at the full midday beam; purging and unscaling her long-abused sight at the fountain itself of heavenly radiance; while the whole noise of timorous and flocking birds, with those also that love the twilight, flutter about, amazed at what she means, and in their envious gabble would prognosticate a year of sects and schisms.

8. Armor.
9. Cf. Jesus' words to his disciples in John 4.35: "Say not ye, There are yet four months, and then cometh harvest? behold, I say unto you, Lift up your eyes, and look on the fields; for they are white already to harvest."
1. Moulting—hence "renewing."

What should ye do then? Should ye suppress all this flowery crop of knowledge and new light sprung up and yet springing daily in this city? Should ye set an oligarchy of twenty engrossers[2] over it, to bring a famine upon our minds again, when we shall know nothing but what is measured to us by their bushel? Believe it, Lords and Commons, they who counsel ye to such a suppressing, do as good as bid ye suppress yourselves.

* * *

For who knows not that Truth is strong, next to the Almighty. She needs no policies, nor stratagems, nor licensings to make her victorious—those are the shifts and the defenses that error uses against her power. * * *

Yet is it not impossible that she may have more shapes than one. What else is all that rank of things indifferent, wherein Truth may be on this side, or on the other, without being unlike herself? What but a vain shadow else is the abolition of those ordinances, that handwriting nailed to the cross;[3] what great purchase is this Christian liberty which Paul so often boasts of?[4] His doctrine is, that he who eats, or eats not, regards a day, or regards it not, may do either to the Lord.[5] How many other things might be tolerated in peace and left to conscience, had we but charity, and were it not the chief stronghold of our hypocrisy to be ever judging one another. I fear yet this iron yoke of outward conformity hath left a slavish print upon our necks; the ghost of a linen decency[6] yet haunts us. We stumble, and are impatient at the least dividing of one visible congregation from another, though it be not in fundamentals; and through our forwardness to suppress, and our backwardness to recover, any enthralled piece of truth out of the grip of custom, we care not to keep truth separated from truth, which is the fiercest rent and disunion of all. We do not see that while we still affect by all means a rigid external formality, we may as soon fall again into a gross conforming stupidity, a stark and dead congealment of "wood, and hay, and stubble"[7] forced and frozen together, which is more to the sudden degenerating of a church than many subdichotomies of petty schisms.

Not that I can think well of every light separation, or that all in a church is to be expected "gold and silver and precious stones." It is not possible for man to sever the wheat from the tares,[8] the good fish from the other fry; that must be the angels' ministry at the end of mortal things. Yet if all cannot be of one mind,—as who looks they should be?—this doubtless is more wholesome, more prudent, and more Chris-

2. Monopolists—in this case, the twenty publishers who would control the licensing.
3. Cf. Col. 2.14.
4. Cf. Gal. 5.1.
5. Cf. Rom. 14.6.
6. The old belief in the need for propriety, tradition, fitness, convention, and "outward conformity" in the practice of religion. The Church of England clergy had insisted on proper regalia (e.g., linen vestments).
7. 1 Cor. 3.12.
8. Matt. 13.24–30.

tian, that many be tolerated, rather than all compelled. I mean not tolerated popery and open superstition, which, as it extirpates all religions and civil supremacies, so itself should be extirpate, provided first that all charitable and compassionate means be used to win and regain the weak and the misled; that also which is impious or evil absolutely, either against faith or manners, no law can possibly permit that intends not to unlaw itself; but those neighboring differences, or rather indifferences, are what I speak of, whether in some point of doctrine or of discipline, which though they may be many, yet need not interrupt "the unity of spirit," if we could but find among us the "bond of peace."[9]

* * *

Sonnet 15[†]

Fairfax, whose name in arms through Europe rings,
    Filling each mouth with envy, or with praise,
    And all her jealous monarchs with amaze,
    And rumors loud, that daunt remotest kings,
Thy firm unshaken virtue ever brings   5
    Victory home, though new rebellions raise
    Their Hydra heads, and the false North displays
    Her broken league to imp their serpent wings.
O yet a nobler task awaits thy hand;
    For what can war but endless war still breed,   10
    Till truth and right from violence be freed,
And public faith cleared from the shameful brand
    Of public fraud. In vain doth valor bleed
    While avarice and rapine share the land.

9. Eph. 4.3.
 † Published posthumously; presumably written in August 1648, after the fall of Colchester.
1. *Fairfax*: The brilliant military career of Thomas Fairfax is noted on p. 331, in Masson's account of Milton's life, above.
5. *virtue*: courage.
7. *Hydra heads*: The hydra was a mythical winged water serpent with nine heads. When a head was cut off it was replaced by two. Destroying the hydra was one of Hercules' nine labors. *False North*: the Scots, who had broken a peace treaty. *displays*: spreads out its troops to make a more extended line. But the figure may be that the Scots army spread its "wings" to supply feathers to imp the wings of various rebellions, as falconers "imped" the wings of injured falcons by replacing broken feathers.

Sonnet 16†

*On the proposals of certain ministers at the Committee for
Propagation of the Gospel*

Cromwell, our chief of men, who through a cloud
    Not of war only, but detractions rude,
    Guided by faith and matchless fortitude,
    To peace and truth thy glorious way hast ploughed,
And on the neck of crowned Fortune proud   5
    Hast rear'd God's trophies and his work pursued,
    While Darwen stream with blood of Scots imbrued,
    And Dunbar field resounds thy praises loud,
And Worcester's laureate wreath; yet much remains
    To conquer still; peace hath her victories   10
    No less renowned than war; new foes arise
Threat'ning to bind our souls with secular chains:
    Help us to save free conscience from the paw
    Of hireling wolves whose gospel is their maw.

† In the spring of 1652, Cromwell was a member of the Committee for the Propagation of the
Gospel, which was considering the establishment of a national church to include all sects that
would agree to a set of fifteen tenets. It would be freer than the old Church of England or the
Presbyterian church of Scotland; but it would not be sufficiently independent to please Crom-
well, who, like Milton, wanted a church open to all dissenters. Milton, in fact, wanted no
national church at all, but he held his peace till he heard that in the new established church
the clergymen would all be paid by the state. Hence his plea in the couplet: let us have no
ministers under the power of anyone but God and the congregations they serve: free shepherds,
not subsidized wolves. It was a crucial point in the reformation Cromwell and Milton both
hoped to realize, and Milton finally broke with Cromwell on the issue of a national church
of any kind. The sonnet was published posthumously; Milton did not write the subtitle.
5. *on the neck of*: immediately following. *crowned Fortune proud*: your being crowned by good
fortune of which you can be proud [?].
7–9. *Darwen . . . Dunbar . . . Worcester*: allusions to three of Cromwell's victories, in August
1648, September 1650, and September 1651.

Sonnet 19†

When I consider how my light is spent,
   Ere half my days, in this dark world and wide,
   And that one talent which is death to hide
   Lodged with me useless, though my soul more bent
To serve therewith my Maker, and present   5
   My true account, lest he returning chide,
   "Doth God exact day labor, light denied?"
   I fondly ask; but patience, to prevent
That murmur, soon replies: "God doth not need
   Either man's work or his own gifts; who best   10
   Bear his mild yoke, they serve him best. His state
Is kingly: thousands at his bidding speed,
   And post o'er land and ocean without rest;
   They also serve who only stand and wait."

† If the subject of this poem is Milton's blindness (as asserted in the familiar title Milton did not give it—"On His Blindness), then "light" in line 1 must mean "eyesight," and its date must be about 1652, the year we know Milton became totally blind. But the metaphorical use of "light" for "power of vision" is strained, uncommon, and inconsistent with the style of Milton's imagery, which is scientifically precise. Even if we do not stumble on this metaphor, we still may be puzzled by "Ere half my days." How could Milton have thought at the age of forty-four that he had not yet reached the midpoint in his life?

No one has found a generally satisfactory solution to the puzzle. If, however, one assumes the likelihood that Milton alluded to the biblical "three score years and ten" as man's allotted span, and meant that he had not yet reached the age of thirty-five, then the date of the poem must be about 1640–42. If that is so, "light" must have its more common meaning of inspiration or understanding.

There is good evidence that Milton knew from an early age that his "talent" was that of an extraordinary poet who would write a poem that would become a classic. Loss of his eyesight, though it would make composition a bit more difficult, would not prevent him from serving his "maker" by exploiting his poetic talent. But loss of inspiration, loss of vision or understanding or faith in himself—or simply not discovering "a great argument," story, or subject—would certainly prevent him from presenting his "true account" to the master in the parable of the talents in Matt. 25.14–30.

If the occasion for Sonnet 19 was an attack of fear that though he had been entrusted with a great talent, he had nothing to say, then Milton could have written it in 1643 as well as a dozen years later. Perhaps he did not include it in the 1645 collection because it was similar to Sonnet 7, "How soon hath time," a poem he may have preferred (no matter how posterity has judged them), and he did not wish to publish them in the same volume. Both allude to the parable of the talents, both express impatience to achieve, both are resolved by assertions of confidence in God's providence and the virtue of patience. In Sonnet 7 the disturbing question about why he is so slow in reaching full maturity is answered by his remembering that when the time comes, he will be equal to the task. In Sonnet 19 the reassurance sounds wiser and more convincing. But the replies are both imagined replies to the master in the parable of the talents in Matt. 25. Though Milton experienced doubts, defeats, and distractions, his was a rare example of a life in which integrity of purpose, abiding self-confidence, and, it would seem, religious conviction made him equal to all contingencies.

1. *spent*: used up.
8. *fondly*: foolishly. *prevent*: forestall.
11. *mild yoke*: See Jesus' words in Matt. 11.30: "For my yoke is easy, and my burden is light."

Sonnet 22

Cyriack, this three years' day these eyes, though clear
   To outward view of blemish or of spot,
   Bereft of light their seeing have forgot;
   Nor to their idle orbs doth sight appear
Of sun or moon or star throughout the year,   5
   Or man or woman. Yet I argue not
   Against Heav'n's hand or will, nor bate a jot
   Of heart or hope, but still bear up and steer
Right onward. What supports me, dost thou ask?
   The conscience, friend, to have lost them overplied   10
   In liberty's defense, my noble task,
Of which all Europe talks from side to side.
   This thought might lead me through the world's vain mask.
   Content though blind, had I no better guide.

Sonnet 23†

Methought I saw my late espousèd saint
   Brought to me like Alcestis from the grave,
   Whom Jove's great son to her glad husband gave,
   Rescued from death by force, though pale and faint.
Mine, as whom, washed from spot of child-bed taint,   5
   Purification in the old Law did save,
   And such as yet once more I trust to have
   Full sight of her in heaven without restraint,
Came vested all in white, pure as her mind.
   Her face was veiled, yet to my fancied sight   10
   Love, sweetness, goodness in her person shined
So clear as in no face with more delight.
   But O as to embrace me she inclined,
   I waked, she fled, and day brought back my night.

7. *bate*: diminish.
8. *bear up*: (nautical) set the helm so as to sail before (i.e., against) the wind.
10. *conscience*: awareness. *overplied*: overworked.
† There is no way to know whether the occasion for this sonnet was the death of Milton's first wife, Mary, in 1652, or of his second wife, Katherine, whom Milton married six years after Mary died and Milton became totally blind, in 1658—just as there is no way to know for sure that he dreamed of anyone, or to know when the sonnet was written. But his saying that "her face was veiled" has convinced many readers that the sonnet is about the wife whom the blind man had never seen. Perhaps more than Mary she can be compared with Alcestis, who sacrificed her life to save her husband. But ingenious arguments have been proposed in favor of Mary.
1. *late espousèd saint*: dead, especially recently deceased, wedded person, now among the blessed.
2–4. *Alcestes . . . faint*: In Euripides' tragedy *Alcestis*, Hercules wrestles with death and brings back from the grave Alcestis, wife of Admetus, whose life she had saved by her own death.
6. *Purification in the old Law*: See Lev. 12.

From The Ready and Easy Way to Establish a Free Commonwealth and the Excellence thereof Compared with the Inconveniences and Dangers of Readmitting Kingship in This Nation†

* * *

I have no more to say at present: few words will save us, well considered; few and easy things, now seasonably done. But if the people be so affected as to prostitute religion and liberty to the vain and groundless apprehension that nothing but kingship can restore trade, not remembering the frequent plagues and pestilences that then wasted this city, such as through God's mercy we never have felt since;[1] and that trade flourishes nowhere more than in the free commonwealths of Italy, Germany, and the Low Countries, before their eyes at this day; yet if trade be grown so craving and importunate through the profuse living of tradesmen, that nothing can support it but the luxurious expenses of a nation upon trifles or superfluities; so as if the people generally should betake themselves to frugality, it might prove a dangerous matter, lest tradesmen should mutiny for want of trading; and that therefore we must forego and set to sale religion, liberty, honor, safety, all concernments divine or human, to keep up trading: if, lastly, after all this light among us, the same reason shall pass for current, to put our necks again under kingship, as was made use of by the Jews to return back to Egypt,[2] and to the worship of their idol queen, because they falsely imagined that they then lived in more plenty and prosperity; our condition is not sound, but rotten, both in religion and all civil prudence; and will bring us soon, the way we are marching, to those calamities which attend always and unavoidably on luxury, all national judgments under foreign or domestic slavery: so far we shall be from mending our condition by monarchizing our government, whatever new conceit now possesses us.

However, with all hazard I have ventured what I thought my duty to speak in season, and to forewarn my country in time wherein I doubt not but there be many wise men in all places and degrees, but am sorry

---

† This conclusion of the essay constitutes about 5 percent of the total work. The first edition appeared about a month after General Monk addressed the "Rump" Parliament in such a way as to suggest that the "republican" form of government that had replaced Richard Cromwell's Protectorate a year before would not endure. A second edition was published about two months later, only days before the Restoration of Charles II.

1. Actually there had been no return of the plague since 1625, but some Englishmen agreed with Milton that freedom from the plague during the years since the death of Charles I was a sign of God's pleasure.

2. See Num. 11, for the story of how, having escaped from Egypt, on the long journey to the Promised Land, the Israelites complained to Moses about the dull diet of manna, and remembered "the fish which we did eat in Egypt freely; the cucumbers, and the melons, and the leeks, and the onions, and the garlic: but now our soul is dried away. . . ."

the effects of wisdom are so little seen among us. Many circumstances and particulars I could have added in those things whereof I have spoken: but a few main matters now put speedily in execution, will suffice to recover us and set all right: and there will want at no time who are good at circumstances; but men who set their minds on main matters, and sufficiently urge them, in these most difficult times I find not many.

What I have spoken is the language of that which is not called amiss "The good old Cause:"[3] if it seem strange to any, it will not seem more strange, I hope, than convincing to backsliders. Thus much I should perhaps have said, though I were sure I should have spoken only to trees and stones, and had none to cry to, but with the prophet,[4] "O earth, earth, earth!" to tell the very soil itself, what her perverse inhabitants are deaf to. Nay, though what I have spoke should happen (which thou suffer not, who didst create mankind free! nor thou next, who didst redeem us from being servants of men!)[5] to be the last words of our expiring liberty. But I trust I shall have spoken persuasion to abundance of sensible and ingenuous men; to some, perhaps, whom God may raise of these stones to become children of reviving liberty;[6] and may reclaim, though they seem now choosing them a captain back for Egypt, to bethink themselves a little, and consider whither they are rushing; to exhort this torrent also of the people not to be so impetuous, but to keep their due channel; and at length recovering and uniting their better resolutions, now that they see already how open and unbounded the insolence and rage is of our common enemies, to stay these ruinous proceedings, justly and timely fearing to what a precipice of destruction the deluge of this epidemic madness would hurry us, through the general defection of a misguided and abused multitude.

From Christian Doctrine†

[Sometime in the 1640s Milton began to collect notes in preparation for this work, and shortly after he became blind, he began the text, dictating it in Latin. He was probably well along in the undertaking when he began to write *Paradise Lost,* in the early 1650s, and it seems likely that he finished the treatise some years before he finished the poem. Little is known of the history of the 735-page manuscript of *Christian Doctrine* before 1825, when

---

3. A popular phrase for the Puritan cause.
4. See Jer. 22.29.
5. "Which (i.e., 'what I have spoke') I pray you will not allow to happen, you who created man free, nor thou [Christ] who saved us from being servants of men!) [i.e., subject in matters of conscience to the old Law or to priests of any kind].
6. See Luke 3.8: "God is able of these stones to raise up children unto Abraham."
† The selections here reprinted are from the translation by John Carey, in vol. 6 of *Complete Prose Works of John Milton,* ed. Maurice Kelley (New Haven, 1973), and are reprinted by the kind permission of Yale University Press.

it was discovered in London in the Old State Paper Office by Charles R. Summer, who translated it into English and published it in 1826.

In his prefatory Epistle, Milton referred to the work as his "best and richest possession," and in its opening sentence he deliberately used a formula used by St. Paul in his doctrinal epistles to the members of various churches—at Rome and Corinth and Ephesus, and so on. Assuming, with other Protestants, that the Bible contained the whole truth, and that it was up to individual Christians to find that truth for themselves, Milton aimed to find answers to all the questions it was within the power of human beings to answer. He depended upon logic, on the exercise of his reason, to reach his conclusions, but he supported them by quotations from the Bible (called "proof-texts"), in the manner commonly used in theological, or doctrinal, discourses.

In *De Doctrina Christiana* Milton set down some heretical beliefs, such as that the idea of the Trinity was not supported by the Scriptures: God created Christ, was not coequal with him—or with the Holy Spirit, an entity not clearly identified in the Bible. Another was that God created the universe out of something—not, as the orthodox doctors held, out of nothing. Another was that the body and soul were created simultaneously and died simultaneously. But most of what he found in the Bible was what most of his audience would have agreed was necessarily so.]

John Milton

ENGLISHMAN

To All the Churches of Christ and to All in any part of the world who profess the Christian Faith, Peace, Knowledge of the Truth, and Eternal Salvation in God the Father and in our Lord Jesus Christ.

The process of restoring religion to something of its pure original state, after it had been defiled with impurities for more than thirteen hundred years, dates from the beginning of the last century. Since that time many theological systems have been propounded, aiming at further purification, and providing sometimes brief, sometimes more lengthy and methodical expositions of almost all the chief points of Christian doctrine. This being so, I think I should explain straight away why, if any work has yet been published on this subject which is as exhaustive as possible, I have been dissatisfied with it, and why, on the other hand, if all previous writers have failed in this attempt, I have not been discouraged from making the same attempt myself.

If I were to say that I had focused my studies principally upon Christian doctrine because nothing else can so effectually wipe away those two repulsive afflictions, tyranny and superstition, from human life and the human mind, I should show that I had been concerned not for religion but for life's well-being.

But in fact I decided not to depend upon the belief or judgment of others[1] in religious questions for this reason: God has revealed the way of eternal salvation only to the individual faith of each man, and demands of us that any man who wishes to be saved should work out his beliefs for himself. So I made up my mind to puzzle out a religious creed for myself by my own exertions, and to acquaint myself with it thoroughly. In this the only authority I accepted was God's self-revelation, and accordingly I read and pondered the Holy Scriptures themselves with all possible diligence, never sparing myself in any way.

I shall mention those methods that proved profitable for me, in case desire for similar profit should, perhaps, lead someone else to start out upon the same path in the future. I began by devoting myself when I was a boy to an earnest study of the Old and New Testaments in their original languages, and then proceeded to go carefully through some of the shorter systems of theologians. I also started, following the example of these writers, to list under general headings all passages from the scriptures which suggested themselves for quotation, so that I might have them ready at hand when necessary. At length, gaining confidence, I transferred my attention to more diffuse volumes of divinity, and to the conflicting arguments in controversies over certain heads of faith. But, to be frank, I was very sorry to find, in these works, that the authors frequently evaded an opponent's point in a thoroughly dishonest way, or countered it, in appearance rather than in reality, by an affected display of logical ingenuity or by constant linguistic quibbles. Such writers, moreover, often defended their prejudices tooth and nail, though with more fervor than force, by misinterpretations of biblical texts or by the false conclusions which they wrung from these. Hence, they sometimes violently attacked the truth as error and heresy, while calling error and heresy truth and upholding them not upon the authority of the Bible but as a result of habit and partisanship.

So I considered that I could not properly entrust either my creed or my hope of salvation to such guides. But I still thought that it was absolutely necessary to possess a systematic exposition of Christian teaching, or at any rate a written investigation of it, which could assist my faith or my memory or both. It seemed, then, safest and most advisable for me to make a fresh start and compile for myself, by my own exertion and long hours of study, some work of this kind which might be always at hand. I should derive this from the word of God and from that alone, and should be scrupulously faithful to the text, for to do otherwise would be merely to cheat myself. After I had painstakingly persevered in this work for several years, I saw that the citadel of reformed religion was

---

1. Cf. *PL* XII. 527–28. This and the following notes are those of Maurice Kelley, from his edition of *Christian Doctrine*, cited above. Kelley's many references to passages in *PL* make it possible to see how Milton's religious beliefs are reflected in his epic.

adequately fortified against the Papists. Through neglect, however, it was open to attack in many other places where defences and defenders were alike wanting to make it safe. In religion as in other things, I discerned, God offers all his rewards not to those who are thoughtless and credulous, but to those who labor constantly and seek tirelessly after truth. Thus I concluded that there was more than I realized which still needed to be measured with greater strictness against the yardstick of the Bible, and reformed with greater care. I pursued my studies, and so far satisfied myself that eventually I had no doubt about my ability to distinguish correctly in religion between matters of faith and matters of opinion. It was, furthermore, my greatest comfort that I had constructed, with God's help, a powerful support for my faith, or rather that I had laid up provision for the future in that I should not thenceforth be unprepared or hesitant when I needed to give an account of my beliefs.

God is my witness that it is with feelings of universal brotherhood and good will that I make this account public. By so doing I am sharing, and that most willingly, my dearest and best possession with as many people as possible. I hope, then, that all my readers will be sympathetic, and will avoid prejudice and malice, even though they see at once that many of the views I have published are at odds with certain conventional opinions. I implore all friends of truth not to start shouting that the church is being thrown into confusion by free discussion and inquiry. These are allowed in academic circles, and should certainly be denied to no believer. For we are ordered to find out the truth about all things, and the daily increase of the light of truth fills the church much rather with brightness and strength than with confusion. I do not see how anyone should be able or is able to throw the church into confusion by searching after truth, any more than the heathen were thrown into confusion when the gospel was first preached. For assuredly I do not urge or enforce anything upon my own authority. On the contrary, I advise every reader, and set him an example by doing the same myself, to withold his consent from those opinions about which he does not feel fully convinced, until the evidence of the Bible convinces him and induces his reason to assent and to believe. I do not seek to conceal any part of my meaning. Indeed I address myself with much more confidence to learned than to untutored readers or, if the very learned are not always the best judges and critics of such matters, at any rate to mature, strong-minded men who thoroughly understand the teaching of the gospel. Most authors who have dealt with this subject at the greatest length in the past have been in the habit of filling their pages almost entirely with expositions of their own ideas. They have relegated to the margin, with brief reference to chapter and verse, the scriptural texts upon which all that they teach is utterly dependent. I, on the other hand, have striven to cram my pages even to overflowing, with quotations drawn from all parts of the Bible and to leave as little space as possible for my own words, even when they arise from the putting together of actual scriptural texts.

I intend also to make people understand how much it is in the interests of the Christian religion that men should be free not only to sift and winnow any doctrine, but also openly to give their opinions of it and even to write about it, according to what each believes. This I aim to achieve not only by virtue of the intrinsic soundness and power of the arguments, new or old, which my readers will find me bringing forward, but much more by virtue of the authority of the Bible, upon very frequent citations of which these arguments are based. Without this freedom to which I refer, there is no religion and no gospel. Violence alone prevails; and it is disgraceful and disgusting that the Christian religion should be supported by violence. Without this freedom, we are still enslaved: not, as once, by the law of God but, what is vilest of all, by human law, or rather, to be more exact, by an inhuman tyranny. There are some irrational bigots who, by a perversion of justice, condemn anything they consider inconsistent with conventional beliefs and give it an invidious title—"heretic" or "heresy"—without consulting the evidence of the Bible upon the point. To their way of thinking, by branding anyone out of hand with this hateful name, they silence him with one word and need take no further trouble. They imagine that they have struck their opponent to the ground, as with a single blow, by the impact of the name heretic alone. I do not expect that my unprejudiced and intelligent readers will behave in this way: such conduct would be utterly unworthy of them. But to these bigots I retort that, in apostolic times, before the New Testament was written, the word heresy, whenever it was used as an accusation, was applied only to something which contradicted the teaching of the apostles as it passed from mouth to mouth. Heretics were then, according to Roman. xvi. 17, 18, only those people who *caused divisions of opinion and offences contrary to the teaching of the apostles: serving not our Lord Jesus Christ but their own belly*. On the same grounds I hold that, since the compilation of the New Testament, nothing can correctly be called heresy unless it contradicts that. For my own part, I devote my attention to the Holy Scriptures alone. I follow no other heresy or sect. I had not even studied any of the so-called heretical writers, when the blunders of those who are styled orthodox, and their unthinking distortions of the sense of scripture, first taught me to agree with their opponents whenever they agreed with the Bible. If this is heresy, I confess, as does Paul in Acts xxiv. 14, that *following the way which is called heresy I worship the God of my fathers, believing all things that are written in the law and the prophets* and, I add, whatever is written in the New Testament as well. In common with the whole Protestant Church I refuse to recognise any other arbiters of or any other supreme authorities for Christian belief, or any faith not independently arrived at but "implicit," as it is termed. For the rest, brethren, cherish the truth with love for your fellow men. Assess this work as God's spirit shall direct you. Do not accept or reject what I say unless you are absolutely convinced by the clear evidence of the Bible. Lastly, live in the spirit of our Lord and Savior Jesus Christ, and so I bid you farewell.

J.M.

THE ENGLISHMAN

JOHN MILTON'S

TWO BOOKS OF INVESTIGATIONS
INTO

Christian Doctrine

DRAWN FROM THE SACRED SCRIPTURES ALONE

* * *

[Book I, Chapter ii]

OF GOD

That there is a God, many deny: *for the fool says in his heart, There is no God*, Psal. xiv. 1. But he has left so many signs of himself in the human mind, so many traces of his presence through the whole of nature, that no sane person can fail to realise that he exists. Job xii. 9: *who does not know from all these things?*; Psal. xix. 2: *the heavens declare the glory of God*; Acts xiv. 17: *he did not allow himself to exist without evidence*, and xvii. 27, 28: *he is not far from every one of us*; Rom. i. 19, 20: *that which can be known about God is obvious*, and ii. 14, 15: *the Gentiles show the work of the law written in their hearts; their conscience is evidence of the same thing*; I Cor. i. 21: *because, in accordance with God's wisdom, the world failed to know God by its wisdom, it pleased God to save those who believe by the foolishness of preaching.*[2] It is indisputable that all the things which exist in the world, created in perfection of beauty and order for some definite purpose, and that a good one, provide proof that a supreme creative being existed before the world, and had a definite purpose of his own in all created things.

There are some who prattle about nature or fate, as if they were to

___

2. Such collections of "proof-texts," common in *Christian Doctrine*, have been extensively abridged for this selection.

be identified with this supreme being. But nature or *natura* implies by its very name that it was *natam*, born. Strictly speaking it means nothing except the specific character of a thing, or that general law in accordance with which everything comes into existence and behaves.[3] Surely, too, fate[4] or *fatum* is only what is *fatum*, spoken, by some almighty power.

Moreover, those who want to prove that all things are created by nature, have to introduce the concept of chance as well, to share godhead with nature. What, then, do they gain by their theory? In place of one God, whom they find intolerable, they are forced to set up as universal rulers two goddesses who are almost always at odds with each other. In fact, then, many visible proofs, the fulfillment of many prophecies and the narration of many marvels have driven every nation to the belief that either God or some supreme evil power of unknown name presides over the affairs of men. But it is intolerable and incredible that evil should be stronger than good and should prove the true supreme power. Therefore God exists.

Further evidence for the existence of God is provided by the phenomenon of Conscience, or right reason. This cannot be altogether asleep, even in the most evil men. If there were no God, there would be no dividing line between right and wrong. What was to be called virtue, and what vice, would depend upon mere arbitrary opinion. No one would try to be virtuous, no one would refrain from sin because he felt ashamed of it or feared the law, if the voice of Conscience or right reason did not speak from time to time in the heart of every man, reminding him, however unwilling he may be to remember it, that a God does exist, that he rules and governs all things, and that everyone must one day render to him an account of his actions, good and bad alike.

* * *

It is safest for us to form an image of God in our minds which corresponds to his representation and description of himself in the sacred writings. Admittedly, God is always described or outlined not as he really is but in such a way as will make him conceivable to us. Nevertheless, we ought to form just such a mental image of him as he, in bringing himself within the limits of our understanding, wishes us to form. Indeed he has brought himself down to our level expressly to prevent our being carried beyond the reach of human comprehension, and outside the written authority of scripture, into vague subtleties of speculation.[5]

In my opinion, then, theologians do not need to employ anthropopathy, or the ascription of human feelings to God. This is a rhetorical device thought up by grammarians to explain the nonsense poets write

3. *PL* XI.48–49; X.804–7.
4. *PL* VII.273.
5. *PL* VIII.119–22; VII.118–30, 639–40; VIII.70–75, 105–6, 163–73, 180–97; XII.557–60, 575–76; II.555–65.

about Jove. Sufficient care has been taken, without any doubt, to ensure that the holy scriptures contain nothing unfitting to God or unworthy of him. This applies equally to those passages in scripture where God speaks about his own nature. So it is better not to think about God or form an image of him in anthropopathetic terms, for to do so would be to follow the example of men, who are always inventing more and more subtle theories about him. Rather we should form our ideas with scripture as a model, for that is the way in which he has offered himself to our contemplation. We ought not to imagine that God would have said anything or caused anything to be written about himself unless he intended that it should be a part of our conception of him. On the question of what is or what is not suitable for God, let us ask for no more dependable authority than God himself. If *Jehovah repented that he had created man*, Gen. vi. 6, *and repented because of their groanings*, Judges ii. 18, let us believe that he did repent. But let us not imagine that God's repentance arises from lack of foresight, as man's does, for he has warned us not to think about him in this way: Num. xxiii. 19: *God is not a man that he should lie, nor the son of man that he should repent.* The same point is made in 1 Sam. xv. 29. If *he grieved in his heart* Gen. vi. 6, and if, similarly, *his soul was grieved*, Judges x. 16, let us believe that he did feel grief. For those states of mind which are good in a good man, and count as virtues, are holy in God. If it is said that God, after working for six days, *rested and was refreshed*, Exod. xxxi. 17, and if he *feared his enemy's displeasure*, Deut. xxxii. 27, let us believe that it is not beneath God to feel what grief he does feel, to be refreshed by what refreshes him, and to fear what he does fear. For however you may try to tone down these and similar texts about God by an elaborate show of interpretative glosses, it comes to the same thing in the end. After all, if *God is said to have created man in his own image, after his own likeness*, Gen. i. 26, and not only his mind but also his external appearance (unless the same words mean something different when they are used again in Gen. v. 3: *Adam begot his son after his own likeness; in his own image*), and if God attributes to himself again and again a human shape and form, why should we be afraid of assigning to him something he assigns to himself, provided we believe that what is imperfect and weak in us is, when ascribed to God, utterly perfect and utterly beautiful? We may be certain that God's majesty and glory were so dear to him that he could never say anything about himself which was lower or meaner than his real nature, nor would he ever ascribe to himself any property if he did not wish us to ascribe it to him. Let there be no question about it: they understand best what God is like who adjust their understanding to the word of God, for he has adjusted his word to our understanding, and has shown what kind of an idea of him he wishes us to have.

* * *

I.iii.

OF DIVINE DECREE

* * *

From the concept of freedom, then, all idea of necessity must be removed. No place must be given even to that shadowy and peripheral idea of necessity based on God's immutability and foreknowledge. If any idea of necessity remains, as I have said before, it either restricts free agents to a single course, or compels them against their will, or assists them when they are willing, or does nothing at all. If it restricts free agents to a single course, this makes man the natural cause of all his actions and therefore of his sins, just as if he were created with an inherent propensity towards committing sins. If it compels free agents against their will, this means that man is subject to the force of another's decree, and is thus the cause of sins only *per accidens*, God being the cause of the sin *per se*. If it assists free agents when they are willing, this makes God either the principal or the joint cause of sins. Lastly, if it does nothing at all, no necessity exists. By doing nothing it reduces itself to nothingness. For it is quite impossible that God should have made an inflexible decree about something which we know man is still at liberty to do or not to do. It is also impossible that a thing should be immutable which afterwards might or might not take place.

Whatever was a matter of free will for the first created man, could not then have been immutably or absolutely decreed from all eternity. Obviously, either nothing ever was in the power of man, or if anything was, God cannot be said to have made a firm decree about it.

* * *

The matter or object of the divine plan was that angels and men alike should be endowed with free will, so that they could either fall or not fall. Doubtless God's actual decree bore a close resemblance to this, so that all the evils which have since happened as a result of the fall could either happen or not: if you stand firm, you will stay; if you do not, you will be thrown out: if you do not eat it, you will live; if you do, you will die.[6]

Those, then, who argue that man's freedom of action is subordinate to an absolute decree by God, wrongly conclude that God's decree is the cause of his foreknowledge and antecedent to it. But really, if we must discuss God in terms of our own habits and understandings, it seems more consonant with reason to foresee first and then decree, and indeed this is more in keeping with scripture, and with the nature of God himself, since, as I have just proved, he decreed everything with supreme wisdom in accordance with his foreknowledge.

I do not deny that God's will is the first cause of everything. But

6. *PL* III.98–102; V.535–38; IV.66–67; VI.911–12.

neither do I divorce his foreknowledge and wisdom from his will, much less pretend that the latter is antecedent. In short, God's will is no less the first cause of everything if he decrees that certain things shall depend upon the will of man, than if he had decreed to make all things inevitable.

To sum up these numerous arguments in a few words, this is briefly how the matter stands, looked at from a thoroughly reasonable angle. By virtue of his wisdom God decreed the creation of angels and men as beings gifted with reason and thus with free will.[7] At the same time he foresaw the direction in which they would tend when they used this absolutely unimpaired freedom. What then? Shall we say that God's providence or foreknowledge imposes any necessity upon them? Certainly not: no more than if some human being possessed the same foresight. For an occurrence foreseen with absolute certainty by a human being will no less certainly take place than one foretold by God. For example, Elisha foresaw what evils King Hazael would bring upon the Israelites in a few years' time: II Kings viii. 12. But no one would claim that these happened inevitably as a result of Elisha's foreknowledge: for these events, no less than any others, clearly arose from man's will, which is always free. Similarly, nothing happens because God has foreseen it, but rather he has foreseen each event because each is the result of particular causes which, by his decree, work quite freely and with which he is thoroughly familiar. So the outcome does not rest with God who foresees it, but only with the man whose action God foresees. As I have demonstrated above, there can be no absolute divine decree about the action of free agents. Moreover, divine foreknowledge can no more affect the action of free agents than can human foreknowledge, that is, not at all, because in both cases the foreknowledge is within the mind of the foreknower and has no external effect. Divine foreknowledge definitely cannot itself impose any necessity, nor can it be set up as a cause, in any sense, of free actions. If it is set up in this way, then liberty will be an empty word, and will have to be banished utterly not only from religion but also from morality and even from indifferent matters. Nothing will happen except by necessity, since there is nothing God does not foresee.

* * *

7. *PL* IX. 351–52.

Chapter IV

OF PREDESTINATION

The principal SPECIAL DECREE[8] of God which concerns men is called PREDESTINATION: by which GOD, BEFORE THE FOUNDATIONS OF THE WORLD WERE LAID, HAD MERCY ON THE HUMAN RACE, ALTHOUGH IT WAS GOING TO FALL OF ITS OWN ACCORD, AND, TO SHOW THE GLORY OF HIS MERCY, GRACE AND WISDOM, PREDESTINED TO ETERNAL SALVATION, ACCORDING TO HIS PURPOSE or plan IN CHRIST, THOSE WHO WOULD IN THE FUTURE BELIEVE AND CONTINUE IN THE FAITH.

In academic circles the word "predestination" is habitually used to refer to reprobation as well as to election.[9] For the discussion of such an exacting problem, however, this usage is too slapdash. Whenever the subject is mentioned in scripture, specific reference is made only to election.

* * *

It seems, therefore, that most commentators are wrong in interpreting the foreknowledge of God in these passages as meaning prescience. For God's prescience seems to have nothing to do with the principle or essence of predestination. God has predestined and elected each person who believes and persists in his belief. What is the point of knowing whether God had prescience about who in the future would believe or not believe? For no man believes because God had prescience about it, but rather God had prescience about it because the man was going to believe. It is hard to see what purpose is served by introducing God's prescience or foreknowledge about particular individuals into the doctrine of predestination, except that of raising useless and utterly unanswerable questions. For why should God foreknow particular individuals? What could he foreknow in them which might induce him to predestine them in particular, rather than all in general, once the general condition of belief had been laid down? Suffice it to know, without investigating the matter any further, that God, out of his supreme mercy and grace in Christ, has predestined to salvation all who shall believe.[1]

---

8. Compare with John Wollebius, *The Abridgement of Christian Divinity* (1650), I, iv, pp. 31–32: 'God's Decree, with respect of the Creatures, is either general or special. The general Decree is that by which he appointed to declare the glory of his power, wisdom and goodness, in the creation and conservation of all things. The special Decree, called Predestination, is that by which he appointed to manifest the glory of his grace, mercy, and justice, in the Election and Reprobation of the reasonable Creatures.

9. *Reprobation* indicates damnation; *election*, salvation.

1. *PL* XII.424–27.

＊   ＊   ＊

Chapter V

PREFACE

I am now going to talk about the Son of God and the Holy Spirit, and I do not think I should broach such a difficult subject without some fresh preliminary remarks. The Roman Church demands implicit obedience on all points of faith. If I professed myself a member of it, I should be so indoctrinated, or at any rate so besotted by habit, that I should yield to its authority and to its mere decree even if it were to assert that the doctrine of the Trinity, as accepted at present, could not be proved from any passage of scripture. As it happens, however, I am one of those who recognize God's word alone as the rule of faith; so I shall state quite openly what seems to me much more clearly deducible from the text of scripture than the currently accepted doctrine. I do not see how anyone who calls himself a Protestant or a member of the Reformed Church, and who acknowledges the same rule of faith as myself, could be offended with me for this, especially as I am not trying to browbeat anyone, but am merely pointing out what I consider the more credible doctrine. This one thing I beg of my reader: that he will weigh each statement and evaluate it with a mind innocent of prejudice and eager only for the truth. For I take it upon myself to refute, whenever necessary, not scriptural authority, which is inviolable, but human interpretations. That is my right, and indeed my duty as a human being. Of course, if my opponents could show that the doctrine they defend was revealed to them by a voice from heaven, he would be an impious wretch who dared to raise so much as a murmur against it, let alone a sustained protest. But in fact they can lay claim to nothing more than human powers and that spiritual illumination which is common to all men. What is more just, then, than that they should allow someone else to play his part in the business of research and discussion: someone else who is hunting the same truth, following the same track, and using the same methods as they, and who is equally anxious to benefit his fellow men? Now, relying on God's help, let us come to grips with the subject itself.

OF THE SON OF GOD

*   *   *

Whatever certain modern scholars may say to the contrary, it is certain that the Son existed in the beginning, under the title of the Word or Logos, that he was the first of created things,[2] and that through him all other things, both in heaven and earth, were afterwards made. John i. 1–3. *in the beginning was the Word, and the Word was with God and the Word was God,* etc., and xvii. 5.

When all the above passages, especially the second Psalm, have been compared and digested carefully, it will be apparent that, however the Son was begotten, it did not arise from natural necessity, as is usually maintained, but was just as much a result of the Father's decree and will as the Son's priesthood, kingship, and resurrection from the dead. The fact that he is called "begotten," whatever that means, and God's *own Son,* Rom. viii. 32, does not stand in the way of this at all. He is called God's own Son simply because he had no other Father but God, and this is why he himself said that God was his Father, John v. 18. For to Adam, formed out of the dust, God was creator rather than Father; but he was in a real sense Father of the Son, whom he made of his own substance. It does not follow, however, that the Son is of the same essence as the Father. Indeed, if he were, it would be quite incorrect to call him Son. For a real son is not of the same age as his father, still less of the same numerical essence: otherwise father and son would be one person. This particular Father begot his Son not from any natural necessity but of his own free will: a method more excellent and more in keeping with paternal dignity, especially as this Father is God.[3] For it has already been demonstrated from the text of scripture that God always acts with absolute freedom, working out his own purpose and volition. Therefore he must have begotten his Son with absolute freedom.

God could certainly have refrained from the act of generation and yet remained true to his own essence, for he stands in no need of propagation.[4] So generation has nothing to do with the essence of deity. And if a thing has nothing to do with his essence or nature, he does not do it from natural necessity like a natural agent. Moreover, if natural necessity was the deciding factor, then God violated his own essence by begetting, through the force of nature, an equal. He could no more do this then deny himself. Therefore he could not have begotten the Son except of his own free will and as a result of his own decree.

*   *   *

2. *PL* III.383.
3. *PL* X.760–65.
4. *PL* XIII.419–20.

Chapter VII

OF THE CREATION

The second[5] kind of external efficiency is commonly called CREA-TION. Anyone who asks what God did before the creation of the world is a fool; and anyone who answers him is not much wiser. Most people think they have given an account of the matter when they have quoted I Cor. ii.7: *that he preordained, before the creation of the world, his wisdom, hidden in a mystery,* which they take to mean that he was occupied with election and reprobation, and with deciding other related matters. But it would clearly be disproportionate for God to have been totally occupied from eternity in decreeing things which it was to take him only six days to create: things which were to be governed in various ways for a few thousand years, and then finally either received into an unchanging state with God for ever, or else for ever thrown away.

That the world was created, must be considered an article of faith: Heb. xi. 3: *through faith we understand that the world was made by God's word.*

CREATION is the act by which GOD THE FATHER PRODUCED EVERYTHING THAT EXISTS BY HIS WORD AND SPIRIT, that is, BY HIS WILL, IN ORDER TO SHOW THE GLORY OF HIS POWER AND GOODNESS.

* * *

There is a good deal of controversy, however, about what the original matter was. On the whole the moderns are of the opinion that everything was formed out of nothing (which is, I fancy, what their own theory is based on!) In the first place it is certain that neither the Hebrew verb בָּרָא nor the Greek κτίφειν, nor the Latin *creare* means "to make out of nothing." On the contrary, each of them always means "to make out of something." Gen.i. 21, 27: *God created . . . which the waters brought forth abundantly, he created them male and female*; Isa. liv. 16: *I have created the maker, I have created the destroyer.* Anyone who says, then, that "to create" means "to produce out of nothing," is, as logicians say, arguing from an unproved premise. The passages of scripture usually quoted in this context do not at all confirm the received opinion, but tend to imply the contrary, namely that all things were not made out of nothing, II Cor. iv. 6: *God who commanded light to shine out of darkness.* It is clear from Isa. xlv. 7 that this darkness was far from being a mere nothing: *I am Jehovah,* etc. *I form the light and create the darkness.* If the darkness is nothing, then when God created the darkness

---

5. Milton's anti-trinitarianism dictates this numbering. According to orthodox theologians, the external efficiency of God manifests itself in creation, by which he produces, and providence, by which he governs that which he produces. To these Milton adds an earlier species, the generation of the Son, so that creation and providence become the second and third rather than the standard first and second species of the Father's external efficiency.

he created nothing, that is he both created and did not create, which is a contradiction in terms. Again, Heb. xi. 3, all we are required *to understand through faith* about *earthly times*, that is, about the world, is that *the things which are seen were not put together from the things which appear.* Now because things do not appear, they must not be considered synonymous with nothing. For one thing, you cannot have a plural of nothing, and for another, a thing cannot be *put together* from nothing as it can from a number of components. The meaning is, rather, that these things are not as they now appear. I might also mention the apocryphal writers, as closest to the scriptures in authority: Wisdom xi. 17: *who created the world out of formless matter;* II Macc. vii. 28: *out of things that were not.* But it is said of Rachel's children in Matt. ii. 18, *they are not,* and this does not mean *they are nothing* but, as frequently in the Hebrew language, they are not among the living.

It is clear, then, that the world was made out of some sort of matter.[6] For since "action" and "passivity" are relative terms, and since no agent can act externally unless there is something, and something material, which can be acted upon, it is apparent that God could not have created this world out of nothing. *Could* not, that is, not because of any defect of power or omnipotence on his part, but because it was necessary that something should have existed previously, so that it could be acted upon by his supremely powerful active efficacy. Since, then, both the Holy Scriptures and reason itself suggest that all these things were made not out of nothing but out of matter, matter must either have always existed, independently of God, or else originated from God at some point in time. That matter should have always existed independently of God is inconceivable. In the first place, it is only a passive principle, dependent upon God and subservient to him; and, in the second place, there is no inherent force or efficacy in time or eternity, and more than there is in the concept of number. But if matter did not exist from eternity, it is not very easy to see where it originally came from. There remains only this solution, especially if we allow ourselves to be guided by scripture, namely, that all things came from God.

Most people argue that the angels should be understood as included in and created along with "the heavens" at the creation of the world. We may well believe that the angels were, in fact, created at a particular time, see Num. xvi. 22: *God of spirits,* and similarly xxvii. 16; Heb. i. 7; Col. i. 16: *through him were invisible things made, whether they be thrones.* . . . . But that they were created on the first or on any one of the six days is asserted by the general mob of theologians with, as usual, quite unjustifiable confidence, chiefly on the authority of the repetition

6. *PL* VII.166–69.

in Gen. ii. 1: *thus the heavens and the earth were finished, and all the army of them:* quite unjustifiable, that is, unless we are supposed to pay more attention to this conclusion than to the preceding narrative, and to interpret this *army* which inhabits the visible heavens as a reference to the angels. The fact that they *shouted for joy* before God at the creation, as we read in Job xxxviii. 7, proves that they were then already created, not that they were first created at that time. Certainly many of the Greek Fathers, and some of the Latin, were of the opinion that angels, inasmuch as they were spirits, existed long before this material world. Indeed it seems likely that that apostasy, as a result of which so many myriads of them fled, beaten, to the lowest part of heaven, took place before even the first beginnings of this world. There is certainly no reason why we should conform to the popular belief that motion and time, which is the measure of motion, could not, according to our concepts of "before" and "after," have existed before this world was made. For Aristotle, who taught that motion and time are inherent only in this world, asserted, nevertheless, that this world was eternal.[7]

* * *

Chapter IX

OF THE SPECIAL GOVERNMENT OF ANGELS

We have been discussing GENERAL PROVIDENCE. SPECIAL PROVIDENCE is concerned particularly with angels and men, as they are far superior to all other creatures.

There are, however, both good and evil angels. Luke ix. 26 and viii. 2, for it is well known that a great many of them revolted from God of their own free will[8] before the fall of man: John viii. 44: *he did not stand firm in the truth, for there is no truth in him, he speaks like what he is, the father of lies;* II Pet. ii. 4: *he did not spare the angels who sinned;* * * *

* * *

It seems . . . reasonable . . . to suppose that the good angels stand by their own strength, no less than man did before his fall, and that they are called "elect" only in the sense that they are beloved or choice: also that they desire to contemplate the mystery of our salvation simply out of love,[9] and not from any interest of their own, that they are not included in any question of reconciliation, and that they are reckoned as being under Christ because he is their head, not their Redeemer.[1]

In addition, they stand around the throne of God as ministers. Deut.

7. *PL* V.580–82.
8. *PL* III.129–30.
9. *PL* VIII.224–26, 639–40.
1. *PL* V.163.

xxxiii. 2: *he came with a crowd of myriads of saints;* I Kings xxii. 19: *I saw Jehovah sitting on his throne and the whole host of heaven on his right hand and on his left.* * * *

Praising God: Job xxxviii. 7: *all the sons of God shouted aloud;* Psal. cxlviii. 2: *praise him all his angels.*

* * *

Their chief ministry concerns believers: Heb. i. 14: *they are all ministering spirits who are sent out to minister for the sake of the heirs of salvation.* * * *

And seven of them particularly patrol the earth: Zech. iv. 10: *these seven are the eyes of Jehovah which go to and from over the earth,* compared with Rev. v. 6: *who are those seven spirits of God sent forth into the whole earth,* see also i. 4 and iv. 5.[2]

It is probable, too, that angels are put in charge of nations, kingdoms and particular districts.[3] * * *

Sometimes they are ministers of divine vengeance,[4] sent from heaven to punish mortal sins. They destroy cities and peoples: Gen. xix. 13; II Sam. xxiv. 16; I Chron. xxi. 16: *David saw the angel of Jehovah threatening Jerusalem with a drawn sword.* They strike down whole armies with unexpected calamity: II Kings xix. 35, and similar passages.

As a result they often appeared looking like soldiers.

* * *

There seems to be a leader among the good angels, and he is often called Michael: Josh. vi. 2: *I am the leader of Jehovah's soldiery;* Dan. x. 13: *Michael is the first of the chief princes,*[5] and xii. 1: *the greatest prince;* Rev. xii. 7, 8: *Michael with his angels.*

A lot of people are of the opinion that Michael is Christ. But whereas Christ alone vanquished Satan and trod him underfoot, Michael is introduced as leader of the angels and Ἀντίπαλος (antagonist) of the prince of the devils: their respective forces were drawn up in battle array and separated after a fairly even fight,

The good angels do not see into all God's thoughts, as the Papists pretend. They know by revelation only those things which God sees fit to show them, and they know other things by virtue of their very high intelligence, but there are many things of which they are ignorant.[6] For we find an angel full of curiosity and asking questions: Dan. viii. 13: *how long is this vision?,* and xii. 6: *how far off is its end.* * * *

Bad angels are kept for punishment: Matt. viii. 29: *have you come here to torment us before the appointed time?;* II Pet. ii. 4: *he thrust them down to hell and chained them in dark chains, to be kept for damnation.* * * *

2. *PL* III.648–55.
3. *PL* IV.561–63.
4. *PL* I.70.
5. *PL* VI.44; XI.295–98.
6. *PL* VII.112–13; XI.67–69; III.681–85.

But sometimes they are able to wander all over the earth, the air, and even heaven, to carry out God's judgments:[7] Job i. 7: *from going to and fro on the earth.* * * * They even come into the presence of God: Job i. 6 and ii. 1; I Kings xxii. 21: *a certain spirit came forth*; Zech. iii. 1: *he showed me Joshua standing in the presence of the angel of Jehovah, and Satan standing at his right hand to oppose him*; Luke x. 18: *I saw Satan falling like lightning out of heavens.* * * *

But there proper place is hell, which they cannot leave without permission. * * * Rev. xx. 3: *he threw him into hell and closed it up.* They cannot do anything unless God commands them: Job i. 12: *look, let them be in your power*; Matt. viii. 31: *allows us to go away into this herd of swine.* * * *

Their knowledge is great, but it is a torment to them rather than a consolation; so that they utterly despair of their salvation: Matt. viii. 29: *what have we to do with you, Jesus? Have you come here to torment us before the appointed time?*, similarly Luke iv. 34; James ii. 19: *the devils believe and are horrified*[8]—because they are kept for punishment, as I said before.

The devils have their prince too: Matt. xii. 24: *Beelzebub prince of devils*, similarly Luke xi. 15; Matt. xxv. 41: *for the devil and his angels*; Rev. xii. 9: *that great dragon and his angels.*

They also keep their ranks: Col. ii. 15: *having plundered principalities and powers*; Eph. vi. 12: *against powers and principalities.*

Their chief is the author of all wickedness and hinders all good:[9] Job i and ii; Zech. iii. 1: *Satan*; John viii. 44: *the father of lies*; I Thess. ii. 18: *Satan hindered us*; Acts v. 3: *Satan has filled your heart*; Rev. xx. 3, 8: *to lead the nations astray*; Eph. ii. 2: *the spirit now working in arrogant men.*

As a result he has been given a number of titles, which suit his actions. He is frequently called *Satan*, that is, enemy or adversry, Job i. 6, I Chron. xxi. 1: also *the great dragon, the old serpent, the devil*, that is, the calumniator, Rev. xii. 9: also κατήγορος τῶν ἀδελφῶν [*the accuser of the brothers*], xii. 10; and *the unclean spirit*, Matt. xii. 43; and *the tempter*, Matt. iv. 3; and *Abaddon, Apollyon*, that is, destroyer, Rev. ix. 11; and *a great red dragon*, xii. 3.

* * *

7. *PL* I. 209–13; II. 1023; VII. 233–39.
8. *PL* I. 53–56, 66–67, 125–26; IV. 73–74, 505–11.
9. *PL* VI. 262; II. 380–82; I. 159–60.

Chapter X

OF THE SPECIAL GOVERNMENT OF MAN
BEFORE THE FALL

The providence of God which governs man relates either to man's prelapsarian or to his fallen state.

The providence which relates to his prelapsarian state is that by which God placed man in the garden of Eden and supplied him with every good thing necessary for a happy life. And, so that there might be some way for man to show his obedience, God ordered him to abstain only from the tree of the knowledge of good and evil, and threatened him with death if he disobeyed:[1] Gen. i. 28; ii. 15, 16, 17. * * *

Some people call this "the covenant of works," though it does not appear from any passage of scripture to have been either a covenant or of works. Adam was not required to perform any works; he was merely forbidden to do one thing. It was necessary that one thing at least should be either forbidden or commanded, and above all something which was in itself neither good nor evil, so that man's obedience might in this way be made evident.[2] For man was by nature good and holy, and was naturally disposed to do right, so it was certainly not necessary to bind him by the requirements of any covenant to something which he would do of his own accord. And he would not have shown obedience at all by performing good works, since he was in fact drawn to these by his own natural impulses, without being commanded. Besides a command, whether it comes from God or from a magistrate, should not be called a covenant just because rewards and punishments are attached: it is rather a declaration of power.

The tree of the knowledge of good and evil was not a sacrament, as is commonly thought, for sacraments are meant to be used, not abstained from; but it was a kind of pledge or memorial of obedience.[3]

It was called the tree of knowledge of good and evil because of what happened afterwards: for since it was tasted, not only do we know evil, but also we do not even know good except through evil.[4] For where does virtue shine, where is it usually exercised, if not in evil?

I do not know whether the tree of life ought to be called a sacrament, rather than a symbol of eternal life or even perhaps the food of eternal life: Gen. iii. 22: *lest he eat and live for ever;*[5] Rev. ii. 7: *to the victor I will give food from the tree of life.*

Man was made in the image of God, and the whole law of nature

---

1. *PL* IV.412–30, 690–92, 883–84; I.28–32; V.503–5, 514–18; VI.7–47; IX.344–47; X.13.
2. That the fruit was in itself neither good nor evil and forbidden merely as a test of man's fidelity was a common view. See C. A. Patrides, "The Tree of Knowledge in the Christian Tradition," *Studia Neophilologica* 30 (1962): 239–40.
3. *PL* III.94–95; VIII.323–25.
4. *PL* IX.1070–73: IV.221–22; XI.84–89.
5. *PL* XI.93–96; IV.194–201.

was so implanted and innate in him that he was in need of no command. It follows, then, that if he received any additional commands, whether about the tree of knowledge or about marriage, these had nothing to do with the law of nature, which is itself sufficient to teach whatever is in accord with right reason (i.e., whatever is intrinsically good). These commands, then, were simply a matter of what is called positive right. Positive right comes into play when God, or anyone else invested with lawful power, commands or forbids things which, if he had not commanded or forbidden them, would in themselves have been neither good nor bad, and would therefore have put no one under any obligation.

* * *

Chapter XI

OF THE FALL OF OUR FIRST PARENTS, AND OF SIN

The PROVIDENCE of God with regard to the fall of man may be discerned both in man's sin and the misery which followed it, and also in his restoration.

SIN, as defined by the apostle, is ἀνομία or the breaking of the law, I John iii. 4.

Here the word *law* means primarily that law which is innate and implanted in man's mind; and secondly it means the law which proceeded from the mouth of God; Gen. ii. 17: *do not eat of this:* for the law written down by Moses is of a much later date. So it is written, Rom. ii. 12: *those who have sinned without law will perish without law.*

SIN is either THE SIN COMMON TO ALL MEN or THE SIN OF EACH INDIVIDUAL.

THE SIN COMMON TO ALL MEN IS THAT WHICH OUR FIRST PARENTS, AND IN THEM ALL THEIR POSTERITY[6] COMMITTED WHEN THEY ABANDONED THEIR OBEDIENCE AND TASTED THE FRUIT OF THE FORBIDDEN TREE.

OUR FIRST PARENTS: Gen. iii. 6: *the woman took some of the fruit and ate it, and gave some to her husband, and he ate it.* Hence I Tim. ii. 14: *Adam was not deceived, but the woman was deceived and was the cause of the transgression.* This sin was instigated first by the devil,[7] as is clear from the course of events, Gen. iii and I John iii. 8: *the man who commits sin is of the devil; for the devil sins from the beginning.* Secondly it was instigated by man's own inconstant nature,[8] which meant that he, like the devil before him *did not stand firm in the truth,* John viii. 44. He did not keep his original state, but left his home, Jude 6. Anyone who examines this sin carefully will admit, and

---

6. *PL* X.817–18; III.290.
7. *PL* I.Argument, 33–34.
8. *PL* V.236–37, 524.

rightly, that it was a most atrocious offence, and that it broke every part of the law.[9] For what fault is there which man did not commit in committing this sin? He was to be condemned both for trusting Satan[1] and for not trusting God;[2] he was faithless, ungrateful, disobedient, greedy, uxorious;[3] she, negligent of her husband's welfare;[4] both of them committed theft, robbery with violence, murder against their children (i.e., the whole human race);[5] each was sacrilegious and deceitful, cunningly aspiring to divinity[6] although thoroughly unworthy of it, proud and arrogant. * * *

AND IN THEM ALL THEIR POSTERITY: for they are judged and condemned in them, although not yet born, Gen. iii. 16, etc. * * *

For Adam, the parent and head of all man, either stood or fell as a representative of the whole human race.

* * *

THE SIN OF EACH INDIVIDUAL is THE SIN WHICH EACH MAN COMMITS ON HIS OWN ACCOUNT, QUITE APART FROM THAT SIN WHICH IS COMMON TO ALL. All men commit sin of this kind: Job ix. 20: *if I were to call myself righteous, my own mouth would condemn me . . .* , and x. 15: *even if I am righteous, I cannot lift up my head.* * * *

Each type of sin, common and personal, has two subdivisions, whether we call them degrees or parts or modes of sin, or whether they are related to each other as cause and effect. These subdivisions are evil desire, or the will to do evil, and the evil deed itself. James i. 14, 15: *every man is tempted when he is drawn on and enticed by his own lust: then, when lust has conceived, it brings forth sin.* This same point is neatly expressed by the poet.

Mars sees her; seeing desires her; desiring enjoys her

It was evil desire that our first parents were originally guilty of. Then they implanted it in all their posterity, since their posterity too was guilty of that original sin, in the shape of a certain predisposition towards, or, to use a metaphor, a sort of tinder to kindle sin.

This is called in scripture *the old man* and *the body of sin*, Rom. vi. 6, Eph. iv. 22, Col. iii. 9: or simply *sin*, Rom. vii. 8: *sin seized its opportunity by means of that commandment; sin dwelling in me*, Rom. vii. 17, 20; *evil which is present*, vii. 21; *the law in my members*, vii. 23; *this body of death*, vii. 24; *the law of sin and of death*, viii. 2.

Apparently Augustine, in his writings against Pelagius was the first to

9. *PL* X.16.
1. *PL* IX.643–44, 733–34.
2. *PL* IX.773–75, 928–29, 6–7.
3. *PL* III.95–98; I.1; IX.7–8; XI.514–16, 475–77; IX.Argument.
4. *PL* X.673–77.
5. *PL* VIII.635–38.
6. *PL* III.206; IX.790, 863–66.

call this ORIGINAL SIN. He used the word *original*, I suppose, because in the *origin* or generation of man this sin was transmitted to posterity by our first parents. But if that is what he meant, the term is too narrow, because this evil desire, this law of sin, was not only inbred in us, but also took possession of Adam after his fall,[7] and from his point of view it could not be called *original*.[8]

The depravity which all human minds have in common, and their propensity to sin, are described in Gen. vi. 5: *that all the thoughts of his heart were always evil and evil alone*; viii. 21: *the devices of a man's heart are evil from childhood.* * * *

Our first parents implanted it in us: Job xiv. 4: *who produces purity from impurity?*, and xv. 14: *what is mortal, and pure? what is born of woman, and righteous?*; Psal. li. 7: *I was formed in iniquity and my mother nursed me in sin*; and lviii. 4: *from the womb*; Isa. xlviii. 8: *a sinner from the womb*; John iii. 6: *that which is born from flesh, is flesh*; Eph. ii. 3: *we were by nature children of anger, like the others*—even those who were born of regenerate parents, for although faith removes each man's personal guilt, it does not altogether root out the vice which dwells within us. So it is not man as a regenerate creature, but man as an animal, that begets man; just as the seed, though cleansed from straw and chaff, produces not only the ear or the grain but also the stalk and the husk. Christ alone was free from this contagion, since he was produced by supernatural generation, although descended from Adam: Heb. vii. 26: *holy, spotless*.

Some interpret this term original sin primarily as guiltiness. But guiltiness is not a sin, it is the imputation of sin, called elsewhere *the judgment of God*: Rom. i. 32: *knowing the judgment of God*. As a result of this sinners are held *worthy of death*, and ὑπόδικοι, that is, *liable to condemnation and punishment*, Rom. iii. 19, and *are under sin*, iii. 9. Thus as soon as the fall occurred, our first parents became guilty, though there could have been no original sin in them. Moreover all Adam's descendants were included in the guilt, though original sin had not yet been implanted in them. Finally, guilt is taken away from the regenerate, but they still have original sin.

Others define original sin as the loss of original righteousness and the corruption of the whole mind. But this loss must be attributed to our first parents before it is attributed to us, and they could not have been subject to original sin, as I said before. Their sin was what is called "actual" sin, which these same theologians, as part of their theory, distinguish from original sin. Anyway their loss was a consequence of sin, rather than a sin itself; or if it was a sin, it was only a sin of ignorance, because they did not expect for a moment that they would lose anything good by eating the fruit, or that they would be worse off in any way at

7. *PL* IX.1077–78.
8. In spite of this objection, Milton does employ the term once, in *PL* IX.1003–4.

all.[9] So I shall not consider this loss under the heading of sin, but under that of punishment in the next chapter.

The second subdivision of sin, after evil desire, is the evil action or crime itself, which is commonly called "actual" sin.[1] It can be committed not only through actions, as such, but also through words and thoughts and even through the omission of a good action.

It is called "actual" not because sin is really an action, on the contrary it is a deficiency, but because it usually exists in some action. For every action is intrinsically good; it is only its misdirection or deviation from the set course of law which can properly be called evil. So action is not the material out of which sin is made, but only the ὑποκείμενον, the essence or element in which it exists.

* * *

Chapter XII

OF THE PUNISHMENT OF SIN

So far I have spoken of sin. After sin came death, as its affliction or punishment. Gen. ii. 17: *on the day you eat it, you will die*; Rom. v. 12: *through sin is death*, and vi. 23: *the wages of sin is death*, and vii. 5: *the effects of sin, to bring forth fruit to death*.

But in scripture every evil, and everything which seems to lead to destruction, is indeed under the name of *death*. For physical death, as it is called, did not follow *on the same day as* Adam's sin, as God had threatened.[2]

So four degrees of death may conveniently be distinguished. First, as I said above, come ALL EVILS WHICH TEND TO DEATH AND WHICH, IT IS AGREED, CAME INTO THE WORLD AS SOON AS MAN FELL. I will here set out the most important of these. First: guiltiness, which, although it is a thing inputed to us by God, is nevertheless a sort of partial death or prelude to death in us, by which we are fettered to condemnation and punishment as by some actual bond: Gen. iii. 7: *then both their eyes opened, and they knew that they were naked;*[3] Lev. v. 2, etc: *although it was hidden from him, nevertheless he is unclean and guilty*; Rom. iii. 19: *the whole world is liable to God's condemnation*. As a result guiltiness is either accompanied or followed by terrors of conscience:[4] Gen. iii. 8: *they heard the voice of God, and Adam hid himself: he said, I was afraid*; * * * also by the loss of divine protection and favor, which results in the lessening of the majesty of the human

9. *PL* X.334–36.
1. *PL* X.586–88.
2. *PL* I.1–3; VII.329–33; X.49–53, 808–13.
3. *PL* IX.12–13, 1113–14.
4. *PL* X.842–43, 849–50.

countenance, and the degredation of the mind:[5] Gen. iii. 7: *they knew that they were naked.* Thus the whole man is defiled: Tit. i. 15: *both their mind and their conscience is defiled.* Hence comes shame:[6] Gen. iii. 7: *they sewed leaves together and made themselves aprons;* Rom. vi. 21: *for which you are now ashamed, for the end of those things is death.*

The second degree of death is called SPIRITUAL DEATH. This is the loss of that divine grace and innate righteousness by which, in the beginning, man lived with God:[7] Eph. ii. 1: *since you were dead in trespasses and sins,* and iv. 18: *alienated from the life of God;* Col. ii. 13: *dead in sins;* Rev. iii. 1: *you have a name for being alive, but are dead.* And this death took place at the same moment as the fall of man, not merely on the same day. Those who are delivered from it are said to be regenerated and born again and created anew. As I will show in my chapter on Regeneration, this is not the work of God alone.

This death consists, first, in the loss or at least the extensive darkening of that right reason, whose function it was to discern the chief good, and which was, as it were the life of the understanding:[8] * * * secondly, in that extinction of righteousness and of the liberty to do good, and in that slavish subjection to sin and the devil which is, as it were, the death of the will.[9] John viii. 34: *whoever commits sin is the slave of sin.* We have all committed sin in Adam, therefore we are born slaves; Rom. vii. 14: *sold to be subject to sin.* * * *

Lastly sin is its own punishment, and the death of the spiritual life; especially when sins are heaped upon sins: Rom. i. 26: *for this reason he has given them up to filthy desires.* The reason for this is not hard to see. As sins increase so they bind the sinners to death more surely, make them more miserable and constantly more vile, and deprive them more and more of divine help and grace, and of their own former glory. No one should have the least doubt that sin is in itself alone the gravest evil of all, for it is opposed to the chief good, that is, to God. Punishment, on the other hand, seems to be opposed only to the good of the creature, and not always to that.

However, it cannot be denied that some traces of the divine image still remain in us, which are not wholly extinguished by this spiritual death.[1] This is quite clear, not only from the holiness and wisdom in both word and deed of many of the heathens, but also from Gen. ix. 2: *every beast shall have fear of you,* and ix. 6: *who sheds man's blood . . . because God made man in his image.* These traces remain in our intellect, Psal. xix. 2: *the heavens declare . . .* —obviously they do not

5. *PL* IX.1077–78, 1011–15, 1053–54, 1122–26, 1138–39; XI.504–8.
6. *PL* X.336–37; IX.1095–98, 1079.
7. *PL* IX.1054–57, 1062–63, 1074–76.
8. *PL* IX.1127–31.
9. *PL* XII.83–90.
1. *PL* XI.508–10.

declare it to beings who cannot hear. Rom. i. 19, 20: *that which can be known about God . . . the invisible things are evident from the creation of the world,* and i. 32: *knowing the judgment of God,* and ii. 15: *which show the work of the law written in their hearts.*

* * *

As a vindication of God's justice,[2] especially when he calls man, it is obviously fitting that some measure of free will should be allowed to man, whether this is something left over from his primitive state, or something restored to him as a result of the call of grace. It is also fitting that this will should operate in good works or at least good attempts, rather than in things indifferent. For if God rules all human actions, both natural and civil, by his absolute command, then he is not doing anything more than he is entitled to do, and no one need complain. But if he turns man's will to moral good or evil just as he likes, and then rewards the good and punishes the wicked, it will cause an outcry against divine justice from all sides. It would seem then that God's general government of all things, which is so often referred to, should be understood as operating in natural and civil matters and in things indifferent and in chance happenings—in fact in anything rather than in moral or religious concerns. There are several scriptural texts which corroborate this. II Chron. xv. 12, 14: *they entered into a covenant to seek Jehovah the God of their ancestors with all their heart and with all their soul: and they swore to Jehovah;* Psal. cxix. 106: *I have sworn (and I will perform it), to keep your righteous judgments.* Obviously if religious matters were not under our control, or to some extent within our power and choice, God could not enter into a covenant with us, and we could not keep it, let alone swear to keep it.

* * *

Chapter XIV

OF MAN'S RESTORATION AND OF CHRIST THE REDEEMER

* * *

Christ, then, although he was God, put on human nature, and was made flesh, but did not cease to be numerically one Christ. Theologians are of the opinion that this incarnation is by far the greatest mystery of our religion, next to that of the three persons existing in one divine essence.[3] There is, however, not a single word in the Bible about the

---

2. *PL* I.25–26.
3. "It may seem surprising that Milton should reject with scorn the notion that there are three persons in one Godhead, and then accept without a qualm the doctrine that in Christ two natures unite in one being. The explanation, however, is not far to seek. The Incarnation is a true mystery, an event that surpasses the reach of man's reason, while the Trinity is a false mystery created by human ingenuity. The basis for such a distinction is found in Scripture,

mystery of the Trinity,[4] whereas the incarnation is frequently spoken of as a mystery.   * * *

As this is such a great mystery, let its very magnitude put us on our guard from the outset, to prevent us from making any rash or hasty assertions or depending upon the trivialities of mere philosophy. Let it prevent us from adding anything of our own, or even from placing weight upon any scriptural text which can be easily invalidated. Instead, let us make do with the most unambiguous of texts, even though these may be few. If we pay attention only to texts of this kind, and are willing to be satisfied with the simple truth, ignoring the glosses of metaphysicians, how many prolix and monstrous controversies we shall put an end to! How many opportunities for heresy we shall remove: how much of the raw material for heresy we shall cut away! How many huge volumes, the works of dabblers in theology, we shall fling out of God's temple as filth and rubbish! If teachers, teachers even of the reformed church, had learned by now to rely on divine authorities alone where divine matters are concerned, and to concentrate upon the contents of the Bible, then nothing would be more straightforward than what the Christian faith propounds as essential for our salvation. Nothing would be more reasonable, or more adapted to the understanding even of the least intelligent. We should easily see the essentials, once they were disentangled from the windings of controversy, and we should let mysteries alone and not tamper with them. We should be afraid to pry into things further than we were meant.

* * *

Chapter XXVI

OF THE MANIFESTATION OF THE COVENANT OF GRACE: ALSO OF THE LAW OF GOD

* * *

The LAW OF GOD is either written or unwritten.

The unwritten law is the law of nature given to the first man. A kind of gleam or glimmering of it still remains in the hearts of all mankind. In the regenerate this is daily brought nearer to a renewal of its original perfection by the operation of the Holy Spirit. Rom. i. 19: *he has shown it to them*, and i. 32: *who knowing the judgment of God (that is, that those who do such things are worthy of death) nevertheless not only do*

which speaks frequently of the mystery of the Incarnation, but never of the mystery of the Trinity" (H. R. MacCallum, "The Role of The Son," *"Paradise Lost": A Tercentenary Tribute*, p. 91).

4. Milton's view of this mystery rests on the antitrinitarian tenets that he advances [in Book 1, Chapter 5 (see p. 407, above)]. . . . He denies the full divinity of Christ, and holds that his two-fold generation took place within time. The orthodox view asserts the full divinity of Christ and maintains a separate eternal and temporal generation of the Son.

these things but also conspire with those who do them, and ii. 14, 15:
*the Gentiles, who have not the law, do by nature the things contained
in the law, for they are their own law: they show the work of the law
written in their hearts.*

Thus *the law* may often be taken to mean merely religious doctrine,
or alternatively it may mean the will of God as expressed in the law or
in the gospel. Jer. xxxi. 33: *I will put my law in their mind*; John x. 34:
is it not written in your law, I have said you are gods? Actually this
quotation occurs in the Psalms, not in the law.

* * *

THE MOSAIC LAW WAS A WRITTEN CODE, CONSISTING
OF MANY STIPULATIONS, AND INTENDED FOR THE ISRAE-
LITES ALONE. IT HELD A PROMISE OF LIFE FOR THE OBE-
DIENT AND A CURSE FOR THE DISOBEDIENT. ITS AIM WAS
TO MAKE THE ISRAELITES HAVE RECOURSE TO THE
RIGHTEOUSNESS OF THE PROMISED CHRIST, THROUGH A
RECOGNITION OF MANKIND'S, AND THEREFORE OF THEIR
OWN DEPRAVITY. ITS AIM, ALSO, WAS THAT ALL WE
OTHER NATIONS SHOULD AFTERWARDS BE EDUCATED
FROM THIS ELEMENTARY, CHILDISH AND SERVILE DISCI-
PLINE TO THE ADULT STATURE OF A NEW CREATURE, AND
TO A MANLY FREEDOM UNDER THE GOSPEL, WORTHY OF
GOD'S SONS.

* * *

The imperfection of the law was made apparent in the person of
Moses himself. For Moses, who was the type of the law, could not lead
the children of Israel into the land of Canaan, that is, into eternal rest.
But an entrance was granted to them under Joshua, that is, Jesus.[5]

* * *

Chapter XXVII

OF THE GOSPEL, AND CHRISTIAN LIBERTY

THE GOSPEL is THE NEW DISPENSATION OF THE COVE-
NANT OF GRACE. IT IS MUCH MORE EXCELLENT AND
PERFECT THAN THE LAW. IT WAS FIRST ANNOUNCED, OB-
SCURELY, BY MOSES AND THE PROPHETS, AND THEN
WITH ABSOLUTE CLARITY BY CHRIST HIMSELF AND HIS
APOSTLES AND THE EVANGELISTS. IT HAS BEEN WRITTEN
IN THE HEARTS OF BELIEVERS THROUGH THE HOLY
SPIRIT, AND WILL LAST UNTIL THE END OF THE WORLD.
IT CONTAINS A PROMISE OF ETERNAL LIFE TO ALL MEN

5. *PL* XII.307–14.

OF ALL NATIONS WHO BELIEVE IN THE REVEALED CHRIST,
AND A THREAT OF ETERNAL DEATH TO UNBELIEVERS.[6]

* * *

Once the gospel, the new covenant through faith in Christ, is intro-
duced, then all the old covenant, in other words the entire Mosaic law,
is abolished. Jer. xxxi. 31–33, as above; Luke xvi. 16: *the law and the
prophets existed until John*; Acts xv. 10: *so now why do you tempt God
to put a yoke on the neck of the disciples, which neither our fathers nor
we were able to bear*; Rom. iii. 21, 22: *but now God's righteousness is
revealed without the law,* and vi. 14: *you are not under the law but
under grace,* and vii. 4: *you have become dead to the law in the body of
Jesus Christ; that you should be another's, his, that is, who is raised from
the dead, that you may bear fruit to God,* and vii. 6: *but now we are
delivered from the law, since that in which we were held is dead, so that
we may serve in newness of spirit, and not in the oldness of the letter.*
At the beginning of the same chapter Paul shows that we are released
from the law in the same way as a wife is released from her dead husband.
Also vii. 7: *I did not know sin except through the law*: that is, the whole
law, *for I should not have known lust if the law had not said, Do not
lust. . . .* The law referred to here is the decalogue, so it follows that
we are released from the decalogue too. See also viii. 15: *you have not
received the spirit of slavery again in fear,* and xiv. 20: *indeed all things
are pure . . . ,* compared with Tit. i. 15: *to the pure, all things are pure:
but to the polluted and the unbelieving nothing is pure, but both their
mind and their conscience is defiled*; I Cor. vi. 12: *all things are lawful
for me, but not all things are for my good; all things are lawful for me,
but I will not let anything take control of me,* and x. 23: *all things are
lawful for me, but not all things are good for me; all things are lawful
for me, but not all things constructive*; II Cor. iii. 3: *not on tablets of
stone but on the fleshly tablets of the heart,* and iii. 6–8: *ministers of the
new covenant, not of the letter but of the spirit: for the letter kills but
the spirit gives life.*

* * *

The usual retort is that all these passages should be taken to refer to
the abolition of the ceremonial code only. This argument can be quickly
refuted, firstly, by the definition of the law itself, as given in the previous

6. Milton's unorthodox dogma regarding abrogation of the whole Mosaic law and the complete
freedom of Christian liberty is fundamental to his Christian humanism and theory of toleration.
Luther, Calvin, and orthodox theologians generally hold that Christ's sacrifice abolished the
ceremonial and civil portions of the Mosaic law but left the moral part binding on Christians.
(Luther holds the entire Mosaic law abrogated but retains the moral part as useful for self-
examination.) The gift of Christian liberty, the orthodox further hold, is limited to the spiritual
life of believers, and has no bearing on civil and political matters. In contrast, Milton argues
that Christ's sacrifice abrogated the total Mosaic law, moral as well as ceremonial and civil,
and bestowed on believers a complete Christian liberty that frees them from the judgments of
men and from civil or ecclesiastical coercion in religious matters.

chapter, which contains all the reasons for the law's enactment. When all the causes of the law, considered as a whole, have been removed or have become obsolete, then the whole law must be annulled too. The principal reasons given for the enactment of the law as a whole, are as follows: to stimulate our depravity, and thus cause anger; to inspire us with slavish fear, as a result of the enmity and the written accusation directed against us; to be a schoolmaster to bring us to the righteousness of Christ, and so on.[7] Now the texts quoted above prove not only that every one of these reasons has now been removed, but also that they have nothing at all to do with ceremonies.

First, then, the law is abolished above all because it is the law of works, and in order that it may give place to a law of grace. Rom. iii. 27: *By what law? The law of works? No: but by the law of faith*, and xi. 6: *if through grace, then no longer from works; otherwise grace is not grace*. Now the law of works was not only the ceremonial law but the whole law.

*   *   *

In addition, this law not only cannot justify, it disturbs believers and makes them waver. It even tempts God, if we try to fulfil it. It contains no promise, in fact it breaks and puts an end to all promises—of inheritance, of adoption, of grace itself and even of the spirit. What is more, it makes us accursed.[8] The law which does all this is surely repealed. Now it was not only the ceremonial law but the whole law, the law of works, which did these things. Therefore the whole law is repealed.

*   *   *

The substance of the law, love of God and of our neighbor, should not, I repeat, be thought of as destroyed. We must realize that only the written surface has been changed, and that the law is now inscribed on believers' hearts by the spirit. At the same time, however, it sometimes appears that, where particular commandments are concerned, the spirit is at variance with the letter. This happens when by breaking the letter of the law we behave in a way which conforms better with our love of God and of our neighbor. Thus Christ himself broke the letter of the law, Mark ii. 27: look at the fourth commandment, and then compare his words, *the sabbath was made for man, not man for the sabbath*. Paul did the same when he said that marriage with an unbeliever was not to be dissolved, contrary to the express injunction of the law. I Cor. vii. 12: *I, not the Lord*. In interpreting both these commandments, the commandment about the Sabbath and that about marriage, attention to the requirements of charity is given precedence over any written law. The other commandments should all be treated in the same way.

*   *   *

7. *PL* XII.287–94.
8. *PL* XII.416.

The law of slavery having been abrogated through the gospel, the result is Christian Liberty. It is true that liberty is primarily the fruit of adoption, and was consequently not unknown in the time of the law, as I said in Chapter xxiii. However, our liberty could not be perfect or manifest before the advent of Christ, our liberator. Therefore liberty is a matter relevant chiefly to the gospel, and is associated with it.[9] This is so, first, because truth exists chiefly under the gospel, John i. 17: *grace and truth are present through Jesus Christ*, and truth liberates, viii. 31, 32: *if you remain in my word, then you will really be my disciples, and you will know the truth, and the truth will make you free*, and viii. 36: *so if the son liberates you, you will really be free.* Secondly, because the peculiar gift of the gospel is the Spirit and: *where the Spirit of the Lord is, there is liberty*, II Cor. iii. 17.

CHRISTIAN LIBERTY means that CHRIST OUR LIBERATOR FREES US FROM THE SLAVERY OF SIN AND THUS FROM THE RULE OF THE LAW AND OF MEN, AS IF WE WERE EMANCIPATED SLAVES. HE DOES THIS SO THAT, BEING MADE SONS INSTEAD OF SERVANTS[1] AND GROWN MEN INSTEAD OF BOYS, WE MAY SERVE GOD IN CHARITY THROUGH THE GUIDANCE OF THE SPIRIT OF TRUTH. Gal. v. 1: *stand fast, then, in the liberty by which Christ has freed us, and do not be entangled again in the yoke of slavery*; Rom. viii. 2: *the law of the spirit of life which is in Christ Jesus has freed me from the law of sin and of death*, and viii. 15: *for you have not received the spirit of slavery again in fear, but you have received the spirit of adoption, through which we cry Abba, Father*; Gal. iv. 7: *you are not a slave any more, but a son*; Heb. ii. 15: *that he might free all those who through fear of death were condemned to slavery all their lives*; I Cor. vii. 23: *you are bought with a price, do not be slaves of men*; James i. 25: *who looks into that perfect law of liberty*, and ii. 12: *speak and act like those who are to be judged by the law of liberty.*

*   *   *

Chapter XXX

OF THE HOLY SCRIPTURE

*   *   *

Thus the scriptures are, both in themselves and through God's illumination absolutely clear. If studied carefully and regularly, they are an ideal instrument for educating even unlearned readers in those matters which have most to do with salvation. Psal. xix. 8: *the doctrine of Jehovah is perfect, restoring the soul; the testimony of Jehovah is true, making the*

9. PL XII.524–26.
1. PL XII.305–6.

unlearned wise . . . , and cxix. 105: *your word is a lamp to my feet and a light to my path,* * * * *that no prophecy of the scriptures is susceptible of particular interpretation: for, at the time when it came, the prophecy was not brought by the will of man. . . .* The prophecy, then, must not be interpreted by the intellect of a particular individual, that is to say, not by his merely human intellect, but with the help of the Holy Spirit, promised to each individual believer.[2] Hence the gift of prophecy, I Cor. xiv.

The scriptures, then, are plain and sufficient in themselves. Thus they *can make a man wise and fit for salvation through faith,* and *through them the man of God may be fully prepared and fully provided for every good work.* Through what madness is it, then, that even members of the reformed church persist in explaining and illustrating and interpreting the most holy truths of religion, as if they were conveyed obscurely in the Holy Scriptures? Why do they shroud them in the thick darkness of metaphysics? Why do they employ all their useless technicalities and meaningless distinctions and barbarous jargon in their attempt to make the scriptures plainer and easier to understand, when they themselves are continually claiming how supremely clear they are already? As if scripture did not contain the clearest of all lights in itself: as if it were not in itself sufficient, especially in matters of faith and holiness: as if the sense of the divine truth, itself absolutely plain, needed to be brought out more clearly or more fully, or otherwise explained, by means of terms imported from the most abstruse of human sciences—which does not, in fact, deserve the name of a science at all!

* * *

Each passage of scripture has only a single sense, though in the Old Testament this sense is often a combination of the historical and the typological, take Hosea xi. 1, for example, compared with Matt. ii. 15: *I have called my son out of Egypt.* This can be read correctly in two senses, as a reference both to the people of Israel and to Christ in his infancy.

* * *

The right method of interpreting the scriptures has been laid down by theologians. This is certainly useful, but no very careful attention is paid to it. The requisites are linguistic ability, knowledge of the original sources, consideration of the overall intent, distinction between literal and figurative language, examination of the causes and circumstances, and of what comes before and after the passage in question, and comparison of one text with another. It must always be asked, too, how far the interpretation is in agreement with faith. * * *

Lastly, no inferences should be made from the text, unless they follow necessarily from what is written. This precaution is necessary, otherwise

2. *PL* XII.511–13.

we may be forced to believe something which is not written instead of something which is, and to accept human reasoning, generally fallacious, instead of divine doctrine, thus mistaking the shadow for the substance. What we are obliged to believe are the things written in the sacred books, not the things debated in academic gatherings.

Every believer is entitled to interpret the scriptures; and by that I mean interpret them for himself. He has the spirit, who guides truth, and he has the mind of Christ. Indeed, no one else can usefully interpret them for him, unless that person's interpretation coincides with the one he makes for himself and his own conscience.

* * *

No visible church, then, let alone any magistrate, has the right to impose its own interpretation upon the consciences of men as matters of legal obligation, thus demanding implicit faith.

* * *

Nowadays the external authority for our faith, in other words, the scriptures, is of very considerable importance and, generally speaking, it is the authority of which we first have experience. The pre-eminent and supreme authority, however, is the authority of the Spirit, which is internal, and the individual possession of each man.

* * *

OF MAN'S RECIPROCAL DUTIES TOWARDS HIS NEIGHBOR, PARTICULARLY PRIVATE DUTIES

So far I have spoken of our special virtues or duties towards our neighbor *qua* neighbor. Now I shall deal with our duties TOWARDS OUR NEIGHBOR, WHEN HE IS RELATED TO US IN SOME PARTICULAR WAY.

These are either private or public.

The private duties are either domestic or concern those not of our own household. Gen xviii. 19: *I know him, and he will teach his children and his household, and they will observe . . .* ; I Tim. v. 8: *if anyone does not make provision for his relations, and especially for members of his own household, he has denied the faith and is worse than an unbeliever.*

Domestic duties are generally reciprocal and include those of husband and wife, parents and children, brothers, kinsfolk, masters and servants.

THE DUTIES OF HUSBAND AND WIFE are either common to both or peculiar to one of them.

Those common to both are outlined in I Cor. vii. 3: *let the husband show due kindness to the wife, and the wife to the husband.*

Duties peculiar to one are peculiar either to husband or to wife.

First, to the husband; Exod. xxi, 10, 11: *he shall not diminish her food, her clothing, or her portion of time. If he does not maintain these*

three things . . . ; Prov. v. 18, 19: *be joyful with the wife of your youth
. . .* ; Esther i. 22: *that each man might be ruler in his own house
. . .* ; I Cor. xi. 3: *I would have you know that Christ is the head of every
man, but woman's head is man;* Eph. v. 25: *husbands, love your wives
as Christ loved his church;* Col. iii. 19: *husbands, love your wives and
do not be bitter with them;* I Pet. iii. 7: *in the same way, husbands should
live with their wives as befits intelligent beings, paying honor to the
woman as the weaker vessel. . . .*

Behavior which runs counter to these instructions is deprecated. Mal.
ii. 13–15: *Jehovah has been a witness between you and the wife of your
youth, towards whom you behave deceitfully . . .* ; Prov. v. 20, 21: *why,
my son, do you go astray with a strange woman. . . .*

The wife's duties. Prov. xiv. 1: *every wise woman builds, her house,*
and xix. 14: *an intelligent wife is Jehovah's gift,* and xxxi. 11, etc.; *her
husband's heart trusts in her . . .* ; I Cor. xi. 3, etc.: *a woman is man's
glory: for man was not made from woman, but woman from man . . .* ;
Eph. v. 22–24: *wives, submit to your own husbands as to the Lord, for
the husband is the head of the wife as Christ is the head of the church
and it is he that gives salvation to the body: so . . . in everything;* Col.
iii. 18: *wives, submit to your husbands, as befits those who are in the
Lord;* Tit. ii. 4, 5: *that they may teach the young women to be wise, and
to love their husbands and children, and be temperate, chaste, busy at
home, good, obedient to their own husbands. Thus God's word will not
be blasphemed;* I Pet. iii. 1, etc.: *let wives subject themselves to their
husbands, so that. . . .* The very creation of woman implies that this
should be so, Gen. ii. 22: *he made that rib which he had taken from
Adam into a woman.* It is wrong for one single part of the body—and
not one of the most important parts—to disobey the rest of the body,
and even the head. This, at any rate, is the opinion of God: Gen. iii.
16: *he shall rule over you.*[3]

3. *PL* X.195–96.

Selections from the Bible†

The Book of Genesis

CHAPTER 1

In the beginning God created the heaven and the earth. And the earth was without form, and void; and darkness was upon the face of the deep. And the spirit of God moved upon the face of the waters. And God said, "Let there be light": and there was light. And God saw the light, that it was good: and God divided the light from the darkness. And God called the light Day, and the darkness he called Night. And the evening and the morning were the first day.

6 And God said, "Let there be a firmament in the midst of the waters, and let it divide the waters from the waters." And God made the firmament, and divided the waters which were under the firmament from the waters which were above the firmament: and it was so. And God called the firmament Heaven. And the evening and the morning were the second day.

9 And God said, "Let the waters under the heaven be gathered together unto one place, and let the dry land appear": and it was so. And God called the dry land Earth; and the gathering together of the waters called he Seas: and God saw that it was good. And God said, "Let the earth bring forth grass, the herb yielding seed, and the fruit tree yielding fruit after his kind, whose seed is in itself, upon the earth": and it was so. And the earth brought forth grass, and herb yielding seed after his kind, and the tree yielding fruit, whose seed was in itself, after his kind: and God saw that it was good. And the evening and the morning were the third day.

14 And God said, "Let there be lights in the firmament of the heaven to divide the day from the night; and let them be for signs, and for seasons, and for days, and years: and let them be for lights in the

† Milton was three years old when the Authorized Version of the Bible was first published, in 1611, and throughout his life he used a copy printed in 1612. Of course he had read and consulted many translations of the Scriptures. The hundreds of quotations used as "proof texts" in his *Christian Doctrine*, for example, are his translations of passages from the Junius-Tremelius Latin Bible in a Geneva edition of 1630, though Milton must have owned a copy of the Vulgate as well. He read the Old Testament in Hebrew and the New Testament in Greek, but most of the verbal echoes of the Bible in *Paradise Lost* are in the words of the King James Version, from which the following selections have been made.

firmament of the heaven to give light upon the earth": and it was so. And God made two great lights; the greater light to rule the day, and the lesser light to rule the night: he made the stars also. And God set them in the firmament of the heaven to give light upon the earth, and to rule over the day and over the night, and to divide the light from the darkness: and God saw that it was good. And the evening and the morning were the fourth day.

20 And God said, "Let the waters bring forth abundantly the moving creature that hath life, and fowl that may fly above the earth in the open firmament of heaven." And God created great whales, and every living creature that moveth, which the waters brought forth abundantly, after their kind, and every winged fowl after his kind: and God saw that it was good. And God blessed them, saying, "Be fruitful, and multiply, and fill the waters in the seas, and let fowl multiply in the earth." And the evening and the morning were the fifth day.

24 And God said, "Let the earth bring forth the living creature after his kind, cattle, and creeping thing, and beast of the earth after his kind": and it was so. And God made the beast of the earth after his kind, and cattle after their kind, and every thing that creepeth upon the earth after his kind: and God saw that it was good. And God said, "Let us make man in our image, after our likeness: and let them have dominion over the fish of the sea, and over the fowl of the air, and over the cattle, and over all the earth, and over every creeping thing that creepeth upon the earth." So God created man in his own image, in the image of God created he him; male and female created he them. And God blessed them, and God said unto them, "Be fruitful, and multiply, and replenish the earth, and subdue it: and have dominion over the fish of the sea, and over the fowl of the air, and over every living thing that moveth upon the earth." And God said, "Behold, I have given you every herb bearing seed, which is upon the face of all the earth, and every tree, in the which is the fruit of a tree yielding seed; to you it shall be for meat. And to every beast of the earth, and to every fowl of the air, and to every thing that creepeth upon the earth, wherein there is life, I have given every green herb for meat": and it was so. And God saw every thing that he had made, and, behold, it was very good. And the evening and the morning were the sixth day.

CHAPTER 2

Thus the heavens and the earth were finished, and all the host of them. And on the seventh day God ended his work which he had made, and he rested on the seventh day from all his work which he had made. And God blessed the seventh day, and sanctified it: because that in it he had rested from all his work which God created and made.

4 These are the generations of the heavens and of the earth when

they were created, in the day that the Lord God made the earth and the heavens, and every plant of the field before it was in the earth, and every herb of the field before it grew: for the LORD God had not caused it to rain upon the earth, and there was not a man to till the ground. But there went up a mist from the earth, and watered the whole face of the ground. And the LORD God formed man of the dust of the ground, and breathed into his nostrils the breath of life; and man became a living soul. And the LORD God planted a garden eastward in Eden; and there he put the man whom he had formed. And out of the ground made the LORD God to grow every tree that is pleasant to the sight, and good for food; the tree of life also in the midst of the garden, and the tree of knowledge of good and evil. 10 And a river went out of Eden to water the garden; and from thence it was parted, and became into four heads. The name of the first is Pison: that is it which compasseth the whole land of Havilah, where there is gold; and the gold of that land is good: there is bdellium and the onyx stone. And the name of the second river is Gihon: the same is it that compasseth the whole land of Ethiopia. And the name of the third river is Hiddekel: that is it which goeth toward the east of Assyria. And the fourth river in Euphrates. And the LORD God took the man, and put him into the garden of Eden to dress it and to keep it. And the LORD God commanded the man, saying, "Of every tree of the garden thou mayest freely eat: but of the tree of the knowledge of good and evil, thou shalt not eat of it: for in the day that thou eatest thereof thou shall surely die."

18 And the LORD God said, "It is not good that the man should be alone; I will make him an help meet for him." And out of the ground the LORD God formed every beast of the field, and every fowl of the air; and brought them unto Adam to see what he would call them: and whatsoever Adam called every living creature, that was the name thereof. And Adam gave names to all cattle, and to the fowl of the air, and to every beast of the field; but for Adam there was not found an help meet for him. And the LORD God caused a deep sleep to fall upon Adam, and he slept: and he took one of his ribs, and closed up the flesh instead thereof; and the rib, which the LORD God had taken from man, made he a woman, and brought her unto the man. 23 And Adam said, "This is now bone of my bones, and flesh of my flesh: she shall be called Woman, because she was taken out of Man." Therefore shall a man leave his father and his mother, and shall cleave unto his wife: and they shall be one flesh. And they were both naked, the man and his wife, and were not ashamed.

CHAPTER 3

Now the serpent was more subtil than any beast of the field which the LORD God had made. And he said unto the woman, "Yea, hath

God said, 'Ye shall not eat of every tree of the garden'?" And the woman said unto the serpent, "We may eat of the fruit of the trees of the garden: but of the fruit of the tree which is in the midst of the garden, God hath said, 'Ye shall not eat of it, neither shall ye touch it, lest ye die.' " And the serpent said unto the woman, "Ye shall not surely die: for God doth know that in the day ye eat thereof, then your eyes shall be opened, and ye shall be as gods, knowing good and evil." And when the woman saw that the tree was good for food, and that it was pleasant to the eyes, and a tree to be desired to make one wise, she took of the fruit thereof, and did eat, and gave also unto her husband with her; and he did eat. And the eyes of them both were opened, and they knew that they were naked; and they sewed fig leaves together, and made themselves aprons. And they heard the voice of the LORD God walking in the garden in the cool of the day: and Adam and his wife hid themselves from the presence of the LORD God amongst the trees of the garden. 10 And the LORD God called unto Adam, and said unto him, "Where art thou?" And he said, "I heard thy voice in the garden, and I was afraid, because I was naked; and I hid myself." And he said, "Who told thee that thou wast naked? Hast thou eaten of the tree, whereof I commanded thee that thou shouldest not eat?" And the man said, "The woman whom thou gavest to be with me, she gave me of the tree, and I did eat." And the LORD God said unto the woman, "What is this that thou hast done?" And the woman said, "The serpent beguiled me, and I did eat." And the LORD God said unto the serpent, "Because thou hast done this, thou art cursed above all cattle, and above every beast of the field; upon thy belly shalt thou go, and dust shalt thou eat all the days of thy life: and I will put enmity between thee and the woman, and between thy seed and her seed; it shall bruise thy head, and thou shalt bruise his heel." Unto the woman he said, "I will greatly multiply thy sorrow and thy conception; in sorrow thou shalt bring forth children; and thy desire shalt be to thy husband, and he shall rule over thee." And unto Adam he said, "Because thou hast hearkened unto the voice of thy wife, and hast eaten of the tree, of which I commanded thee, saying, Thou shalt not eat of it: cursed is the ground for thy sake; in sorrow shalt thou eat of it all the days of thy life; thorns also and thistles shall it bring forth to thee; and thou shalt eat the herb of the field; in the sweat of thy face shalt thou eat bread, till thou return unto the ground; for out of it wast thou taken: for dust thou art, and unto dust shalt thou return." And Adam called his wife's name Eve; because she was the mother of all living. Unto Adam also and to his wife did the LORD God make coats of skins, and clothed them.

22 And the LORD God said, "Behold, the man is become as one of us, to know good and evil; and now, lest he put forth his hand, and take also of the tree of life, and eat, and live for ever": therefore the LORD God sent him forth from the garden of Eden, to till the ground

from whence he was taken. So he drove out the man; and he placed at the east of the garden of Eden Cherubims, and a flaming sword which turned every way, to keep the way of the tree of life.

CHAPTER 11.1–9, 31–32

And the whole earth was of one language, and of one speech. And it came to pass, as they journeyed from the east, that they found a plain in the land of Shinar; and they dwelt there. And they said one to another, "Go to, let us make brick, and burn them thoroughly." And they had brick for stone, and slime had they for morter. And they said, "Go to, let us build us a city and a tower, whose top may reach unto heaven; and let us make us a name, lest we be scattered abroad upon the face of the whole earth." And the LORD came down to see the city and the tower, which the children of men builded. And the LORD said, "Behold, the people is one, and they have all one language; and this they begin to do: and now nothing will be restrained from them, which they have imagined to do. Go to, let us go down, and there confound their language, that they may not understand one another's speech." So the LORD scattered them abroad from thence upon the face of all the earth: and they left off to build the city. Therefore is the name of it called Babel; because the LORD did there confound the language of all the earth: and from thence did the LORD scatter them abroad upon the face of all the earth.

* * *

And Terah took Abram his son, and Lot the son of Haran his son's son, and Sarai his daughter in law, his son Abram's wife; and they went forth with them from Ur of the Chaldees, to go into the land of Canaan; and they came unto Haran, and dwelt there. And the days of Terah were two hundred and five years: and Terah died in Haran.

CHAPTER 12.1–7

Now the LORD had said unto Abram, "Get thee out of thy country, and from thy kindred, and from thy father's house, unto a land that I will shew thee: and I will make of thee a great nation, and I will bless thee, and make thy name great; and thou shalt be a blessing: and I will bless them that bless thee, and curse him that curseth thee: and in thee shall all families of the earth be blessed." So Abram departed, as the LORD had spoken unto him; and Lot went with him: and Abram was seventy and five years old when he departed out of Haran. And Abram took Sarai his wife, and Lot his brother's son, and all their substance that they had gathered, and the souls that they had gotten in Haran; and they went forth to go into the land of Canaan; and into the land of Canaan they came. And Abram passed through the land unto the place

of Sichem, unto the plain of Moreh. And the Canaanite was then in
the land. And the LORD appeared unto Abram, and said, "Unto thy
seed will I give this land": and there builded he an altar unto the LORD,
who appeared unto him.

The Book of Exodus

CHAPTER 13.17–22

And it came to pass, when Pharaoh had let the people go, that God
led them not through the way of the land of the Philistines, although
that was near; for God said, "Lest peradventure the people repent when
they see war, and they return to Egypt": but God led the people about,
through the way of the wilderness of the Red sea: and the children of
Israel went up harnessed out of the land of Egypt. And Moses took the
bones of Joseph with him: for he had straitly sworn the children of Israel,
saying, "God will surely visit you; and ye shall carry up my bones away
hence with you." And they took their journey from Succoth, and en-
camped in Etham, in the edge of the wilderness. And the LORD went
before them by day in a pillar of a cloud, to lead them the way; and by
night in a pillar of fire, to give them light; to go by day and night: he
took not away the pillar of the cloud by day, nor the pillar of fire by
night, from before the people.

CHAPTER 14.5–31

And it was told the king of Egypt that the people fled: and the heart
of Pharaoh and all of his servants was turned against the people, and
they said, "Why have we done this, that we have let Israel go from
serving us?" And he made ready his chariot, and took his people with
him: and he took six hundred chosen chariots, and all the chariots of
Egypt, and captains over every one of them. And the LORD hardened
the heart of Pharaoh king of Egypt, and he pursued after the children
of Israel: and the children of Israel went out with an high hand. But
the Egyptians pursued after them, all the horses and chariots of Pharaoh,
and his horsemen, and his army, and overtook them encamping by the
sea, beside Pi-hahiroth, before Baal-zephon. And when Pharaoh drew
nigh, the children of Israel lifted up their eyes, and, behold, the Egyp-
tians marched after them; and they were sore afraid: and the children
of Israel cried out unto the LORD. And they said unto Moses, "Because
there were no graves in Egypt, hast thou taken us away to die in the
wilderness? wherefore hast thou dealt thus with us, to carry us forth out
of Egypt? Is not this the word that we did tell thee in Egypt, saying, Let
us alone, that we may serve the Egyptians? For it had been better for

us to serve the Egyptians, than that we should die in the wilderness." And Moses said unto the people, "Fear ye not, stand still, and see the salvation of the LORD, which he will shew to you to day: for the Egyptians whom ye have seen to day, ye shall see them again no more for ever. The LORD shall fight for you, and ye shall hold your peace."

15 And the Lord said unto Moses, "Wherefore criest thou unto me? speak unto the children of Israel, that they go forward: but lift thou up thy rod, and stretch out thine hand over the sea, and divide it: and the children of Israel shall go on dry ground through the midst of the sea. And I, behold, I will harden the hearts of the Egyptians, and they shall follow them: and I will get me honour upon Pharaoh, and upon all his host, upon his chariots, and upon his horsemen. And the Egyptians shall know that I am the LORD, when I have gotten me honour upon Pharaoh, upon his chariots, and upon his horsemen." And the angel of God, which went before the camp of Israel, removed and went behind them; and the pillar of the cloud went from before their face, and stood behind them: and it came between the camp of the Egyptians and the camp of Israel; and it was a cloud and darkness to them, but it gave light by night to these: so that the one came not near the other all the night. And Moses stretched out his hand over the sea; and the LORD caused the sea to go back by a strong east wind all that night, and made the sea dry land, and the waters were divided. And the children of Israel went into the midst of the sea upon the dry ground: and the waters were a wall unto them on their right hand, and on their left. And the Egyptians pursued, and went in after them to the midst of the sea, even all Pharaoh's horses, his chariots, and his horsemen. And it came to pass, that in the morning watch the LORD looked unto the host of the Egyptians through the pillar of fire and of the cloud, and troubled the host of the Egyptians, and took off their chariot wheels, that they drave them heavily: so that the Egyptians said, "Let us flee from the face of Israel; for the LORD fighteth for them against the Egyptians."

26 And the LORD said unto Moses, "Stretch out thine hand over the sea, that the waters may come again upon the Egyptians, upon their chariots, and upon their horsemen." And Moses stretched forth his hand over the sea, and the sea returned to his strength when the morning appeared: and the Egyptians fled against it; and the LORD overthrew the Egyptians in the midst of the sea. And the waters returned, and covered the chariots, and the horsemen, and all the host of Pharaoh that came into the sea after them; there remained not so much as one of them. But the children of Israel walked upon dry land in the midst of the sea; and the waters were a wall unto them on their right hand, and on their left. Thus the LORD saved Israel that day out of the hand of the Egyptians; and Israel saw the Egyptians dead upon the sea shore. And Israel saw that great work which the LORD did upon the Egyptians: and the people feared the LORD, and believed the LORD, and his servant Moses.

CHAPTER 19. 1–9, 16–25

In the third month, when the children of Israel were gone forth out of the land of Egypt, the same day came they into the wilderness of Sinai. For they were departed from Rephidim, and were come to the desert of Sinai, and had pitched in the wilderness; and there Israel camped before the mount. And Moses went up unto God, and the LORD called unto him out of the mountain, saying, "Thus shalt thou say to the house of Jacob, and tell the children of Israel; 'Ye have seen what I did unto the Egyptians, and how I bare you on eagles' wings, and brought you unto myself. Now therefore, if ye will obey my voice indeed, and keep my covenant, then ye shall be a peculiar treasure unto me above all people: for all the earth is mine: and ye shall be unto me a kingdom of priests, and an holy nation.' These are the words which thou shalt speak unto the children of Israel." And Moses came and called for the elders of the people, and laid before their faces all these words which the LORD commanded him. And all the people answered together, and said, "All that the LORD hath spoken we will do." And Moses returned the words of the people unto the LORD. And the LORD said unto Moses, "Lo, I come unto thee in a thick cloud, that the people may hear when I speak with thee, and believe thee for ever." And Moses told the words of the people unto the LORD.

* * *

And it came to pass on the third day in the morning, that there were thunders and lightnings, and a thick cloud upon the mount, and the voice of the trumpet exceeding loud; so that all the people that was in the camp trembled. And Moses brought forth the people out of the camp to meet with God; and they stood at the nether part of the mount. And mount Sinai was altogether on a smoke, because the LORD descended upon it in fire: and the smoke thereof ascended as the smoke of a furnace, and the whole mount quaked greatly. And when the voice of the trumpet sounded long, and waxed louder and louder, Moses spake, and God answered him by a voice. And the LORD came down upon mount Sinai, on the top of the mount: and the LORD called Moses up to the top of the mount; and Moses went up. And the LORD said unto Moses, "Go down, charge the people, lest they break through unto the LORD to gaze, and many of them perish. And let the priests also, which come near to the LORD, sanctify themselves, lest the LORD break forth upon them." And Moses said unto the LORD, "The people cannot come up to mount Sinai: for thou chargedst us, saying, 'Set bounds about the mount, and sanctify it.' " And the LORD said unto him, "Away, get thee down, and thou shalt come up, thou, and Aaron with thee: but let not the priests and the people break through to come up unto the LORD, lest he break forth upon them." So Moses went down unto the people, and spake unto them.

CHAPTER 20.1–21

And God spake all these words, saying,

"I am the LORD thy God, which have brought thee out of the land of Egypt, out of the house of bondage.

"Thou shalt have no other gods before me.

"Thou shalt not make unto thee any graven image, or any likeness of any thing that is in heaven above, or that is in the earth beneath, or that is in the water under the earth: thou shalt not bow down thyself to them, nor serve them: for I the LORD thy God am a jealous God, visiting the iniquity of the fathers upon the children unto the third and fourth generation of them that hate me; and shewing mercy unto thousands of them that love me, and keep my commandments.

"Thou shalt not take the name of the LORD thy God in vain; for the LORD will not hold him guiltless that taketh his name in vain.

9 "Remember the sabbath day, to keep it holy. Six days shalt thou labour, and do all thy work: but the seventh day is the sabbath of the LORD thy God: in it thou shalt not do any work, thou, nor thy son, nor thy daughter, thy manservant, nor thy maidservant, nor thy cattle, nor thy stranger that is within thy gates: for in six days the LORD made heaven and earth, the sea, and all that in them is, and rested the seventh day: wherefore the LORD blessed the sabbath day, and hallowed it.

"Honour thy father and thy mother: that thy days may be long upon the land which the LORD thy God giveth thee.

"Thou shalt not kill.

"Thou shalt not commit adultery.

"Thou shalt not steal.

"Thou shalt not bear false witness against thy neighbour.

"Thou shalt not covet thy neighbour's house, thou shalt not covet thy neighbour's wife, nor his manservant, nor his maidservant, nor his ox, nor his ass, nor any thing that is thy neighbour's."

18 And all the people saw the thunderings, and the lightnings, and the noise of the trumpet, and the mountain smoking: and when the people saw it, they removed, and stood afar off. And they said unto Moses, "Speak thou with us, and we will hear: but let not God speak with us, lest we die." And Moses said unto the people, "Fear not: for God is come to prove you, and that his fear may be before your faces, that ye sin not." And the people stood afar off, and Moses drew near unto the thick darkness where God was.

CHAPTER 24

And he said unto Moses, "Come up unto the LORD, thou, and Aaron, Nadab, and Abihu, and seventy of the elders of Israel; and worship ye afar off. And Moses alone shall come near the LORD: but they shall not

come nigh; neither shall the people go up with him." And Moses came
and told the people all the words of the LORD, and all the judgments:
and all the people answered with one voice, and said, "All the words
which the LORD hath said will we do." And Moses wrote all the words
of the LORD, and rose up early in the morning, and builded an altar
under the hill, and twelve pillars, according to the twelve tribes of Israel.
5 And he sent young men of the children of Israel, which offered burnt
offerings, and sacrificed peace offerings of oxen unto the LORD. And
Moses took half of the blood, and put it in basons; and half of the blood
he sprinkled on the altar. And he took the book of the covenant, and
read in the audience of the people: and they said, "All that the LORD
hath said will we do, and be obedient." And Moses took the blood, and
sprinkled it on the people, and said, "Behold the blood of the covenant,
which the LORD hath made with you concerning all these words." Then
went up Moses, and Aaron, Nadab, and Abihu, and seventy of the elders
of Israel: and they saw the God of Israel: and there was under his feet
as it were a paved work of a sapphire stone, and as it were the body of
heaven in his clearness. And upon the nobles of the children of Israel
he laid not his hand: also they saw God, and did eat and drink.

12 And the LORD said unto Moses, "Come up to me into the mount,
and be there: and I will give thee tables of stone, and a law, and com-
mandments which I have written; that thou mayest teach them." And
Moses rose up, and his minister Joshua: and Moses went up into the
mount of God. And he said unto the elders, "Tarry ye here for us, until
we come again unto you: and, behold, Aaron and Hur are with you: if
any man have any matters to do, let him come unto them." And Moses
went up into the mount, and a cloud covered the mount. And the glory
of the LORD abode upon mount Sinai, and the cloud covered it six days:
and the seventh day he called unto Moses out of the midst of the cloud.
And the sight of the glory of the LORD was like devouring fire on the
top of the mount in the eyes of the children of Israel. And Moses went
into the midst of the cloud, and gat him up into the mount: and Moses
was in the mount forty days and forty nights.

CHAPTER 40.34–38

Then a cloud covered the tent of the congregation, and the glory of
the LORD filled the tabernacle. And Moses was not able to enter into
the tent of the congregation, because the cloud abode thereon, and the
glory of the LORD filled the tabernacle. And when the cloud was taken
up from over the tabernacle, the children of Israel went onward in all
their journeys: but if the cloud were not taken up, then they journeyed
not till the day that it was taken up. For the cloud of the LORD was
upon the tabernacle by day, and fire was on it by night, in the sight of
all the house of Israel, throughout all their journeys.

The Book of Psalms

PSALM 2

Why do the heathen rage,
And the people imagine a vain thing?
The kings of the earth set themselves.
And the rulers take counsel together,
Against the Lord, and against his anointed, saying,
Let us break their bands asunder,
And cast away their cords from us.
He that sitteth in the heavens shall laugh:
The Lord shall have them in derision.
5   Then shall he speak unto them in his wrath.
And vex them in his sore displeasure.
Yet have I set my king upon my holy hill in Zion.
I will declare the decree:
The Lord hath said unto me, Thou art my Son;
This day have I begotten thee.
Ask of me, and I shall give thee
The heathen for thine inheritance,
And the uttermost parts of the earth for thy possession.
Thou shalt break them with a rod of iron;
Thou shalt dash them in pieces like a potter's vessel.
10 Be wise now, O ye kings:
Be instructed, ye judges of the earth.
Serve the Lord with fear, and rejoice with trembling.
Kiss the Son, lest he be angry, and ye perish from the way.
When his wrath is kindled but a little.
Blessed are all they that put their trust in him.

PSALM 104

Bless the Lord, O my soul.
O Lord my God, thou art very great;
Thou art clothed with honour and majesty.
Who coverest thyself with light as with a garment:
Who stretchest out the heavens like a curtain:
Who layeth the beams of his chambers in the waters:
Who maketh the clouds his chariot:
Who walketh upon the wings of the wind:
Who maketh his angels spirits;
His ministers a flaming fire:
5 Who laid the foundations of the earth,
That it should not be removed for ever.
Thou coveredst it with the deep as with a garment:

The waters stood above the mountains.
At thy rebuke they fled:
At the voice of thy thunder they hasted away.
They go up by the mountains; they go down
    by the valleys
Unto the place which thou hast founded for them.
Thou hast set a bound that they may not pass over;
That they turn not again to cover the earth.
10 He sendeth the springs into the valleys,
Which run among the hills.
They give drink to every beast of the field:
The wild asses quench their thirst.
By them shall the fowls of the heaven have
    their habitation,
Which sing among the branches.
He watereth the hills from his chambers:
The earth is satisfied with the fruit of thy works.
He causeth the grass to grow for the cattle,
And herb for the service of man:
That he may bring forth food out of the earth;
15 And wine that maketh glad the heart of man,
And oil to make his face to shine,
And bread which strengtheneth man's heart.
The trees of the LORD are full of sap;
The cedars of Lebanon, which he hath planted;
Where the birds make their nests:
As for the stork, the fir trees are her house.
The high hills are a refuge for the wild goats;
And the rocks for the conies.
He appointed the moon for seasons:
The sun knoweth his going down.
20 Thou makest darkness, and it is night:
Wherein all the beasts of the forest do creep forth.
The young lions roar after their prey,
And seek their meat from God.
The sun ariseth, they father themselves together,
And lay them down in their dens.
Man goeth forth unto his work
And to his labour until the evening.
O LORD, how manifold are thy works!
In wisdom hast thou made them all:
The earth is full of thy riches.
25 So is this great and wide sea,
Wherein are things creeping innumerable,
Both small and great beasts.
There go the ships:
There is that leviathan, whom thou hast made

to play therein.
These wait all upon thee:
That thou mayest give them their meat in
    due season.
That thou givest them they gather:
Thou openest thine hand, they are filled with good.
Thou hidest thy face, they are troubled:
Thou takest away their breath, they die,
And return to their dust.
30 Thou sendest forth thy spirit, they are created:
And thou renewest the face of the earth.
The glory of the LORD shall endure for ever:
The LORD shall rejoice in his works.
He looketh on the earth, and it trembleth:
He toucheth the hills, and they smoke.
I will sing unto the LORD as long as I live:
I will sing praise to my God while I have my being.
My meditation of him shall be sweet:
I will be glad in the LORD.
Let the sinners be consumed out of the earth,
And let the wicked be no more.
Bless thou the LORD, O my soul.
Praise ye the LORD.

PSALM 148

Praise ye the LORD.
Praise ye the LORD from the heavens:
Praise him in the heights.
Praise ye him, all his angels:
Praise ye him, all his hosts.
Praise ye him, sun and moon:
Praise him, all ye stars of light.
Praise him, ye heavens of heavens.
And ye waters that be above the heavens.
5 Let them praise the name of the LORD:
For he commanded, and they were created.
He hath also stablished them for ever and ever:
He hath made a decree which shall not pass.
Praise the LORD from the earth,
Ye dragons, and all deeps:
Fire, and hail; snow, and vapour;
Stormy wind fulfilling his word:
Mountains, and all hills;
Fruitful trees, and all cedars:
10 Beasts, and all cattle;
Creeping things, and flying fowl:

Kings of the earth, and all people;
Princes, and all judges of the earth:
Both young men, and maidens;
Old men, and children:
Let them praise the name of the LORD:
For his name alone is excellent;
His glory is above the earth and heaven.
14   He also exalteth the horn of his people,
The praise of all his saints;
Even of the children of Israel, a people near unto him.
Praise ye the LORD.

The Book of Isaiah

CHAPTER 6.1–9

In the year that king Uzziah died I saw also the LORD sitting upon a throne, high and lifted up, and his train filled the temple. Above it stood the seraphims: each one had six wings, with twain he covered his face, and with twain he covered his feet, and with twain he did fly. And one cried unto another, and said,

> "Holy, holy, holy, is the LORD of hosts:
> The whole earth is full of his glory."

And the posts of the door moved at the voice of him that cried, and the house was filled with smoke. Then said I, "Woe is me! for I am undone; because I am a man of unclean lips, and I dwell in the midst of a people of unclean lips: for mine eyes have seen the King, the LORD of hosts." Then flew one of the seraphims unto me, having a live coal in his hand, which he had taken with the tongs from off the altar: and he laid it upon my mouth, and said, "Lo, this hath touched thy lips; and thine iniquity is taken away, and thy sin purged." Also I heard the voice of the LORD, saying, "Whom shall I send, and who will go for us?" Then said I, "Here am I; send me." And he said, "Go, and tell this people,

> 'Hear ye indeed, but understand not;
> And see ye indeed, but perceive not.' "

CHAPTER 7.10–14

Moreover the LORD spake again unto Ahaz, saying,

> "Ask thee a sign of the LORD thy God;
> Ask it either in the depth, or in the height above."

But Ahaz said, "I will not ask, neither will I tempt the LORD." And he said,

"Hear ye now, O house of David;
Is it a small thing for you to weary men,
    but will ye weary my God also?
Therefore the Lord himself shall give you a sign;
Behold, a virgin shall conceive, and bear a son,
And shall call his name Immanuel."

CHAPTER 9. 2–7

The people that walked in darkness
    have seen a great light:
They that dwell in the land of the shadow of death,
    upon them hath the light shined.
Thou hast multiplied the nation,
    and not increased the joy;
They joy before thee according to the joy in harvest,
And as men rejoice when they divide the spoil.
For thou hast broken the yoke of his burden,
    and the staff of his shoulder,
The rod of his oppressor, as in the day of Midian.
For every battle of the warrior is with confused noise,
And garments rolled in blood;
But this shall be with burning and fuel of fire.
for unto us a child is born, unto us a son is given:
And the government shall be upon his shoulder:
And his name shall be called Wonderful, Counsellor,
    The Mighty God,
The Everlasting Father, The Prince of Peace.
Of the increase of his government and peace
    there shall be no end,
Upon the throne of David, and upon his kingdom,
To order it, and to establish it with judgment
    and with justice.
From henceforth even for ever.
The seal of the LORD of hosts will perform this.

CHAPTER 14. 1–21

For the LORD will have mercy on Jacob,
And will yet choose Israel,
And set them in their own land:
And the strangers shall be joined with them,
And they shall cleave to the house of Jacob.
And the people shall take them, and bring them
    to their place:
And the house of Israel shall possess them in the land

of the LORD
For the servants and handmaids:
And they shall take them captives,
    whose captives they were;
And they shall rule over their oppressors.

And it shall come to pass in the day that the LORD shall give thee rest
from thy sorrow, and from thy fear, and from the hard bondage wherein
thou wast made to serve, that thou shalt take up this proverb against the
king of Babylon, and say,

"How hath the oppressor ceased! the golden city ceased!
The LORD hath broken the staff of the wicked, and
    the sceptre of the rulers.
He who smote the people in wrath with a continual stroke,
He that ruled the nations in anger, is persecuted, and
    none hindereth.
The whole earth is at rest, and is quiet: they break
    forth into singing.
Yea, the fir trees rejoice at thee, and the cedars
    of Lebanon, saying,
'Since thou art laid down, no feller is come up against us.'
Hell from beneath is moved for thee to meet thee at
    thy coming:
It stirreth up the dead for thee, even all the chief ones
    of the earth;
It hath raised up from their thrones all the kings
    of the nations.
All they shall speak and say unto thee,
'Art thou also become weak as we?
    art thou becomes like unto us?'
The pomp is brought down to the grave, and the noise
    of thy viols:
The worm is spread under thee, and the worms cover thee.
How art thou fallen from heaven. O Lucifer,
    son of the morning!
How art thou cut down to the ground, which didst
    weaken the nations!
For thou hast said in thine heart, 'I will ascend into heaven,
I will exalt my throne above the stars of God:
I will sit also upon the mount of the congregation,
    in the sides of the north:
I will ascend above the heights of the clouds; I will be
    like the Most High.'
Yet thou shalt be brought down to hell, to the
    sides of the pit.
They that see thee shall narrowly look upon thee,

and consider thee, saying,
'Is this the man that made the earth to tremble,
    that did shake kingdoms;
That made the world as a wilderness, and destroyed
    the cities thereof;
That opened not the house of his prisoners?'
All the kings of the nations, even all of them,
Lie in glory, every one in his own house.
But thou art cast out of thy grave like an abominable
    branch,
And as the rainment of those that are slain, thrust through
    with a sword,
That go down to the stones of the pit;
    as a carcase trodden under feet.
20   Thou shalt not be joined with them in burial,
Because thou hast destroyed thy land, and slain thy people:
The seed of evil doers shall never be renowned.
Prepare slaugher for his children for the
    iniquity of their fathers;
That they do not rise, nor possess the land,
Nor fill the face of the world with cities."

CHAPTER 40

"Comfort ye, comfort ye my people," saith your God.
"Speak ye comfortably to Jerusalem, and cry unto her,
That her warefare is accomplished,
That her iniquity is pardoned:
For she hath received of the LORD's hand double
    for all her sins."

3   The voice of him that crieth in the wilderness, "Prepare
    ye the way of the LORD,
Make straight in the desert a highway for our God.
Every valley shall be exalted,
And every mountain and hill shall be made low:
And the crooked shall be made straight,
And the rough places plain:
And the glory of the LORD shall be revealed,
And all flesh shall see it together:
For the mouth of the LORD hath spoken it."
The voice said, "Cry."
And he said, "What shall I cry?"
"All flesh is grass.
And all the goodliness thereof is as the flower of the field:
The grass withereth, the flower fadeth:
Because the spirit of the LORD bloweth upon it:

Surely the people is grass.
The grass withereth, the flower fadeth:
But the word of our God shall stand for ever."

9   O Zion, that bringest good tidings, get thee up into
        the high mountain;
O Jerusalem, that bringest good tidings, lift up thy voice
        with strength;
Lift it up, be not afraid;
Say unto the cities of Judah, "Behold your God!"
Behold, the LORD GOD will come with strong hand,
And his arm shall rule for him:
Behold, his reward is with him,
And his work before him.
He shall feed his flock like a shepherd:
He shall gather the lambs with his arm,
And carry them in his bosom,
And shall gently lead those that are with young.

12   Who hath measured the waters in the hollow of his hand,
And meted out heaven with the span,
And comprehended the dust of the earth in a measure,
And weighed the mountains in scales,
And the hills in a balance?
Who hath directerd the spirit of the LORD,
Or being his counsellor hath taught him?
With whom took he counsel, and who instructed him,
And taught him in the path of judgment,
And taught him knowledge,
And shewed to him the way of understanding?
Behold, the nations are as a drop of a bucket,
And are counted as the small dust of the balance:
Behold, he taketh up the isles as a very little thing.
And Lebanon is not sufficient to burn,
Nor the beasts thereof sufficient for a burnt offering.
All nations before him are as nothing:
And they are counted to him less than nothing, and vanity.

18   To whom then will ye liken God?
Or what likeness will ye compare unto him?
The workman melteth a graven image,
And the goldsmith spreadeth it over with gold,
And casteth silver chains.
He that is so impoverished that he hath no oblation
        chooseth a tree that will not rot;
He seeketh unto him a cunning workman
To prepare a graven image, that shall not be moved.

21 Have ye not known? have ye not heard?
Hath it not been told you from the beginning?
Have ye not understood from the foundations of the earth?
It is he that sitteth upon the circle of the earth,
And the inhabitants thereof are as grasshoppers;
That stretcheth out the heavens as a curtain,
And spreadeth them out as a tent to dwell in:
That bringeth the princes to nothing;
He maketh the judges of the earth as vanity.
Yea, they shall not be planted;
Yea, they shall not be sown:
Yea, their stock shall not take root in the earth:
And he shall also blow upon them, and they shall wither,
And the whirlwind shall take them away as stubble.

25 "To whom then will ye liken me, or shall I be equal?"
        saith the Holy One.
Lift up your eyes on high.
And behold who hath created these things,
That bringeth out their host by number:
He calleth them all by names
By the greatness of his might, for that he is
        strong in power;
Not one faileth.

27 Why sayest thou, O Jacob, and speakest, O Israel,
"My way is hid from the LORD,
And my judgment is passed over from my God"?
Hast thou not known? hast thou not heard,
That the everlasting God, the LORD,
The Creator of the ends of the earth,
Fainteth not, neither is weary?
There is no searching of his understanding.
He giveth power to the faint;
And to them that have no might he increaseth strength.
Even the youths shall faint and be weary,
And the young men shall utterly fall:
But they that wait upon the LORD shall
        renew their strength;
They shall mount up with wings as eagles;
They shall run, and not be weary;
And they shall walk, and not faint.

The Book of Ezekiel

CHAPTER 1

Now it came to pass in the thirtieth year, in the fourth month, in the fifth day of the month, as I was among the captives by the river of Chebar, that the heavens were opened, and I saw visions of God. In the fifth day of the month, which was the fifth year of king Jehoiachin's captivity, the word of the LORD came expressly unto Ezekiel the priest, the son of Buzi, in the land of the Chaldeans by the river Chebar; and the hand of the LORD was there upon him.

4 And I looked, and, behold, a whirlwind came out of the north, a great cloud, and a fire unfolding itself, and a brightness was about it, and out of the midst thereof as the colour of amber, out of the midst of the fire. Also out of the midst thereof came the likeness of four living creatures. And this was their appearance; they had the likeness of a man. And every one had four faces, and every one had four wings. And their feet were straight feet; and the sole of their feet was like the sole of a calf's foot: and they sparkled like the colour of burnished brass. And they had the hands of a man under their wings on their four sides; and they four had their faces and their wings. Their wings were joined one to another; they turned not when they went; they went every one straight forward. As for the likeness of their faces, they four had the face of a man, and the face of a lion, on the right side: and they four had the face of an ox on the left side; they four also had the face of an eagle. Thus were their faces: and their wings were stretched upward; two wings of every one were joined one to another, and two covered their bodies. And they went every one straight forward: whither the spirit was to go, they went; and they turned not when they went. As for the likeness of the living creatures, their appearance was like burning coals of fire, and like the appearance of lamps: it went up and down among the living creatures; and the fire was bright, and out of the fire went forth lightning. And the living creatures ran and returned as the appearance of a flash of lightning.

16 Now as I beheld the living creatures, behold one wheel upon the earth by the living creatures, with his four faces. The appearance of the wheels and their work was like unto the colour of a beryl: and they four had one likeness: and their appearance and their work was as it were a wheel in the middle of a wheel. When they went, they went upon their four sides: and they turned not when they went. As for their rings, they were so high that they were dreadful; and their rings were full of eyes round about them four. And when the living creatures went, the wheels went by them: and when the living creatures were lifted up from the earth, the wheels were lifted up.

20 Whithersoever the spirit was to go, they went, thither was their spirit to go; and the wheels were lifted up over against them: for the spirit of the living creature was in the wheels. When those went, these went; and when those stood, these stood; and when those were lifted up from the earth, the wheels were lifted up over against them: for the spirit of the living creature was in the wheels.

22 And the likeness of the firmament upon the heads of the living creature was as the colour of the terrible crystal, stretched forth over their heads above. And under the firmament were their wings straight, the one toward the other: every one had two, which covered on this side, and every one had two, which covered on that side, their bodies. And when they went, I heard the noise of their wings, like the noise of great waters, as the voice of the Almighty, the voice of speech, as the noise of an host: when they stood, they let down their wings. And there was a voice from the firmament that was over their heads, when they stood, and had let down their wings.

26 And above the firmament that was over their heads was the likeness of a throne, as the appearance of a sapphire stone: and upon the likeness of the throne was the likeness as the appearance of a man above it. And I saw as the colour of amber, as the appearance of fire round about within it, from the appearance of his loins even upward, and from the appearance of his loins even downward, I saw as it were the appearance of fire, and it had brightness round about. As the appearance of the bow that is in the cloud in the day of rain, so was the appearance of the brightness round about. This was the appearance of the likeness of the glory of the LORD. And when I saw it, I fell upon my face, and I heard a voice of one that spake.

The Gospel According to St. Matthew†

CHAPTER 1.18–25

Now the birth of Jesus Christ was on this wise: When as his mother Mary was espoused to Joseph, before they came together, she was found with child of the Holy Ghost. Then Joseph her husband, being a just man, and not willing to make her a publick example, was minded to put her away privily. But while he thought on these things, behold, the angel of the LORD appeared unto him in a dream, saying, "Joseph, thou son of David, fear not to take unto thee Mary thy wife: for that which is conceived in her is of the Holy Ghost. And she shall bring forth a son, and thou shalt call his name JESUS: for he shall save his people

---

† The gospels are accounts of the life and teachings of Jesus. The word *gospel* derives from the Middle English *god* good + *spel* tale.

from their sins." Now all this was done, that it might be fulfilled which
was spoken of the Lord by the prophet, saying,

"Behold, a virgin shall be with child, and shall bring forth a son,
And they shall call his name Emmanuel,"

which being interpreted is, God with us. Then Joseph being raised from
sleep did as the angel of the Lord had bidden him, and took unto him
his wife: and knew her not till she had brought forth her firstborn son:
and he called his name JESUS.

[*The Sermon on the Mount,* 5–7]

CHAPTER 5

And seeing the multitudes, he [Jesus] went up into a mountain: and
when he was set, his disciples came unto him: and he opened his mouth,
and taught them saying,
Blessed are the poor in spirit: for theirs is the kingdom of heaven.
Blessed are they that mourn: for they shall be comforted.
Blessed are the meek: for they shall inherit the earth.
Blessed are they which do hunger and thirst after righteousness: for
they shall be filled.
Blessed are the merciful: for they shall obtain mercy.
Blessed are the pure in heart: for they shall see God.
Blessed are the peacemakers: for they shall be called the children of
God.
Blessed are they which are persecuted for righteousness' sake: for theirs
is the kingdom of heaven.
Blessed are ye when men shall revile you [,] and persecute you, and
shall say all manner of evil against you falsely, for my sake.
Rejoice, and be exceeding glad: for great is your reward in heaven,
for so persecuted they the prophets which were before you.
13 Ye are the salt of the earth: but if the salt have lost his savor,
wherewith shall it be salted? it is thenceforth good for nothing, but to
be cast out, and to be trodden under foot of men. Ye are the light of
the world. A city that is set on an hill cannot be hid. Neither do men
light a candle, and put it under a bushel, but on a candlestick; and it
giveth light unto all that are in the house. Let your light so shine before
men, that they may see your good works, and glorify your Father which
is in heaven.
17 Think not that I am come to destroy the law, or the prophets: I
am not come to destroy, but to fulfil. For verily I say unto you, Till
heaven and earth pass, one jot or one tittle shall in no wise pass from
the law, till all be fulfilled. Whosoever therefore shall break one of these

least commandments, and shall teach men so, he shall be called the least in the kingdom of heaven: but whosoever shall do and teach them, the same shall be called great in the kingdom of haven. For I say unto you, That except your righteousness shall exceed the righteousness of the scribes and Pharisees, ye shall in no case enter into the kingdom of heaven

21 Ye have heard that it was said by them of old time, Thou shalt not kill; and whosoever shall kill shall be in danger of the judgment: But I say unto you, That whosoever is angry with his brother without a cause shall be in danger of the judgment: and whosoever shall say to his brother, Raca, shall be in danger of the council: but whosoever shall say, Thou fool, shall be in danger of hell fire. Therefore if thou bring thy gift to the altar, and there rememberest that thy brother hath ought against thee; Leave there thy gift before the altar, and go thy way; first be reconciled to thy brother, and then come and offer thy gift. Agree with thine adversary quickly, whiles thou art in the way with him; lest at any time the adversary deliver thee to the judge, and the judge deliver thee to the officer, and thou be cast into prison. Verily I say unto thee, Thou shalt by no means come out thence, till thou hast paid the uttermost farthing.

27 Ye have heard that it was said by them of old time, Thou shalt not commit adultery: But I say unto you, That whosoever looketh on a woman to lust after her hath committed adultery with her already in his heart. And if thy right eye offend thee, pluck it out, and cast it from thee: for it is profitable for thee that one of thy members should perish, and not that thy whole body should be cast into hell. And if thy right hand offend thee, cut it off, and cast it from thee: for it is profitable for thee that one of thy members should perish, and not that thy whole body should be cast into hell. It hath been said, Whosoever shall put away his wife, let him give her a writing of divorcement: But I say unto you, That whosoever shall put away his wife, saving for the cause of fornication, causeth her to commit adultery: and whosoever shall marry her that is divorced committeth adultery. Again, ye have heard that it hath been said by them of old time, Thou shalt not forswear thyself, but shalt perform unto the Lord thine oaths: But I say unto you, Swear not at all; neither by heaven; for it is God's throne: Nor by the earth; for it is his footstool: neither by Jerusalem; for it is the city of the great King. Neither shalt thou swear by thy head, because thou can't not make one hair white or black. But let your communication be, Yea, yea; Nay, nay: for whatsoever is more than these cometh of evil.

38 Ye have heard that it hath been said, An eye for an eye, and a tooth for a tooth: But I say unto you, That ye resist not evil: but whosoever shall smite thee on thy right cheek, turn to him the other also. And if any man will sue thee at the law, and take away thy coat, let him have

thy cloke also. And whosoever shall compel thee to go a mile, go with him twain. Give to him that asketh thee, and from him that would borrow of thee turn not thou away.

43 Ye have heard that it hath been said, Thou shalt love thy neighbour, and hate thine enemy. But I say unto you, Love your enemies, bless them that curse you, do good to them that hate you, and pray for them which despitefully use you, and persecute you; That ye may be the children of your Father which is in heaven: for he maketh his sun to rise on the evil and on the good, and sendeth rain on the just and on the unjust. For if ye love them which love you, what reward have ye? do not even the publicans the same? And if ye salute your brethren only, what do ye more than others? do not even the publicans so? Be ye therefore perfect, even as your Father which is in heaven is perfect.

CHAPTER 6

Take heed that ye do not your alms before men to be seen of them: otherwise ye have no reward of your Father which is in heaven. Therefore when thou doest thine alms, do not sound a trumpet before thee, as the hyprocrites do in the synagogues and in the streets, that they may have glory of men. Verily I say unto you, They have their reward. But when thou doest alms, let not thy left hand know what thy right hand doeth: That thine alms may be in secret: and thy Father which seeth in secret himself shall reward thee openly.

5 And when thou prayest, thou shalt not be as the hypocrites are: for they love to pray standing in the synagogues and in the corners of the streets, that they may be seen of men. Verily I say unto you. They have their reward. But thou, when thou prayest, enter into thy closet, and when thou hast shut thy door, pray to thy Father which is in secret; and thy Father which seeth in secret shall reward thee openly. But when ye pray, use not vain repetitions, as the heathen do: for they think that they shall be heard for their much speaking. Be not ye therefore like unto them: for your Father knoweth what things ye have need of, before ye ask him. After this manner therefore pray ye: Our Father which art in heaven, Hallowed be thy name. Thy kingdom come. Thy will be done in earth, as it is in heaven. Give us this day our daily bread. And forgive us our debts, as we forgive our debtors. And lead us not into temptation, but deliver us from evil: For thine is the kingdom, and the power, and the glory, for ever. Amen. For if ye forgive men their trespasses, your heavenly Father will also forgive you: But if ye forgive not men their trespasses, neither will your Father forgive your trespasses.

16 Moreover when ye fast, be not, as the hypocrites, of a sad countenance: for they disfigure their faces, that they may appear unto men to fast. Verily I say unto you, They have their reward. But thou, when thou fastest, anoint thine head, and wash thy face; That thou appear

not unto men to fast, but unto thy Father which is in secret: and thy Father, which seeth in secret, shall reward thee openly.

19 Lay not up for yourselves treasures upon earth, where moth and rust doth corrupt, and where thieves break through and steal: But lay up for yourselves treasures in heaven, where neither moth nor rust doth corrupt, and where thieves do not break through nor steal: For where your treasure is, there will your heart be also. The light of the body is the eye: if therefore thine eye be single, thy whole body shall be full of light. But if thine eye be evil, thy whole body shall be full of darkness. If therefore the light that is in thee be darkness, how great is that darkness!

24 No man can serve two masters: for either he will hate the one, and love the other; or else he will hold to the one, and despise the other. Ye cannot serve God and mammon. Therefore I say unto you, Take no thought for your life, what ye shall eat, or what ye shall drink; nor yet for your body, what ye shall put on. Is not the life more than meat, and the body than raiment? Behold the fowls of the air: for they sow not, neither do they reap, nor gather into barns; yet your heavenly Father feedeth them. Are ye not much better than they? Which of you by taking thought can add one cubit unto his stature? And why take ye thought for raiment? Consider the lilies of the field, how they grow; they toil not, neither do they spin: And yet I say unto you, That even Solomon in all his glory was not arrayed like one of these. Wherefore, if God so clothe the grass of the field, which to day is, and to morrow is cast into the oven, shall he not much more clothe you, O ye of little faith? Therefore take no thought, saying, What shall we eat? or, What shall we drink? or, Wherewithal shall we be clothed? (For after all these things do the Gentiles seek) for your heavenly Father knoweth that ye have need of all these things. But seek ye first the kingdom of God, and his righteousness; and all these things shall be added unto you. Take therefore no thought for the morrow: for the morrow shall take thought for the things of itself. Sufficient unto the day is the evil thereof.

CHAPTER 7

Judge not, that ye be not judged. For with what judgment ye judge, ye shall be judged: and with what measure yet mete, it shall be measured to you again. And why beholdest thou the mote that is in thy brother's eye, but considerest not the beam that is in thine own eye? Or how wilt thou say to thy brother, Let me pull out the mote out of thine eye; and, behold, a beam is in thine own eye? Thou hypocrite, first cast out the beam out of thine own eye; and then shalt thou see clearly to cast out the mote out of thy brother's eye.

6 Give not that which is holy unto the dogs, neither cast ye your pearls before swine, lest they trample them under their feet, and turn again and rend you.

7 Ask, and it shall be given you; seek, and ye shall find; knock, and it shall be opened unto you. For every one that asketh receiveth; and he that seeketh findeth; and to him that knocketh it shall be opened. Or what man is there of you, whom if his son ask bread, will he give him a stone? Or if he ask a fish, will he give him a serpent? If ye then, being evil, know how to give good gifts unto your children, how much more shall your Father which is in heaven give good things to them that ask him? Therefore all things whatsoever ye would that men should do to you, do ye even so to them: for this is the law and the prophets.

13 Enter ye in at the strait gate: for wide is the gate, and broad is the way, that leadeth to destruction, and many there be which go in thereat: Because strait is the gate, and narrow is the way, which leadeth unto life, and few there be that find it.

15 Beware of false prophets, which come to you in sheep's clothing, but inwardly they are ravening wolves. Ye shall know them by their fruits. Do men gather grapes of thorns, or figs of thistles? Even so every good tree bringeth forth good fruit; but a corrupt tree bringeth forth evil fruit. A good tree cannot bring forth evil fruit, neither can a corrupt tree bring forth good fruit. Every tree that bringeth not forth good fruit is hewn down, and cast into the fire. Wherefore by their fruits ye shall know them.

21 Not every one that saith unto me, Lord, Lord, shall enter into the kingdom of heaven; but he that doeth the will of my Father which is in heaven. Many will say to me in that day, Lord, Lord, have we not prophesied in thy name? and in thy name have cast out devils? and in thy name done many wonderful works? And then will I profess unto them, I never knew you: depart from me, ye that work iniquity.

24 Therefore whosoever heareth these sayings of mine, and doeth them, I will liken him unto a wise man, which built his house upon a rock: And the rain descended, and the floods came, and the winds blew, and beat upon that house; and it fell not: for it was founded upon a rock. And every one that heareth these sayings of mine, and doeth them not, shall be likened unto a foolish man, which built his house upon the sand: And the rain descended, and the floods came, and the winds blew, and beat upon that house; and it fell: and great was the fall of it. And it came to pass, when Jesus had ended these sayings, the people were astonished at his doctrine: For he taught them as one having authority, and not as the scribes.

The Gospel According to St. Mark

CHAPTER 12.28–31

And one of the scribes came, and having heard them reasoning together, and perceiving that he had answered them well, asked him, "Which is the first commandment of all?" And Jesus answered him, "The first of all the commandments is 'Hear, O Israel: The Lord our God is one Lord: and thou shalt love the Lord thy God with all thy heart, and with all thy soul, and with all thy mind, and with all thy strength': this is the first commandment. And the second is like, namely this, " 'Thou shalt love thy neighbour as thyself.' There is none other commandment greater than these."

CHAPTER 13.24–27

But in those days, after that tribulation, the sun shall be darkened, and the moon shall not give her light, and the stars of heaven shall fall, and the powers that are in heaven shall be shaken. And then shall they see the Son of man coming in the clouds with great power and glory. And then shall he send his angels, and shall gather together his elect from the four winds, from the uttermost part of the earth to the uttermost part of heaven.

The Gospel According to St. Luke

CHAPTER 1.26–35

And in the sixth month the angel Gabriel was sent from God unto a city of Galilee, named Nazareth, to a virgin espoused to a man whose name was Joseph, of the house of David, and the virgin's name was Mary. And the angel came in unto her, and said, "Hail, thou that art highly favoured, the Lord is with thee: blessed art thou among women." And when she saw him, she was troubled at his saying, and cast in her mind what manner of salutation this should be. And the angel said unto her, "Fear not, Mary: for thou hast found favour with God. And, behold, thou shalt conceive in thy womb, and bring forth a son, and shalt call his name JESUS. He shall be great and shall be called the Son of the Highest: and the Lord God shall give unto him the throne of his father David: and he shall reign over the house of Jacob for ever; and of his kingdom there shall be no end." Then said Mary unto the angel, "How shall this be, seeing I know not a man?" And the angel answered and said unto her, "The Holy Ghost shall come upon thee, and the power of the Highest shall overshadow thee: therefore also that holy thing which shall be born of thee shall be called the Son of God."

The Gospel According to St. John

CHAPTER 1. 1–4

In the beginning was the Word, and the Word was with God, and the Word was God. The same was in the beginning with God. All things were made by him; and without him was not any thing made that was made. In him was life, and the life was the light of men.

CHAPTER 3. 16–21

For God so loved the world, that he gave his only begotten Son, that whosoever believeth in him should not perish, but have everlasting life. For God sent not his Son into the world to condemn the world, but that the world through him might be saved. He that believeth on him is not condemned: but he that believeth not is condemned already, because he hath not believed in the name of the only begotten Son of God. And this is the condemnation, that light is come into the world, and men loved darkness rather than light, because their deeds were evil. For every one that doeth evil hateth the light, neither cometh to the light, lest his deeds should be reproved. But he that doeth truth cometh to the light, that his deeds may be made manifest, that they are wrought in God.

The Acts of the Apostles

CHAPTER 13. 16–37

Then Paul stood up, and beckoning with his hand said, "Men of Israel, and ye that fear God, give audience. The God of this people of Israel chose our fathers, and exalted the people when they dwelt as strangers in the land of Egypt, and with an high arm brought he them out of it. And about the time of forty years suffered he their manners in the wilderness. And when he had destroyed seven nations in the land of Chanaan, he divided their land to them by lot. And after that he gave unto them judges about the space of four hundred and fifty years, until Samuel the prophet. And afterward they desired a king: and God gave unto them Saul the son of Cis, a man of the tribe of Benjamin, by the space of forty years. And when he had removed him, he raised up unto them David to be their king; to whom also he gave testimony, and said, 'I have found David the son of Jesse, a man after mine own heart, which shall fulfil all my will.' Of this man's seed hath God according to his promise raised unto Israel a Savior, Jesus: When John had first preached before his coming the baptism of repentance to all the people of Israel. And as John fulfilled his course, he said, Whom think ye that I am? I am not he. But, behold, there cometh one after me, whose shoes of his feet I am not worthy to loose. Men and brethren, children of the stock of Abraham, and whosoever among you feareth God, to you is the word of this salvation sent. For they that dwell at Jerusalem, and their rulers, because they knew him not, nor yet the voices of the prophets which are read every sabbath day, they have fulfilled them in condemning him. And though they found no cause of death in him, yet desired they Pilate that he should be slain. And when they had fulfilled all that was written of him, they took him down from the tree, and laid him in a sepulchre. But God raised him from the dead: And he was seen many days of them which came up with him from Galilee to Jerusalem, who are his witnesses unto the people. And we declare unto you glad tidings, how that the promise which was made unto the fathers. God hath fulfilled the same unto us their chidren, in that he hath raised up Jesus again; as it is also written in the second psalm, 'Thou art my Son, this day have I begotten thee.' And as concerning that he raised him up from the dead, now no more to return to corruption, he said on this wise, 'I will give you the sure mercies of David.' Wherefore he saith also in another psalm, Thou shalt not suffer thine Holy One to see corruption. For David, after he had served his own generation by the will of God, fell on sleep, and was laid unto his fathers, and saw corruption: But he, whom God raised again, saw no corruption."

The First Letter of Paul to the Corinthians

CHAPTER 7.1–16

Now concerning the things whereof ye wrote unto me: It is good for a man not to touch a woman. Nevertheless, to avoid fornication, let every man have his own wife, and let every woman have her own husband. Let the husband render unto the wife due benevolence: and likewise also the wife unto the husband. The wife hath not power of her own body, but the husband: and likewise also the husband hath not power of his own body, but the wife. Defraud ye not one the other, except it be with consent for a time, that ye may give yourselves to fasting and prayer; and come together again, that Satan tempt you not for your incontinency. But I speak this by permission, and not of commandment. For I would that all men were even as I myself. But every man hath his proper gift of God, one after this manner, and another after that.

8 I say therefore to the unmarried and widows, It is good for them if they abide even as I. But if they cannot contain, let them marry: for it is better to marry than to burn. And unto the married I command, yet not I, but the Lord, Let not the wife depart from her husband: But and if she depart, let her remain unmarried, or be reconciled to her husband: and let not the husband put away his wife.

12 But to the rest speak I, not the Lord: If any brother hath a wife that believeth not, and she be pleased to dwell with him, let him not put her away. And the woman which hath an husband that believeth not, and if he be pleased to dwell with her, let her not leave him. For the unbelieving husband is sanctified by the wife, and the unbelieving wife is sanctified by the husband: else were your children unclean; but now are they holy. But if the unbelieving depart, let him depart. A brother or a sister is not under bondage in such cases: but God hath called us to peace. For what knowest thou, O wife, whether thou shalt save thy husband? or how knowest thou, O man, whether thou shalt save thy wife?

17 But as God hath distributed to every man, as the Lord hath called every one, so let him walk. And so ordain I in all churches.

CHAPTER 11.3–12

But I would have you know, that the head of every man is Christ; and the head of the woman is the man; and the head of Christ is God. Every man praying or prophesying, having his head covered, dishonoureth his head. But every woman that prayeth or prophesieth with her head uncovered dishonoureth her head: for that is even all one as if she were shaven. For if the woman be not covered, let her also be shorn: but if it be a shame for a woman to be shorn or shaven, let her be covered. For a man indeed ought not to cover his head, forasmuch as he is the image and glory of God: but the woman is the glory of the man. For the man is not of the woman; but the woman of the man. Neither was the man created for the woman; but the woman for the man. For this cause ought the woman to have power on her head because of the angels. Nevertheless neither is the man without the woman, neither the woman without the man in the Lord. For as the woman is of the man, even so is the man also by the woman; but all things of God.

CHAPTER 15.21–28, 51–58

For since by man came death, by man came also the resurrection of the dead. For as in Adam all die, even so in Christ shall all be made alive. But every man in his own order: Christ the firstfruits; afterward they that are Christ's at his coming. Then cometh the end, when he shall have delivered up the kingdom to God, even the Father; when he shall have put down all rule and all authority and power. For he must reign, till he hath put all enemies under his feet. The last enemy that shall be destroyed is death. For he hath put all things under his feet. But when he saith all things are put under him, it is manifest that he is excepted, which did put all things under him. And when all things shall be subdued unto him, then shall the Son also himself be subject unto him that put all things under him, that God may be all in all.

* * *

51 Behold, I show you a mystery; We shall not all sleep, but we shall all be changed. In a moment, in the twinkling of an eye, at the last trump: for the trumpet shall sound, and the dead shall be raised incorruptible, and we shall be changed. For this corruptible must put on incorruption, and this mortal must put on immortality. So when this corruptible shall have put on incorruption, and this mortal shall have put on immortality, then shall be brought to pass the saying that is written, "Death is swallowed up in victory." "O death, where is thy sting? O grave, where is thy victory?" The sting of death is sin; and the strength of sin is the law. But thanks be to God, which giveth us the victory through our Lord Jesus Christ.

Therefore, my beloved brethren, be ye stedfast, unmoveable, always abounding in the work of the Lord, forasmuch as ye know that your labor is not in vain in the Lord.

The First Letter of Paul to Timothy

CHAPTER 2.7–15

Whereunto I am ordained a preacher, and an apostle, (I speak the truth in Christ, and lie not;) a teacher of the Gentiles in faith and verity.

8 I will therefore that men pray everywhere, lifting up holy hands, without wrath and doubting. In like manner also, that women adorn themselves in modest apparel, with shamefacedness and sobriety; not with broided hair, or gold, or pearls, or costly array; but (which becometh a woman professing godliness) with good works. Let the woman learn in silence with all subjection. But I suffer not a woman to teach, nor to usurp authority over man, but to be in silence. For Adam was first formed, then Eve. And Adam was not deceived, but the woman being

deceived was in the transgression. Notwithstanding she shall be saved in childbearing, if they continue in faith and charity and holiness with sobriety.

The General Epistle of James

CHAPTER 1.12–15

Blessed is the man that endureth temptation: for when he is tried, he shall receive the crown of life, which the Lord hath promised to them that love him. Let no man say when he is tempted, "I am tempted of God": for God cannot be tempted with evil, neither tempteth he any man: But every man is tempted, when he is drawn away of his own lust, and enticed.

The Revelation of St. John the Divine

CHAPTER 12.3–12

And there appeared another wonder in heaven; and behold a great red dragon, having seven heads and ten horns, and seven crowns upon his heads. And his tail drew the third part of the stars of heaven, and did cast them to the earth: and the dragon stood before the woman which was ready to be delivered, for to devour her child as soon as it was born. And she brought forth a man child, who was to rule all nations with a rod of iron: and her child was caught up unto God, and to his throne. And the woman fled into the wilderness, where she hath a place prepared of God, that they should feed her there a thousand two hundred and threescore days.

7 And there was war in heaven: Michael and his angels fought against the dragon; and the dragon fought and his angels, and prevailed not; neither was their place found any more in heaven. And the great dragon was cast out, that old serpent, called the Devil, and Satan, which deceiveth the whole world: he was cast out into the earth, and his angels were cast out with him. And I heard a loud voice saying in heaven, "Now is come salvation, and strength, and the kingdom of our God, and the power of his Christ: for the accuser of our brethren is cast down, which accused them before our God day and night. And they overcame him by the blood of the Lamb, and by the word of their testimony; and they loved not their lives unto the death. Therefore rejoice, ye heavens, and ye that dwell in them. Woe to the inhabiters of the earth and of the sea! for the devil is come down unto you, having great wrath, because he knoweth that he hath but a short time."

Important Concepts and Topics in *Paradise Lost*

The Universe

The world of *Paradise Lost* was created out of that part of chaos which was ensphered by God's act of turning a great pair of golden compasses. The resulting spherical shell, made of an impenetrable and immobile substance, was suspended from heaven by a golden chain fastened to heaven's floor at a point near heaven's gate and at the head of a flight of retractable stairs that led down to the top of the sphere. There the chain was fastened at a point near an opening, through which God could look down into the universe from his heavenly throne and through which would pass all traffic between earth and heaven or hell. Hell was a separate enclosure within chaos situated below the universe at a distance equal to the diameter of the universe.

Milton did not believe that the universe was created from nothing. It was made from whatever was contained in what the Bible called "the deep," a synonym for *abyss* (a Greek word meaning "bottomless," therefore infinite). *Chaos* also meant a "yawning gulf," and carried the connotations of emptiness and formlessness. But Milton conceived of it as containing something out of which matter could be formed, and he thought of the process of *ordering*, a word whose root means "to begin." Forces or primordial matter were ordered. The first phenomenon within the universe was light. The next was the separation of the waters into two concentric spheres by means of the "firmament," a word which in Hebrew is related to the idea of expansion and to the idea of a vault. Milton followed convention in using *sky, vault, expanse, heaven* or *heavens*, and *firmament* synonymously. The inner sphere of waters contained what would become the earth; the outer sphere of waters became the "chrystalline waters" that formed a cover for the outer shell of the universe. Both the universe and the earth floated, so to speak, in a kind of uterine fluid, the outer waters protecting the universe from chaos, the inner furnishing nourishment for the earth.

Next, the continents emerged from the waters covering the earth, and vegetation was created. Then, within the firmament, the space between earth and the outer shell of the universe, God put ten concentric transparent and immaterial spheres. Milton did not pretend to know whether the center of this set of spheres was the earth or the sun, and none of his astronomical descriptions or allusions commits him to one or the other of the possibilities.

As earthbound readers we tend to imagine the easier Ptolemaic arrangement, which puts our standpoint, the earth, at the center, surrounded by the spheres of the moon, Mercury, Venus, the sun, Mars, Jupiter, and Saturn. Beyond Saturn is the sphere of the "fixed stars," among them the twelve constellations that constitute the signs of the zodiac. Before the Fall this zone (meaning "belt"), about 18° wide, revolved around the earth parallel with the equator, and within its boundaries moved (as they still do) the sun and all the "other" planets—each at a different speed (and in some cases, apparently, not always in the same direction). The twelve constellations that stud this belt are set about 30° apart, and during the course of a year the sun, revolving at a different speed from that of the zodiac, passes through each of the twelve signs. At creation the sun was thought to have been "in" Aries, that is to have been traveling in a position between earth and the constellation of Aries. Aries is the sign in which (until recently) the sun traveled from March 21 to April 20—in the northern hemisphere, the first month of spring.

But Eden was perpetually in spring because before the Fall the plane of the earth's equator coincided with the plane of the sun's orbit (or, in a heliocentric system, the plane of the earth's equator would always intersect the sun)—hence there were no solstices, but perpetual equinox and, at the latitude of Eden, perpetual temperate or springlike weather. After the Fall, the earth was tipped on its axis, and the cycle of seasons was introduced—with its painful extremes of temperature. The sun continued to travel in the zodiac, but now, for the earthly observer, that path across the heavens moved slowly during the year from south to north to south, so that at noon in January in our hemisphere the sun, and the constellation of Capricorn (the Goat), with which it is in conjunction, were "low" in the sky, and in June the sun and Cancer (the Crab) were "high." Before the Fall all astrological patterns of relationships between the planets and the stars were benign; after the Fall, God sent angels down to instruct the stars and planets how in certain astrological relationships to rain down on earth various malign "influences"—meteorological, natural, physiological, and psychological.

Beyond the sphere of the fixed stars were two more spheres: the "crystalline" (III. 482)—invented by a thirteenth-century astronomer to account for a celestial phenomenon that later proved to be an error in observation—and the *primum mobile*, or "rhomb" (VIII. 134), which somehow moved all the spheres within it.

The space between the surface of the earth and the shell of the universe was conceived of by the ancients as consistsing of two main divisions separated by the sphere of the moon. What was within that sphere (sublunar) was made of the four elements of earth, air, fire, and water. What was above or beyond the moon's sphere was made of a fifth element called "quintessence." The planets and stars were made of this "most pure" element, as was the atmosphere or ether of the upper world. The sublunar atmosphere of the earth was bounded by a sphere (or "region") of fire, and between this region and the surface of the earth there were three regions of air, the one nearest the region of fire being very hot and the one nearest the earth being warm from the heat of the sun reflected from the earth's surface. The middle, very cold region, barely penetrated by the tallest mountains, was the home of the imaginary Greek gods, and was the source of weather: clouds, rain and snow, winds, thunder, and lightning. Meteors were generated in the upper, or third, region of air.

When on the last two days of Creation God made animals and human life, he continued the basic process of ordering forces and sublunar elements of water, earth, air, and fire (See "Physiology and Psychology," below).

The universe (meaning "the whole turning") revolved on an axis running parallel to the floor of heaven so that when God looked down through the opening at the "top" of the stationary shell he was directly above the Garden of Eden. And the revolving planets and constellations, the clockwork, marked time in units of days, months, and years.

From man's point of view the most compelling of all the parts of his universe was the sun, in which on the fourth day of Creation God concentrated the light that he created on the first day, and *Paradise Lost* is full of evidence of man's ancient belief that the sun was the immediate source of all physical energy, the maker or sire of all phenomena: mineral, vegetable, and animal.

Physiology and Psychology

Just as the cosmology of *Paradise Lost* allowed for the possible truth of the discoveries of Galileo and Copernicus, none of the poem's assumptions about human physiology does violence to the implications of Harvey's discoveries of the circulation of the blood. One of the four humors (literally "fluids") of the body, blood was the means of distributing the other three humors (black bile, yellow bile, and phlegm), as well as the spirits ("vapors") that performed the functions of what we might now call the nervous system. A person's temper (or humor) depended on how the humors in him were tempered (literally "mixed"). Melancholy, for example, was the result of a disproportionally large amount of black bile. As in the creation of the universe, so in the creation of life, heat and moisture were determining factors, and all organisms consisted of variously proportioned and arranged elements. The four humors were associated with the four elements in that each humor was either moist (water) or dry (air) and cold (earth) or hot (fire). Both temperamentally and physiologically phlegmatic people were cold and moist; sanguine, hot and moist; choleric, hot and dry; melancholy, cold and dry. The art (practice) of medicine and the science (knowledge) of biology developed elaborate theories of pathology based on the theory of the humors.

Spirits or vapors, the active principles of life, were of three kinds—natural, animal, and intellectual. Natural spirits (generated in animals in the liver) controlled the basic vital functions of the body (e.g., digestion); animal spirits (generated in the heart) carried sense perceptions to the brain, and directions from the brain to the muscles; intellectual spirits controlled and communicated to the body the commands of the faculties of reason and will. The souls of vegetable life had only natural, vital spirits to work with. In animal souls, both vital and sensitive spirits operated. Human souls had all three—vital, sensitive, and intellectual.

The psychology of Milton's time was similarly neat and simple. The brain, seat of mental *faculties* (literally the "powers to act"), consisted of three cells. To the first cell, that of the fancy (literally *phantasia*, or "imagination") the spirits communicated the messages from the five senses. The fancy passed these impressions on to the second cell, that of reason, which acted upon the image (creating perhaps what we might call an idea) before passing it on to the third cell, that of the faculty of memory. Sleep was a condition in which the second faculty ceased to operate, and dreams were a product of the first and third faculties, uncensored or unrationalized by the reason, which in healthy wakefulness was what controlled the will. (Cf. V.100–113) Milton did not believe in the existence of a human soul apart from the live body in which it operated. (Cf. X782–93n.)

One way to describe the Fall and its consequences is to call them a distempering and a disturbance of the perfect balance in the mixture of elements and forces in all aspects of the world, which God created perfect. When Nature sighed "through all her works" (IX.783 and 1001) at the time of the Fall, storms as well as stomach-aches, earthquakes as well as shivers, extremes of heat and cold as well as manic and depressive states of mind— all forms of disequilibrium—began to plague mankind.

Reason

The Cambridge Platonists, a group of thinkers contemporary with Milton, who opposed the mechanistic, deterministic, atheistic ideas of Thomas Hobbes, called reason "the candle of the Lord," and believed that this light was innate in every man. The light was not only what we call conscience in ethical matters but also that intuitive intelligence by means of which we discern the laws of nature—as distinct from what Raphael calls "discursive" reason, or what we loosely call logic, or the human faculty by which we figure things out, or arrive at conclusions from a set of data. Milton's Raphael agrees with the Cambridge Platonists that the difference between faith and reason is only a matter of degree. He tells Adam that man depends most on discursive reason, whereas angels depend most on intuition, "Differing but in degree." Even after the Fall man was left with enough unimpaired reason (of both kinds) to know God's will, to see the difference between right and wrong. Sir Philip Sidney was thinking of *ratio recta*, or right reason, when he said, "Our erected wit maketh us know what perfection is, and yet our infected will keepeth us from reaching unto it." See also "Freedom," below.

The Scale of Nature

Nature, meaning sometimes the forces and processes that produce everything according to the laws of nature (which include what we call physical laws), sometimes simply those laws, and sometimes all that nature produces— nature, after the Fall, did not wholly lose her original power to produce and control natural, perfect, ordered phenomena, any more than Satan lost all his original brightness or man all his power to reason or to intuit natural law and God's will. What was left to fallen man was all the glories of the natural world and of humanity as we know them—that is, the glories that help us understand the perfection of the paradise we lost.

Milton's concept of nature, animate and inanimate, is not so mechanical as our simplifications of seventeenth-century "science" make it sound. The force in Mother Nature is identical with the force of God the Father as Abdiel suggests (VI.174) when he argues that wise and happy angels "serve whom God ordains,/Or nature; God and nature bid the same." Both are benevolent, or in Milton's diction, provident (i.e., seeing or planning ahead—exercising loving care and guardianship). And in this best of all possible universes everything had been thought of—no thing, being, or force had been omitted. This idea of perfection as completeness goes back to Plato, and as elaborated by the Renaissance Platonists was well known to Milton. Sometimes called the concept of plenitude, it is a help to the understanding of the idea of good in *Paradise Lost*. God's goodness was in giving every conceivable thing. The gift was not a static complex, or inorganic mechanism. Its chief characteristic was not its matter, but its activity and, in one of Milton's favorite words, its variety. As Raphael tells Adam, God made of one primordial matter, "various forms, various degrees/Of substance, and in things that live, of life."

The arrangement of all the things in the universe, their articulation with one another, had been conceived as a dynamic hierarchy, from lowest or simplest or least good (not of course to be confused with bad or not good) to the highest, the perfect (full or complete) or best, which was God Himself. In the scale of nature each form or creature (created thing) incorporated the virtues of all the forms beneath it. Satan knew that in man were "summed up" all the lower forms of "growth, sense, reason"—that is, of all vegetable, animal, and human life (IX.112). Everything, therefore, was served by what was below it and in turn served what was above it. The two most common metaphors for this arrangement were a chain and a ladder or stairway (the basic meaning of *scale*—as in a musical scale). The golden chain of II.1005 and 1051, by which the universe hangs from heaven, symbolized "the universal concord and sweet union of all things which Pythagoras poetically figures as harmony." The history and meaning of ideas about the scale of nature are the subject of Arthur O. Lovejoy's famous book, *The Great Chain of Being*.

The scale, or ladder, or stairs as a symbol appears near the chain as a second connection between heaven and the universe. Milton associated it with the ladder on which Jacob dreamed he saw "Angels ascending and descending" (III.510). The stairway was an appropriate symbol for the ascending scale on which, before the Fall, natural forms might by a sort of evolution change to a higher form, as God intended human beings eventually to evolve into angels ("Each stair was mysteriously meant"). The completeness, variety, and upward motion of all the phenomena on nature's scale are clearly implied by Raphael in his lectures to Adam in Book V (404ff., and 469ff.).

From the point of view of man the two most interesting positions on the scale of nature were those directly below and above him. Though Milton tells us that what distinguishes men from other animals is that men stand up straight (and can thereby look up toward heaven) and that they can smile, one of the central themes of *Paradise Lost* is that man's reason is his most godlike and distinguishing characteristic ("smiles from reason flow" IX.239).

Angels

Adam is humanly curious about the nature of the creatures who are just a little above him on the divine scale, and the angelology of *Paradise Lost* is contained chiefly in Raphael's responses to Adam's questions. In these descriptive passages (cf. V.401ff., 461ff., VI.344ff., VIII.614ff.), Milton again drew eclectically upon the large body of theory that had been accumulating for centuries, and added a few speculations of his own. The scale of nature is extended beyond the boundary of the universe; angels are a link between human beings and God. They are "pure/Intelligential substances" as distinct from "rational" beings. In their preponderance of intuitive reason they include all the discursive reason of mankind. They have bodies, but these are not made of earth, air, fire, and water, but of the "fifth" element, called "ether"; like everything beyond the lunar sphere, including heaven itself, they are quintessential and ethereal. Compared with men they are pure spirit; compared with God they are natural (his creatures). But in their fiery or airy bodies, in their form as pure spirit ("liquid texture" meaning nonsolid), they retain all the qualities and powers of human beings. They eat, make love (a notion original with Milton), and enjoy all the sensations of the five senses, but the seats, or the mechanisms, of their senses are not localized in organs: angels feel, see, hear, taste, and smell with their whole being. Like prelapsarian Adam they are immortal, but unlike men they are in their insubstantiality literally invulnerable. Tending as they do toward the unity of God, they are in their relative perfection simpler in organization than man. Unlike God, they cannot be in two places at the same time, but unlike man they can travel with unimaginable speed, and can assume either sex and any size or shape. They move freely from heaven to earth and, like Plato's daemons, or "attendant spirits," they can inhabit planets. They may in fact be stars. Their dance is like the movement of the heavenly bodies, and their song is like the Platonic harmony of the spheres. As they are ministered unto by God, so they minister unto men—as agents of divine providence. Or as fallen angels or evil spirits, they try to pervert man.

To Adam (and to Milton and his Muse) they appear as they are described in the Bible—shining, beautiful, winged. In asserting that God created them before he created the universe and that his purpose in creating man was to fill the ranks vacated by the fallen angels, Milton followed theological speculations well-known to his readers. Even his conviction that the good angels remained loyal by an act of their own free will, though a minority opinion, was not original.

In the chapter on angels in his *Christian Doctrine*, Milton collected all the facts the Bible supplies: angels are either good or evil; they stand "dispersed around the throne of God in the capacity of ministering agents"; Michael seems to be the chief of the good angels; all bad angels will be punished, but some are allowed to execute God's judgment on men; bad angels are ruled by Satan, and they retain in hell their respective ranks. Though *Paradise Lost* goes far beyond the Bible in describing the nature, history, and personalities of the angels, Milton rejected or modified most of the theories that were the product of centuries of speculation by Jewish and Christian writers of the occult. He did not accept the standard hierarchial ordering of the ranks of angels into three degrees, or "choirs," each consisting of three ranks: Seraphim, Cherubim, Thrones; Dominions, Virtues, Powers; Principalities, Archangels, Angels. This hierarchy descending from Seraphim to Angels was the invention of an early Christian writer and had been the subject of centuries of speculation made possible by the lack of scriptural authority. Angels, Seraphim, and Cherubim appear throughout the Bible; but Thrones, Dominions, Virtues, Powers and Principalities occur chiefly in the letters of St. Paul and are not there defined or distinguished; Archangels are mentioned only twice in the Bible.

Milton referred to certain leading or commanding angels as Archangels —Michael, first in command of God's Army, Gabriel, second in command, and Satan in the battle in heaven, as well as Uriel, the viceroy of the sun, and Raphael, God's chief minister. But there seems to be no reason for the titles assigned to the other angels, some of whom are called by several titles. The five New Testament titles, Thrones, Dominions (or Dominations), Virtues, Powers, and Principalities (or Princedoms), which Satan was so fond of rolling off his tongue when addressing his followers, are all words for power and authority, and all the angels in *Paradise Lost*, in heaven and hell, seem to live in societies where everyone has a title, a province, and a responsibility to a superior lord and ultimately to a king, but nothing quite that explicit appears in *Paradise Lost*.

Most of the given names of the angels in *Paradise Lost* come from the Bible or the Apocrypha, but some appear only in early Jewish and Christian occult writings. The names of the twelve chief followers of Satan are annotated in this text of *Paradise Lost*; Beelzebub, Moloch, Belial, Mammon, Chemos, Astoreth, Thammuz, Dagon, Rimmon, Osiris, Isis, and Orus. The seven other fallen angels in *Paradise Lost* are *Andramalec*, a sun-god; *Ariel*, a version of Mars; *Arioc*, identified by commentators as a "spirit of revenge"; *Asmadai*, or *Asmadeus*, a devil mentioned in the Book of Tobit; *Azazel*, whose name, mentioned in the Old Testament, means "scapegoat," and who was said by commentators to be one of Satan's four standard-bearers; *Nizroch*, an Assyrian idol named in the Old Testament; and *Ramiel*, one of the angels who had intercourse with "the daughters of men" (apocryphal Book of Enoch I, vi. 7).

Of the good angels only nine appear in *Paradise Lost: Michael*, a great prince whom Daniel, in the Old Testament, sees in a vision as the deliverer of the Children of Israel, becomes an archangel in Jude, in the New Testament, and in Rev. 12.7 he "and his angels fought against the dragon"; *Gabriel*, an interpreter of one of Daniel's visions and, in Luke 1.19 and 26, an angel and messenger of God, was made by commentators a military leader, and guardian of Paradise; *Raphael* appears in the apocryphal Book of Tobit as a helpful angel; *Uriel*, meaning "light of God," is named only in the Apocrypha, but commentators had identified him as one of the "eyes of the Lord." These four archangels were said by the commentators to rule the four corners of the earth—about all of them there was a certain amount of occult speculation. The five other loyal angels are *Abdiel*, a seraph, whose name (meaning "servant of God") appears as that of a human being in the Old Testament; *Ithuriel*, like the remaining three, a cherub, does not appear in the Bible or the Apocrypha—the word means "discovery of God"; *Uzziel* ("strength of God") appears as a human being in the Old Testament, but commentators had made him, like Uriel, one of the seven "eyes of the Lord"; *Zephon* ("searcher of secrets") is a human being in the Old Testament; and *Zophiel* means "spy of God," but not much else is known about him. Angelology began with the Jewish commentators and was made more confusing by Christian commentators.

God

Milton's God personifies "eternal providence." He foresees—cf. Latin *pro* before + *videre* to see—and provides everything, including his son, Christ, by whose agency God's will was manifested in the creation of the world, and by whose love God's justice and mercy and grace are manifested and man's salvation is effected. The Christian concept of the Trinity (by which the Father, Son, and Holy Spirit are both three and one) was not important in Milton's theology, and the mystery of the incarnation, crucifixion, and resurrection of Christ, though alluded to in *Paradise Lost*, is not part of the narrative.

Milton had little patience with metaphysical speculation of the kind practiced by Scholastic philosophers, or with other "vague cogitations and subtleties." Nonetheless, in justifying God's ways, Milton could not avoid being theological, and hence could not help asserting or implying things about God that were just as debatable in Milton's time as they had been for centuries before and are still today, three centuries later. Some of these are not crucial to the understanding or enjoyment of the poem, but a few that are central to its argument deserve to be understood and in our time may need explanation. The first of these is the relationship of God's foreknowledge to man's freedom.

In foreknowing all events God did not cause them. He made man capable of falling, knew he would fall, but did not make him fall. Thus foreknowledge is not the same as predestination in its general sense. (Milton did not believe in predestination in its special Calvinistic sense—that God decided from the beginning which individuals would be damned and which saved.) Next to the gift of life itself, Milton thought God's greatest gift to man was reason and the freedom to exercise that reason in the act of choosing. A man incapable of making a mistake would have been a man incapable of significant decisions, incapable of enjoying a sense of achievement, and incapable of the God-like pleasure of freely making a gift—as in the joy of giving thanks. Such a man, incapable of true obedience to God, would have no human dignity, or worth, as Milton defined those terms.

It would have been illogical to make man free to choose and at the same time not free to make wrong choices. And Milton believed God incapable of acting illogically. This argument seems sophistical to those who feel that a good God would not have made man capable of doing anything that would have undesirable consequences—that a good God would not have spoiled Paradise by planting the Tree and requiring obedience—or have allowed Satan to revolt—or Christ to suffer. Milton was, of course, aware of such objections. In fact, *Paradise Lost* is an attempt to meet them. (Cf. *Christian Doctrine* I.iii)

Freedom

Man's liberty before and after the Fall depended upon his following the dictates of the twofold, God-given power (i.e., virtue) of reason (XII.79ff.), which must govern his will. In *Paradise Lost* when Abdiel, the faithful angel, returned to heaven after his encounter with Satan, God characterized the fallen angels as those who "refuse/Right reason for their law." And though in the war in heaven the good angels employ force against the rebel angels, the victory is achieved only by Christ, the personification of reason, the *Logos*. Reason, like love, is a form of obedience. As Abdiel tells Satan, servitude or slavery is simply a state in which men "serve the unwise"; and Gabriel in his preview of postlapsarian history expresses Milton's own protestant liberal conviction that no man should forfeit his God-given freedom to any other man, but should preserve his liberty to serve God according to the dictates of his reason and in the light of the candle of the Lord. When, after Raphael's instruction, Adam tries to make Eve understand the nature of their freedom in Paradise, he applies the same freedom-through-obedience formula to the relationship between the will and the reason (or judgment). Man's will is free as long as it obeys reason, but it may become enslaved to irrational forces if it disobeys reason. When reason errs, misjudges, mistakes, it will misinform and misdirect the will, but in following the false dictates of reason the will does not cease to be free.

Justifying his own ways, God says in Book III that both acts of reason and acts of will are forms of choice, implying that when human beings choose, both will and reason are involved, whereas choice in animals is simply an act of will. Therefore, presumably, if animals can be said to obey, their obedience is irrational—predetermined, so to speak—and their lives are not blessed with the freedom (or the responsibility) that is a corollary of the gift of reason.

Covenant

Covenant is the word used by translators of the Old Testament for the Hebrew word *berith*, meaning a relationship between two parties and the terms thereof. God's covenants with the patriarchs Noah, Abraham, Isaac, and Jacob, and through Moses with Israel (Gen. 6.18, 9.9, 17.1ff.; Exod. 24.7, 8) were collectively called by Christian writers the Old Covenant—with special reference to the institution of the Mosaic Law as well as to the Law itself and its observance. The Greek word *diatheke*, used to translate the

Hebrew *berith*, carried the meaning of *testament*, as in "last will and testament," and hence the New Covenant, prophesied by Jeremiah (31.31) and interpreted by Luke and Paul in the Greek New Testament as God's promise of salvation to all believers in Christ, was called the New Testament. Eventually, the Christian books of the Bible were called the New Testament, and the pre-Christian books, the Old Testament. The New Covenant (that all believers in Christ would be saved by faith) was thought by Protestants to have superseded, or "renewed" (XI.116), though not entirely to have replaced, the Old Covenant, which applied only to the Jews and was fulfilled by obedience to the Law.

Knowledge

Though in the poem Milton follows the Bible in calling the forbidden tree the Tree of Knowledge, in *Christian Doctrine* he said he thought the tree was so named from the event. The consequence of eating was knowledge of a certain kind—knowledge of good that could be gained only by knowing evil. God did not forbid Adam and Eve from knowledge of anything that was within their power to understand, and what that limitation meant Adam seemed generally to know even before Raphael tried to make it more explicit (see VII.126 and VIII.119, 188). Milton recognized in perfect Adam a thirst for knowledge that is best understood as a passion for contemplating God's works for the right purpose—that of knowing God and glorifying him. Part of the sin in the act of the Fall was a desire for a knowledge equal to God's, or a knowledge of things purposely placed beyond man's comprehension. It was not the desire to know, but the aggressive attempt to exceed their own humanity that was sinful. How much knowledge was open to men and angels, and under what conditions, was clear to Uriel (see III.694). In *Christian Doctrine* Milton said that "love and obedience are always the best guides to knowledge." When the thirst for knowledge was motivated and limited by love and obedience, it could not be excessive nor could God be said to have forbidden it. What was forbidden was simply eating the fruit of the Tree and, by implication, the disobedient motives that perverted Adam's and Eve's God-given desire to know as much as they could about God's works.

The Fortunate Fall

Instead of the kind of knowledge they sought when they fell, Adam and Eve gained two other kinds: the knowledge of evil and the knowledge of God's providence, to which Adam responds when he wonders at the end of the poem whether he should be sorry or glad about his fall.

> Full of doubt I stand,
> Whether I should repent me now of sin
> By me done and occasioned, or rejoice

> Much more, that much more good thereof shall spring,
> To God more glory, more good will to men
> From God, and over wrath grace shall abound.

That is Milton's version of the idea expressed in the Mass for Holy Saturday: *O felix culpa quae talem ac tantum meruit habere redemptorum*—"O blessed sin (or crime) that was rewarded by so good and so great a redeemer!" In a famous essay Arthur O. Lovejoy calls it "The Paradox of the Fortunate Fall," but Milton makes it less a paradox by having Adam say only that he is uncertain how he should feel. The poem does not convince us that Adam should be glad he fell—only that Christians may be glad that the consequences were so good for mankind. The final justification of God's ways is the manifestation of his grace in the redemption of man through the incarnation and crucifixion of Christ—"whereby man, being delivered from sin and death . . . is raised to a far more excellent state of grace and glory than that from which he had fallen" (*CD* I.xiv). The words *pay, price, ransom,* and *redeem* are part of the biblical metaphor in which Christ's death is seen as the price paid as ransom to free man from the bondage of Satan, sin, and death into which Adam sold himself and all his progeny by his disobedience. But according to a less primitive metaphor, also biblical, the divine court of justice demanded that someone pay the penalty for breaking the law. The act of reparation must be equal to the crime—only the greatness of Christ's goodness could compensate for the greatness of Adam's crime. So by his death Christ was believed to have fulfilled the law (cf. "satisfaction," III.212) and to have paid "the required price for all mankind" (*CD* I.xvi— cf. "deadly forfeiture and ransom set," *PL* III.221). In this act of atonement, Christ restored to man the possibility of eternal life (as in Paradise), freed him from the inherited guilt of Adam's sin, and made him more aware of God's infinite love than he had been before.

The word *grace* has a complicated history, having in earlier forms meant praise, favor, charm, and thanks. In its Christian sense it is related to the idea in the title used for certain noblemen, as in "His Grace," for Christian grace is among other things a characteristic of an action done out of magnanimity and generosity by a person of power and position without regard to the merits of the person who benefits from the act. God's grace is a gift, which by definition is something that does not have to be given and something that makes the receiver grateful, or for which he may "say grace"— and in the possession of which he may be said to be in a "state of grace." So in the poem God's providence is made to seeem just by the conclusion of the *great argument*, or story: Satan fell because he thought he merited more than he got, and Adam in his redemption got more than he merited. As Addison said long ago, in the end "Satan is represented as miserable in the heights of his triumph, and Adam triumphant in the heights of his misery."

Paradise

The visual image of Paradise is highly generalized, but its outlines are fairly clear, even from the shifting point of view of Satan, who either walks or flies low as he moves into Eden. It is an elevated, enclosed garden or park occupying the level top (*champaign head*) of a steep, rugged (*savage*) circular hill whose sides are covered by a *brake, wilderness*, or *thicket* consisting of *shrubs and tangling bushes*, over which grow trees of various kinds (cf. *woody mountain*, VIII.303) arranged in rows and tiers (*ranks*) like the seats in amphitheatres (except that they curve the wrong way). A natural earth wall covered by vegetation in such a way as to look like a hedge row (*rural mound*) surrounds the plateau at its edge. The *hairy* sides of the *shaggy hill* (which have reminded one unfortunate critic of the *mons veneris*) are a part of a metaphorical head wearing a colorful crown consisting of the green band of the wall and, within that, a circle of fruit trees whose blossoms and golden fruit are mixed with *gay enameled colors* (*enameled* meant both "variegated" and "glossy"), the whole work of natural art illuminated by the blazing light of the sun. The image suggests the wealth and power of Adam (who rules over his *nether empire* [145], as well as the beauty and security of his pastoral garden. Milton's description, as Fowler says, "assimilates and refines upon the whole European tradition of paradises, gardens, pleasances, fortunate isles, and lands of the blessed. . . ." Parts of the description are taken from the description of gardens in Sidney's *Arcadia* and Spenser's *Faerie Queene*. European gardens in the seventeenth century were private parks on estates, carefully and ingeniously planted in geometrical patterns, and stocked for the pleasure of their privileged owners. They had become among other things, idealized settings for contemplation and philosophical dialogue. But in the older, middle-Eastern tradition they carried associations of sensual pleasure, and in the Bible the physical pleasures of sex are described in "garden" imagery; see the Song of Solomon 4.1–16 [*NEB*]:

> How beautiful are your breasts, my sister, my bride!
>   Your love is more fragrant than wine,
>   and your perfumes sweeter than any spices.
> Your lips drop sweetness like the honeycomb, my bride,
>   syrup and milk are under your tongue,
>   and your dress has the scent of Lebanon.
>   Your two cheeks are an orchard of pomegranates,
>   an orchard full of rare fruits:
> spikenard and saffron, sweet-cane and cinnamon
>   with every incense-bearing tree,
>   myrrh and aloes
>   with all the choicest spices.
> My sister, my bride, is a garden close-locked,
> a garden close-locked, a fountain sealed.

Bride

> The fountain in my garden is a spring of running water
>   pouring down from Lebanon.
> Awake, north wind, and come, south wind;
> blow upon my garden that its perfumes may pour forth,
>   that my beloved may come to his garden
>   and enjoy its rare fruits.

Milton echoes this metaphor in *enclosure,* and in the *native perfumes, balmy spoils,* and *Sabean odors from the spicy shore.*

Truth and Poetry

Milton did not believe that the biblical commentators on whose works he drew for certain details in *Paradise Lost* were authoritative. In fact at one point he mentions his disagreement with "the common gloss/Of theologians." Their speculations and their elaborations and extensions of the Bible were, like pagan myths, secular history, and popular science, simply material that a poet could feel free to use when it did not conflict with anything in the Bible. Like practically everyone else in his time, Milton had no doubt of the literal, factual, historical truth of everything in the Bible. And nothing in *Paradise Lost* disagrees with anything in the Bible. But of course there is much in the poem that is not in the Bible. He undertook to do what the Bible was not intended to do and what no one before him had done—to put the whole story of man in an epic poem. And in adding all the detail necessary for this imaginative elaboration of the biblical history he knew he was not committing an impiety. It had been a commonplace among religious teachers that the truth had often to be accommodated to the understanding of men—even as Christ had told the truth by telling parables. And many of the Greek and Roman myths had long been interpreted as simply pagan corruptions of biblical truth: the revolt of the Greek gods was a pagan version of the revolt of the angels; Hercules, a pagan version of Samson; Deucalion, of Noah; Prometheus, of Adam; Apollo, of Christ, and so on. Raphael's rationale for his narrative method in the "epic poem" he sings to Adam is essentially Milton's (see V.563). If we can know supernatural things by assuming that natural things are imperfect representations of them, we can know characters and events in history by assuming that they were much like those of the present. And if events narrated in the Old Testament are only shadows or types of the truth revealed in the New Testament (see "From shadowy types to truth, from flesh to spirit," XII.303), then the imagined detail of the poem may convey general truths of a higher order. Milton hoped that his prayers to the divine Muse were answered—that what he was inspired to write was as true as the story that Moses, the first historical poet, was inspired by God to write, in the first five books of the Bible. To entertain such hopes was not, of course, to believe that *Paradise Lost* had the authority of the Bible.

As for the truth of the implied religious doctrine of the poem, Milton believed that it could all be substantiated by the Scriptures, in the manner in which he substantiated all his conclusions in his own theological treatise, *Christian Doctrine.* In that prose work Milton arrived at some conclusions that would have been considered heresy by the Church of England as well as other churches. But the heresies that theological scholars may be able to discover in *Paradise Lost* are not obvious to the common reader.

CRITICISM

Great Writers on Milton, 1688–1929

JOHN DRYDEN

Epigram on Milton
(1688)

Three poets, in three distant ages born,
Greece, Italy, and England did adorn.
The first in loftiness of thought surpass'd,
The next in majesty, in both the last:
The force of Nature could no farther go;
To make a third, she join'd the former two.

VOLTAIRE

[Milton]†
(1727)

* * *

If the difference of genius between nation and nation ever appeared in its full light, 'tis in Milton's *Paradise Lost*.

The French answer with a scornful smile when they are told there is in England an epic poem the subject whereof is the Devil fighting against God, and Adam and Eve eating an apple at the persuasion of a snake. As that topic hath afforded nothing among them but some lively lampoons, for which that nation is so famous, they cannot imagine it possible to build an epic poem upon the subject of their ballads. And indeed such an error ought to be excused, for if we consider with what freedom the politest part of mankind throughout all Europe, both Catholics and Protestants, are wont to ridicule in conversation those consecrated his-

† From *An Essay Upon the Civil Wars of France. . . . And also Upon the Epick Poetry of the European Nations From Homer to Milton* (London, 1727) 70–88.

tories; nay, if those who have the highest respect for the mysteries of the Christian religion, and who are struck with awe at some parts of it, yet cannot forbear now and then making free with the Devil, the Serpent, the frailty of our first parents, the rib which Adam was robbed of, and the like; it seems a very hard task for a profane poet to endeavor to remove those shadows of ridicule, to reconcile together what is divine, and what looks absurd, and to command a respect that the sacred writers could hardly obtain from our frivolous minds.

What Milton so boldly undertook he performed with a superior strength of judgment, and with an imagination productive of beauties not dreamt of before him. The meanness (if there is any) of some parts of the subject is lost in the immensity of the poetical invention. There is something above the reach of human forces to have attempted the creation without bombast; to have described the gluttony and curiosity of a woman without flatness; to have brought probability and reason amidst the hurry of imaginary things belonging to another world, and as far remote from the limits of our notions as they are from our earth; in short, to force the reader to say, "If God, if the Angels, if Satan would speak, I believe they would speak as they do in Milton."

I have often admired how barren the subject appears, and how fruitful it grows under his hands.

The *Paradise Lost* is the only poem wherein are to be found in a perfect degree, that uniformity which satisfies the mind, and that variety which pleases the imagination—all its episodes being necessary lines which aim at the center of a perfect circle. Where is the nation who would not be pleased with the interview of Adam and the Angel? With the Mountain of Vision, with the bold strokes which make up the relentless, undaunted and sly character of Satan? But above all, with that sublime wisdom which Milton exerts whenever he dares to describe God and to make him speak? He seems indeed to draw the picture of the Almighty as like as human nature can reach to through the mortal dust in which we are clouded.

The heathens always, the Jews often, and our Christian priests sometimes, represent God as a tyrannt infinitely powerful. But the God of Milton is always a creator, a father, and a judge; nor is his vengeance jarring with his mercy, nor his predeterminations repugnant to the liberty of man. These are the pictures which lift up indeed the soul of the reader. Milton in that point, as well as in many others, is as far above the ancient poets as the Christian religion is above the heathen fables.

But he hath especially an undisputable claim to the unanimous admiration of mankind when he descends from those high flights to the natural description of human things. It is observable that in all other poems love is represented as a vice; in Milton only 'tis a virtue. The pictures he draws of it are naked as the persons he speaks of, and as venerable. He removes with a chaste hand the veil which covers everywhere else the enjoyments of that passion. There is softness, tenderness, and warmth without lasciviousness; the poet transports himself and us into that state of innocent happiness in which Adam and Eve continued for a short time. He soars not above human, but above corrupt, nature; and as there is no instance of such love, there is none of such poetry.

* * *

To come to more essential points, and more liable to be debated: I dare affirm that the contrivance of the Pandemonium would have been entirely disapproved of by critics like Boileau, Racine, etc.

That seat built for the parliament of the devils seems very preposterous, since Satan has summoned them all together and harangued them just before in an ample field. The council was necessary, but where it was to be held 'twas very indifferent. The poet seems to delight in building his Pandemonium in Doric order, with frieze and cornice, and a roof of gold. Such a contrivance favors more of the wild fancy of our father Le Moine, than of the serious spirit of Milton.

But when afterwards the devils turn dwarfs to fill their places in the house, as if it was impracticable to build a room large enough to contain them in their natural size, it is an idle story, which would match the most extravagant tales. And to crown all, Satan and the chief lords preserving their own monstrous forms, while the rabble of the devils shrink into pigmies, heightens the ridicule of the whole contrivance to an inexpressible degree. Methinks the true criterion for discerning what is really ridiculous in an epic poem is to examine if the same thing would not fit exactly the mock-heroic. Then I dare say that nothing is so adapted to that ludicrous way of writing as the metamorphosis of the devils into dwarfs.

The fiction of Death and Sin seems to have in it some great beauties and many gross defects. In order to canvass this matter with order, we must first lay down that such shadowy beings as Death, Sin, Chaos are intolerable when they are not allegorical, for fiction is nothing but truth in disguise. It must be granted too that an allegory must be short, decent, and noble. For an allegory carried too far or too low is like a beautiful woman who wears always a mask. An allegory is a long metaphor, and to speak too long in metaphors must be tiresome because unnatural. This being premised, I must say that in general those fictions, those imaginary beings, are more aggreeable to the nature of Milton's poem than to any other, because he has but two natural persons for his actors, I mean Adam and Eve. A great part of the action lies in imaginary worlds, and must of course admit of imaginary beings.

Then, Sin springing out of the head of Satan seems a beautiful allegory of pride, which is looked upon as the first offense committed against God. But I question if Satan getting his daughter with child is an invention to be approved of. I am afraid that fiction is but a mere quibble; for if sin was of a masculine gender in English, as it is in all the other languages, that whole affair drops, and the fiction vanishes away. But suppose we are not so nice, and we allow Satan to be in love with Sin, because this word is made feminine in English (as death passes also for masculine), what a horrid and loathsome idea does Milton present to the mind in this fiction? Sin brings forth Death; this monster, inflamed with lust and rage, lies with his mother, as she had done with her father. From that new commerce, springs a swarm of serpents, which creep in and out of their mother's womb, and gnaw and tear the bowels they are born from.

Let such a picture be ever so beautifully drawn, let the allegory be ever so obvious, and so clear, still it will be intolerable on the account of its foulness. That complication of horrors, that mixture of incest, that heap of monsters, that loathsomeness so far fetched, cannot but shock a reader of delicate taste.

But what is more intolerable, there are parts in that fiction which, bearing no allegory at all, have no manner of excuse. There is no meaning in the communication between Death and Sin, 'tis distasteful without any purpose; or if any allegory lies under it, the filthy abomination of the thing is certainly more obvious than the allegory.

I see with admiration Sin, the portress of Hell, opening the gates of the Abyss, but unable to shut them again: that is really beautiful, because 'tis true. But what signifies Satan and Death quarrelling together, grinning at one another, and ready to fight?

* * *

Now the sublimest of all the fictions calls me to examine it. I mean the war in heaven. The Earl of Roscommon, and Mr. Addison (whose judgment seems either to guide, or to justify the opinion of his countrymen) admire chiefly that part of the poem. They bestow all the skill of their criticism, and the strength of their eloquence, to set off that favorite part. I may affirm that the very things they admire would not be tolerated by the French critics. The reader will perhaps see with pleasure in what consists so strange a difference and what may be the ground of it.

First, they would assert that a war in heaven, being an imaginary thing which lies out of the reach of our nature, should be contracted in two or three pages, rather than lengthened out into two books, because we are naturally impatient of removing from us the objects which are not adapted to our senses.

According to that rule they would maintain that 'tis an idle task to give the reader the full character of the leaders of that war, and to describe Raphael, Michael, Abdiel, Moloch, and Nisroch as Homer paints Ajax, Diomede, and Hector.

For what avails it to draw at length the picture of these beings, so utterly strangers to the reader, that he cannot be affected any way towards them? By the same reason, the long speeches of these imaginary warriors, either before the battle or in the middle of the action, their mutual insults, seem an injudicious imitation of Homer.

The aforesaid critics would not bear with the angels plucking up the mountains with their woods, their waters, and their rocks, and flinging them on the heads of their enemies. Such a contrivance (they would say) is the more puerile, the more it aims at greatness. Angels armed with mountains in heaven resemble too much the Dipsodes in Rabelais, who wore an armor of Portland stone six foot thick.

The artillery seems of the same kind, yet more trifling, because more useless.

To what purpose are these engines brought in? Since they cannot wound the enemies, but only remove them from their places, and make them tumble down. Indeed (if the expression may be forgiven) 'tis to play at nine-pins. And the very thing which is so dreadfully great on earth, becomes very low and ridiculous in heaven.

* * *

I leave it to the readers to pronounce if these observations are right, or ill-grounded, and if they are carried too far. But in case these exceptions are just, the severest critic must however confess there are perfections enough in Milton to atone for all his defects.

I must beg leave to conclude this article on Milton with two observations. His hero (I mean Adam, his first personage) is unhappy. That demonstrates against all the critics that a very good poem may end unfortunately, in spite of all their pretended rules. Secondly, *Paradise Lost* ends completely. The thread of the fable is spun out to the last. Milton and Tasso have been careful of not stopping short and abruptly. The one does not abandon Adam and Eve till they are driven out of Eden. The other does not conclude before Jerusalem is taken. Homer and Virgil took a contrary way: the *Iliad* ends with the death of Hector, the *Aeneid* with that of Turnus. The tribe of commentators have upon that enacted a law that a house ought never to be finished, because Homer and Virgil did not complete their own, but if Homer had taken Troy, and Virgil married Lavinia to Aeneas, the critics would have laid down a rule just the contrary.

SAMUEL JOHNSON

[*Paradise Lost*]†

I am now to examine *Paradise Lost*; a poem, which, considered with respect to design, may claim the first place, and with respect to performance the second, among the productions of the human mind.

By the general consent of critics, the first praise of genius is due to the writer of an epic poem, as it requires an assemblage of all the powers which are singly sufficient for other compositions. Poetry is the art of uniting pleasure with truth, by calling imagination to the help of reason. Epic poetry undertakes to teach the most important truths by the most pleasing precepts, and therefore relates some great event in the most affecting manner. History must supply the writer with the rudiments of narration, which he must improve and exalt by a nobler art, animate by dramatic energy, and diversify by retrospection and anticipation; morality must teach him the exact bounds, and different shades, of vice and virtue: from policy, and the practice of life, he has to learn the discriminations of character, and the tendency of the passions, either single or combined; and physiology must supply him with illustrations and images. To put these materials to poetical use, is required an imagination capable of painting nature, and realizing fiction. Nor is he yet a poet till he has attained the whole extension of his language, distinguished all the delicacies of phrase, and all the colors of words, and learned to adjust their different sounds to all the varieties of metrical modulation.

Bossu[1] is of opinion that the poet's first work is to find a *moral*, which his fable is afterwards to illustrate and establish. This seems to have been the process only of Milton; the moral of other poems is incidental and consequent; in Milton's only it is essential and intrinsic. His purpose was the most useful and the most arduous; *to vindicate the ways of God to man*;[2] to shrew the reasonableness of religion, and the necessity of obedience to the Divine Law.

To convey this moral there must be a *fable*, a narration artfully constructed, so as to excite curiosity, and surprise expectation. In this part of his work, Milton must be confessed to have equalled every other poet. He has involved in his account of the Fall of Man the events which preceded, and that were to follow it: he has interwoven the whole system of theology with such propriety, that every part appears to be

---

† From "Milton," in *The Lives of the Most Eminent English Poets*, rev. ed. (London, 1783). The footnotes for this selection are by the editor.
1. René le Bossu, author of *Traité du Poème Epique* (1675).
2. Johnson confuses Milton's line with Pope's, in *Essay on Man* 1.16.

necessary; and scarcely any recital is wished shorter for the sake of quickening the progress of the main action.

The subject of an epic poem is naturally an event of great importance. That of Milton is not the destruction of a city, the conduct of a colony, or the foundation of an empire. His subject is the fate of worlds, the revolutions of heaven and of earth; rebellion against the Supreme King, raised by the highest order of created beings; the overthrow of their host, and the punishment of their crime; the creation of a new race of reasonable creatures; their original happiness and innocence, their forfeiture of immortality, and their restoration to hope and peace.

Great events can be hastened or retarded only by persons of elevated dignity. Before the greatness displayed in Milton's poem, all other greatness shrinks away. The weakest of his agents are the highest and noblest of human beings, the original parents of mankind; with whose actions the elements consented; on whose rectitude, or deviation of will, depended the state of terrestrial nature, and the condition of all the future inhabitants of the globe.

Of the other agents in the poem, the chief are such as it is irreverence to name on slight occasions. The rest were lower powers;

> ———of which the least could wield
> Those elements, and arm him with the force
> Of all their regions.

powers, which only the control of Omnipotence restrains from laying creation waste, and filling the vast expanse of space with ruin and confusion. To display the motives and actions of beings thus superior, so far as human reason can examine them, or human imagination represent them, is the task which this mighty poet has undertaken and performed.

In the examination of epic poems much speculation is commonly employed upon the *characters*. The characters in the *Paradise Lost*, which admit of examination, are those of angels and of man; of angels good and evil; of man in his innocent and sinful state.

Among the angels, the virtue of Raphael is mild and placid, of easy condescension and free communication; that of Michael is regal and lofty, and, as may seem, attentive to the dignity of his own nature. Abdiel and Gabriel appear occasionally, and act as every incident requires; the solitary fidelity of Abdiel is very amiably painted.

Of the evil angels the characters are more diversified. To Satan, as Addison observes,[3] such sentiments are given as suit *the most exalted and most depraved being*. Milton has been censured, by Clark,[4] for the impiety which sometimes breaks from Satan's mouth. For there are

---

3. Joseph Addison's essays on *PL* appeared weekly in the *Spectator* from Jan. 5 to May 3, 1712. Johnson's reference here is to the essay of Feb. 16, 1712.
4. John Clarke, author of *An Essay upon Study* (1731).

thoughts, as he justly remarks, which no observation of character can justify, because no good man would willingly permit them to pass, however transiently, through his own mind. To make Satan speak as a rebel, without any such expressions as might taint the reader's imagination, was indeed one of the great difficulties in Milton's undertaking, and I cannot but think that he has extricated himself with great happiness. There is in Satan's speeches little that can give pain to a pious ear. The language of rebellion cannot be the same with that of obedience. The malignity of Satan foams in haughtiness and obstinacy; but his expressions are commonly general, and no otherwise offensive than as they are wicked.

The other chiefs of the celestial rebellion are very judiciously discriminated in the first and second books; and the ferocious character of Moloch appears, both in the battle and the council, with exact consistency.

To Adam and to Eve are given, during their innocence, such sentiments as innocence can generate and utter. Their love is pure benevolence and mutual veneration; their repasts are without luxury, and their diligence without toil. Their addresses to their Maker have little more than the voice of admiration and gratitude. Fruition left them nothing to ask, and Innocence left them nothing to fear.

But with guilt enter distrust and discord, mutual accusation, and stubborn self-defense; they regard each other with alienated minds, and dread their Creator as the avenger of their transgression. At last they seek shelter in his mercy, soften to repentance, and melt in supplication. Both before and after the Fall, the superiority of Adam is diligently sustained.

* * *

It is justly remarked by Addison, that this poem has, by the nature of its subject, the advantage above all others, that it is universally and perpetually interesting. All mankind will, through all ages, bear the same relation to Adam and to Eve, and must partake of that good and evil which extend to themselves.

* * *

The questions, whether the action of the poem be strictly *one*, whether the poem can be properly termed *heroic*, and who is the hero, are raised by such readers as draw their principles of judgment rather from books than from reason. Milton, though he intituled *Paradise Lost* only a *poem*, yet calls it himself *heroic song*. Dryden,[5] petulantly and indecently, denies the heroism of Adam, because he was overcome; but there is no reason why the hero should not be unfortunate, except established practice, since success and virtue do not go necessarily together. Cato

5. John Dryden, in "A Discourse Concerning the Original and Progress of Satire" (1693).

is the hero of Lucan;[6] but Lucan's authority will not be suffered by Quintilian[7] to decide. However, if success be necessary, Adam's deceiver was at last crushed; Adam was restored to his Maker's favor, and therefore may securely resume his human rank.

After the scheme and fabric of the poem, must be considered its component parts, the sentiments and the diction.

The *sentiments*, as expressive of manners, or appropriated to characters, are, for the greater part, unexceptionably just.

Splendid passages, containing lessons of morality, or precepts of prudence, occur seldom. Such is the original formation of this poem that, as it admits no human manners till the Fall, it can give little assistance to human conduct. Its end is to raise the thoughts above sublunary cares or pleasures. Yet the praise of that fortitude, with which Abdiel maintained his singularity of virtue against the scorn of multitudes, may be accommodated to all times; and Raphael's reproof of Adam's curiosity after the planetary motions, with the answer returned by Adam, may be confidently opposed to any rule of life which any poet has delivered.

The thoughts which are occasionally called forth in the progress, are such as could only be produced by an imagination in the highest degree fervid and active, to which materials were supplied by incessant study and unlimited curiosity. The heat of Milton's mind might be said to sublimate his learning, to throw off into his work the spirit of science, unmingled with its grosser parts.

He had considered creation in its whole extent, and his descriptions are therefore learned. He had accustomed his imagination to unrestrained indulgence, and his conceptions therefore were extensive. The characteristic quality of his poem is sublimity. He sometimes descends to the elegant, but his element is the great. He can occasionally invest himself with grace; but his natural port is gigantic loftiness. He can please when pleasure is required; but it is his peculiar power to astonish.

He seems to have been well acquainted with his own genius, and to know what it was that nature had bestowed upon him more bountifully than upon others; the power of displaying the vast, illuminating the splendid, enforcing the awful, darkening the gloomy, and aggravating the dreadful; he therefore chose a subject on which too much could not be said, on which he might tire his fancy without the censure of extravagance.

The appearances of nature, and the occurrences of life, did not satiate his appetite of greatness. To paint things as they are, requires a minute attention, and employs the memory rather than the fancy. Milton's delight was to sport in the wide regions of possibility; reality was a scene

6. I.e., of Lucan's epic *Pharsalia* (first century A.D.).
7. A contemporary of Lucan, whose work on rhetoric and literary criticism was well known by Milton as well as Johnson and later English critics.

too narrow for his mind. He sent his faculties out upon discovery, into worlds where only imagination can travel, and delighted to form new modes of existence, and furnish sentiment and action to superior beings, to trace the counsels of hell, or accompany the choirs of heaven.

But he could not be always in other worlds: he must sometimes revisit earth, and tell of things visible and known. When he cannot raise wonder by the sublimity of his mind, he gives delight by its fertility.

Whatever be his subject, he never fails to fill the imagination. But his images and descriptions of the scenes or operations of nature do not seem to be always copied from original form, nor to have the freshness, raciness, and energy of immediate observation. He saw nature, as Dryden expresses it, *through the spectacles of books;*[8] and on most occasions calls learning to his assistance. The garden of Eden brings to his mind the vale of *Enna*, where Proserpine was gathering flowers. Satan makes his way through fighting elements, like *Argo* between the *Cyanean* rocks, or *Ulysses* between the two *Sicilian* whirlpools, when he shunned *Charybdis* on the *larboard*. The mythological allusions have been justly censured, as not being always used with notice of their vanity; but they contribute variety to the narration, and produce an alternate exercise of the memory and the fancy.

His similes are less numerous, and more various, than those of his predecessors. But he does not confine himself within the limits of rigorous comparison: his great excellence is amplitude, and he expands the adventitious image beyond the dimensions which the occasion required. Thus, comparing the shield of Satan to the orb of the moon, he crowds the imagination with the discovery of the telescope, and all the wonders which the telescope discovers.

Of his moral sentiments it is hardly praise to affirm that they excel those of all other poets; for this superiority he was indebted to his acquaintance with the sacred writings. The ancient epic poets, wanting the light of Revelation, were very unskilful teachers of virtue: their principal characters may be great, but they are not amiable. The reader may rise from their works with a greater degree of active or passive fortitude, and sometimes of prudence; but he will be able to carry away few precepts of justice, and none of mercy.

From the Italian writers it appears, that the advantages of even Christian knowledge may be possessed in vain. Ariosto's pravity is generally known; and though the *Deliverance of Jerusalem* may be considered as a sacred subject, the poet has been very sparing of moral instruction.

In Milton every line breathes sanctity of thought, and purity of manners, except when the train of the narration requires the introduction of the rebellious spirits; and even they are compelled to acknowledge

8. *An Essay of Dramatic Poetry* (1668): Shakespeare "needed not the spectacles of books to read nature."

their subjection to God, in such a manner as excites reverence and confirms piety.

Of human beings there are but two; but those two are the parents of mankind, venerable before their fall for dignity and innocence, and amiable after it for repentance and submission. In their first state their affection is tender without weakness, and their piety sublime without presumption. When they have sinned, they show how discord begins in natural frailty, and how it ought to cease in mutual forbearance; how confidence of the divine favor is forfeited by sin, and how hope of pardon may be obtained by penitence and prayer. A state of innocence we can only conceive, if indeed, in our present misery, it be possible to conceive it; but the sentiments and worship proper to a fallen and offending being, we have all to learn, as we have all to practice.

The poet, whatever be done, is always great. Our progenitors, in their first state, conversed with angels; even when folly and sin had degraded them, they had not in their humiliation *the port of mean suitors*; and they rise again to reverential regard, when we find that their prayers were heard.

As human passions did not enter the world before the Fall, there is in the *Paradise Lost* little opportunity for the pathetic; but what little there is has not been lost. That passion which is peculiar to rational nature, the anguish arising from the consciousness of transgression, and the horrors attending the sense of the Divine displeasure, are very justly described and forcibly impressed. But the passions are moved only on one occasion; sublimity is the general and prevailing quality in this poem; sublimity variously modified, sometimes descriptive, sometimes argumentative.

* * *

The plan of *Paradise Lost* has this inconvenience, that it comprises neither human actions nor human manners. The man and woman who act and suffer, are in a state which no other man or woman can ever know. The reader finds no transaction in which he can be engaged; beholds no condition in which he can by any effort of imagination place himself; he has, therefore, little natural curiosity or sympathy.

We all, indeed, feel the effects of Adam's disobedience; we all sin like Adam, and like him must all bewail our offences; we have restless and insidious enemies in the fallen angels, and in the blessed spirits we have guardians and friends; in the redemption of mankind we hope to be included; and in the description of heaven and hell we are surely interested, as we are all to reside hereafter either in the regions of horror or of bliss.

But these truths are too important to be new; they have been taught to our infancy; they have mingled with our solitary thoughts and familiar conversation, and are habitually interwoven with the whole texture of life. Being therefore not new, they raise no unaccustomed emotion in the mind; what we knew before we cannot learn; what is not unexpected cannot surprise.

Of the ideas suggested by these awful scenes, from some we recede with reverence, except when stated hours require their assocation; and from others we shrink with horror, or admit them only as salutary inflictions, as counterpoises to our interests and passions. Such images rather obstruct the career of fancy than incite it.

Pleasure and terror are indeed the genuine sources of poetry; but poetical pleasure must be such as human imagination can at least conceive, and poetical terror such as human strength and fortitude may combat. The good and evil of eternity are too ponderous for the wings of wit; the mind sinks under them in passive helplessness, content with calm belief and humble adoration.

Known truths, however, may take a different appearance, and be conveyed to the mind by a new train of intermediate images. This Milton has undertaken, and performed with pregnancy and vigor of mind peculiar to himself. Whoever considers the few radical positions which the Scriptures afforded him, will wonder by what energetic operation he expanded them to such extent, and ramified them to so much variety, restrained as he was by religious reverence from licentiousness of fiction.

Here is a full display of the united force of study and genius; of a great accumulation of materials, with judgment to digest, and fancy to combine them: Milton was able to select from nature, or from story, from ancient fable, or from modern science, whatever could illustrate or adorn his thoughts. An accumulation of knowledge impregnated his mind, fermented by study, and exalted by imagination.

It has been therefore said, without an indecent hyperbole, by one of his encomiasts, that in reading *Paradise Lost* we read a book of universal knowledge.[9]

But original deficience cannot be supplied. The want of human interest is always felt. *Paradise Lost* is one of the books which the reader admires and lays down and forgets to take up again. None ever wished it longer than it is. Its perusal is a duty rather than a pleasure. We read Milton for instruction, retire harassed and overburdened, and look elsewhere for recreation; we desert our master, and seek for companions.

Another inconvenience of Milton's design is, that it requires the description of what cannot be described, the agency of spirits. He saw that immateriality supplied no images, and that he could not show angels acting but by instruments of action; he therefore invested them with form and matter. This, being necessary, was therefore defensible; and he should have secured the consistency of his system, by keeping immateriality out of sight, and enticing his reader to drop it from his

---

9. See the second paragraph of Northrop Frye's essay, p. 510, below.

thoughts. But he has unhappily perplexed his poetry with his philosophy. His infernal and celestial powers are sometimes pure spirit, and some-times animated body. When Satan walks with his lance upon the *burning marle*, he has a body; when, in his passage between hell and the new world, he is in danger of sinking in the vacuity, and is supported by a gust of rising vapors, he has a body; when he animates the toad, he seems to be mere spirit, that can penetrate matter at pleasure; when he *starts up in his own shape*, he has at least a determined form; and when he is brought before Gabriel, he has a *spear and shield*, which he had the power of hiding in the toad, though the arms of the contending angels are evidently material.

The vulgar inhabitants of Pandaemonium, being *incorporeal spirits*, are *at large, though without number*, in a limited space; yet in the battle, when they were overwhelmed by mountains, their armor hurt them, *crushed in upon their substance, now grown gross by sinning*. This like-wise happened to the uncorrupted angels, who were overthrown *the sooner for their arms*, for *unarmed they might easily as spirits have evaded by contraction, or remove*. Even as spirits they are hardly spiritual; for *contraction* and *remove* are images of matter; but if they could have escaped without their armor, they might have escaped from it, and left only the empty cover to be battered. Uriel, when he rides on a sun-beam, is material: Satan is material when he is afraid of the prowess of Adam.

The confusion of spirit and matter which pervades the whole narration of the war of heaven fills it with incongruity; and the book, in which it is related, is, I believe, the favorite of children, and gradually neglected as knowledge is increased. * * *

After the operation of immaterial agents, which cannot be explained, may be considered that of allegorical persons, which have no real exis-tence. To exalt causes into agents, to invest abstract ideas with form, and animate them with activity, has always been the right of poetry. But such airy beings are, for the most part, suffered only to do their natural office, and retire. Thus Fame tells a tale, and Victory hovers over a general, or perches on a standard; but Fame and Victory can do no more. To give them any real employment, or ascribe to them any material agency, is to make them allegorical no longer, but to shock the mind by ascribing effects to nonentity. In the *Prometheus of Aese-chylus*, we see *Violence* and *Strength*, and in the *Alcestis* of Euripides, we see *Death* brough upon the stage, all as active persons of the drama; but no precedents can justify absurdity.

Milton's allegory of Sin and Death is undoubtedly faulty. Sin is indeed the mother of Death, and may be allowed to be the portress of hell; but when they stop the journey of Satan, a journey described as real, and when Death offers him battle, the allegory is broken. That Sin and Death should have shown the way to hell might have been allowed; but they cannot facilitate the passage by building a bridge, because the difficulty of Satan's passage is described as real and sensible, and the bridge ought to be only figurative. The hell assigned to the rebellious spirits is described as not less local than the residence of man. It is placed in some distant part of space, separated from the regions of harmony and order by a chaotic waste and an unoccupied vacuity; but Sin and Death worked up a *mole* of *aggregated soil*, cemented with *asphaltus*; a work too bulky for ideal architects.

This unskilful allegory appears to me one of the greatest faults of the poem; and to this there was no temptation, but the author's opinion of its beauty.

To the conduct of the narrative some objections may be made. Satan is with great expectation brought before Gabriel in Paradise, and is suffered to go away unmolested. The creation of man is represented as the consequence of the vacuity left in heaven by the expulsion of the rebels, yet Satan mentions it as a report *rife in heaven* before his departure.

To find sentiments of the state of innocence, was very difficult; and something of anticipation perhaps is now and then discovered. Adam's discourse of dreams seems not to be the speculation of a new-created being. I know not whether his answer to the angel's reproof for curiosity does not want something of propriety: it is the speech of a man acquainted with many other men. Some philosophical notions, especially when the philosophy is false, might have been better omitted. The angel, in a comparison, speaks of *timorous deer*, before deer were yet timorous, and before Adam could understand the comparison.

Dryden remarks, that Milton has some flats among his elevations.[1] This is only to say that all the parts are not equal. In every work, one part must be for the sake of others; a palace must have passages; a poem must have transitions. It is no more to be required that wit should always be blazing, than that the sun should always stand at noon. In a great work there is a vicissitude of luminous and opaque parts, as there is in the world a succession of day and night. Milton, when he has expatiated in the sky, may be allowed sometimes to revisit earth; for what other author ever soared so high, or sustained his flight so long?

* * *

Such are the faults of that wonderful performance *Paradise Lost*; which he who can put in balance with its beauties must be considered not as nice but as dull, as less to be censured for want of candor than pitied for want of sensibility.

* * *

Through all his greater works there prevails an uniform peculiarity of *diction*, a mode and cast of expression which bears little resemblance

1. Preface to *Sylvae* (1685).

to that of any former writer, and which is so far removed from common use, that an unlearned reader, when he first opens his book, finds himself surprised by a new language.

This novelty has been, by those who can find nothing wrong in Milton, imputed to his laborious endeavors after words suitable to the grandeur of his ideas. *Our language*, says Addison, *sunk under him*. But the truth is, that, both in prose and verse, he had formed his style by a perverse and pedantic principle. He was desirous to use English words with a foreign idiom. This in all his prose is discovered and condemned; for there judgment operates freely, neither softened by the beauty nor awed by the dignity of his thoughts; but such is the power of his poetry, that his call is obeyed without resistance, the reader feels himself in captivity to a higher and a nobler mind, and criticism sinks in admiration.

Milton's style was not modified by his subject: what is shown with greater extent in *Paradise Lost*, may be found in *Comus*. One source of his peculiarity was his familiarity with the Tuscan poets: the disposition of his words is, I think, frequently Italian; perhaps sometimes combined with other tongues. Of him, at last, may be said what Jonson says of Spenser, that *he wrote no language*, but has formed what Butler calls a *Babylonish dialect*,[2] in itself harsh and barbarous, but made by exalted genius, and extensive learning, the vehicle of so much instruction and so much pleasure, that, like other lovers, we find grace in its deformity.

Whatever be the faults of his diction, he cannot want the praise of copiousness and variety: he was master of his language in its full extent; and has selected the melodious words with such diligence, that from his book alone the Art of English Poetry might be learned.

After his diction, something must be said of his *versification*. *The measure*, he says, *is the English heroic verse without rhyme*. Of this mode he had many examples among the Italians, and some in his own country. The Earl of Surry is said to have translated one of Virgil's books without rhyme; and, besides our tragedies, a few short poems had appeared in blank verse; particularly one tending to reconcile the nation to Raleigh's wild attempt upon Guiana, and probably written by Raleigh himself. These petty performances cannot be supposed to have much influenced Milton, who more probably took his hint from Trisino's *Italia Liberata*; and, finding blank verse easier than rhyme, was desirous of persuading himself that it is better.

Rhyme, he says, and says truly, *is no necessary adjunct of true poetry*. But perhaps, of poetry as a mental operation, meter or music is no necessary adjunct: it is however by the music of meter that poetry has been discriminated in all languages; and in languages melodiously constructed, by a due proportion of long and short syllables, meter is sufficient. But one language cannot communicate its rules to another:

2. Ben Jonson in *Timber, or Discoveries* (1641) and Samuel Butler in *Hudibras* (1662–78).

where meter is scanty and imperfect, some help is necessary. The music of the English heroic line strikes the ear so faintly that it is easily lost, unless all the syllables of every line cooperate together: this cooperation can be only obtained by the preservation of every verse unmingled with another, as a distinct system of sounds; and this distinctness is obtained and preserved by the artifice of rhyme. The variety of pauses, so much boasted by the lovers of blank verse, changes the measures of an English poet to the periods of a declaimer; and there are only a few skilful and happy readers of Milton, who enable their audience to perceive where the lines end or begin. *Blank verse*, said an ingenious critic, *seems to be verse only to the eye.*

Poetry may subsist without rhyme, but English poetry will not often please; nor can rhyme ever be safely spared but where the subject is able to support itself. Blank verse makes some approach to that which is called the *lapidary stile*; has neither the easiness of prose, nor the melody of numbers, and therefore tires by long continuance. Of the Italian writers without rhyme, whom Milton alleges as precedents, not one is popular; what reason could urge in its defence, has been confuted by the ear.

But, whatever be the advantage of rhyme, I cannot prevail on myself to wish that Milton had been a rhymer; for I cannot wish his work to be other than it is; yet, like other heroes, he is to be admired rather than imitated. He that thinks himself capable of astonishing, may write blank verse; but those that hope only to please, must condescend to rhyme.

The highest praise of genius is original invention. Milton cannot be said to have contrived the structure of an epic poem, and therefore owes reverence to that vigor and amplitude of mind to which all generations must be indebted for the art of poetical narration, for the texture of the fable, the variation of incidents, the interposition of dialogue, and all the strategems that surprise and enchain attention. But, of all the borrowers from Homer, Milton is perhaps the least indebted. He was naturally a thinker for himself, confident of his own abilities, and disdainful of help or hindrance: he did not refuse admission to the thoughts or images of his predecessors, but he did not seek them. From his contemporaries he neither courted nor received support; there is in his writings nothing by which the pride of other authors might be gratified, or favor gained; no exchange of praise, nor solicitation of support. His great works were performed under discountenance, and in blindness, but difficulties vanished at his touch; he was born for whatever is arduous, and his work is not the greatest of heroic poems, only because it is not the first.

WILLIAM BLAKE

From The Marriage of Heaven and Hell
(1793)

Note: The reason Milton wrote in fetters when he wrote of Angels &
God, and at liberty when of Devils & Hell, is because he was a true
Poet and of the Devil's party without knowing it.

WILLIAM WORDSWORTH

London
(1802)

Milton! thou shouldst be living at this hour:
England hath need of thee: she is a fen
Of stagnant waters: altar, sword, and pen,
Fireside, the heroic wealth of hall and bower,
Have forfeited their ancient English dower
Of inward happiness. We are selfish men;
Oh! raise us up, return to us again;
And give us manners, virtue, freedom, power.
Thy soul was like a Star, and dwelt apart;
Thou hadst a voice whose sound was like the sea:
Pure as the naked heavens, majestic, free,
So didst thou travel on life's common way,
In cheerful godliness; and yet thy heart
The lowliest duties on herself did lay.

SAMUEL TAYLOR COLERIDGE

[Milton]†
(1818)

If we divide the period from the accession of Elizabeth to the Protectorate
of Cromwell into two unequal portions, the first ending with the death
of James I, the other comprehending the reign of Charles and the brief
glories of the Republic, we are forcibly struck with a difference in the

† "Lecture X," in Lectures of 1818, from *Coleridge's Miscellaneous Criticism*, ed. Thomas
Middleton Raysor (Cambridge, Mass., Harvard University Press, 1936) 157–65. Some of
Raysor's notes to this essay have been deleted. The editor's additions appear in brackets.

character of the illustrious actors, by whom each period is rendered severally memorable. Or rather, the difference in the characters of the great men in each period, leads us to make this division. Eminent as the intellectual powers were that were displayed in both; yet in the number of great men, in the various sorts of excellence, and not merely in the variety but almost diversity of talents united in the same individual, the age of Charles falls short of its predecessor; and the stars of the Parliament, keen as their radiance was, in fulness and richness of lustre, yield to the constellation at the court of Elizabeth;—which can only be paralleled by Greece in her brightest moment, when the titles of the poet, the philosopher, the historian, the staesman and the general not seldom formed a garland round the same head, as in the instances of our Sidneys and Raleighs. But then, on the other hand, there was a vehemence of will, an enthusiasm of principle, a depth and an earnestness of spirit, which the charms of individual fame and personal aggrandisement could not pacify,—an aspiration after reality, permanence, and general good,—in short, a moral grandeur in the latter period, with which the low intrigues, Machiavellic maxims, and selfish and servile ambition of the former, stand in painful contrast. [1]

The causes of this it belongs not to the present occasion to detail at length; but a mere allusion to the quick succession of revolutions in religion, breeding a political indifference in the mass of men to religion itself, the enormous increase of the royal power in consequence of the humiliation of the nobility and the clergy—the transference of the papal authority to the crown;—the unfixed state of Elizabeth's own opinions, whose inclinations were as popish as her interests were protestant—the controversial extravagance and practical imbecility of her successor—will help to explain the former period; and the persecutions that had given a life and soul-interest to the disputes so imprudently fostered by James,—the ardour of a conscious increase of power in the commons, and the greater austerity of manners and maxims, the natural product and most formidable weapon of religious disputation, not merely in conjunction, but in closest combination, with newly awakened political and republican zeal, these perhaps account for the character of the latter aera.

In the close of the former period, and during the bloom of the latter, the poet Milton was educated and formed; and he survived the latter, and all the fond hopes and aspirations which had been its life; and so in evil days, standing as the representative of the combined excellence of both periods, he produced the Paradise Lost as by an after-throe of nature. "There are some persons (observes a divine, a contemporary of Milton's) of whom the grace of God takes early hold, and the good spirit

1. Cf. Coleridge's *Shakespearean Criticism* [ed. T. M. Raysor] ii. 115–16, for another treatment of this subject.

inhabiting them, carries them on in an even constancy through inno-
cence into virtue, their Christianity bearing equal date with their man-
hood, and reason and religion, like warp and woof, running together,
make up one web of a wise and exemplary life. This (he adds) is a most
happy case, wherever it happens; for, besides that there is no sweeter or
more lovely thing on earth than the early buds of piety, which drew
from our Saviour signal affection to the beloved disciple, it is better to
have no wound than to experience the most sovereign balsam, which,
if it work a cure, yet usually leaves a scar behind." Although it was and
is my intention to defer the consideration of Milton's own character to
the conclusion of this Lecture, yet I could not prevail on myself to
approach the Paradise Lost without impressing on your minds the con-
ditions under which such a work was in fact producible at all, the original
genius having been assumed as the immediate agent and efficient cause;
and these conditions I find in the character of the times and in his own
character. The age in which the foundations of his mind were laid, was
congenial to it as one golden aera of profound erudition and individual
genius;—that in which the superstructure was carried up, was no less
favorable to it by a sternness of discipline and a show of self-control,
highly flattering to the imaginative dignity of an heir of fame, and which
won Milton over from the dear-loved delights of academic groves and
cathedral aisles to the anti-prelatic party. It acted on him, too, no doubt,
and modified his studies by a characteristic controversial spirit, (his
presentation of God is tinted with it)—a spirit not less busy indeed in
political than in theological and ecclesiastical dispute, but carrying on
the former almost always, more or less, in the guise of the latter. And
so far as Pope's censure of our poet,—that he makes God the Father a
school divine[2]—is just, we must attribute it to the character of his age,
from which the men of genius, who escaped, escaped by a worse disease,
the licentious indifference of a Frenchified court.

Such was the *nidus* or soil, which constituted, in the strict sense of
the word, the circumstances of Milton's mind. In his mind itself there
were purity and piety absolute; an imagination to which neither the past
nor the present were interesting, except as far as they called forth and
enlivened the great ideal, in which and for which he lived; a keen love
of truth, which, after many weary pursuits, found a harbor in a sublime
listening to the still voice in his own spirit, and as keen a love of his
country, which, after a disappointment still more depressive, expanded
and soared into a love of man as a probationer of immortality. These
were, these alone could be, the conditions under which such a work as
the Paradise Lost could be conceived and accomplished. By a life-long
study Milton had known—

2. "And God the Father turns a school divine." Imitations of Horace, First Epistle of the Second
Book, 1.102.

What was of use to know,
What best to say could say, to do had done.
His actions to his words agreed, his words
To his large heart gave utterance due, his heart
Contain'd of good, wise, fair, the perfect shape;
[Cf. *PR*, III. 7–11]

and he left the imperishable total, as a bequest to the ages coming, in the PARADISE LOST.

Difficult as I shall find it to turn over these leaves without catching some passage, which would tempt me to stop, I propose to consider, 1st, the general plan and arrangement of the work;—2ndly, the subject with its difficulties and advantages; 3rdly, the poet's object, the spirit in the letter, the ἐνθύμιον ἐν μύθῳ, the true school-divinity; and lastly, the characteristic excellencies of the poem, in what they consist, and by what means they were produced.

1. As to the plan and ordonnance of the Poem.

Compare it with the Iliad, many of the books of which might change places without any injury to the thread of the story. Indeed, I doubt the original existence of the Iliad as one poem; it seems more probable that it was put together about the time of the Pisistratidae. The Iliad—and, more or less, all epic poems, the subjects of which are taken from history—have no rounded conclusion; they remain, after all, but single chapters from the volume of history, although they are ornamental chapters. Consider the exquisite simplicity of the Paradise Lost. It and it alone really possesses a beginning, a middle, and an end; it has the totality of the poem as distinguished from the *ab ovo* birth and parentage, or straight line, of history.

2. As to the subject.

In Homer, the supposed importance of the subject, as the first effort of confederated Greece, is an after-thought of the critics; and the interest, such as it is, derived from the events themselves, as distinguished from the manner of representing them, is very languid to all but Greeks. It is a Greek poem. The superiority of the Paradise Lost is obvious in this respect, that the interest transcends the limits of a nation. But we do not generally dwell on this excellence of the Paradise Lost, because it seems attributable to Christianity itself;—yet in fact the interest is wider than Christendom, and comprehends the Jewish and Mohammedan worlds;—nay, still further, inasmuch as it represents the origin of evil, and the combat of evil and good, it contains matter of deep interest to all mankind, as forming the basis of all religion, and the true occasion of all philosophy whatsoever.

The FALL of Man is the subject; Satan is the cause; man's blissful state the immediate object of his enmity and attack; man is warned by an angel who gives him an account of all that was requisite to be known, to make the warning at once intelligible and awful; then the temptation ensues, and the Fall; then the immediate sensible consequence; then the consolation, wherein an angel presents a vision of the history of men with the ultimate triumph of the Redeemer. Nothing is touched in this vision but what is of general interest in religion; anything else would have been improper.

* * *

But notwithstanding the advantages in Milton's subject, there were concomitant insuperable difficulties, and Milton has exhibited marvellous skill in keeping most of them out of sight. High poetry is the translation of reality into the ideal under the predicament of succession of time only. The poet is an historian, upon condition of moral power being the only force in the universe. The very grandeur of his subject ministered a difficulty to Milton. The statement of a being of high intellect, warring against the supreme Being, seems to contradict the idea of a supreme Being. Milton precludes our feeling this, as much as possible, by keeping the peculiar attributes of divinity less in sight, making them to a certain extent allegorical only. Again, poetry implies the language of excitement; yet how to reconcile such language with God? Hence Milton confines the poetic passion in God's speeches to the language of scripture; and once only allows the *passio vera*, or *quasihumana* to appear, in the passage, where the Father contemplates his own likeness in the Son before the battle:—

> Go then, thou Mightiest, in thy Father's might,
> Ascend my chariot, guide the rapid wheels
> That shake Heaven's basis, bring forth all my war,
> My bow and thunder; my almighty arms
> Gird on, and sword upon thy puissant thigh;
> Pursue these sons of darkness, drive them out
> From all Heaven's bounds into the utter deep:
> There let them learn, as likes them, to despise
> God and Messiah his anointed king.
>   [*PL*, VI. 710–18]

3. As to Milton's object:—

It was to justify the ways of God to man! The controversial spirit observable in many parts of the poem, especially in God's speeches, is immediately attributable to the great controversy of that age, the origination of evil. The Arminians considered it a mere calamity. The Calvinists took away all human will. Milton asserted the will, but declared for the enslavement of the will out of an act of the will itself. There are three powers in us, which distinguish us from the beasts that perish;— 1, reason; 2, the power of viewing universal truth; and 3, the power of contracting universal truth into particulars. Religion is the will in the reason, and love in the will.

The character of Satan is pride and sensual indulgence, finding in self the sole motive of action. It is the character so often seen *in little* on the political stage. It exhibits all the restlessness, temerity, and cunning which have marked the mighty hunters of mankind from Nimrod and Napoleon. The common fascination of men is, that these great men, as they are called, must act from some great motive. Milton has carefully marked in his Satan the intense selfishness, the alcohol of egotism, which would rather reign in hell than serve in heaven. To place this lust of self in opposition to denial of self or duty, and to show what exertions it would make, and what pains endure to accomplish its end, is Milton's particular object in the character of Satan. But around this character he has thrown a singularity of daring, a grandeur of sufferance, and a ruined splendor, which constitute the very height of poetic sublimity.

Lastly, as to the execution:—

The language and versification of the Paradise Lost are peculiar in being so much more necessarily correspondent to each than those in any other poem or poet. The connexion of the sentences and the position of the words are exquisitely artificial; but the position is rather according to the logic of passion or universal logic, than to the logic of grammar. Milton attempted to make the English language obey the logic of passion as perfectly as the Greek and Latin. Hence the occasional harshness in the construction.

Sublimity is the pre-eminent characteristic of the Paradise Lost. * * * There is a greatness arising from images of effort and daring, and also from those of moral endurance; in Milton both are united. The fallen angels are human passions, invested with a dramatic reality.

The apostrophe to light at the commencement of the third book is particularly beautiful as an intermediate link between Hell and Heaven; and observe, how the second and third book support the subjective character of the poem. In all modern poetry in Christendom there is an under consciousness of a sinful nature, a fleeting away of external things, the mind or subject greater than the object, the reflective character predominant. In the Paradise Lost the sublimest parts are the revelations of Milton's own mind, producing itself and evolving its own greatness; and this is so truly so, that when that which is merely entertaining for its objective beauty is introduced, it at first seems a discord.

In the description of Paradise itself you have Milton's sunny side as a man; here his descriptive powers are exercised to the utmost, and he draws deep upon his Italian resources. In the description of Eve, and throughout this part of the poem, the poet is predominant over the theologian. Dress is the symbol of the Fall, but the mark of intellect; and the metaphysics of dress are, the hiding what is not symbolic and displaying by discrimination what is. The love of Adam and Eve in Paradise is of the highest merit—not phantomatic, and yet removed from every thing degrading. It is the sentiment of one rational being towards another made tender by a specific difference in that which is essentially the same in both; it is a union of opposites, a giving and receiving mutually of the permanent in either, a completion of each in the other.

Milton is not a picturesque, but a musical, poet; although he has this merit that the object chosen by him for any particular foreground always remains prominent to the end, enriched, but not incumbered, by the opulence of descriptive details furnished by an exhaustless imagination. I wish the Paradise Lose were more carefully read and studied than I can see any ground for believing it is, especially those parts which, from the habit of always looking for a story in poetry, are scarcely read at all,—as for example, Adam's vision of future events in the 11th and 12th books. No one can rise from the perusal of this immortal poem without a deep sense of the grandeur and the purity of Milton's soul, or without feeling how susceptible of domestic enjoyments he really was, notwithstanding the discomforts which actually resulted from an apparently unhappy choice in marriage. He was, as every truly great poet has ever been, a good man; but finding it impossible to realize his own aspirations, either in religion, or politics, or society, he gave up his heart to the living spirit and light within him, and avenged himself on the world by enriching it with this record of his own transcendant ideal.

The reader of Milton must be always on his duty; he is surrounded with sense; it rises in every line; every word is to the purpose. There are no lazy intervals: all has been considered, and demands and merits observation. If this be called obscurity, let it be remembered 'tis such a one as is complaisant to the reader: not that vicious obscurity, which proceeds from a muddled head.[3]

I dare not pronounce such passages as these [from *Romeo and Juliet*] to be absolutely unnatural, not merely because I consider the author a much better judge than I can be, but because I can understand and allow for an effort of the mind, when it would describe what it cannot satisfy itself with the description of, to reconcile opposites and qualify contradictions, leaving a middle state of mind more strictly appropriate to the imagination than any other, when it is, as it were, hovering between images. As soon as it is fixed on one image, its becomes understanding; but while it is unfixed and wavering between them, attaching itself permanently to none, it is imagination. Such is the fine description of Death in Milton:—[II.666–73]

The grandest efforts of poetry are where the imagination is called forth, not to produce a distinct form, but a strong working of the mind,

3. An entry of about 1796 in a notebook of Coleridge's; from Raysor, *Miscellaneous Criticism*, 169–70 [*Editor*].

still offering what is still repelled, and again creating what is again rejected; the result being what the poet wishes to impress, namely, the substitution of a sublime feeling of the unimaginable for a mere image. I have sometimes thought that the passage just read might be quoted as exhibiting the narrow limit of painting, as compared with the boundless power of poetry: painting cannot go beyond a certain point; poetry rejects all control, all confinement. Yet we know that sundry painters have attempted pictures of the meeting between Satan and Death at the gates of Hell; and how was Death represented? Not as Milton has described him, but by the most defined thing that can be imagined—a skeleton, the dryest and hardest image that it is possible to discover; which, instead of keeping the mind in a state of activity, reduces it to the merest passivity,—an image, compared with which a square, a triangle, or any other mathematical figure, is a luxuriant fancy.[4]

But neither can reason or religion exist or co-exist as reason and religion, except as far as they are actuated by the will (the Platonic υμος,) which is the sustaining, coercive and ministerial power, the functions of which in the individual correspond to the officers of war and police in the ideal Republic of Plato. In its state of immanence or indwelling in reason and religion, the will appears indifferently as wisdom or as love: two names of the same power, the former more intelligential, the latter more spiritual, the former more frequent in the Old, the latter in the New Testament. But in its utmost abstraction and consequent state of reprobation, the will becomes Satanic pride and rebellious self-idolatry in the relations of the spirit to itself, and remorseless despotism relatively to others; the more hopeless as the more obdurate by its subjugation of sensual impulses, by its superiority to toil and pain and pleasure; in short, by the fearful resolve to find in itself alone the one absolute motive of action, under which all other motives from within and from without must be either subordinated or crushed.

This is the character which Milton has so philosophically as well as sublimely embodied in the Satan of his Paradise Lost.[5]

In my judgment, an epic poem must either be national or mundane. As to Arthur, you could not by any means make a poem on him national to Englishmen. What have we to do with him? Milton saw this, and with a judgment at least equal to his genius, took a mundane theme—one common to all mankind. His Adam and Eve are all men and women inclusively. Pope satirises Milton for making God the Father talk like a school divine. Pope was hardly the man to criticise Milton. The truth

---

4. From Coleridge's *Seven Lectures on Shakespeare and Milton*, delivered in 1811–12, and first published in 1856. The text is from *Coleridge's Shakespearean Criticism*, ed. Thomas Middleton Raysor (Cambridge: Harvard, 1930) 2.138–39 [*Editor*].
5. From Appendix B, to Coleridge's *The Statesman's Manual* (1816), in *Lay Sermons* (3rd ed., London, 1852) 68–69 [*Editor*].

is, the judgment of Milton in the conduct of the celestial part of his story is very exquisite. Wherever God is represented as directly acting as Creator, without any exhibition of his own essence, Milton adopts the simplest and sternest language of the Scriptures. He ventures upon no poetic diction, no amplification, no pathos, no affection. It is truly the Voice or the Word of the Lord coming to, and acting on, the subject Chaos. But, as some personal interest was demanded for the purposes of poetry, Milton takes advantage of the dramatic representation of God's address to the Son, the Filial Alterity, and in *those addresses* slips in, as it were by stealth, language of affection, or thought, or sentiment. Indeed, although Milton was undoubtedly a high Arian in his mature life, he does in the necessity of poetry give a greater objectivity to the Father and the Son, than he would have justified in argument. He was very wise in adopting the strong anthropomorphism of the Hebrew Scriptures at once.[6]

JOHN KEATS

[Milton][†]
(1818)

* * *

You say "I fear there is little chance of any thing else in this life." you seem by that to have been going through with a more painful and acute zest the same labyrinth that I have—I have come to the same conclusion thus far. My Branchings out therefrom have been numerous: one of them is the consideration of Wordsworth's genius and as a help, in the manner of gold being the meridian Line of worldly wealth,—how he differs from Milton.—And here I have nothing but surmises, from an uncertainty whether Miltons apparently less anxiety for Humanity proceeds from his seeing further or no than Wordsworth: And whether Wordsworth has in truth epic passion, and martyrs himself to the human heart, the main region of his song. . . . We feel the "burden of the Mystery," To this Point was Wordsworth come, as far as I can conceive when he wrote 'Tintern Abbey' and it seems to me that his Genius is explorative of those dark Passages. Now if we live, and go on thinking, we too shall explore them—he is a Genius and superior [to] us, in so far as he can, more than we, make discoveries, and shed a light in

6. Entry for September 4, 1833, in Coleridge's *Table Talk* (1835), from Raysor, *Miscellaneous Criticism*, 429–30 [*Editor*].
† From letters of Keats to John Hamilton Reynolds, May 3, 1818; Benjamin Bailey, August 14, 1819; John Hamilton Reynolds, September 21, 1819; and George and Georgiana Keats, September 21, 1819, from *The Letters of John Keats*, ed. Maurice Buxton Forman, 4th ed. (Oxford, 1932) 140–44, 368, 384, 424–25.

them—Here I must think Wordsworth is deeper than Milton—though
I think it has depended more upon the general and gregarious advance
of intellect, than individual greatness of Mind—From the *Paradise Lost*
and the other Works of Milton, I hope it is not too presuming, even
between ourselves to say, that his Philosophy, human and divine, may
be tolerably understood by one not much advanced, in years. In his
time englishmen were just emancipated from a great superstition—and
Men had got hold of certain points and resting places in reasoning which
were too newly born to be doubted, and too much opposed by the Mass
of Europe not to be thought etherial and authentically divine—who
could gainsay his ideas on virtue, vice, and Chastity in Comus, just at
the time of the dismissal of Cod-pieces and a hundred other disgraces?
who would not rest satisfied with his hintings at good and evil in the
Paradise Lost, when just free from the inquisition and burning in Smith-
field? The Reformation produced such immediate and great benefits,
that Protestantism was considered under the immediate eye of heaven,
and its own remaining Dogmas and superstitions, then, as it were,
regenerated, constituted those resting places and seeming sure points of
Reasoning—from that I have mentioned, Milton, whatever he may have
thought in the sequel, appears to have been content with these by his
writings—He did not think into the human heart, as Wordsworth has
done—Yet Milton as a Philosopher, had sure as great powers as
Wordsworth—What is then to be inferr'd? O many things—It proves
there is really a grand march of intellect—, It proves that a mighty
providence subdues the mightiest Minds to the service of the time being,
whether it be in human Knowledge or Religion.

*   *   *

I am convinced more and more every day that (excepting the human
friend Philosopher) a fine writer is the most genuine Being in the World.
Shakspeare and the paradise Lost every day become greater wonders to
me.

*   *   *

I have given up Hyperion—there were too many Miltonic inversions
in it—Miltonic verse can not be written but in an artful or rather artist's
humour. I wish to give myself up to other sensations.

*   *   *

I shall never become attach'd to a foreign idiom so as to put it into
my writings. The Paradise lost though so fine in itself is a curruption
of our language—it should be kept as it is unique—a curiosity—a
beautiful and grand Curiosity. The most remarkable Production of the
world. A northern dialect accommodating itself to greek and latin in-
versions and intonations. The purest english I think—or what ought to
be the purest—is Chatterton's. The Language had existed long enough
to be entirely uncorrupted at Chaucer's gallicisms, and still the old words

are used. Chatterton's language is entirely northern. I prefer the native
music of it to Milton's cut by feet. I have but lately stood on my guard
against Milton. Life to him would be death to me. Miltonic verse cannot
be written but it [*for* in] the verse of art—I wish to devote myself to
another sensation.

WALTER SAVAGE LANDOR

[Milton]†
(1846)

* * *

Surely it is a silly and stupid business to talk mainly about the moral of
a poem, unless it professedly be a fable. A good epic, a good tragedy,
a good comedy, will inculcate several. . . . Why should the machinery
of the longest poem be drawn out to establish an obvious truth, which
a single verse would exhibit more plainly, and impress more memorably?
Both in epic and dramatic poetry it is action, and not moral, that is first
demanded. The feelings and exploits of the principal agent should excite
the principal interest. The two greatest of human compositions are here
defective: I mean the *Iliad* and *Paradise Lost*. . . . In the *Paradise Lost*
no principal character seems to have been intended. There is neither
truth nor wit however in saying that Satan is hero of the piece, unless,
as is usually the case in human life, he is the greatest hero who gives
the widest sway to the worst passions. It is Adam who acts and suffers
most, and on whom the consequences have most influence. This con-
stitutes him the main character; although Eve is the more interesting,
Satan is the more energetic, and on whom the greater force of poetry
is displayed. The Creator and his angels are quite secondary. . . .

> Yielded with coy submission, modest pride,
> And sweet, reluctant, amorous, delay.

I would rather have written these two lines than all the poetry that
has been written since Milton's time in all the regions of the earth. We
shall see again things equal in their way to the best of them: but here
the sweetest of images and sentiments is seized and carried far away from
all pursuers. . . .

It appears then on record that the first overt crime of the refractory
angels was *punning*: they fell rapidly after that. . . .

It is impossible not to apply to Milton himself the words he has
attributed to Eve:

† From "Southey and Landor," *Imaginary Conversations*, 1846.

From thee
How shall I part? and whither wander down
Into a lower world?

My ear, I confess it, is dissatisfied with everything, for days and weeks, after the harmony of *Paradise Lost*. Leaving this magnificent temple, I am hardly to be pacified by the fairy-built chambers, the rich cupboards of embossed plate, and the omnigenous images of Shakespeare. . . .

After I have been reading the *Paradise Lost*, I can take up no other poet with satisfaction. I seem to have left the music of Handel for the music of the streets, or at best for drums and fifes. Although in Shakespeare there are occasional bursts of harmony no less sublime, yet, if there were many such in continuation, it would be hurtful, not only in comedy, but also in tragedy. . . . In our English heroic verse, such as Milton has composed it, there is a much greater variety of feet, of movement, of musical notes and bars, than in the Greek heroic; and the final sounds are incomparably more diversified. My predilection in youth was on the side of Homer; for I had read the *Iliad* twice, and the *Odyssea* once, before the *Paradise Lost*. Averse as I am to everything relating to theology, and especially to the view of it thrown open by this poem, I recur to it incessantly as the noblest specimen in the world of eloquence, harmony, and genius.

ALFRED, LORD TENNYSON

Milton
(1863)

O mighty-mouth'd inventor of harmonies,
O skill'd to sing of Time or Eternity,
   God-gifted organ-voice of England,
      Milton, a name to resound for ages;
Whose Titan angels, Gabriel, Abdiel,
Starr'd from Jehovah's gorgeous armories,
   Tower, as the deep-domed empyrean
      Rings to the roar of an angel onset!
Me rather all that bowery loneliness,
The brooks of Eden mazily murmuring,
   And bloom profuse and cedar arches
      Charm, as a wanderer out in ocean,
Where some refulgent sunset of India
Streams o'er a rich ambrosial ocean isle,
   And crimson-hued the stately palm-woods
      Whisper in odorous heights of even.

MATTHEW ARNOLD

Milton†
(1888)

* * *

The mighty power of poetry and art is generally admitted. But where the soul of this power, of this power at its best, chiefly resides, very many of us fail to see. It resides chiefly in the refining and elevation wrought in us by the high and rare excellence of the great style. We may feel the effect without being able to give ourselves clear account of its cause, but the thing is so. Now, no race needs the influences mentioned, the influences of refining and elevation, more than ours; and in poetry and art our grand source for them is Milton.

To what does he owe this supreme distinction? To nature first and foremost, to that bent of nature for inequality which to the worshippers of the average man is so unacceptable; to a gift, a divine favor. "The older one grows," says Goethe, "the more one prizes natural gifts, because by no possibility can they be procured and stuck on." Nature formed Milton to be a great poet. But what other poet has shown so sincere a sense of the grandeur of his vocation, and a moral effort so constant and sublime to make and keep himself worthy of it? The Milton of religious and political controversy, and perhaps of domestic life also, is not seldom disfigured by want of amenity, by acerbity. The Milton of poetry, on the other hand, is one of those great men "who are modest"—to quote a fine remark of Leopardi, that gifted and stricken young Italian, who in his sense for poetic style is worthy to be named with Dante and Milton—"who are modest, because they continually compare themselves, not with other men, but with that idea of the perfect which they have before their mind." The Milton of poetry is the man, in his own magnificent phrase, of "devout prayer to that Eternal Spirit that can enrich with all utterance and knowledge, and sends out his Seraphim with the hallowed fire of his altar, to touch and purify the lips of whom he pleases." And finally, the Milton of poetry is, in his own words again, the man of "industrious and select reading." Continually he lived in companionship with high and rare excellence, with the great Hebrew poets and prophets, with the great poets of Greece and Rome. The Hebrew compositions were not in verse, and can be not inadequately represented by the grand, measured prose of our English Bible. The verse of the poets of Greece and Rome no translation can adequately reproduce. Prose cannot have the power of verse; verse-translation may give whatever of charm is in the soul and talent of the

† From *Essays in Criticism*, 2nd series (London, 1908) 63–66.

translator himself, but never the specific charm of the verse and poet translated. In our race are thousands of readers, presently there will be millions, who know not a word of Greek and Latin, and will never learn those languages. If this host of readers are ever to gain any sense of the power and charm of the great poets of antiquity, their way to gain it is not through translations of the ancients, but through the original poetry of Milton, who has the like power and charm, because he has the like great style.

VIRGINIA WOOLF

[Some Remarks on Milton]†

Our quarrel is not at all with the words [in a passage from a poem by John Davidson], which might very well take their place in poetry, or with the subject, which is magnificent, but with the proselytising spirit, which makes the truth of the facts of more importance than the poetry, and with the growing arrogance and acerbity of manner, as of one dinning the Gospel into the heads of an indifferent public. It is an open question how far Milton and Dante believed the truth of the doctrines which they sang, and it is possible to enjoy them to the utmost without agreeing with them. [From a review in the *Times Literary Supplement*, Aug. 16, 1917]

I read the Greeks [Sophocles], but I am extremely doubtful whether I understand anything they say; also I have read the whole of Milton, without throwing any light upon my own soul, but that I rather like. Don't you think it very queer though that he entirely neglects the human heart? Is that the result of writing one's masterpiece at the age of 50? [From a letter to Lytton Strachey, Oct. 12, 1918]

Though I am not the only person in Sussex who reads Milton, I mean to write down my impressions of Paradise Lost while I am about it.

† Excerpts from *The Essays of Virginia Woolf*, Volume II: 1912–1918, edited by Andrew McNellie, copyright © 1987 by Quentin Bell and Angelica Garnett; *The Essays of Virginia Woolf*, Volume III: 1919–1924, edited by Andrew McNellie, copyright © 1988 by Quentin Bell and Angelica Garnett; *The Letters of Virginia Woolf*, Volume II: 1919–1922, edited by Nigel Nicolson, copyright © 1976 by Quentin Bell and Angelica Garnett; *The Letters of Virginia Woolf*, Volume IV: 1929–1931, edited by Nigel Nicolson and Joanne Trautmann, copyright © 1978 by Quentin Bell and Angelica Garnett; *The Diary of Virginia Woolf*, Volume I: 1915–1919, edited by Anne Olivier Bell, copyright © 1977 by Quentin Bell and Angelica Garnett; *The Diary of Virginia Woolf*, Volume II: 1920–1924, edited by Anne Olivier Bell, copyright © 1978 by Quentin Bell and Angelica Garnett; *A Room of One's Own* by Virginia Woolf, copyright [sic] 1929 by Harcourt Brace Jovanovich, Inc. and renewed 1957 by Leonard Woolf; all excerpts reprinted by permission of Harcourt Brace Jovanovich, Inc. and The Hogarth Press.

Impressions fairly well describes the sort of thing left in my mind. I have left many riddles unread. I have slipped on too easily to taste the full flavor. However I see, and agree to some extent in believing, that this full flavor is the reward of highest scholarship. I am struck by the extreme difference between this poem and any other. It lies, I think, in the sublime aloofness and impersonality of the emotions. * * * The substance of Milton is all made of wonderful, beautiful, and masterly descriptions of angels bodies, battles, flights, dwelling places. He deals in horror and immensity and squalor and sublimity, but never in the passions of the human heart. Has any great poem ever let in so little light upon ones own joys and sorrows? I get no help in judging life; I scarcely feel that Milton lived or knew men and women; except for the peevish personalities about marriage and the woman's duties. He was the first of the masculinists; but his disparagement rises from his own ill luck, and seems even a spiteful last word in his domestic quarrels. But how smooth, strong and elaborate it all is! What poetry! I can conceive that even Shakespeare after this would seem a little troubled, personal, hot and imperfect. I can conceive that this is the essence, of which almost all other poetry is the dilution. The inexpressible fineness of the style, in which shade after shade is perceptible, would alone keep one gazing in to [it], long after the surface business in progress has been despatched. Deep down one catches still further combinations, rejections, felicities, and masteries. Moreover, though there is nothing like Lady Macbeth's terror or Hamlet's cry, no pity or sympathy or intuition, the figures are majestic; in them is summed up much of what men thought of our place in the universe, of our duty to God, our religion. [From a diary entry for Tuesday, Sept. 10, 1918]

I dined with the Sangers last night, and enjoyed society. I wore my new black dress, and looked, I daresay, rather nice. That's a feeling I very seldom have; and I rather intend to enjoy it oftener. I like clothes, if I can design them. So Bertie Russell [Bertram Russell, celebrated philosopher and mathematician] was attentive, and we struck out like swimmers who knew their waters. One is old enough to cut the trimmings and get to the point. Bertie is a fervid egoist—which helps matters. And then, what a pleasure—this mind on springs. I got as much out of him as I could carry.

"For I should soon be out of my depth," I said. I mean, I said, "all this" and I waved my hand round the room, where by this time were assembled Mr and Miss Amos, Rosaline Toynbee, a German, and Mrs Lucas—"All this is mush; and you can put a telescope to your eye and see through it."

"If you had my brain you would find the world a very thin, colorless place" he said.

But my colors are so foolish I replied.

You want them for your writing, he said. Do you never see things impersonally?

Yes. I see literature like that; Milton, that is.

The choruses in Samson are pure art, he said.

But I have a feeling that human affairs are impure.

God does mathematics. That's my feeling. It is the most exalted form of art.

Art? I said.

Well theres style in mathematics as there is in writing, he said. I get the keenest aesthetic pleasure from reading well written mathematics. [From a diary entry for Saturday, Dec. 3, 1921]

These instances, however, are all of a simple character; the men have been supposed to remain men, the women women when they write. They have exerted the influence of their sex directly and normally. But there is a class which keeps itself aloof from any such contamination. Milton is their leader; with him are [Walter Savage] Landor, Sappho, Sir Thomas Browne, Marvell. Feminists or anti-feminists, passionate or cold—whatever the romances or adventures of their private lives, not a whiff of that mist attaches itself to their writing. It is pure, uncontaminated, sexless as the angels are said to be sexless. [From "Indiscretions," *The Essays of Virginia Woolf*]

Directly I go back [to London, from the country] I am badgered and worried; a thousand sucking vampires attach themselves to my ribs and if I snatch up Milton once in a blue moon, its about all the reading for pleasure I ever do. [From a letter to her sister, Vanessa Bell, Dec. 30, 1929]

[*"Milton's bogey"*]

* * * by degrees fear and bitterness modified themselves into pity and toleration; and then in a year or two, pity and toleration went, and the greatest release of all came, which is freedom to think of things in themselves. That building, for example, do I like it or not? Is that picture beautiful or not? Is that in my opinion a good book or a bad? Indeed my aunt's legacy unveiled the sky to me, and substituted for the large and imopsing figure of a gentleman, which Milton recommended for my perpetual adoration, a view of the open sky. [From *A Room of One's Own* (1929)]

* * * For my belief is that if we live another century or so—I am talking of the common life which is the real life and not of the little separate lives which we live as individuals—and have five hundred a year each of us and rooms of our own; if we have the habit of freedom and the courage to write exactly what we think; if we escape a little from the common sitting-room and see human beings not always in their relation to each other but in relation to reality; and the sky, too, and the trees or whatever it may be in themselves; if we look past Milton's bogey, for no human being should shut out the view; if we face the fact, for it is a fact, that there is no arm to cling to, but that we go alone and that our relation is to the world of reality and not only to the world of men and women, then the opportunity will come and the dead poet who was Shakespeare's sister will put on the body which she has so often laid down. Drawing her life from the lives of the unknown who were her forerunners, as her brother did before her, she will be born [From A *Room of One's Own*, 198–99]

Recent Criticism

NORTHROP FRYE

The Story of All Things†

I suppose anyone proposing to deliver a series of lectures on *Paradise Lost* ought to begin with some explanation of why he is not deterred from doing so by the number of his predecessors. If my predecessors had all failed, I could at least claim the merit of courage, like the youngest adventurer of so many folk tales who is also the brashest and most bumptious of the whole series. But many of them have succeeded better than I expect to do, and I have no knowledge of Milton sufficiently detailed to add to the body of Milton scholarship or sufficiently profound to alter its general shape. I am talking about Milton because I enjoy talking about Milton, and while I may have begun the subject of these lectures late, it was not long in choosing. Huron College is a hundred years old, and though I find, on checking the dates, that I have not been teaching Milton for quite that long, I have been teaching him long enough to have incorporated him as a central part of my own literary experience. Consequently I feel that I can approach Milton with some sense of proportion based on the fact that his proportions are gigantic.

† From *The Return of Eden: Five Essays on Milton's Epics* (Toronto, 1965) 3–31. By permission of the University of Toronto Press.

Every student of Milton has been rewarded according to his efforts and
his ability: the only ones who have abjectly failed with him are those
who have tried to cut him down to size—their size—and that mistake
at least I will not make.

The second edition of *Paradise Lost* opened with two complimentary
poems addressed to Milton, one in English by Andrew Marvell and one
in Latin by Samuel Barrow. The Barrow poem begins with a rhetorical
question. When you read this wonderful poem, he says, what do you
read but the story of all things? For the story of all things from their
first beginnings to their ultimate ends are contained within this book:

> Qui legis Amissam Paradisum, grandia magni
> Carmina Miltoni, quid nisi cuncta legis?
> Res cunctas, et cunctarum primordia rerum,
> Et fata, ef fines continet iste liber.

Implicit in what Barrow says is a standard Renaissance critical theory.
It will be familiar to most readers, but I need it again because its elements
reappear as structural principles in *Paradise Lost*. It was generally as-
sumed that in literature there were inherently major genres and minor
genres. Minor poets should stick to the minor genres, and should confine
themselves to pastorals or to love lyrics. Minor genres were for poets of
minor talents, or for professional poets learning their trade, or for poets
too high in social rank to be much interested in publication or in any
kind of poetic utterance beyond the kind of graceful conventional verse
that is really a form of private correspondence. The major poets were
those for whom the major genres were reserved; and of these, the most
important in Renaissance theory were epic and tragedy.

The epic, as Renaissance critics understood it, is a narrative poem of
heroic action, but a special kind of narrative. It also had an encyclopaedic
quality in it, distilling the essence of all the religious, philosophical,
political, even scientific learning of its time, and, if completely suc-
cessful, the definitive poem for its age. The epic in this sense is not a
poem by a poet, but that poet's poem: he can never complete a second
epic unless he is the equal of Homer, and hence the moment at which
the epic poet chooses his subject is the crisis of his life. To decide to
write an epic of this kind is an act of considerable courage, because if
one fails, one fails on a colossal scale, and the echo of ridicule may last
for centuries. One thinks of what the name "Blackmore" still suggests
to students of English literature, many of whom have not read a line of
Blackmore's epics. Further, the epic can only be completed late in life,
because of the amount of sheer scholarship it is compelled to carry. In
Gabriel Harvey's phrase, major poets should be "curious universal schol-
ars," but it takes time to mature a scholar and still more time to unite
scholarship with poetic skill. Of course this theory implies that Homer
was a poet of encyclopaedic learning, but it was almost a critical com-

monplace to assume that he was: William Webbe, for example, speaks of "Homer, who as it were in one sum comprehended all knowledge, wisdom, learning and policy that was incident to the capacity of man."

The epic, as a poem both narrative and encyclopaedic, is to be distinguished from the long poem which is simply one or the other. A narrative poet, as such, is a story-teller, and a story-teller is in the position of a modern novelist: the more stories he tells the more successful he is. One thinks of Ariosto's *Orlando Furioso* and of the question addressed to the author by the Cardinal who was supposed to be his patron: "Where did you find all these silly stories, Messer Lodovico?" This remark, however inadequate as criticism, does indicate something of the quality of the romance genre that Ariosto was using, for the romance tends to become an endless poem, going on from one story to another until the author runs out of stories to tell. The encyclopaedic poem, again, was a favorite genre of the Renaissance. The two poets of this group whom we should now rank highest, Lucretius and Dante, were somewhat disapproved of in Protestant England on ideological grounds, and a more tangible influence on Milton was *La Sepmaine* of du Bartas, which displayed so much knowledge of the creation that its author was compelled to expand the divine activity into two weeks. Some other encyclopaedic poems, such as Palingenius' *Zodiac of Life*, which, as translated by Barnabe Googe, may have been one of Shakespeare's school books, were based on rather facile organizing schemes—in other words their scholarship was a matter of content rather than of poetic structure. Romances, particularly *The Faerie Queene*, could also achieve an encyclopaedic quality by virtue of being allegorical, when they not only told stories but when their stories meant things in moral philosophy and political history—"Where more is meant than meets the ear," as Milton says.

But although there were many encyclopaedic poems and many romances and narratives, and although the authors of both genres were highly respected, still the central form with the greatest prestige was the epic. And the ideal, the huge, impossible ideal, would be a poem that derived its structure from the epic tradition of Homer and Virgil and still had the quality of universal knowledge which belonged to the encyclopaedic poem and included the extra dimension of reality that was afforded by Christianity. Now, says Samuel Barrow, who would ever have thought that anyone could actually bring off such a poem? But it's been done, and by an English poet too:

> Haec qui speraret quis crederet esse futurum?
> Et tamen haec hodie terra Britanna legit.

For in the seventeenth century, writing such a poem in English was still a patriotic act, with a certain amount of conscious virtue about it, as writing poetry on this side of the American border has now. The first critical statement ever made about *Paradise Lost*, therefore, tells us that *Paradise Lost* is among other things a technical *tour de force* of miraculous proportions.

That Milton was fully aware of the size and scope of what he was attempting, and that he shared the assumptions of his age about the importance of the epic, hardly need much demonstrating. For him, of course, the responsibilities entailed by the possession of major poetic talent were only incidentally literary: they were primarily religious. The word "talent" itself is a metaphor from a parable of Jesus that seems to associate the religious and the creative aspects of life, a parable that was never long out of Milton's mind. The analogy between the Christian and the creative life extends even further. A Christian has to work hard at living a Christian life, yet the essential act of that life is the surrender of the will; a poet must work hard at his craft, yet his greatest achievements are not his, but inspired.

Milton's first major poem, the one we know as the Nativity Ode, ends its prelude with the self-addressed exhortation:

> And join thy voice unto the angel choir
> From out his secret altar touched with hallowed fire.

In a sense this is the key signature, so to speak, of Milton's poetry: his ambition as a poet is to join the tradition of inspired prophetic speech that began with the great commission to Isaiah. When he speaks in *Paradise Lost* of wanting to justify the ways of God to men, he does not mean that he wishes to do God a favor by rationalizing one of God's favorite parables: he means that *Paradise Lost* is a sacrificial offering to God which, if it is accepted, will derive its merit from that acceptance. The Nativity Ode is closely related to the Sixth Elegy, addressed to Diodati, where Milton distinguishes the relaxed life permitted the minor poet who writes of love and pleasure from the austerity and rigorous discipline imposed by major powers. One is a secular and the other a priestly or dedicated life. The reason for the discipline is not so much moral as spiritually hygienic. To be a fit vessel of inspiration the poet must be as genuinely pure as the augur or pagan priest was ceremonially pure:

> Qualis veste nitens sacra, ete lustralibus undis
> Surgis ad infensos augur iture Deos.
>   [Elegy VI, ll. 65–66]

After the first period of Milton's poetry had reached its climax with the two great funeral elegies, *Lycidas* and *Epitaphium Damonis*, Milton started making plans for poetry in the major genres—perhaps part of the meaning of the "fresh woods and pastures new" at the end of *Lycidas*. His *Reason of Church Government*, in a famous passage, mentions in particular three genres, the tragedy, the "diffuse" or full-length epic, and the "brief" epic. This last is still a somewhat undeveloped conception in criticism, though examples of it in English literature stretch from *Beowulf* to *The Waste Land*. One cannot help noticing the similarity between this list of three major genres and the *Samson Agonistes*, *Paradise Lost* and *Paradise Regained* produced so many years later. At that time, Milton tells us, he was thinking of Arthur as the subject for his "diffuse" epic. But of course he had still many years to wait before he could give his full attention to writing it. The simultaneous pull in Milton's life between the impulse to get at his poem and finish it and the impulse to leave it until it ripened sufficiently to come by itself must have accounted for an emotional tension in Milton of a kind that we can hardly imagine. That the tension was there seems certain from the way in which the temptation to premature action remains so central a theme in his poetry. The tension reached a crisis with his blindness, yet his blindness, as he had perhaps begun to realize by the time he wrote *Defensio Secunda*, eventually gave him, as deafness did Beethoven, an almost preternatural concentration, and was what finally enabled him to write of heaven, hell and the unfallen world on his own terms.

In the same passage of *The Reason of Church Government* Milton speaks of doing something for his own nation of the same kind as Homer and Virgil, "with this over and above, of being a Christian." This additional advantage means for him partly a technical poetic advantage as well. For what gave the encyclopaedic poem such prestige in Christian civilization was the encyclopaedic shape of Christian philosophy and theology, a shape derived ultimately from the shape of the Bible. The Bible, considered in its literary aspect, is a definitive encyclopaedic poem starting with the beginnings of time at the creation, ending with the end of time at the Last Judgment, and surveying the entire history of man, under the symbolic names of Adam and Israel, in between. Explicitly Christian poetry had moved within this framework from earliest times. Bede's *Ecclesiastical History*, one of the authorities used by Milton for his history of Britain, tells how English poetry began with the poet Caedmon, who was ordered by an angel to sing him something. Being inspired by a Christian muse, Caedmon began promptly with a paraphrase of the first verses of Genesis on the creation, worked his way down through the Exodus and the main episodes of the Old Testament to the Incarnation, and went on to the Last Judgment and the life eternal. The dramatic cycles of the Middle Ages are another example of the effect of the shape of the Bible on English literature.

The sermon, in Milton's day, constituted a kind of oral epic tradition dealing with the same encyclopaedic myth. The proverbially long Puritan sermons, divided into anything from eighteen to twenty-five divisions, usually owed their length to a survey of the divine plan of salvation as it unrolled itself from the earliest prelapsarian decrees to the eventual consummation of all things. This oral tradition has been embedded in *Paradise Lost* in the four hundred lines of the third book which constitute a sermon of this type preached by God himself. The speech of Michael, which takes up most of the last two books of *Paradise Lost*, is a summary of the Bible from the murder of Abel to the vision of John in Patmos in which the biblical myth takes the form of a miniature epic or epyllion, and as such pulls together and restates all the major themes of the poem, like a stretto in a fugue.

Renaissance critics believed that there were major and minor genres for prose as well as for poetry, as they made much less of the technical distinction between prose and verse than we do. In prose the major genres were mainly those established by Plato: the Socratic dialogue form, and the description of the ideal commonwealth. Such works as Sidney's *Arcadia* were highly praised because they were felt to belong to this tradition, as we can see in the discussion of the *Arcadia* in the opening chapter of Fulke Greville's biography of Sidney. But the Renaissance was above all a great age of educational theory, and its educational theory, to which Milton contributed, was based squarely on the two central facts of Renaissance society, the prince and the courtier or magistrate. Hence the educational treatise, which normally took the form of the ideal education of prince, courtier or magistrate, had even greater prestige in Renaissance eyes than the description of the ideal commonwealth.

The Classical pattern for the treatise on the ideal education of the prince had been established by Xenophon in the *Cryopaedia*, which Sidney describes as "an absolute heroical poem," thus implying that it represents the prose counterpart of the encyclopaedic epic. Spenser, in the letter to Raleigh which introduces *The Faerie Queene*, makes it clear that this encyclopaedic prose form is also a part of the conception of his poem, and speaks of his preference for Xenophon's form to Plato's, for a practicable as compared to an impossible ideal. Milton also shows a touch of impatience with Plato and with what he calls Plato's "airy burgomasters," and we should expect him to be of Spenser's mind in this matter. And just as the encyclopadic shape of the Bible is condensed into the speech of Michael, so the speech of Raphael versifies a major prose genre, for the colloquy of Raphael and Adam is a Socratic dialogue without irony, a symposium with unfermented wine, a description of an ideal commonwealth ending with the expulsion of undesirables, and (for Adam is the king of men) a cyropaedia, or manual or royal discipline. It is essentially the education of Adam, and it covers a vast amount of knowledge, both natural and revealed.

The tradition of the epic was, of course, established by Homer in the *Iliad* and the *Odyssey*, but these two epics represent different structural principles. Many Classical scholars have noted that the *Iliad* is closer in form to Greek tragedy than it is to the *Odyssey*. The *Odyssey*, the more typically epic pattern, is the one followed more closely by Virgil in the *Aeneid* and by Milton in *Paradise Lost*. Of the characteristics which the *Odyssey*, the *Aeneid* and *Paradise Lost* have in common, three are of particular importance.

In the first place, there are, in the form in which we have them, twelve books, or a multiple of twelve. Milton published the first edition of *Paradise Lost* in ten books to demonstrate his comtempt for tradition, and the second edition in twelve to illustrate the actual proportions of the poem. He had been preceded in his conversion to a duodecimal system by Tasso, who had expanded the twenty cantos of *Gerusalemme Liberata* into the twenty-four of *Gerusalemme Conquistata.* Spenser, too, is preoccupied with twelves: each book has twelve cantos and the total number of books planned was either twelve or twenty-four. We shall try to suggest in a moment that the association of Milton's epic with this sacred and zodiacal number may be less arbitrary then it looks.

Secondly, the action of both the *Odyssey* and the *Aeneid* splits neatly in two. The first twelve books of the *Odyssey* deal with the wanderings of the hero, with the journey through wonderlands of marvels and terrors, the immemorial quest theme. The next twelve books never leave Ithaca (except for the Katabasis at the end, in a part of the poem often considered a later addition), and their action is that of a typical comedy of recognition and intrigue, as the unknown and ridiculed beggar eventually turns out to be the returning hero. The first six books of the *Aeneid* have a similar quest pattern; the next six, the account of the struggle of Aeneas with the Italian warlords, also has the structure of romantic comedy, full of compacts, ordeals and other traditional features of comic action, and ending in success, marriage, and the birth of a new society. In both epics the main interest shifts half way from the hero's private perils to his social context. In the letter to Raleigh, Spenser, with a reference to Tasso, also distinguishes private or princely from public or kingly virtues in the epic theme. This division of narrative between a quest theme and a theme of the settling of a social order has a biblical parallel in the story of the Exodus, where forty years of Isarel's wandering in the wilderness are followed by the conquest and settlement of the Promised Land. Milton preserves the traditional feature of a split in the middle of the action when, at the beginning of Book Seven, he says that the action for the second half of the poem will be confined to the earth. The order in *Paradise Lost* is the reverse of the biblical one, as it starts with the Promised Land and ends in the wilderness; but the biblical order is preserved when we add *Paradise Regained* to the sequence.

But of course of all the traditional epic features, the most important is that of beginning the action in *medias res*, in Horace's phrase, at a dramatically well-advanced point and then working back simultaneously to the beginning and forward to the end. If we ask beginning and end of what, the answer is, beginning and end of the total action, of which only a part may be presented in the actual poem. This total action is cyclical in shape: it almost has to be because of the nature of the quest theme. The hero goes out to do something, does it, and returns. In the *Odyssey*, the total action begins when Odysseus leaves Ithaca and goes off to the Trojan War, and it ends when he gets back to Ithaca as master of his house again. Matters are less simple in the *Iliad*, but even there the total movement of the Greeks out to Troy and back home again is clearly in the background. In the *Aeneid* there is what from Milton's point of view is a most important advance in this conception of a total cyclical action. Here the total action begins and ends, not at precisely the same point, but at the same point renewed and transformed by the heroic action itself. That is, the toal action of the *Aeneid* begins when Aeneas leaves Troy collapsing in flames, losing his wife; and it ends with the new Troy established at Rome, Aeneas remarried and the household gods of the defeated Troy set up once again in a new home. The end is the beginning as recreated by the heroism of Aeneas.

We notice that the trick of beginning the action at a dramatically well-advanced point is not done entirely at random. The *Odyssey* begins with Odysseus at the furthest point from home, on the island of Calypso, subjected to the temptations of Penelope's only formidable rival. The action of the *Aeneid* similarly begins with Aeneas' shipwreck on the shores of Carthage, the *Erbfeind* or hereditary enemy of Rome and the site of the citadel of Juno, Aeneas' implacable enemy. Similarly, the action of *Paradise Lost* begins at the furthest possible point from the presence of God, in hell. The cycle which forms the total background action of *Paradise Lost* is again the cycle of the Bible. It begins where God begins, in an eternal presence, and it ends where God ends, in an eternal presence. The foreground action begins *in medias res*, translated by Milton in his Argument as "in the midst of things," with Satan already fallen into hell, and it works from there back to the beginning and forward to the end of the total action. The foreground action deals with the conspiracy of Satan and the fall of Adam and Eve, and the two speeches of the two angels deal with the rest of the cycle. Raphael begins with what is chronologically the first event in the poem, the showing of Christ to the angels, and brings the action down to a point at which the poem begins. After Adam's fall, Michael picks up the story and summarizes the biblical narrative through to the Last Judgment, which brings us back again to the point at which God is all in all. The epic narrative thus consists of a foreground action with two great flanking speeches where the action is reported by messengers (*aggeloi*) putting it in its proper context.

We notice that in the Classical epics there are two kinds of revelation. There is the kind that comes from the gods above, when Athene or Venus appears to be the hero at a crucial point with words of comfort or advice. There is nothing mysterious about these appearances: they happen in broad daylight and their function is to illuminate the present situation. Athene appears in the disguise of Mentor to give Telemachus the kind of advice that a wise and kindly human being would also give. There is another kind of revelation which is sought from gods below. Telemachus gains it by disguising himself as a seal and catching Proteus; Odysseus gains it by a complicated and sinister ritual of sacrifice, the spilling of blood, ghosts and darkness. There are strong hints that knowledge obtained in this way is normally forbidden knowledge, and it does not illuminate a present situation: it is specifically knowledge about the future. It is knowledge about his own future that Odysseus seeks when he calls up Teiresias from hell; it is knowledge of the future of Rome that Aeneas gets when he descends, though with less ritual elaboration, into the cave guarded by the Sibyl. The association of future and forbidden knowledge is carried even further in Dante's *Inferno*, because the people in Dante's hell have knowledge of the future but not of the present.

The kind of knowledge given to Adam in Michael's speech is essentially a knowledge of the future, of what is going to happen. It is intended to be consoling, although Adam collapses twice under the ordeal of being consoled, and the fact that knowledge of the future is possible means of course that the freedom of human will has been mortally injured. The suggestion is clearly that such knowledge of the future is a part of the forbidden knowledge which Adam should never have had in the first place, knowledge which God is willing to give him but which Satan would have cheated him out of. Human life now is in large part a dialectic between revelation and the knowledge of good and evil, and this dialectic is represented in *Paradise Lost* by the contrast between God the Father and Adam after his fall. God the Father sits in heaven and foreknows what will happen, but, as he carefully explains, not forcing it to happen. Below him is Adam in a parody of that situation, foreknowing what is going to happen to the human race in consequence of his fall, but unable in the smallest degree to interfere with or alter the course of events.

The foreground action, the conspiracy of Satan and its consequences, forms a kind of mock-Telemachia in counterpoint to the main epic action to be considered in a moment, a parable of a prodigal son who does not return. Technically, however, the foreground action presents a sharp focusing of attention which brings it close to dramatic forms. The fall itself is conceived in the form of tragedy, the great rival of epic in Renaissance theory, yet almost the antithesis of the epic, as it demanded a concentrated unity of action which seems the opposite of the epic's encyclopaedic range. The ninth book represents a crystallization of Milton's earlier plans for treating the fall of man in tragic form, with Satan as a returning spirit of vengeance persuading Eve into a foreshortened compliance much as Iago does Othello. Nature, sighing through all her works, occupies the place of the chorus.

At the opening of the poem we find ourselves plunged into the darkness of hell and eventually, after our pupils have expanded, look around and see one or two lights glaring. We then realize that these are eyes, and a number of huge clouded forms begin to come out of a kind of sea and gather on a kind of shore. Throughout the first two books we move through shadowy and indefinite gloom, and then, at the opening of the third, are plunged quite as suddenly into blinding light, where only after our pupils have contracted again can we observe such details as the pavement of heaven which "Impurpled with celestial roses smiled." We feel that such intensities are appropriate to a poet who is not only blind but baroque, and who, if he never saw the shadows of Rembrandt or the sunlight of Claude, still reflects his age's interest in chiaroscuro. But the principle *ut pictura poesis* can only be expressed in verbal spectacle, and we should also realize the extent to which the dramatic form of the Jonsonian masque has informed these first three books, a dark and sinister antimasque being followed by a splendid vision of ordered glory. The masque vision moves slowly from heaven down through the starry spheres to Eden; the antimasque modulates into the ludicrous disorder of the Limbo of Vanities, and disappears until it is recalled by Raphael's narrative of an earlier expulsion from heaven.

There is, then, with the dramatic foreground action and the speeches of Raphael and Michael filling in the beginning and end of the total background action, a kind of formal symmetry of a type that we might not expect in a poem that we have just called baroque. I think that this formal symmetry can be carried much further, and I should like to divide the total action in a way which I think best illustrates it. Some of the divisions take up several books and others only a few lines, but that is of no importance. Most of the shorter ones are from the Bible, and Milton expected his reader to be able to give them their due importance. Let us visualize the dial of a clock, with the presence of God where the figure 12 is. The first four figures of the dial represent the four main events of the speech of Raphael. First comes the first epiphany or manifestation of Christ, when God the Father shows his Son to the angels and demands that they worship him. This is the chronological beginning of the total action, as already remarked. Next, at 2 on the dial, comes the second epiphany of Christ at the end of the war in heaven, when on the third day he tramples on the rebel angels and manifests himself in triumph and wrath. The third stage is the creation of the natural order, as described by Milton in his extraordinarily skilful paraphrase of the Genesis account. The fourth phase is the creation of the human order, with the forming of the bodies of Adam and Eve, in the account of which Adam takes over from Raphael.

After this the foreground action moves across the lower part of the dial. At the figure 5 comes the conspiracy of Satan, ending in his pact with Sin and Death. The generations of Death from Satan is a parody of the generation of the Son from the Father which starts off the action, Death being, so to speak, the Word of Satan. At 6, the nadir of the action, comes the tragic catastrophe, the fall of Adam and Eve, the fall, that is, of the human order established by God. Next, at 7, comes the fall of the natural order, which is really a part of the fall of Adam and Eve, and is described in Book Ten as the triumph of Sin and Death, corresponding to Satan's pact with them at 5.

The next four stages are the ones covered by the speech of Michael: they correspond to the four that we found in the speech of Raphael, but are in roughly the reverse order. First, at 8, comes the re-establishing of the natural order at the time of the flood, when it is promised with the symbol of the rainbow that seedtime and harvest will not fail until the end of the world. Next, at 9, comes the re-establishing of the human order, when the law is given to Israel and the prototype of Jesus, Joshua, who has the same name as Jesus, takes possession of the Promised Land. Next, at 10, comes the third epiphany of Christ, the Incarnation properly speaking, which again is an epiphany ending with the triumph over death and hell in a three-day battle. Next, at 11, comes the fourth epiphany of Christ, the Last Judgment, again an epiphany of triumph and wrath, when the final separation is made between the orders of heaven and of hell. At 12, we come back again to the point prophesied by God himself in his speech in Book Three, when he says that there will come a time when he will lay by his sceptre and "God shall be all in all." The final point in the vast cycle is the same point as the beginning, yet not the same point, because, as in the *Aeneid*, the ending is the starting point renewed and transformed by the heroic quest of Christ. Thus there can by only one cycle, not an endless series of them. To summarize:

1. First epiphany of Christ: generation of Son from Father.
2. Second epiphany of Christ: triumph after three-day conflict.
3. Establishment of the natural order in the creation.
4. Establishment of the human order: creation of Adam and Eve.
5. Epiphany of Satan, generating Sin and Death.
6. Fall of the human order.
7. Fall of the natural order: triumph of Sin and Death.
8. Re-establishment of the natural order at the end of the flood.
9. Re-establishment of the human order with the giving of the law.
10. Third epiphany of Christ: the Word as gospel.
11. Fourth epiphany of Christ: the apocalypse or Last Judgment.

There are four orders of existence in *Paradise Lost*, the divine order, the angelic order, the human order and the demonic order. Being an epic, *Paradise Lost* has to deal with the traditional theme of the epic, which is the theme of heroic action. In order to understand what heroic action was to Milton we have to think what a Christian poet would mean by the conception of heroic action: that is, we have to ask ourselves what for Milton a hero was, and, even more important, what an act was. Milton says clearly in *The Christian Doctrine* what he means by an act. An act is the expression of the energy of a free and conscious being. Consequently all acts are good. There is no such thing, strictly speaking, as an evil act; evil or sin implies deficiency, and implies also the loss or lack of the power to act. There is a somewhat unexpected corollary of this: if all acts are good, then God is the source of all real action. At the same time, as Milton says, or rather as his sentence structure says in spite of him, it is almost impossible to avoid speaking of evil acts:

> It is called actual sin, not that sin is properly an action, for in reality it implies defect; but because it commonly consists in some act. For every act is in itself good; it is only its irregularity, or deviation from the line of right, which properly speaking is evil.

What happens when Adam eats the forbidden fruit, then, is not an act, but the surrendering of the power to act. Man is free to lose his freedom, and there, obviously, his freedom stops. His position is like that of a man on the edge of a precipice—if he jumps it appears to be an act, but it is really the giving up of the possibility of action, the surrendering of himself to the law of gravitation which will take charge of him for the brief remainder of his life. In this surrendering of the power to act lies the key to Milton's conception of the behavior of Adam. A typically fallen human act is something where the word "act" has to be in quotation marks. It is a pseudo-act, the pseudo-act of disobedience, and it is really a refusal to act at all.

Implied in this argument is a curious paradox between the dramatic and the conceptual aspects of the temptation scenes in Milton's poetry. In a temptation somebody is being persuaded to do something that looks like an act, but which is really the loss of the power to act. Consequently, the abstaining from this kind of pseudo-activity is often the sign that one possesses a genuine power of action. The Lady in *Comus*, for example, has a somewhat uninteresting dramatic role: she is, in fact, paralyzed, and, dramatically, says little except an eloquent and closely reasoned paraphrase of "no." Comus attracts a good deal more of our sympathy because his arguments are specious, and therefore dramatically more interesting. Yet we have to realize that the real situation is the opposite of the dramatic one. It is Comus who represents passion, which is the opposite of action; it is the Lady who holds to the source of all freedom of action. The same situation is even more sharply manifested in the role of Jesus in *Paradise Regained*, where Jesus behaves, for four books, like a householder dealing with an importunate salesman. Yet again what is actually going on is the opposite of what appears to be going on. Satan, who seems so lively and resourceful, is the power that moves toward the cessation of all activity, a kind of personal entropy that transforms all energy into a heat-death.

The typical demonic "act" is not a real act either, but it is a much more concentrated parody of divine action. It has the quality not of disobedience but of rebellion, and it differs from the human act in that it involves rivalry, or attempted rivalry, with God. The appearance of Nimrod at the beginning of the last book of *Paradise Lost* represents the coming into human life of the demonic, of the ability to worship devils, of turning to Satan for one's conception of the kingdom and the power and the glory, instead of to God. What Satan himself manifests in *Paradise Lost* is this perverted quality of parody-heroism, of which the essential quality is destructiveness. Consequently it is to Satan and his followers that Milton assigns the conventional and Classical type of heroism. Satan, like Achilles, retires sulkily in heaven when a decision appears to be favoring another Son of God, and emerges in a torrent of wrath to wreak vengeance. Like Odysseus, he steers his way with great cunning between the Scylla-like Sin and the Charybdis-like Death; like the knights errant of romance, he goes out alone on a perilous quest to an unknown world. The remark the devils make about the war in heaven, that they have sustained the war for a day "And, if one day, why not eternal days?" opens up a perverted vision of eternity as a Valhalla of endless strife.

It it only the divine that can really act, by Milton's own definition of an act, and the quality of the divine act reveals itself in *Paradise Lost* as an act of creation, which becomes an act of recreation or redemption after the fall of man. Christ, therefore, who creates the world and then recreates or redeems man, is the hero of *Paradise Lost* simply because, as the agent or acting principle of the Father, he is ultimately the only actor in the poem.

The angelic order is there to provide models for human action. They have superior intellectual and physical powers which man may eventually attain, but in *Paradise Lost* they are moral models only. They form a community of service and obedience, often doing things meaningless to them except that as the will of God they have meaning. They are ministers of responsibility (Gabriel), instruction (Raphael), command (Michael) or vigilance (Uriel). The figure of the tense, waiting angels, listening for the Word to speak and motionless until it does, appears in the last line of the Nativity Ode and again in the last line of the sonnet on the poet's blindness. Such angels are, as the angel says to John at the end of the Bible, fellow servants of mankind: there is nothing in Milton of Rilke's "schrecklich" angel.

More important than any of these, for the theme of heroism, is Abdiel, who remains faithful to God in the midst of the revolted angels. Abdiel, like many people of unimpeachable integrity, is not a very attractive character, but everything he says in the poem is of the highest importance. The speech which he makes to Satan at the time of the war in heaven indicates that he is establishing the pattern of genuine heroism that is later to be exhibited in the life of Christ, the "better part of fortitude" which consists primarily in obedience and endurance and in the kind of courage that is willing to suffer under ridicule and contempt and a chorus of opposition. As Abdiel says to Satan, after being restored to the faithful angels, "My sect thou seest." This pattern is followed in the biblical visions which Michael shows to Adam: in the story of Enoch, the one just man who stands out against all the vice of his time, and receives the angelic reward of direct transportation to heaven, and in Noah, who is similarly the one just man of his time and is saved from an otherwise total destruction. It could have been exemplified by Lot in Sodom, which is referred to briefly by Milton. This is the pattern which is followed by the prophets and apostles, and nobody else is entitled to be called heroic.

Doubtless the faithful angels could have defeated the rebels by themselves, but the symbolism of the three-day war in heaven is designed to show that the total angelic power of action is contained in the Son of God. The angels have no strength that does not come from God, and the devils have no strength against God at all. It is difficult not to feel that the entire war in heaven is a huge practical joke to the Father, all the more of one because of the seriousness with which the devils take it. The admiring description of the size of Satan's spear and shield in Book One has two perspectives: from man's point of view Satan is incalculably strong, but from God's point of view he is only a lubber fiend. God's own conception of strength is represented by the infant Christ of the Nativity Ode, the genuine form of Hercules strangling the serpent in his cradle, physically weak and yet strong enough to overcome the world.

In this world spiritual strength, being a direct gift of God, is not necessarily accompanied by physical strength, though it is normally accompanied by physical invulnerability. This condition is the condition of chastity, traditionally a magical strength in romance, and the theme of the magic of chastity runs all through Milton. The Lady cannot be hurt by Comus because of the "hidden strength" of her chastity. Samson owes his physical strength to his chastity, to his observance of his Nazarite vow: as he says bitterly, God hung his strength in his hair. He loses his chastity when he tells Delilah what his secret is. Such chastity does not in his case imply virginity or even continence: two marriages to Philistine women do not affect it, nor apparently does even a visit to a Philistine harlot, which Milton ignores, though he read about it in the Book of Judges. Adam and Eve have been given more than mortal strength by their chastity, which is also not affected by sexual intercourse: they lose their chastity only by eating of the forbidden tree. A reference to Samson in Book Nine establishes the link in the symbolism of chastity between the two.

Like most morally coherent writers, Milton is careful to distinguish the human from the demonic, even when what he is showing is the relation between them. As it may be difficult to feel this distinction without examples we may take an analogy from Shakespeare. Cleopatra in Shakespeare is all the things that the critics of Milton say Eve is. She is vain and frivolous and light-minded and capricious and extravagant and irresponsible and a very bad influence on Antony, who ought to be out chasing Parthians instead of wasting his time with her. She is morally a most deplorable character, yet there is something about her which is obstinately likable. Perhaps that makes her more dangerous, but it's no good: we cannot feel that Cleopatra is evil in the way that Goneril and Regan are evil. For one thing, Cleopatra can always be unpredictable, and as long as she can be that she is human. Goneril and Regan are much closer to what is meant in religion by lost souls, and what that means dramatically is that they can no longer be unpredictable. Everything they do or say is coarse and ugly and cruel, but still it also has about it something of the stylized grandeur of the demonic, something of the quality that Milton's devils have and that his human beings do not have. At the same time Cleopatra is a part of something far more sinister than herself: this comes out in the imagery attached to Egypt, if not in the characterization attached to her. Putting the two together, what we see is the human contained by the demonic, a fascinating creature of infinite variety who is still, from another point of view, sprung from the equivocal generation of the Nile.

It is the same with Adam and Eve. Theologically and conceptually, they have committed every sin in the calendar. In *The Christian Doctrine* Milton sets it all down: there was nothing bad that they omitted to do when they ate that wretched apple:

> It comprehended at once distrust in the divine veracity, and a proportionate credulity in the assurances of Satan; unbelief; ingratitude; disobedience; gluttony; in the man excessive uxoriousness, in the woman a want of proper regard for her husband, in both an insensibility to the welfare of their offspring, and that offspring the whole human race; parricide, theft, invasion of the rights of others, sacrilege, deceit, presumption in aspiring to divine attributes, fraud in the means employed to attain the object, pride, and arrogance.

Yet this is something that it is wholly impossible for us to feel or realize dramatically, nor does Milton attempt to make us do so. Eve may have been a silly girl but she is still our general mother, still quite obviously the same kind of human being that we are. What has happened is that human life is now attached to the demonic, this being one of the points made by Michael, especially in the vision of Nimrod, the archetypal tyrant, the tyrant being one of the clearest examples of a human being who has given himself up to the demonic.

The fact that conventional heroism, as we have it in Classical epic and medieval and Renaissance romance, is associated with the demonic in Milton means, of course, that *Paradise Lost* is a profoundly anti-romantic and anti-heroic poem. Most of us live our lives on a roughly human level, but if we meet with some setback, snub, imposed authority or other humiliation we are thrown back on something that will support and console us, and unless we are saints that something is likely to be the ego. The sombre, brooding, humourless ego, with its "high disdain from sense of injured merit" drives us to look for compensation, perhaps by identifying ourselves with some irresistable hero. If in this state we read Milton, we shall find his Satan, so far from being the author of evil, a congenial and sympathetic figure. If we later regain a better sense of proportion, we may understand something of the profundity and accuracy of Milton's conception of evil.

Satan is a rebel, and into Satan Milton has put all the horror and distress with which he contemplated the egocentric revolutionaries of his time, who stumbled from one party to another and finally ended precisely where they had started, in a cyclical movement with no renewal. There is an almost uncanny anticipation of some of the moods of later Romanticism, also an age of egocentric revolutionaries. In particular, there is a quality in Milton's treatment of the demonic world that can only be called Wagnerian: in the unvarying nobility of the rhetoric, in the nihilistic heroic action that begins and ends in the lake of fire, in the *Götterdämmerung* motif in the music of hell:

> Others, more mild,
> Retreated in a silent valley, sing
> With notes angelical to many a harp
> Their own heroic deeds, and hapless fall
> By doom of battle, and complain that Fate
> Free virtue should enthrall to force or chance.

This is not to say that Wagner is a demonic artist, any more than that Milton is a Satanist, only that there are demonic elements portrayed in Wagner that some very evil people have found, as many have found Satan, irresistibly attractive.

The anti-heroic tendency in Milton is, however, less complicated than his attitude to myth, of which it forms part. When a literary critic says that the story of the fall of man is a myth, he is not making any statement about the truth of its content, merely that it is a certain kind of story; but still his feeling about its truth is colored by this very shift of attention from its content to its form. But Milton is never tired of stressing the difference in ethical content between the truth of the Bible and the fables of the heathen, and obviously the story of the fall would never have interested him if he had not believed it to be as literally true as the events of his own life. The story of *Paradise Lost* is a myth in the sense that the action or narrative movement (*mythos*) is provided by a divine being: the essential content is human, and as credible and plausible as Milton's source would allow him to make it. The marvels and grotesqueries of the poem, such as the building of Pandemonium or the Limbo of Vanities, are mostly demonic, and form a contrast to the central action. In modern literature a writer may use a mythical subject because it affords him an interesting and traditional story pattern, as Cocteau does in *Orphée* or Giraudoux in *Antigone*. In Tolstoy's *Resurrection* we have a purely realistic narrative which assumes a shape with the religious significance indicated in the title. Milton's attitude to myth in *Paradise Lost* is much closer, temperamentally and technically, to Tolstoy than it is to Cocteau or Giraudoux.

Myths differ from folk tales or legends in having a superior kind of importance attached to them, and this in turn makes them stick together and form mythologies. A fully developed mythology thus tends, as the Bible does, to take an encyclopaedic shape. Ovid's *metamorphoses*, for example, starts with creation and flood stories and works its way down to Julius Caesar as the Bible does to Jesus. Milton's exhaustive use of Ovid is often sympathetic, but evidently he finds in the Ovidian theme of metamorphosis, the identifying of a human figure with an object in nature, the point at which polytheism becomes obvious idolatry. The demonic action of *Paradise Lost* ends with an Ovidian metamorphosis in which the devils are changed to serpents. Satan has taken the form of the serpent; he finds in hell that he cannot get rid of it, but is still a serpent; the devils in looking at him become serpents too:

> what they saw
> They felt themselves now changing.

There is a clear recall of the remark about idols in the 115th Psalm: "they that make them are like unto them."

For us, the mythological imagination is really part of the poetic imagination: the instinct to identify a human figure with a natural object, which gives mythology its sun gods and tree gods and ocean gods, is the same instinct that is described by Whitman:

> There was a child went forth every day,
> And the first object he look'd upon, that object he became,
> And that object became part of him for the day or a certain part
>   of the day,
> Or for many years or stretching cycles of years.

The author of *Lycidas* would have understood this very well; but a question not relevant to Whitman is relevant to Milton: is this identifying consciousness centered in the ego, as Satan's intelligence is, or not? To identify one's consciousness directly with the works of God in our present world, for Milton, is to enter the forest of Comus on Comus' own terms, to unite ourselves to a sub-moral, sub-conscious, sub-human existence which is life to the body but death to the soul. The free intelligence must detach itself from this world and unite itself to the totality of freedom and intelligence which is God in man, shift its centre of gravity from the self to the presence of God in the self. Then it will find the identity with nature it appeared to reject: it will participate in the Creator's view of a world he made and found good. This is the relation of Adam and Eve to Eden before their fall. From Milton's point of view, the poly-theistic imagination can never free itself from the labyrinths of fantasy and irony, with their fitful glimpses of inseparable good and evil. What Milton means by revelation is a consolidated, coherent, encyclopaedic view of human life which defines, among other things, the function of poetry. Every act of the free intelligence, including the poetic intelli-gence, is an attempt to return to Eden, a world in the human form of a garden, where we may wander as we please but cannot lose our way.

STANLEY EUGENE FISH

Discovery as Form in *Paradise Lost*†

I

Recently I have argued that the true center of *Paradise Lost* is the reader's consciousness of the poem's *personal* relevance, and that the arc of the poem describes, in addition to the careers of the characters, the education of its readers.[1] This education proceeds in two stages: in the first, the reader is brought face to face with the corruption within him, as he is made aware of the confusion reigning in his scale of values and of the inadequacy of his perceptions; in the second, he is invited to cooperate with the poem's effort to effect his regeneration, invited, in Milton's words, to purge hiis "intellectual ray" until it is once more "fit and proportionable to Truth the object, and end of it, as the eye of the thing visible."[2] These stages correspond to the stages of Plato's dialectc, the inducing in the respondent of a "healthy perplexity" followed by the refinement of his inner eye to the point where it recognizes and embraces the Supreme Good;[3] and the poem's operation is analogous to that of

† From *New Essays on "Paradise Lost,"* ed. Thomas Kranidas (Berkeley, 1971) 1–14. Reprinted with the kind permission of the author. The author's footnotes have been renumbered and one has been deleted.
1. *Surprised by Sin: The Reader in Paradise Lost* (London and New York, 1967).
2. Milton, *Complete Prose Works*, Vol. I, ed. D. M. Wolfe, New Haven, 1953), p. 566.
3. See Robert Cushman, *Therapeia* (Chapel Hill, N.C., 1958), p. 89.

the Mosaic Law which, we are told in *The Christian Doctrine*, calls
forth "our natural depravity, that by this means it might . . . bring us
to the righteousness of Christ."[4] In its potential effect, then, *Paradise
Lost* may claim the status of what Bunyan calls a "work of grace" in the
soul; for it gives the sinner "conviction of sin, especially of the defilement
of his nature, and the sin of unbelief."[5]

This description of *Paradise Lost*, as a poem concerned with the self-
education of its readers, if it is accepted, throws a new light on some
old questions. Specifically, it dictates a reorientation of the debate con-
cerning the structure or form of the poem; for if the meaning of the
poem is to be located in the reader's experience of it, the form of the
poem is the form of that experience; and the outer or physical form, so
obtrusive, and, in one sense, so undeniably there, is, in another sense,
incidental and even irrelevant. This is a deliberately provocative thesis,
the defense of which will be the concern of the following pages; and I
would like to begin by explaining more fully what is meant by the phrase
"the form of the reader's experience."

The stages of this experience mark advances in the reader's under-
standing, in the refining of his vision rather than in the organization of
material. In *Paradise Lost*, *things* are not being clarified or ordered;
rather, *eyes* are being made capable of seeing things as they truly are
already in the clarity of God's order. The process, and its relationship
to a truth that is evident to those who have eyes to see it, is adumbrated
in this passage from *Of Reformation*.

> The very essence of Truth is plainnesse, and brightnes; the
> darknes and crookednesse is our own. . . . If our *understanding*
> have a film of *ignorance* over it, or be blear with gazing on
> other false glisterings, what is that to Truth? If we will but
> purge with sovrain eyesalve that intellectual ray which God
> hath planted in us, then we would beleeve the Scriptures
> protesting their own plainnes.[6]

In Augustine's *On Christian Doctrine* the Scriptures themselves are the
instrument by which the understanding can be made proportional to
their plainness; and Augustine's description of what happens to the at-
tentive reader of God's word is not unlike my description of the reader's
experience in *Paradise Lost*:

> The student first will discover in the Scriptures that he has
> been enmeshed in the love of this world. . . . Then . . . that
> fear which arises from the thought of God's judgment . . .
> will force him to lament his own situation. . . . And by means

4. See p. 422, above [*Editor*].
5. *The Pilgrim's Progress*, ed. J. B. Wharey, rev. R. Sharrock (Oxford, 1960), pp. 82–83.
6. Milton, *Complete Prose Works*, I, 566.

> of this affection of the spirit he will extract himself from all
> mortal joy in transitory things . . . and turn toward the love
> of eternal things . . . he purges his mind, which is rising up
> and protesting in the appetite for inferior things, of its
> contaminations.[7]

Augustine then describes five steps or stages leading to a sixth where the
aspirant "cleanses that eye through which God may be seen, in so far
as He can be seen by those who die to the world as much as they are
able." "From fear to wisdom," he concludes, "the way extends through
these steps."

To some extent Augustine's "steps" suggest a regular and predictable,
that is, linear, progression to wisdom; but, of course, the movement
from one step to the next cannot be predicted or charted since the
operative factor is the "purging of the mind" or "the cleansing of the
eye"; and the extent to which the mind is distracted by the appeal of
transitory things, and, consequently, the period of time which must
elapse before the eys are made clear, will vary with the individual, who
dies to the world as much as *he* is able. Nor will progress be regular
(linear) within the discrete stages enumerated by Augustine. In how
many differing contexts must the eye be challenged to distinguish true
beauty from the "false glisterings" of "fair outsides" before it is able to
see what is and is not truly beautiful *immediately?* No one answer will
serve for all eyes. In Plato's dialectic, A. E. Taylor explains, the appre-
hension of Reality "comes as a sudden 'revelation' though it is not to
be had without the long preliminary process of travail of thought."[8]
Taylor's point is that the relationship between the "travail of thought"
and the "revelation" is indeterminate, partly because the thing to be
known cannot be known by "discursive knowledge about it," and partly
because, as Robert Cushman observes, the effort that must be expended
"to disengage the mind from preoccupation with sensibiles" will be in
proportion to the strength of the "fetters" binding the individual mind
to earthly perception.[9]

Consider the case of Samson, whose experience in Milton's verse
drama parallels that of the reader in *Paradise Lost.* When Manoa quarrels
with God's dispensing of justice—"methinks whom God hath chosen
once/ . . . He should not so o'erwhelm" (11.368–370)—Samson answers
firmly "Appoint not heavenly disposition" (1.373). But within a few lines
he too begins to appoint heavenly disposition when he declares himself
ineligible for service to God in his present condition—"To what can I
be useful?"—for, in effect, he is putting limits on God's ability to use
him. No straight line can describe Samson's spiritual journey. At times,

---

7. *On Christian Doctrine*, trans. D. W. Robertson (New York, 1958), pp. 39–40.
8. *Plato: The Man and his Work* (Meridian Books, New York, 1957), p. 231.
9. Cushman, *op. cit.*, pp. 163, 166.

as in this instance, he seems to make an advance toward understanding, only in the next minute to embrace in another guise the error he has just rejected. When clarity of vision does come to Samson, we can look back and see a series of starts (gestures) toward it—intimations, partial illuminations—but no chartable and visible progression. Let me here anticipate a later argument by pointing out that since the concern of the play is Samson's regeneration, Dalila, Harapha, the messenger, the Chorus, and Manoa are important, not for themselves, but for the opportunities they bring to Samson's laboring mind.

In *Paradise Lost*, the reader is repeatedly forced to acknowledge the unworthiness of values and ideals he had precisely admired, yet, like Samson, he will often fall into the same admiration when the context changes slightly. To take as an example something I have treated at length elsewhere, in the early books: Satan's false heroism draws from the reader a response that is immediately challenged by the epic voice, who at the same time challenges the concept of heroism in which the response is rooted. Subsequently, Satan's apparent heroism is discredited by covert allusions to other heroes in other epics, by his ignoble accommodation to the "family" he meets at the gates of Hell, by his later discoveries squatting at the ear of Eve in the form of a toad, and, most tellingly, by his own self-revelations in the extended soliloquy that opens Book IV. At *some point* during this sequence of actions, the reader becomes immune to the Satanic appeal because he has learned what it is, or to be more precise, what it is not. "Some point," however, will be a different point for each reader, depending on the extent to which he is committed to the false ideal Satan exemplifies. Nor will the progress of any reader—of whatever capacity—be regular, since the learning of an individual lesson is not a guarantee against falling into a generic error. The reader who in Book I is led to resist the sophistries of the Satanic line when they are offered directly, may not recognize them in Book II when they are put forward in the Grand Council, especially if he has surrendered too much of his attention to the thrust and parry of the debate, that is, to the strategy rather than to the morality of the scene. And this same reader, when he is presented with a true hero in the person of Abdiel, is likely to admire him for the wrong reasons. That is to say, his response to Abdiel's action at the close of Book V will be a response to the melodramatic aspect of the situation—a lone figure rising to assert himself against innumerable foes—and therefore a response not enough differentiated from that originally given to the now discredited Satan. In Book VI, during the War in Heaven, the reader is given the opportunity to distinguish Abdiel's heroism from the *incidental* circumstances of its exercise. So that, at *some point* in the course of his struggles with the interpretative problems raised by the battle, the reader discovers the naked essence of heroism itself. It is important to realize that the poem does not move to this revelation; it has been there from the first, plainly visible to the eye capable of seeing it. It is the reader who moves, or advances, until his cleansed eye can see what has always been there. At least the reader is given the *opportunity* to advance. He may not take it, and so remain a captive of his clouded vision. It follows, then, that between Books I and VI Satan does not change at all. His degradation is a critical myth. The reader's capacity to see him clearly changes, although that change is gradual and fitful, uneven unchartable, to some extent invisible, not easily separated from parallel changes in the reader's capacity to see other things clearly— virtue, heroism, love, beauty. (I am thinking, for example, of the contrast between the good and bad poetry of Satan's and God's speeches. I leave you to apply the labels.)

If Satan has not moved or altered, the only alteration being the reader's, it follows that the episodes in which Satan appears are not important for any light they throw on *him*, or for the challenges they present to *him*, but for the function they serve as a whetstone to the reader's laboring mind. Moreover the action of the poem is taking place in that mind, not in the narrative, whose world is static. For, strictly speaking, the plot of *Paradise Lost*, in the sense of a linear movement toward a dramatic and moral climax—the Fall—does not exist; simply because the concept of free will, as Milton defines it, precludes the usual process of decision—the interplay between circumstance, motivation, and choice— which in other works fills up a plot. The decision of an absolutely free will cannot be determined by forces outside it, and, in a casual sense, such a decision has no antecedents. I would suggest that the point of the scenes in Paradise from Book IV to Book IX is their irrelevance, as determining factors, to the moment of crisis experienced by the characters; and the action taking place in these scenes is the reader's discovery or comprehension of that irrelevance. In the middle books, and especially at those points where Milton has been accused of "necessary faking"— the phrase is Tillyard's[1]—the reader is presented with a series of "interpretative choices." On the surface, the account of Eve's infatuation with her reflected image, and the fact of her dream, and of Adam's admissions to Raphael of his weakness, seem to deny the freedom of the unfallen will by circumscribing our first parents in what Watkins[2] has termed a "network of circumstances." Yet in each instance Milton provides evidence that makes it possible for the reader to disengage these incidents from the Fall—I am thinking for example of Adam's statement, "Evil into the mind of God or Man/May come and go . . . and leave/ No spot . . . behind"—and finally to see them as moving away from, rather than toward, that crisis. This is the poet's solution to the problem of building a poem around an event that has no antecedents. He gives us a plot without a middle—Adam and Eve fall spontaneously—but he

---

1. E. M. W. Tillyard, *Studies in Milton* (London, 1951) 10 [*Editor*].
2. W. B. C. Watkins, *An Anatomy of Milton's Verse* (Baton Rouge, 1955) [*Editor*].

allows for a *psychological* middle, a middle to the reading experience, by leaving it to us to discover that the narrative middle does not, indeed could not, exist.

II

Now, for the obvious question: if the poem does not move, but the reader moves, if there is no plot except for the plot of the reader's education, and if the true form of the poem is the form of the individual reader's experience rather than the visible form represented by the division into twelve books; if, in sum, the action is interior, taking place inside the reader's mind, what is the function of the exterior form? Why is it there? What do we say, for instance, about the intricate patterning of words and phrases continually being uncovered by modern criticism? There are several answers to this question. The divisions in the narrative, in the physical artifact called *Paradise Lost*, mark out areas within which the process of regeneration can go forward, while the instances of parallelism provide "stations" at which the progress of the process can be checked. When the reader comes across a word or a phrase that recalls him to an earlier point in the poem, he is not being asked to compare the contents of two scenes now juxtaposed in his mind, but to apply whatever insights he has gained in the *psychological* interim to the single content these two scenes share. That is to say, the meaning of the parallel is determined not by its existence but by the success the reader has had in purging his intellectual ray. Anyone, even a computer, can point out echoes. Only a reader who has learned, only a reader with a cleansed eye, can create their meaning. *He* does it, not the poem. Echoes and cross-references are not saying, "Look at this." They are saying, "Do you know what to make of this *now*?"[3] The important time in the poem is psychological time. In the time consumed while reading, the poem is not developing, the reader is (or he isn't). And any significance one can attach to the sequence of events is to be found not in their relationship to the narrative situation—whose temporal structure, as many have observed, is confused—but to the reader's situation. Milton in effect tells us this when God sends Raphael down to warn Adam in Book V. In this way, the epic voice explains, "God fulfills all justice." But God here fulfills more than justice if Adam is meant, because Adam is sufficient to his test without Raphael's warning. Justice is being done to the reader, who is being given the opportunity. Adam does not need, although what Adam will do in Book IX created the imperfection that makes it necessary for the reader to *now* have the opportunity. When at the end of Book VI the phrase "nine days they fell" returns us to the

---

3. Again we find an analogue in the dialectic of Plato, where apparent progressions and/or digressions unexpectedly return to the point of origin, and the hapless respondent is asked to reasses his original position in the light of the truth he has ascended to, or, as is the case in most of the dialogues, in the light of the truth Socrates has drawn out of him.

opening lines of Book I, our attention is not being called to what has happened to Satan since he was first expelled (of course nothing has happened to Satan), but to what has happened to ourselves. Satan is in the same place; we, one hopes, are not. Thus, this halfway point in *Paradise Lost* (in its outer form, that is) *is* there for a reason; it does mark the end of something, not, however, of something going on in the world of the characters (in that context we are right back where we started), but of something going on in the world of the reader. This, in fact, is the end of the poet's attempt to refine the reader's sense of what true heroism is. And later in Book IX the superficial nobility of Adam's gesture will pose once again the same question, "Do you understand now?" And in his response the reader will give his answer.

What I have said here with reference to the single problem of heroism applies to other problems and to other patternings. In Book III, God delivers a speech whose arguments, if they are understood, assure a correct reading of the crucial scene in Book IX. At irregular intervals, phrases from this "ur speech" are repeated (I am thinking especially of "sufficient to have stood, though free to fall"), and each repetition asks a silent question, "Do you understand *now*?" In the intervals between repetitions, the same question is posed indirectly by the events of the narrative. When Eve questions the perfection of her situation ("frail is our happiness if this be so"), she betrays a complete misunderstanding of the concepts God has been at pains to define, and thus her speech becomes a negative test of the reader. That is, the reader's ability to perceive the fallacies in her argument measures the extent to which he *now* understands God's logic. And once again we return to a point made earlier: since the misconceptions Eve entertains here cannot affect her performance at the moment of temptation ("the seat of temptation is in the will, not in the understanding"), her speech is more important for the reader's state of mind than for her own; in relationship to the Fall, her state of mind does not matter. It is the reader who has the most at stake in the scenes preceding the crisis; and the patterns, the repetitions, the time passing—they are all for him.

In addition to providing the reader with stations at which he may check his progress, and with cases or problems whose consideration is the vehicle of that progress, the poem's Aristotelian superstructure— beginning, middle, end—has a negative value as one form of a way of knowing Milton believes to be inferior or secondary. Plato makes a distinction between knowledge "by way of division," that is, knowledge whose end is the clarification of objects in the material world (*dianoia*), and knowledge by illumination, knowledge whose end is the recognition of a suprasensible reality (*episteme*); and this distinction corresponds to that made by Augustine and other theologians between *scientia* and *sapientia*. In one sphere, the mind, with the help of certain aids— deductive logic, enumeration, denotation—performs a refining operation on the data of experience; in the other, the mind itself is led to transcend the flux of experience and to interpret it in the light of the reality to which it has ascended. True knowledge, then, is not reached by following a chain of inferences or by accurately labeling *things* (although inference and labeling may have some part in the attainment of it), but is the possesion of the mind that has been made congruent with it; true knowledge cannot be brought to the mind (it is not transmissable), the mind must be brought to it; to the point where there is no longer any need for the aid logical inference can offer. One must take care not to extend illegitimately the province of *scientia* and so fail to distinguish between that which can be seen and measured by the physical eye and that which reveals itself only to the inner eye of the aspiring soul. It is this danger to which Milton deliberately exposes his rader when he suggests in the opening lines that the purpose of his poem is to provide a verifiable answer to the question "What cause?"; in its position, this question holds out a promise that proves in the course of the poem to be false, the promise that if the reader follows Milton's argument, from its beginning to its middle to its end, he will find the answer and along with it a rational justification of God's ways, awaiting him, as it were, at the end of a syllogism. But this is not the case. The promise is given so that its falseness can be more forcefully exposed and so that the reader can learn not to rely on the way of knowing it assumes, but to rely instead on illumination and revelation. Just as the search for cause and for a rational justification is an attempt to confine God within the limits of formal reasoning, and is thus a temptation, so is the temporal-spatial structure of the poem, by means of which that search is supposedly to be conducted, a temptation, since the reader may fall into the error of looking to *it* as a revealer of meaning: that is, to the limited and distorting, though organized, picture of reality it presents, rather than to the inner light developing within him. (The more the inner light develops, of course, the less a temptation the outer formal structure will offer, since the reader's need of it, or of anything else, will progressively lessen.) The reader's situation parallels Adam's and Eve's, who are also tempted to look to the organization of experience, and to the meaning conferred on things by accidents of time and space, for guidance, rather than to revelation. So that, in summary, what we can call the outer form of the poem—twelve books, a regular plot line, the illusion of cause and effect—is (1) unnecessary (finally) to correct perception, and (2) a temptation, since dependence on it is enslavement to it and to the earthly (rational) perspective of which it is one manifestation. In other words, part of the poem's lesson is the superfluousness of the mold of experience—of space and time—to the perception of what is true; and thus the epic's outer form, inasmuch as it is the area within which the inner eye is purified, is the vehicle of its own abandonment. Like the hierarchical structure of the early Church as it is described in *The Reason of Church-government*, the outer form of the poem is a "scaffolding" which "so soon as the building is finished" is but a "troublesome disfigurement" that is to be cast aside.[4] And this casting aside is imitated in the *conceptual* movement of *Paradise Lost* by the rejection of the external trappings of a public heroism in favor of a better heroism whose successes are not visible to the physical eye.

III

And what does the reader who has reached this point discover at the end of his labors? The truth, of course, or Truth, as it awaits those who have climbed the Platonic ladder: the Supreme Good concerning which nothing can be predicated, since it is the basis of all predication; "a principle that requires justification and explanation by reference to nothing besides itself,"[5] because it is the basis of justification and that in the light of which all else is to be explained; a good whose value cannot be measured because it is the measure (or norm) of value. In Milton's poem, the position occupied by Plato's Supreme Good is occupied by Christ, whose action in Book XII—taking place not there but everywhere, not at one point in time, but at all points—is the measure of all other actions and the embodiment of everything that is truly valuable.

I began this paper by suggesting that the physical form of *Paradise Lost* has only an oblique relationship to its true form, which I identified with the form of the reader's experience. That experience, however, does not lend itself to the kind of description one usually associates with the word "formal"; here are no readily discernible beginning, middle, and end, no clearly marked transitions, no moments of crisis at which issues are preeminently resolved; instead, the form, if it can be called that, follows the convolutions of the reader's education, now describing an advance, now a backsliding, at one moment pointing upward, at another, downward, at a third, in both directions at once. Still, there is a pattern into which the experiences of all successful readers fall (although there are as many variations within it as there are readers) and we are now in a position to trace out that pattern:

(1) During the poem, the reader is being forced by the verse to sharpen his moral and spiritual perceptions to the point where they are answerable to those essences of which he has hitherto had only an imperfect and partial knowledge. This refining process is desultory and wandering, concerned randomly with the entire range of moral abstractions.

(2) At regular intervals, the reader is asked to assess his progress, asked if he is able to recognize the true form of one of these abstractions.

(3) There are in the poem two places where the answerability of the reader's vision to the *unity* of the conceptions he has been considering

4. Milton, *Complete Prose Works*, I. 791.
5. Cushman, *op. cit.*, p. 177. See *Symposium*, 211b.

singly is tested: first in Book IX where Adam violates all of the values with whose identification the poem has been concerned—significantly he sins in their name and this "misnaming" becomes the legacy he leaves his sons—and again in Book XII when Christ restores to these much abused terms their true, that is spiritual, meaning.

The experience of the entire poem, then, moves toward this moment when the arc of the narrative action and the end of the reader's education coincide. (It is no accident that Adam's understanding is made perfect at the point where Christ is brought before his eyes at the end of a process very much like the education of the reader.) Knowledge of Christ is the end of all the smaller investigations and searches that go on in the body of the poem, investigations of the nature of heroism, love, beauty, innocence, happiness. He is the measure of them all and His essence *informs* them all. He gives form to the universe and to everything in it, including the things in this poem, including the poem itself. In an ultimate sense, *He* is the poem's true form,[6] and His relationship to the temporal-spatial structure of the poem is a reflection of His relationship to the temporal-spatial structure of post-Edenic experience. He enters both structures at once to fulfill them and to supersede them as conveyors of meaning by making good on the promises they could not keep. The promise to justify God's ways to men, for instance, cannot, we discover, be fulfilled within the rational and linear framework of the physical *Paradise Lost*; but it is fulfilled when the reader, who has been led to an intuitive understanding of Christ's significance, understands, at that moment, how much the mercy of God exceeds the requirements of reason. (Mercy, the word taking flesh and sacrificing itself, is unreasonable.)

For the reader who has been so led, the poem no longer has any parts; rather, like the universe God sees from his prospect high, it constitutes a unity, infused at every point with a single stable meaning. This meaning is apprehended through what become its parts when one is limited to anything but an all-inclusive glance. As the reader moves (irregularly) toward this illuminative height, the divisions into books and episodes, and all other markers indicating subordination and emphasis, recede into the background and reveal themselves finally as artificial heighteners of what is self-evident to the purged eye.[7] The units of the

6. William Madsen makes a similar point in a review of Frye's *The Return of Eden*: "If it is formal symmetry we are looking for in *Paradise Lost*, the nearest approach to it is provided by the image of Christ which radiates from the exact center of the poem" (*Criticism* [Fall, 1966], p. 393). See also C. A. Patrides, *Milton and the Christian Tradition* (Oxford, 1966), p. 260: "I am persuaded that the God-man in *Paradise Lost* . . . renders coherence to the entire epic."

7. In this overview the argument concerning the poem's crisis is resolved, or, to be more precise, dismissed. Since every moment at which there is the possibility of seeing or not seeing truly (that is, every moment) is a crisis—that statement applies also to Adam and Eve—the concept becomes meaningless. Some "crises" are merely (and accidentally) made spectacular. See Jackson Cope's description of the poem as having no "center from which one might measure

poem are now interchangeable, one with another, receptables all of the good and merciful news Christ proclaims in Book XII. The illusion of a multiplicity of parts, or even of a clash of values (i.e., love vs. obedience), is now seen to have been the creation of the distorting perspective of local contexts, a perspective that no longer delimits the horizons of the reader's vision. In short, the reader who finally knows Christ will experience none of the difficulties associated with Milton's poem; although, paradoxically, it is these difficulties (tests, trials, temptations) as they have been encountered in those (illusory) parts which have led him to that knowledge.[8]

This leads me naturally to the question some of my readers will have been asking. If knowledge of Christ is sufficient to all our needs, including the needs *Paradise Lost* speaks to, what claim does the poem have on us beyond a successful first reading? The answer is bound up in the inability of the fallen mind to prolong the moment of vision to which dialectical self-examination can occasionally bring it. Augustine's spiritual history is a case in point.

> And now came I to have a sight of those invisible things of thee, which are understood by those things which are made. But I was not able to fix mine eye long upon them: but my infirmity being beaten back again, I was turned to my wonted fancies; carrying along with me no more but a liking of those new thoughts in my memory, and an appetite, as it were, to the meat I had smelt.[9]

The perishability of the insight that awaits us at the end of *Paradise Lost* assures the poem's continuing relevance. We may have succeeded to some degree in purging our intellectual ray, but the "film of ignorance" is not so easily removed, and a "sovrain eyesalve" may be needed again. And in that (certain) event, the first reading holds out the promise of another success. In the meantime, the abandoned outer form—which has been the vehicle for the apprehension of meaning, although meaning is not imbedded *in* it—remains as an area within which the interior journey can be renegotiated. With Adam, we exit from the poem into experience; but we can return to it, as he returns to the memory of Paradise, for strength and sustenance.

the distances relating beginning, middle, end, or 'crisis' " (*The Metaphoric Structure of Paradise Lost* [Baltimore, 1962], p. 77). See also G. A. Wilkes, *The Thesis of Paradise Lost* (Melbourne, 1961), p. 42: "The weight of Milton's conception is not poised on one episode . . . its weight is distributed through the whole structure."

8. Wilkes argues that these local difficulties are finally "submerged" in the wholeness of the "great argument." What he does not see is that they do exist for the reader while he is *inside* the poem, and that they *lead* him to comprehend the "great argument."

9. Quoted by Louis Martz, *The Paradise Within* (New Haven, 1964), p. 50.

CHRISTOPHER RICKS

Milton's Grand Style†

[*The Successful Metaphor*]

The dignity of the epic is not compatible with such metaphors as are boldly and explosively new. But there is more than one kind of verbal life, and both his temperament and his respect for literary decorum impelled Milton to choose to bring ancient metaphors back to life rather than to forge new ones. The magnificent powers of Donne and Hopkins are sometimes in danger of making us silently assume that all our respect should go to the pioneer and none to the historian. Sometimes it even seems to be implied that it is only the pioneer who is 'sincere'. But each has value, and each has his apt style. Milton, like all epic poets, is concerned mainly to lead us back, not to blaze new trails. And the vigor of his words is a matter of his leading us back to the riches buried in them.

At its simplest, such a use of language does no more (and no less) than make words mean what they ought to mean. Dr. Davie has pointed out how often the verbal activity of the eighteenth-century poets is a matter of bringing dead metaphors to life. The poet takes a word or a phrase which has become slack or empty, and puts it into a context which suddenly brings back to life the original force. So any of us can now talk of 'goading' someone into a fury—but it is for Pope to say how his wit will 'goad the prelate slumbering in his stall', where the double aptness of *stall* (to prelate and to ox) tautens the whole line and puts the sting back into *goad*. Such a use of words might be thought to be particularly the method of those who seek to be original with the minimum of alteration—but it is very common in Milton, and ought to remind us of the balance between his notable idiosyncrasy of style and his observance of decorum. His admiration for the traditional is as much a matter of language as of epic machinery or convention.

Milton's Grand Style, in other words, has something in common with Goldsmith as well as with Hopkins. Dr. Davie points out how 'Goldsmith enlivens the metaphor gone dead in the locution "smiling land" (where smiling is 'beautiful', as in the Latin *ridere*):

> While scourg'd by famine from the smiling land,
> The mournful peasant leads his humble band

---

† Reprinted from *Milton's Grand Style* (1963) by permission of Oxford University Press. The author's footnotes have been renumbered, and one has been deleted. All changes by the editor appear in brackets.

—where the land is 'seen to smile with heartless indifference on the ruined peasant'.[1] But Milton, too, had seen the ominous possibilities in the beautiful convention of the 'smiling' of nature. It is explicit in Eve's words after the Fall:

> for see the Morn,
> All unconcern'd with our unrest, begins
> Her rosie progress smiling. (XI. 173–75)[2]

And it is implicit at that earlier tragic moment when Adam's faltering heart divines the ill which Eve is to conceal under a blithe countenance:

> Of knowledge he must pass, there he her met,
> Scarse from the Tree returning; in her hand
> A bough of fairest fruit that downie smil'd. (IX. 848–51)

Once again the smile is 'all unconcern'd with our unrest', or (in Dr. Davie's words) one of 'heartless indifference'. And once again the metaphor is enlivened, without shock and with the dignity suited to the Grand Style.

The metaphor is usually faded, too, when *transport* is given the extended sense of 'to carry away with emotion'. In Milton's hands, indeed in any poet's, it often might seem to mean no more than 'with one's emotions out of control'. But Milton re-establishes the power of the original metaphor, by setting the word in a context which stresses the physical roots of the emotional meaning, so that we see a *transport* as something that does literally and powerfully *move* you. So it is when God sees Satan 'coasting the wall of Heav'n'.

> Onely begotten Son, seest thou what rage
> Transports our adversarie, whom no bounds
> Prescrib'd, no barrs of Hell, nor all the chains
> Heapt on him there, nor yet the main Abyss
> Wide interrupt can hold; so bent he seems
> On desperat revenge, that shall redound
> Upon his own rebellious head. And now
> Through all restraint broke loose he wings his way
> Not farr off Heav'n . . . (III. 80–88)

God at this moment is not concerned primarily with Satan's emotions, but with the desperate physical energy of his journey. And the whole passage is superbly expressive of such energy. In diction: 'broke loose he wings his way'. And in syntax: notice how the crucial verb *can hold* flies triumphantly free, at the very end of its clause, from the grip of the previous twenty-two words of heaped chains. It is the superb syntax of

1. *The Deserted Village*, lines 299–300; [Donald Davie,] *Purity of Diction in English Verse* (1952), pp. 50–51.
2. There is a similar effect at v. 122–24.

'can hold' which is prior to, and the condition of, the lines' magnificent sound which Mr. Empson praised.[3]

The result of these effects is that when God says

> seest thou what rage
> Transports our adversarie,

the words compress his knowledge of Satan's single motive with his observation of his escape from Hell. After all, it is literally true that rage *transports* Satan.

This may seem over-ingenious, but there is substantiation in another famous passage where once again the powerful physical meaning reinforces the emotional one—emotion itself being a form of motion. Satan is entranced by the beauty of Eve, and for a moment he stands abstracted from his own evil. Then,

> Thoughts, *whither have ye led me*, with what sweet
> Compulsion thus *transported* to forget
> What *hither brought us* . . . (IX. 473–75)

Surely the italicized sequence insists on our taking 'transported' as very much more than a synonym for 'out of control'. And 'compulsion', too, renews its original *drive*.

That Milton was particularly fond of this complex of ideas is clear from Adam's tribute to Eve, when 'transported', 'commotion', and 'unmov'd' all renew their original movement:

> But here
> Farr otherwise, transported I behold,
> Transported touch; here passion first I felt,
> Commotion strange, in all enjoyments else
> Superiour and unmov'd. (VIII. 528–32)

The words have a similar unobtrusive and dignified energy when, during the temptation of Eve, Satan is described as 'the spirited sly Snake' (IX. 613). Obviously the main meaning is 'possessed by a spirit', for which the O.E.D. quotes the phrase. And spirited is used elsewhere in the poem to mean exactly that (III. 717). But the other meaning ('brisk, blithe') is not left out. Plainly the meanings co-exist in a synonym like 'animated', and Milton is taking advantage of both of them. The very next mention of the snake describes it as 'the wilie Adder, blithe and glad', *spirited* in the modern sense. And the 'evil Spirit' returns explicitly in the simile which follows, that of the *ignis fatuus*.

The degeneration of the transcendent brightness of Satan to that of a will-of-the-wisp is summed up in the way that Milton uses the word 'glory'. By stressing the sense of 'brightness, halo', he makes it clear that there is no true glory except that of God's goodness, and that Satan has

3. [William Empson,] *Milton's God*, p. 119.

only what—in a superbly shrivelling phrase—he calls 'permissive glory' (X. 451),[4] that is, 'false glitter'. We need to see the halo in the *glory* of the famous lines on Satan:

> his form had yet not lost
> All her Original brightness, nor appear'd
> Less than Arch Angel ruind, and th' excess
> Of Glory obscur'd: As when the Sun new ris'n
> Looks through the Horizontal misty Air
> Shorn of his Beams . . . (I. 591–96)[5]

There the context all bears on *glory*, insisting that it is literal as well as moral. So it is too when Beelzebub despairs of 'all our Glory extinct' (I.141). It was Patrick Hume, in 1695, who made the apt comment: 'put out, as a Flame, or any thing that burns and shines, a word well expressing the loss of that Angelick Beauty, which like a Glory attended on their Innocency, which by their foul Rebellion they had forfeited. . . . *Extinctus* is used in the same Metaphorical manner by *Virgil*.'[6]

It was the eighteenth-century editors who grasped the nature of the style, perhaps because the eighteenth-century poets owed so much to it. (The poets who merely imitated it are another and sadder matter.) Jonathan Richardson insisted that Milton's 'Sense is Crouded So Close, that Those who have been us'd to be indulg'd with Words and Sentences to Play withall, will find no Such Here; they must Attend Diligently, or Somthing Material will pass away'.[7]

So when we hear that the heathen gods 'with their darkness durst *affront* his light' (I. 391), Richardson brings out the force: 'This Word Carries a Stronger Sense than what is Commonly intended by it, though it also has That; it is from the *Italian Affrontare*, to Meet Face to Face; an Impudent Braving.'[8]

'Front' is still used by Milton in the sense of forehead, face to face; and the 'Stronger Sense' returns when Eve—as often—makes explicit what the poet had elsewhere muted. Her confidence rings with too emphatic a set of repetitions when she says that it will not matter even if the devil does tempt her:

> onely our Foe
> Tempting affronts us with his foul esteem
> Of our integritie: his foul esteeme
> Sticks no dishonor on our Front, but turns
> Foul on himself. (IX. 327–31)

4. For a similar effect compare 'Forc't Halleluiahs' (II. 243).
5. Cleanth Brooks analyses this passage, 'Milton and the New Criticism', *Sewanee Review* (1951).
6. *Poetical Works of Milton, Annotations by P.H.* (1695), p. 11.
7. *Explanatory Notes and Remarks on Milton's "Paradise Lost"* (1734), p. clxxvii [*Editor*].
8. P. 29.

There one can notice the precision which the word 'integrity' still had. For Milton it really does mean completeness, unity, wholeness—just as the world *whole* has the same root as the word holy. 'Our integritie': it is that innocent unity which Eve breaks when she wilfully withdraws her hand from her husband's. In the same way, when Satan corrupts the angels in Heaven, Milton brings out the full force of integrity by setting it against 'ambiguous': Satan

> casts between
> Ambiguous words and jealousies, to sound
> Or taint integritie . . . (V. 699–701)

Such mastery of the context does more than anything else can to invigorate language while still preserving decorum.

The inspiration of words that would otherwise be half-dead is inseparable from Milton's famous liking for using words with their original Latin meaning. Of course one must first put aside those 'Latinisms' which are no more than completely normal seventeenth-century English (say, *admire* as 'wonder at'); and then concentrate on what seem acts of choice by Milton. Sometimes a Miltonic usage may be of extreme rarity; and the question is simple. At other times, his deviation may be slight; but one should not put aside as critically irrelevant those moments when he seems to prefer what was apparently by then an unusual or a less usual application. Any critic is in danger of finding unique beauty in what was a casual or common usage; but any linguist is in danger of implying that in the past everybody wrote equally well.

Milton's Latinate usages are curiously open both to Mark Pattison's irrelevant praise (reading Milton as 'the last reward of consummated scholarship'), and to Dr. Leavis's equally irrelevant blame ('a callousness to the intrinsic nature of English'). Everything depends, as usual, on the particular case; on whether there is anything gained, in terms of meaning as well as sound, by his choosing to be Latinate. Is he simply being pedantic? Landor commented darkly, 'He soon begins to give the learned and less obvious signification to English words'.[9]

The extra meaning which Milton finds comes clearly from the fact that he does not discard the English meaning. As Raleigh said, 'He was not content to revive the exact classical meaning in place of the vague or weak English acceptation; he often kept both senses, and loaded the word with two meanings at once.'[1] What we have is not a pompous substitution, or an antiquarian delight in a remoter meaning, but an addition to the meaning, sometimes one of emphasis, sometimes one of refinement. Such Anglo-Latinisms are not the property of Milton alone, and often they are simple enough. So every schoolboy knows

9. *Works*, ed. Welby, v. 238.
1. [Walter Raleigh,] *Milton*, p. 209.

that when Satan falls 'With hideous ruine and combustion down' (I. 46), *ruine* includes the literal falling of the Latin. Or that when the reed for the gunpowder is described as 'pernicious with one touch to fire' VI. 520), *pernicious* is both 'destructive' and 'swift'.

But the effect can be much subtler. Dr. Davie's point about metaphor was anticipated by Thomas Newton in 1749, in commenting on the moment when Satan and the other devils turn into serpents:

> His Armes clung to his Ribs, his Leggs entwining
> Each other, till *supplanted* down he fell.   (X. 512–13)

'We may observe here', said Newton, 'a singular beauty and elegance in Milton's language, and that is his using words in their strict and litteral sense, which are commonly apply'd to a metaphorical meaning, whereby he gives peculiar force to his expressions, and the litteral meaning appears more new and striking than the metaphor itself. We have an instance of this in the world *supplanted*, which is deriv'd from the Latin *supplanto*, to trip up one's heels or overthrow . . . and there are abundance of other examples in several parts of this work, but let is suffice to have taken notice of it here once and for all.'[2]

This is a very fine critical comment, but it is perhaps not explicit enough as to why Milton here uses *supplanted* with its physical meaning. The applied moral meaning is in the background, and provides the grim irony with which Satan is always seen—Satan, on whom always evil 'recoils', on whose head revenge 'redounds'. Satan is the great supplanter: 'He set upon our fyrst parentes in paradyse, and by pride supplanted them' (More, 1522).[3] In *Paradise Regained* (IV. 607), too, the word itself reminds us of this. So 'supplanted' here is a succinct and telling comment on the reason for Satan's being overthrown (hoist with his own petard), at the very same moment as it tells us that he *was* overthrown:

> Immediate are the Acts of God, more swift
> Then time or motion, but to human ears
> Cannot without process of speech be told.   (VII. 17–68)

Milton's process of speech is so compact that it can even reflect divine immediacy, the divine moment that instantaneously judges crime *and* punishment. Milton's phrase has what Raphael, in an excellent phrase, called 'Speed almost Spiritual'.

An equally acute comment by Newton (expanding a note by Hume)

2. ii. 252. Compare Arnold Stein on the release of the original metaphor in 'By Haralds voice *explain'd*'. 'Compared with the more primitive meaning, the derived meaning tends to be abstract, the accepted equivalent of the familiar result or even process of an action, but with no physical or imaginative sense of the very happening of that process' (*Answerable Style*, p. 147).
3. *O.E.D.* 2: 'To cause to fall', from 1340. It also cites *c.* 1610, *Women Saints*: 'The divell envying these her vertuous studies, thought to supplant her.'

brings home that Milton's reaching down to the roots is certainly not limited to Latinisms. During the council in Hell, Beelzebub yearns to destroy God's

> whole Creation, or possess
> All as our own, and drive as we were driven,
> The punie habitants. (II. 365–67)

Hume's gloss ran: 'The weak infirm Possessors, the late made Inmates of this new World: *Puisné*, born since, created long since us, Angelick Beings boasting Eternity.'[4] And Newton developed the point: 'It is possible that the author by *puny* might mean no more than weak or little; but yet if we reflect how frequently he uses words in their proper and primary signification, it seems probable that he might include likewise the sense of the French (from whence it is deriv'd) *puis né*, born since, created long after us.'[5] Again it is only a matter of making more explicit the double meaning which Hume and Newton so admirably fasten on. That Man was 'born since' the fallen angels is precisely the great reason why they hate him. The hatred and its cause were clear enough from the way in which Beelzebub introduced the subject of Man in this same speech:

> some new Race call'd Man, about this time
> To be created like to us, though less
> In power and excellence, but favour'd more
> Of him who rules above. (II. 348–51)

The mixture of envy and contempt comes out in the bitter placing of 'less' and 'more'. And the same feelings stir Satan to cry out against

> this new Favorite
> Of Heav'n, this Man of Clay, Son of despite,
> Whom us the more to spite his Maker rais'd
> From dust: spite then with spite is best repaid. (IX. 175–78)

That men are 'the punie habitants', then, superbly compresses Beelzebub's contemptuous reasons for hating them (new favourites) *and* his reasons for revenge: they are weak. To the fallen angels, men are weak just because they are a sort of divine afterthought, a poor attempt, to make up the numbers in Heaven. The comment of Hume and Newton on this one word radiates into the whole of the poem—a mark of good criticism and of a great poem.

* * *

4. P. 65.
5. [Thomas Newton, ed. *Paradise Lost* (1749),] i. 105. The survival of the form 'puisne' make a ready awareness of the derivation of *puny* likely. Moreover, the seventeenth-century sense of 'junior' will have pointed towards Milton's usage.

[*Simile and Cross-Reference*]

* * *

Macaulay has an excellent commentary on the Miltonic style: 'The most striking characteristic of the poetry of Milton is the extreme remoteness of the associations by means of which it acts on the reader. Its effect is produced, not so much by what it expresses, as by what it suggests; not so much by the ideas which it directly conveys, as by other ideas which are connected with them. He electrifies the mind through conductors.'

This is certainly to the point. But unfortunately the examples of the principle at work which Macaulay offered reduce the process to a kind of divine wool-gathering. Of the allusions, for instance, he says: 'A third [name] evokes all the dear classical recollections of childhood, the schoolroom, the dog-eared Virgil, the holiday, and the prize.'[6] This may pass as autobiography, but not as criticism of Milton. To understand the particular moments when Milton 'electrifies the mind through conductors', we do better to turn to the eighteenth century.

It was clear to Richardson that Milton's allusions often merited close and imaginative examination. For one thing, it was Richardson's general belief that 'he Expresses himself So Concisely, Employs Words So Sparingly, that whoever will Possess His Ideas must Dig for them, and Oftentimes pretty far below the Surface.'[7] And Richardson was able to put the principle to work in the service of subtle examples. As when the corner of Eden cultivated by Eve is compared to three famous gardens:

> Spot more delicious then those Gardens feign'd
> Or of reviv'd Adonis, or renowned
> Alcinous, host of old Laertes Son,
> Or that, not Mystic, where the Sapient King
> Held dalliance with his faire Egyptian Spouse.   (IX. 439–43)

Richardson fastened on *Adonis*: 'The Circumstance of these Gardens of *Adonis* being to Last but a very little while, which even became a Proverb among the Ancients, adds a very Pathetick propriety to the Simile: Still More, as that 'tis not the Whole Garden of *Eden* which is Now spoken of, but that *One Delicious Spot* where *Eve* was, This *Flowrie Plat* and This was of her Own Hand, as those Gardens of *Adonis* were always of the Hands of those *Lovely Damsels*, Less Lovely yet than She.'[8]

This is finely said. Yet the most important of the gardens is the last: that which, not mythical, refers to Solomon and Pharaoh's daughter. Its main purpose is to invoke the beauties of that garden—yet this seems to be very perfunctorily performed, since there is not a word of description. If the beauty of the garden were the sole reason for the allusion,

6. *Literary and Historical Essays* (1934), pp. 9–11.
7. p. cxliv.
8. p. 416.

we might be tempted to think that here is epic allusion of the rather empty kind—Milton finding it easier to refer than to create.

But it is significant that the passage which moved Bentley to just such a protest should be the comparison of Paradise and the field of Enna: 'And then, in stead of painting out their several Beauties, as a Pretense for their rivaling Paradise; you give us their bare Names, with some fabulous Story to them, not denoting at all any Beauty.'[9] The answer to this is Mr. Lewis's observation that the real point of the comparison is that Eve is like Proserpin. And there is the same 'subterranean virtue' in the mention of Solomon's garden. The allusion includes more than beauty: it recalls how a man of great wisdom showed his famous inability to resist a woman. Solomon is a type of Adam, and the allusion has the oblique but powerful purpose of predicting the Fall.

Solomon was traditionally linked with Adam—as at the end of *Sir Gawain and the Green Knight*. Indeed, in Milton's Trinity College manuscripts, one of the entries in the list of subjects for tragedy refers to 'Salomon Gynæcocratomenus', Solomon Woman-governed. Moreover, the account of the heathen gods includes an emphatic mention of

> that uxorious King, whose heart though large,
> Beguil'd by fair Idolatresses, fell
> To Idols foul. (I. 444–46)

Here the aptness to the Fall hardly needs underlining. 'Solomon is "Beguil'd by fair Idolatresses" just as Adam will be by Eve.'[1] Adam, too, was large of heart but uxorious; and he reproaches Eve for beguiling him:

> with the Serpent meeting
> Fool'd and beguil'd, by him thou, I by thee. (X. 879–80)

And Eve is a fair idolatress; after her fall,

> from the Tree her step she turnd,
> But first low Reverence don, as to the power
> That dwelt within. (IX. 834–36)

If the allusion to Solomon in Book I does not reflect on Adam, then there are a strange number of coincidences. That the allusion in Book IX is linked with the earlier one is suggested by the fact that a reference to Adonis follows 'that uxorious King' just as it precedes 'the Sapient King'.

More support can be found in *Paradise Regain'd*. There Satan dismisses the idea of setting women in Christ's eye, not (as one might expect) because the second Adam is stronger than the first, but because

9. [Richard Bentley, ed., *Paradise Lost* (1732).] p. 115 (misnumbered 215).
1. [John] Peter, A *Critique of P.L.*, p. 37.

he is stronger than Solomon. 'Women, when nothing else, beguil'd the heart/Of wisest Solomon'; but 'Solomon he liv'd at ease', and 'he whom we attempt is wiser far/Then Solomon'.[2]

But the verbal points are crucial. 'The Sapient King held dalliance with his faire Egyptian Spouse': twice, Eve is 'his fair Spouse'.[3] Much more importantly, neither *Sapient* nor *dalliance* is a common word, and their recurrence together after the Fall (in this same Book) would be a most remarkable coincidence:

> in Lust they burne:
> Till Adam thus 'gan Eve to dalliance move.
> Eve, now I see thou art exact of taste,
> And elegant, of Sapience no small part . . .   (IX. 1015–18)

At which Adam unfolds the importance of *taste* and *sapience*, combining as they do the two great themes of the poem, knowledge gained by tasting (the Latin *sapere*):

> of Sapience no small part,
> Since to each meaning savour we apply,
> And Palate call judicious . . .

Indeed Eve herself had seen sapience as the great quality of the fruit she had just tasted:

> O Sovran, vertuous, precious of all Trees
> In Paradise, of operation blest
> To Sapience.   (IX. 795–97)

The allusion to Solomon, then, ominously and beautifully hints at the Fall. But in that case what of the single-line sentence which follows? It is apparently usually taken as returning us to the serpent watching Eve.[4] But it is also strangely and brilliantly apt *within* the allusion:

> where the Sapient King
> Held dalliance with his faire Egyptian Spouse.
> *Much hee the Place admir'd, the Person more.*
> As one who long in populous City pent . . .

Is it merely a coincidence that the line is so apt to Solomon and to Adam? That indeed it provides so terse a summary of the whole poem? Adam was struck with wonder by paradise, 'this happie place'. But he was even more struck by Eve. It is not until the closing lines of the poem that we see the true balancing of person and place, in Eve's moving penitence:

2. *P.R.*, II. 169–70, 201, 205–6.
3. IV. 742; v. 129.
4. Editors are silent, but James Paterson in 1744 paraphrased it: '*He*, i.e. *Satan*, admired *Paradise*, but much more *Eve*' (*A Commentary on P.L.*, p. 393).

> thou to mee
> Art all things under Heav'n, all places thou.   (XII. 617–18)

It is interesting, but no more, that Christopher Pitt's reminiscence of
the line should concern Dido and Aeneas, and so be more apt to Sol-
omon than to the serpent:

> Charm'd with his Presence, Dido gaz'd him o'er,
> Admir'd his Fortune much, his Person more.[5]

More relevant is the fact that Adam's sin is twice seen as a matter of
too *much admiring* Eve. Raphael, in a very important speech, rebukes
him for

> attributing overmuch to things
> Less excellent, as thou thy self perceav'st.
> For what admir'st thou, what transports thee so,
> An outside? fair no doubt . . .   (VIII. 565–68)

The conjunction of *much* and *admire* is closer when after the Fall Adam
admits that

> I also err'd in overmuch admiring
> What seemd in thee so perfet.   (IX. 1178–79)

But there is another way of getting at whether or not it is completely
satisfactory to take 'Much hee the Place admir'd, the Person more' as
going simply with the lines that follow it. Does Milton ever begin a new
sequence of thought with a single-line sentence? Or, more strictly, does
he ever use a single-line sentence entirely detached from what precedes
it?

Such sentences are rare and emphatic in Milton, because they so
obviously conflict with his basic principle of 'the sense variously drawn
out from one Verse into another'. And, as far as I can see, he never
uses such a sentence without some continuity with the previous lines.[6]

In other words, if we take this line as simply and solely returning us
to the serpent, we are postulating not only a very harsh break (in the

5. *An Essay on Virgil's Aeneid, Being a Translation of the First Book* (1728), p. 49.
6. Single-line questions, such as 'Who first seduc'd them to that foul revolt?', are not relevant
—in any case they come naturally in a current train of thought, rather than as the start of a
new one. Nor are the single-line stage-directions relevant ('Whereto with speedy words th'
Archfiend reply'd'). But they too never show a complete break with the previous lines. The
continuity is always provided by words like 'whereto', 'to whom', or 'whom thus'. There
remain, then, the comparable single-line sentences. Not counting the line under discussion,
there seem to be thirteen in *Paradise Lost*. In no case is one of them completely detached
from the previous lines. Seven of them, on the contrary, are used to end a speech: 'Awake,
arise, or be for ever fall'n' (I. 330. Also III. 735; IX. 566, 732; XI. 180, 633, 835). Three of
them are embedded in the continuing argument: 'This was that caution giv'n thee; be advis'd'
(V. 523. Also VIII. 490; X. 54). Two show the reciprocation of dialogue—a very different
thing from what would be postulated here Eve 'thus abasht repli'd. / The Serpent me beguil'd
and I did eate' (X. 162). And: 'I yield it just, said Adam, and submit' (XI. 526). The remaining
one of the thirteen sentences does, admittedly, begin a new narrative phase, but without
snapping the continuity: 'So all was cleard, and to the Field they haste' (V. 136).

work of a poet who is a master of transitions), but also a unique usage of the single-line sentence. Not only is the line extremely apt within the allusion, but Milton's practice would suggest that it belongs there.

Does this mean that the line *cannot* refer to the serpent? It is certainly very apt there too; it fits exactly both with the following simile and narrative, and the fact that it is so often read as belonging to the serpent means that one should not lightly transfer it. In fact, the reasons for treating the line as *within* the allusion are powerful, and so are the more obvious reasons for treating it as outside.

But Milton is a master of syntactical fluidity. He achieves some of his finest effects precisely by leaving it possible for a word or a clause to look backward or forward. And what Mr. Prince says of the rhyme-scheme in *Lycidas* could well be applied to Miltonic syntax: 'The rhetoric of rhyme derived from the *canzone* has thus provided Milton with an invaluable instrument—a type of rhyme which looks both back and forward.' The six-syllable lines 'not only always rhyme with a previous longer line (thus looking back), but they give the impression of a con-tracted movement which must be compensated by a full movement in the next line (which is always of full length), and they thus look forward. This effect is most marked when, as in most cases, these short lines rhyme with the line immediately preceding them.'[7]

It is at any rate possible that this line is Milton's masterpiece of syntactical fluidity. It stands as a self-contained sentence between two sentences each ten lines long; and it acts as a hinge, with a hinge's property of belonging to both sides, to the preceding allusion and to the following narrative:

> Nature that hateth emptiness,
> Allows of penetration less.

But this would be a supreme feat of penetration, in which two sentences occupy exactly the same space. If this is so—and one should say no more, and no less, than that it may be—then the only way of unfolding the syntax would be to say the line twice:

> Or that, not Mystic, where the Sapient King
> Held dalliance with his faire Egyptian Spouse.
> (Much hee the Place admir'd, the Person more.)
> Much hee the Place admir'd, the Person more.
> As one who long in populous City pent . . .

*   *   *

Since the use of these cross-connexions has been well studied recently, I want to comment on only one such image, in an attempt to show that this kind of allusion can radically alter our attitude even to passages

7. *The Italian Element*, pp. 86–87.

usually thought of as laughably bad. Adam and Eve's gardening has often been laughed at; Dr. Tillyard, who calls their work 'ridiculous', has said that 'Adam and Eve are in the hopeless position of Old Age Pensioners enjoying perpetual youth'.[8] At the very least, the gardening is usually thought of as an intractable corner of the myth that Milton could do no more than tidy up.

Certainly he is bound to be involved in many difficulties when he has to show the nature of labor before the Fall. I can think of only one really successful treatment of the paradox, the closing lines of Marvell's 'Bermudas'. The Bermudas were traditionally thought of as Paradise—as Waller said,

> Heaven sure has kept this spot of earth uncursed,
> To show how all things were created first.[9]

Marvell's poem describes this Paradise, ending with a brilliantly un-obtrusive insight into labor before the Fall:

> Thus sung they, in the *English* boat,
> An holy and a chearful Note,
> And all the way, to guide their Chime,
> With falling Oars they kept the time.

In fact, the point is made so unobtrusively that some readers never seem to notice it at all; without any nudge, Marvell tells us that they *rowed* in order to keep time in their song—not, as we would expect in this fallen world, that they sang in order to keep time in their rowing. Before the Fall, man worked simply in order to praise God with 'an holy and a chearful Note'—now life is the other way round. It is a brilliant poetic summing-up of the paradox of prelapsarian labor.

It would be foolish to argue that Milton achieves anything like the same success with Adam and Eve's gardening; but he faces very different problems from Marvell. Marvell could rely on a moment of poetic intuition; but Milton is writing a long narrative poem, and the problem cannot be seized once and for all. Yet to me the gardening is far from ridiculous if we are fully aware of what Milton is saying.

This is a case where it is essential to consider, not the separable problem, but the actual words in which Milton presents it. And just as in alluding to the field of Enna, the real focus of the allusion was not on the beauty of the field but on the drama of Eve and Satan, so the gardening is not primarily a matter of horticulture, but is at every point enmeshed with the imminent tragedy.

8. *Milton* (1930), p. 282.
9. *The Battle of the Summer Islands*, Canto I.

Let me take Eve's first speech to Adam when she suggests going off
on her own:

> Adam, well may we labour still to dress
> This Garden, still to tend Plant, Herb and Flour,
> Our pleasant task enjoy'nd, but till more hands
> Aid us, the work under our labour grows,
> Luxurious by restraint; what we by day
> Lop overgrown, or prune, or prop, or bind,
> One night or two with wanton growth derides
> Tending to wilde. Thou therefore now advise
> Or hear what to my mind first thoughts present,
> Let us divide our labours, thou where choice
> Leads thee, or where most needs, whether to wind
> The Woodbine round this Arbour, or direct
> The clasping Ivie where to climb, while I
> In yonder Spring of Roses intermixt
> With Myrtle, find what to redress till Noon:
> For while so near each other thus all day
> Our task we choose, what wonder if so near
> Looks intervene and smiles, or object new
> Casual discourse draw on, which intermits
> Our dayes work brought to little, though begun
> Early, and th' hour of Supper comes unearn'd. (IX. 205–25)

First, a brief mention of the psychological acuteness here. There is
the grave presentation of Eve's self-will, still disguised by words about
Adam's superior wisdom and authority (words that do not pause):

> Thou therefore now advise
> Or hear what to my mind first thoughts present . . .

And subtly making the same point is the contrast between the prolif-
eration of choice for Adam and the direct decision for herself; she doesn't
care what he does, and she knows very well what she will do. After all,
there follow more than a hundred and fifty lines of argument between
them; then she leaves; and when we, and the serpent, next see her, it
is exactly where she had insisted she was going when she first mentioned
the subject: in the thicket of roses tying up the flowers with myrtle.

But my present concern is not with deft psychology, but with the
emblematic correspondences between the gardening and the Fall. The
work, says Eve, 'under our labour grows,/Luxurious by restraint'. *Lux-
urious* is before the Fall a harmless horticultural word, but its fallen
meaning jostles against it here; luxury is not only one of the most
important results of the Fall, it is the first ('in Lust they burne'). And
'luxurious *by restraint*' is also grim with anticipation. Milton at the very
beginning of his poem had called on his muse to

> say first what cause
> Mov'd our Grand Parents in that happy State,
> Favour'd of Heav'n so highly, to fall off
> From their Creator, and transgress his Will
> *For one restraint*, Lords of the World besides? (I. 28–32)

Eve's obstinacy is to lead very soon to the Fall, since abandoning the one restraint means abandoning all restraints: 'Greedily she ingorg'd without restraint' (IX. 791).

So that we should be prepared for her words to Adam to tighten from detail to sombre generality:

> what we by day
> Lop overgrown, or prune, or prop, or bind,
> One night or two with wanton growth derides
> Tending to wilde.

'Wanton' begins etymologically as 'undisciplined, disobedient', and ends as 'lustful', so that it compresses the reason for the Fall and the immediate effects of it. Then to describe the garden as 'tending to wilde' finely thrusts home the point. Not that Eve can shuffle off her responsibility, and claim that sin was a natural tendency.[1] But with Eve in it, the garden will certainly tend to wild; so that Adam cries out when he hears that she has fallen—her sin and the thought of losing her shatter the leaves:

> How can I live without thee, how forgoe
> Thy sweet Converse and Love so dearly joyn'd,
> To live again in these wilde Woods forlorn? (IX. 908–10)

There is a similarly subtle hint in the word *redress*: 'find what to redress till Noon'. This is a technical application, to horticulture, of the ancient meaning: 'To set a person or thing upright again; to raise again to an erect position '[2] But it seems improbable that Milton is unaware of the moral resonance in the word—its moral meaning is also ancient, and found in Chaucer. Eve may believe that she is going to set the plants upright and erect. In fact, she 'her self, though fairest unsupported Flour', will be 'drooping unsustained'. It is a bitter irony that seizes on the word 'redress'.

The poet turns the notes to tragic, too, when Eve says that if she stays near Adam, some *object new* may

> Casual discourse draw on, which intermits
> Our dayes work brought to little.

1. Mrs. I. G. MacCaffrey: 'the wilderness is there, waiting to encroach at the slightest neglect' (*P.L. as 'Myth'*, p. 154).
2. *O.E.D.* I, from Chaucer on. Examples include the horticultural application—one from Sylvester's Du Bartas.

What in fact is the 'object new' on this fatal day? What but the snake? For as Adam says,

> Reason not impossibly may meet
> Some specious object by the Foe subornd. (IX. 360–61)

And the snake draws on, not casual discourse, but the most pregnant conversation in the history of mankind. There is grim irony, almost parody even, in the echo of God's instructions to Raphael to warn Adam:

> such discourse bring on,
> As may advise him of his happie state,
> Happiness in his power left free to will . . . (V. 233–35)

Casual, moreover, means not only 'which befalls', but also 'which falls', as Milton shows elsewhere in the poem.[3] And the discourse certainly will have *brought* their *day's work to little*.

What is essential, then, is to insist on the huge web of anticipation and echo. So that when Adam in his reply says

> for nothing lovelier can be found
> In woman, then to studie houshold good,
> And good workes in her Husband to promote,

the appropriate comment is not biographical, that Milton is showing his usual 'Turkish contempt of females', but critical—that Adam speaks unwittingly to an Eve who is not exactly going to study household *good*, and who is about to promote in her husband not good works, but the first act of evil.

Milton's demands are very great, and the most important of all is that we should know his poem well enough to be able to see when a phrase, a line, or a moment is touched by tinctures or reflections. His sublimities are superbly direct, but his subtleties depend on our receiving not only the delicacies of simile and allusion, but also those of allusion within the poem itself.

As Milton's earliest commentators saw, his Grand Style is as remarkable for its accurate delicacy as for its power. MIltonic criticism since then, whether hostile or friendly, has tended to dwell most on its power; so that the case for the other virtues has often gone by default. One of the main points to make is that there is more than one 'traditional' way of reading Milton, and that Mr. Empson's choice of the eighteenth-century editors was not capricious or peripheral. Not that the Victorian tradition is wrong. It points to something very important in Milton, but with a dangerously exclusive gesture. His earliest editors were open to more various powers.

But isn't there also something dangerously exclusive in concentrating

---

3. XI. 562, where 'casual fire' is lightning.

on Milton's *style* alone? Surely there can be no satisfactory divorce of style from content? In general terms one might reply that for any critical argument to get off the ground, one must reluctantly select from the poem. But certainly the points about the Grand Style ought now to be related briefly to the poem itself.

It seems to me that there is a very close analogy between the successes of the style and the wider successes of the poem. The more closely one looks at the style, the clearer it seems that Milton writes at his very best only when something prevents him from writing with total directness. And the same is true of what is good or bad in *Paradise Lost* in other terms.

Milton's Grand Style is delicately suggestive, very much more flexible or supple than is sometimes thought. To Milton, a man of great conviction, great energy, and great emotion, the danger was of being too direct, of stunning or bludgeoning us. But as Richardson insisted, Milton's felicities 'when they Awaken the Mind, do it not with a Sudden Crash, but as with Musick; if they Surprize, they don't Startle Us'.[4] Naturally we are in favour of a poet's words having 'masculine persuasive force'—but masculinity is not enough. At its very best, Milton's style is remarkable for its simultaneous combination of what is energetically strong with what is winning soft and amiably mild. It is this which undoes Mr. Eliot's comparison of Milton's style with Henry James's, since indirectness is to James the congenial excess which directness is to Milton. How often we wish that Milton would not affirm too directly and powerfully. And how often we long for an affirmation of some kind from James.

This is not to say that either in style or in content Milton is never successful in directness. But as a rule it seems that his greatest effects are produced when he is compelled to be oblique as well as direct. The analogy with the wider successes of the poem is clear. For example, it seems to me that there are two descriptions of Paradise which soar above all Milton's other accounts of it; and what they have in common is that neither directly confronts Paradise. The first begins:

> Not that faire field
> Of Enna, where Proserpin gathring flours
> Her self a fairer Floure by gloomie Dis
> Was gatherd . . . (IV. 268–71)

It is, I believe, the very fact that Milton's gaze is *not* directly on Paradise which makes these lines among the most haunting he ever wrote. And the *not* of 'Not that faire field . . .' is itself an opportunity for Milton to release his full feelings while still gaining all the advantages of the oblique. It seems to me similarly remarkable that if asked to point to the most moving account of Eve in the poem, it is once again these

4. P. cli.

lines that I would quote. Eve is never more powerfully and tragically herself than when Milton glimpses her as Proserpin. Mr. Empson, in the notes to one of his poems, points out that 'a star just too faint to be seen directly can still be seen out of the corners of your eyes'; and his poem itself emphasizes the limited reach of 'the stoutest heart's best direct yell', while at the same time wryly defining the right kind of indirection:

> the spry arts
> Can keep a steady hold on the controls
> By seeming to evade.

The other outstanding description of Paradise seems to me this:

> then shall this Mount
> Of Paradise by might of Waves be moovd
> Out of his place, pushd by the horned floud,
> With all his verdure spoil'd, and Trees adrift
> Down the great River to the op'ning Gulf,
> And there take root an Iland salt and bare,
> The haunt of Seales and Orcs, and Sea-mews clang.
>
> (XI. 825–31)

Nowhere else in the poem, not even at the magnificent moments when Milton lavishes his full luxuriance on the Garden, do we so yearn for Paradise. And of all Milton's touching oxymorons, perhaps the greatest is the title of his epic.

The finest successes of the poem in larger terms all seem to me to have been created when total directness was impossible. Hell is more memorable than Heaven, because Hell resists directness. Not that it gets out of hand, or that Milton is lax with it; merely that, at any rate in the first two books, its inhabitants are irreducible. Pandæmonium is both beautiful and desperate. In the content of the poem, as well as in its style, Milton is at his best when his directness is at one with indirections. The vibrant understanding which we occasionally feel when we see Satan or Adam and Eve is due to the fact that here Milton is grappling with things that strength alone will not be able to open, things that need delicacy too. A balance that is not precarious and is the result of a strength manifesting itself in innumerable tiny, significant, internal movements—this is the balance of Milton's Grand Style.

HAROLD BLOOM

Milton and His Precursors†

No poet compares to Milton in his intensity of self-consciousness as an artist and in his ability to overcome all negative consequences of such concern. Milton's highly deliberate and knowingly ambitious program necessarily involved him in direct competition with Homer, Virgil, Lucretius, Ovid, Dante and Tasso, among other major precursors. More anxiously, it brought him very close to Spenser, whose actual influence on *Paradise Lost* is deeper, subtler and more extensive than scholarship so far has recognized. Most anxiously, the ultimate ambitions of *Paradise Lost* gave Milton the problem of expanding Scripture without distorting the Word of God.

A reader, thinking of Milton's style, is very likely to recognize that style's most distinctive characteristic as being the density of its allusiveness. Perhaps only Gray compares to Milton in this regard, and Gray is only a footnote, though an important and valuable one, to the Miltonic splendor. Milton's allusiveness has a distinct design, which is to enhance both the quality and the extent of his inventiveness. His handling of allusion is his highly individual and original defense against poetic tradition, his revisionary stance in writing what is in effect a tertiary epic, following after Homer in primary epic and Virgil, Ovid and Dante in secondary epic. Most vitally, Miltonic allusion is the crucial revisionary ratio by which *Paradise Lost* distances itself from its most dangerous precursor, *The Faerie Queene*, for Spenser had achieved a national romance, of epic greatness, in the vernacular, and in the service of moral and theological beliefs not far from Milton's own.

The map of misprision charted in Chapter 5 moved between the poles of *illusio*—irony as a figure of speech, or the reaction-formation I have termed *clinamen*—and allusion, particularly as the scheme of transumption or metaleptic reversal that I have named *apophrades* and analogized to the defenses of introjection and projection. As the common root of their names indicates, *illusio* and allusion are curiously related, both being a kind of mockery, rather in the sense intended by the title of Geoffrey Hill's poem on Campanella, that "Men are a mockery of Angels." The history of "allusion" as an English word goes from an initial meaning of "illusion" on to an early Renaissance use as meaning a pun, or word-play in general. But by the time of Bacon it meant any symbolic likening, whether in allegory, parable or metaphor, as when in *The Advancement of Learning* poetry is divided into "narrative, rep-

† From *A Map of Misreading* by Harold Bloom. Copyright © 1975 by Oxford University Press, Inc. Reprinted by permission.

resentative, and allusive." A fourth meaning, which is still the correct modern one, follows rapidly by the very early seventeenth century, and involves any implied, indirect or hidden reference. The fifth meaning, still incorrect but bound to establish itself, now equates allusion with direct, overt reference. Since the root meaning is "to play with, mock, jest at," allusion is uneasily allied to words like "ludicrous" and "elusion," as we will remember later.

Thomas McFarland, formidably defending Coleridge against endlessly repetitive charges of plagiarism, has suggested that "plagiarism" ought to be added as a seventh revisionary ratio. Allusion is a comprehensive enough ratio to contain "plagiarism" also under the heading of *apophrades*, which the Lurianic Kabbalists called *gilgul*, as I explained in the Introduction. Allusion as covert reference became in Milton's control the most powerful and successful figuration that any strong poet has ever employed against his strong precursors.

Milton, who would not sunder spirit from matter, would not let himself be a receiver, object to a subject's influencings. His stance against dualism and influence alike is related to his exaltation of unfallen *pleasure*, his appeal not so much to his reader's senses as to his reader's yearning for the expanded senses of Eden. Precisely here is the center of Milton's own influence upon the Romantics, and here also is why he surpassed them in greatness, since what he could do for himself was the cause of their becoming unable to do the same for themselves. His achievement became at once their starting point, their inspiration, yet also their goad, their torment.

Yet he too had his starting point: Spenser. Spenser was "the soothest shepherd that e'er piped on plains," "sage and serious." "Milton has acknowledged to me, that Spenser was his original," Dryden testified, but the paternity required no acknowledgment. A darker acknowledgment can be read in Milton's astonishing mistake about Spenser[1] in *Areopagitica*, written more than twenty years before *Paradise Lost* was completed:

> . . . It was from out the rind of one apple tasted, that the knowledge of good and evil, as two twins cleaving together, leaped forth into the world. And perhaps this is that doom which Adam fell into of knowing good and evil, that is to say of knowing good by evil. As therefore the state of man is, what wisdom can there be to choose, what continence to forbear, without the knowledge of evil? He that can apprehend and consider vice with all her baits and seeming pleasures, and yet abstain, and yet distinguish, and yet prefer that which is truly better, he is the true warfaring Christian. I cannot praise a

---

1. See Ernest Sirluck, "Milton Revises *The Faerie Queene*," *Modern Philology*, XLVIII (1950), pp. 90–96 [*Editor*].

fugitive and cloistered virtue, unexercised and unbreathed, that never sallies out and sees her adversary, but slinks out of the race, where that immortal garland is to be run for, not without dust and heat. Assuredly we bring not innocence into the world, we bring impurity much rather; that which purifies us is trial, and trial is by what is contrary. That virtue therefore which is but a youngling in the contemplation of evil, and knows not the utmost that vice promises to her followers, and rejects it, is but a blank virtue, not a pure; her whiteness is but an excremental whiteness; which was the reason why our sage and serious poet Spenser, whom I dare be known to think a better teacher than Scotus or Aquinas, describing true temperance under the person of Guyon, brings him in with his palmer through the cave of Mammon, and the bower of earthly bliss, that he might see and know, and yet abstain. . . .

Spenser's cave of Mammon is Milton's Hell; far more than the descents to the underworld of Homer and Virgil, more even than Dante's vision, the prefigurement of Books I and II of *Paradise Lost* reverberates in Book II of *The Faerie Queene*. Against Acrasia's bower, Guyon enjoys the moral guidance of his unfaltering Palmer, but necessarily in Mammon's cave Guyon has to be wholly on his own, even as Adam and Eve must withstand temptation in the absence of the affable Raphael. Guyon stands, though at some cost; Adam and Eve fall, but both the endurance and the failure are independent. Milton's is no ordinary error, no mere lapse in memory, but is itself a powerful misinterpretation of Spenser, and a strong defense against him. For Guyon is not so much Adam's precursor as he is Milton's own, the giant model imitated by the Abdiel of *Paradise Lost*. Milton re-writes Spenser so as to *increase the distance* between his poetic father and himself. St. Augustine identified memory with the father, and we may surmise that a lapse in a memory as preternatural as Milton's is a movement against the father.

Milton's full relation to Spenser is too complex and hidden for any rapid description or analysis to suffice, even for my limited purposes in this book. Here I will venture that Milton's transumptive stance in regard to all his precursors, including Spenser, is founded on Spenser's re sourceful and bewildering (even Joycean) way of subsuming his precursors, particularly Virgil, through his labyrinthine syncretism. Spenserian allusiveness has been described by Angus Fletcher as collage: "Collage is parody drawing attention to the *materials* of art and life." Fletcher follows Harry Berger's description of the technique of *conspicuous allusion* in Spenser: "the depiction of stock literary motifs, characters, and genres in a manner which emphasizes their conventionality, displaying at once their debt to and their existence in a conventional climate— Classical, medieval, romance, etc.—which is archaic when seen from

Spenser's retrospective viewpoint." This allusive collage or conspicu-
ousness is readily assimilated to Spenser's peculiarly metamorphic ele-
giacism, which becomes the particular legacy of Spenser to all his poetic
descendants, from Drayton and Milton down to Yeats and Stevens. For
Spenser began that internalization of quest-romance that is or became
what we call Romanticism. It is the Colin Clout of Spenser's Book VI
who is the father of Milton's *Il Penseroso*, and from Milton's visionary
stem the later Spenserian transformations of Wordsworth's Solitary, and
all of the Solitary's children in the wanderers of Keats, Shelley, Brown-
ing, Tennyson and Yeats until the parodistic climax in Stevens' co-
median Crispin. Fletcher, in his study of Spenser, *The Prophetic
Moment*, charts this genealogy of introspection, stressing the intervention
of Shakespeare between Spenser and Milton, since from Shakespeare
Milton learned to contain the Spenserian elegiacism or "prophetic strain"
within what Fletcher calls "transcendental forms." In his study of *Comus*
as such a form, *The Transcendental Masque*, Fletcher emphasizes the
"enclosed vastness' in which Milton, like Shakespeare, allows reverber-
ations of the Spenserian resonance, a poetic diction richly dependent
on allusive echoings of precursors. *Comus* abounds in *apophrades*, the
return of many poets dead and gone, with Spenser and Shakespeare
especially prominent among them. Following Berger and Fletcher, I
would call the allusiveness of *Comus* still "conspicuous" and so still
Spenserian, still part of the principle of echo. But, with *Paradise Lost*,
Miltonic allusion is transformed into a mode of transumption, and poetic
tradition is radically altered in consequence.

Fletcher, the most daemonic and inventive of modern allegorists, is
again the right guide into the mysteries of *transumptive allusion*, through
one of the brilliant footnotes in his early book, *Allegory: The Theory of
a Symbolic Mode* (p. 241, n. 33). Studying what he calls "difficult
ornament" and the transition to modern allegory, Fletcher meditates on
Johnson's ambivalence towards Milton's style. In his *Life of Milton*,
Johnson observes that "the heat of Milton's mind might be said to
sublimate his learning." Hazlitt, a less ambivalent admirer of Milton,
asserted that Milton's learning had the effect of intuition. Johnson,
though so much more grudging, actually renders the greater homage,
for Johnson's own immense hunger of imagination was overmatched by
Milton's, as he recognized:

> Whatever be his subject, he never fails to fill the imagi-
> nation. But his images and descriptions of the scenes or op-
> erations of Nature do not seem to be always copied from
> original form, nor to have the freshness, raciness, and energy
> of immediate observation. He saw Nature, as Dryden expresses
> it, *through the spectacles of books*; and on most occasions calls
> learning to his assistance. . . .

. . . But he does not confine himself within the limits of
rigorous comparison: his great excellence is amplitude, and
he expands the adventitious image beyond the dimensions
which the occasion required. Thus, comparing the shield of
Satan to the orb of the Moon, he crowds the imagination with
the discovery of the telescope, and all the wonders which the
telescope discovers.

This Johnsonian emphasis upon allusion in Milton inspires Fletcher
to compare Miltonic allusion to the trope of transumption or metalepsis,
Puttenham's "far-fetcher":

Johnson stresses allusion in Milton: "the spectacles of books"
are a means of sublimity, since at every point the reader is led
from one scene to an allusive second scene, to a third, and
so on. Johnson's Milton has, we might say, a "transumptive"
style. . . .

Here is the passage that moved Johnson's observation, *Paradise Lost*,
Book I, 283–313. Beelzebub has urged Satan to address his fallen legions,
who still lie "astounded and amazed" on the lake of fire:

> He scarce had ceas't when the superior Fiend
> Was moving toward the shore; his ponderous shield
> Ethereal temper, massy, large and round,
> Behind him cast; the broad circumference
> Hung on his shoulders like the Moon, whose Orb
> Through Optic Glass the *Tuscan* Artist views
> At Ev'ning from the top of *Fesole*,
> Or in *Valdarno*, to descry new Lands,
> Rivers or Mountains in her spotty Globe.
> His Spear, to equal which the tallest Pine
> Hewn on *Norwegian* hills, to be the Mast
> Of some great Ammiral, were but a wand,
> He walkt with to support uneasy steps
> Over the burning Marl, not like those steps
> On Heaven's Azure, and the torrid Clime
> Smote on him sore besides, vaulted with Fire;
> Nathless he so endur'd, till on the Beach
> Of that inflamed Sea, he stood and call'd
> His Legions, Angel Forms, who lay intrans't
> Thick as Autumnal Leaves that strow the Brooks
> In *Vallombrosa*, where th'*Etrurian* shades
> High overarch't imbow'r; or scatter'd sedge
> Afloat, when with fierce Winds *Orion* arm'd
> Hath vext the Red-Sea Coast, whose waves o'erthrew
> *Busiris* and his *Memphian* Chivalry,
> While with perfidious hatred they pursu'd

> The Sojourners of *Goshen*, who beheld
> From the safe shore thir floating Carcasses
> And broken Chariot Wheels, so thick bestrown
> Abject and lost lay these, covering the Flood,
> Under amazement of thir hideous change.

The transumption of the precursors here is managed by the juxta-position between the far-fetching of Homer, Virgil, Ovid, Dante, Tasso, Spenser, the Bible and the single near-contemporary reference to Gal-ileo, "the Tuscan artist," and his telescope. Milton's aim is to make his own belatedness into an earliness, and his tradition's priority over him into a lateness. The critical question to be asked of this passage is: why is Johnson's "adventitious image," Galileo and the telescope, present at all? Johnson, despite his judgment that the image is extrinsic, implies the right answer: because the expansion of this apparently extrinsic image crowds the reader's imagination, by giving Milton the true priority of *interpretation*, the powerful reading that insists upon its own uniqueness and its own accuracy. Troping upon his forerunners' tropes, Milton compels us to read as he reads, and to accept his stance and vision as our origin, his time as true time. His allusiveness introjects the past, and projects the future, but at the paradoxical cost of the present, which is not voided but is yielded up to an experiential darkness, as we will see, to a mingling of wonder (discovery) and woe (the fallen Church's imprisonment of the discoverer). As Frank Kermode remarks, *Paradise Lost* is a wholly contemporary poem, yet surely its sense of the present is necessarily more of loss than of delight.

Milton's giant simile comparing Satan's shield to the moon alludes to the shield of Archilles in the *Iliad*, XIX, 373–80:

> . . . and caught up the great shield, huge and heavy
> next, and from it the light glimmered far, as from the moon.
> And as when from across water a light shines to mariners
> from a blazing fire, when the fire is burning high in the mountains
> in a desolate standing, as the mariners are carried unwilling
> by storm winds over the fish-swarming sea, far away from their
>   loved ones;
> so the light from the fair elaborate shield of Achilleus
> shot into the high air.
>
> > [Lattimore version]

Milton is glancing also at the shield of Radigund in *The Faerie Queene*, V, v, 3:

> > And on her shoulder hung her shield, bedeckt
> > Upon the bosse with stones, that shined wide,
> > As the faire Moone in her most full aspect,
> > That to the Moone it mote be like in each respect.

Radigund, Princess of the Amazons, is dominated by pride and anger, like Achilles. Satan, excelling both in his bad eminence, is seen accurately through the optic glass of the British artist's transumptive vision, even as Galileo sees what no one before him has seen on the moon's surface. Galileo, when visited by Milton (as he tells us in *Areopagitica*), was working while under house arrest by the Inquisition, a condition not wholly unlike Milton's own in the early days of the Restoration. Homer and Spenser emphasize the moonlike brightness and shining of the shields of Achilles and Radigund; Milton emphasizes size, shape, weight as the common feature of Satan's shield and the moon, for Milton's post-Galilean moon is more of a world and less of a light. Milton and Galileo are *late*, yet they see more, and more significantly, than Homer and Spenser, who were *early*. Milton gives his readers the light, yet also the true dimensions and features of reality, even though Milton, like the Tuscan artist, must work on while compassed around by experiential darkness, in a world of woe.

Milton will not stop with his true vision of Satan's shield, but transumes his precursors also in regard to Satan's spear, and to the fallen-leaves aspect of the Satanic host. Satan's spear evokes passages of Homer, Virgil, Ovid, Tasso and Spenser, allusions transumed by the contemporary reference to a flagship ("ammiral") with its mast made of Norwegian fir. The central allusion is probaby to Ovid's vision of the Golden Age (Golding's version, I, 109–16):

The loftie Pyntree was not hewen from mountaines where it stood,
In seeking straunge and forren landes to rove upon the flood.
Men knew none other countries yet, than where themselves did
    keepe:
There was no towne enclosed yet, with walles and ditches deepe.
No home nor trumpet was in use, no sword nor helmet worne.
The worlde was suche, that souldiers helpe might easly be
    forborne.
The fertile earth as yet was free, untoucht of spade or plough,
And yet it yeelded of it selfe of every things inough.

Ovid's emblem of the passage from Golden Age to Iron Age is reduced to "but a wand," for Satan will more truly cause the fall from Golden to Iron. As earlier Satan subsumed Achilles and Radigund, now he contains and metaleptically reverses the Polyphemus of Homer and of Virgil, the Tancredi and Argantes of Tasso, and the proud giant Orgoglio of Spenser:

a club, or staff, lay there along the fold—
an olive tree, felled green and left to season
for Kyklops' hand. And it was like a mast
a lugger of twenty oars, broad in the beam—

a deep-sea-going-craft—might carry:
so long, so big around, it seemed.
[*Odyssey*, IX, 322–27, Fitzgerald version]

upon a peak the shepherd Polyphemus;
he lugged his mammoth hulk among the flocks,
searching along familiar shores—an awful
misshapen monster, huge, his eyelight lost.
His steps are steadied by the lopped-off pine
he grips. . . .
[*Aeneid*, III, 660–66; Mandelbaum version, 849–55]

These sons of Mavors bore, instead of spears,
    Two knotty masts, which none but they could lift;
Each foaming steed so fast his master bears,
    That never beast, bird, shaft, flew half so swift:
Such was their fury, as when Boreas tears
    The shatter'd crags from Taurus' northern clift:
Upon their helms their lances long they brake,
And up to heav'n flew splinters, sparks, and smoke.
[*Jerusalem Delivered*, VI, 40; Fairfax version]

So growen great through arrogant delight
    Of th'high descent, whereof he was yborne,
And through presumption of his matchlesse might,
    All other powres and knighthood he did scorne.
Such now he marcheth to this man forlorne,
    And left to losse: his stalking steps are stayde
Upon a snaggy Oke, which he had torne
    Out of his mothers bowelles, and it made
His mortall mace, wherewith his foemen he dismayde.
[*Faerie Queene*, I, vii, x]

The Wild Men, Polyphemus the Cyclops and the crudely proud Orgoglio, as well as the Catholic and Circassian champions, Tancredi and Argantes, all become late and lesser versions of Milton's earlier and greater Satan. The tree and the mast become interchangeable with the club, and all three become emblematic of the brutality of Satan as the Antichrist, the fallen son of God who walks in the darkness of his vainglory and perverts nature to the ends of war-by-sea and war-by-land, Job's Leviathan and Behemoth. Milton's present age is again an experiential darkness—of naval warfare—but his backward glance to Satanic origins reveals the full truth of which Homer, Virgil, Tasso give only incomplete reflections. Whether the transumption truly overcomes Spenser's Orgoglio is more dubious, for he remains nearly as Satanic as Milton's Satan, except that Satan is more complex and poignant, being a son of heaven and not, like the gross Orgoglio, a child of earth.

The third transumption of the passage, the fiction of the leaves, is surely the subtlest, and the one most worthy of Milton's greatness. He tropes here on the tropes of Isiah, Homer, Virgil and Dante, and with the Orion allusion on Job and Virgil. The series is capped by the references to Exodus and Ovid, with the equation of Busiris and Satan. This movement from fallen leaves to starry influence over storms to the overwhelming of a tyrannous host is itself a kind of transumption, as Milton moves from metonymy to metonymy before accomplishing a final reduction.

Satan's fallen hosts, poignantly still called "angel forms," most directly allude to a prophetic outcry of Isaiah 34:4:

> And all the host of heaven shall be dissolved, and the heavens shall be rolled together as a scroll; and all their host shall fall down, as the leaf falleth off from the vine, and as a falling fig from the fig tree.

Milton is too wary to mark this for transumption; his trope works upon a series of Homer, Virgil, Dante:

> . . . why ask of my generation?
> As is the generation of leaves, so is that of humanity
> The wind scatters the leaves on the ground, but the fine timber
> burgeons with leaves again in the season of spring returning.
> So one generation of men will grow while another dies. . . .
> [*Iliad*, VI, 145–50, Lattimore version]

> thick as the leaves that with the early frost
> of autumn drop and fall within the forest,
> or as the birds that flock along the beaches,
> in flight from frenzied seas when the chill season
> drives them across the waves to lands of sun.
> They stand; each pleads to be the first to cross
> the stream; their hands reach out in longing for
> the farther shore. But Charon, sullen boatman,
> now takes these souls, now those; the rest he leaves;
> thrusting them back; he keeps them from the beach.
> [*Aeneid*, VI, 310–19; Mandelbaum version, 407–16]

> . . . But those forlorn and naked souls changed color, their teeth chattering, as soon as they heard the cruel words. They cursed God, their parents, the human race, the place, the time, the seed of their begetting and of their birth. Then, weeping loudly, all drew to the evil shore that awaits every man who fears not God. The demon Charon, his eyes like glowing coals, beckons to them and collects them all, beating with his oar whoever lingers.
> As the leaves fall away in autumn, one after another, till

the bough sees all its spoils upon the ground, so there the evil
seed of Adam: one by one they cast themselves from that shore
at signals, like a bird at its call. Thus they go over the dark
water, and before they have landed on the other shore, on this
side a new throng gathers.

[*Inferno*, III, 100–120, Singleton version]

Homer accepts grim process; Virgil accepts yet plangently laments,
with his unforgettable vision of those who stretch forth their hands out
of love for the farther shore. Dante, lovingly close to Virgil, is more
terrible, since his leaves fall even as the evil seed of Adam falls. Milton
remembers standing, younger and then able to see, in the woods at
Vallombrosa, watching the autumn leaves strew the brooks. His char-
acteristic metonymy of shades for woods allusively puns on Virgil's and
Dante's images of the shades gathering for Charon, and by a metalepsis
carries across Dante and Virgil to their tragic Homeric origin. Once
again, the precursors are projected into belatedness, as Milton introjects
the prophetic source of Isaiah. Leaves fall from trees, generations of
men die, because once one-third of the heavenly host came falling down.
Milton's present time again is experiential loss; he watches no more
autumns, but the optic glass of his art sees fully what his precursors saw
only darkly, or in the vegetable glass of nature.

By a transition to the "scattered sedge" of the Red Sea, Milton calls
up Virgil again, compounding two passages on Orion:

> Our prows were pointed there when suddenly,
> rising upon the surge, stormy Orion
> drove us against blind shoals . . .
> 　[*Aeneid*, I, 534–36; Mandelbaum version, 753–55]

> 　　　　　. . . he marks Arcturus,
> the twin Bears and the rainy Hyades,
> Orion armed with gold; and seeing all
> together in the tranquil heavens, loudly
> he signals. . . .
> [*Aeneid*, III. 517–21; Mandelbaum version, 674–78]

Alstair Fowler notes the contrast to the parallel Biblical allusions:

> He is wise in heart, and mighty in strength: who hath hard-
> ened himself against him, and hath prospered?
> 　. . . Which alone spreadeth out the heavens, and treadeth
> upon the waves of the sea.
> 　Which maketh Arcturus, Orion, and Pleiades, and the
> chambers of the south.
> 　　　　　　　　　　　　　　　　　　[Job 9:4, 8–9]

> Seek him that maketh the seven stars and Orion, and turneth the shadow of death into the morning, and maketh the day dark with night: that calleth for the waters of the sea, and poureth them out upon the face of the earth: The LORD is his name. . . .
>
> [Amos, 5:8]

In Virgil, Origin rising marks the seasonal onset of storms. In the Bible, Orion and all the stars are put into place as a mere sign-system, demoted from their pagan status as powers. Milton says "hath vexed" to indicate that the sign-system continues in his own day, but he says "o'erthrew" to show that the Satanic stars and the host of Busiris the Pharaoh fell once for all, Pharaoh being a type of Satan. Virgil, still caught in a vision that led Orion as a potency, is himself again transumed into a sign of error.

I have worked through this passage's allusions in some detail so as to provide one full instance of a transumptive scheme in *Paradise Lost*. Johnson's insight is validated, for the "adventitious image" of the optic glass is shown to be not extrinsic at all, but rather to be the device that "crowds the imagination," compressing or hastening much transumption into a little space. By arranging his precursors in series, Milton figuratively reverses his obligation to them, for his stationing crowds them between the visionary truth of his poem (carefully aligned with Biblical truth) and his darkened present (which he shares with Galileo). Transumption murders time, for by troping on a trope, you enforce a state of rhetoricity or word-consciousness, and you negate fallen history. Milton does what Bacon hoped to do; Milton and Galileo become ancients, and Homer, Virgil, Ovid, Dante, Tasso, Spenser become belated moderns. The cost is a loss in the immediacy of the living moment. Milton's meaning is remarkably freed of the burden of anteriority, but only because Milton himself is already one with the future, which he introjects.

It would occupy too many pages to demonstrate another of Milton's transumptive schemes in its largest and therefore most powerful dimensions, but I will outline one, summarizing rather than quoting the text, and citing rather than giving the allusions. My motive is not only to show that the "optic glass" passage is hardly unique in its arrangement, but to analyze more thoroughly Milton's self-awareness of both his war against influence and his use of rhetoricity as a defense. Of many possibilities, Book I, lines 670–798, seems to me the best, for this concluding movement of the epic's initial book has as its hidden subject both the anxiety of influence and an anxiety of morality about the secondariness of any poetic creation, even Milton' own. The passage describes the sudden building, out of the deep, of Pandaemonium, the palace of Satan, and ends with the infernal peers sitting there in council.

This sequence works to transume the crucial precursors again—Homer, Virgil, Ovid and Spenser—but there are triumphant allusions here to Lucretius and Shakespeare also (as Fowler notes). In some sense, the extraordinary and reverberating power of the Pandaemonium masque (as John Hollander terms it, likening it to transformation scenes in court masques) depends on its being a continuous and unified allusion to the very idea of poetic tradition, and to the moral problematic of that idea. Metalepsis or transumption can be described as an extended trope with a missing or weakened middle, and for Milton literary tradition is such a trope. The illusionistic sets and complex machinery of the masque transformation scene are emblematic, in the Pandaemonium sequence, of the self-deceptions and morally misleading machinery of epic and tragic convention.

Cunningly, Milton starts the sequence with a transumption to the fallen near-present, evoking the royal army in the Civil War as precise analogue to the Satanic army. Mammon leads on the advance party, in an opening allusion to Spenser's Cave of Mammon canto, since both Mammons direct gold-mining operations. With the next major allusion, to the same passage in Ovid's *Metamorphoses* I that was evoked in the Galileo sequence. Milton probes the morality of art:

> Let none admire
> That riches grow in Hell; that soil may best
> Deserve the precious bane. And here let those
> Who boast in mortal things, and wond'ring tell
> Of *Babel*, and the works of *Memphian* Kings,
> Learn how thir greatest Monuments of Fame,
> And Strength and Art are easily outdone
> By Spirits reprobate, and in an hour
> What in an age they with incessant toil
> And hands innumerable scarce perform.

Milton presumably would not have termed the *Iliad* or the *Aeneid* "precious bane," yet the force of his condemnation extends to them, and his anxiety necessarily touches his own poem as well. Pandaemonium rises in baroque splendor, with a backward allusion to Ovid's Palace of the Sun, also designed by Mulciber (*Metamorphoses* II, 1–4), and with a near-contemporary allusion to St. Peter's at Rome and, according to Fowler, to Bernini's colonnade in the piazza of St. Peter's. Mulciber, archetype not only of Bernini but more darkly of all artists, including epic poets, becomes the center of the sequence:

> Men call'd him *Mulciber*; and how he fell
> From Heav'n, they fabl'd, thrown by angry *Jove*
> Sheer o'er the Crystal Battlements: from Morn
> To Noon he fell, from Noon to dewy Eve,
> A Summer's day; and with the setting Sun
> Dropt from the Zenith like a falling Star,

> On *Lemnos* th'*Ægæan* Isle: thus they relate,
> Erring: for he with this rebellious rout
> Fell long before; nor aught avail'd him now
> To have built in Heav'n high Towrs; nor did he scape
> By all his Engines, but was headlong sent
> With his industrious crew to build in hell.

The devastating "Erring" of line 747 is a smack at Homer by way of the *errat* of Lucretius (*De rerum natura*, I, 393, as Fowler notes). The contrast with Homer's passage illuminates the transumptive function of Milton's allusiveness, for Homer's Hephaistos (whose Latin name was Vulcan or Mulciber) gently fables his own downfall:

> . . . It is too hard to fight against the Olympian.
> There was a time once before now I was minded to help you,
> and he caught me by the foot and threw me from the magic threshold,
> and all day long I dropped helpless, and about sunset
> I landed in Lemnos. . . .
>
> > [*Iliad*, I, 589–93; Lattimore version]

Milton first mocks Homer by over-accentuating the idyllic nature of this fall, and then reverses Homer completely. In the dark present, Mulciber's work is still done when the bad eminence of baroque glory is turned to the purposes of a fallen Church. So, at line 756, Pandaemonium is called "the high capital" of Satan, alluding to two lines of Virgil (*Aeneid*, VI, 836 and VIII, 348), but the allusion is qualified by the complex simile of the bees that continues throughout lines 768–75, and which relies on further allusions to *Iliad*, II, 87–90 and *Aeneid*, 430–36, where Achaian and Carthaginian heroes respectively are compared to bees. One of the most remarkable of Milton's transumptive returns to present time is then accomplished by an allusion to Shakespeare's *Midsummer Night's Dream*, II, i, 28ff. A "belated peasant" beholds the "Faery Elves" even as we, Milton's readers, see the giant demons shrink in size. Yet *our* belatedness is again redressed by metaleptic reversal, with an allusion to *Aeneid*, VI, 451–54, where Aeneas recognizes Dido's "dim shape among the shadows (just as one who either sees or thinks he sees . . . the moon rising)." So the belated peasant "sees, or dreams he sees" the elves, but like Milton we *know* we see the fallen angels metamorphosed from giants into pygmies. The Pandaemonium sequence ends with the great conclave of "a thousand demi-gods on golden seats," in clear parody of ecclesiastical assemblies re-convened after the Restoration. As with the opening reference to the advance-party of the royal army, the present is seen as fallen on evil days, but it provides vantage for Milton's enduring vision.

So prevalent throughout the poem is this scheme of allusion that any possibility of inadvertence can be ruled out. Milton's design is wholly definite, and its effect is to reverse literary tradition, at the expense of the presentness of the present. The precursors return in Milton, but only at his will, and they return to be corrected. Perhaps only Shakespeare can be judged Milton's rival in allusive triumph over tradition, yet Shakespeare had no Spenser to subsume, but only a Marlowe, and Shakespeare is less clearly in overt competition with Aeschylus, Sophocles, Euripides than Milton is with Homer, Virgil, Ovid, Dante, Tasso.

Hobbes, in his *Answer to Davenant's Preface* (1650), had subordinated wit to judgment, and so implied also that rhetoric was subordinate to dialectic:

> From knowing much, proceedeth the admirable variety and novelty of metaphors and similitudes which are not possibly to be lighted on in the compass of a narrow knowledge. And the want whereof compelleth a writer to expressions that are either defaced by time or sullied with vulgar or long use. For the phrases of poesy, as the airs of music, with often hearing become insipid; the reader having no more sense of their force, than our flesh is sensible of the bones that sustain it. As the sense we have of bodies, consisteth in change and variety of impression, so also does the sense of language in the variety and changeable use of words. I mean not in the affectation of words newly brought home from travel, but in new (and withal, significant) translation to our purposes, of those that be already received, and in far fetched (but withal, apt, instructive, and comely) similitudes. . . .

Had Milton deliberately accepted this as challenge, he could have done no more both to fulfill and to refute Hobbes than *Paradise Lost* already does. What Davenant and Cowley could not manage was a complete translation to their own purposes of received rhetoric; but Milton raised such translation to sublimity. In doing so, he also raised rhetoric over dialectic, *contra* Hobbes, for his farfetchedness (Puttenham's term for transumption) gave similitudes the status and function of complex arguments. Milton's wit, his control of rhetoric, was again the exercise of the mind through all her powers, and not a lower faculty subordinate to judgment. Had Hobbes written his *Answer* twenty years later, and after reading *Paradise Lost*, he might have been less confident of the authority of philosophy over poetry.

BARBARA LEWALSKI

The Genres of *Paradise Lost*:
Literary Genre as a Means
of Accommodation†

That *Paradise Lost* is an epic whose closest structural affinities are to
Virgil's *Aeneid*, and that it undertakes to redefine classical epic heroism
in Christian terms are truisms about the poem's genre.[1] Widely recog-
nized also is the importance of epic traditions and epic features other
than Virgilian. *Paradise Lost* has an Iliadic subject involving the loss
and woe resulting from an act of disobedience, together with an Achil-
lean hero motivated by a sense of injured merit; that same hero is also
an Odyssean hero of wiles and craft, who undertakes a perilous journey
in order to find (like Aeneas) a new homeland.[2] *Paradise Lost* has also
a Hesiodic gigantomachia with Homeric battle scenes; numerous Ovi-
dian metamorphoses; an Ariostan Paradise of Fools; a pair of Spenserian
allegorical figures (Sin and Death); a romance garden in which a hero
and heroine must withstand a dragon of sorts; and a poetic hexameron
in the tradition of Du Bartas.[3] Moreover, because heroic values have
been so profoundly transvalued in *Paradise Lost*, the poem is sometimes

---

† This work originally appeared as "The Genres of *Paradise Lost*: Literary Genre as a Means of
 Accommodation," by Barbara K. Lewalski, in *Milton Studies, Volume XVII (Composite
 Orders: The Genre of Milton's Last Poems)*, R. S. Ide and Joseph Wittreich, guest editors.
 Published in 1983 by the University of Pittsburgh Press. Reprinted by permission of the
 publisher.
1. See especially C. M. Bowra, *From Virgil to Milton* (London, 1944); Davis P. Harding, *The
 Club of Hercules: Studies in the Classical Background of Paradise Lost*, Illinois Studies in
 Language and Literature, L (Urbana, 1962); John M. Steadman, *Milton and the Renaissance
 Hero* (Oxford, 1967); K. W. Gransden, "*Paradise Lost* and the *Aeneid*," *Essays in Criticism*,
 XVII (1967), 281–303; Mario A. Di Cesare, "*Paradise Lost* and Epic Tradition," in *Milton
 Studies*, I, ed. James D. Simmonds (Pittsburgh, 1969), pp. 31–50; Francis C. Blessington,
 "*Paradise Lost*" and the Classical Epic (Boston, 1979).
2. See, e.g., Martin Mueller, "*Paradise Lost* and the *Iliad*," *Comparative Literature Studies*, VI
 (1969), 292–316; John M. Steadman, *Milton and the Renaissance Hero*, and *Milton's Epic
 Characters: Image and Idol* (Chapel Hill, 1968); Manoocher Aryanpur, "*Paradise Lost* and
 the *Odyssey*," *TSLL*, IX (1967), 151–66; Blessington, "*Paradise Lost*" and the Classical Epic.
3. See, e.g. Merritt Y. Hughes, "Milton's Celestial Battles and the Theogonies," in his *Ten
 Perspectives on Milton* (New Haven, 1965), pp. 196–219; Stella Purce Revard, *The War in
 Heaven: "Paradise Lost" and the Tradition of Satan's Rebellion* (Ithaca, 1980); Davis P.
 Harding, *Milton and the Renaissance Ovid* (Urbana, 1946); Louis L. Martz, "*Paradise Lost*:
 Figurations of Ovid," in his *Poet of Exile: A Study of Milton's Poetry* (New Haven, 1980),
 pp. 203–44; A. Bartlett Giamatti, *The Earthly Paradise and the Renaissance Epic* (Princeton,
 1966); Merritt Y. Hughes, "Milton's Limbo of Vanities," and Wayne Shumacher, "*Paradise
 Lost* and the Italian Epic Tradition," in *Th'Upright Heart and Pure*, ed. Amadeus P. Fiore
 (Pittsburgh, 1967), pp. 7–24, 87–100; Irene Samuel, *Dante and Milton: "The Commedia"
 and "Paradise Lost"* (Ithaca, 1966); Edwin Greenlaw, "Spenser's Influence on *Paradise Lost*,"
 XVII (1920), 320–59; A. Kent Hieatt, *Chaucer, Spenser, Milton: Mythopoeic Continuities
 and Transformations*" (Montreal, 1975), pp. 153–270; Kathleen Williams, "Milton, Greatest
 Spenserian," in *Milton and the Line of Vision*, ed. Joseph A. Wittreich, Jr. (Madison, 1975),
 pp. 25–55; George C. Taylor, *Milton's use of Du Bartas* (Cambridge, Mass., 1967); J. M.
 Evans, "*Paradise Lost*" and the Genesis Tradition (Oxford, 1968).

assigned to categories beyond epic: pseudomorph, prophetic poem, apoc-
alypse, anti-epic, transcendent epic.[4]

Within the epic or epiclike structure, many dramatic elements have
also been identified, including some vestiges of Milton's early sketches
for a drama entitled "Adam unparadiz'd," some structural resemblances
to contemporary heroic epics in five acts such as Davenant's *Gondibert*,
and a tragic figure (Adam) who falls from happiness to misery through
hamartia. We find also tragic soliloquies by Satan and Adam which
recall those of Dr. Faustus and Macbeth; a morality play "Parliament
of Heaven" episode; a scene of domestic farce in which Satan first
vehemently repudiates and then fawns upon his reprehensible offspring
Sin and Death; scenes of domestic tragedy modulating to tragicomedy
which present Adam and Eve's quarrel, fall, mutual recrimination, and
later, reconciliation; and tragic masques or pageants portraying the sins
and miseries of human history.[5]

Pastoral forms are hardly less important: landscape description; an
Arcadian happy rural seat of various view" (IV, 247); a pastoral idyl with
Adam and Eve at their supper fruits engaging in eclogue-like dialogue;
scenes of light georgic gardening activity.[6] Lyric forms of all kinds are
also embedded in the poem and have received some attention: celebratory
odes, psalmic hymns of praise and thanksgiving, epithalamia, love lyrics
including Adam's aubade and Satan's nocturnal serenade to Eve, sub-

4. See, e.g., John Steadman, "The Epic as Pseudomorph: Methodology in Milton Studies," in *Milton Studies*, VII, ed. Albert C. Labriola and Michael Leib (Pittsburgh, 1973), pp. 3–25; Joseph A. Wittreich "A Poet Amongst Poets: Milton and the Tradition of Prophecy," in *Milton and the Line of Vision*, pp. 97–142; Michael Fixler, "The Apocalypse Within *Paradise Lost*," in *New Essays on "Paradise Lost"*, ed., Thomas Kranidas (Berkeley and Los Angeles, 1969), pp. 131–78; T. J. B. Spencer, "*Paradise Lost*: The Anti-Epic," in *Approaches to "Paradise Lost": The York Tercentenary Lectures*, ed. C. A. Patrides (Toronto, 1968); Harold E. Toliver, "Milton's Household Epic," in *Milton Studies*, IX, ed. James D. Simmonds (Pittsburgh, 1976), pp. 105–20; Joan Webber, *Milton and His Epic Tradition* (Seattle, 1979).
5. See, e.g., James Holly Hanford, "The Dramatic Element in *Paradise Lost*," SP, XIV (1917), 178–95; Arthur E. Barker, "Structural Pattern in *Paradise Lost*," PQ, XXVIII (1949), 16–36; Ernest Sirluck, "*Paradise Lost*: A Deliberate Epic (Cambridge, 1967); Roger E. Rollin, "*Paradise Lost*: Tragical-Comical-Historical-Pastoral,' " in *Milton Studies*, V, ed. James D. Simmonds (Pittsburgh, 1973), pp. 3–37; John M. Steadman, *Epic and Tragic Structure in "Paradise Lost"* (Chicago, 1976); F. T. Prince, "Milton and the Theatrical Sublime," in *Approaches to "Paradise Lost,"* ed. Patrides, pp. 53–63; John G. Demaray, *Milton's Theatrical Epic: The Invention and Design of "Paradise Lost"* (Cambridge, Mass., 1980); Thomas Kranidas, "Adam and Eve in the Garden: A Study of *Paradise Lost*, Book V." SEL, IV (1964), 71–83; Irene Samuel, "The Dialogue in Heaven: A Reconsideration of *Paradise Lost* III.1–417," PMLA, LXXII (1957), 601–11; Alwin Thaler, "Shakespearean Recollections in Milton: A Summing Up," in his *Shakespeare and Our World* (Knoxville, 1966), 139–227.
6. The major study is John R. Knott, *Milton's Pastoral Vision: An Approach to "Paradise Lost"* (Chicago, 1971). See also Joseph E. Duncan, *Milton's Earthly Paradise: A Historical Study of Eden* (Minneapolis, 1972); William Empson, "Milton and Bentley: The Pastoral of the Innocence of Man and Nature," in his *Some Versions of Pastoral* (London, 1935), pp. 149–94; Northrop Frye, *The Return of Eden* (Toronto, 1965); Roy Daniells, "A Happy Rural Seat of Various View," in "*Paradise Lost*": A Tercentenary Tribute, ed. B. Rajan (Toronto, 1967), pp. 3–17; G. Stanley Koehler, "Milton and the Art of Landscape," in *Milton Studies*, VIII, ed. James D. Simmonds (Pittsburgh, 1975), pp. 3–40; Barbara K. Lewalski, "Innocence and Experience in Milton's Eden," in *New Essays on "Paradise Lost,"* ed. Kranidas, pp. 86–117; Roger B. Rollin, "*Paradise Lost*: "Tragical-Comical-Historical-Pastoral," *Milton Studies*, V (1973), 3–37.

merged sonnets, complaints, laments.[7] Rhetorical and discursive forms also abound: Satan's several speeches of political oratory; God's lengthy theological disquisition or sermon on free will; a parliamentary debate in hell over what to do next and another between Satan and Abdiel in heaven over God's right of governance; a treatise on astronomical systems; a dialogue about human nature between God and Adam and a dialogue about love between Raphael and Adam, an interpretative account of biblical history; and of course Satan's temptation speeches to Eve in the style and manner of "som Orator renound / In *Athens* or free *Rome*" (IX, 670–71).[8]

If we ask why Milton incorporated so complete a spectrum of literary forms and genres in *Paradise Lost*, a partial answer must be that much Renaissance critical theory supports the notion of the epic as a heterocosm or a compendium of subjects, forms, and styles. As Rosalie Colie has noted, Homer was widely recognized as the source and origin of all the arts and sciences—philosophy, mathematics, history, geography, military art, religion, oratory, hymnic praise, rhetoric, and much more—and by that token he was regarded as the source of all literary forms.[9] Out of Homer, said his great English Renaissance translator George Chapman (citing Petrarch), "are all Arts deduced, confirmed or illustrated," and by reason of this inclusiveness Homer can best instruct all kinds of people—kings, soldiers, counsellors, fathers, husbands, wives, lovers, friends.[1]

* * *

7. See, e.g., Joseph Summers, "Grateful Vicissitude," in his *The Muse's Method: An Introduction to "Paradise Lost,"* (Cambridge, Mass., 1962), pp. 71–86; Donald Davie, "Syntax and Music in *Paradise Lost,*" in *The Living Milton,* ed. Frank Kermode (London, 1960), pp. 70–84; William Haller, "Hail Wedded Love," *ELH,* XIII (1946), 79–97; Gary M. McCown, "Milton and the Epic Epithalamium," in *Milton Studies,* V. pp. 39–66; John Demaray, "Love's Epic Revel in *Paradise Lost*: A Theatrical Vision of Marriage," *MLQ,* XXXVIII (1977), 3–20; Lee M. Johnson, "Milton's Blank Verse Sonnets, in *Milton Studies,* V, pp. 129–53; Anna K. Nardo, "The Submerged Sonnet as Lyric Moment in Miltonic Epic," *Genre,* IX (1976), 21–35; Richard M. Bridges, "Milton's Original Psalm," *Milton Quarterly,* XIV (1980), 12–21; Judy L. Van Sickle, "Song as Structure and Symbol in Four Poems of John Milton," Ph.D. diss., Brown University, 1980, pp. 190–267.
8. See, e.g., J. B. Broadbent, *Some Graver Subject: An Essay on "Paradise Lost"* (London, 1960), pp. 110–20; and "Milton's Rhetoric," *MP,* LVI (1958–59), 224–42; John M. Steadman, " 'Semblance of Worth': Pandaemonium and Deliberative Oratory," *Neophilologus,* XLVIII (1964), 159–76, rpt. in Steadman, *Milton's Epic Characters: Image and Idol* (Chapel Hill, 1968), pp. 241–62; Steadman, "Ethos and Dianoia: Character and Rhetoric in *Paradise Lost,*" in *Language and Style in Milton,* ed. R. D. Emma and J. T. Shawcross (New York, 1967), 193–232; Dennis Burden, *The Logical Epic: A Study of the Argument of "Paradise Lost"* (London, 1967); Samuel, "Dialogue in Heaven," pp. 601–11; Stanley E. Fish, *Surprised by Sin: The Reader in "Paradise Lost"* (Berkeley and Los Angeles, 1967), pp. 57–157; H. R. Macallum, "Milton and Sacred History, Books XI–XII of *Paradise Lost,* in *Essays in English Literature from the Renaissance to the Victorian Age, Presented to A. S. P. Woodhouse,* ed. M.Maclure and F. W. Watt (Toronto, 1964), pp. 149–68.
9. Rosalie L. Colie, *The Resources of Kind: Genre-Theory in the Renaissance,* ed. Barbara K. Lewalski (Berkeley and Los Angeles, 1973), pp. 22–23.
1. Chapman, "The Preface to the Reader," *Homer's Iliad,* in *Chapman's Homer,* ed. Allardyce Nicoll, 2 vols. (Princeton, 1957), I, 14; "To the Understander," *Achilles Shield,* in *Chapman's Homer,* 1, 549.

In addition to this general idea of epic inclusiveness, many Renaissance theorists called attention to specific analgams in the great poems of the tradition. Aristotle's close paralleling of epic and tragedy, together with his identification of the plot of the *Iliad* as "pathetic," laid the groundwork for the common Renaissance view of the *Iliad* as a tragic epic. * * * And the major English Renaissance narratives with claims to epic status before *Paradise Lost*—Sidney's *New Arcadia* and Spenser's *Faerie Queene*—were quite obviously mixtures of epic, romance, pastoral, allegory, and song.

This Renaissance theory and practice helps us understand how Milton came to resolve as he did the genre questions he was pondering in *The Reason of Church-Government* (1642):

> Whether that Epick from whereof the two poems of Homer, and those other two of *Virgil* and *Tasso* are a diffuse, and the book of *Job* a brief model: . . . Or whether those Dramatick constitutions, wherein *Sophocles* and *Euripides* raigne shall be found more doctrinal and exemplary to a Nation, the Scripture also affords us a divine pastoral Drama in the *Song of Solomon* consisting of two persons and a double *Chorus*, as *Origen* rightly judges. And the Apocalyps of Saint *John* is the majestick image of a high and stately Tragedy, shutting up and intermingling her solemn Scenes and Acts with a sevenfold *Chorus* of halleluja's and harping symphonies: and this my opinion the grave autority of *Pareus* commenting that booke is sufficient to confirm. Or if occasion shall lead to imitat those magnifick Odes and Hymns wherein *Pindarus* and *Callimachus* are in most things worthy, some others in their frame judicious, in their matter most an end faulty: But those frequent songs throughout the law and prophets beyond all these, not in their divine argument alone, but in the very critical art of composition may be easily made appear over all the kinds of Lyrick poesy to be incomparable. (YP, I, 813–16)

Contemporary theory, it seems clear, gave Milton ample warrant to conclude that an epic incorporating the entire spectrum of kinds and subjects would be most doctrinal and exemplary and would also have the best claim to inclusion in the company he expressly sought for it— the *Iliad*, the *Odyssey*, the *Aeneid*, *Gerusalemme Liberata*, and the Bible.

Recognizing that Milton would want his poem to have the comprehensiveness attributed to the greatest epics, we need to ask a further question: just how did Milton employ generic inclusiveness to accomplish his specific poetic purposes? My general proposition is that for Milton, genre choices, changes, and transformations serve as a primary vehicle of artistic perception and of conscious accommodation to the reader, affording that reader a range of perspectives upon the Miltonic subject. This suggestion invites some revision in two currently fashionable views of Milton: that he saw himself as a prophet directly inspired by the Spirit of God, seeking to present his prophetic visions of divine truth to his audience; or, that he took on the role of rigorous and punitive teacher, engaging his reader in a strenuous dialectic intended to force the reader into frequent and inevitable mistakes in reading, thereby causing the reader to recognize and reenact his or her own fallenness.[2] The formidable array of conventional genres in *Paradise Lost* indicates, I suggest, that Milton can only see and tell of things invisible by using the familiar forms art supplies to his own imagination and that of his readers. It also indicates that he can teach most effectively by building upon and letting his readers refine their developed repsonses to the values and assumptions about man, nature, language, heroism, virtue, pleasure, work, and love which have long been associated with the various genres and literary modes.

As a guide to Milton's poetic method and intention, I propose to examine the two poets/prophets/teachers he creates in the poem as subordinate narrators—Raphael and Michael. Both of them have to teach and to mediate divine truth to a sometimes not-so-fit audience, Adam and Eve, and both of them do so by literary accommodation, "inventing" precisely those literary genres which are most appropriate to their several subjects and to the special needs of the audience. Milton's angelic narrators invent the prototypes, as it were, of several genres we know, setting them forth in their pristine, ideal forms to teach, delight, and move Adam and Eve in the ways commonly attributed to those genres. The bard's audience, conscious of literary tradition as Adam and Eve are not, must learn from the angelic narratives in more complex ways, by comparing the angelic archetypal poems with their literary progenies in regard to the human goods and values presented.

Both of Milton's angelic narrators are prophets in the broad seventeenth-century sense of the term. According to the Cambridge Platonist John Smith, prophecy encompasses all forms of divine illumination of the mind, chiefly about divine things but sometimes about the natural order as well.[3] * * * Going beyond this notion, Milton presents his angelic prophets as Renaissance poets who meet the problem of accommodation in part by inventing literary genres suited to their own capacities, the height and variety of the subjects they treat, and the needs and condition of the audience; like Milton himself, these angelic prophet/poets clearly believe that decorum is the grand masterpiece to observe.

2. Cf. Stanley Fish, *Surprised by Sin: The Reader in Paradise Lost* (London, 1967) (or "Discovery as Form in *Paradise Lost*," pp. 526–36, above; and Joseph A. Wittreich, Jr., ed., *Milton and the Line of Vision* (Madison, 1975) [*Editor*].
3. John Smith, "Of Prophesie," in his *Select Discourses* (London, 1660), pp. 169–71.

Raphael is a prophet in Smith's most general sense: his understanding has been informed by God, he enlightens Adam about natural things as well as divine truth, but he is not himself dependent upon direct, continuous divine illumination, except (perhaps) in recounting the Creation story. God, we note, gave Raphael general directives concerning his manner, tone, and basic purpose: Raphael was to advise Adam about his own happiness and the threat to it from Satan. But God permitted the angel artistic license in devising appropriate forms of discourse to accomplish this mission:

> "Go therefore, half this day as friend with friend
> Converse with *Adam*, in what Bowre or shade
> Thou find'st him from the heat of Noon retir'd.
>
> . . . .
>
> and such discourse bring on,
> As may advise him of his happie state,
> Happiness in his power left free to will,
>
> . . . .
>
> tell him withall
> His danger, and from whom.
>
> (V, 229–39)

As a skillful teacher will, Raphael allows Adam's questions and initiatives to determine the particular subjects discussed; and as a true poet must, he finds for those subjects fitting generic forms which reinforce the truths he is charged to set forth. At one point Adam accords Raphael the title "Divine / Hystorian" (VIII, 6–7), recognizing thereby that the angel discourses chiefly of past events and of the nature of things and that he draws for the most part upon his own firsthand experience and observation—supplemented, we may suppose, by the reports of others, especially as regards the war in heaven. Since this is so, the poet Raphael usually seems confident that his own knowledge is adequate to his subject matter, though worried at times about how to accommodate it to his intelligent but inexperienced audience.

Responding to Adam's hospitable offer of food and queries about the comparison of earthly and heavenly food, Raphael invents his first literary work—a brief disquisition in verse on ontology, the nature of things (V, 404–33, 469–505). Though its concepts derive from Plato's *Timaes* and from Lucretius, Lipsius, Fludd, and others,[4] its form, as a miniature philosophic poem, is closest to Lucretius' *De rerum natura*. Lucretius' poem (along with Empedocles' Περί φύσεως, Virgil's *Georgics*, and some others) became the basis for Renaissance critical disputes about

---

4. For discussion of some intellectual sources for these ideas, see Denis Saurat, *Milton: Man and Thinker* (New York, 1925), pp. 301–09; W. C. Curry, *Milton's Ontology, Cosmogony and Physics* (Lexington, Ky., 1966), pp. 114–43, 158–82; Kester Svendsen, *Milton and Science* (Cambridge, Mass., 1956), pp. 9–42; 114–36; Lee A. Jacobus, *Sudden Apprehension: Aspects of Knowledge in "Paradise Lost"* (The Hague, 1976), pp. 45–88.

the status of the philosophical-scientific poem as poetry. Those who followed Aristotle closely in making imitation the sine qua non of poetry excluded such works; others, like Scaliger and Minturno, who defined and categorized poetry according to verse forms or subject matter, identified Lucretius' poem as a philosophical epic or a variety of heroic poem.[5] Puttenham ranked Lucretius and poets of his type who treat "such doctrines and arts as the commonwealth fared the better by" next after historical (epiclike) poems, noting that these poets employed verse *Exameter* savouring the Heroicall."[6] Sidney proposed to leave to grammarians the dispute as to whether such philosophical poems can properly be termed poems or no, while he praised the "sweet food of sweetly uttered knowledge" to be found in them.[7]

Lucretius' poem is a passionate and eloquent argument for the philosophy of Epicurus, grounded upon a version of Democritean atomism. As the thematic statement in the first book indicates, the poem seeks to explain the nature of the universe, the origins of all life and change, the human condition, and human freedom as alike resulting from the constant, fortutious collision of atoms, which, in various degrees of refinement, make up the substratum of all being, including the gods and the soul. * * * Lucretius' purpose is to free his addressee, Memnius, from superstition about the gods and from fear of death through knowledge of "the aspect and law of nature," so that he will base his choices in life upon true and profound understanding of man's place in the processes of nature. * * *

Raphael's miniature *De rerum natura* recalls statements both in its form and in its emphasis upon certain concepts—the heavenly source of all life, the common material substratum of all being, the ongoing processes of change in the universe. And Raphael also intends to lead his addressee, Adam, to make sound choices in life on the basis of a true apprehension of his place in nature. But Raphael's protypical Lucretian epic is based on teleological rather than atomistic principles, recognizing God as the source and end of all the natural processes and emphasizing human choice rather than the fortutious collision of atoms as a principal determinant of the direction of change:

> O *Adam*, one Almightie is, from whom
> All things proceed, and up to him return,
> If not deprav'd from good, created all
> Such to perfection, one first matter all,
> Indu'd with various forms, various degrees
> Of substance, and in things that live, of life;
> But more refin'd, more spiritous, and pure,

---

5. See, e.g., Antonio Sebastiano Minturno, *De Poeta* (Venice, 1559), p. 417; Scaliger, *Poetices libri septem* (I, 2), pp. 16–17.
6. *Arte of English Poesie*, p. 35.
7. *Defence of Poesie*, sig. C2.

As neerer to him plac't or neerer tending
Each in thir several active Sphears assignd,
Till body up to spirit work, in bounds
Proportiond to each kind.

(V, 469–79)

* * *

Raphael next invents the genre of the classical epic. Adam, responding to Raphael's apparently casual remark about disobedient angels, asks for a "full relation" of that story (V, 556). This request causes Raphael to confront a difficult problem of literary accommodation. The subject is "High matter" involving "th'invisible exploits / Of warring Spirits," while the audience is limited to "human sense." Moreover, his own emotions may prove difficult to control: "how shall I relate / . . . without remorse / The ruin of so many glorious once." Finally, these "secrets of another world" are perhaps not lawful to reveal. The last problem is solved by a dispensation allowing the revelation for Adam's good, and Raphael proposes to deal with the limitations of his audience "by lik'ning spiritual to corporal forms"—leaving open the question of whether such corporal forms are in fact Platonic shadows of spiritual reality or not (V, 563–76).

Acting upon this decision, Raphael presents the war in heaven as a miniature *Iliad*, based upon a true history yet with large scope for invention. Raphael's epic, like Homer's, begins with a ceremony (the elevation of the Son) at which an Achillean hero feels his honor affronted and withdraws with his forces to his own regions. From the reader's comparatist perspective, Satan is seen to be a debased Achilles, as Francis Blessington observes:[8] his claims of equality with his ruler are without any basis whatsoever, his council of war is in fact a temptation, and his withdrawal of allegiance escalates to open warfare against his erstwhile comrades. We recognize also that the warfare in heaven is Homeric, complete with single combats, epic boasts, mockery of foes, flytings, chariot clashes, and legions attacking legions with spears and shields. But the hill-hurlings from Hesiod's *Theogony* and the diabolical cannon and gunpowder from later epics such as Erasmo di Valvasone's *Angeleida* and Spenser's *Faerie Queene*[9] identify this celestial battle as the source of the epic-warfare topos in literature wherever it is used.

* * *

In addition to the loyal angels whose obedience and faith were tested in battle and found heroic, Raphael's epic focuses upon two heroes whose deeds flank and thereby provide a touchstone for the military actions. One is Abdiel, the moral hero, who alone defended the right

---

8. *"Paradise Lost" and the Classical Epic,* esp. pp. 8–14.
9. *Angeleida* (Venice, 1590), (II, 20), trans. Watson Kirkconnell, in his *The Celestial Cycle* (Toronto, 1952), p. 81; *Faerie Queene* (I, vii,13), ed. J. C. Smith and E. De Selincourt (Oxford, 1970), p. 35. See the discussion in Revard, *War in Heaven*, pp. 186–90.

in the camp of the enemy and who attempted by heroic argument to persuade his fellows from their evil course. The other is the Son, the agent of God's omnipotence, who engaged the entire Satanic army in single combat but derided his enemies, even as he conquered them, for measuring all worth by physical strength:

> they may have thir wish, to trie with mee
> In Battel which the stronger proves, they all,
> Or I alone against them, since by strength
> They measure all, of other excellence
> Not emulous, nor care who them excells.
>
> (VI, 818–22)

Moreover, before the battle the Son displayed his own preferred use of power in restoring the heavenly landscape. By its conception and design Raphael's prototypical epic (rather like Milton's own) undertakes to display to its audience, Adam and Eve, the dangerous lure of evil, the deceptive rhetoric of temptation, the danger of power severed from right, the chaos attendant upon sin, and the nature of true moral heroism and true epic glory.

Adam's next query concerns the origin of heaven and earth, and it elicits additional "revealed" knowledge—the Creation story from Genesis. Though Adam assures Raphael that he does not ask in order to explore God's secrets but only to magnify his works, the form of Adam's question—"what cause / Mov'd the Creator in his holy Rest / Through all Eternitie so late to build / In *Chaos*" (VII, 90–93)—shows Adam making a precarious beginning in theological speculation. Besides the implication of divine mutability and laziness in Adam's words, his curiosity about God's activity before the Creation has long been seen as the very hallmark of presumptive inquiry into God's secret ways.[1] The genre Raphael chooses for his response is nicely calculated to lead Adam from such fruitless and dangerous inquiries into hidden mysteries by underscoring the necessarily radical accommodation of all knowledge of God to human understanding. Accordingly, Raphael does not merely summarize or paraphrase the first two chapters of Genesis: he creates a poetic hexameron, a brief biblical epic which we should recognize as a prototype of Tasso's *Il Mondo Creato* and especially Du Bartas' *La Semaine ou creation du monde*.

Du Bartas' *Semaine*, as Susan Snyder observes, is set forth as an encyclopedic epic—"an epic of the divine plan in the physical universe, with God the Maker as its epic hero"—and contemporaries acclaimed

---

1. See, e.g., Augustine, *Confessions* in *Basic Writings of Saint Augustine*, ed. Whitney J. Oates, 2 vols. (New York, 1948), I, 202; Calvin, *Institutes* (I, xiv), ed. John T. McNeill, Library of Christian Classics XX (Philadelphia, 1960), p. 160. Milton, in *CD* (I, vii) declared that "Anyone who asks what God did before the creation of the world is a fool; and anyone who answers him is not much wiser (YP, VI, 299). For further discussion of the interplay between Raphael and Adam on this point, see Lewalski, "Innocence and Experience," pp. 106–08.

it as such both in the original and in Sylvester's extemely popular translation, which had been published in nine editions by 1641.[2] Scattering his superlatives broadcast, Gabriel Harvey compares Du Bartas with Homer, Virgil, Dante, and the Holy Spirit itself: "Bartas [is] . . . for the highnesse of his subject and the majesty of his verse nothing inferiour unto Dante (whome some Italians preferre before Virgil or Homer), a right inspired and enravished Poet, full of chosen, grave, profound, venerable, and stately matter, even in the next Degree to the sacred and reverend stile of heavenly Divinity it selfe.[3]

* * *

Raphael's prototypical hexameral epic meets [Adam's] formidable challenge with a design and style vastly superior to what we find in the poems we are to recognize as its literary progeny, and it is precisely suited to Adam and Eve's situation. In the first place, Raphael eschews the lengthy catalogs and the encyclopedic lore so characteristic of the genre for a sharply focused description of the wonders and processes of creation. Second, while scholars have identified echoes from passages in Sylvester's *DuBartas* and in Lucretius. Ovid, and others describing nature's luxuriant creativity. Raphael's prototypical *Semaine* presents as it were the original from which such passages were derived—a magnificently unified vision of the divine creative power and energy, rendered through pervasive and vibrant imagery of procreation and generation.[4] The Spirit broods and infuses his vital virtue and vital warmth into the fluid mass; the earth is first an embryon in the womb of waters and then itself the womb which brings forth the "tumid Hills," the "tender grass" and all manner of vegetation, bursting with life and seeds of new life:

> Forth flourish't thick the clustering Vine, forth crept
> The smelling Gourd, up stood the cornie Reed
> Embattell'd in her field: and the humble Shrub,
> And Bush with frizl'd hair implicit: last
> Rose as in Dance the stately Trees, and spred

2. Susan Snyder, ed., *The Divine Weeks and Works of Guillaume De Saluste, Sieur Du Bartas, translated by Josuah Sylvester*, 2 vols. (Oxford, 1979), I, 2, 5. *La Semaine* was published in 1578; the unfinished sequel, *La Seconde Semaine*, dealing with the seven ages of biblical history, was first published in 1584. The standard edition of Du Bartas is *The Works of Guillaume de Salluste, Sieur du Bartas*, ed. U. T. Holmes, J. C. Lyons, and R. W. Linker, 3 vols. (Chapel Hill, 1953–40).

3. Pierce's *Supererogation*, in Smith, *Elizabethan Critical Essays*, I, 265.

4. See esp. Sylvester's *Du Bartas*, "First Week, First Day," 285–90, and *PL* VIII, 276–80; Sylvester's *Du Bartas*, "Third Day," 533–44, and *PL* VII, 313–19; Sylvester's *Du Bartas*, "Fifth Day," 879–88, and *PL* VII, 442–46. See also Lucretius, *De rerum natura* V, 783–825. For an extended discussion of echoes from Sylvester's *Du Bartas*, see Taylor, *Milton's Use of Du Bartas*; Grant McColley, *Paradise Lost: An Account of Its Growth and Major Origins, with a Discussion of Milton's Use of Sources and Literary Patterns* (Chicago, 1940). For suggestive discussions of the imagery of *PL* VII, see Summers, *Muse's Method*, pp 137–46, and Michael Lieb, *The Dialectics of Creation* (Amherst, Mass., 1969), pp. 56–63.

> Thir branches hung with copious Fruit, or gemm'd
> Thir blossoms.
>
> (VII, 320–26).

The sea generates "Frie innumerable," the caves and fens hatch from an egg "Bursting with kindly rupture" a numerous brood of birds, and then the Earth "Op'ning her fertil Woomb teem'd at a Birth / Innumerous living Creatures" (VII, 400, 419, 454–55):

> The grassie Clods now Calv'd, now half appeer'd
> The Tawnie Lion, pawing to get free
> His hinder parts, then springs as broke from Bonds,
> And Rampant shakes his Brinded main; the Ounce,
> The Libbard, and the Tyger, as the Moale
> Rising, the crumbl'd Earth above them threw
> In Hillocks; the swift Stag from under ground
> Bore up his branching head: scarse from his mould
> *Behemonth* biggest born of Earth upheav'd
> His vastness: Fleec't the Flocks and bleating rose,
> As Plants.
>
> (VII, 463–73).

By couching his poetic hexameron in the imagery of sexual generation, Raphael accommodates it brilliantly to Adam and Eve: besides making the subject comprehensible to them, he reinforces their awareness of their own dignity and happiness by inviting them to recognize their own mode of creation by sexual generation as an imitation of and participation in the divine act.

* * *

The final genre Raphael invents is the speculative scientific treatise, a prototype in verse of Galileo's *Dialogue Concerning the Two Chief World Systems*—Ptolemaic & Copernican.[5] Prompted perhaps by Raphael's description of the angelic creation hymn with its reference to "Starrs / Numerous, and every Starr perhaps a World / Of destind habitation" (VII, 620–22), Adam poses to Raphael a question concerning the design of the cosmos and its motion, "Which onely thy solution can resolve" (VIII, 14). Raphael, however, presents his response in a genre which will not resolve the question but will instead provide a model for scientific speculation, then and later. Just how deliberate and significant Raphael's genre choice is will be apparent when we recall that this question was commonly treated in the hexameral literature (and by Du Bartas) as an aspect of the fourth day's creation of the planets and in that context resolved in biblical literalist terms, on divine authority. Raphael, by refusing to resolve the issue on his angelic authority and by inventing a distinct genre for scientific discourse, removes such

---

5. [*Dialogo . . . soprai due massime sistemi del mondo, Tolemaico, e Copernicano*], trans. Stillman Drake, 2d. ed. (Berkeley and Los Angeles, 1967).

inquiry from the province of revelation and places it squarely in the realm of human speculation. Raphael's genre choice provides the underpinning for his "Benevolent and facil" opening words to Adam, "To ask or search I blame thee not, for Heav'n / Is as the Book of God before thee set, / Wherein to read his wondrous Works" (VIII, 65–68).

Galileo's dialogue has as interlocutors three friends met together to discuss the Ptolemaic and Copernican systems in a spirit of friendly inquiry. Salviati, who undertakes to "act the part of Copernicus in our arguments and wear his mask,"[6] supports the Copernican system with cogent reasoning, careful astronomical observation (aided by the telescope), and elaborate mathematical calculations. Simplicio, stout defender of Aristotelian physics and Ptolemaic astronomy, grounds his arguments chiefly upon ancient authority and piety. Sagredo is an urbane, open-minded, intelligent layman who desires to be informed about the two systems so that he may decide rationally which to credit. Galileo's dialogue leaves no question whatsoever that Salviati's arguments carry the day: the inconclusiveness of the ending and Simplicio's final appeal to the unsearchable way of God (along with a few other disclaimers) were a transparent, and in the event futile, attempt to satisfy the censors.

In Raphael's prototypical dialogue, these positions are all represented, but with large differences. Adam occupies the position of Sagredo, the intelligent layman striving to make sense of the cosmos and fully conscious of the irrationality of the planetary system as the naked eye (and Ptolemy) perceive it: "Has Nature, then, produced and directed all these enormous, perfect, and most noble celestial bodies, invariant, eternal, and divine, for no other purpose than to serve the changeable, transitory, and mortal earth? . . . Take away this purpose of serving the earth, and the innumerable host of celestial bodies is left useless and superfluous.[7] As he initiates the discussion with Raphael, Adam voices in similar terms his sense of irrationality and absurdity in the geocentric cosmos he perceives. The entire firmament seems to move with incorporeal speed through incomprehensible space,

> meerly to officiate light
> Round this opacous Earth, this punctual spot,
> One day and night; in all thir vast survey
> Useless besides, reasoning I oft admire,
> How Nature wise and frugal could commit
> Such disproportions, with superfluous hand
> So many nobler Bodies to create,
> Greater so manifold to this one use,
> For aught appeers, and on thir Orbs impose
> Such restless revolution day by day
> Repeated, while the sedentarie Earth,

6. Ibid., p. 131.
7. Ibid., pp. 59–60.

That better might with farr less compass move,
Serv'd by more noble than her self, attaines
Her end without least motion.   (VIII, 22–35)

To explore Adam's inquiry, Raphael develops what is formally an evenhanded dialogue in which he plays both the Ptolemaic and the Copernican roles, though his perspective is as clearly Copernican as Galileo's. He begins by defining sharply for Adam the issue to be discussed, "Whether Heav'n move or Earth"—though Adam has not actually supposed that the earth might move—and he proceeds to indicate that the resolution of this question "Imports not" to the recognition that God's works are indeed wonderful. He then sets aside other questions as beyond the ken of man or angel: "the rest / From Man or Angel the great Architect / Did wisely to conceal" (VIII, 70–73). Such matters are, presumably, God's secret reasons for disposing as he does in the cosmos, and as Raphael later specifies (VIII, 169–70, 175–76), God's ways toward other worlds and other creatures in the universe.

Raphael's Ptolemaic argument is a far cry from Simplicio's. There are no appeals to authority, or to the need for higher illumination, or to Aristotelian physics; indeed, from the sample of Adam's reasoning he has just heard, Raphael associates with Adam's progeny the specific follies of the Ptolemaic apologists, guessing "how they will . . . /build, unbuild, contrive / To save appeerances, how gird the Sphear / With Centric and Eccentric scribbl'd o're, / Cycle and Epicycle, Orb in Orb" (VIII, 81–84). Raphael simply offers a critique of the false values implicit in Adam's complaint of disproportion in a geocentric universe (and the aspersions Adam thereby, albeit unintentionally, casts upon its Maker). Raphael's critique makes these points: the greatness and brightness of the other planets do not make them superior to the fertile earth; the noble planets at any rate do not serve the earth itself but man, who is more noble still; and (contrary to Simplicio's notions)[8] man is not the focus of the cosmic system but is rather "Lodg'd in a small partition, and the rest / Ordain'd for uses to his Lord best known" (VIII, 105–06).

As he prepares to shift to his Copernican argument, Raphael suggests that the cosmic system one credits depends on one's vantage point. To Adam on earth the universe seems Ptolemaic and thereby irrational: Raphael states that he developed his previous Ptolemaic argument "to shew / Invalid that which thee to doubt it mov'd; / Not that I so affirm, thoug so it seem / To thee who hast thy dwelling here on Earth" (VIII, 115–16). To angels who move among the planets the cosmos evidently seems Copernican, for Raphael proceeds to describe such a cosmos through a series of provocative suggestions, highlighting several topics explored at length by Salviati: that the sun may be a stationary center

8. Ibid., p. 61: "In brief, if we proceed to examine and weigh carefully all these things, we shall find that the goal to which all are directed is the need, the use, the comfort and the delight of men."

to the world; that the seemingly steadfast earth might move "Insensibly three different Motions," fetching day and night by her travels; that the earth might enlighten the moon by day as the moon enlightens earth by night; that the spots on the moon might be atmospheric clouds, possibly producing food for moon-dwellers, if any. Then, moving considerably beyond the topics addressed by Salviati, Raphael introduces Adam to advanced scientific speculations about life on other planets and unknown galaxies throughout the universe—dizzying speculations which are quite beyond Adam's wildest imaginings, though couched in the animistic, sexual imagery so precisely suited to Adam's comprehension:

> and other Suns perhaps
> With thir attendant Moons thou wilt descrie
> Communicating Male and Femal Light,
> Which two great Sexes animate the World,
> Stor'd in each Orb perhaps with some that live.
>   (VIII, 148–52)

Raphael's prototypical Galilean dialogue is not designed (like Galileo's) to demonstrate and argue for a theory, but rather to help Adam discover, as no other genre could, the appropriate terms and attitudes which should govern scientific inquiry into the cosmos. Raphael's sudden shift from human to angelic perspective should encourage Adam to distrust naive sense impressions and to abandon the notion that human concerns must be the focus and end of the entire cosmos—attitudes which Salviati also urged upon his friends as essential to scientific discourse.[9] Raphael's dialogue of one, in which he plays the roles both of Ptolemaic apologist and daring modern theorist, makes Adam confront his inevitable limitations in the study of astronomical science. Adam's sons must wait some centuries before the telescope—or space probes and moon landings—bring them somewhat closer to Raphael's angle of vision (itself limited), and they will then be thinking in terms of the relativity of space and time, and black holes. In preparation for all this, Adam is to learn from Raphael's dialogue that he should not rashly conclude nature defective and God's ways imperfect on the basis of his earthbound and necessarily inadequate understanding of God's purpose in the cosmos, nor yet assume that the scientific orthodoxy of the moment—Ptolemaic or otherwise—can explain the whole order of things for all time. Finally, Raphael's choice of genre reinforces the scale of human values. By at once indulging and refusing to satisfy Adam's scientific curiosity, while at the same time demonstrating the limitations pertaining to the human condition, Raphael underscores his advice that Adam's primary attention, care, and joy should be directed to human things: "thy being," "this Paradise / And thy fair *Eve*" (VIII, 170–74). Adam and his progeny are to learn from Raphael's dialogue

9. Ibid., pp. 256, 367–71.

that scientific speculation or activity must not displace or violate the human person, the human environment, and human society.

The other subordinate narrator, the archangel Michael, is charged to reveal the course of biblical history to fallen Adam. Like Raphael, Michael has his mission and manner prescribed by God in very general terms, but unlike Raphael he is to derive his subject matter from God by direct illumination: God charges him to drive Adam and Eve from Paradise "not disconsolate" and to "reveale / To *Adam* what shall come in future dayes, / As I shall thee enlighten, intermix / My Cov'nant in the womans seed renewd" (XI, 113–16). In that Michael receives this subject matter by means of visionary scenes and then mediates it to Adam, he is a prophet in the strict, technical sense of the term, whereas Raphael is a prophet only in the broad sense that he is authorized by God to reveal divine truth. Summarizing the tradition of Hebrew exegesis to explain the stricter kind of prophecy, John Smith declares:

> In all proper *Prophesie* . . . they [the Hebrew prophets] supposed the *Imaginative* power to be set forth as a *Stage* upon which certain *Visa* and *Simulacra* were represented to their Understandings, just indeed as they are to us in our common Dreams; only that the Understandings of the Prophets were alwaies kept awake and strongly acted by God in the midst of these apparitions, to see the intelligible Mysteries in them, and so in these Types and Shadows, which were Symbols of some spiritual things, to behold the Antitypes themselves.[1]

Michael enacts quite precisely the role of prophets such as Isaiah, Elijah, Ezekiel, and especially John of Patmos, whose Book of Revelation was described in the Geneva Bible as "a summe of those prophecies, which were written before, but shulde be fulfilled after the comming of Christ."[2] Adam, accordingly, addresses Michael as "Seer blest" (XII, 553). It is worth noting, however, that the mode which both Michael and Adam experience as prophecy the Miltonic bard and his audience perceive as history—the biblical record of all our woe and of the course of providential history through the ages.

Like Raphael, Michael is a poet as well as a prophet: though he draws his subject matter from visionary scenes—present rather than past experience—he too must choose the appropriate literary genres to accommodate that subject matter to his audience. From one perspective, Michael's entire narrative may be seen as a prototype of the Book of

---

1. Smith, "Of Prophets," pp. 178–79.
2. 41. *The Bible and Holy Scriptures Conteyned in the Olde and Newe Testament* (Geneva, 1560), Argument to the Book of Revelation, fol. 114ᵛ. For discussion from various perspectives of Milton's use of the Book of Revelation and development of a poetics of prophecy, see, e.g., William Kerrigan, *The Prophetic Milton* (Charlottesville, Va., 1974); Wittreich, *Visionary Poetics*; Fixler, "Apocalypse within *Paradise Lost*" and *Milton and the Kingdoms of God* (Evanston, Ill., 1964).

Revelation, incorporating the mixture of literary genres—epic, tragedy, history—commonly associated with that book in Milton's day. The Book of Revelation was understood to present the epic conflict of Christ and Antichrist, God and Satan throughout history and at the end of time; in this conflict the elect are portrayed "fighting or a warfaring" in spiritual combat against the forces of evil.[3] The Book of Revelation was also taken to be a "most long and doleful Tragedy, which shall overflow with scourges, slaughters, and destructions," as well as "an ecclesiastical history of the troubles and persecutions of the Church."[4] In similar terms, Michael introduces his narrative with an epic statement of theme identifying that narrative as the counterpoint in the fallen human world to Raphael's Homeric brief epic, and as an illustration of the "better fortitude / Of Patience and Heroic Martyrdom" (IX, 31–32) which the Miltonic bard has claimed as the true heroic subject: "Expect to hear, supernal Grace contending / With sinfulness of Men; thereby to learn / True patience" (XI, 359–61). Michael's narrative is also history and tragedy—the history of the few just and the many wicked from the first age to the last, presented as tragic scenes and stories of sin and suffering.

Within this apocalyptic, mixed-genre narrative, Michael disposes his material into two segments, comprising two distinct genres which are differentiated by conception of subject and manner of presentation in accordance with Adam's needs. The first segment is a series of tragic masques or pageants, interpreted as emblems.[5] Because Adam has been blind to sin and its effects, Michael first purges his eyes and then points out to him from the Hill of Speculation several scenes from antediluvian history: the murder of Abel; a lazar house full of loathsome diseases; the deceptively attractive but actually sinful society of the sons of God and the daughters of Cain; the wholesale destruction wrought by the giant offspring of that union; the luxurious riot of the ensuing generation; and finally, God's destruction of the entire world by flood, saving only Noah and his family.

* * *

The second segment of Michael's discourse is a narrative of biblical history from Abraham to the end of time set forth as the providential design of God. Michael changes his manner of presentation in response to a change in Adam's condition—"I perceave / Thy mortal sight to faile; objects divine / Must needs impaire and wearie human sense" (XII, 8–10)—and also to the demands of his new subject, providential history. Michael himself continues to receive his subject from God in the vi-

3. See e.g., Franciscus Junius, *The Apocalypse, or Revelation of St. John*, trans. T. Barbar (Cambridge, 1596), p. 247.

4. See, e.g., Thomas Brightman, *A Revelation of the Apocalypse*, in *Works* (London, 1644), p. 234; Henry Bullinger, *A Hundred Sermons upon the Apocalypse* London, 1573), sig. Aiii. See also Barbara K. Lewalski, "*Samson Agonistes* and the 'Tragedy' of the Apocalypse," *PMLA*, LXXXV (1970), 1050–62.

5. Demaray, *Milton's Theatrical Epic*, pp. 102–15, explorers the masque dimension and backgrounds of Michael's prophecy.

sionary mode of prophecy—"I see him, but thou canst not" (XII, 128)—but he now mediates these visions to Adam in the common mode of revealed Scripture. In substance, Michael's narrative is an expansion of Hebrews, chaper xi, presenting a résumé and interpretation of the typological progression of exemplary Old Testament heroes of faith, culminating in and fulfilled by Christ's redemptive sacrifice. * * *

But again, Michael does not simply offer a verse paraphrase of or a commentary upon Hebrews, chapter xi. His accommodation is literary as well as theological, as once again he invents a literary genre appropriate to his material and his audience. In conceptual terms, Michael's second narrative may be seen as a prototype of that classic of Christian historiography, Augustine's *City of God*. Augustine traces the perpetual opposition and conflict between the earthly and the heavenly city, tracing their respective origins to the companies of rebel and loyal angels in heaven, and on earth to Cain and Abel. But there is warrant in Augustine for the choice of Nimrod and Abraham as the starting point of Michael's prophesied history: Augustine observes that with Abraham the City of God "begins to be more conspicuous, and the divine promises which are now fulfilled in Christ are more fully revealed"; he also identifies Nimrod as both the builder of Babel and the founder of Babylon, that quintessential historical manifestation of the earthly city.[6] Michael's prototypical *City of God* presents Nimrod and Abraham at the outset as the founders of the two cities considered as historical and political entities. Nimrod, the "mightie Hunter," instituted tyrannical government on earth, and Abraham, the man of faith, founded the elect nation convenanted to God and saved by faith in the Promises. Michael's narrative, like Augustine's, culminates in an account of the Apocalypse and Millennium, but in both narratives the terms are essentially typological rather than apocalyptic. By means of his prophetic-historical narrative Michael leads Adam by stages to understand the covenant of grace and to read in the Old Testament types their Christic and apocalyptic fulfillments. Moreover, Michael's account renders the values of the two cities very much as Augustine articulates them:

> Two cities have been formed by two loves: the earthly by the love of self, even to the contempt of God; the heavenly by the love of God, even to the contempt of self. . . . The one seeks glory from men; but the greatest glory of the other is God, the witness of conscience. . . . In the one, the princes and the nations it subdues are ruled by the love of ruling; in the other, the princes and the subjects serve one another in love. . . . The one delights in its own strength, represented in the persons of its rulers; the other says to its God, "I will love Thee, O Lord, my strength." And therefore the wise men of the one

6. *City of God*, trans. Marcus Dods (New York, 1950), pp. 526–27, 537.

city [are vain], . . . glorying in their own wisdom, and being possessed by pride. . . . But in the other city there is no human wisdom, but only godliness, which offers due worship to the true God, and looks for its reward in the society of the saints.[7]

At the close of Michael's narrative, Adam's affirmation makes clear that he now understands and accepts the value of the city of God:

> Henceforth I learne, that to obey is best,
> And love with fear the onely God, to walk
> As in his presence, ever to observe
> His providence, and on him sole depend,
> Mercifull over all his works, with good
> Still overcoming evil, and by small
> Accomplishing great things, by things deemd weak
> Subverting worldly strong, and worldly wise
> By simply meek; that suffering for Truths sake
> Is fortitude to highest victorie,
> And to the faithful Death the Gate of Life;
> Taught this by his example whom I now
> Acknowledge my Redeemer ever blest.   (XII, 561–73)

In formal terms, the second segment of Michael's discourse is a prototype of the brief epic based on biblical history—a miniature and completed version of Du Bartas' incomplete *Seconde Semaine*. Du Bartas proposed to trace the Providence of God as it shaped the history of the Church from Paradise to the Last Judgment: his new hexameron, complementing the seven days of Creation, is based upon the scheme of the seven historical eras as outlined by Augustine. Du Bartas' epic conception of his subject is indicated by his combined thematic statement and invocation:

> Grant me the story of thy Church to sing,
> And gests of kinges: Let me this Totall bring
> From thy first Sabaoth to his fatall toombe,
> My stile extending to the day of doombe.[8]

But the intended unity and teleological direction are not realized in the poem. Du Bartas lived to complete only four of his projected seven days; his use of typology, though considerable, is sporadic; and his diffuseness and disgressions blur the pattern he would define. Also, Du Bartas attempts to assimiliate his biblical narratives to epic by pervasive use of epic and romance topoi and conventions: the numerous Old Testament battles and skirmishes are elaborated into epic warfare with heroes and heroines, challenges, vaunts, addresses to troops, councils of war; there are also allegorical interludes, councils in heaven, soliloquies, ecphrases,

---

7. Ibid., p. 477.
8. Sylvester's *Du Bartas*, "Second Week, First Day," 9–12, (Snyder, I, 316).

passionate declarations of love, apostrophes, catalogues, epic similes. By contrast, Michael's prototypical *Seconde Semaine* achieves conceptual rigor and structural cohesion from its Pauline and Augustinian models, and it wholly eliminates conventional epic apparatus. Michael's poem in Book XII of *Paradise Lost* is accordingly a true counterpoint to Raphael's Homeric brief epic in Book VI: it is a fully achieved epic of providential history in which all the elect are called upon, in tragic circumstances, to display some version of the new Christian heroism— unwavering faith and love, moral courage, "the better fortitude / Of Patience and Heroic Martyrdom."

As we have seen, the subordinate narrators Milton creates in *Paradise Lost* are imagined as poets inventing literary forms—chiefly varieties of epic—as a means to accommodate particular subjects to a specific audience, Adam and Eve. They present, as it were, the ideal forms of these genres in miniature: the "Lucretian" philosophical poem, the Homeric epic, the hexameron, the scientific treatise in verse, the apocalyptic epic comprised of tragic pageants, the epic of biblical history. In so doing, the angelic poets may be presumed to realize the highest potential of the various genres, to teach, move, and delight Adam and Eve; at another level, these angelic poems provide a standard against which the bard's audience is expected to measure the values conveyed by other noteworthy poems in the several genres. If Milton's subordinate narrators use such literary strategies, I think we may fairly expect to find that the Miltonic bard—the all-encompassing narrative voice of the poem—employs generic choices and changes in similar ways. Unlike Raphael and Michael, who have to invent literary forms as yet unknown to their audience, the bard addresses an audience knowledgeable about the literary tradition and the values exhibited in particular kinds and works. He can therefore use genre changes and permutations to provide multiple perspectives upon the personages and incidents of the poem and to engage the reader continually in a process of comparison and evaluation, thereby developing and exercising the reader's moral sense. The poetics exhibited by Milton's angelic poets lends supports to a hypothesis which I am exploring elsewhere: that it is by humanistic and literary means (notably, genre), rather than primarily by prophetic authority or verbal entrapment, that Milton leads his readers from partial to more complete, from simple to more complex, understanding of the human condition.

FRANK KERMODE

Adam Unparadised†

*   *   *

We may conclude that there is a reason to suppose that we shall miss the force of Milton's poem if we assume that he was strictly limited by the *naïveté* of his theme or the inerrancy of its biblical expression. His method is to affect the senses of his audience and not its reason directly. He could not have hoped for total control over the affective power of the poem, for that is not consistent with the nature of poetry; and in this particular poem the material is common property, so that there must be many aspects of it which interest other people and not Milton, yet cannot be excluded. The original myth is a myth of total explanation, and therefore infinitely explicable; the poet can only say some of the things about it but the rest of it is still in men's minds, or indeed below them—Joyce's umbilical telephone line to Edenville. It is not of course doubted that Milton does offer interpretations, that he gets at the reader in many ways; the theology of Book iii, for example, is made to sound very dogmatic, though only to prevent irrelevant speculation; and we are always being told the proper way to think about Satan. As well as presenting the human predicament the poet suggests ways of understanding and accepting it. It should even be admitted that the general design of the poem is governed by this double purpose of presentation and interpretation; and that not only in the strategic theologizing of the third book and the loaded education of Adam between Books iv and ix. For although it is commonly said that Milton, on the ancient epic pattern, proceeds *in medias res*, he in fact strikes into his subject nothing like so near the middle as Virgil and Homer; he starts not in the Garden but with the fall of the angels, which is why some schoolchildren, having read Books i and ii, go through life thinking it was Satan who lost paradise. The reason for this, one guesses, is that Milton wanted us to think of events in this order: the Fall from heaven, the Fall from Paradise, and finally the effect of the Fall in the life of humanity in general, just in the manner of Ignatian meditation on these subjects.[1] But it is important that we should not allow considerations of this sort to lead to a conviction that there is at all times a design upon us. So deceived, we can easily miss something far more obvious and important to the structure of the poem: namely, that it is based on a series of massive antitheses,

---

† From *The Living Milton: Essays by Various Hands,* collected and edited by Frank Kermode (London, Routledge & Kegan Paul Ltd., 1960) 98–106, 109–23. Reprinted by permission of the publisher. The author's footnotes have been renumbered.
1. See for example *The Sermons and Devotional Writings of Gerard Manley Hopkins,* ed. C. Devlin (1959), pp. 131 ff.

or if you like huge structural pseudo-rhymes, and the central pseudo-rhyme is *delight/woe*. The delight and woe are here and now, which is the real point of all the squeezing together of the time-sequence that Milton carries on in his similes, in upsetting allusions to clerical corruption, in using expressions like 'never since created man' or 'since mute'; in a hundred other ways, some of which I will discuss later. The poem is absolutely contemporary, and its subject is human experience symbolized in this basic myth, and here made relevant in a manner not so different from that to which our own century has accustomed us.

The Themes

Miss Rosemond Tuve, in her magnificent and too brief book, has persuasively expounded Milton's treatment in the minor poems of certain great central themes. They lie at the heart of each poem and govern its secondary characteristics of imagery and diction; given the theme, the poet thinks in the figures appropriate to it, and in every case the theme and the figures have a long and rich history. The subject of *L'Allegro* is every man's Mirth, our Mirth, the very Grace herself with all she can include';[2] the *Hymn on the Morning of Christ's Nativity* proliferates images of harmony because its theme is the Incarnation. I now take a step of which Miss Tuve would probably not approve, and add that beneath these figures and themes there is Milton's profound and personal devotion to an even more radical topic, potentially coextensive with all human experience: the loss of Eden. In the *Hymn* there is a moment of peace and harmony in history—the 'Augustan peace', which looks back to human wholeness and incorruption, as well as forward to a time when, after generations of human anguish, the original harmony will be restored. The same moment of stillness, poised between past and future, is there in 'At a Solemn Musick', for music remembers as well as prefigures. In *Comus* too there is presented that moment of harmony, of reunion and restitution, that prefigures the final end, and in *Comus* as in the others there is an emphasis on the long continuance of grief and suffering; for in the much misunderstood Epilogue Adonis is still not cured of his wound and Venus 'sadly sits.' Only in the future will Cupid be united with Psyche and the twins of Paradise, Youth and Joy, be born. *Lycidas* tells of disorder, corruption, false glory as incident to life here and now, with order, health, and the perfect witness of God to come. All of them speak of something that is gone.

Paradise Lost deals most directly with this basic theme, the recognition of lost possibilities of joy, order, health, the contrast between what we can imagine as human and what is so here and now; the sensuous import of the myth of the lost Eden. To embody this theme is the main business of *Paradise Lost*; thus will life be displayed in some great symbolic attitude

2. *Images and Themes in Five Poems by Milton* (1957), p. 20.

and not by the poet's explanations of the how and the why. His first task is to get clear the human experience of the potency of delight, and its necessary frustration, and if he cannot do that the poem will fail no matter what is added of morality, theology or history.

My difficulty in establishing this point is that some will think it too obvious to be thus laboured, and others will think it in need of much more elaborate defence. What is rare is to find people who read *Paradise Lost* as if it were true that the power of joy and its loss is its theme; and though it is true that for certain well-known and important reasons Milton's poem is not accessible to the same methods of reading as Romantic literature, it is also true that this is the theme of *The Prelude*, and that we can do some harm by insisting too strongly upon differences at the expense of profound similarities. Anyway, I think I can make my point in a somewhat different way by a reference to Bentley,[3] and in particular to his observations on the last lines of *Paradise Lost*, stale as this subject may seem.

Adam, hearing Michael's promise of a time when 'Earth/Shall all be Paradise, far happier place/Than this of *Eden*' xii. 463–65 is 'replete with joy and wonder' (468) and replies with the famous cry of *felix culpa*:

> full of doubt I stand,
> Whether I should repent me now of sin
> By mee done and occasiond, or rejoice
> Much more, that much more good thereof shall spring . . .
> (473–76)

Michael says that the Comforter will watch over and arm the faithful; Adam, benefiting by Michael's foretelling of the future (in which 'time stands fixt' as it does in the poem) has now all possible wisdom (575–76); and Eve is well content with her lot. And thus matters stand when Eden is closed, and Adam and Eve move away

> The World was all before them, where to choose
> Thir place of rest, and Providence thir guide:
> They hand in hand with wandring steps and slow,
> Through *Eden* took thir solitarie way.
> (xii. 646–49)

'Why' asks Bentley, 'does this distich dismiss our first parents in anguish, and the reader in melancholy? And how can the expression be justified, *with wandring steps and slow? Why wandring?* Erratick steps? Very improper, when, in the line before, they were *guided by Providence*. And why slow? even when Eve has professed her readiness and alacrity for the journey:

---

3. Richard Bentley, whose edition of *Paradise Lost* was published in 1732 [*Editor*].

> but now lead on;
> In me is no delay.

And why their *solitarie way*? All words to represent a sorrowful parting?
when even their former walks in Paradise were as solitary as their way
now; there being nobody besides them two both here and there. Shall
I therefore, after so many prior presumptions, presume at last to offer
a distich, as close as may be to the author's words, and *entirely agreeable
to his scheme*?

> Then hand in hand with *social* steps their way
> Through Eden took, *with heavenly comfort cheer'd.*'

Bentley assumes that he has exact knowledge of Milton's 'scheme', and
quarrels with the text for not fitting it. He seems to be forgetting God's
instructions to Michael—'so send them forth, though sorrowing, yet in
peace' (xi. 117), and also Adam's knowledge of the events leading up to
the happy consummation; yet it remains true that if Milton's 'scheme'
was simply to show that everything would come out right in the end,
and that this should keenly please both Adam and ourselves, Bentley is
not at all silly here; or if he is, so are more modern commentators who,
supported by all that is now known about the topic *felix culpa*, tend to
read the poem in a rather similar way though without actually rewriting
it, by concentrating on Milton's intention, somewhat neglected in the
past, to present this belated joy of Adam's as central to the whole poem.
There is, of course, such an intention or 'scheme'; the mistake is to
suppose that it is paramount. It is in fact subsidiary, *Paradise Lost* being
a poem, to the less explicable theme of joy and woe, which has to be
expressed in terms of the myth, as a contrast between the original justice
of Paradise and the mess of history: between Paradise and Paradise Lost.
The poem is tragic. If we regard it as a document in the history of ideas,
ignoring what it does to our senses, we shall of course find ideas, as
Bentley did, and conceivably the closing lines will seem out of true.
But our disrespect for Bentley's Milton, and in this place particularly,
is proof that the poem itself will prevent our doing this unless we are
very stubborn or not very susceptible to poetry. The last lines of the
poem are, we *feel*, exactly right, for all that Adam has cried out for
pleasure; death denounced, he has lost his Original Joy. The tragedy is
a matter of *fact*, of life as we feel it; the hope of restoration is a matter
of faith, and faith is 'the substance of things hoped for, the evidence of
things unseen'—a matter altogether less simple, sensuous, and passion-
ate, altogether less primitive. We are reminded that 'the conception that
man is mortal, by his nature and essence, seems to be entirely alien to
mythical and primitive religious thought'.[4] In the poem we deplore the

4. E. Cassirer, *An Essay on Man* (1944), pp. 83–84.

accidental loss of native immortality more than we can applaud its gracious restoration.

Adam Imparadised

One of the effects of mixing up Milton with the Authorized Version, and of intruding mistaken ideas of Puritanism into his verse, is that it can become very hard to see what is made absolutely plain: that for Milton the joy of Paradise is very much a matter of the senses. The Authorized Version says that 'the Lord God planted a garden' (Gen. ii. 8) and that he 'took the man and put him into the garden of Eden to dress it and keep it' (i. 15). But even in Gen. ii. 8 the Latin texts usually have *in paradisum voluptatis* 'into a paradise of pleasure'—this is the reading of the Vulgate currently in use. And the Latin version of ii. 15 gives *in paradiso deliciarum*. Milton's Paradise is that of the Latin version; in it, humanity without guilt is 'to all delight of human sense expos'd' (iv. 206), and he insists on this throughout. Studying the exegetical tradition on this point, Sister Mary Corcoran makes it plain that Milton pushes this sensuous pleasure much harder than his 'scheme' as Bentley and others might conceive it, required. For example, he rejected the strong tradition that the first marriage was not consummated until after the Fall, choosing to ignore the difficulty about children conceived before but born after it. For this there may be an historical explanation in the Puritan cult of married love; but it could not account for what has been called Milton's 'almost Dionysiac treatment'[5] of sexuality before the Fall; Sister Corcoran is sorry that she can't even quite believe the assertion that 'in those hearts/Love unlibidinous reignd (v. 449–50).[6]

In fact Milton went to great trouble to get this point firmly made; had he failed no amount of finesse in other places could have held the poem together; and it is therefore just as well that nothing in the poem is more beautifully achieved.

Why was innocent sexuality so important to Milton's poem? Why did he take on the task of presenting an Adam and an Eve unimaginably privileged in the matter of sensual gratification 'to all delight of human sense expos'd'? There is a hint of the answer in what I have written earlier about his view of the function of poetry. Believing as he did in the inseparability of matter and form, except by an act of intellectual abstraction, Milton could not allow a difference of kind between soul and body; God

> created all
> Such to perfection, one first matter all,
> Indu'd with various forms, various degrees
> Of substance, and in things that live, of life;

5. Harris Fletcher, *Milton's Rabbinical Readings* (1930), p. 185.
6. *Paradise Lost with reference to the Hexameral Background* (1945), pp. 76 ff.

But more refin'd, more spiritous and pure,
As nearer to him plac't or nearer tending
Each in thir several active Sphears assignd,
Till body up to spirit work, in bounds
Proportiond to each kind. So from the root
Springs lighter the green stalk, from thence the leaves
More aerie, last the bright consummat flowre
Spirits odorous breathes: flowrs and thir fruit
Mans nourishment, by gradual scale sublim'd
To vital Spirits aspire, to animal,
To intellectual, give both life and sense,
Fancie and understanding, whence the Soule
Reason receives, and reason is her being,
Discursive or Intuitive; discourse
Is Oftest yours, the latter most is ours . . .

(v. 471–89)

An acceptance of Raphael's position involves, given the cosmic scale of the poem, a number of corollaries which Milton does not shirk. Matter, the medium of the senses, is continuous with spirit; or 'spirit, being the more excellent substance, virtually and essentially contains within itself the inferior one; as the spiritual and rational faculty contains the corporeal, that is, the sentient and vegetative faculty' (*De Doctrina Christiana* I, vii). It follows that the first matter is of God, and contains the potentiality of form;[7] so the body is not to be thought of in disjunction from the soul, of which 'rational', 'sensitive and 'vegetative' are merely aspects. Raphael accordingly goes out of his way to explain that the intuitive reason of the angels differs only in degree from the discursive reason of men; and Milton that there is materiality in angelic spirit. It is a consequence of this that part of Satan's sufferings lie in a deprivation of sensual pleasure. Milton's thought is penetrated by this doctrine, which, among other things, accounts for his view of the potency of poetry for good or ill; for poetry works through pleasure, by sensuous delight; it can help 'body up to spirit work' or it can create dangerous physiological disturbance. Obviously there could be no more extreme challenge to the power and virtue of his art than this: to require of it a representation of ecstatic sensual pleasure, a *voluptas* here and only here not associated with the possibility of evil: 'delight to Reason join'd' (ix. 243). The loves of Paradise must be an unimaginable joy to the senses, yet remain 'unlibidinous.'

If we were speaking of Milton rather than of his poem we might use this emphasis on materiality, on the dignity as well as the danger of sense, to support a conclusion similar to that of De Quincey in his account of Wordsworth: 'his intellectual passions were fervent and strong;

7. See W. B. Hunter, Jr., 'Milton's Power of Matter', *Journal of the History of Ideas*, xiii (1952), 551–62.

but they rested upon a basis of preternatural animal sensibility diffused through *all* the animal passions (or appetites); and something of that will be found to hold of all poets who have been great by original force and power . . .' (De Quincey was thinking about Wordsworth's facial resemblance to Milton). And it would be consistent with such an account that Milton also had, like Wordsworth, a constant awareness of the dangers entailed by a powerful sensibility. This gives us the short reason why, when Milton is representing the enormous bliss of innocent sense, he does not do so by isolating it and presenting it straightforwardly. He sees that we must grasp it at best deviously; we understand joy as men partially deprived of it, with a strong sense of the woeful gap between the possible and the actual in physical pleasure. And Milton's prime device for ensuring that we should thus experience his Eden is a very sophisticated, perhaps a 'novelistic' one: we see all delight through the eyes of Satan.

* * *

The Garden of Love

The degree of literary sophistication in Milton's treatment of the biblical account of Adam and Eve in Paradise is a reasonably accurate index of his whole attitude to what I have called the myth. I have already mentioned the incorporation of other literary and mythological gardens in this Eden; they are significant shadows of it. But the full exploration of the literary context of Milton's Paradise would be a very large inquiry, and here there is occasion only for a brief and tentative sketch of it, touching only upon what affects the present argument.

When Milton comes to treat of the inhabitants of the garden he plunges us at once into a dense literary context. The Bible says: 'And they were both naked, the man and his wife, and were not ashamed' (Genesis ii. 25). According to Milton, however, they were 'with native Honour clad/In naked Majestie' (289–90); and a little later he moralizes this:

> Nor those mysterious parts were then conceal'd,
> Then was not guiltie shame, dishonest shame
> Of Natures works: honor dishonorable,
> Sin-bred, how have ye troubl'd all mankind
> With shews instead, mere shows of seeming pure . . .
> (312–15)

This is in open allusion to a literary topic so often treated in Renaissance and seventeenth-century writing as to be unwieldy in its complexity. First one needs to understand the general primitivistic position which held that custom and honour were shabby modern expedients unnecessary in a Golden Age society, with all its corollaries in Renaissance 'naturalism'. Then one has to consider the extremely complex subject of literary gardens and their connection with the Earthly Paradise and the Golden Age, not only in Renaissance, but also in classical and mediaeval literature. Of the first of these I now say nothing. The easy way to approach the second is through the *locus classicus*, the chorus *O bella età de l'oro* in Tasso's *Aminta*. In the Golden Age, as in Eden, the earth bore fruit and flowers without the aid of man; the air was calm and there was eternal spring. Best of all, there was continual happiness because—in the translation of Henry Reynolds—

> Because that vain and ydle name,
> That couz'ning Idoll of unrest,
> Whom the madd vulgar first did raize,
> And call'd it Honour, whence it came
> To tyrannize o're ev'ry brest,
> Was not then suffred to molest
> Poore lovers hearts with new debate. . . .
> The Nymphes sate by their Paramours,
> Whispring love-sports, and dalliance. . . .

It was Honour that ruined Pleasure,

> And lewdly did instruct faire eyes
> They should be nyce, and scrupulous. . . .
> (*Torquato Tassos Aminta Englisht*, 1628)

This is the Honour, a tyrant bred of custom and ignorant opinion, which inevitably intrudes into Milton's argument when he uses the word in forcible oxymoron, 'honor dishonorable.' But he is not using the idea as it came sometimes to be used in poetry Milton would have called dishonest; his Honour is 'sin-bred,' a pathetic subterfuge of the fallen, and not, as it is in libertine poems, an obstacle to sexual conquest that must yield to primitivist argument.[8] Of these ambiguities Milton must have been fully aware, since the poetry of his time contains many libertine attacks on Honour which imply that reason and 'native Honour' will be satisfied only by an absolute surrender to pleasure. Furthermore, many of these poems are set in gardens, and we should not overlook the difficulties Milton had to overcome before he could be reasonably satisfied that his garden of love was the right kind. The garden of love has a long history, and the topic nowadays called the *locus amoenus*[9] is as old as the garden of Alcinous in the *Odyssey*; the expression *locus amoenus* meant to Servius 'a place for lovemaking', and *amoenus* was derived by a false etymology from *amor*. This tradition, mingling with

8. I have said part of my say about this in 'The Argument of Marvell's Garden', *Essays in Criticism*, ii (1952), 225–41.
9. See E. R. Curtius, *European Literature in the Latin Middle Ages* (1952), Cap. 10, especially pp. 195 ff. And among the growing literature on this theme, E. G. Kern, 'The Gardens of the Decameron Cornice," *PMLA*, LXVI (1951), 505–23.

the continuous traditions of the Earthly Paradise, and modified by the allegorical skills of the Middle Ages, sometimes conformed and sometimes conflicted with the garden of Genesis; gardens could be the setting for all kinds of love, just as Venus herself could preside over all kinds of love and all kinds of gardens. Milton needed a *paradisus voluptatis*, but it must not be the same as a 'naturalist' or libertine garden, and it must not be connected with 'courtly love'—hence the disclaimers in II. 7 ff. and II. 769–70. Whatever the dishonest and sophisticate, or for that matter the falsely philosophical, might do with imaginary Edens, he was dealing with the thing itself, and must get innocent delight into it. So he uses these conventions, including the usual attack upon Honour, with his customary boldness, as if his treatment, though late, were the central one, and all the others mere shadows of his truth; the same method, in fact, as that used for pagan mythology. In Book ix, having risked all the difficulties of his contrast between love unlibidinous and love libidinous by showing them both in the experience of Adam and Eve, he is able to enlarge upon the oxymoron 'honor dishonorable,' saying that

> innocence, that as a veil
> Had shaddowd them from knowing ill, was gon,
> Just confidence and native righteousness,
> And honour from about them. . . .
>
> (ix. 1054–57)

And Adam sees that the fruit of knowledge was bad, 'if this be to know,/ Which leaves us naked thus, of Honour void' (1073–74); here the fig-leaves are assimilated to the literary tradition. As for *locus amoenus*, Milton also contrives to give two versions of it: in Book iv it is worked into the account of 'unreprov'd' lovemaking (see especially II. 1034 ff.) as the scene of the first fallen act of love. Pope first saw another link between these two passages, and Douglas Bush has recently written upon this link a brilliant page of commentary:[1] each derives a good deal, and the manner of derivation is ironical, from a single episode in the *Iliad*, the lovemaking of Zeus and Hera in Book xiv.

So, erudite and delicate, yet so characteristic a device might find, among fit audience, someone to value it for itself; but Milton's object was to exploit, with what force all the literature in the world could lend, the contrast between the true delight of love and the fallacious delight which is a mere prelude to woe; between possible and actual human pleasure. And however complex the means, the end is simply to show Adam and Eve as actually enjoying what to us is a mere imagination, and then explain how they lost it, and what was then left. In this sense their simple experience contains the whole of ours, including that which we feel we might but know we cannot have; and in this sense they

---

1. *Paradise Lost in Our Time* (1948), pp. 105–6.

include us, they are what we are and what we imagine we might be.
This inclusiveness is given remarkably concrete demonstration in lines
so famous for their unidiomatic English that the reason for the distorted
word-order has been overlooked:

> the lovliest pair
> That ever since in loves inbraces met,
> *Adam* the goodliest man of men since born
> His Sons, the fairest of her Daughters *Eve*.
>
> (iv. 321–24)

The syntax may be Greek, but the sense is English, and inclusiveness
could hardly be more competely presented; Adam and Eve here literally
include us all. The illogic of the expression serves the same end as the
illogic of those mythological parallels inserted only to be denied, or of
those continuous reminders that the whole of history 'since created man'
is somehow being enacted here and now in the garden. What must
never be underestimated is the sheer absorbency of Milton's theme;
everything will go into it, and find itself for the first time properly placed,
completely explained. Todd[2] has a note on the passage (iv. 458 ff.) in
which Milton adapts to the awakening of Eve Ovid's account of Narcissus
first seeing himself in the pool: he cites one commentator who enlarges
upon Milton's enormous improvement of Ovid's lines, and another who
adds that 'we may apply to Milton on this occasion what Aristotle says
of Homer, that he taught poets how to lie properly'. Lying properly
about everything is a reasonable way of describing the poet's achievement
in *Paradise Lost*, if a proper lie is one that includes the *terra incognita*
of human desires, actual love and possible purity.

That is why we see Adam and Eve in the garden of love not directly,
but through many glasses; and the darkest of these is the mind of Satan.
He looks at his victims with passionate envy and even regret:

> Ah gentle pair, ye little think how nigh
> Your change approaches, when all these delights
> Will vanish and deliver ye to woe,
> More woe, the more your taste is now of joy;
> Happie, but for so happie ill secur'd
> Long to continue, and this high seat your Heav'n
> Ill fenc't for Heav'n to keep out such a foe
> As now is enterd.
>
> (iv. 366–73)

He is reluctant to harm them; he pleads necessity (Milton calls this 'The
Tyrants plea' (394) and neatly gives it to Adam in x. 131 ff.). But what
he must take away from them is *delight*, physical pleasure in innocence;
his dwelling in Hell 'haply may not please/Like this fair Paradise, your

2. H. J. Todd, whose edition of *The Poetical Works of John Milton* first appeared in 1801 [*Editor*].

sense' (iv. 378–79). They are to 'taste' something other than Joy; and one remembers how frequently, at critical moments, the word 'taste' occurs in *Paradise Lost,* from the second line on. The shadow of Satan falls most strikingly over the pleasures of the garden when he watches Adam and Eve making love. It is not merely that the absolutely innocent and joyous act is observed as through a peep-hole, as if the lovers had been tricked into a bawdy-house; Satan himself acquires some of the pathos of an old *voyeur.* Pursuing his equation of delight with innocence, Milton boldly hints that the fallen angel is sexually deprived. He has forfeited the unfallen delights of sense. There is, we are to learn, love-making in heaven, but not in hell; the price of warring against omni-potence is impotence.

> Sight hateful, sight tormenting! thus these two
> Imparadis't in one anothers arms
> The happier *Eden,* shall enjoy their fill
> Of bliss on bliss, while I to Hell am thrust,
> Where neither joy nor love, but fierce desire,
> Among our other torments not the least,
> Still unfulfilld with pain of longing pines . . .
> (iv. 505–11)

Satan is so sure of their sexual joy that he anticipates later love poetry in making the body of the beloved a paradise in itself—his 'happier Eden' is not the same as that promised later to Adam (xii. 587)—and he uses a word, 'imparadis't', which was to have its place in the vocab-ulary of fallen love. But at this moment only Satan can feel desire without fulfilment, and Milton reminds us that he resembles in this fallen men; thus he actualizes the human contrast between innocence and experi-ence, and between love and its counterfeits—the whole 'monstruosity of love', as Troilus calls it.

Milton, in short, provides an illogical blend of purity and impurity in the first delightful lovemaking. He does not present an isolated purity and then its contamination, as the narrative might seem to require, but interferes with this order just as he does with word-order, and for similar reasons. Not ony does he show us the unfallen Adam and Eve in such a way that we can never think of their delight without thinking of its enemies; he also establishes such links between the fourth and ninth books that we can never think of his account of unfallen love without remembering the parallel passages on lust. It is here relevant to em-phasize the unpraised brilliance of one of the linking devices, Milton's use of the theme of physiological perturbation. At the opening of Book iv Uriel observes that Satan is affected by unregulated passions, as the unfallen Adam and Eve cannot be; he is the first person on earth to experience this. But by the end of the Book he has established by an act of demonic possession that Eve is physiologically capable of such a disturbance (iv. 799 ff.; v. 9–11); and the effect of the Fall in Book ix can be measured by the degree to which the humours of the lovers are distempered by the fruit:

> Soon as the force of that fallacious Fruit,
> That with exhilerating vapour bland
> About thir spirits had playd, and inmost powers
> Made err, was now exhal'd, and grosser sleep
> Bred of unkindly fumes, with conscious dreams
> Encumberd, now had left them, up they rose
> As from unrest. . . .
>
> (ix. 1046–52)

We happen to know what Milton, as theologian, believed to be the significance of the eating of the fruit. He regarded the tree of the knowledge of good and evil as merely 'a pledge, as it were, and memorial of obedience.' The tasting of its fruit was an act that included all sins: 'it comprehended at once distrust in the divine veracity, and a proportionate credulity in the assurances of Satan; unbelief, ingratitude; disobedience; gluttony; in the man excessive uxoriousness, in the woman a want of proper regard for her husband, in both an insensibility to the welfare of their offspring, and that offspring the whole human race; parricide, theft, invasion of the rights of others, sacrilege, deceit, presumption in aspiring to divine attributes, fraud in the means employed to attain the object, pride, and arrogance' (De Doctrina Christiana I, xi, Sumner's translation). But none of this stemmed from the intoxicating power of the fruit; God was testing fidelity by forbidding 'an act of its own nature indifferent.' In other words Milton the poet establishes the theme of perturbation as a structural element in the poem, using it as an index of fallen nature, of the disaster brought upon Joy by Woe, by means which must have earned the disapproval of Milton the theologian, namely the attribution of intoxicating powers to the forbidden fruit. Joy and Woe in the poem take precedence over theological niceties; Milton's theology is in the De Doctrina, not in Paradise Lost.

Adam Unparadised

Joy and Woe, the shadow of one over the other, the passage from one to the other, are the basic topic of the poem. We turn now to Adam unparadised, to Joy permanently overshadowed by Woe, light by dark, nature by chaos, love by lust, fecundity by sterility. Death casts these shadows. It is not difficult to understand why a very intelligent Italian, reading Paradise Lost for the first time, should have complained to me that he had been curiously misled about its subject; for, he said, 'it is a poem about Death'.

For who would lose
Though full of pain, this intellectual being?
(ii. 146–47)

Belial asks the question, as Claudio had done; it is a human reaction, and most of the time we do not relish the thought of being without 'sense and motion' (ii. 151); nor can we help it if this is to be called 'ignoble' (ii. 227). In the same book, Milton gives Death allegorical substance, if 'substance might be calld that shaddow seemd' (669); for it is all darkness and shapelessness, a 'Fantasm' (743), all lust and anger, its very name hideous (788). The only thing it resembles is Chaos, fully described in the same book; and it stands in relation to the order and delight of the human body as Chaos stands to Nature. So, when Satan moved out of Chaos into Nature, he not only 'into Nature brought/ Miserie' (vi. 267), but into Life brought Death, and into Light (which is always associated with order and organic growth) darkness. At the end of Book ii he at last, 'in a cursed hour' (1055), approaches the pendant world, having moved towards it from Hell through Chaos; and the whole movement of what might be called the *sensuous* logic of the poem so far—the fall into darkness and disorder, the return to light and order— is triumphantly halted at the great invocation to Light which opens Book iii. But the return is of course made with destructive intent. We see the happiness of a man acquainted with the notion of Death but having no real knowledge of it—'So neer grows Death to Life, what e're Death is,/Som dreadful thing no doubt' (iv. 425–26); and then, after the long interruption of Books v–viii, which represent the everything which stretched between life and death, we witness the crucial act from which the real knowledge of Death will spring, when Eve took the fruit, 'and knew not eating Death' (ix. 792). The syntax, once again, is Greek; but we fill it with our different and complementary English senses: 'she knew not that she was eating death'; 'she knew not Death even as she ate it'; 'although she was so bold as to eat Death for the sake of knowledge, she still did not know—indeed she did not even know what she had known before, namely that this was a sin'. Above all she *eats* Death, makes it a part of her formerly incorruptible body, and so explains the human sense of the possibility of incorruption, so tragically belied by fact. The function of Death in the poem is simple enough; it is 'to destroy, or unimmortal make/All kinds' (x. 611–12). There is, of course, the the-ological explanation to be considered, that the success of Death in this attempt is permissive; but in terms of the poem this is really no more than a piece of dogmatic cheering-up, and Milton, as usual, allows God himself to do the explaining (x. 616 ff.). From the human point of view, the intimation of unimmortality takes priority over the intellectual com-fort of God's own theodicy, simply because a man can feel, and can feel the possibility of immortality blighted.

Milton saw the chance, in Book ix, of presenting very concretely the impact of Death on Life; and it would be hard to think of a fiction more completely achieved. The moment is of Eve's return to Adam, enormously ignorant and foolishly cunning, 'with Countnance blithe. . . . But in her Cheek distemper flushing glowd' (ix. 886–87). This flush is a token of unimmortality; and then, since 'all kinds' are to be affected, the roses fade and droop in Adam's welcoming garland. He sees that Eve is lost, 'Defac't, deflowrd, and now to Death devote' (901). He retreats into Eve's self-deception; but all is lost.

The emphasis here is on *all*; from the moment of eating the fruit to that of the descent of 'prevenient grace' (end of Book x and beginning of xi) Adam and Eve have lost everything, and are, without mitigation, to death devote. If one bears this steadily in mind the tenth book is a lot easier to understand; it seems often to be misread. Adam, 'in a troubl'd Sea of passion tost' (718) cries out 'O miserable of happie!' (720) and laments the end of the 'new glorious World' (721). He feels particularly the corruption of love:

> O voice once heard
> Delightfully, *Encrease and multiply*,
> Now death to hear!
>
> (729–31)

and sums up in a couplet using the familiar pseudo-rhyme: 'O fleeting joyes/Of Paradise, deare bought with lasting woes!' (741–42). He has knowledge of the contrast between then and now, but of nothing else. Deprived of Original Justice, he is now merely natural; hence the importance of remembering that he is here simply a human being in a situation that is also simple, and capable of being felt naturally, upon our pulses. Deprived as he is, Adam finds life 'inexplicable' (754); knowing nothing of the great official plan by which good will come of all this, his speculations are by the mere light of nature. Rajan made something of this in his explanation of how Milton got his heterodox theology into the poem—mortalism, for example, is not very tendentious if proffered as the opinion of a totally corrupt man.[3] But, much more important, Adam is here for the first time true kindred to the reader. The primary appeal of poetry is to the natural man; that is why it is called simple, sensuous and passionate. When Eve proposes that they should practise a difficult abstinence in order not to produce more candidates for unimmortality, or Adam considers suicide (x. 966 ff.) we should be less conscious of their errors than of their typicality. Whatever the mind may make of it, the sensitive body continues to feel the threat of unimmortality as an outrage:

3. B. Rajan, *Paradise Lost and the Seventeenth Century Reader* (1947), Cap. ii.

> Why is life giv'n
> To be thus wrested from us? rather why
> Obtruded on us thus? who, if we knew
> What we receive, would either not accept
> Life offerd, or soon beg to lay it down,
> Glad to be so dismisst in peace.
>
> (xi. 502–7)

Michael's treatment of the same topic that the Duke inflicts upon Claudio in *Measure for Measure* can only strengthen such sentiments:

> thou must outlive
> Thy youth, thy strength, thy beauty, which will change
> To witherd weak and gray; thy Senses then
> Obtuse, all taste of pleasure must forgo,
> To what thou hast, and for the Air of youth
> Hopeful and cheerful, in thy blood will reign
> A melancholly damp of cold and dry
> To weigh thy spirits down, and last consume
> The Balm of Life.
>
> (xi. 538–46)

Whatever the consolation offered by Death—no one would wish to 'eternize' a life so subject to distempers of every kind—it is not pretended that this makes up for the loss of the 'two fair gifts . . . Happiness/And Immortalitie' (xi. 56–8). Most criticism of the verse of Book x and xi amounts to a complaint that it is lacking in sensuousness; but this is founded on a misunderstanding of the poem. *Paradise Lost* must be seen as a whole and whoever tries to do this will see the propriety of this change of tone, this diminution of *sense* in the texture of the verse.

A striking example of this propriety is the second of the formal salutations to Eve, Adam's in xi. 158 ff. * * * Here Adam sees that Eve is responsible not only for death but for the victory over it; as she herself says, 'I who first brought Death on all, am grac't/The source of life' (xi. 168–9). This paradox, considered as part of the whole complex in which Milton places it, seems to me much more central to the mood of the poem that the famous *felix culpa*, because it is rooted in nature, and related to our habit of rejoicing that life continues, in spite of death, from generation to generation. Yet Adam is still under the shadow of death, and his restatement of the theme Venus-Eve-Mary is very properly deprived of the sensuous context provided for Raphael's salutation; and since the second passage cannot but recall the first, we may be sure that this effect was intended.

There is, indeed, another passage which strongly supports this view of the centrality of the paradox of Eve as destroyer and giver of life, and it has the same muted quality, casts the same shadow over the power and delight of love. This is the curious vision of the union between the

sons of Seth and the daughters of Cain (xi. 556–636). The Scriptural
warrant for this passage is extremely slight, though there were precedents
for Milton's version. Adam rejoices to see these godly men united in
love with fair women:

> Such happy interview and fair event
> Of love and youth not lost, Songs, Garlands, Flowrs
> And charming Symphonies attachd the heart
> Of *Adam*, soon enclin'd to admit delight,
> The bent of Nature. . . .
>
> (593–97)

And he thanks the angel, remarking that 'Here Nature seems fulfilld in
all her ends' (602). He is at once coldly corrected; these women, against
the evidence of Adam's own senses, are 'empty of all good' (616), and
nothing but ill comes from the 'Sons of God' (622) yielding up all their
virtue to them. Milton remembered how much of Pandora there was
in Eve. From women Adam is taught to expect woe; but, more impor-
tant, this change in the divine arrangements means that the evidence
of the senses, the testimony of pleasure, is no longer a reliable guide:

> Judge not what is best
> By pleasure, though to Nature seeming meet . . .
>
> (603–4)

   Paradise Lost is a poem about death, and about pleasure and its
impairment. It is not very surprising that generations of readers failed
to see the importance to Milton's 'scheme' of Adam's exclamation upon
a paradox which depends not upon the senses but upon revelation; I
mean the assurance that out of all this evil good will come as testimony
of a benevolent plan.

> more wonderful
> Than that which by creation first brought forth
> Light out of darkness.
>
> (xii. 471–73)

The senses will not recognize that out of their own destruction will come
forth 'Joy and eternal Bliss' (xii. 551). In that line Milton echoes the
Comus Epilogue—Joy will come from the great wound the senses have
suffered, but it is a joy measured by what we have had and lost. And
the sense of loss is keener by far than the apprehension of things unseen,
the remote promise of restoration. The old Eden we know, we can
describe it, inlay it with a thousand known flowers and compare it with
a hundred other paradises; throughout the whole history of loss and
deprivation the poets have reconstructed it with love. The new one may
be called 'happier farr', but poetry cannot say much more about it
because the senses do not know it. The paradise of Milton's poem is the

lost, the only true, paradise; we confuse ourselves, and with the same subtlety confuse the 'simple' poem, if we believe otherwise.

Shelley spoke of Milton's 'bold neglect of a direct moral purpose', and held this to be 'the most decisive proof of the supremacy of Milton's genius'. 'He mingled, as it were', Shelley added, 'the elements of human nature as colours upon a single pallet, and arranged them in the composition of his great picture according to the laws of epic truth; that is, according to the laws of that principle by which a series of actions of the external universe and of intelligent and ethical beings is calculated to excite the sympathy of succeeding generations of mankind.'[4] This passage follows upon the famous observations on Satan, and is itself succeeded by and involved with a Shelleyan attack on Christianity; and perhaps in consequence of this it has not been thought worth much attention except by those specialized opponents who contend for and against Satan in the hero-ass controversy. Theirs is an interesting quarrel, but its ground ought to be shifted; and in any case this is not the occasion to reopen it. But the remarks of Shelley I have quoted seem to be substantially true; so, rightly understood, do the much-anathematized remarks of Blake. I say 'substantially' because Milton himself would perhaps have argued that he accepted what responsibility he could for the moral effect of his poem, and that in any case he specifically desiderated a 'fit' audience, capable of making its own distinctions between moral good and evil. Yet in so far as poetry works through the pleasure it provides—a point upon which Milton and Shelley would agree—it must neglect 'a direct moral purpose'; and in so far as it deals with the passions of fallen man it has to do with Blake's hellish energies. And however much one may feel that they exaggerated the truth in applying it to Milton, one ought to be clear that Shelley and Blake were not simply proposing naughty Romantic paradoxes because they did not know enough. Indeed they show us a truth about *Paradise Lost* which later commentary, however learned, has made less and less accessible.

With these thoughts in my mind, I sometimes feel that the shift of attention necessary to make friends out of some of Milton's most potent modern enemies is in reality a very small one. However this may be, I want to end by citing Mr. Robert Graves; not because I have any hope of persuading him from his evidently and irrationally powerful distaste for Milton, but to give myself the pleasure of quoting one of his poems. It is called 'Pure Death', and in it Mr. Graves speculates on a theme that he might have found, superbly extended, in Milton's epic:

> We looked, we loved, and therewith instantly
> Death became terrible to you and me.
> By love we disenthralled our natural terror

---

4. A *Defence of Poetry*, in *Shelley's Literary and Philosophical Criticism*, ed. J. Shawcross (1909), p. 146.

From every comfortable philosopher
Or tall grey doctor of divinity:
Death stood at last in his true rank and order.[5]

Milton gives us this perception, but 'according to the laws of epic truth';
which is to say, he exhibits life in a great symbolic attitude.

WILLIAM EMPSON

Milton's God†

* * * The motive of the Father in crucifying the Son is of course left
in even deeper obscurity.

Milton did however I think mean to adumbrate a kind of motive by
his picture of the Last Things. Professor C. S. Lewis[1] once kindly came
to a lecture I was giving on the half-finished material of this book; and
at question time, after a sentence of charitable compunction, recognizing
that the speaker wasn't responsible for this bit, he said "Does Phelps
Morand[2] think God is going to abdicate, then?" I tried to explain that
M. Morand regarded this as the way Milton's dramatic imagination
worked, after it had been corrupted by his patriotic labours, not as part
of his theological system. The answer felt weak, and soon afterwards
another difficulty drove me back to the book of M. Saurat,[3] which I
had probably not read since I was an undergraduate; I thus suddenly
realized, what M. Saurat was not intending to prove, that Milton did
expect God to abdicate. At least, that is the most direct way to express
the idea; you may also say that he is an emergent or evolutionary deity,
as has been believed at times by many other thinkers, for example
Aeschylus and H. G. Wells.

There has been such a campaign to prove that only the coarsely worldly
Victorians would even want the world to get better that I had better
digress about that, or I may be thought to be jeering at Milton. We are
often told that In Memoriam is bad because Tennyson tries to palm off
progress in this world as a substitute for Heaven. But he says in the poem
that he would stop being good, or would kill himself, if he stopped
believing he would go to Heaven; it is wilful to argue that he treats the
progress of the human race as an adequate alternative. Indeed, he seems
rather too petulant about his demand for Heaven, considering that Ti-

5. Collected Poems (1959), p. 71.
   † From Milton's God by William Empson, pp. 130–37, 140, 142–43, 144–46, 204–10. Re-
   printed by permission of New Directions Publishing Corporation, Lady Empson, and The
   Hogarth Press. The footnotes for this selection are by the editor.
1. Author of A Preface to Paradise Lost (London, 1942).
2. Author of De Comus & Satan (Paris, 1939).
3. Denis Saurat, Milton: Man and Thinker (London, 1925).

thonus, written about the same time (according to Stopford Brooke) though kept from publication till later, appreciates so nobly the hunger of mankind for the peace of oblivion. But the underlying logic of *In Memoriam* is firm. The signs that God is working out a vast plan of evolution are treated as evidence that he is good, and therefore that he will provide Heaven for Tennyson. To believe that God's Providence can be seen at work in the world, and that this is evidence for his existence and goodness, is what is called Natural Theology; it is very traditional, and the inability of neo-Christians to understand it casts an odd light on their pretensions. Tennyson has also been accused of insincerity about progress because in another poem he expressed alarm at the prospect of war in the air; but he realized the time-scale very clearly; while maintaining that the process of the suns will eventually reach a good end, it is only sensible to warn mankind that we are likely to go through some very bad periods beforehand. Now, when mankind seems almost certain to destroy itself quite soon, we cannot help wincing at a belief that progress is inevitable; but this qualification seems all that is needed. I think that reverence *ought* to be aroused by the thought that so long and large a process has recently produced ourselves who can describe it, and other-worldly persons who boast of not feeling that seem to me merely to have cauterized themselves againt genuine religious feeling. The seventeenth century too would have thought that so much contempt for Providence verged upon the Manichean. Milton claimed to get his conception of progress from the Bible; but he would have found corroboration, one would think, in the *Prometheus*, which was well known. There is only one reference to the myth in the epic, and it is twisted into a complaint against women (iv. 717); but Mr. R. J. Z. Werblowsky, in his broad and philosophical *Lucifer and Prometheus* (1952), may well be right to think that Milton tried to avoid direct comparison between Prometheus and his Satan.

At the point which seemed to me illuminating, M. Saurat was calling Milton 'the old incorrigible dreamer' (p. 165, 1944 edition), apparently just for believing in the Millennium on earth, though that only requires literal acceptance of Revelation xx; but he was quoting part of Milton's commentary in Chapter XXXIII of the *De Doctrina*, "Of Perfect Glorification", and no doubt recognized that Milton was somehow going rather further. Milton says:

> It may be asked, if Christ is to deliver up the kingdom to God and the Father, what becomes of the declarations [quotations] from Heb. i. 8, Dan. vii. 14, and Luke i. 33] "of his kingdom there shall be no end". I reply, there shall be no end of his kingdom . . . till time itself shall be no longer, Rev. x. 6, until everything which his kingdom was intended to effect shall be accomplished . . . it will not be destroyed, nor will

its period be a period of dissolution, but rather of perfection
and consummation, like the end of the law, Matt. v. 18.

The last clause seems to recall the precedent of an earlier evolutionary
step, whereby the New Dispensation of Jesus made the Mosaic Law
unnecessary; it is clear that the final one, which makes even the Mil-
lennium unnecessary, must be of an extremely radical character. The
Father, I submit, has to turn into the God of the Cambridge Platonists
and suchlike mystical characters; at present he is still the very disagreeable
God of the Old Testament, but eventually he will dissolve into the
landscape and become immanent only. The difficulty of fitting in this
extremely grand climax was perhaps what made Milton uncertain about
the controverted time-scheme of the Millennium. The doctrine of the
end of time, if one takes it seriously, is already enough to make anything
but Total Union (or else Total Separateness from God) hard to conceive.

The question which Milton answers here is at least one which he
makes extremely prominent in the speech of rejoicing by the Father
after the speech of sacrifice by the Son (III. 320). The Father first says
he *will* give the Son all power, then in the present tense "I give thee";
yet he had given it already, or at least enough to cause Satan and his
followers to revolt. Without so much as a full stop, the Father next says
that the time when he will give it is the Day of Judgement, and the
climax of the whole speech is to say that immediately after that 'God
shall be All in All". The eternal gift of the Father is thus to be received
only on the Last Day, and handed back the day after. This has not been
found disturbing, because the paradox is so clear that we assume it to
be deliberate; nor are interpretations of it hard to come by. But Milton
would see it in the light of the passage in the *De Doctrina*; there "God
shall be All in All" ends the Biblical quotation which comes just before
Milton's mystical "reply":

> Then cometh the end . . . but when he saith, all things are
> put under him, it is manifest that he is expected which did
> put all things under him; and when all things are subdued
> unto him, then shall the Son himself also be subject unto him
> that put all things under him, that God may be all in all. (I
> Corinthians xv. 24–28)

St Paul is grappling with earlier texts here in much the same scholarly
way that Milton did, which would give Milton a certain confidence
about re-interpreting his results even though they were inspired because
Biblical. After hearing so much from M. Morand about the political
corruption of Milton's mind, one is pleased to find it less corrupt than
St Paul's; Milton decided that God was telling the truth, and that he
would keep his promise literally. At the end of the speech of the Father,
Milton turns into poetry the decision he had reached in prose:

The World shall burn, and from her ashes spring
New Heav'n and Earth, wherein the just shall dwell
. . .
Then thou thy regal Sceptre shalt lay by,
For regal Sceptre then no more shall need,
God shall be All in All. But all ye Gods
Adore him, who to compass all this dies,
Adore the Son, and honour him as me.   (III. 340)

I grant that the language is obscure, as is fitting because it is oracular;
and, besides, Milton wanted the poem to be universal, so did not want
to thrust a special doctrine upon the reader. But the doctrine is implied
decisively if the language is examined with care. St Paul presumably
had in mind a literal autocracy, but Milton contrives to make the text
imply pantheism. The O.E.D. records that the intransitive use of the
verb *need* had become slightly archaic except for a few set phrases; the
general intransitive use needed here belongs to the previous century—
e.g. "stopping of heads with lead shall not need now" 1545. But a reader
who noticed the change of grammar from *shalt* to *shall* could only impute
the old construction: "Authority will then no longer be needed"—not,
therefore, from the Father, any more than from the Son. There is much
more point in the last two lines quoted if the Father has just proposed,
though in an even more remote sense than the Son, that he too shall
die. *All* is rather a pet word in Milton's poetry but I think he never gives
it a capital letter anywhere else, and one would expect that by writing
"All in All" he meant to imply a special doctrine, as we do by writing
"the Absolute". Then again, this is the only time God calls the angels
Gods, with or without a capital letter. He does it here meaning that
they will in effect become so after he has abdicated. The reference has
justly been used as a partial defence of Satan for calling his rebels Gods,
but we are meant to understand that his claim for them is a subtle misuse
of the deeper truth adumbrated here. Taking all the details together, I
think it is clear that Milton wanted to suggest a high mystery at this
culminating point.

There was a more urgent and practical angle to the question; it was
not only one of the status of the Son, but of mankind. You cannot think
it merely whimsical of M. Morand to call God dynastic if you look up
the words *heir* and *inherit* in the concordance usually given at the end
of a Bible. Milton was of course merely quoting the text when he made
the Father call the Son his heir (as in vi. 705); but the blessed among
mankind are also regularly called 'heirs of God's kingdom' and suchlike.
The word *heir* specifically means one who will inherit; it would be
comical to talk as if M. Morand was the first to wonder what the Bible
might mean by it. The blessed among mankind are heirs of God through
their union with Christ; Milton's Chapter XXIV is 'Of Union and Fel-

lowship with Christ and the Saints, wherein is considered the Mystical or Invisible Church', and he says it is 'not confined to place or time, inasmuch as it is composed of individuals of widely separated countries, and of all ages from the foundation of the world'. He would regard this as a blow at all priesthoods, but also regard the invisible union as a prefiguring of the far distant one. We can now see that it is already offered in the otherwise harsh words by which the Father appointed the Son:

> Under his great Vice-regent reign abide
> United as one individual Soul
> For ever happy   (V. 610)

As a means of achieving such unity the speech is a remarkable failure; but God already knew that men would be needed as well as angels before the alchemy could be done. When the unity is complete, neither the loyal angels nor the blessed among mankind will require even the vice-regency of the Son, still less the rule of the Father; and only so can they become 'heirs and inheritors of God's Kingdom'.

The texts prove, I submit, that Milton envisaged the idea, as indeed so informed a man could hardly help doing; but the poetry must decide whether it meant a great deal to him, and the bits so far quoted are not very good. Milton however also ascribes it to God in the one really splendid passage allotted to him. This is merely an earlier part of the same speech, but the sequence III. 80–345 is full of startling changes of tone. The end of the speech happens to let us see Milton's mind at work, because we can relate it to the *De Doctrina*, but the main feeling there is just immense pride; Milton could never let the Father appear soft, and his deepest yielding must be almost hidden by a blaze of glory. Just before advancing upon thirty lines of glory, he has rejoiced that his Son:

> though thron'd in highest bliss,
> Equal to God, and equally enjoying
> God-like fruition, quitted all to save
> A world from utter loss, and hast been found
> By Merit more than Birthright Son of God,
> Found worthiest to be so by being Good,
> Far more than Great or High; because in thee
> Love hath abounded more than Glory abounds,
> Therefore thy Humiliation shall exalt
> With thee thy Manhood also to this Throne;
> Here shalt thou sit incarnate, here shalt Reign
> Both God and Man, Son both of God and Man,
> Anointed universal King; all Power
> I give thee, reign for ever, and assume

Thy Merits; under thee as Head Supreme
Thrones, Princedoms, Powers, Dominions I reduce: (III. 305)

It is a tremendous moral cleansing for Milton's God, after the greed for power which can be felt in him everywhere else, to say that he will give his throne to Incarnate Man, and the rhythm around the word *humiliation* is like taking off in an aeroplane. I had long felt that this is much the best moment of God in the poem, morally as well as poetically, without having any idea why it came there. It comes there because he is envisaging his abdication, and the democratic appeal of the prophecy of God is what makes the whole picture of him just tolerable.

* * *

Thus, by combining the views of M. Saurat and M. Morand, the one attributing to Milton thoughts beyond the reaches of our souls and the other a harsh worldliness, we can I think partly solve the central problem about the poem, which is how Milton can have thought it to justify God. I think the 'internal' evidence of Milton's own writing enough to decide that he meant what I have tried to describe, because it makes our impression of the poem and indeed of the author much more satisfactory; but, even so, external evidence is needed to answer the objection that Milton could not have meant that, or could not have thought of it. I had best begin by saying what I learned from M. Saurat and where I thought his view inadequate. His main interest, as I understand, was to show that the European Renaissance could not have occurred without an underground influence from Jewish mystics beginning two or three centuries before Milton; the main reason for supposing that Milton had read the *Zohar*, even after textual evidence had been found, was that he was a man who habitually went to the sources of the ideas which he had already found floating about. The doctrine that matter was not created from nothing but was part of God M. Saurat considered fundamental to the Renaissance, because it allowed enough trust in the flesh, the sciences, the arts, the future before man in this world. Milton undoubtedly does express this doctrine, but it does not strike me as prominent in other poets of the time, except for the paradoxes of Donne's love-poetry.

* * *

The trouble with M. Saurat's position, I think, is that he welcomes the liquefaction of God the father, making him wholly immanent in his creation, and argues that Milton intended that in his epic, without realizing that Milton and his learned contemporaries would think the liquefaction of all the rest of us a prior condition. The idea of the reabsorption of the soul into the Absolute does get hinted at a good deal in the literature, if only in the form of complete self-abandonment to God; whereas the idea that God himself is wholly immanent in his creation belonged mainly to the high specialized output of the Cambridge Platonists. Marlowe's Faustus, in his final speech, desires to return his soul like a raindrop to the sea rather than remain eternally as an individual in Hell, and this is a crucial image for grasping the Far-Eastern position; the same idea is quite noisy in the supposedly orthodox peroration of *Urn-Burial*: "if any have been so happy as truly to understand Christian annihilation . . . liquefaction . . . ingression into the divine shadow". When Lovewit at the end of *The Alchemist* rebuffs a superstitious fool by saying "Away, you Harry Nicholas" (the founder of the mystical Family of Love which maintained that any man can become Christ), the now remote figure is presumed to be familiar to a popular audience. The ideas which Milton hinted at in the bits of his epic which I have picked out were therefore not nearly so learned and unusual as they seem now; indeed, he probably treated them with caution because they might suggest a more Levelling, more economic-revolutionary, political stand than he in fact took. But the Cambridge Platonists were not dangerous for property-owners in this way; they were a strand of recent advanced thought which deserved recognition in his epic; also they allowed of a welcome contrast to the picture of God which the Bible forced him to present, and gave a bit more body to the mysterious climax of the Fortunate Fall. The abdication of the Father was thus quite an important part of his delicately balanced structure, and not at all a secret heresy; and of course not 'unconscious' if it needed tact. At bottom, indeed, a quaintly political mind is what we find engaged on the enormous synthesis. Milton knows by experience that God is at present the grindingly harsh figure described in the Old Testament; after all, Milton had long been printing the conviction that his political side had been proved right because God had made it win, so its eventual defeat was a difficult thing to justify God for. But it was essential to retain the faith that God has a good eventual plan; well then, the Cambridge Platonists can be allowed to be right about God, but only as he will become in the remote future. It seems to me one of the likeable sides of Milton that he would regard this as a practical and statesmanlike proposal.

* * *

The well-argued view of M. Morand, that the purblind Milton described God from his experience of Cromwell, also allows of an unexpectedly sublime conclusion. Milton's own political record, as I understand, cannot be found contemptible; he backed Cromwell and his Independents in the army against the Presbyterians in Parliament because he wanted religious freedom, but always remained capable of saying where he thought Cromwell had gone wrong; for example, in refusing to disestablish the Church. However, on one point Cromwell was impeccable, and appears to be unique among dictators; his admitted and genuine bother, for a number of years, was to find some way of establishing a Parliament under which he could feel himself justified in

stopping being dictator. When Milton made God the Father plan for
his eventual abdication, he ascribed to him in the high tradition of
Plutarch the noblest sentiment that could be found in an absolute ruler;
and could reflect with pride that he had himself seen it in operation,
though with a tragic end. Milton's God is thus to be regarded as like
King Lear and Prospero, turbulent and masterful characters who are
struggling to become able to renounce their power and enter peace; the
story makes him behave much worse than they do, but the author allows
him the same purifying aspiration. Even the lie of God "Die he or
Justice must", we may now charitably reflect, is partly covered when
Milton says that Satan

> with necessity
> The Tyrant's plea, excused his devilish deeds.   (IV. 395)

It must be added at once that we cannot find enough necessity; the
poem, to be completely four-square, ought to explain why God had to
procure all these falls for his eventual high purpose. Such is the basic
question as it stood long before Milton handled it; but he puts the mystery
in a place evidently beyond human knowledge, and he makes tolerably
decent, though salty and rough, what is within our reach.

This I think answers the fundamental objection of Yvor Winters, with
which it seemed right to begin the chapter;[4] Milton's poetical formula
for God is not simply to copy Zeus in Homer but, much more dra-
matically, to cut out everything between the two ends of the large body
of Western thought about God, and stick to Moses except at the high
points which anticipate Spinoza. The procedure is bound to make God
interesting; take the cae of his announcing to the loyal angels that he
will create mankind to spite the devil. God must be supposed to intend
his words to suggest to the angels what they do to us, but any angel
instructed in theology must realize that God has intended throughout
all eternity to spite Satan, so that when he presents this plan as new he
is telling a lie, which he has also intended to tell throughout all eternity.
No wonder it will be 'far happier days' after he has abdicated (XII. 465).
Milton was well able to understand these contradictions, and naturally
he would want to leave room for an eventual solution of them.

Perhaps I find him like Kafka merely because both seem to have had
a kind of foreknowledge of the Totalitarian State, whether or not this

---

4. "It requires more than a willing suspension of disbelief to read Milton; it requires a willing
suspension of intelligence. A good many years ago I found Milton's procedure more nearly
defensible than I find it now; I find that I grow extremely tired of the meaningless inflation,
the tedious falsification of the materials by way of excessive emotion. . . . [Comparison to the
gods in Homer] . . . Milton, however, is concerned with a deity and with additional supernatural
agents who are conceived in extremely intellectual terms; our conceptions of them are the
result of more than 2000 years of the most profound and complex intellectual activity in the
history of the human race. Milton's form is such that he must first reduce these beings to
something much nearer the form of the Homeric gods than their proper form, and then must
treat his ridiculously degraded beings in heroic language." *Hudson Review* (1956).

was what C. S. Lewis praised as his beautiful sense of the idea of social order. The picture of God in the poem, including perhaps even the high moments when he speaks of the end, is astonishingly like Uncle Joe Stalin; the same patience under an appearance of roughness, the same flashes of joviality, the same thorough unscrupulousness, the same real bad temper. It seems little use to puzzle ourselves whether Milton realized he was producing this effect, because it would follow in any case from what he had set himself to do.

* * *

I hope these extracts[5] will be enough to make clear that Milton genuinely considered God in need of defence, and indeed that, when Milton said at the beginning of his epic he intended to justify God, he was so far from expecting a reader to think the phrase poetical rhetoric that he was not even steppping out of the usual procedure of his prose. A curious trick has been played on modern readers here; they are told: 'Why, but of course you must read the poem taking for granted that Milton's God is good; not to do that would be absurdly unhistorical. Why, the first business of a literary critic is to sink his mind wholly into the mental world of the author, and in a case like this you must accept what they all thought way back in early times.' I think this literary doctrine is all nonsense anyhow; a critic ought to use his own moral judgement, for what it is worth, as well as try to understand the author's, and that is the only way he can arrive at a 'total reaction'. But in a case like this the argument is also grossly unhistorical. No doubt Milton would only have snorted if a Victorian had come up and praised him for making Satan good, but anyone who told him he had made God wicked would find his mind surprisingly at home; there would be some severe cross-questioning (is this a Jesuit or merely an Arminian?), but if that passed off all right he would ask the visitor to sit down and discuss the point at length. Nor was it only the later Milton, after the disillusion of the Fall of the Commonwealth, who felt God to need defence; he can be shown feeling it both before and after a major change in this theology. In *The Doctrine and Discipline of Divorce* (1643), writing as a believer in predestination, he remarks of Jesuits and Arminians that, if they could only understand the argument he has just propounded, 'they might, methinks, be persuaded to absolve both God and us' (*us* meaning the Calvinists). Near the end of Chapter III of the *De Doctrina* we find he has abandoned predestination, and his reason for it is still that he is anxious to absolve God:

> free causes are not impeded by any law of necessity arising from the decrees or prescience of God. There are some who, in their zeal to oppose this doctrine, do not hesitate even to assert that God himself is the cause and origin of evil. Such

5. From Milton's *De Doctrina Christiana*.

men, if they are not to be looked upon as a misguided rather than mischievous, should be ranked among the most abandoned of all blasphemers. An attempt to refute them would be nothing more than an argument to prove that God was not the evil spirit.

This exasperation against his opponents, this extreme readiness to see that they are making God into the Devil, while the point of distinction he wants to insist upon is really so very slight, makes evident that Milton himself was sensitive and anxious about the danger of finding that he too was worshipping the Devil. When Milton gets round to his own pronouncement on this point, in Chapter VIII, after listing the crucial texts, he is hardly able to do more than issue a rule of decorum:

But though in these, as well as in many other passages of the Old and New Testaments, God distinctly declares it is himself who impels the sinner to sin, who binds his understanding, and leads him into error; yet, on account of the infinite holiness of the Deity, it is not allowable to consider him as in the smallest instance the author of sin.

What first struck me, when I began to nose about in the English translation of the *De Doctrina*, rather belatedly, was that its tone is very unlike what the learned critics who summarize it had led me to expect. But maybe, I thought, having no judgement of Latin style, this is only a result of translation; the work was done by Sumner, later an Anglican bishop, who must have been working fairly rapidly; it was printed (and reviewed by Macaulay) in 1825, two years after the Latin text had been discovered. One can imagine a translator making it sound like Gibbon, partly because that was an easy formula but also through feeling a certain impatience with this heretic. But the following passage, from Chapter VII, 'Of the Creation', another discussion of the effects of the Fall, seemed to me enough to refute the suspicion; it rises above the variations of tone available to a translator:

But, it is contended, God does not create souls impure, but only impaired in their nature, and destitute of original righteousness; I answer that to create pure souls, destitute of original righteousness—to send them into contaminated and corrupt bodies—to deliver them up in their innocence and helplessness to the prison house of the body, as to an enemy, with understanding blinded and with will enslaved—in other words, wholly deprived of sufficient strength for resisting the vicious propensities of the body—to create souls thus cicumstanced, would argue as much injustice, as to have created them impure would have argued impurity; it would have argued as much injustice, as to have created the first man Adam himself impaired in his nature, and destitute of original righteousness.

Surely, in the face of this burning sense of the injustice of God, which Milton only just manages to drag into line, it was rather absurd of C. S. Lewis to say that nobody had ever doubted Milton's account of the Fall until Romantics made rebellion fashionable. A sympathetic reader of Milton's prose is accustomed to feel that he writes like a lawyer or a politician, concerned to convince his reader by any argument which would serve, though really more humane or enlightened arguments are what have made Milton himself choose the side he is arguing on. But in discussing the justice of God Milton admits that the conscience of every decent man is against what he has to maintain; there is an 'outcry' against it; but what he has found in the Bible is the horrible truth about the justice of God, and men had much better learn to face it.

I shall end these quotations from the *De Doctrina* with an example which seems to me coldly hair-raising, though Sewell does not appear to find it so, and perhaps Milton did not either. In Chapter XVI, 'Of the Ministry of Redemption', the section *By Payment of the Required Price* consisted of a list of texts and then one sentence claiming that they refute any Socinian view, that is, any theory that Christ died not to pay for us but merely to set us an example to follow. The idea of payment is indeed deeply embedded in the system, as we too are paying all the time for Adam; what Satan reaches as rock bottom, after abandoning his suspicion that God is a usurper, is that he could not in any case submit to a God who is a usurper. Some while after writing this section, Milton must have told his secretary to read it out to him, and then he dictated one further Latin sentence:

At the time I confess myself unable to perceive how those who consider the Son of the same essence with the Father can explain either his incarnation or his satisfaction.

Maybe the shock comes partly from putting the sentence into English; the English word *satisfaction* has its own suggestions beside the central achievement of the Christ, 'a full oblation, remission and satisfaction for the sins of the whole world'. But these seem to me to act as a just satire. What Milton is thinking has to be: 'God couldn't have been satisfied by torturing himself to death, not if I know God; you could never have bought him off with that money; he could only have been satisfied by torturing somebody else to death.' Until I tried to follow the mind of Milton, I did not realize why the doctrine of the Trinity had been considered so important. Surely, if you regard God the Father as Milton had come to do here, he cannot possibly be justified. Milton when he embarked upon his epic was exactly in the position of the Satan he presents, overwhelmingly stubborn and gallant but defending a cause inherently hopeless from the start.

It is a difficult matter to try to sum up. The quotations I think make clear that Milton only just managed, after spiritual wrestling and the introduction of a certain amount of heresy, to reconcile his conscience or keep his temper with his God. When he says that the Holy Spirit dictated the poem to him, we can readily believe that, as the problems at issue had been gone over so long and anxiously, it was by a fairly direct process that the blind man at once invented and learned by heart a whole paragraph, commonly at night, and then waited as he said to be 'milked' of it; what is surprising is that the parts of the narrative fit together as well as they do. Even so, it is clear that he could have recognized the more alarming aspects of the narrative, merely by switching his attention; and his character makes him unlikely not to have recognized them. I should think that, with his usual nerve, he just refused to be rattled. Perhaps the main point is that when composing he felt like a defending counsel; such a man is positively wanted to realize at what points his client's case is weak, and he does not feel personally disgraced if his client still loses after he has gone as far as he can. Adding a little human interest to the admittedly tricky client God, by emphasizing his care to recover the reputation of his son, and giving a glimpse of the deeper side of his nature which makes him prepare for his latter end, is about all that can be done to swing the jury when the facts of the case are so little in dispute. On the other hand, when he made the case as strong as he could for Satan, Eve and Adam, he somehow did not mind driving home the injustice of God, because God was not at the moment his client. This picture is very inadequate because the problems about God are never out of sight in the poem; but still, being such a good advocate was what made the poetry so dramatic and in a way so broad. He understood how all contemporary sects would react to the words and situations he arranged for God, or the contradictions with which he had himself wrestled; it seems fair to add, he knew what he could get away with in the poem, even when it was necessarily very dickey. Though apparently isolated, he thus became an echoing-chamber for the whole mind of his period. The fact that he went on to make out a strong case for Delilah, even though in a narrower and fiercer frame of mind, proves I think that the moral generosity of *Paradise Lost* is not due to accident, muddle-headedness or split personality.

* * *

ROBERT M. ADAMS

A Little Look into Chaos

This is a topic without a bibliography and a paper almost without foot-notes. I say this not out of bravado, but momentarily. It would have been nice to find other people's definitions, descriptions, and doctrines of Milton's Chaos, for guidance and support, as well as the always welcome occasions of polemic. But I was unable to find more than passing remarks on the subject, and will welcome suggestions as to where else I should look. And it would have been nice to get in a reference or two to my favorite Miltonic source. Rupertus Tuitensis or some other suitably occult figure. But my interest is not in where Milton got his Chaos but in what he did when he got it. So this rather limits the erudition one can display without making ostentation an end in itself. Hence the poor, sparse, speculative paper which follows—a paper over which I would like to inscribe a spectacular and gigantic question mark, emblematic of all the open questions I feel clustering around the paper. Can the poem usefully be seen from such a special angle? Why hasn't anybody ever tried it before? What authority can an "outside" interpretation like this have against the Christian humanist morality that has held the strong right-center position in Miltonic criticism for so long against so many antag-onists? It would be nice if these questions could be asked from some safe, neutral position—noncommitally, as it were. But as we don't know what a question can do till we put some heart and energy into asking it, I've chosen to take my chances.

In talking about Chaos in Milton's great poem, it's probably prudent to start by locating it along a couple of different coordinates, by trying to say what it is and where it is and when it is, in the cosmos that Milton imagined as well as in the poem he wrote. A lot of this preliminary material will be familiar, and for that I apologize; but it's a topic that's generally peripheral to the focus of our interests as we read *Paradise Lost*; and a quick reminder of the circumstances may get our collective feet under us.

Chaos, then, is situated in one of Milton's universes—in the big universe, with Heaven at the top, Hell at the bottom, and no other determinate shape at all—Chaos occupies in this universe a middle

† From *Illustrious Evidence: Approaches to English Literature of the Early Seventeenth Century*, ed. Earl Miner (Berkeley: University of California Press, 1975) 71–89. Reprinted by per-mission of the University of California Press. A list of other studies of Milton's Chaos appears in a footnote to the excellent, original study by Regina Schwartz "Milton's Hostile Chaos: '. . . and The Sea Was No More,'" in *ELH* 52 (1985): 337–74.

position. Heaven is on top, as presumably it always was; Hell is on the bottom. Since it was prepared for the fallen angels—

> Such place eternal justice had prepared
> For those rebellious, here their prison ordained
> In utter darkness—
>
> [I, 70–72]

Hell can hardly have been in existence before there were any rebels. That would involve attributing to God almost too much foresight, and too malicious a character. Yet Milton does specify "eternal justice," and this reminds us that God rules the whole cosmos, from top to bottom, from beginning to end. (It may help with the passage if we read the word "utter" as "complete," not as "outer," since Hell is in no sense outside God's providence.) If He did not create Hell for the bad angels before they fell, to be ready for them when they did fall, He certainly foresaw the necessity of doing so. Hell therefore is a subtraction from Chaos, which probably had no lower boundary at all. Speaking to Satan, the Anarch himself complains that his kingdom has been diminished by two recent subtractions:

> first Hell
> Your dungeon stretching far and wide beneath;
> Now lately Heaven and Earth, another World
> Hung o'er my realm.
>
> [II, 1002–1005]

We notice, in passing, that "Heaven" has been newly created too, as Chaos sees the matter—"Heaven and Earth." He is not only echoing Genesis I, but distinguishing the nine empyreal spheres of the created cosmos from the eternal heaven of God's presence.

So Chaos is a large, elastic, disorderly place between two fixed and essentially unchanging planes of existence. Hell is immutably and unremittingly evil; it is dark and low, as dark as you can get ("utter darkness") and as low as you can go. When Satan in his soliloquy atop Niphates contemplates a deeper hell than that in which he now suffers, it isn't physical depth (because I think there isn't anything lower than the fiery soil on which Pandemonium stands), it's psychological depth of suffering that he envisages:

> Which way I fly is hell, myself am hell;
> And in the lowest deep a lower deep
> Still threatening to devour me opens wide,
> To which the hell I suffer seems a heaven.
>
> [IV, 75–78]

Heaven is immutably and eternally good; it is bright and high. Chaos is the area of change and struggle in between. The created cosmos (heaven and earth together) is actually hung in the midst of Chaos; God created it out of Chaos, and at the end of recorded history it will revert to Chaos, when heaven and hell are closed up, the world consumed with fire, and nature comes to an end. Chaos, Milton tells us in a tremendous line, is

> The womb of nature and perhaps her grave.[1]

That is, to explicate what is perhaps already clear enough, Chaos contained from the beginning the seeds of those elements (earth, air, water, fire) of which the natural world was created by the imposition of divine order, and to which it will ultimately revert. Chaos is the baseline or norm from which the special purposes of God raised the cosmos, and to which (so far as the special purposes of God will allow) the cosmos will automatically relapse after the Last Judgment. Let us note that Chaos, though spatially at the center of Milton's largest universe (between the limiting districts of Heaven and Hell), is temporally at the outer limits. It bounds the temporal extent of the cosmos, and for that matter of the poem. We cannot see beyond it, either before or after. "Beyond is all abyss," says Adam (XII, 555); the word is constantly associated with Chaos (as in II, 917, 969, 1027 and VII, 211, 234); and indeed if we add darkness to disorder, there is not need to look or imagine further. "Et sine fine Chaos, & sine fine Deus," says S. B., M. D., in one of the two poems dedicatory to *Paradise Lost*, the second edition. In time, if not in space, the two powers are coextensive.

Whether Chaos provided the original raw material for God's Heaven (in the precreation dimension) we do not know and are not encouraged to guess; but, Heaven apart, it is quite explicit that everything else in the cosmos is disguised (i.e., organized) Chaos, which could be jolted back, with relative ease, into Chaos again. Milton steers clear of specifying Chaos overtly as a possible outcome of the war in heaven, but he hints at it:

> and now all heaven
> Had gone to wrack, with ruin overspread,
> Had not th' Almighty Father, etc.
> [VI, 669–71]

The bridge that Sin and Death build over Chaos seems to be another encroachment on the Anarch's kingdom, and as Satan passes down the bridge, Chaos snarls resentlfully at him:

> on either side
> Disparted Chaos over-built exclaimed,

1. It is customary to cite as the classical analogue for this line Lucretius, V, 260: "Omniparens, eaden rerum commune sepulchrum."

> And with rebounding surge the bars assailed
> That scorned his indignation.
>
>   [X, 415–18]

But in bringing Sin and Death to the world, the bridge fulfills almost to the word the last prophetic words of Chaos to Satan:

> Havoc and spoil and ruin are my gain.
>   [II, 1009]

It has long been remarked that Satan, in reporting back to the cohorts awaiting him in Pandemonium, exaggerates the obstacles he had faced, and exaggerates by implication his own accomplishments, in saying that "Chaos wild/. . . fiercely opposed/My journey strange" (X, 477–79). In fact Chaos in his own person actually helped Satan along. The point may be scored off against Satan (he is a *miles gloriosus*), or else it is a way of softening the evident circumstance that in the warfare between God and Satan, though neither particpant wants this outcome, Chaos is the one immediate and obvious gainer. Satan's victory on earth has not been a thwarting of Chaos, but an expansion of his ancient empire. Chaos, out of which the Ptolemaic "heaven and earth" were created no longer ago than Book VII, and which has bounded and surrounded that Ptolemaic cosmos ever since, has largely reestablished itself already in Book X—as if to provide a paradigm of the way in which the larger universe also will pass, over a somewhat longer period of time, from Chaos to Chaos, with a little period of partial order in between.

Chaos as ancient Emperor of a nonempire, anarch not monarch, is a figure of grim Miltonic paradox, strong only in his weakness. All other empires grow by extending their controls and powers, his only by letting go. He is not even positive enough to claim empire for himself, for it is the standard of his consort Night that he proposes to advance—Night, "eldest of things" (II, 962), "unoriginal Night" (X, 477). The epithets strongly reemphasize that Night in this poem is not daughter of Chaos (as she is in Hesiod, who tells us directly, "From Chaos came forth Erebus and black Night," verse 123); if anything, the parental relation runs the other way. If Night were the mother of Chaos, as well as his consort, she would parallel Sin in her relation to Death and emphasize darkness as the ultimate enemy of divine light; but Chaos himself, containing seeds of light as well as darkness, is interestingly ambivalent in his relation to the warfare between the poem's more "positive" powers.

More positive powers? Curiously, when we look at Chaos for a while, we start to see some surprisingly positive aspects of Satan—he looks more like an opponent, a dramatic antagonist, even a foil, than like an enemy. But before we start pursuing this tantalizing rabbit, let's dispose of the last of our preliminaries by noting that the composition of Milton's poem *does* make it necessary for us to look at Chaos, or think of Chaos, again and again. In this respect, Milton's poem is quite unlike those of his two classical predecessors in chaotic description, Hesiod and Ovid. Both use Chaos as a kind of starting point in their poems, depart from it, and never come back. But Milton's poem, whether by accident or design (and with Milton that's never a real option) returns to Chaos over and over. There is of course the great panorama of Book II, when Satan is about to venture forth, followed by the encounter in the pavilion; there is an equivalent description, involving some parallels, in Book VII, when God ventures into Chaos in order to create the Ptolemaic universe. Sin and Death venture into it very graphically in Book X, the angels fall through it, hurtling out of control in Books I and VI. Literally described, it recurs again and again—of the first ten books only IV and IX fail to mention it specifically. And by implication, innuendo, recall, metaphor—that is quite a long story, to which we shall come later.

Chaos is present or potentially present throughout Milton's poem, and it represents a very deeply felt image of evil as essential weakness. Saint Augustine tells us somewhere that the devil himself is an advocate of peace; he must have certain varieties and areas and levels of peace, in order to be more effectually malicious. But Chaos is neutral as between good and evil; all he likes is disorder. That inclines him to evil, of course, but not all the way, for evil is itself a principle of order; and Chaos, is, so to speak, beyond good and evil. I do not think anyone before Milton represented Chaos as he did, under the guise of a feeble, tongue-tied old monarch unable to command even his own features. "With faltering speech and visage uncomposed"—it is an image of utter breakdown and loss of control. For a poet whose epic aspirations call for him to make his way across vast physical and imaginative distances, to organize immense bodies of material, to poise a fictive world in the void, the figure of Chaos could represent an authentic psychic menace.

But I want to consider in the poem the two positive forces who are common enemies of Chaos, and whose hostility to each other has been so lavishly emphasized, has absorbed so much partisan energy, that even to talk of their cooperation smacks of paradox. Satan is, I propose, in service to God in a variety of ways that mostly involve their common enmity to Chaos. A first and very simple way of seeing this is in the matter of space. I hope it's not too obvious to say that Satan by establishing his headquarters in Hell—Down There—creates a range of physical and moral possibility for man; he structures the cosmos. A universe consisting of just two parts, Heaven and Chaos, is essentially undirected and incomprehensible. In Heaven, a state of absolute bliss and perfect fulfillment, one feels no deficiency, hence no desire or purpose. In Chaos, one is out of touch with everything; one can't see or conceive or desire (with a fixed purpose) Heaven or anything else. One can't fear a fall because there is no down to fall to. It is a place, or rather than a place, a condition.

> Without dimension, where length, breadth, and height
> And time and place are lost.
>
> [II, 893–94]

If it weren't for Hell, Chaos would be bound to imply a state of weight-lessness, as there would be nothing below to exert gravitational force. Satan, by falling, gives the cosmos a bottom and a sense of moral and physical distance. By not only giving the cosmos an up and down (one inconceivable without the other), but by tying that up and down to a moral dimension, Satan gives the universe a shape. Simply by falling, he measures distance and points a direction; he is God's first plumb-bob. And by tying morality in with our sense of vertical direction, he triggers an automatic, an instinctive reaction. Fear of falling is, we are told, one of man's first and deepest instincts.[2] Adam doesn't fall phys-ically at all. It's obvious that his fall is a very serious act, but equally obvious that it doesn't take such a deep and terrifying form as Satan's. Satan falls in terror, out of control, Adam at most in dismay. To make another comparison (for my intent is simply to show how much Satan's physical fall into Hell adds to the emotional tone of the poem), only compare the depth and complexity of our feeling about Hell with our feelings about Heaven in the poem. We know vividly how one gets into Hell—by falling violently and helplessly for nine days and nights. How to get into Heaven is a much more mysterious, much less definite process. For one thing, we never see anyone do it; we see them only after they are already there, and what they experience we are forced to imagine for ourselves. Satan adds a physical dimension to Milton's moral universe, making up be really up, down be absolutely way far down, and good be all the better because it is diametrically *not* evil. He knots our moral feelings tightly to our basic physical instincts—serving in all this didactic ends which are both Miltonic and (so to speak) divine.

Satan not only structures the world spatially, he does so temporally; at the very moment when he seems to be defying God most vig-orously, he serves God's ends, and the ends of the poem, by an act of definition in time. The question concerns simply the point of Satan's own origin. It is not easy to work out, from the several assertions and counterassertions of the poem, what precisely consituted Milton's "doc-trine" in this matter, if he had one. In a passage of his first soliloquy atop Mount Niphates, Satan speaks remorsefully of his own ingratitude toward God:

---

2. We note in the matter of Satan the serpent, vulture, and toad how concerned Milton is to connect his devil with creatures from which we feel instinctive revulsion. Our love for God and attraction to Him are based on high, "spiritual" principles—a large perspective, an en-lightened point of view, logic, gratitude. Our responses to evil are intuitional.

> he deserv'd no such return
> From me, whom he created what I was
> In that bright eminence.
>
> [IV, 42–44]

But in public debate with Abdiel before the masses of revolted angels, Satan has quite another story:

> We know no time when we were not as now;
> Know none before us, self-begot, self-raised
> By our quickening power, when fatal course
> Had circled his full orb, the birth mature
> Of this our native heaven, ethereal sons.
>
> [V, 859–63]

Commentary has traditionally contrasted these private and public postures of Satan in order to emphasize the sinful arrogance of the latter. In declaring his independence of his Maker, Satan is said to be guilty of a kind of hubris for which, to the reader's edification, he will shortly be punished. And the conscientious annotator sends us off to rummage through the *Christian Doctrine* in search of that passage (it is I, vii) where Milton, on the very shaky authority of Numbers 16:22 and 27:16, declares roundly that the angels were created "at some particular period."

So this is evidently Milton's "doctrine," delivered in his own literal person, and Satan, in claiming to be independent of God, is a bad fellow, a boaster, and a hypocrite. He denies his Maker in a way that we would be most ill-advised to imitate. Morally, I daresay this is right; from a narrative point of view, Milton may even have wanted to score the point against Satan. But in terms of the Miltonic "argument" ("to justify the ways of God to men"), the more vigorously Satan asserts his independence, especially in the act of revolt, the better he serves his function in the economy of the poem and the economy of God's cosmos. That function is to remove from God responsibility for the evil in the world by assuming that responsibility himself. Only suppose that, in the act of revolt, Satan were to pursue that line of thought which he began in the soliloquy atop Niphates: "God created me what I was—bright, eminent, and doomed to fall. I am his creature; he made me: at any moment he can destroy me; whatever I do, I do, not only by his permission but with powers of his granting, the full consequences of which he foreknew at the time of my creation. I am not only his creature, but his agent." A creaturely devil, delivering himself of mealy-mouthed sentiments like that, and shifting the blame for the imperfect cosmos onto his Maker, would be worse, from Milton's point of view, than no devil at all. For one of Satan's major functions in the poem is to *stop* that line of questioning which leads back ineluctably from the present evil, whatever it may be—back from ancestor to ancestor, from wrong to wrong, back down the trail of history, all the way to Adam, who blamed Eve, who blamed the serpent, who would have blamed Satan had he been able to speak. And if Satan will not stop the line of blame there, what is to prevent it from going back all the way to the maker of all things, to God himself? Satan has to be an opaque, self-generated, self-sustained figure, at least in his own conceit. He has to be a figure without the dimension of inner questioning that would lead him into the pit of his own motivation—a figure who absorbs our questions and stops them through a kind of inner blindness—who is given so much momentum to begin with that the reader never pauses to ask what is the source of his first energy. By being such a figure, Satan becomes the chief bulwark of God, a lightning rod for his protection from the only enemy he has to fear in the poem, a resentful human conscience. "Who's to blame for this awful mess in which we see the world?" A great deal that has been dismissed as "sinful" in Satan's character serves in fact to fit him for an important and difficult role in relation to this question: he is a scapegoat. Symbolically, we hate the scapegoat. We load on him all the sins of the tribe, and to demonstrate our aversion, we drive him out into the wilderness, we separate ourselves from him every way possible. But there is another inevitable component in our feelings about him; it is not admiration or hero worship by any means; it is relief, it is gratitude. He carries off an element of ourselves that we want to purge, to excrete, to dispose of.[3] Without trying to define at all precisely what is very difficult to put into words, we may speak sketchily of the static electricity of life that we must, so to speak, "ground" some-where. Satan is a ground for these feelings in us, as well as for a good deal else in the poem—including our resentful sense that someone besides ourselves must be "to blame" for the way things are.

Satan is probably a very bad fellow to deny that he is the son of God, but he is also a very good fellow for the same reason. And it must be added that neither God nor Milton nor anybody else in the poem insists very warmly that Satan *is* the creation of God—if indeed he is. Repeated description of the Son as "only begotten Son" effectually keeps one from feeling that any of the angels, good or bad, are properly children of God the Father. Created they may have been, begotten they were not: we are left to imagine, as idle speculation moves us, what curious process of fabrication brought them all into being, with their differing poten-tialities for good and evil.

In taking responsibility for the sum of evil in the world—taking it boldly, without seeming to be aware of the tremendous sacrifice he is making—Satan grounds the reverse lightning of blame. In passing, he removes much of the load of guilt from the two human actors. From

3. Cf. Denis Saurat, *Milton, Man and Thinker* (New York, 1925), p. 220: "Milton had Satan in him and wanted to drive him out."

the point of view of Adam and Eve, the Fall is an episode that was all over before either of them knew it had happened; from Satan's point of view, the scene in the garden is the climax of a long-laid plot, which we have seen devised and proposed and carried out, in spite of enormous difficulties, with malicious evil as its deliberate end. So, inevitably, we attribute to Satan most of the blame for the Fall; not only so, man by departing from the Satanic example of reaction after the fall can limit rather easily the consequences of his own disaster. In other words, Satan, by taking the heavy rap, shows the seriousness of the crime; man, by appealing to the clemency of the judge, shows the basic benevolence of the establishment. It is relatively easy to obtain mercy when someone else has provoked and established the rigorous process of justice.

I have been thus large in setting forth the mock contest or collusion (game?) between God and Satan as it might appear from the viewpoint of the old Anarch, Chaos, in order to suggest how warily Milton must have proceeded with his two great contestants lest the only victor be too patently the third empire of weakness and contradiction. The imperial parallel between God and Satan is reinforced throughout the poem: they are rival emperors, sitting on "equal" and opposite thrones, ruling by means of a close council through a general assembly; they hold consults, issue edicts, man the battlements, review the troops, decide on imperial policies. A persistent strain of imagery identifies Satan with the Turkish Sophi; the empire of Heaven is just as distinctly based on Revelations and Ezekiel. But they are both organized empires; and, as with most imperial conflicts, theirs are full of absurdity. Neither participant wishes to abolish the other, or can even envisage such an outcome, since that would involve assuming full responsibility for the governance of things. God wants Satan to be responsible for the wrong and evil in the world, and Satan, with surprisingly little resistance, accepts the responsibility. The result of their mingled intentions and self-restrictions, is a partial, muted, and metaphorical reassertion of the sway of Chaos in the last books of the poem. With prophetic insight, no less a personage than Mammon had suggested something like such an outcome during the Great Consult:

> him to unthrone we then
> May hope when everlasting fate shall yield
> To fickle chance, and chaos judge the strife.
>   [II, 231–33]

God is not unthroned, of course, nor does everlasting fare yield unconditionally to fickle chance. But God's providence is in some major way withdrawn from our little world as a result of the fall; disorder and chance take the place of design in the shape of it; and as the focus of the poem narrows and lengthens to fit the dimensions of human history, the war of the two empires (which had organized the cosmos, divided it, and arranged it) disappears in the distance. Man's fate is now to struggle with

that limited Chaos which the indecisive and apparently indefinite con-
flict of God and Satan has allowed to seep back into the immediate affairs
of men. Chaos in this last part of the epic is nowhere named, nor specifi-
cally described; it has become part of the air we breathe. Its presence is felt
in three contexts particularly: in the exterior structure of the world, in the
history of man, and in his most inward workings, his psyche.

A notable instance of Chaos asserting itself in the external cosmos
occurs when the angels, at God's behest (but that behest was itself dictated
by Satan's successful seduction of man), disorder the structure of the
solar system so as to allow the planets to shed now benign and now
malignant influence on man and his earth. It's reasonably clear that
Milton felt that astrology was a mathematical science, enabling men to
predict if not to control the influence of the planets. Raphael had rebuked
Adam's vain and fruitless curiosity about the working of the stars and so
he might when their influence was unfailingly benign; but after the fall,
a knowledge of astrology is apparently going to be crucial to the prudent
conduct of human life. More striking even than this charge, is the action
of the angels in modifying the earth's weather:

> to the winds they set
> Their corners, when with bluster to confound
> Sea, air, and shore, the thunder when to roll
> With terror through the dark aerial hall.
> [X, 664–67]

This is surely to bring back some element of that Chaos which consisted

> Of neither sea, nor shore, nor air, nor fire
> But all these in their pregnant causes mixed
> Confusedly, and which thus must ever fight.
> [II, 912–14]

It is the same thing, the mixing of the elements; yet Milton has taken
a little edge off the parallel by almost leaving out the fourth element of
fire. *Almost* I say, because it's there by implication in connection with
the thunder roll. Earth, air, and water are confounded by the winds,
with fire flashing just offstage; and this is Chaos itself. We recall, in this
matter of winds, how much of Satan's journey through Chaos consisted
of a struggle through conflicting winds, how often we hear of the

> ever-threatening storms
> Of Chaos blustering round, inclement sky.
> [III, 425–26]

When we were first introduced to Chaos, there was a proviso that the
fight of elements must continue forever,

Unless th'Almighty maker them ordain
His dark materials to create more worlds.
                    [II, 915–16]

But in Book X the unleashing of the winds to confound the elements
is a way of surrendering to chaos part of an already-created world.

I don't suppose I have to labor the various ways in which Chaos is
involved in stories like those of the Flood and the Tower of Babel; what's
strikingly different in them is that the architect of confusion is the Lord
himself. Doubtless he is justified many times over in punishing the
wickedness of man; yet this puts him in the middle of the chain of
blame, doing one evil because of another, and out of this logic only
Chaos can profit. The curse of Babel is an impressive instance of a major
human disorder, the immediate source of which is God's deliberate
decree. Instead of Satan taking the blame and saving God from it, God
must stand in the foreground and save Satan, in the remote background,
from blame. There couldn't be a clearer instance of how Chaos seeps
into the postlapsarian Miltonic world, despite the intentions of either
the forces of good or the forces of evil. And as we look at the recurrent
action of human history in the last books of *Paradise Lost*, we see it to
be a constant slumping into weakness and confusion. Satan doesn't
directly contribute to this falling off, Chaos is never mentioned; but the
utmost heroism is demanded, again and again, of some isolated Christian
hero who is called on to redeem the time from its inherent tendency to
corruption. Such an impersonal phenomenon as the tangle of diseases
with which Adam is confronted in Book XI is not the work of a single
personal agent; all the ailments are comprehensible as a single condition,
intemperance, which is disorder and disproportion in the economy of
the body. Man himself has created them, man in the corrupted state
for which Satan is, doubtless, ultimately responsible. But no specific
force in the macrocosmos is made directly responsible for man's cata-
strophic state. It is the new consitition of things, or the old constitution
just allowed to reassert itself (Satan was sick before man was created).
In withdrawing the picket line of angels around the Garden, and letting
Adam and Eve wander forth into the gross, impure air of a lower world,
does God create a new balance of forces or simply free an old one to
assert itself? Milton does not say with any decisiveness. Our feeling, as
readers with a human, not an angelic perspective, can only be that the
withdrawal of heavenly protection (against disease and bad weather, for
example) is the termination of a special exemption, and the resumption
of an ordinary condition, within which Chaos has a certain matter-of-
course role to play. No plots or apparatus are required; when the delib-
erately interposed shield is lifted, things crumble of their own "natural
impulse." Adam's agonized cry—

> Both Death and I
> Am found Eternal, and incorporate both—

sounds at the depth of his remorseful monologue (X, 815–16). He could
just as well cry that Chaos and he are now incorporate, except that death
is the special exquisite privilege of the animate world—Chaos is less
fiercely felt because it is now incorporate with the inanimate as well as
the animate world. It has become mingled with the substance of
things—homogenized chaos.

Finally, in the realm of psychology, the Fall has long been understood
as an explicit reversal of ideal order, an upheaval and invasion of emo-
tional, irrational chaos into the ordered processes of Adam and Eve as
they were created. When our great parents fall first to lust and then to
quarreling, once more it's conflicting winds that image forth their inner
chaos:

> Nor only tears
> Rained at their eyes, but high winds worse within
> Began to rise, high passions—anger, hate,
> Mistrust, suspicion, discord—and shook sore
> Their inward state of mind, calm region once
> And fullof peace, now tost and turbulent.
> [IX, 1121–26]

The parallel with other blustering and turbulent winds is too obvious
and deliberate to need enforcing; at the root of it is, of course, the old
physiology of the humors, according to which moods and emotional
states were the consequence of interior winds, ill-compounded and ill-
managed. Beyond this immediate occasion, moreover, we can hardly
help noticing, over the last two books of the poem, a curious and surely
deliberate excess in Adam's emotional responses to the historical events
he is shown or told about. He is delighted with the idyllic existence of
the Sethites—Milton excuses him as "soon inclined to admit delight,/
The bent of nature" (XI, 596–97)—and has to be warned against judging
by the mere appearance of things. He is in abject despair at the vision
of the Flood, and has to be encouraged to see the brighter side of things.
In dramatic terms, this is perfectly understandable. Starting from a state
of almost perfect innocence, Adam is required to understand and assume
the weight of all human history, and given very little time in which to
do it. The purpose of his education is precisely to give him some per-
spective on things—to temper him toward a nice blend of assurance
and humility. By erring, first in the direction of complacency, then in
the direction of despair, he works his way toward a difficult emotional
balance. His conscience, he learns, must be a vigilant and scrupulous
warrior against the world's continual forays on his peace of mind. After
the angelic guard around Paradise strikes camp, only the sentinel con-

science remains on lonely guard. And the evil against which it remains alert is no longer a big dark flying man in a suit of armor—it is built into the very structure of the cosmos, of society, of the mind within which conscience itself patrols. It is not an empire, to be fought by ranked battalions; it is discord, passivity, weakness—Chaos, in other words, seen not from the outside as a stuttering, moping old man with a facial tic, but from the inside, as a constant ingredient of the Christian life, an intimate, and ultimately invincible enemy.

Reactions to a scholarly paper generally involve two traditional elements in uneasy combination:

(1) it's a pack of nonsense, and
(2) we knew it all the time.

Looking back over what I've said so far, I'm inclined to agree with both these comments, and to see in the making of them the salvation of my argument. If I have any insight to bring to the reading of *Paradise Lost*, it derives from applying both these useful clichés at once to the discussion I've laid out so far.

My paper about Chaos is essentially a pack of nonsense because it goes pervasively against the grain and structure of *Paradise Lost* itself, making primary and consecutive what Milton, for excellent reasons of his own, left intermittent and peripheral. I sin here in pretty good company, but I sin nonetheless. A skeptic could shrink the matter over which I've made such ado to small proportions indeed. Milton, he would say, had certain inescapable geographical facts to cope with: Hell, Earth, and Heaven are bound to lie at some distance from one another, and to have some minimal, representable stuff in between; Creation, to be shown in a poem, has to be creation from some basic substance. Chaos was simply Milton's way of killing these two birds with one stone. Having it already there, he used it wherever else he needed it in the poem; but he gave it no universal allegorical significance, and there's no particular reason to think Milton meant Chaos to be felt in the last two books, silently encroaching on those three fields of existence. If he had any such intentions, he might as well have mentioned Chaos or used the adjective "chaotic"—in other words, made explicit what he deliberately left unexpressed. Writing a paper about "Chaos" in *Paradise Lost* is almost as mechanical, as computerly a process, as writing a paper about Milton's use of the color green, the quality of hardness, or triangular shapes. All you need to write this sort of paper is monomania.

So far with the first objector. The second one is also right. Nobody reads *Paradise Lost* without feeling the power and terror of the Chaos whom Satan encounters out there in intergalactic space; and no half-wakeful reader has failed to see that Chaos, as a concept if not a figure, continues to exert pressure on the latter part of the poem. How far precisely that pressure extends may be questioned; but we've all felt it, as what Milton plainly intended, a marginal element. You, therefore, who have always treated it as a marginal element, are in a better position to assess its importance than is someone who focuses on it, and strains to see it wherever there's the least hint of its potential existence. The man who sees the nuances of a text in their proper light can never be a man who's concentrating on nuances.

I'm not unaware that there are ways to turn these methodological arguments around, upside down, and insight out; for the moment, what we open up here is a problematic which focuses on a relatively simple question: for the purposes of the poem, how much weight should we allow to the figure of Chaos and the perspectives which an awareness of his presence unfolds? I'm happy to concede that in this paper, I've overstated the case for his presence, and traced out the implications of his logic as vigorously as I could—too vigorously for the good of the poem. We must suppress Chaos a little bit, mute him, sit (maybe) on his head, so that the poem as a whole may maintain its intended balance. On the other hand, it may help to be made aware of his unsettling presence, if only to appreciate better Milton's art in managing the other energies of his fable. Chaos is an operative element in the balance if only by being himself so radically unstable an element.

There are reasons, thus, to push Chaos forward in the poem, and reasons to push him back; to which I would add, as a fundamental consideration, that he may serve to recall a special quality of Milton's mind—its ability to pursue its moral ends across several complex mythic structures and metaphors in close succession. There's a way of saying this that makes it sound like an accusation of mental confusion. I mean no such thing. I mean only that none of the many metaphors Milton used expressed his moral insight as largely as Dante's central spatial metaphors expressed *his* moral insight. Warfare, for example, expresses part, but only part, of Milton's vision of how a saint serves God in this world. Abstention from temptation is another form of service; so is delight in the natural richness of the world and gratitude for its beauty. Life is a quest, a race, a battle; it is service to cause, pursuit of a pattern. No image is more deeply rooted in Milton's mind as a metaphor of spiritual insight, than the image of light. The radiance of God's grace illumines man's darkened mind; through the Gospels and the Book of Creatures alike, his light pours upon us. Our role is to clear our eyes, open our hearts, purify our senses, and accept the divine infusions as sincerely as we can. A mighty nation cannot have too much light; and in a famous passage, Milton compares England to "an Eagle muing her mighty youth, and kindling her undazl'd eyes at the full midday beam; purging and unscaling her long-abused sight at the fountain itself of heav'nly radiance." Yet at the same time, and in the same splendid piece of prose, there is another metaphor for truth, one that implies very different attitudes toward it, and very different behavior in its regard. The myth that Milton adopts momentarily, with no apparent sense of its incongruity with that which he uses so liberally elsewhere, is a deeply "chaotic" fable; it assumes the presence of chaos and disorder at the very heart of religious light—the near-indistinguishability of saving truth and grievous error:

> Truth indeed came once into the world with her divine Master, and was a perfect shape most glorious to look on: but when he ascended, and his Apostles after him were laid asleep, then strait arose a wicked race of deceivers, who as that story goes of the *Aegyptian Typhon* with his conspirators, how they dealt with the good *Osiris*, took the virgin Truth, hewd her lovely form into a thousand pieces, and scatter'd them to the four winds. From that time ever since, the sad friends of Truth, such as durst appear, imitating the careful search that *Isis* made for the mangl'd body of *Osiris*, went up and down gathering up limb by limb still as they could find them. We have not found them all, Lords and Commons, nor ever shall doe till her Masters second comming: he shall bring together every joynt and member, and shall mould them into an immortall feature of loveliness and perfection. Suffer not these licensing prohibitions to stand at every place of opportunity, forbidding and disturbing them that continue seeking, that continue to do our obsequies to the torn body of our martyr'd Saint.[4]

If we let the second myth carry over into the first, it would seem to say that we must painfully assemble the sun before we can rise like an eagle to stare undazzled at the full midday beam. If we let the first myth carry over into the second, it minimizes the difficulty of assembling the god, because every piece would be as radiant as the sun itself—would carry its own instant hallmark of bright divinity. Each of the myths is true to a fragment of Milton's experience, Milton's intent. It seems idle to try to legislate here. Milton has left us an open space, for which, as readers, we should be duly grateful; it is an area where we can adjust values and assign relative weights to the elements of his thought, as seems most convenient to ours. If our reading of *Paradise Lost* strikes a poised and natural balance without any necessity of bringing Chaos explicitly into the account, well, so much the better. But if we find William Empson and A. J. A. Waldock at frantic odds with T. S. Eliot and C. S. Lewis, the moral readings of the poem being used to dull the aesthetic highlights, and discussion of the great poem deteriorating here and there toward a slanging match between God's Own Boys and the Devil's Disciples, then a little look into Chaos may serve a reconciling purpose.

4. *Areopagitica: Complete Prose Works of John Milton*, ed. Ernest Sirluck et al., Vol. II (New Haven and London), pp. 549–550, 558.

In this whole business we may get a momentary perspective on critical alternatives by alluding to a pair of northern California colleagues. Only one of them is a professed Miltonist, so far, but since our interest is methodology that's no great matter. Paul Alpers repeatedly tells us, in his long and fascinating book on *The Faerie Queene* that we must "trust the verse"; Stanley Fish tells us, in an equally provocative book on *Paradise Lost*, that we mustn't on any account trust the verse—that the verse traps us into a response against the sinfulness of which Milton already has prepared a lecture. Personally, and for no better reasons perhaps than those of temperament, I'm inclined to trust the verse; and my glimpse into Chaos reinforces this instinct. It teaches me that I'm not all wrong in admiring Satan's abrupt and independent energy; it encourages me to see that in the decline of that God-Satan polarity which structures so powerfully the early books of *Paradise Lost*, Chaos presents a hidden third force leading toward The-Way-Things-Are which is more acceptable to sincere religious feeling than if either God or Satan (each qualified only by the conscious energy of the other) were allowed to control the closing energies of the poem. The Way Things Are is No Damn Good; Milton knows that, and his deftness in allowing the negative power of Chaos to assert itself, muffling and muting the active imperial rhetoric on both sides, can be appreciated as an extraordinary touch of art. There was more to his spiritual economy, I would argue, than that "egotistical sublime" which has been so generously appreciated. In this poem where history has had to be so incredibly foreshortened, there isn't really much space for the *lacrymae rerum*, but for this too Milton has found room. Chaos insinuates it; and his agency, precisely because it isn't tied to explicit benevolence or malice, makes easier that response of ours, which mingles rueful regret, reaffirmation to the "right" cause, and an awareness that nobody's intention corresponds very closely to what we have to live with.

CHRISTOPHER HILL

The Relevance of Milton†

> Counter-culture radicalism *is* in some respects more personal and in-
> trospective than past radicalisms normally have been. . . . This . . .
> reflects the perception that the revolutionary theory and practice of the
> past have placed too much faith in economic and institutional changes,
> and have neglected the need to change people's way of thought and
> modes of personal behaviour.
>   Anthony Arblaster, *Times Literary Supplement*, 6 June 1975

I. *Milton Agonistes*

Mr. Arblaster might have excepted Milton from the charge against 'past
radicalisms'. Milton's political experience led him to attach more im-
portance to changes in people's modes of thought and conduct, less to
political manipulation and institutional change. This would seem to
give him a certain modern relevance.

But we have to work a little to grasp Milton's relevance. We cannot
just 'let the poetry speak for itself' Some of it will, most of the ideas
will not; and Milton is nothing if not a poet of ideas. To understand his
relevance we must see him as a man of total political commitment. Like
Wordsworth, he started out with extravagantly high hopes: unlike Words-
worth, he strove to cling on to them. Like Yeats, Milton wrote his
greatest poetry when he was over the age of fifty. Like Blake, unlike
Wordsworth and Auden, Milton did not renege on the political con-
victions which had inspired him in his younger days. When Milton's
revolution had turned sour, he did not seek the facile way out of saying
that his God had failed. He knew that any human beings who thought
God had failed them must have idolatrously set up as an object of worship
their own desires and fancies. Believers were included in the failure:
self-respect prevented Milton from looking for a divine scapegoat. Defeat
of his cause left him not bewailing and lamenting but probing deeper
into his own nature and that of others, in order to find out what was
needed for the good cause to succeed. Milton wrestled with God for the
blessing which had so signally been withheld, convinced that it was not
unattainable. His most mature writings were aimed at the politically
dedicated minority, fit though few, who could with him face defeat
without whining, without self-exculpation.

But Milton's relevance can hardly be grasped without some under-
standing of his theology, through which his initial radicalism and his
final synthesis were expressed. If we regard the theology as merely out-

† From *Milton and the English Revolution* (New York: Viking, 1978) 459–70. Reprinted with
the permission of Christopher Hill and the publisher.

of-date lumber—which on the surface it is—or, worse still, if we regard it as something we have to believe if we are to appreciate the poetry, then Milton is mostly dead for us. We must see, for instance, the Fall of Man as a myth or metaphor through which Milton (and not only Milton) expresses determination to change *this* world: only so can we grasp the relevance of his poetry to men and women living in a world which still needs transforming but which is not going to be transformed except by human effort. Above all Milton *fought*: this determination not to surrender what he believes to be right, however complete the apparent defeat of his cause, makes Milton every age's contemporary. Properly understood, he will be outdated only when the millennium arrives. And that, he would have grimly agreed, is long enough.

I have spoken of Milton as an individualist. But the this-worldliness of his thought makes him far less concerned with his own soul or with the after life than many of his contemporaries. There is no evidence that Milton ever underwent the conversion that was almost *de rigueur* among certain Puritan groups. There is in him none of the fevered search for personal salvation that we find in Vaughan on the one hand, in Bunyan on the other. Milton is concerned with Christ's kingdom, the good society, rather than with personal consolations or rewards. Even in *Lycidas*, where it would have been most appropriate, the reference to personal immortality is perfunctory: the real consolation is the two-handed engine, ready like Samson to smite the enemies of the church, of Christ's kingdom. Milton's virtual abandonment of the idea of sacrificial atonement, his failure to emphasize the miracles of the New Testament, including the incarnation, the resurrection, the ascension and pentecost, all make his approach verge on the secular.

The dominant characters in Milton's last three great poems are not merely individuals: they are public persons, representatives. This role is traditional for Adam and Jesus Christ in the Christian scheme of salvation. ('Adam, the parent and head of all men, either stood or fell as a representative of the whole human race.'[1]) The Son of God is the second Adam throughout *Paradise Regained*, though at the very end 'he unobserved/Home to his mother's house private returned' (IV. 638–9), divesting himself of his public persona as he had earlier divested himself of his divinity. Milton also emphasizes that Samson was 'no private' but a public person, that the fate of Israel is totally linked with his fate. The role of 'perfect men' throughout history is to save their people by their example—Moses, Enoch, Noah, Abraham, Job, Samson, Jesus—or Abdiel on a different plane. It is a shallow view which sees Milton as the hero of *Paradise Lost*. Milton is included in Adam, the informed conscience of humanity. Samson of course recalls Milton, who had hoped to liberate his people and who had suffered defeat and blindness;

1. *CD, XI*, see pp. 415–18, above [*Editor*].

but we must not allow this to obscure the representative character which Samson shares with Adam, and with the Son in *Paradise Regained*. The seventeenth century invented the new science of 'political economy': Milton's is almost a political theology.

Milton was not an original thinker, about politics or theology. He synthesized other people's ideas, and he spoke out fearlessly. His attack on Constantine in 1641, his defence of Familism in 1642, his advocacy of divorce, of the accountability of kings to their peoples, his defence of republicanism in 1660, were all acts of great courage. He was a profoundly political character, dedicated to the cause which he believed to be right. But he tried also to be a realist. *Areopagitica* in 1644, *The Ready and Easy Way* in 1660, *Of True Religion, Heresy, Schism, Toleration* in 1673, all show considerable political shrewdness. The Leveller and Digger appeal to a wider democracy is attractive to modern eyes, but Milton was more realistic in his refusal to attach any revolutionary régime that he hoped could be radicalized.

Even Milton's silences were often politically significant. Between 1641 and 1649, as the conflict between Presbyterian City, Independent Grandees and Leveller rank and file shook the unity of the Parliamentarian cause, Milton published nothing. He never attacked Oliver Cromwell as long as the latter lived to unite the Good Old Cause. In 1659–60 Milton tried desperately to popularize his schemes for reunion, and he returned to this activity just as soon as the political climate permitted it in the sixteen-seventies. His enemies remained constant—tyranny and superstition, always allied to one another.[2] The defects to which his own side were liable were avarice and ambition, also always twinned.[3]

His heresies were the common currency of radical circles, with their powerful emphasis on this world. Where Milton was unique was in his vast attempt to combine these heresies into a coherent system, and to put it forward in Latin with a view to reuniting the Protestant world. His ambition, his dedication, where what he believed to be God's cause was at stake, knew no bounds. In the *De Doctrina Christiana* and in the last pamphlets we find him still repaying the international obligations which he had incurred in Italy in the thirties. The optimism of the forties, focused on England as the chosen nation, had been succeeded by the beleaguered defensive nationalism of the fifties, the near-despair of the sixties when he felt he had no country. In the seventies hope stirred again.

The failure of Milton's audience was not, as it turned out, unmitigated disaster. Together with the reimposition of the censorship, it enabled and forced him to abandon left-handed prose propaganda and return to poetry. Now he could write for a select audience, no longer worrying about problems of communication, no longer trying ever new styles,

2. *Complete Prose Works of John Milton*, I, p. 107; VI, p. 118.
3. See C.P.W., VI, p. 598.

none of them totally to his satisfaction. Now he couled listen to the Muse and write as she dictated, confident that those would hear who were fit to hear. In poetry he no longer had to pretend that grey was white because it was whiter than black. He could give the devil his due, be as ambiguous and ambivalent as he knew the 'real world was, without feeling that he was betraying the good cause. Poetry had its own logic and its own rhetoric, and into poetry he could pour all the conflicts, the doubts, the uncertainties that had racked him as he played the propagandist. But in it too he could express the moral certainty, far beyond rational prose argument, of what he knew to be right: Adam's love for Eve, the assurance that worldly strong will be subverted by things deemed weak, that the perfect man will miraculously stand in face of all temptations, that even a failed leader can make good by standing and waiting for the moment in which the Lord delivers the Philistines into his hands, made strong again, as he had delivered the Scots into those of Oliver Cromwell at Dunbar.

Into the last poems Milton could pour, too, his astonishingly surviving sensuous delight in the plenitude of God's creation, in the overgrown thickets of the earthly Paradise and in the burning brightness of the tigress Dalila, as well as in words, their sonority, their overtones, their ambiguities, their use to conceal as well as to communicate. F. T. Prince illustrates Milton's 'armoury of puns and jingles' in *Paradise Lost*.[4] The sheer vitality of the blind man in his late fifties and sixties is astonishing, the man who had worked so hard and suffered so much, who should have been cynical or self-defensive, and who instead summons God to judgment and finally pronounces him not guilty. I cannot think of Milton as a tragic figure in those last years when, in defeat, he wrote *Paradise Lost*, *Paradise Regained* and *Samson Agonistes*. He was not only affirming the survival of a remnant; he was proclaiming that from these would grow an hundredfold, that victory would still come in the end, however tragic the present, provided we do not lose our heads or our hearts.

Milton's radicalism, I have suggested, had its limits. On occasion it was cut short by social considerations of which he was only partly aware. This relates to the paradox of his passionate and simultaneous belief in both liberty and discipline. Counterposing liberty to licence assumes certain social stabilities as a check on the intellectual iconoclasm which also attracted him. Milton's rejections of conservative views are rational: his rejections to the left are emotional, social. 'For who loves that must first be wise and good' raises questions of definition, which Milton consistently begged. His contemporary Thomas Hobbes had a short way with those who used words like 'justice', 'reason', 'liberty', 'goodness' in Milton's manner. 'Their moral philosophy is but a description of their

4. *The Italian Element in Milton's Verse* (1954), pp. 123–26.

own passions', Hobbes wrote. 'Whatsoever is the object of any man's appetite or desire, that is it which he for his part calleth good.[5] Milton's Whiggish use of such words covers a Whiggish double-think about equality.

Part of the difficulty in assessing Milton is that some of his ideas are so advanced that we tend to treat him as though he were our contemporary. Unfortunately, the three areas in which he rightly felt that he was striking blows for freedom are areas in which he now seems old-fashioned. His superb advocacy of religious liberty seems deficient in that it is restricted to Protestants. But this is because international Catholicism no longer poses the threat which it did in the seventeenth century. Catholic emancipation now seems to us the acid test of sincerity and consistency in this respect. But Catholic emancipation is a nineteenth-century phrase. 'The emancipation of Antichrist' would not have seemed a good slogan to the English revolutionaries, nor indeed to many Englishmen so long as Louis XIV's France appeared to threaten national independence. In the sphere of domestic liberty, Milton's advocacy of divorce for incompatibility now seems excessively male-orientated. Again we have to put Milton back into the seventeenth century (and to remember *Jane Eyre* and *Jude the Obscure*) to see how advanced he was in his day. In the sphere of political liberty Milton suffers in twentieth-century eyes because he was no democrat. I have tried to explain the seventeenth-century (and not only seventeenth-century) problem of republicans faced with an uneducated electorate, specifically a politically uneducated electorate.

Recognizing Milton's contradictions, and placing them in their social context, is essential to understanding the poet. 'When a man tells us unprovoked lies about himself,' Tillyard mildly observed, 'you may reasonably infer that his emotions are seriously involved.' By saying in *Paradise Lost* that he was unskilled in and unstudious of the literary artifices of the romances, Milton 'betrays the deep feelings which made him turn against them'.[6] We should look out for all the points at which Milton is fiercest—in attacking his former allies among the Presbyterian clergy or the Long Parliament, in denouncing mere humanist culture in *Paradise Regained*, in his contemptuous references to the common people or in his discussion of the relation of the sexes. Here Milton is arguing with himself, or feels that his ideals or standards have let him down. His anger springs from disappointment; it may be anger with himself rather than with those it was ostensibly directed against.

Milton never resolved his tensions—between liberty and discipline, passion and reason, human love and God's providence, the necessity of individualism and the necessity of society, radicalism and élitism. They ultimately perhaps seemed insoluble on earth: the pressures of the every-

5. Hobbes, *Leviathan* [Penguin ed.], pp. 686, 720.
6. E. M. W. Tillyard, *The Miltonic Setting* (1947), p. 20.

day world worked against the intensity of Milton's inner vision. But he tried again and again—in *Areopagitica*, in defending and warning Cromwell, in his appeal to the virtuous few in *The Ready and Easy Way*. At the end he was forced into withdrawal from all churches, despite his continuing belief in the godly remnant. In the great poems he tried to face up to the brute facts which he called God. It seemed that only divine intervention could solve the problems of the English Revolution: near hopelessness about effective political action underlies both *Paradise Regained* and *Samson Agonistes*. Yet if no one but God can produce the solutions, what becomes of human freedom? And had God shown himself worthy of this trust? Milton's is a tension between decorum and right reason on the one hand, and on the other the radical revolutionariness of individual consciences through which right reason was expressed. The mediating term was 'the middling sort', among whom he had seen the greatest hope of finding good men who would love freedom. Milton's ideological contradictions must all be related to his social position, and to the nature of the revolution in which he took part. When even the middling sort let him down in 1660, he still wanted to fight on: but he could see no solution beyond concentrating on small things in the hope that great may come of them when God gives the sign. Reformism was forced on him by the failure of the Revolution; he no longer hoped that the masses of the population might bring about the sort of revolution he wanted to see. Moses Wall proved right: centuries of economic development were necessary before solutions were possible on earth without divine intervention.[7]

I tried to suggest, I hope not too schematically, that after the eclipse of the traditional culture of court and bishops, Milton found his allegiance divided between the culture of the Protestant ethic and the lower-class third culture; and that this may underlie many of the tensions revealed in his writings. Newton and Locke, who shared many of Milton's secret heresies and tensions, were of a younger generation, and lived on into the world of triumphant Whiggery. But they still, like Milton, censored themselves before publication. Milton concealed his views so successfully that in the eighteenth and nineteenth centuries he came to be regarded as the orthodox Puritan poet. Newton—secret anti-Trinitarian and millenarian—was seen by Blake as the personification of rational science; Locke—anti-Trinitarian and millenarian, Arminian and mortalist—as the personification of rational philosophy. Against them Blake looked upon Milton as a potential ally. But in fact all three were furtively attracted by many of the ideas of the radical underground which were not to survive the triumph of 'Newtonian' science and 'Lockean' philosophy and politics. There are many ironies here to be

7. Cf. Brian Manning, *The English People and the English Revolution* (1976), pp. 314–17.

incorporated in the history of English popular culture when it comes to
be written.

In 1642 Milton used prophetic words which he must have recalled
in 1659–60: 'Timorous and ungrateful, the church of God is now again
at the foot of her insulting enemies: and thou bewailest. What matters
is for thee or thy bewailing? When time was, thou couldst not find a
syllable of all that thou hadst read or studied to utter in her behalf. Yet
ease and leisure was given thee for thy retired thoughts out of the sweat
of other men.'[8] 'Of other men': the reference is not just to his father,
but social. Milton was as aware of his responsibilities to society as any
guilt-ridden intellectual of to-day.

Milton had passed his own test, had not spared himself. 'If I be not
heard nor believed, the event will bear me witness to have spoken truth;
and I in the meanwhile have borne witness, not out of season, to the
church and to my country.'[9] He early came to see his role as that of
the dedicated national poet. In *Of Reformation* he shows himself in the
wings, ready to come on stage and celebrate successful revolutionary
action. In *Areopagitica* he anticipated a more positive leading role for
learned men, and felt a greater confidence in popular creativity. He
certainly did not think of himself then as an aloof and austere scholar.
Disappointment at the reception of his divorce pamphlets made him
want to cut himself off from his too radical admirers; he was more
isolated in his self-portraits than in reality. In *Eikonoklastes* and the
Defences of the People of England he seemed to have attained the position
of leader, smashing the idols, defending 'the most heroic and exemplary
achievements since the foundation of the world',[1] those of the English
republican nation. Even in the *De Doctrina Christiana* he still aspired
to teach European Protestants in the traditional English manner. *Par-
adise Regained* renounces some of this. Where is this great deliverer
now? But we must not exaggerate the renunciation: the brief epic ends
with the Son of God entering on his active mission of preaching. In
Samson Agonistes the emphasis is again on action after preparatory
waiting; perhaps Milton looked forward to publication of the *De Doctrina*
as his destruction of the Temple, a secret time-bomb which would
ultimately explode in the face of the orthodox. He was not to know how
long it would be before it saw the light of day, or how near it came to
never being published at all. But he must have smiled with grim irony
as men praised *Paradise Lost* who would have recoiled in horror at the
heresies of the *De Doctrina*.

The word Agonistes, we are told, means not only wrestler, struggler,

8. *The Reason of Church Government, Complete Prose Works*, I, p. 804.
9. *Considerations Touching the Likeliest Means to Remove Hirelings out of the Church, The Works
of John Milton* (New York, Columbia University Press, 1932), VI, p. 100.
1. *Complete Prose Works*, IV, p. 549. Christ's life on earth was less heroic and exemplary?

but also one who deceives whilst entertaining. Saurat saw Milton Agonistes, 'wrecked in hope, blind and poor, . . . meditating and perfecting the glorious revenge of *Paradise Lost'*. Milton, like Samson, was deceiving his audience whilst entertaining them; he was God's fool at the same time as he was God's wrestler and champion. Job, so influential for the structure and tone of *Samson Agonistes*, was also depicted as a wrestler.[2] Agonistes is a fittingly ambiguous word to describe Milton's relation to his public in the first century and a half after publication of *Paradise Lost*. Now that nearly as long again has elapsed since the appearance of the *De Doctrina*, we might begin to see Milton's point.

II. *Milton and Posterity*

I have called Milton a Whig, a revolutionary but no democrat. But though this places him in one respect, it does scant justice to his heretical radicalism. Milton was used by the Whigs in 1688 and after, but not all Whigs applauded regicide. It all depended in whose pocket the King was. Milton's revolutionary principles may have inspired the Calves' Head Club; they had no serious appeal for men of reason and compromise. But if, for instance, the *De Doctrina Christiana* had achieved publication in 1676, what would have been its effect on intellectual history? *Paradise Lost* could never have been built up as the classic of orthodoxy, and the image of Milton would have looked very different. It was exceptionally bad luck for the poet that the accident of historical development made *Paradise Lost* as bad a model for later poets as T. S. Eliot himself has been; and that Milton's dearest and best possession was published too late, when religious heresy was no longer revolutionary. That it should have been translated and edited by a bishop was only the last twist of the knife. The dynamite of the sixteen-sixties became the damp squib of the eighteen-twenties—an embarrassment to Milton's respectable admirers, but one that could be ignored. By this time Milton seemed out of the main stream of republican radicalism. He was no less opposed to clericalism than Voltaire, but since Voltaire those who wished to crush *l'infâme* had different alternatives. Milton's radicalism was still rooted in the Bible, in Christian heresy, in the dialectical thinking of the pre-Newtonian age. Only through Blake was this element communicated to the nineteenth century.

So we must not see Milton only as a precursor of eighteenth-century unitarians and deists, of Priestley and Paine; not only of the radical Whig republicans, the Commonwealthsmen, a man to whom Francis Place

2. D. Saurat, *Milton, Man and Thinker* (1944) (first published 1925), p. 198. P. R. Sellin, "Milton's Epithet Agonistes," *Studies in English Literature*, IV (1964), pp. 157–62. Barbara Lewalski, *Milton's Brief Epic: The Genre, Meaning and Art of Paradise Regained*, pp. 22, 105.

and the Chartists looked back with affection and admiration;[3] not only
a figure in the international history of revolution, influencing Jefferson
and the American revolutionaries, Mirabeau and the French revolu-
tionaries. He also influenced Herzen and the Russian romantic revo-
lutionaries, and this reminds us that Voltaire said that no one before
Milton had spoken in favour of romantic love.[4] Even if not strictly
true, it was a striking thing for Voltaire to say: and it links *Paradise
Lost* with the English romantic poets, with Blake again, with Words-
worth, Keats and Shelley.[5] As against the selfishness, hypocrisy and
fear of death taught by priests and churches, Blake saw Milton's role as
being

> to teach men to despise death and to go on
> In fearless majesty annihilating self, laughing to scorn
> Thy laws and terrors, shaking down thy synagogues as webs.[6]

Just because Milton participated in the dialogue between the two cultures
in seventeenth-century England, he looks forward to Blake as well as to
Paine, to romanticism as well as to deistic rationalism. Shelley reunited
something of the two revolutionary traditions. Milton was Freud's fa-
vourite poet.

The curve of Milton's posthumous reputation is not entirely haphaz-
ard. 'Works of inspiration are always being annexed by orthodoxy, which
hardens itself against every new incursion of the spirit': Joseph Wick-
steed's words are applied to Milton by J. A. Wittreich, who speaks of
commentators 'surreptitiously snaring the poet in their own net of or-
thodoxy'. During the century and more after the defeat and suppression
of the third culture Milton became the great Puritan poet. Every decade
of the eighteenth century saw on average ten editions of *Paradise Lost*
and seven of Milton's complete poems.[7] A change came only with the
revival of political activity among the lower and middle classes. Dr.
Johnson smelt danger and roundly denounced Milton's ideas. But the
radicals picked them up and emphasized unorthodoxies which had been
ignored since the revolutionary decades. Blake, who certainly knew about
the Ranter past,[8] picked Milton out as the historical figure with whom
the radicals' argument must be continued. He gave them the last word
against Milton by claiming that he was of the devil's party without

3. *The White Hat*, I (1819), pp. 42, 96; *The Chartist Circular*, 13 March 1841; A. K. Stevens,
   "Milton and Chartism," *P.Q.*, XII (1933), pp. 377–88.
4. J. T. Shawcross, ed., *Milton: The Critical Heritage* (1970), p. 250.
5. S. S. Curran, "The Mental Pinnacle: *Paradise Regained* and the Four-Book Epic," in J. A.
   Wittreich, ed., *The Romantics on Milton* (1970), pp. 133–62.
6. *Poetry and Prose* (Nonesuch edn.), p. 541.
7. J. A. Wittreich, *Angel of Apocalypse: Blake's Idea of Milton* (1975), p. 148. W. J. Bate, *The
   Burden of the Past and the English Poet* (1971), p. 22. Isabel Rivers tells me that Wesley
   urged his lay preacher to read *Paradise Lost*: and Methodism contributed to the labor movement
   as well as to Puritan piety.
8. A. L. Morton, *The Matter of Britain* (1966), pp. 83–121.

knowing it;[9] Shelley called Satan the hero of *Paradise Lost*, though in a sense different from Dryden and Dennis. The reforming Major Cartwright associated enthusiasm with love of liberty and hatred of corruption.

The revival of Milton's radical reputation was accompanied by similar revivals of trends which had been suppressed for over a century. Sociological history was picked up by the Scottish school where Harrington had left it, political economy by Adam Smith where Petty had left it. The advance of chemistry, checked since Boyle, was resumed by Priestley and Lavoisier. Political radicals, from Wilkes to the Chartistrs, looked back to their seventeenth-century precursors, to the Levellers and Milton. After a long struggle, the Reform Bill of 1832 re-enacted something very like the Parliamentary franchise of 1654. Robert Owen and some Chartists rediscovered ideas of communal production, though there is no evidence that they read Winstanley: men did not need to read Milton to reject tithes.[1] English society in the age of the French Revolution had caught up with the teeming freedom of the English Revolution. The publication in 1825 of the *De Doctrina Christiana* ought to have been a match to gunpowder; but by that date political radicalism had left religious heresy behind.

Chartism failed no less than Levellers, Diggers and Fifth Monarchists. Samson's hair was trimmed again. From Macaulay onwards Milton was re-annexed to orthodoxy, this time to English liberalism. In our own day the heirs of the third culture are waving their locks again. The attempt to dislodge Milton having failed, the neo-Christians tried to annex him. In the nineteen-fifties, the decade of the coldest war, which proclaimed the end of ideology, which saw Shakespeare as a Christian humanist and not much else, an effort was made to deny that Milton had really been a heretic at all. History has shown up the superficiality of pretending that ideology can cease to exist in a class-divided society (though, to do them justice, some of the end-of-ideologists imagined that the welfare state had abolished class divisions too—alas!). Shakespeare and Milton have escaped from the little nets which were cast around them. Saurat, Caudwell, Wolfe, Kelley, Empson, Ricks,[2] have all helped to restore Milton to his proper place in the English tradition.

Milton was *sui generis*, wedded and glued to no forms, the great eclectic. But he was open to the left and closed to the right—intolerant

---

9. Cf. J. A. Wittreich, who argues that the Whigs were often called "the diabolical party," *Angel of the Apocalypse*, p. 214.
1. 'Every man has a right to have what priest he chooses and to pay him what recompense he chooses, but no man of government has a right to force his God down my throat or his priestly hand into my pocket' ("The People's Paper," 9 July 1853, quoted by John Saville, *Ernest Jones, Chartist* [1952], p. 222).
2. See their works listed in the Selected Bibliography below, except Christopher Caudwell's *Illusion and Reality: A Study of the Sources of Poetry* (London, 1937), an early and interesting example of Marxist literary criticism [*Editor*].

of papists though embracing all varieties of Protestantism, merciless to
the Philistine aristocracy and priests but merciful to the excluded vulgar,
linking himself with the radicals just as far as his strong sense of the
necessity of bourgeois society would permit.

JAMES GRANTHAM TURNER

Passion and Subordination†

Milton's vision of pre-lapsarian sexuality, like the landscape of Paradise
where it unfolds, is distinguished from all others by its capacity for
'growth and compleating'. Our sense of Milton's erotic universe grows
throughout the central books of *Paradise Lost*, not only by accumulation
of detail, but by an increasing awareness of complexity; each successive
episode involves confrontation with a new form of erotic sensibility
(Satan, Raphael) or a new aspect of the self revealed by passion, and
the horizons of innocence expand to include the problematic. The
discovery of redeemed sensuousness is part of a taxing enquiry into the
'prime institution' of Paradisal marriage, into the nature of human sex-
uality and its relation to the divine—the most important task for fallen
humanity, condemned to sift like Psyche through the mingled grains of
good and evil.[1] But the same struggle for truth—to foster rather than to
recover their righteous pleasures—confronts the first couple. Under-
standing their sexual love, and discovering how to preserve it in a Paradise
that must be shared with Satan, is therefore a central action of the poem,
for the characters as much as for the readers.

The effect of continual discovery is generated by the narrative design
itself, which builds up a texture of overlapping viewpoints, and thus
subjects the passion of Adam and Eve to a refined scrutiny that anticipates
the epistolary novel. Even the first description of the couple, a dramatic
and didactic *tableau vivant* of Genesis 1 and 2, is framed by the presence
of Satan, fluctuating between love, desire, and envy, straining to discover
details that he can put to evil use: the obvious ideological function of
lines such as 'Hee for God only, shee for God in him' and 'Not equal,
as their sex not equal seemd' is undermined when we reflect that the
only observer, the only subject to whom these qualities 'seemed' a prod-
uct of 'their sex', is Satan himself. Indeed, the subjective impression of
the couple receives an emphasis unusual even in Milton—'seemed' is

---

† Excerpted from "Love Made in the First Age," reprinted from *One Flesh* by James Grantham
Turner, by permission of Oxford University Press. Copyright © 1987 by James Grantham
Turner.
1. *The Complete Prose Works*, II (New Haven, 1959), pp. 528, 587, 514. [See *Areopagitica*, pp.
382–91, above—*Editor.*] The image of the grains is one of several incompatible models of
good and evil in *Areopagitica*; M sometimes assumes a dialectic interchange between good
and evil, sometimes a simple 'mingling' of essentially distinct and immutable essences.

repeated three times in the sentence introducing them, each time as a main verb—and the Satanic association of the word is increased by the remark that, since the fall, true sexual purity has been replaced by 'mere shows of seeming pure' (IV. 290–9, 316). The possibility of competing models of sexual identity, stirring even within this ostensibly monolithic description, is increased shortly afterwards when Eve recounts the first crisis of her life, the scene by the lake; she is forced to decide between two 'images' of erotic love, one 'watery' and narcissistic, the other substantial and reciprocal. As we have seen, the sexual bond emerges from this episode as a profounder and more complex phenomenon than was suggested in the original separation and limitation of functions ('For contemplation hee and valour formd, / For softness shee and sweet attractive grace'): both male and female are led by intense desire, both feel incomplete without a partner, and both devote their contemplative and active powers to realizing this drive. This sense of the reciprocity of the lovers and the interpenetration of intelligence, energy, and eroticism, absent from any other version of the Eden-myth, is confirmed in the dream-episode—where the problem is solved with exemplary lucidity and deepening affection—and in the successive events of Raphael's visit, including Adam's own account of his encounter with Eve and the 'commotion strange' of sexual passion.

[II]

The long scene with Raphael (Books V–VIII) serves not only to feed audience and characters with necessary information, but to provide a social encounter in which the paradoxical attractiveness and innocence of unfallen sexuality can be tested, and its problems illuminated both in practice and in conversation. Milton is quite aware that the presence of an observer could impose a strain on his sexual idyll, and he is not afraid to evoke these tensions in order to shape them to his poetic purpose. The first evening's 'dalliance' is defined by contrast with the response of Satan, who grows more verminous the closer he edges to Eve; now she is approached by an unfallen archangel. In both cases the supernatural visitor is considered as an erotic subject, capable of a reaction that Milton characterizes as specifically male. (Female sensuousness is not ignored by Milton, as we have seen, but he renders it more indirectly.) The male reader's self-scrutiny, sometimes explicitly directed by the author, forms a counterpoint to the unfolding narrative of erotic discovery. Raphael's visit thus continues the complicated drama of Book IV, in which the triangular situation of Adam, Eve, and the newcomer is itself observed by the epic audience, which must include not only the solitary youth but also, given Milton's insistence on godly marriage as the highest form of human life, the couple reading together.

The confrontation of woman and angel involved a special hermeneutic problem—one that was all the deeper because it concerned primeval sexuality and the origin of evil. In some Hebrew scriptures, we have seen in chapter 1, the original fall occurs when the angels ('Sons of God') make love to the daughters of men and beget giants on them; a fragment of this story survives in Genesis 6:1–2, where it seems to provide the motive for exterminating the entire human race apart from Noah's family. The ingenuity of commentators was greatly taxed by this stupendous episode; most of them (though Donne is an exception) followed Augustine in wrongly interpreting 'Sons of God' as the elect, the godly part of the human race— though like Augustine they also asserted that devils could and often did copulate with wicked women.[2] But St. Paul, in a passage that greatly influenced Milton's depiction of Eve, might suggest that angels are meant: 'if a woman have long hair', he explains in 1 Corinthians 11:15, 'it is a glory to her, for her hair is given her for a covering,' and she needs to be covered—with a veil or similar sign of subjection if her own hair is cut—'because of the angels'.

Milton was quite uncertain about the meaning of this passage in Genesis 6, and the efforts of modern scholars to reduce him to orthodoxy are unsatisfactory. In *Paradise Lost* XI. 580–636 the seduction of the Sons of God, in their standard Augustinian meaning, provides an important episode in which Michael teaches Adam the need for sexual temperance. But in *De Doctrina* Milton quotes Genesis 6:1 approvingly, as an example of sound moral judgement in love. In the Limbo of *Paradise Lost* Book III the offspring of those 'ill-joyn'd Sons and Daughters' appear closely associated with births 'abortive, monstrous, or unkindly mixt' and with 'middle Spirits . . . Betwixt th'Angelical and Human Kind', though the connection may be intended as a delusion. But in *Paradise Regain'd* Milton assumes quite unequivocally that the unholy couplings of Genesis 6 were in fact done by the supernatural Belial and his 'lusty crew', who then falsely named the perpetrators 'Sons of God'; since the character of evil, in Milton's universe, is a perversion of the good, then a purer version of such propensities must exist in all angels. Milton tells us explicitly that angels enjoy diffuse sexual intercourse among themselves, and that they can take on either sex and 'limb themselves' for their encounters with other beings. 'Sons of God' is thus a term which could refer to upright men, or to fallen angels, or to the highest spiritual beings—indeed, one of Satan's chief purposes in *Paradise Regain'd* is to find out which of these meanings applies to Christ,

2. Cf. Watson Kirkconnell, *The Celestial Cycle: The Theme of Paradise Lost in World Literature, with Translations of the Major Analogues* (Toronto, 1952), pp. 486, 507–9; St. Augustine, *City of God* III.5 and XIV.23. *De Trinitate*. XII.vii.10; Martin Luther, *Lectures on Genesis, Luther's Works*, ed. Jaroslav Pelikan (St. Louis, 1958–   ), II.10–11; John Donne, *Sermons*, ed. Evelyn M. Simpson and George R. Potter (Berkeley, 1953–62), VIII.107; Arnold Williams, *The Common Expositor* (Chapel Hill, 1948), pp. 117, 152.

for 'Sons of God both Angels are and Men', and the phrase 'bears no single sence'.[3]

There are hints of this multiple signification at several points in *Paradise Lost*. The first description of the happy pair, in which Eve's 'wanton' hair, arranged 'as a vail down to the slender waist . . . implied subjection,' concludes by linking their unveiled nakedness with the angels: 'So pass'd they naked on, nor shund the sight / Of God or Angel, for they thought no ill' (IV. 319–20). And when Raphael first meets Eve in all her splendour, lovelier than Venus displaying herself to Paris, a similar point is made: 'no vail / Shee needed, Vertue-proof' (V. 383–4). The primary stress, of course, is on the inner purity of the naked Eve (Adam's nudity passes without comment in the second example), but both descriptions evoke the possibility of a 'thought infirm' or susceptible response. Milton is apparently fascinated by the paradox of the veil that hides and reveals at once, simultaneously enhancing innocence and desirability. He found this piquant effect in a favourite episode of *The Faerie Queene*, where it is used by the wicked nymphs to inflame Sir Guyon; here it is reappropriated for innocence.[4] Just as Eve here is decked and undecked ('Undeckt, save with her self'), so she is somehow veiled and not veiled—veiled for the fallen but virtuous Sons of God who read the poem and appreciate the metaphorical allusion to what St. Paul would have to make literal, but unveiled for the angels who meet her in the flesh.

We are likely to wonder, as Adam does, what Raphael feels during the visit. The parallel with Venus on Mount Ida announces this as another scene of judgement, but the identity of the judge remains elusive. Is it the reader, the voyeur of three naked beings, or Adam, whose choice of Eve will soon set off an epic catastrophe worse than the Trojan war, or is it the newly-arrived Raphael himself? Even if we are unaware of the sexual capacity of the 'Sons of God', Milton has several times reminded us of the erotic associations of this archangel. Raphael is a seraph, whose natures were particularly suited to Love; he is selected for the visit because of his special interest in marital success (his later help to Tobit, already evoked when Satan first meets the scents of Paradise, is emphasized again at V. 221–3); and his arrival in Eden is heralded by an astonishing burst of sensuous imagery, a 'pouring forth' of 'enormous bliss' in the landscape (V. 296–7). He arrives, on the stroke of noon, just as 'the mounted Sun / Shot down direct his fervid Raies

3. *Prose* VI. 720 (Col. edn. XVII.203) and cf. 1.552; *PL* III. 461 3, VI. 352; *PR* II. 178–81.IV. 197 and 517. For scholarly opinion, see notes on these passages in Fowler (which contradict the identification of 'Sons of God' with angels at V. 446–50) and A *Variorum Commentary on the Poems of John Milton*, IV, ed. Walter MacKellar (New York, 1975), p. 117.

4. *FQ* II. xii. 63–8, esp. 64; several details of M's erotic Eden are borrowed from, and hence rebuild, Spenser's Bower of Bliss. For some fruitful speculation on the relation of M to Spenser, and of both poets to their female patronesses mortal and celestial, cf. Maureen Quilligan, *Milton's Spenser* (Ithaca, 1983) ch. 4, 'The Gender of the Reader and the Problem of Sexuality'.

to warm / Earths inmost womb' (V. 300–2). Raphael's entrance is thus charged with sexual energy, and he leaves, with a noble exhortation to happiness and love, after a glowing response to Adam's frank curiosity about angelic Eros. And we have seen that at the midpoint of the conversation, when Eve leaves to go gardening, 'all Eyes'—which must include Raphael's—are struck with 'Darts of desire . . . to wish her still in sight'.

The characters in this naked *déjeuner sur l'herbe* are not waxwork figures of innocence, then, but powerful breathing beings who may inspire sensuous empathy and curiosity, as well as shame and tension at the contrast between their state and our own. Though the female reader is not necessarily excluded from this scene, which presents Eve as a creative and self-motivated artist as well as a passive object of desire—imaginative readers can in any case participate in the experience of the opposite gender vicariously, if not uncritically—Milton is here absorbed by an erotic response normally associated with the male: the frenzy caused by the submission of a beautiful woman. At one point this becomes quite explicit. The occasion is another of Milton's revisions of Spenser's Bower of Bliss, in which a moment of erotic sorcery is transplanted to Paradise with its sensuous root-structure intact. Whereas in Spenser it was the bathing nymphs who blush and display their nakedness, and 'Excesse' who offers the gentlemen an enchanted cup, now

> at Table *Eve*
> Ministerd naked, and their flowing cups
> With pleasant liquors crown'd: O innocence
> Deserving Paradise! if ever, then,
> Then had the Sons of God excuse t'have been
> Enamour'd at the sight; but in those hearts
> Love unlibidinous reign'd, nor jealousie
> Was understood, the injurd Lovers Hell.   (V. 443–50)

The emotional vehemence of this extraordinary passage does not exempt us from interpretative struggle. We are not allowed to fall back on the simple opposition of heavenly love to fallen lust, nor to rely on simple definitions of 'enamour'd' and 'Sons of God'. At first it seems that Love-unlibidinous and being-enamoured are mutually exclusive and morally polarized terms. We then recall, however, that Adam only a few hours earlier had 'hung over [Eve] enamour'd' (V. 13): it is possible of course that we assent to the murmuring voice that calls Adam foppish, uxorious, and already fallen, thus accusing either God or Milton of incompetence; but as regenerate readers we should have rescued the word from these associations and restored it to the state of innocence. (Augustine, we saw in chapter 2, believed that even words as tainted as *libido* and

Concupiscentia could be redeemed.) Since Adam can be innocent, 'un-libidinous', and 'enamour'd' at the same time, we are forced to replace our static dichotomy with a more complex dialectic.

The allusion to the 'Sons of God' is similarly multivalent and compressed. In the immediate context the phrase apparently refers to angelic as well as human susceptibility. The plural 'those hearts' shows that Milton is thinking of feelings shared by more than one admirer, and 'jealouise' is therefore applied first to both witnesses: Milton evokes, even as he denies it, a scenario like that of *Amphitryon*. We must assume in Raphael a loving but innocent desire for Eve, compared explicitly to the imprudent angels of Genesis 6, and implicitly to the jealousy and 'fierce desire' of Satan, the demonic copulator and Courtly Amorist— the sarcastic allusion to 'the injured Lover's Hell' encompasses both these roles. In the larger context, which includes the sober lesson of Book XI, 'Sons of God' refers to the upright man in a fallen world, the tribe of the author himself and the masculine part of his fit audience. In this quasi-confessional moment, Milton seems to be saying that Eve's 'sweet attractive grace' could have filled the highest beings, as well as the ordinary *homme moyen sensuel*, with a rush of amorous feeling, and that at the high points of his description such lunacy might be excused.[5]

In powerful outbursts of yearning such as this, Milton suffuses the Genesis-story with more personal, Proustian dreams of vanished happiness and an ideal mistress—a process already begun in the prose, but now given fuller voice. His tributes to an imagined Eve derive their special urgency from emotive repetition: her 'Subjection' (a fetish in the divorce tracts as well as here) is 'by her yielded, by him best receivd, / Yielded with coy submission . . .'; her food (increasingly important to Milton himself in successive marriages) is designed to bring 'Taste after taste upheld with kindliest change'. The climactic moment when Eve serves as cupbearer or Ganymede, and the Sons of God are excused their passion, again produces a critically placed repetition, overflowing the line-ending and drowning out the conditional phrase: 'if ever, then, / Then . . .' At these peaks of excitement we see a naïve, transparent Milton, not the manipulator of fallen responses but the agent of unexamined passions. His presentation of Eve, a kind of surrogate courtship, is thus as personal as the invocations that tell of his blindness and misfortune, or the sonnet on his dead wife, or the private speculation that the desire of the Sons of God might have been entirely good.[6] As in his reckless divorce tracts, Milton bares his own emotion in order to revitalize the Paradise myth for the Sons of God among his own people. Here he seems to speak from a position of uneasy intimacy, both priv-

---

5. Peter Lindenbaum, in "Love-making in Milton's Paradise" (*MS* VI [1974], p. 287), treats this episode perceptively.
6. *PL* IV.309–10, V.336, 446–7: Milton included specific culinary demands in his third marriage-contract.

ileged and abashed; he is not quite a stranger in Paradise, and not quite a member of the innocent party, but he offers himself as the leader of the intruding group and the orchestrator of their tensions.

[III]

The latent confessional impulse in Milton's relation of Edenic sexuality becomes explicit in Adam's conversation with Raphael (VIII. 251–630). Adam follows Eve's lead in reconstructing the pleasures and discoveries of his first waking hours: she first told of the triumph of love over hesitancy in their first meeting, crowned with immediate consummation; now Adam retells the same moment in similar terms, first diffident, then rising to a rapturous display of nuptial imagery. He then proceeds, with astonishing boldness, to tell Raphael how it feels to make love to Eve:

> [I] must confess to find
> In all things else delight indeed, but such
> As us'd or not, works in the mind no change,
> Nor vehement desire, these delicacies
> I mean of Taste, Sight, Smell, Herbs, Fruits, and Flowrs,
> Walks, and the melodie of Birds; but here
> Farr otherwise, transported I behold,
> Transported touch. Here passion first I felt,
> Commotion strange. (VIII. 523–31)

Adam's critical analysis and defence of his own passion comes at the climax of the most idyllic part of *Paradise Lost*; it is the intimate core to which the conversation with Raphael gradually moves. In his conversations with Eve Adam would 'solve high dispute / With conjugal Caresses' (VIII. 55–6); but now the same caresses *generate* high dispute, and reveal problems of their own. Eros and female subordination turn out to be doubly problematic, moreover: not only must Adam struggle with the same dialectic of emotion as the reader, but the 'solutions' of the poem do not quite match the complexity of its awareness of human sexuality, and do not quite reconcile the original contradictions of Genesis, now hatched by Milton's powerful imagination.

In all other enjoyments Adam describes himself as 'superior and unmov'd'; he means that he is distinct from and more advanced than the object that provides the delight, and that he is not 'moved' in his whole being, or 'transported' to a different realm of existence. This is quite in keeping with the dominion over the environment granted to mankind in Genesis 1. But in the presence of his fellow-human his very mind is changed, and he cannot separate his sensuous delight from his admiration for Eve's specifically human qualities—not just her beauty, but her dignity, intelligence, and completeness (VIII. 531–59). It is important to recall at this point that the text of Genesis says nothing whatever about male superiority or rule over the female, until the latter is imposed as a punishment after the fall. And the exegetical tradition, though it repeatedly violated the Scripture by assigning male dominance to the state of nature, was not unanimous; as we have seen in chapter 3, Chrysostom insisted that Eve was not subordinated until her punishment, as did several English radicals, and the Lutheran *Enarrationes* describe primal equality in great detail—though they contradict themselves in different parts of the text. Milton was working with a divided heritage, and this is reflected in Adam's attempt to understand his love for Eve.[7]

Adam begins, like any apprentice in the mysteries of Eros, by trying an inadequate dichotomy. Intellectually he 'understands' her to be what the divorce tracts say she is—an 'inferior', inwardly less gifted and outwardly less like God than he is, a being made 'occasionally' as an afterthought; but in the penumbra of love he experiences her as intelligent, dignified, and 'absolute', 'in herself compleat', a being 'intended first', an autonomous and fully human counterpart to himself (VIII. 540–55). This latter vision, though it alarms the suprematist in Raphael and Milton, fits perfectly well with the 'fit help' promised in Genesis. Nor does Adam quite call her a superior. But he does lavish superlatives on her that balance ambiguously between what Eve ought to be and what she seems to be, between how he feels and what he knows he should be thinking; he then widens it by carelessly using a vocabulary of extreme moral turpitude, and digs it deeper with alarming explanations that seem to accuse God more than himself. He even toys with the idea that God had deliberately weakened him when He extracted Eve from his side, a notion that any Christian should find blasphemous—though Donne, as we saw in chapter 3, used it to adorn a wedding-sermon.

By creating an Adam who is conscious of being 'weak / Against the charm of Beauties powerful glance' (VIII. 532–3), Milton again focuses on a problem that had unwittingly compromised other versions of Genesis. In Loredano as well as in Milton Adam finds in Eve 'the summe of all his desires', but when Loredano attempts to praise God's handiwork in Eve, and pay tribute to her beauty and glory, he falls into a distinctively worldly and fallen attitude, a kind of gallant humanism with misogynistic undertones:

> Women have derived from heaven so sweet a Tyranny into
> their faces, that the denying them the subjection of all hearts
> is an effect rather of stupidity than of prudence. He that can
> resist the inchantments of a feminine beauty, either is no man,
> or is indued with qualities superiour to those of a Man.

---

7. *In Primum Librum Mose Enarrationes* (1544), ed G. Koffmane and O. Reichert, in *Werke*, Kritische Gesamtausgabe (Weimar, 1883–), XLII (1911).

Loredano effectively antedates the fall, accuses God of entrapment, and 'pleads Adam's excuse'. His condemnation of the fall is softened by a similar indulgence.[8] At these moments the author's attitude is indistinguishable from the flippancy of Adam's own reply to God's accusation: ' "Who can resist the power of beauty? . . . He that can withstand the importunate solicitude of the fairest piece (cosa) that ever came out of thy hands, either knows not how to Love or deserves not to be Beloved." ' The fierce condemnation that Loredano showers on this speech of Adam's has very little moral authority, since he has already practically endorsed it in his own descriptions of Eve. In Milton a similar surrender to gallantry is 'placed' dramatically, checked by Raphael's frown, and scrutinized by Adam himself: he is not 'stupified' by his amorous experiences, but stimulated to keener self-analysis. Nevertheless, this process of discrimination—in Adam himself and in the reader—is achieved with difficulty, and the episode remains precariously poised on the edge of simplistic moralism and authorial confusion.

Adam's description of his passion presents us with a very mingled grain. Adam pours out his feelings in a torrent of praise for Eve, an overflow of the cup of earthly blessings; he ends, not by formulating a question about a problem, but by returning to the angelic radiance of his beloved. Nevertheless, what began as an indulgent 'confession' between friends soon takes on the tone of a real confession—confess, weak, Nature faild in mee, too much of Ornament, degraded, folly.[9] The vocabulary seems so wildly incompatible with the state of innocence, and so remote from the conversations we have actually witnessed between Adam and Eve, that we labour to apply the special mode of reading that we have already practised with 'dalliance', 'attractive grace', 'liquid lapse of falling streams', 'wanton', and 'enamoured'. We rescue passion and commotion from their Satanic associations by recalling that in Areopagitica 'passions' are the God-given seeds of virtue and 'commotions' are the marks of divine healing—and even 'vehemence' exists in a heroic Christ-like form.[1]

Other parts of Adam's confession resist improvement, however. His blame of 'Nature' for not making him more superior seems unduly fallen, especially when we notice that, even earlier in his narration, he had equated 'Nature' with the possibility of sinful thoughts in Eve. He seems to have been deluded into crude anthropomorphism when he says that

8. "What cannot women do in an amorous soule? What fortitude will not she conquer, what constancy will not she subdue, what Will will she not pervert, what impossibility will not she effect? He that, loving, is able to resist the violences of Woman, is either a God or hath the power of a God' (pp. 42–3); cf. pp. 21, 34–5. For a similar combination of gallantry and moralization, see Francesco Pona, L'Adamo (Verona, 1654), and William Davenant, Gondibert VI.64.

9. PL VIII. 523–59, and cf. IX.2 'as with his Friend'. Just as M's Paradise can contain blushing without shame and wantonness without lust, so it can have confession without sin.

1. Prose II. 527, 566; among the frequent praises of 'vehemence' in the prose of the 1640s, cf. I.663, 874, 878, and in the divorce tracts II.282, 301, 644, 664.

Eve's 'outward' form is less in the image of God than his; not even Satan made this observation.[2] The terms 'degraded' and 'folly' seem themselves to degrade his partner even when he purports to exalt her. Both possible meanings of '[not] intended first' are dubious: we can agree that Eve is not planned as a ruler over him (as she was in van Helmont), but it is a gross presumption to declare that she was an afterthought, a being 'made / Occasionally' rather than intended from the first. The effect of these multiple doubts is to throw Adam's whole conceptual model into greater disarray than perhaps his author intended.

Does this mean that Raphael's reply is wholly correct? The archangel rebukes some of Adam's assumptions, but he endorses others. He is properly severe on Adam's blame of 'Nature', identical to the pusillanimous excuse he will offer when confronted with his crime. He agrees enthusiastically with Adam's disparagements of Eve, however, and proclaims her worthy of honour but 'less excellent' and of less ultimate value; he would certainly disagree with the critic who explains Eve's position as subordination without devaluation.[3] And he condemns 'Passion' with something of the austere anti-sexuality of the divorce tracts; love-making is no more than 'the sense of touch whereby mankind / Is propagated', and far from being of supreme value must be considered something given also to 'Cattel and each Beast'. (In the *Doctrine and Discipline of Divorce*, we recall, 'God does not principally take care for such cattell.') Passion, in Raphael's view, is entirely incompatible with Love, which here as in the earlier prose is conceived as a Platonic ascent:

> In loving thou dost well, in passion not,
> Wherein true Love consists not; love refines
> The thoughts, and heart enlarges, hath his seat
> In Reason, and is judicious, is the scale,
> By which the heav'nly Love thou maist ascend.
>
> (VIII. 588–92)

Adam must not remain 'sunk in carnal pleasure', which could have been provided by mating him with one of the beasts.

2. *PL* VIII. 506, 543–6; cf. Satan's early observation: 'so lively shines / In *them* divine resemblance, and such grace / The hand that formed *them* on their shape hath poured' (IV.363–5, my emphasis). M did perhaps assume that God had the appearance of a human male: certainly He always appears to Adam as a male, as does Raphael (whence Adam could deduce in his fallen anger that Heaven is peopled with 'Spirits Masculine', X. 890). But Adam's (and M's) uncertainty about how God appeared to Eve before she met Adam (n. 8 below), and the fact that God communicates directly to Eve while His messenger is instructing Adam in Books XI–XII, could suggest that God's manly looks are put on only for Adam, according to the principle of accommodation (i.e. we must conceive 'Him' the way 'He' chooses to communicate 'Himself' to us; *Prose* VI.133–6). Cf. William Kerrigan, 'The Fearful Accommodations of John Donne', *ELR* IV (1974), esp. 340–6.

3. *PL* VIII. 561–6; [Diane Kelsey McColley, *Milton's Eve* (Urbana, 1983)], ch. 2 and *passim*. McColley argues that Adam and Eve should model their relationship on that of the divine Father and Son, learning submission-in-equality, obedience to a consubstantial being, and sacrificial love: but God deliberately stimulates Adam's sense of the *dis*similarity of God and man in this area (in the testing-scene before the creation of Eve); and sacrificial love, supposing Adam had been told of it, would have encouraged his fall even more.

Adam's response, to this rebuke is complex and divided: he is only 'half abasht', and he is stimulated to a more thorough and discriminating defence of erotic desire. A gulf thus opens between man and angel, and it is by no means certain who has the 'true authority'. Raphael expresses Milton's deeply held beliefs, of course: 'Passion' in the fallen world must be kept under because it is always ready to spring at the higher faculties and tear them down; as another impeccably orthodox speaker later puts it, once Reason is 'obscur'd or not obeyd', 'inordinate desires / And upstart Passions' snatch the government and reduce man to servitude—his previous condition, interestingly enough, having been equality (XII. 86–90). But Milton was just as serious about his vitalistic and experiential ethics, in which virtue is constituted by struggle with excess, and in which passions are implanted by God even in unfallen man, and must be 'known' to the full—'he had bin else a meer artificial *Adam*'. He was serious, too, in his worship of pre-lapsarian Wedded Love. Aquinas had speculated that *passions animae* could have existed in perfect harmony with reason, and that erotic feeling would have been all the more intense; Milton 'hatched' this hypothetical state, and gave it moral credibility by making conflict essential to the 'growth and compleating' of innocence. Adam's reply to Raphael draws on all these Miltonic beliefs.

He justifies himself to Raphael by drawing on the same sensationalist psychology that he used to explain Eve's dream:

> I to thee disclose
> What inward thence I feel, not therefore foild,
> Who meet with various objects, from the sense
> Variously representing; yet still free
> Approve the best. (VIII.607–11)

Approval will still be granted, he assures Raphael, on subordinationist criteria: passion will be kept below reason and woman below man. But then he challenges the archangel's estimation of sexual desire, and so redeems some of the rhapsodic 'Passion' that had inspired his high valuation of Eve and thus caused the frowning interruption. He replies to Raphael's charge with a sense of mild superiority derived from the experience of married love:

> Neither her out-side formd so fair, not aught
> In procreation common to all kinds
> (Though higher of the genial Bed by far,
> And with mysterious reverence I deem)
> So much delights me as those graceful acts,
> Those thousand decencies that daily flow
> From all her words and actions mixt with Love.
> (VIII. 596–602)

Human eroticism is both 'higher' and more complex than the archangel realizes. Adam is right, then, to end this extraordinarily probing conversation by asking his preceptor about angelic sexuality, just as he had asked him about angelic eating at the very beginning. His goal is to discover whether heavenly love (which Raphael *can* describe at first hand) is indeed joined in a Platonic 'scale' to the highest sexual love between man and woman, and if so, whether this vertical dimension provides an adequate model for understanding his own feelings.

Milton knew from Matthew 22:30 that there is no marriage in heaven, and he seems to have agreed with Donne that angels do not and perhaps cannot know the mind of man; both the Chorus in 'Adam Unparadiz'd'[4] and Satan in *Paradise Lost* display a curiosity to know more about the new creature. Angelic apprehension, like that of the pastoral swain, is intense but one-dimensional. Raphael is by no means an infallible guide: he has already vacillated on the important question of 'accommodation', and Book VII has already established that his knowledge is limited to the 'Priestly' part of Genesis, to the biological rather than the human aspect of creation. He there expressed the opinion that Milton denounced as 'crabbed' and 'rustic' in the divorce tracts: 'Male he created thee, but thy consort / Female for Race.[5] Raphael's responses to Adam show us that angelic sexuality is like the angelic mind.

Milton's angels are not inaccessibly different from humans, but are another form of 'one first matter', more spirituous because nearer to God; they have the same digestive needs and the same sexual emotion, though they are not limited by specific organs:

> Whatever pure thou in the body enjoy'st
> (And pure thou wert created) we enjoy
> In eminence, and obstacle find none
> Of membrane, joynt, or limb, exclusive barrs:
> Easier than Air with Air, if Spirits embrace,
> Total they mix, Union of Pure with Pure
> Desiring: nor restrain'd conveyance need
> As Flesh to mix with Flesh, or Soul with Soul.
> (VI. 469–90, VIII. 622–9)

4. A translation of *Adamus Exul*, by Hugo Grotius in Kirkconnell, *The Celestial Cycle* [*Editor*].
5. Donne, *Sermons*, X. 58, 82 (I owe this point to Arthur Barker); Fowler, introd.; *PL* III. 662–76, VII. 529–30; ch. 3 *passim* and 6. 2. iii above. Raphael's oft-quoted doctrine of accommodation (V. 564–74), which relies on the dualism of spirit and body and the ineffability of their connection, is undermined immediately by his own uncertainty (V. 574–6), and contradicted by the monism of his explanations of digestion (V. 404–500) and wounding (VI. 330–53). Several critics recognize that the archangel may not be a simple mouthpiece when the conversation turns to sexuality, e.g. Lindenbaum, pp. 294–5 (a perceptive discussion), David Aers and Bob Hodge, " 'Rational Burning': Milton on Sex and Marriage," *MS*, XIII (1979), pp. 144–8 (God deliberately gives Raphael an inadequate ideology in order to test Adam once again), and J. B. Broadbent (Raphael and Adam are both infuriatingly limited, but this only proves the fundamental seriousness of M's treatment of sexuality; *Some Graver Subject* [1960], pp. 244–6).

These higher physical delights, reminiscent of the climactic aerial min-
gling that Shakespeare's Cleopatra only attains at her death, do indeed
form a continuous scale with human sexuality. But it is not a simple or
homogenous scale: each level of being has its own specific experiences,
not necessarily less or worse than those above. Angels enjoy a distillate
of human eroticism, but without its density and rootedness; their texture
is 'liquid' rather than palpable and mulifarious (VI. 348–52). They can
'limb themselves', but in love-making they evidently choose not to ex-
perience the constraint of limbs, which means they also forego the touch
of breasts meeting through a veil of hair. They do not suffer 'exclusive
barrs', but neither do they enjoy the exclusivity or 'sole propriety' that
enriches the private love-making of Adam and Eve. They have Eros,
but they do not have marriage. Angels—and earnest young men trying
to gain a place at the Wedding-feast of the Lamb by keeping their virginity
until their mid-thirties—are as it were Platonists by nature, but mature
humans need a more complicated model. Unlike Raphael and Satan,
Adam can be 'enamoured' and 'unlibidinous' at the same time; he
glimpses the possibility that in a 'right temper' passion and love might
be interfused rather than kept rigidly apart.

Adam is therefore not 'cleared' after this discussion of sexuality, as he
was 'cleared' after his questions about astronomy, and as 'all was cleared'
after Eve's dream. He is left suspended between two paradigms of the
loving relationship, an embattled hierarchy of Reason and Passion, man
and woman, and a vision of equality-in-difference. Raphael of course
castigates Adam for yielding his very identity to a creature of less value:

> weigh with her thy self;
> Then value: Oft times nothing profits more
> Than self-esteem, grounded on just and right
> Well manag'd; of that skill the more thou know'st
> The more she will acknowledge thee her Head,
> And to realities yield all her shows.   (VIII. 570–5)

Raphael's cynical condemnation is particularly appalling because, in
equating Eve with 'shows', he declares her intrinsically fallen: when we
first encountered her nakedness and sexual purity, Milton had explicitly
contrasted it with 'sin-bred' hypocrisy—'shows instead, mere shows of
seeming pure'; now he seems to agree with the archangel. But the poem
itself allows us to challenge this authority. In the same narration, just
before the nuptial dithyramb that leads to Raphael's interruption, we
learn that Adam's most fervent desire is for an equal—a desire so deeply
rooted in his being that it gives him the astonishing ability to argue
down the Almighty within minutes of his creation; and his most rap-
turous eloquence is reserved for those moments (truly Paradisal to a non-
hierarchic mind) where feeling and thought are harmonized and fused

in sexual fulfilment with an 'absolute' human counterpart. Adam is divided between shame and pride at these feelings. A strict Augustinian would probably call Adam's hierarchic determination *caritas* or 'good love', and dismiss the ecstatic and egalitarian passion as evil *libido*; but it is difficult to dismiss an experience conveyed with such transfiguring poetic power. Adam is only 'half abasht' by Raphael's rebuke because Raphael's model of Love is only half true.

The choice between ecstatic-egalitarian and patriarchal relationships is not simply a choice between good and evil, or between reason and passion; whatever Milton the ideologue would say, the poem itself presents both as moral systems based on self-knowledge and responsibility, and both appear to have been sanctioned by higher beings. Up to this point in the poem, in fact, Adam's experience has mostly encouraged him to think that God intends a fundamental equality and reciprocity between the sexes. At their first appearance, of course, the author's voice tells us that they 'seemed' to Satan 'not equal', because of their 'sex'. In its immediate context the phrase relates, rather loosely, to the image of God or 'true authority' that Satan senses in both man and woman, and in the larger context of the idyllic books, transformed by the semantics of Paradise, it comes to mean 'not identical' rather than essentially and ontologically different in value; as Adam observes. Eve is 'manlike but different sex'—a difference not necessarily marked by hierarchy.[6] Much of the accumulated experience of the poem supports the 'True Leveller' reading of Genesis: 'Man had Domination given him over the Beasts, Birds, and Fishes, but not one word was spoken in the beginning, that one branch of mankind should rule over other'; 'every single man, Male and Female, is a perfect Creature of himself.'[7] Milton's Eve is not 'perfect' in the sense of self-sufficient, of course, any more than Adam is; but compared with every other version she is an autonomous and well-rounded character, with specific counterparts to Adam's mental and physical skills, happily able to out-argue him in matters that concern her own sphere of expertise; even Raphael tells Adam that she 'sees when thou art seen least wise'. Nor can female inferiority be deduced from the 'beasts, birds and fishes' over whom the human couple jointly rule. The vegetable kingdom displays some conventional emblems of female weakness, like the vine and the elm, but otherwise the physical environment is remarkably free of lessons in subordination: male dominance within the animal species is mentioned neither in Adam's first survey of the beasts in Book VIII, nor in the ample descriptions of Book IV,

6. IV. 291–6, VIII. 471; the loose grammatical relationship of 'not equal' to the preceding lines can be seen by contrast with the sentence from *Tetrachordon* that M apparently echoes: woman shares the man's 'empire' over the universe, 'though not equally, yet largely', *Prose*, II, 589.

7. *The True Levellers Standard Advanced* in Gerrard Winstanley, *Works*, ed. George H. Sabine (Ithaca, 1941), p. 251, also quot. (as a 'Leveller' belief, though it is in fact a Digger pamphlet) in McColley, p. 50.

nor in the explicitly didactic Creation-story of Book VII—virtually the only creature to be given a symbolic application is the ant, 'Pattern of just equalitie perhaps'.[8] Most importantly of all, neither Eve nor Adam says a word about subordination or inferiority when they describe the most sacred moment of their lives, when God spoke directly to them and presented them with their mate.

Eve does, of course, provide one striking exception to this relatively egalitarian conception; she begins each of her speeches to Adam with a formal statement of the narrow Pauline interpretation of woman's role. Between her introduction in Book IV when Milton announces her 'submission', and Raphael's interruption in Book VIII, she herself is the only subordinationist voice in the poem. At times she even seems to embroider on her secondary role, attributing God-like features to Adam, and thus deepening the idolatry to which her author unwittingly condemned her from the first ('Hee for God only, shee for God in him'). Though Adam is taller and better at systematic reasoning, he is not 'Praeeminent by so much odds' that he must remain lonely, and he is not the 'Author' of Eve at all, unless the paper is the author of the book. If her formula of submission ('Unargu'd I obey; so God ordains') really does express the ideal, then we must condemn her when she corrects Adam's opinions about food-storage, and we must regard her as hopelessly corrupt when she argues for separate gardening, even though Milton insists she is 'yet sinless'. If God 'ordained' her obedience and inferiority, then He did so in a scene that neither Scripture nor Milton has recorded. 'Ordain' is a solemn word, referring to an eternal law decreed explicitly by God. The 'voice' that leads Eve to her husband (sometimes assumed to be God, sometimes a 'genial angel') is significantly devoid of gender, and defines marriage in terms of partnership and motherhood; and when Adam retells this scene, borrowing from conversations with Eve, he mentions only nuptial sanctity and marriage 'rites'—though the voice combines several roles later assigned to father, priest, and mother, it does not dictate obedience.[9] When Raphael refers to the creation of 'female for race' he says nothing about subordination. And when Adam feels the 'intelligible flame' and demands a consort— the central moment from which grew Milton's entire conception of marriage both in the divorce tracts and in the epic—the relationship imagined by man and approved by God is described in egalitarian terms.

Adam's primal yearning is for an 'equal' partner. The reader may suspect either a divine trick or an authorial blunder here, remembering that Satan and Milton had conspired to pronounce Adam and Eve 'not equal'. The earlier declaration had been proved by the separation of

8. *PL* V. 321–5, VIII. 578, VII. 487. Raphael's comment on Eve may also have a less flattering meaning: 'she notices your lapses.'
9. *PL* IV. 445–8, 635–6; cf. IV. 467–76, IV. 712 and Fowler's note, VIII. 484–7.

male and female qualities, but in the intervening books this definition receded into the shadows, as contemplation and softness, valour and attractive grace, blend in what Heale had called 'a strange kind of *Metamorphosis*'. Now the concept of equality is established with greater clarity:

> Among unequals what societie
> Can sort, what harmonie or true delight?   (VIII. 383–4)

Adam imagines a relationship not of bland identity but of reciprocity, an equal degree of creative tension, 'fellowship', and 'complacence'— which means not simply an 'object or source of pleasure' but a delight in the awareness of the other's pleasure.[1] In Genesis, moreover, it is God who pronounces it 'not good for man to be alone', but in *Paradise Lost* it is Adam himself who realizes this lack and imagines an equal partner, arguing down God's attempts to talk him out of it. The craving for partnership is so 'deeply graven', and so energetically maintained throughout the long wrestling-match with God, that it seems to define his whole being; he is unfinished without Eve. In the practice of dramatization, though not in his explicit ideological statements, Milton approaches the erotic ontogeny of Karl Barth (ch. 1 n. 2 above), assuming that humanity only exists in the relation of man to woman and woman to man. The notion that Eve is 'occasional', which implies that Adam's loneliness is an inessential mood, can barely stand beside this powerfully imagined vision.

When God congratulates Adam for passing this test, He too equates the urge for equal partnership with the essential discovery of self:

> Thus farr to try thee, *Adam*, I was pleas'd,
> And find thee knowing not of Beasts alone,
> Which thou hast rightly nam'd, but of thy self,
> Expressing well the spirit within thee free.
> (VIII. 437–40)

He then promises to create precisely what Adam has imagined: 'Thy likeness, thy fit help, thy other self, / Thy wish exactly to thy hearts desire' (VIII. 450–1). Female subordination and inferiority are never mentioned in this episode, astonishingly enough. Milton here, however locally, remains true to the original text, to the Lutheran vision of primal freedom for both sexes, and to the love of equality proclaimed in his own political writings (though not in his domestic treatises) and upheld by the archangel Michael in his teaching of Adam.

1. Fowler, note on VIII. 433; Nathaniel Hardy, *Love and Fear the Inseparable Twins of a Blest Matrimony* (1653), p. 8. McColley argues that, though Adam asks for an equal, he actually gets something else (p. 87, and cf. IX. 823); if so, this would bring M's God closer to the trickster of the original fable. It may be objected that M is using the sense recorded in *OED* 'equal' A.3 (fit in quantity, degree, or quality), but this meaning is only found in the construction with *to*.

Proper self-knowledge, then, involves the discovery of the human capacity for egalitarian love, instituted in Paradise. But Raphael assumes, with fallen culture, that the principal business of married life is to obtain acknowledgements of superiority from the wife, and he in turn recommends the proper kind of self-knowledge to achieve this. And Christ, justly rebuking Adam's oily self-exoneration and transference of blame to Eve after the fall, asks

> Was shee thy God, that her thou didst obey
> Before his voice, or was shee made thy guide,
> Superior, or but equal, that to her
> Thou did'st resign thy Manhood, and the Place
> Wherein God set thee above her made of thee,
> And for thee?

'Had'st thou known thy self aright', the judgement continues, Adam would have known that Eve's gifts were those of a subordinate, meant 'to attract thy Love, not thy Subjection' (X. 145–56). Adam has now forfeited the right, and temporarily the ability, to give an honest and courageous answer; but he could have replied, not in exoneration of his sin but in simple truth, that Eve was properly his 'guide' at times, that she was not his 'superior', but that God Himself had 'ordained' her as an equal, and had praised his self-knowledge when he demanded one. The ambiguous phrase 'or but equal' could set off a similar train of thought in the reader.

I am not suggesting that Milton intended to criticize or subvert the judgement of Raphael, Christ, and the divorce tracts; he undoubtedly believed that Eve's inferiority was so self-evident that she herself could spell it out. But his poem sees when he is seen least wise. Pre-subordination is a given, an axiom, an 'ideological imperative' that exists independently of evidence; but the act of expanding Eden into an almost novelistic universe brings it into the empirical sphere, and generates contrary evidence. Milton has succeeded in bringing to life, in the *praxis* of his art, two quite different models of the politics of love: one is drawn from the experience of being in love with an equal, and the mutual surrender of 'due benevolence', the other from the hierarchical arrangement of the universe, and the craving for male supremacy. His treatment of Genesis stands out from all others because his imagination responds generously to both of these, to the ecstatic egalitarian love of 'one flesh' as well as to the patriarchal love of superior and inferior; he has hatched the contradictions in the text and the tradition that elsewhere lie dormant. As Christ later points out, this brings 'Love' and 'Subjection' into potential conflict.

Adam's reply to Raphael attempts to solve the dichotomy his 'confession' has brought to light, by concentrating on the point where Love and Subjection touch. The 'words and actions' that make him enamoured of Eve are not just mixed with love, but 'mixt with Love / And sweet compliance'. Adam thus underlines those over-excited moments in the poem when desire is kindled by the acknowledgement of dominance, and encourages a distorting simplification of his marriage. As far as we can tell, the first couple lie 'side by side' when they make love, and in the morning Adam 'hangs over' his sleeping beloved more like Venus than Mars. But at other times he does assume a more dominant posture, sitting at the door of his bower while the 'mounted Sun' shoots his rays into the womb of the earth and Eve prepares lunch, or talking with his guest while Eve hangs back like a servant. (Milton cannot make up his mind whether Eve could hear Raphael's narrative at all.)[2] These patriarchal attitudes do not sum up the range of amorous emotion in the poem, however, and Adam's reply does not resolve the contradictions between the different modes of love it bodies forth. Indeed, his own impulse to 'say all', in this conversation with Raphael, has forced us to be aware of these discrepancies: we recall, for example, that at one of the most intense moments in Book IV, when Satan boils over with jealousy and desire, Milton has Adam 'Smile with superior Love' at Eve's 'meek surrender'; but we also remember Adam's confession to Raphael, that in the surges of love—precisely at moments like these— he has no feeling of superiority.

This irresolvable doubleness at the heart of Milton's apprehension of wedded love—a contradiction that lies dormant in Genesis and the Pauline tradition—may be traced even in the lines that first introduce the ideal couple. Let us recall again that Genesis gives the 'male and female' joint dominion over all the lower species (in chapter 1), but says nothing about masculine rule until it is imposed as a punishment after the fall. Milton deliberately evokes the former text where he introduces Adam and Eve as 'lords of all'—indeed, the whole account of sexual difference is offered as an explanation of their joint worthiness to rule over Paradise. Syntactically, Eve's 'softness' is as much a form of 'true authority', a manifestation of the image of God, as is Adam's 'valour'. His features and hair-arrangement 'declared / Absolute rule' and hers 'impli'd / Subjection, but requir'd with gentle sway' (IV. 300–8): the parallelism of syntax and allusion tells us that man and woman exercise their dominion in different ways, that Eve rules gently over her animals and Adam sternly—though we may also hear a courtly compliment in her sway over Adam here. Milton's actual meaning is then achieved by

<hr>

2. *PL* VIII. 602–3; IV. 741; V. 13 (cf. Lucretius, *De Rerum Natura*, I. 31–40). 299–302 (cf. Gen. 18:1). Eve sat 'retired in sight' during the conversation (in which Raphael addresses Adam alone, referring to Eve as an absent third person, 'thy consort'), and leaves when she *sees* an abtruse look on Adam's face; later she claims that her entire knowledge of the Satanic threat comes from what Adam has retold her and from what she overheard, hiding behind a bush on her way back from gardening, of the closing stages of the talk on sexuality (VII. 529, VIII. 41, IX. 275–8). But at VII. 50–4 M says that Adam 'with his consorted Eve / The story heard attentive', and refers to the astonishment the war in Heaven provoked in '*their* thought' (my emphasis).

a violent swivelling. The subject of 'requir'd' turns out to be Adam, in defiance of all grammar, and 'Subjection' suddenly becomes the sexual and domestic surrender of Eve to him—'Yeilded' of course, 'with coy submission, modest pride, / And sweet reluctant amorous delay' (IV. 309–11). Rhetorical slipperiness is not confined to Satan; despite Milton's praise of Paradisal 'simplicity' (IV. 318), his version of innocence has its sleights and contortions too. The exultant repetition, swelling epithets and langorous rhythm of these disturbingly beautiful lines may be interpreted, not just as an expression of Milton's ideal of pre-lapsarian love (intensified by his own slightly perverse sensibility), but as an attempt to cloud and soften the divergence between the text of Genesis and the tradition of exegesis—to solve high dispute with conjugal caresses.

JANET E. HALLEY

Female Autonomy in Milton's Sexual Poetics†

The early feminist critics of *Paradise Lost* read Eve as a product of Miltonic misogyny: she is a purely derivative being, a "defect / of Nature,"[1] the rebellious ally of Satan.[2] Their essays initiated a vigorous controversy, in which women critics have rebutted the early feminist analysis. Barbara K. Lewalski wrote a sharp retort to Marcia Landy; Joan Malory Webber rebutted Sandra Gilbert in a posthumously published article; and Diane Kelsey McColley countered the feminist critique of Milton in a book-length defense of his Eve.[3] In the process of this debate, the term "feminist" as a descriptor of Milton criticism has become multivalent, referring both to critics who see Eve as the object of Milton's patriarchal imagination and to others to whom she is the image of a genuine female subjectivity not created but recognized by a progressive, liberal Milton. At least one of the things at stake in this controversy is

† From *Milton and the Idea of Woman*, ed. Julia M. Walker (Champaign: University of Illinois Press, 1988) 230–53. Reprinted with the permission of the University of Illinois Press. At the request of the editor of this Norton Critical Edition, the author kindly abridged the original essay and provided three additional footnotes.
1. *Paradise Lost*, in *John Milton: Complete Poems and Major Prose*, ed. Merritt Y. Hughes (Indianapolis: Odyssey Press, 1957), II. 891–92, p. 427. All subsequent quotations of Milton's poems, and all translations of them, will be from this edition, and will be noted by book and line number as necessary in the text.
2. See, for example, Marcia Landy, "Kinship and the Role of Women in *Paradise Lost*," *Milton Studies*, 4, ed. James D. Simmonds (Pittsburgh: University of Pittsburgh Press, 1972), pp. 3–18, and " 'A Free and Open Encounter': Milton and the Modern Reader," *Milton Studies*, 9 (1976), 3–36; Sandra K. Gilbert, "Patriarchal Poetry and Women Readers: Reflections on Milton's Bogey," *PMLA*, 93 (1978), 368–82. A useful bibliography is provided by Marilyn R. Farwell, "Eve, the Separation Scene, and the Renaissance Idea of Androgyny," *Milton Studies*, 16 (1982), 17, n. 1.
3. Barbara K. Lewalski, "Milton on Women—Yet Once More," *Milton Studies*, 6 (1974), 3–20; Joan Malory Webber, "The Politics of Poetry: Feminism and *Paradise Lost*," *Milton Studies*, 14 (1980), 3–24; Diane Kelsey McColley, *Milton's Eve* (Urbana: University of Illinois Press, 1983).

the involvement of the critics themselves in a history of subjectivity[4] in which, most participants can agree, Milton played an important role. Lewalski, Webber, and McColley alike charge that the application of contemporary feminist thinking to Milton is ahistorical. And they propose, as a historically more accurate strategy, that we link the poem with the development of what Lawrence Stone has called the "companionate marriage.[5] In Eve, they argue, Milton gives poetic expression to the new and improved position of woman in Puritan marriage: as the companion and helpmeet ordained for man by God, she may still be her husband's civil inferior, but she has become his spiritual equal. Milton's epic represents Adam and Eve as free, they argue, both in electing marriage and in continuing to love one another. It thus reflects the historical innovation of the progressive bourgeois marriage, in which even brides were freed from the economic constraints of parental prearrangement, and instead voluntarily entered into marriage as autonomous individuals.[6]

These critics of early feminist essays on Milton argue convincingly that his Eve, far from being a mere image of deficiency and perversion, is endowed with a subjectivity as genuine as Adam's. But paradoxically, in proposing this reading as more truly historical than the feminist ones they oppose, they offer it as a means of transcending history altogether: as Lewalski writes in her conclusion, "great poets have a way of rising like phoenixes from whatever ashes are left in the wake of social and intellectual revolutions, so no doubt it will not be long before we can all again read Milton for what is of enduring importance rather than

4. "Subjectivity" refers to a problem about the self in postmodern critical thinking. On the one hand "subjectivity" is an assumed human potential to perceive one's own situation in the world and one's own desires autonomously, and to exercise one's will on the basis of that autonomy. On the other hand, postmodern theory has concerned itself with the possibility that such a subject is always *subject* to the perceptions and desires of others, or the constraints of historical experience, in the sense that she has no alternative but to mirror those perceptions, reciprocate those desires, or conform to those constraints.

5. Lawrence Stone, *The Family, Sex and Marriage in England*, 1500–1800 (New York: Harper & Row, 1977).

6. In addition to Stone's study, works on the development of Puritan or bourgeois marriage include: Roland Frye, "The Teachings of Classical Puritanism on Conjugal Love," *Studies in the Renaissance*, 2 (1955), 148–59; William Haller and Malleville Haller, "The Puritan Art of Love," *Huntington Library Quarterly*, 5 (1942), 235–72; William Haller, "Hail Wedded Love," *ELH*, 13 (1946), 79–97; James Johnson, *A Society Ordained by God: English Puritan Marriage Doctrine in the First Half of the Seventeenth Century* (Nashville: Abingdon Press, 1970); Joan Larsen Klein, "Women and Marriage in Renaissance England: Male Perspectives," in *Topic 36: The Elizabethan Woman*, intro. Anne Paston (Washington, Pa.: Washington and Jefferson College, 1982), pp. 20–37; Levin L. Schucking, *The Puritan Family* (New York: Schocken, 1970); and Eli Zaretsky, *Capitalism, the Family, and Personal Life* (New York: Harper-Colophon, 1976). Studies specifically focusing on Milton's position in this development include Jackie DiSalvo, "Blake Encountering Milton: Politics and the Family in *Paradise Lost* and *The Four Zoas*," in *Milton and the Line of Vision*, ed. Joseph Anthony Wittreich, Jr. (Madison: University of Wisconsin Press, 1975), pp. 143–84; Cheryl H. Fresch, " 'And brought her unto the man': The Wedding in *Paradise Lost*," *Milton Studies*, 16 (1982), 21–33; Allan H. Gilbert, "Milton on the Position of Women," *MLR*, 15 (1920), 240–64; John Haklett, *Miilton and the Idea of Matrimony: A Study of the Divorce Tracts and Paradise Lost*, Yale Studies in English, 173 (New Haven: Yale University Press, 1970); and Edward Le Comte, *Milton and Sex* (New York: Columbia University Press, 1978).

what is historically conditioned in his conception of man and woman."[7] This double attitude to history—it is both the ground of all valid critical argument and the clog that great art and good readings must shed—is part of an effort to make the female subjectivity historically created by bourgeois marriage as transcendent[8] and enduring as the poem that represents them purportedly is.

The prominent academic women who have taken on this liberal effort in Milton studies attribute to themselves, then, the same autonomy they read in Milton's Eve. Their work is part of a widespread effort, in which antifeminist and liberal feminist work by women has been important, to construct an ideology of professional women's "academic freedom" appropriate to a "postfeminist" era.[9] But feminists cannot merely dismiss their challenge—for it raises a question that has become urgent throughout the feminist community in vitally important debates over the place of heterosexuality and marriage in the feminist movement, over dominance and submission in sexual relations, over pornography and censorship. At its most general, that question might be phrased, "Is autonomous female subjectivity possible?"[1] If the first wave of feminist criticism of Milton, regarding Eve as an object of male imagination and desire, neglected the problematics of her subjectivity, its opponents— not only in their scholarly polemics but also in propria persona—have made that question inescapable. Their reading of Eve reminds us that real women actively participate, with widely varying degrees of consciousness and irony, in forms of subjectivity and desire prepared for us by a history dominated by patriarchal power. Their challenge calls for a reformulation of the feminist project in Milton studies.

History and Heterosexual Reading

The arguments offered by Lewalski (1975), Webber (1980), and McColley (1983) range from the conservative to the liberal, from hu-

7. Lewalski, p. 19.
8. The wish for "transcendence" is the wish to resolve tensions and contradictions, in particular those attending the problem of subjectivity. Such a resolution is usually represented as *rising above* or as *harmonizing* conflicting pressures. Eve's transcendence would be achieved if she could autonomously desire exactly what others desire her to desire. To the extent that apprehending Eve's transcendence is an effect of the poet's or the reader's creative investment in the meaning structures of the poem, this essay analyzes it as a "poetics of transcendence."
9. For an analysis of "postfeminist criticism," see Elaine Tuttle Hansen, "Saving Chaucer's Good Name," in *Feminist Criticism of Chaucer*, ed. S. Tomasch (forthcoming).
1. The radical feminist critique of female consent within political systems that make sex an arena for male power is best represented, perhaps, by Adrienne Rich, "Compulsory Heterosexuality and Lesbian Existence," *Signs*, 5, no. 4 (1980), 631–60, and by Catherine A. MacKinnon, "Feminism, Marxism, Method, and the State: Toward Feminist Jurisprudence," *Signs*, 8, no. 4 (1983), 635–58 (see esp. p. 637, n. 5 and pp. 646–55). These and other works helped to spark a debate over sexuality in which many feminists have argued that modes of female desire and consent can—or, *faut de mieux*, must—be found within the cultural forms of dominance and submission: see *Heresies #12*, 3, no. 4 (1981), the "Sex Issue"; *Powers of Desire: The Politics of Sexuality*, ed. Ann Snitow, Christine Stansell, and Sharon Thompson (New York: Monthly Review Press, 1983); and *Pleasure and Danger: Exploring Female Sexuality*, ed. Carole S. Vance (New York: Routledge & Kegan Paul, 1984).

manist to humanist-feminist—a gradient that may reflect the growing ability of mainstream academic feminism to assimilate originally conservative analyses. For they share a great deal, most notably a finding that the freedom of Eve applies to the reader of *Paradise Lost* as well. Lewalski commends *Paradise Lost* to us as a profound exploration of "a basic human predicament," the conjoining of "full individual responsibility" in each of our first parents with the experience of "the need for the other, the inescapable bonds of human interdependence."[2] In the course of the poem, Adam and Eve discover their sameness and equality as well as a structure of differences that makes each the incomplete part of a heterosexual pair that is the only whole. Lewalski provides a model for Webber and McColley not only in proposing this analysis of the relationship between Adam and Eve, but also in basing an aesthetic for the poem on it: she offers heterosexual interdependence as a strategy for reading *Paradise Lost*. While acknowledging that "our perceptions of art are necessarily affected in important ways by race, class, or sex," Lewalski nevertheless "affirm[s] the capacity of great art to transcend these lesser categories of human experience and speak to our common humanity"[3]—to speak, that is, precisely to that shared posture of individual moral responsibility and inescapable heterosexual interdependence that founds the bourgeois marriage.

Webber extends Lewalski's analysis of the social life of Adam and Eve to a description of the heterosexual constitution of Milton's universe itself. The "two great Sexes [which] animate the World" (*PL* 8.151), like all conflicts and oppositions in the created cosmos, proceed from the fundamental universal principle that opposites coincide in God but are necessarily divorced in his creation. Marriage figures forth both the harmony of differences in the created cosmos and the anticipated apocalyptic assimilation of all differences into God.[4] Webber concludes that "For [Milton] the epic goal was the wholeness that marriage offers, figured also in every part of the universe that grows through its many opposites, and figured ultimately in the visionary time when 'God shall be all in all.' The challenge that confronts us now is whether it is possible to retain that ideal, perhaps the only remaining idea that makes poetry out of life, while reaching beyond the particular poetry that seems to promote male dominance."[5]

In this difficult paragraph, Webber leaves intact the suggestion that transcendent reading may not be possible. Against the pull of actual experience ("life" itself) and of "particular poetry," though, Webber hopes that readers will aspire to an ideal: indeed, they will make *poetry* out of their lives by seeing *Paradise Lost* only in terms of the ideal that

---

2. Lewalski, p. 5.
3. Lewalski, p. 4.
4. On this point, see also Don Parry Norford, " 'My Other Half': The Coincidence of Opposites in *Paradise Lost*," *MLQ*, 36 (1975), 21–53.
5. Webber, p. 15.

it offers. The language of transcendence here masks the material conditions Webber silently posits for reading: the ideal reader of *Paradise Lost* is a married heterosexual, someone who seeks "the wholeness that marriage offers" not only in poetry but also in life. The "inescapable bonds" of heterosexual "interdependence" are applied here to the reader herself (or himself), whose married transcendence provides both a very practical and an aesthetic enactment of Milton's *coincidentia oppositorum*.

McColley's book presents a decidedly Christian version of this correspondence between transcendence in reading and in life. This study proposes that "redeeming" Eve from the reductive readings offered in "our own incoherent and friable age" will result in a "regenerative reading of her role," an understanding of Eve as "a speaking picture of the recreative power of poetry itself."[6] This power is figured, tellingly, in Eve's conscription into heterosexuality in Book 4 of *Paradise Lost*. There, Eve relates to Adam how, newly created, she was transfixed with the admiration of her own reflection in a lake. Called first by God and then by Adam, she turned from the contemplation of her own image to the husband in whose image she was created. McColley argues that Milton represents here "a pattern of response that is a mimetic model, both for the art of marriage and for the art of reading"—and, she later adds, "for a regenerate reading of the poem."[7] Free choice is at the center of that pattern: "the method of Eve's creation . . . requires for its completion the free and deliberate choice that Eve's decision, after she knows whose face is in the lake, supplies. . . . Her moment of hesitation marks her discovery that her will is free."[8] Only because Eve *wills* her acceptance of Adam, only because she freely *responds* to his call to heterosexual love, can she be a model for marriage and for reading.

This aesthetic of transcendence rests on an ideology that woman autonomously, freely elects not only heterosexuality and marriage, but even, McColley holds, the subordination these institutions have historically demanded of her. It is no accident that Lewalski, Webber, and McColley are able to build convincing arguments about Eve's subjectivity—its creation was one of the major ideological projects of the seventeenth century in England, and of Milton himself after his own disastrous first marriage. Milton's antifeminist and liberal feminist readers repeatedly charge that it is ahistorical to approach his work with reading assumptions invented after the seventeenth century—Webber even asserts that the modern reader of Milton should study his representation not of woman but of humanity, because seventeenth-century women did not see their interests as distinct from men's.[9] Against this

6. McColley, pp. 4, 16.
7. McColley, pp. 75–76.
8. McColley, pp. 81–82.
9. Webber, p. 5.

charge we may observe that a poetic ideal of transcendence, though ideologically loaded, represents itself as historically "objective" by virtue of its congruence with the codes of the poem, by virtue of its own historical continuity with seventeenth-century sexual ideology.

Feminist thought and action have broken this continuity, making visible something that Lewalski, Webber, and McColley do not see because, for all the three hundred years that separate them from Milton, they share it with him—a particular moment in the historical construction of the female subject. By opening the gap between (biological) sex and (learned) gender, and by studying the systematic ways in which a "sex/gender system" socially transforms the former into the latter,[1] feminists have shown that female heterosexuality is not natural but socially constructed. Indeed, Adrienne Rich, asking "why such violent strictures should be found necessary to enforce women's total emotional, erotic loyalty and subservience to men," has argued that female heterosexuality is not a "sexual preference" but compulsory.[2]

In a powerfully revisionist essay, Gayle Rubin has argued that human females are "engendered" as women in a system of exchange that requires their heterosexuality not because it is natural to them but because it articulates relations among men. The pattern of interaction she describes was first outlined by Claude Lévi-Straus in *The Elementary Structures of Kinship*. There Lévi-Strauss argues that the exchange of women between men is a basic form of gift-giving, orchestrating relations of trust and rivalry between men and so articulating the social relationships that constitute culture. As Rubin points out, "if it is women who are being transacted, then it is the men who give and take them who are linked, the women being a conduit of a relationship rather than a partner to it. . . . [I]t is men who are the beneficiaries of the product of such exchanges—social organization."[3] The paradigm offered here has profound resonance for the study of male interrelationship, as Eve Kosofsky Sedgwick has demonstrated in her powerful book, *Between Men: English Literature and Male Homosocial Desire*. Sedgwick defines her term "male homosocial desire" very carefully.

> "Homosocial" is a word occasionally used in history and the social sciences, where it describes social bonds between persons of the same sex; it is a neologism, obviously formed by analogy with "homosexual," and just as obviously meant to be distinguished from "homosexual." In fact, it is applied to such activities as "male bonding," which may, as in our society, be

---

1. The quoted term is Gayle Rubin's; see "The Traffic in Women: Notes on the 'Political Economy' of Sex," in *Toward an Anthropology of Women*, ed. Rayna R. Reiter (New York: Monthly Review Press, 1975), p. 159.
2. Rich, pp. 637–48.
3. Claude Lévi-Strauss, *The Elementary Structures of Kinship*, rev. ed., trans. James Harle Bell, John Richard von Sturmer, and Rodney Needham (Boston: Beacon Press, 1969); Rubin, p. 174.

characterized by intense homophobia, fear and hatred of homosexuality. To draw the "homosocial" back into the orbit of "desire," of the potentially erotic, then, is to hypothesize the potential unbrokenness of a continuum between homosocial and homosexual—a continuum whose visibility, for men, in our society, is radically disrupted.[4]

Along the continuum of male homosociality, then, active heterosexuality is only one of the forms in which the partnership and rivalries of men can take shape. In such a dynamic, the hetersexuality enjoined upon women is a mechanism of male identity and interrelationship, not a vehicle of female will.

This context makes it clear that the voluntary participation of seventeenth-century bourgeois women in marriage is ideological in the sense suggested by Louis Althusser: it "represents the imaginary relationship of individuals to their real conditions of existence."[5] For women, those real conditions required marriage—in this they do not differ from earlier forms of arranged marriage—but they required it with the superaddition of desire. The bourgeois form of compulsory heterosexuality "interpellates" woman, as Althusser would say, calls upon her to assume the subjectivity of a *fully assenting* heterosexual, a free agent in the sexual marketplace. We do not know—and *Paradise Lost* cannot tell us—how fully real women of the seventeenth century entered into this subjectivity. Even for ourselves we may not be able to answer this question, so problematic is the issue of consent that it raises. But we can examine Milton's own relationship to the ideological formation of the female subject, and trace in his writing the contradictions that invest the apparently simple notion of heterosexual reading.

Milton's Homosocial Poetics

Milton's great narrative poems—*Comus, Paradise Lost, Paradise Regained, Samson Agonistes*—present us with single women enmeshed in male worlds. They establish sex "triangles" composed of two men and a woman in which the isolated woman is the pivot between two male powers, social groups, or ethical value which can be understood to participate in a homosocial relation through her. In *Comus*, the Lady becomes lost as she travels with her brothers to their father's house: the plot traces her capture by Comus and her restoration to her (motherless and sisterless) family. In *Paradise Lost*, Sin links Satan and Death— one her father and mate, the other her son, brother, and mate—in an incestuous triangle; and Eve articulates the relationship of God and

---

4. Eve Kosofsky Sedgwick, *Between Men: English Literature and Male Homosocial Desire* (New York: Columbia University Press, 1985), pp. 1–2.
5. Louis Althusser, "Ideology and Ideological State Apparatuses (Notes toward an Investigation)," in *Lenin and Philosophy and Other Essays* (London: New Left Books, 1971), pp. 121–73, esp. p. 153.

Adam by being the offspring of them both (in another motherless family), while her subservience to Adam and God is intended to model Adam's filial obedience to his father.[6] Further, she links these two triangles— the depraved and the righteous family—when she allows Satan to tempt Adam through her. In *Paradise Regained*, Mary is the medium through which a divine father begets a human son. And in *Samson Agonistes*, Dalila is an object of exchange through whom Samson and the Philistines conduct their national conflict.

Women bear relation to *other women* in only one kind of Miltonic scenario: the poet's own invocations to sister Muses. In *Paradise Lost*, Milton invokes the obscure figure Urania:

> . . . for thou
> Nor of the Muses nine, nor on the top
> Of old *Olympus* dwell'st, but Heav'nly born,
> Before the Hills appear'd, or Fountain flow'd,
> Thou with Eternal Wisdom didst converse,
> Wisdom thy Sister . . .
>
> (7.5–10)

In *Lycidas*, he invokes the "Sisters of the sacred well, / That from beneath the seat of *Jove* doth spring," to "Begin, and somewhat loudly sweep the string" (ll. 15–17). And *At a Solemn Music* begins:

> Blest pair of *Sirens*, pledges of Heav'n's joy,
> Sphere-born harmoniuos Sisters, Voice and Verse,
> Wed your divine sounds . . .
>
> (ll. 1–3)

By inviting these sisters to "wed" their divine sounds, Milton apparently counters the entire strategy of the traffic in women, by acknowledging a primary and sufficient relationship between two female figures. Whereas the more typical male-female-male triangle establishes the relatedness of its male members, these passages situate the isolated male poet before two women, making him a petitioner who asks that his poetic identity be established on *their* using *him* as a conduit for *their* voice. The traffic relationship has been inverted.

Oddly, it is inverted only when Milton petitions for a perfect langugage, for "lucky words" (*Lycidas*, l. 20), an "answerable style" (*PL* 9.20). In a single anxious figure, Milton associates a challenge to male primacy and autonomy with a recognition that his poem's language will not necessarily be perfectly referential. His poetic construction of the traffic relationship gives special resonance to Lévi-Strauss's evaluation of woman's problematic situation in culture: "For a woman could never

6. On Eve's mediation of Adam's relation with God, see Kathleen M. Swaim, " 'Hee for God only, shee for God in him': Structural Parallelism in *Paradise Lost*," *Milton Studies*, 9 (1976), 121–49.

become just a sign and nothing more, since even in a man's world she is still a person, and since insofar as she is defined as a sign she must be recognized as a generator of signs."[7] As a genuinely autonomous generator of signs, the Muse threatens to disrupt the very fullness of meaning that her exchange makes possible.

* * *

In several early poems, Milton deflects the dangers of the powerful female voice by excluding the Muse from the dynamics of perfect expression. These poems represent a transcendent poetics that is entirely male or even genderless.[8] The Milton who wrote those poems might well have cried out with his Adam, "O why did God, / Creator wise, that peopl'd highest Heav'n / With Spirits Masculine . . . / . . . not fill the World at once / With Men as Angels without Feminine?" (*PL* 10.889–93). But *Paradise Lost* as a whole rebukes this form of misogyny, insisting instead on the incorporation of woman into its picture of social and poetic harmony. It constructs a sexual poetics that can accommodate rather than eliminate the female subject.

If the problem posed by the Siren/Muse is the ability of woman to produce her own signification and so to disrupt the traffic in which she is the sign of male interrelationship, Milton's strategy in *Paradise Lost* is to incorporate into the traffic relationship woman *as a generator of signs*, a "genuine subject." As Sedgwick's analysis of male homosocial desire makes clear, however, the heterosexual bonds that result from such a move do not eliminate but rather reformulate male homosocial relations: thus, the heterosexual transcendence offered in *Paradise Lost*, even though it includes woman as a desiring and speaking subject, repeats the homosocial forms of transcendence found in the early poems.

* * *

Milton's Heterosexual Poetics: Paradise Lost

As the work of Lewalski, Webber, and McColley would suggest, *Paradise Lost* incorporates female subjectivity into its most gorgeous descriptions of harmony, both in the relationship of Adam and Eve and in the poet's intimacy with his Muse. But the result is a newly heterosexual form of transcendence that incorporates the female voice and the female will only by subsuming them in male intention. Far from abandoning history, then, the epic's formulation of sexual poetics belongs to the history of the liberal self. Modeling his relation to the Muse on the husband's proper relation to his wife—for Adam and Eve represent the perfect marriage which Milton envisioned in his political tract entitled the *Doctrine and Discipline of Divorce*—Milton creates an intersubjective

7. Lévi-Strauss, p. 406.
8. For the author's argument that, in *Elegy* V, *Epitaphium Damonis*, and *Lycidas*, Milton figured transcendence as the exclusion of the female figure of the Muse, see the original version of this essay, at pp. 235–242 [*Editor*].

heterosexual encounter that is, nevertheless, the product of his own autonomous mind. Ultimately, however, the homosociality of this transcendence is disguised by the privacy of the nuclear family and of the solitary poet.

The epic repeatedly figures married love as a harmony. Adam adds to Scripture when he rejoices that he and his wife are "one Flesh, one Heart, *one Soul*" (8.499; emphasis mine): they spontaneously sing a prayer in perfect unison, "unanimous" in the root sense of the term (4.736). Commenting on their harmony, Adam praises

> . . . all [Eve's] words and actions, mixt with Love
> And sweet compliance, which declare unfeign'd
> Union of Mind, or in us both one Soul;
> Harmony to behold in wedded pair
> More grateful than harmonious sound to the ear.
> (8.602–6)

Though Adam had originally asked God for an "equal," he realizes by the time he says these lines that the living harmony of married action depends on Eve's "sweet compliance," on her derivation of her will from his.

This asymmetry of male and female will in heterosexual harmony has been the subject of grateful rumination on the part of some male critics,[9] and the target of stern critique by feminist readers like Landy and Gilbert. To Lewalski, Webber, and McColley it is an historical accident which the harmony itself, and the heterosexual reading it invokes, transcend. But the poetics of transcendence in *Paradise Lost* places female participation in a far more complex dynamic than any of these analyses would suggest. Perhaps the poem's most concise rendering of that dynamic occurs when Eve herself defines the terms on which she participates in heterosexual harmony.

The poem allows Eve to voice the story of her conversion to heterosexual love. She relates how, in her first moments of consciousness, she bent down to see and interact with "A Shape within the wat'ry gleam," the image of her own face:

> . . . there I had fixt
> Mine eyes till now, and pin'd with vain desire,
> Had not a voice thus warn'd me, What thou seest,
> What there thou seest fair Creature is thyself,
> With thee it came and goes: but follow me,
> And I will bring thee where no shadow stays
> Thy coming, and thy soft imbraces, hee
> Whose image thou art, him thou shalt enjoy

9. See Northrop Frye, "The Revelation to Eve," in *Paradise Lost: A Trecentenary Tribute*, ed. Balachandra Rajan (Toronto: Toronto University Press, 1969), pp. 18–47; and Norford, " 'My Other Half.' "

Inseparably thine, to him shalt bear
Multitudes like thyself, and thence be call'd
Mother of the human Race: what could I do,
But follow straight, invisibly thus led?

(4.466–76)

Does Eve's question about her induction into heterosexuality—"what could I do, / But follow straight"—reflect her sense that she has been compelled to turn to Adam or that she has engaged in a reasoning interaction with a persuading voice? And when she goes on to relate how she then spurned the sight of Adam, fleeing to "that smooth wat'ry image" (4.480) until she was called back by him, does her narration of the crisis—"with that thy gentle hand / Seiz'd mine, I yielded" (4.488–89; emphasis mine)—emphasize his violent appropriation of her or her willing compliance? The ostensible function of her speech is to confirm to Adam her voluntary participation in heterosexual love, but what meaning can be given to her repeated references to male compulsion in this crucial scene? Or conversely, the clear subtext here is Eve's resentment of the force under which she has acted: what meaning can we give, then, to her repeated affirmations of her active, reasoning assent to it? Adam's interpellation of Eve as his "individual solace dear" (I. 486) suggests that female autonomy is given a contradictory structure here, making any simple answer to these questions untenable. For Adam's term creates Eve both as an autonomous individual in the liberal tradition, and as a being in-dividual, indivisible from the husband whose speech provides her with her true identity.

A failure to recognize the irresolution of this dilemma characterizes two of the strongest feminist analyses of this scene—one offered by Christine Froula, working with great theoretical sophistication in the feminist tradition exemplified by Landy and Gilbert, and the other proposed by McColley in her liberal-feminist defense of Eve and her creator(s).

Froula focuses on God's words, "What there thou seest fair Creature is thyself," concluding: "The reflection is not of Eve: according to the voice, it is Eve." God defines her as a "substanceless image" and invites her to mirror not her own face but that of Adam, that of the man "Whose image thou art." In response, Eve internalizes the utterance of the "voice" and of Adam: her "indoctrination into her own 'identity' is complete at the point at which her imagination is so successfully colonized by patriarchal authority that she literally becomes its voice."[1] The sequence Froula sees here is almost exactly what we would expect from the Doctrine and Discipline of Divorce, in which Milton insisted that marriage was defined by the fully voluntary consent of husband and

---

1. Christine Froula, "When Eve Reads Milton: Undoing the Canonical Economy." Critical Inquiry 10 (December 1983): 328–29.

wife to the conversation of their minds and bodies. As a result, Milton argued, "contrareity of mind" should justify divorce. Though Milton made "mutuall consent" a prerequisite for divorce, he concluded that the wife must be understood to consent when and because her husband does.[2] Froula detects in *Paradise Lost* precisely this subsumption of the woman's will in her husband's—but when Froula concludes that "Eve does not speak patriarchal discourse; it speaks her,"[3] she obscures Milton's historically innovative insistence on female conversation. At least part of the importance of Eve's speech is that she *does* speak patriarchal discourse, *as* an autonomous subject.

McColley, on the other hand, studies this autonomy without acknowledging its embeddedness in a social relation structured by male power. Observing that the scene as Eve relates it follows an educational sequence which activates her free will, McColley provides a needed corrective to Froula's analysis by emphasizing the salience of Eve's autonomy. But her argument ignores not only Eve's references to the constraints she encountered, but also its own language of compulsion: "Eve's narrow escape from narcissism . . . *requir[es]* her to lose herself in order to find herself while leaving her full freedom to fail. . . . [T]he method of Eve's creation is part of what Milton believes to be God's way in creating all things, and *requires* for its completion the free and deliberate choice that Eve's decision, after she knows whose face is in the lake, supplies. . . . It is *important to Milton's concept of domestic liberty* that Eve should respond spontaneously yet preparedly to Adam, . . . in full knowledge of who she is."[4]

McColley's language quite properly points to the backstage presence of a mastermind whose intentions require Eve's autonomy. *Pace* Lewalski, it is this figure who enjoys the only transcendence actually represented in *Paradise Lost*. The poet's invocations of the Muse repeat the sexual harmonics of Adam and Eve: just as Eve's creation remedied Adam's "single imperfection" (8.423), the Muse rescues the poet from "solitude": he is "not alone," he says in the invocation to Book 7, "while thou / Visit'st my slumbers Nightly" (7.28–29). And by incorporating that harmonic's adaptation of the politics of consent expounded in the *Doctrine and Discipline of Divorce*, these invocations reformulate the terms of transcendence. Milton's strategy is no longer to transcend female textuality[5] by driving the Muse from the poem. In the four invocations of *Paradise Lost*, he never abandons his appeal to a female Muse. Instead,

---

2. *The Doctrine and Discipline of Divorce*, in *Complete Prose Works of John Milton*, vol. 2 (New Haven: Yale University Press, 1959), pp. 242, 349. [The author provides a more detailed discussion of female consent in *The Doctrine and Discipline of Divorce* in the original version of this essay, at pp. 242–46—*Editor*.]

3. Froula, p. 329.

4. McColley, pp. 75, 81–82.

5. "Textuality" here indicates the multivocality and autonomy of language, its potential to divert its user's meaning and ultimately to defeat the poet's project.

a prior masculine understanding or meaning both incorporates and tran-
scends the mere imagery of the female figure.

The clearest model for this transcendence appears in the invocation
to Book 1, where Milton calls on the "Heav'nly Muse" but soon revises
his appeal:

> But Chiefly Thou O Spirit, that dost prefer
> Before all Temples th' upright heart and pure,
> Instruct me, for Thou know'st; Thou from the first
> Wast present, and with mightly wings outspread
> Dove-like satst brooding on the vast Abyss
> And mad'st it pregnant. . . .
>
> (1.17–22)

Exactly when maternal brooding becomes paternal impregnation, the
female figure of the "heav'nly Muse" is displaced by a male spirit.[6]
Milton has finally reached the origin—"Thou from the first / Wast
present"—that he has sought throughout the invocation. But the female
is not utterly transcended in the invocations of *Paradise Lost*: the shift
in address—"But chiefly Thou"—rather than abandon the female
Muse, incorporates her into the prior, higher, and more inclusive person
of the male spirit.

The invocation of Urania in Book 7 suggests how this new form of
transcendence resolves the problems that *At a Solemn Music* concen-
trates in the sister-Muse figure. For here Milton invokes Urania as one
of a pair of sisters whose identity is clearly subsumed in that of their
father:

> Thou with Eternal Wisdom didst converse,
> Wisdom thy Sister, and with her didst play
> In presence of th' Almightly Father . . .
>
> (7.9–11)

It is no accident that, in juxtaposition with this super-real "Father," the
sister Muses assume the texture of fable. For Milton has already carefully
delimited Urania to the status of a sign profoundly remote from its divine
signification:

> Descend from Heav'n *Urania*, by that name
> If rightly thou art call'd. . . .
> The meaning, not the Name I call. . . .
>
> (7.1–5)

Textuality and the female are again associated here, but now they are
clearly subordinated to and controlled by a phallocentric "meaning"
whose powers resemble those of the husband envisioned in the *Doctrine*

---

6. For an argument that the Muse here is androgynous, see Virginia R. Mollenkott, "Some
Implications of Milton's Androgynous Muse," *Bucknell Review* 24 (Spring 1978): 27–38.

and Discipline of Divorce. Moreover, it is almost certain that the meaning Milton actually invokes here is the spirit he invoked in Book 1: it knows, and Milton knows it. Milton establishes here a traffic in the female "Name" that orchestrates the relationship between two male signifying powers. Its heterosexual design should not blind us to its homosocial function.

This semiotic transcendence expresses in Christian terms a union of the epic poet with a male God even as it simultaneously elides both woman and textuality. But this invocation continues to address the "Name" of Urania through its thirty-nine lines. At its close, Milton presents a key revision of *Lycidas.* He asks the Muse to drive far off not the "rout that made the hideous roar," the Thracian women who destroyed Orpheus in the earlier poem (1.61)—but their "barbarous dissonance" and "savage clamor." It is not the women but their unharmonious noise that must be driven off: Urania, Eve, the female figure must participate in this text, as a harmonic "other half" whose "meaning" originates in male intention. The truly transcendent element in this aesthetic is not the heterosexual couple that it requires, but the male mind that defines both its members.

John Milton: A Chronology

1534   Act of Supremacy, by which King Henry VIII assumes full authority over the Church of England, passed.

1558–1603   Reign of Queen Elizabeth I. Presbyterians at work to extend the Reformation in England.

1603–25   James VI King of Scotland, reared as a Presbyterian, rules England as James I.

1605   Guy Fawkes, a Roman Catholic, tries to blow up the King, Lords, and Commons.

1608   December 6, Milton born in London.

1609   The Pilgrims (left-wing Puritans) settle in Leyden.

1611   Authorized (King James) Version of the Bible published.

1616   Death of Shakespeare.

1620   Pilgrim Fathers land (Plymouth Rock). Milton enters St. Paul's School about this time.

1625   Milton enters Christ's College, Cambridge. Charles I crowned.

1628   Charles grants Petition of Right, agreeing not to tax without consent of Parliament or imprison without due process.

1629   Milton graduates B.A. in January; at Christmas writes "On the Morning of Christ's Nativity." King Charles dissolves Parliament.

1632   Milton graduates M.A.; begins six years' residence with his parents in the country, first in Hammersmith, later in Horton. William Laud, opponent of Puritanism, appointed Archbishop of Canterbury.

1632–37   Milton studies the history of western civilization: history, philosophy, literature, religion, political theory, geography, astronomy, mathematics, music, etc. Writes "L'Allegro," "Il Penseroso," *Comus*, and "Lycidas."

1637   Milton's mother dies.

1638–39   Milton travels in Italy.

1638   Charles Diodati dies.

1640   Milton settles into a house of his own in Aldersgate Street in London, a few blocks from his birthplace, and begins to teach his two nephews. Completes *Epitaphium Da-*

monis, a 219-line pastoral elegy, in Latin, in memory of his friend Diodati.

1641–42   Milton publishes five tracts urging that the Church of England reform itself by reducing its monopolistic, tyrannical power over the religious lives of the people.

1641   Archbishop Laud impeached and imprisoned.

1642   Civil War begins. Milton marries Mary Powell, whose family supports the king and the hierarchical Church of England. She leaves her husband two months later and returns to her parents, near Oxford, a stronghold of Royalists.

1643–45   Milton publishes three tracts urging that divorce on grounds of incompatibility be allowed.

1644   In response to learning of (unsuccessful) efforts to prevent publication of his *Doctrine and Discipline of Divorce*, Milton publishes *Areopagitica*, against censorship.

1645   Mary Powell Milton returns to her husband. Battle of Naseby; victory of Cromwell and his New Model Army. Milton moves to large house in Barbican; continues to teach school in it till 1647.

1646   Publication of *Poems of Mr. John Milton*. Birth of daughter Anne. The Powells flee from Oxford and take refuge with Miltons in London.

1647   John Milton, Sr. dies. Milton gives up teaching and moves to smaller house in High Holborn.

1648   Birth of daughter Mary.

1649–53   The Commonwealth.

1649   January: Charles I executed. February: Milton's *Of the Tenure of Kings and Magistrates* published. March: Milton appointed Latin Secretary to Council of State at an annual salary of £248 14s 4½d; moves to an apartment in Whitehall.

1651   Milton's *Pro Populo Anglicano Defensio* published. Son, John, born. Milton becomes totally blind; moves to a house nearby in Petty France, Westminster.

1652   May 2: Daughter Deborah born. May 5: Mary Powell Milton dies. June 16?: Son, John, dies.

1653–58   Oliver Cromwell Lord Protector.

1654   *Defensio Secundo* published.

1656   November 12: Milton and Katherine Woodcock married.

1657   October 19: Daughter Katherine born.

1658   February and March: Katherine Woodcock Milton and infant daughter die. September: Cromwell dies; Richard Cromwell Lord Protector till Restoration.

1660   February: *Ready and Easy Way to Establish a Free Com-monwealth* published. May 29: Charles II enters London as king. Milton goes into hiding in Bartholomew Close. June 16: order for Milton's arrest and for the burning of his pamphlets. Sept.–Oct.: Milton arrested, put in custody, and soon discharged; rents a house in Holborn, near Red Lion Fields.

1660–65   Milton writes *Paradise Lost.*

1661   Moves to house in Jewin Street.

1663   February 24: Milton and Elizabeth Minshull married.

1665   During the Great Plague in London, Milton lives at Chalfont St. Giles, Buckinghamshire. The house still stands.

1666   Great Fire in London.

1667   *Paradise Lost,* in ten books, published by Mrs. Mary Simmons and her nephew Samuel, next door to the Golden Lion, in Aldersgate Street, a building that had escaped the fire. Milton paid £5 upon delivery of the MS and another £5 when the first edition of thirteen hundred copies is sold.

1671   *Paradise Regained* and *Samson Agonistes* published.

1669 or

1670   Moves to Artillery Walk, Bunhill Fields.

1674   Second edition of *Paradise Lost* published, in twelve books. November 8?: Milton dies of gout; buried in St. Giles, Cripplegate.

Selected Bibliography

Key to acronyms: ELH: *A Journal of English Literary History*. ELR: *English Literary Renaissance*. MP: *Modern Philology*. MQ: *Milton Quarterly*. MS: *Milton Studies*. PMLA: *Publications of the Modern Language Association*. PQ: *Philological Quarterly*. RES: *Review of English Studies*. SEL: *Studies in English Literature*. SP: *Studies in Philology*.

I. MODERN EDITIONS

Patterson, Frank Allen, gen. ed. [The Columbia edition of] *The Works of John Milton*. 18 vols. New York, 1931–38.

Wolfe, Don M., gen. ed. [The Yale edition of] *The Complete Prose Works of John Milton*. 8 vols. New Haven, 1953–82.

Hughes, Merritt Y., ed. *John Milton. Complete Poems and Major Prose*. New York, 1957.

Bush, Douglas, ed. *The Complete Poetical Works of John Milton*. Boston, 1965.

Fowler, Alastair, ed. *Paradise Lost*. London, 1971.

Hughes, Merritt Y., and John M. Steadman, eds. *A Variorum Commentary on the Poems of John Milton*, vol. 3, *Paradise Lost* [Columbia University Press, New York, in preparation].

II. BIBLIOGRAPHIES, REFERENCE BOOKS, GUIDES

Broadbent, John. Paradise Lost. *Introduction*. Cambridge, 1972.

——, ed. *John Milton: Introductions*. Cambridge, 1973.

Danielson, Dennis. *The Cambridge Companion to Milton*. Cambridge and New York, 1989.

Gilbert, Allen H. *A Geographical Dictionary of Milton*. New Haven, 1919

Hanford, James Holly, and James G. Taaffe. *A Milton Handbook: Fifth Edition*. New York, 1970.

Huckabay, Calvin. *John Milton: A Bibliographical Supplement, 1929–1957*. Pittsburgh, 1960.

Hunter, William B., Jr., ed. *A Milton Encyclopedia*. 9 vols. Lewisburg, PA, 1979–83.

Ingram, William, and Kathleen Swaim. *A Concordance to Milton's English Poems*. Oxford, 1972.

Klemp, Paul. *The Essential Milton: An Annotated Bibliography of Modern Studies*. Boston, 1989.

LeComte, Edward S. *A Milton Dictionary*. New York, 1961.

Lockwood, Laura E. *Lexicon to the English Poetical Works of John Milton*. New York, 1907.

Milton Quarterly, annual bibliography.

MLA International Bibliography (Published annually by the Modern Language Association of America.)

Patrides, C. A. *An Annotated Critical Bibliography of John Milton*. New York, 1987.

Patterson, Frank Allen, and French R. Fogel. *An Index to the Columbia Edition of the Works of John Milton*. 2 vols. New York, 1940. (An index of words, persons, characters, subjects, events, allusions, references, sources, etc., in the works of Milton.)

Shawcross, John T. *Milton: A Bibliography for the Years 1624–1700*. Binghamton, N.Y., 1984.

Stevens, David H. *A Reference Guide to Milton from 1800 to the Present Day*. Chicago, 1930. See also Harris Francis Fletcher, *Contributions to a Milton Bibliography . . . Addenda to Stevens'* Reference Guide to Milton. Urbana, IL, 1931.

Studies in Philology, annual bibliography. "Recent Literature of the English Renaissance."

III. BIOGRAPHY

Diekhoff, John S., ed. *Milton on Himself: Milton's Utterances upon Himself and His Works*. 2nd ed. London, 1965.

Darbishire, Helen, ed. *The Early Lives of Milton.* New York, 1965.

Masson, David. *The Life of John Milton: Narrated in Connexion with the Political, Ecclesiastical, and Literary History of His Time.* 7 vols. London, 1859–94.

Bush, Douglas. *John Milton: A Sketch of His Life and Works.* New York, 1964.

Daiches, David. *Milton.* London, 1957.

Fletcher, Harris Francis. *The Intellectual Development of John Milton.* 2 vols. Urbana, IL, 1956.

French, J. Milton, ed. *The Life Records of John Milton.* 5 vols. New Brunswick, N.J., 1949–58.

Hanford, James Holly. *John Milton, Englishman.* New York, 1949.

Parker, William Riley. *Milton: A Biography.* 2 vols. Oxford, 1968.

Shawcross, John. "Milton and Diodati: An Essay in Psychodynamic Meaning." *MS* 7 (1975): 127–63.

Tillyard, E. M. W. *Milton.* London, 1930.

Wilson, A. N. *The Life of John Milton.* New York, 1983.

Wolfe, Don M. *Milton in the Puritan Revolution.* New York, 1941.

IV. BACKGROUNDS

Barker, Arthur E. *Milton and the Puritan Dilemma, 1641–1660.* Toronto, 1956.

Bush, Douglas. *Mythology and the Renaissance Tradition in English Poetry.* Rev. ed. Minneapolis, 1963.

Clark, Donald L. *John Milton at St. Paul's School, A Study of Ancient Rhetoric in English Renaissance Education.* New York, 1948.

Giamatti, A. Bartlett. *The Earthly Paradise and the Renaissance Epic.* Princeton, 1966.

Greene, Thomas M. *The Descent from Heaven: A Study in Epic Continuity.* New Haven, 1963.

Haller, William. *The Rise of Puritanism; or The Way to the New Jerusalem as Set Forth in Pulpit and Press from Thomas Cartwright to John Wilburne and John Milton, 1570–1643.* New York, 1938.

———. *Liberty and Reformation in the Puritan Revolution.* New York, 1955.

Hill, Christopher. *Puritanism and Revolution; Studies in Interpretation of the English Revolution of the 17th Century.* New York, 1958.

———. *The Century of Revolution, 1603–1714.* 2nd ed. New York, 1982.

———. *Intellectual Origins of the English Revolution.* Oxford, 1965.

———. *The World Turned Upside Down: Radical Ideas During the English Revolution.* New York, 1972.

Kirkconnell, Watson. *The Celestial Cycle: The Theme of Paradise Lost in World Literature, with Translations of the Major Analogues.* New York, 1952.

Langdon, Ida. *Milton's Theory of Poetry and Fine Art.* New Haven, 1924.

Lovejoy, Arthur O. *The Great Chain of Being. A Study of the History of an Idea.* Cambridge, MA, 1936.

Mahood, M. M. *Poetry and Humanism.* New Haven, 1950.

Nicolson, Marjorie Hope. *The Breaking of the Circle: Studies in the Effect of the "New Science" upon Seventeenth-Century Poetry.* Rev. ed. New York, 1960.

Williams, Arnold. *The Common Expositer: An Account of the Commentaries on Genesis, 1527–1633.* Chapel Hill, 1948.

Wolfe, Don M. *Milton and His England.* Princeton, 1971.

V. COLLECTIONS OF CRITICAL ESSAYS

Barker, Arthur E., ed. *Milton: Modern Essays in Criticism.* New York, 1965.

Critical Essays on Milton from ELH. Baltimore, 1968.

Emma, Ronald David, and John T. Shawcross, eds. *Language and Style in Milton.* New York, 1967.

Ferguson, Margaret, and Mary Nyquist, eds. *Re-Membering Milton: Essays on the Texts and Traditions.* New York, 1988.

Fiore, Amadeus P., ed. *Th' Upright Heart and Prose.* Pittsburgh, 1967.

Hunter, William B., Jr., et al. *Bright Essence: Studies in Milton's Theology.* Salt Lake City, 1971.

Kermode, Frank, ed. *The Living Milton: Essays by Various Hands.* London, 1960.

Kranidas, Thomas, ed. *New Essays on Paradise Lost.* Berkeley, 1969.

Loewenstein, David, and James Grantham Turner, eds. *Paradise Lost and the Politics of Rebellion.* Cambridge and New York, 1990.

Martz, Louis L., ed. *Milton: A Collection of Critical Essays.* Englewood Cliffs, N.J., 1966.

Milton Studies. Published annually since 1969, by the University of Pittsburgh Press.
Patrick, J. Max, and Roger H. Sundell, eds. *Milton and the Art of Sacred Song.* Madison, 1979.
Patrides, C. A., ed. *Milton's Epic Poetry: Essays on* Paradise Lost *and* Paradise Regained. Harmondsworth, 1967.
————, ed. *Approaches to* Paradise Lost. London and Toronto, 1968.
Rajan, Balachandra, ed. *"Paradise Lost": A Tercentenary Tribute.* Toronto, 1967.
Rudrum, Alan, ed. *Milton: Modern Judgements.* London, 1968.
Shawcross, John T., ed. *Milton: The Critical Heritage.* New York, 1970.
Thorpe, James Ernest, ed. *Milton Criticism.* New York, 1950.
Walker, Julia M., ed. *Milton and the Idea of Woman.* Champaign, IL, 1988.
Wittreich, Joseph A., Jr., ed. *Milton and the Line of Vision.* Madison, WI, 1975.

VI. STUDIES OF *PARADISE LOST*

Adams, Robert M. *Ikon: Milton and the Modern Critics.* Ithaca, 1955.
Aers, David, and Bob Hodge. " 'Rational Burning': Milton on Sex and Marriage." *MS* 13 (1979): 3–33. Rep. in Aers et al., *Literature, Language and Society in England, 1580–1680.* Dublin, 1981.
Arthos, John. *Dante, Michelangelo and Milton.* London, 1963.
Babb, Lawrence. *The Moral Cosmos of* Paradise Lost. East Lansing, MI, 1970.
Barker, Arthur E. "Structural Pattern in *Paradise Lost.*" *PQ* 23 (1949): 17–30.
Belsey, Catherine. *John Milton: Language, Gender, Power.* New York, 1988.
Bennett, Joan S. "God, Satan, and King Charles: Milton's Royal Portraits." *PMLA* 92 (1977): 441–57.
————. *Reviving Liberty: Radical Christian Humanism in Milton's Great Poems.* Cambridge, MA, and London, 1989.
Berek, Peter. " 'Plain' and 'Ornate' Styles and the Structure of *Paradise Lost.*" *PMLA* 85 (1970): 237–46.
Berry, Boyd M. *Process of Speech; Puritan Religious Writing and* Paradise Lost. Baltimore, 1976.
Blessington, Francis C. Paradise Lost *and the Classical Epic.* London, 1979.
————. Paradise Lost: *Ideal and Tragic Epic.* Boston, 1988.
Bridges, Robert. *Milton's Prosody, with a Chapter on Accentual Verse and Notes.* Oxford, 1921.
Broadbent, J. B. *Some Graver Subject: An Essay on* Paradise Lost. London, 1960.
Budick, Sanford. *The Dividing Muse: Images of Sacred Disjunction in Milton's Poetry.* New Haven, 1985.
————. "Milton and the Scene of Interpretation: From Typology Toward Midrash." *Midrash and Literature.* Eds. Geoffrey Hartman and Sanford Budick. New Haven, 1986. 195–205.
Burden, Dennis H. *The Logical Epic.* Cambridge, MA, 1967.
Christopher, Georgia. *Milton and the Science of the Saints.* Princeton, 1982.
Cohen, Kitty. *The Throne and the Chariot: Studies in Milton's Hebraism.* The Hague, 1975.
Colie, Rosalie L. "Time and Eternity: Paradox and Structure in *Paradise Lost.*" *Journal of the Warburg and Courtauld Institutes* 23 (1960): 127–38.
Cook, Albert. "Milton's Abstract Music." *PMLA* 72 (1957): 601–11. Rep. in first Norton Critical Edition of *PL.* New York, 1975, 433–41.
Cope, Jackson I. *The Metaphoric Structure of* Paradise Lost. Baltimore, 1962.
Corcoran, Mary Irma. *Milton's Paradise with Reference to the Hexameral Background.* Washington, 1945.
Crosman, Robert. *Reading* Paradise Lost. Bloomington, IN, and London, 1980.
Curry, Walter Clyde. *Milton's Ontology, Cosmology and Physics.* Lexington, KY, 1957.
Daniells, Roy. *Milton, Mannerism and Baroque.* Toronto, 1963.
Danielson, Dennis R. *Milton's Good God: A Study in Literary Theodicy.* Cambridge, 1982.
Davie, Donald. "Syntax and Music in *Paradise Lost.*" *The Living Milton.* Ed. Frank Kermode. London, 1960. 70–84.
Davies, Stevie. *The Feminine Reclaimed.* Louisville, KY, 1986.
————. *Milton.* New York, 1991.
Demaray, John G. *Milton's Theatrical Epic: The Invention and Design of* Paradise Lost. Cambridge, MA, 1980.
di Cesare, Mario. "*Paradise Lost* and Epic Tradition." *MS* 1 (1969): 31–50. Also in his *The Altar and the City: A Reading of Vergil's* Aeneid. New York, 1974.
Diekhoff, John S. *Milton's* Paradise Lost: *A Commentary on the Argument.* New York, 1946.
di Salvo, Jackie. "Blake Encountering Milton: Politics and the Family in *Paradise Lost* and *The Four Zoas.*" *Milton and the Line of Vision.* Ed. Joseph Anthony Wittreich, Jr. Madison, WI, 1975. 143–84.
Donoghue, Denis. "God with Thunder." *Thieves of Fire.* London, 1973.

Duncan, Joseph E. *Milton's Earthly Paradise*. Minneapolis, 1972.

Durocher, Richard. *Milton and Ovid*. Ithaca, 1985.

Eliot, T. S. "Milton," and "A Note on the Verse of John Milton." *On Poetry and Poets*. London, 1957.

Emma, Ronald David. *Milton's Grammar*. The Hague, 1964.

Empson, William. *Milton's God*. Rev. ed. London, 1965.

Evans, John Martin. *Paradise Lost and the Genesis Tradition*. Oxford, 1968.

Farwell, Marilyn R. "Eve, the Separation Scene, and the Renaissance Idea of Androgyny." *MS* 16 (1982): 3–20.

Ferry, Ann Davidson. *Milton's Epic Voice*. Cambridge, MA, 1963.

Fiore, Peter A. *Milton and Augustine: Patterns of Augustinian Thought in* Paradise Lost. University Park, PA, 1981.

Fish, Stanley Eugene. *Surprised by Sin: The Reader in* Paradise Lost. London, 1967.

———. "The Temptation to Action in Milton's Poetry." *ELH* 48 (1981): 516–31.

———. "Transmuting the Lump: *Paradise Lost*, 1942–82." *Literature and History: Theoretical Problems and Russian Case Studies*. Ed. Gary Saul Morson. Stanford, 1986. 33–56.

Fixler, Michael. *Milton and the Kingdoms of God*. London, 1964.

Fletcher, Harris Francis. *Milton's Rabbinical Readings*. Urbana, IL, 1930.

Fresch, Cheryl H. "Milton's Eve and the Problem of the Additions to the Command." *MQ* 12 (1978): 83ff.

———. " 'And brought her unto the man': The Wedding in *Paradise Lost*." *MS* 16 (1982): 21–33.

Friedman, Donald. "Galileo and the Art of Seeing." *Milton in Italy*. Ed. Mario di Cesare. Binghamton, N.Y., 1991.

Froula, Christine. "When Eve Reads Milton: Undoing the Canonical Economy." *Critical Inquiry* 10 (1983): 321–47.

———. "Pechter's Specter: Milton's Bogey Writ Small; Or Why is He Afraid of Virginia Woolf?" *Critical Inquiry* 11 (1984): 171–78.

Frye, Northrop. *The Return of Eden: Five Essays on Milton's Epics*. Toronto, 1965.

Frye, Roland Mushat. *God, Man, and Satan: Patterns of Christian Thought and Life in* Paradise Lost, Pilgrim's Progress, *and the Great Theologians*. Princeton, 1960.

———. *Milton's Imagery and the Visual Arts*. Princeton, 1978.

Gardner, Helen Louise. "Milton's 'Satan' and the Theme of Damnation in Elizabethan Tragedy." *Essays and Studies* by Members of the English Association, ns 1 (1948): 46–66.

———. *A Reading of* Paradise Lost. Oxford, 1965.

Gilbert, Allen H. "Milton and Galileo." *SP* 19 (1922): 152–85.

———. "Milton's Textbook of Astronomy." *PMLA* 38 (1923): 297–307

Gilbert, Sandra. "Patriarchal Poetry and Women Readers: Reflections on Milton's Bogey." *PMLA* 93 (1978): 368–92.

Grossman, Marshall. *"Authors to Themselves": Milton and the Revelation of History*. New York, 1987.

Guillory, John. *Poetic Authority: Spenser, Milton, and Literary History*. New York, 1983.

Hagstrum, Jean H. *Sex and Sensibility: Ideal and Erotic Love from Milton to Mozart*. Chicago, 1980.

Halkett, John. *Milton and the Idea of Matrimony*. New Haven, 1970.

Harding, David P. *The Club of Hercules: Studies in the Classical Background of* Paradise Lost. Urbana, IL, 1962.

Hartmann, Geoffrey. "Milton's Counterplot." *ELH* 25 (1958): 1–12.

Herz, Judith Scherer. " 'For whom this glorious sight?': Dante, Galileo and the Galileo Question." *Milton in Italy*. Ed. Mario di Cesare. Binghamton, N.Y., 1991.

Hill, Christopher. *Milton and the English Revolution*. New York, 1977.

———. *The Experience of Defeat: Milton and Some Contemporaries*, New York, 1984.

Hollander, John. *The Figure of Echo: A Mode of Allusion in Milton and After*. Berkeley, 1981.

Hunter, G. K. *Paradise Lost*. London, 1980.

Jacobus, Lee. *Sudden Apprehension: Aspects of Knowledge in* Paradise Lost. The Hague, 1976.

Jameson, Fredric. "Religion and Ideology: A Political Reading of *Paradise Lost*." *Literature, Politics and Theory: Papers from the Essex Conference, 1976–84*. Eds. Francis Barker et al. London, 1986, 35–56.

Kelley, Maurice. *This Great Argument: A Study of Milton's* De Doctrina Christiana *as a Gloss upon* Paradise Lost. Princeton, 1941.

Kendrick, Christopher. *Milton: A Study in Ideology and Form*. New York, 1986.

Kermode, Frank. "Milton's Hero." *RES* ns 4 (1953): 317–30.

Kerrigan, William. *The Prophetic Milton*. Charlottesville, VA, 1974.

———. *The Sacred Complex: On the Psychogenesis of* Paradise Lost. Cambridge, MA, 1983.

———, and Gordon Braden. "Milton's Coy Eve: *Paradise Lost* and Renaissance Love Poetry." *ELH* 53 (1986): 27–51.

Knott, John R. *Milton's Pastoral Vision: An Approach to* Paradise Lost. Chicago, 1971.

Kranidas, Thomas. *The Fierce Equation: A Study of Milton's Decorum.* The Hague, 1965.

Labriola, Albert C. "The Titans and the Giants: *Paradise Lost* and the Tradition of the Renaissance Ovid." *MQ* 12 (1978): 9–16.

Lawry, Jon S. *The Shadow of Heaven: Matter and Stance in Milton's Poetry.* Ithaca, 1968.

Leavis, F. R. "Milton's Verse." *Revaluation.* London, 1936.

———. "Mr. Eliot and Milton," and "In Defence of Milton." *The Common Pursuit.* London, 1952.

LeComte, Edward. *Milton's Unchanging Mind.* Port Washington, N.Y., 1973.

———. *Milton and Sex.* New York, 1978.

———. "Dubious Battle: Saving the Appearances." *English Language Notes* 19 (1982): 177–93.

Leonard, John. *Naming in Paradise.* New York, 1990.

Lewalski, Barbara Kiefer. "Structure and the Symbolism of Vision in Michael's Prophecy, *PL*, XI–XII." *PQ* 42 (1963): 25–35.

———. "Milton on Women—Yet Once More." *MS* 6 (1974): 3–20.

———. *Paradise Lost and the Rhetoric of Literary Forms.* Princeton, 1985.

Lewis, C. S. *A Preface to* Paradise Lost. London, 1942.

Lieb, Michael. *The Dialectics of Creation: Patterns of Birth and Regeneration in* Paradise Lost. Amherst, 1970.

———. *Poetics of the Holy: A Reading of* Paradise Lost. Chapel Hill, 1981.

———. *The Sinews of Ulysses: Form and Convention in Milton's Works.* Pittsburgh, 1989.

———. "Reading God: Milton and the Anthropopathetic Tradition." *MS* 25 (1990): 213–43.

Lovejoy, Arthur O. "Milton and the Paradox of the Fortunate Fall." *ELH* 4 (1937). Rep. in his *Essays in the History of Ideas* (Baltimore, 1948) and in *Critical Essays on Milton from ELH* (Baltimore, 1969).

Loewenstein, David. *Milton and the Drama of History: Historical Vision, Iconoclasm and the Literary Imagination.* Cambridge, 1990.

MacCaffrey, Isabel Gamble. Paradise Lost *as Myth.* Cambridge, MA, 1959.

McColley, Diane. "The Voice of the Destroyer in Adam's Diatribe." *MP* 75 (1977): 18–28.

———. " 'Daughter of Man': The Subordination of Milton's Eve." *Familiar Colloquy: Essays Presented to Edward Arthur Barker.* Ed. Patricia Bruckmann. Ottawa, 1978. 196–208.

———. *Milton's Eve.* Champaign, IL, 1983.

McColley, Grant. "Milton's Dialogue on Astronomy. The Principal Immediate Sources." *PMLA* 52 (1937): 728–62.

———. Paradise Lost: *An Account of Its Growth and Major Origins.* New York, 1963.

Madsen, William G. "The Idea of Nature in Milton's Poetry." *Three Studies in the Renaissance.* New Haven, 1958.

———. *From Shadowy Types to Truth.* New Haven, 1968.

Martindale, Charles. *John Milton and the Transformation of Ancient Epic.* Totowa, N.J., 1986.

Martz, Louis L. *Poet of Exile: A Study of Milton's Poetry.* New Haven, 1980.

Milner, Andrew. *John Milton and the English Revolution: A Study in the Sociology of Literature.* London, 1981.

Miner, Earl. "The Reign of Narrative in *Paradise Lost*." *MS* 17 (1983): 3–25.

Mollenkott, Virginia. "Some Implications of Milton's Androgynous Muse." *Bucknell Review* 24 (1978): 27–38.

Morand, Paul Phelps. *The Effects of His Political Life upon John Milton.* Paris, 1939.

Murrin, Michael. "The Language of Milton's Heaven." *The Allegorical Epic.* Chicago, 1980.

Nicolson, Marjorie Hope. "Milton and the Telescope." *Science and Imagination.* Ithaca, 1956.

Norford, Don Parry. " 'My Other Half': The Coincidence of Opposites in *Paradise Lost*." *MLQ* 36 (1975): 21–33.

Nyquist, Mary. "Reading the Fall: Discourse and Drama in *Paradise Lost*." *ELR* 14 (1984): 199–220.

———. "The Father's Word/ Satan's Wrath." *PMLA* 100 (1985): 187–202.

———. "The Genesis of Gendered Subjectivity in the Divorce Tracts in *Paradise Lost*." *Re-Membering Milton.* Eds. Margaret W. Ferguson and Mary Nyquist. New York, 1987.

Parker, Patricia A. "Eve, Evening, and the Labor of Reading *Paradise Lost*." *ELR* 9 (1979): 319–42.

Patrides, C. A. *Milton and the Christian Tradition.* Oxford, 1966.

Peczenic, F. "Fit Help: The Egalitarian Marriage in *Paradise Lost*." *Mosaic* 17 (1984): 29–48.

Peter, John D. *A Critique of* Paradise Lost. New York, 1960.

Pointon, Marcia R. *Milton and English Art.* Toronto, 1970.

Prince, F. T. *The Italian Element in Milton's Verse.* Oxford, 1954.

Quarnstrom, Gunnar. *The Enchanted Palace.* Stockholm, 1967.

Quilligan, Maureen. *Milton's Spenser: The Politics of Reading.* Ithaca, 1983.

Radzinowicz, Mary Ann. "The Politics of *Paradise Lost*." *Politics of Discourse.* Ed. Kevin Sharpe and Steven N. Zwicker. Berkeley, 1987. 204–29.

————*Milton's Epics and the Book of Psalms.* Princeton, 1989.

Rajan, Balachandra. Paradise Lost *and the Seventeenth-Century Reader.* London, 1962.

————. *The Lofty Rhyme: A Study of Milton's Major Poetry.* London, 1970.

————. "*Paradise Lost:* The Uncertain Epic." *Composite Orders: The Genres of Milton's Last Poems. MS* 17 (1983): 105–19.

Rapaport, Herman. *Milton and the Postmodern.* Lincoln, NE, 1983.

Revard, Stella. "Eve and the Doctrine of Responsibility in *Paradise Lost." PMLA* 88 (1973): 69–78.

————. *The War in Heaven:* Paradise Lost *and the Tradition of Satan's Rebellion.* Ithaca, 1980.

Ricks, Christopher. *Milton's Grand Style.* Oxford, 1963.

Riggs, William G. *The Christian Poet in* Paradise Lost. Berkeley, 1972.

Rosenblatt, Jason P. "The Mosaic Voice in *Paradise Lost." MS* 7 (1975): 207–32.

Ross, Malcolm M. *Milton's Royalism.* Ithaca, 1943.

————. "Milton and the Protestant Aesthetic." In his *Poetry and Dogma.* New Brunswick, N.J., 1954.

Rostvig, Maren-Sofie. *The Hidden Sense.* New York, 1963.

Ryken, Leland. *The Apocalyptic Vision in* Paradise Lost. Ithaca, 1970.

Samuel, Irene. *Plato and Milton.* Ithaca, 1947.

————. "Milton on Learning and Wisdom." *PMLA* 64 (1949): 708–23.

————. "The Dialogue in Heaven: A Reconsideration of *Paradise Lost,* III, 1–417." *PMLA* 72 (1957): 601–11. Rep. in first Norton Critical Edition of *PL.* New York, 1975. 468–78.

————. *Dante and Milton: The* Commedia *and* Paradise Lost. Ithaca, 1966.

Schultz, Howard. *Milton and Forbidden Knowledge.* New York, 1955.

Schwartz, Regina M. *Remembering and Repeating: Biblical Creation in* Paradise Lost. Cambridge and New York, 1988.

————. "From Shadowy Types to Shadowy Types: The Unendings of *Paradise Lost." MS* 24 (1988): 123–39.

Sensabaugh, George F. *The Grand Whig, Milton.* Stanford, 1952.

Sharrat, Bernard. "The Appropriation of Milton." *Essays and Studies* 35 (1982): 30–40.

Shawcross, John T. "The Balanced Structure of *Paradise Lost." SP* 62 (1965): 696–718.

————. "*Paradise Lost* and the Theme of the Exodus." *MS* 2 (1970): 3–26.

————. *With Mortal Voice: The Creation of* Paradise Lost. Lexington, KY, 1982.

————. *John Milton and Influence.* Pittsburgh, 1991.

Shumaker, Wayne. *Unpremeditated Verse: Feeling and Perception in* Paradise Lost. Princeton, 1967.

Sims, James H. *The Bible in Milton's Epics.* Gainesville, FL, 1962.

————, and Leland Ryken. *Milton and Scriptural Tradition: The Bible into Poetry.* Columbia, MO, 1984.

Spaeth, Sigmund G. *Milton's Knowledge of Music.* Ann Arbor, MI, 1963.

Sprott, Ernest S. *Milton's Art of Prosody.* Oxford, 1958.

Stavely, Keith W. F. *Puritan Legacies:* Paradise Lost *and the New England Tradition, 1630–1890.* Ithaca, 1989.

————. "Satan and Arminianism in *Paradise Lost." MS* 25 (1990): 125–39.

Steadman, John M. *Milton and the Renaissance Hero.* Oxford, 1967.

————. *Milton's Epic Characters.* Chapel Hill, 1968.

————. *Epic and Tragic Structure in* Paradise Lost. Chicago, 1976.

————. *Milton and the Renaissance Hero.* Oxford, 1976.

————. *Milton's Biblical and Classical Imagery.* Pittsburgh, 1984.

Stein, Arnold. *Answerable Style: Essays on* Paradise Lost. Minneapolis, 1953.

Stevens, Paul. "Milton and the Icastic Imagination." *MS* 20 (1984): 43–73.

Summers, Joseph H. *The Muse's Method: An Introduction to* Paradise Lost. Cambridge, MA, 1962.

————. "The Embarrassments of *Paradise Lost." Approaches to* Paradise Lost. Ed. C. A. Patrides. Toronto, 1968.

Svendson, Kester. *Milton and Science.* Cambridge, MA, 1956.

Swaim, Kathleen M. " 'He for God only, she for God in him': Structural Parallelism in *Paradise Lost." MS* 9 (1976): 121–49.

————. "The Mimesis of Accommodation in Book 3 of *Paradise Lost." PQ* 63 (1984): 461–75.

Tanner, John S. " 'Say First What Cause': Ricoeur and the Etiology of Evil in *Paradise Lost." PMLA* 103 (1988): 45–56.

Tayler, Edward W. *Milton's Poetry: Its Development in Time.* Pittsburgh, 1979.

Teskey, Gordon. "Milton's Choice of Subject in the Context of Renaissance Critical Theory." *ELH* 53 (1986): 53–71.

————. "Milton and Modernity." *Diacritics* 18 (1988): 42–53.

Tillyard, E. M. W. *Studies in Milton.* London, 1951.

————. *The Miltonic Setting, Past and Present.* London, 1957.

Turner, James Grantham. *One Flesh*. New York, 1987.

Watkins, W. B. C. *An Anatomy of Milton's Verse*. Baton Rouge, LA, 1955.

Webber, Joan Mallory. *Milton and His Epic Tradition*. Seattle, 1979.

———. "The Politics of Poetry: Feminism and *Paradise Lost*." *MS* 14 (1980): 3–24.

West, Robert H. *Milton and the Angels*. Athens, GA, 1955.

Whaler, James. "The Miltonic Simile." *PMLA* 46 (1931): 1034–74.

———. *Counterpoint and Symbol*. Copenhagen, 1956.

Williamson, George. "The Education of Adam." *MP* 61 (1963): 96–109.

Wittreich, Joseph A., Jr. *Visionary Poetics: Milton and His Legacy*. San Marino, CA, 1979.

———. *Feminist Milton*. Ithaca, 1987.

Wollaeger, Mark A. "Apocryphal Narration: Milton, Raphael, and the Book of Tobit." *MS* 21 (1985): 137–56.

Woodhouse, A. S. P. *The Heavenly Muse: A Preface to Milton*. Ed. Hugh MacCullum. Toronto, 1972.

Wright, B. A. *Milton's* Paradise Lost. London, 1962.

NORTON CRITICAL EDITIONS

HARDY *The Mayor of Casterbridge* edited by James K. Robinson
HARDY *The Return of the Native* edited by James Gindin
HARDY *Tess of the d'Urbervilles* edited by Scott Elledge *Third Edition*
HAWTHORNE *The Blithedale Romance* edited by Seymour Gross and Rosalie Murphy
HAWTHORNE *The House of the Seven Gables* edited by Seymour Gross
HAWTHORNE *Nathaniel Hawthorne's Tales* edited by James McIntosh
HAWTHORNE *The Scarlet Letter* edited by Seymour Gross, Sculley Bradley, Richmond Croom Beatty, E. Hudson Long *Third Edition*
HERBERT *George Herbert and the Seventeenth-Century Religious Poets* selected and edited by Mario A. DiCesare
HERODOTUS *The Histories* translated and selected by Walter E. Blanco, edited by Walter E. Blanco and Jennifer Roberts
HOMER *The Odyssey* translated and edited by Albert Cook *Second Edition*
HOWELLS *The Rise of Silas Lapham* edited by Don L. Cook
IBSEN *The Wild Duck* translated and edited by Dounia B. Christiani
JAMES *The Ambassadors* edited by S. P. Rosenbaum
JAMES *The American* edited by James A. Tuttleton
JAMES *The Portrait of a Lady* edited by Robert D. Bamberg
JAMES *Tales of Henry James* edited by Christof Wegelin
JAMES *The Turn of the Screw* edited by Robert Kimbrough
JAMES *The Wings of the Dove* edited by J. Donald Crowley and Richard A. Hocks
JONSON *Ben Jonson and the Cavalier Poets* selected and edited by Hugh Maclean
JONSON *Ben Jonson's Plays and Masques* selected and edited by Robert M. Adams
MACHIAVELLI *The Prince* translated and edited by Robert M. Adams *Second Edition*
MALTHUS *An Essay on the Principle of Population* edited by Philip Appleman
MANN *Death in Venice* translated and edited by Clayton Koelb
MARX *Communist Manifesto* edited by Fredric L. Bender
MELVILLE *The Confidence-Man* edited by Hershel Parker
MELVILLE *Moby-Dick* edited by Harrison Hayford and Hershel Parker
MEREDITH *The Egoist* edited by Robert M. Adams
Middle English Lyrics selected and edited by Maxwell S. Luria and Richard L. Hoffman
MILL *On Liberty* edited by David Spitz
MILTON *Paradise Lost* edited by Scott Elledge *Second Edition*
Modern Irish Drama edited by John P. Harrington
MORE *Utopia* translated and edited by Robert M. Adams *Second Edition*
NEWMAN *Apologia Pro Vita Sua* edited by David J. DeLaura
NORRIS *McTeague* edited by Donald Pizer
Restoration and Eighteenth-Century Comedy edited by Scott McMillan
RICH *Adrienne Rich's Poetry and Prose* edited by Barbara Charlesworth Gelpi and Albert Gelpi
ROUSSEAU *Rousseau's Political Writings* edited by Alan Ritter and translated by Julia Conway Bondanella
ST. PAUL *The Writings of St. Paul* edited by Wayne A. Meeks
SHAKESPEARE *Hamlet* edited by Cyrus Hoy *Second Edition*
SHAKESPEARE *Henry IV, Part I* edited by James J. Sanderson *Second Edition*
SHAW *Bernard Shaw's Plays* edited by Warren Sylvester Smith
SHELLEY *Shelley's Poetry and Prose* selected and edited by Donald H. Reiman and Sharon B. Powers
SMOLLETT *Humphry Clinker* edited by James L. Thorson
SOPHOCLES *Oedipus Tyrannus* translated and edited by Luci Berkowitz and Theodore F. Brunner
SPENSER *Edmund Spenser's Poetry* selected and edited by Hugh Maclean and Anne Lake Prescott *Third Edition*
STENDHAL *Red and Black* translated and edited by Robert M. Adams
STERNE *Tristram Shandy* edited by Howard Anderson
STOWE *Uncle Tom's Cabin* edited by Elizabeth Ammons
SWIFT *Gulliver's Travels* edited by Robert A. Greenberg *Second Edition*
SWIFT *The Writings of Jonathan Swift* edited by Robert A. Greenberg and William B. Piper
TENNYSON *In Memoriam* edited by Robert Ross
TENNYSON *Tennyson's Poetry* selected and edited by Robert W. Hill, Jr.
THOREAU *Walden and Resistance to Civil Government* edited by William Rossi *Second Edition*
TOLSTOY *Anna Karenina* (the Maude translation) edited by George Gibian
TOLSTOY *Tolstoy's Short Fiction* edited and with revised translations by Michael R. Katz
TOLSTOY *War and Peace* (the Maude translation) edited by George Gibian
TOOMER *Cane* edited by Darwin T. Turner
TURGENEV *Fathers and Sons* edited with a thoroughly revised translation by Ralph E. Matlaw *Second Edition*
VOLTAIRE *Candide* translated and edited by Robert M. Adams *Second Edition*
WATSON *The Double Helix: A Personal Account of the Discovery of the Structure of DNA* edited by Gunther S. Stent
WHARTON *The House of Mirth* edited by Elizabeth Ammons
WHITMAN *Leaves of Grass* edited by Sculley Bradley and Harold W. Blodgett
WILDE *The Picture of Dorian Gray* edited by Donald L. Lawler
WOLLSTONECRAFT *A Vindication of the Rights of Woman* edited by Carol H. Poston *Second Edition*
WORDSWORTH *The Prelude: 1799, 1805, 1850* edited by Jonathan Wordsworth, M. H. Abrams, and Stephen Gill